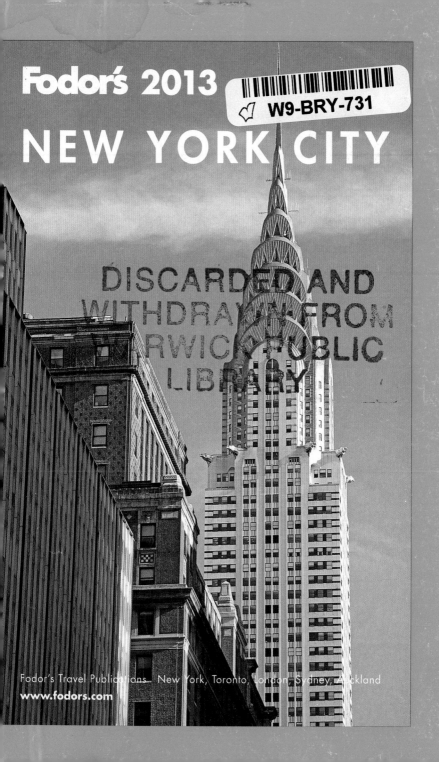

Fodor's 2013

NEW YORK CITY

W9-BRY-731

Fodor's Travel Publications   New York, Toronto, London, Sydney, Auckland
www.fodors.com

FODOR'S NEW YORK CITY 2013

Editorial Contributors: Lynne Arany, Alexander Basek, Arthur Bovino, Robert Brenner, Samantha Chapnick, David Farley, Jacinta O'Halloran, Anja Mutić, John Rambow, Adeena Sussman, Christina Valhouli

Editor: Caroline Trefler

Production Editor: Jennifer DePrima
Maps & Illustrations: Mark Stroud, David Lindroth, *cartographers;* Rebecca Baer, *map editor;* William Wu, *information graphics*
Design: Fabrizio La Rocca, *creative director;* Tina Malaney, Chie Ushio, Jessica Ramirez, *designers;* Melanie Marin, *associate director of photography;* Jennifer Romains, *photo research*
Cover Photo: (Aerial view of Wall Street): Cameron Davidson/Corbis
Production Manager: Angela L. McLean

ISBN 978-0-307-92929-7

ISSN 0736-9395

SPECIAL SALES

This book is available at special discounts for bulk purchases for sales promotions or premiums. Special editions, including personalized covers, excerpts of existing books, and corporate imprints, can be created in large quantities for special needs. For more information, write to Special Markets/Premium Sales, 1745 Broadway, MD 3-1, New York, NY 10019, or e-mail specialmarkets@randomhouse.com.

AN IMPORTANT TIP & AN INVITATION

Although all prices, opening times, and other details in this book are based on information supplied to us at press time, changes occur all the time in the travel world, and Fodor's cannot accept responsibility for facts that become outdated or for inadvertent errors or omissions. So **always confirm information when it matters**, especially if you're making a detour to visit a specific place. Your experiences—positive and negative— matter to us. If we have missed or misstated something, **please write to us**. Share your opinion instantly through our online feedback center at fodors.com/contact-us.

PRINTED IN COLOMBIA

10 9 8 7 6 5 4 3 2 1

CONTENTS

ABOUT
THIS GUIDE

Fodor's Ratings

Everything in this guide is worth doing—we don't cover what isn't—but exceptional sights, hotels, and restaurants are recognized with additional accolades. **Fodor's Choice** ★ indicates our top recommendations; ★ highlights places we deem highly recommended; and **Best Bets** call attention to notable hotels and restaurants in various categories. Care to nominate a new place? Visit Fodors.com/contact-us.

Trip Costs

We list prices wherever possible to help you budget well. Hotel and restaurant price categories from **$** to **$$$$** are noted alongside each recommendation. For hotels, we include the lowest cost of a standard double room in high season. For restaurants, we cite the average price of a main course at dinner or, if dinner isn't served, at lunch. For attractions, we always list adult admission fees; discounts are usually available for children, students, and senior citizens.

Hotels

Our local writers vet every hotel to recommend the best overnights in each price category, from budget to expensive. Unless otherwise specified, you can expect private bath, phone, and TV in your room. For expanded hotel reviews, facilities, and deals visit Fodors.com.

TripAdvisor ⊙⊙

Our expert hotel picks are reinforced by high ratings on TripAdvisor. Look for representative quotes in this guide, and the latest TripAdvisor ratings and feedback at Fodors.com.

Ratings		Hotels & Restaurants	
★	Fodor's Choice	🏠	Hotel
★	Highly recommended	⤴	Number of rooms
☾	Family-friendly	⏐⏐	Meal plans
Listings		✕	Restaurant
✉	Address	⟲	Reservations
✉	Branch address	👔	Dress code
🏠	Mailing address	▭	No credit cards
☎	Telephone	$	Price
🖶	Fax	**Other**	
🌐	Website	⇨	See also
✉	E-mail	☞	Take note
🏷	Admission fee	🏌	Golf facilities
☉	Open/closed times		
Ⓜ	Subway		
✛	Directions or Map coordinates		

Restaurants

Unless we state otherwise, restaurants are open for lunch and dinner daily. We mention dress code only when there's a specific requirement and reservations only when they're essential or not accepted. To make restaurant reservations, visit Fodors.com.

Credit Cards

The hotels and restaurants in this guide typically accept credit cards. If not, we'll say so.

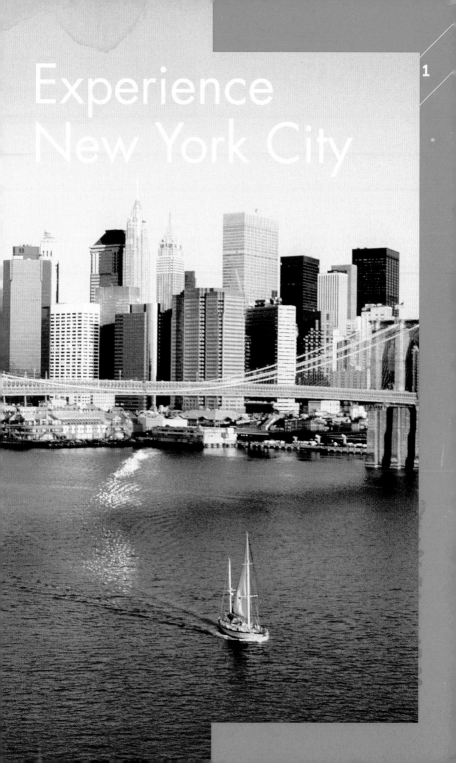

Experience
New York City

NEW YORK CITY TODAY

The phrase "in a New York minute" is cliché for a reason: in this wonderful, frenetic, and overwhelming city, things really do change in a flash. Even for those of us who live here, keeping up with the latest in news, art, music, food, sports, and politics can be exhausting. It can also be riveting. In 2011, New York saw the fall of a rising New York City congressman after he revealed a little too much of himself on Twitter, and the resignation of the head of the International Monetary Fund after he assumed room service in NYC includes the maid (it doesn't). We were battered by a hurricane and rattled by an earthquake (in the same week!); saw the historic passage of a same-sex marriage law; and watched the rise and reach of the Occupy Wall Street movement. There was MoMa's PopRally, the Met's Alexander McQueen, Broadway's *Book of Mormon,* and the Bronx Zoo's escaped Egyptian cobra. And of course, there was the day we stopped to mark the 10th anniversary of 9/11.

A lot can happen in a New York minute; even more in a year. With 2012 well under way, here's what's on our radar for 2013:

Politics

No doubt there will be the usual sex, lies, and videotape political antics to challenge the headline writers of the local media, but there's also no doubt that the main story in New York City politics in 2013 will be the mayoral race. Mayor Michael R. Bloomberg is on the last leg of his third and final (unless he has another change of mind) term as mayor, and the city will eagerly watch as would-be mayors duke it out for the title.

Economy

Maybe we're optimistic, or maybe we just can't move so fast if you bog us down with economic statistics; either way, we don't want to whine about the economy. A few quick positive indicators: the city's unemployment numbers are slightly better than national averages, there are more restaurants opening than closing, and there were 45 new hotels under construction in Manhattan in 2012—up from just eight hotels in 2011. The Manhattan real estate market is strong, especially the luxury real estate market; a penthouse apartment on Central Park West recently sold for a record $88 million, so things can't be that bad, right? Enough about the economy already!

WHAT'S NEW?

New York City is looking to become the new Paris or Copenhagen with a public bike-sharing system that will provide on-demand bikes to locals and visitors. This may be the year that New Yorkers embrace this cheap and easy transportation option and get off their cynical butts and onto bikes.

With its final phase due to open in early 2014, the High Line Park is still the subject of much New York chatter and attention. That said, some New Yorkers are turning their attentions to the next big thing—a proposal to develop an abandoned trolley station below Delancey Street on the Lower East Side. Known as the Low Line, this underground

Sports

If there's something the quintessential New Yorker can't get enough of, its sports, so if you're looking to make small talk with a local, just pick a team. And what's new with local teams? Well, the New Jersey Nets became the Brooklyn Nets for the 2012–13 season and moved to brand-new digs in Downtown Brooklyn, a move christened by a series of concerts from homegrown rap icon—and part owner of the Brooklyn Nets—Jay Z.

The NY Giants will look to defend their 2012 Super Bowl title in early 2013, but "Tebowmania"—the hoopla surrounding quarterback Tim Tebow, who joined the Jets roster in 2012—might continue to get the lion's share of attention.

With the resignation of legendary catcher Jorge Posada, and constant speculation about the resignation of another legend, Mariano Rivera, New York Yankee fans will be watching A-Rod solidify his legend status as he bats his way up the all-time home-run list. (At press time, he was chasing Willie Mays's title of fourth all-time HR hitter.) Also on the New York sports radar in 2013 is talk about extending the New York City marathon to a two-day event, rising hopes that the New York Red Bulls will continue to do their—or rather, Thierry (Henry)—thing in American Major League Soccer, and anticipation that "Linsanity" and Jeremy Lin will resume as a main attraction for the New York Knicks in 2013.

The Arts

Vermeer's *Girl with a Pearl Earring* will be a hot ticket at the Frick in late 2013 when the so-called Dutch Mona Lisa visits as part of the exhibit *Vermeer, Rembrandt, and Hals: Masterpieces of Dutch Paintings from the Mauritshuis*. The Met will exhibit several hundred pieces of jewelry from New York–born jewelry designer Joel A. Rosenthal in the first retrospective of his work, while artist Jeff Koons hopes to suspend his art piece *Train*, an operational full-size replica of a 1943 steam locomotive over the High Line Park.

London's Royal Shakespeare Company's hit musical *Matilda* will arrive on Broadway in early 2013 along with a revival of the Aaron Sorkin military-courtroom drama, *A Few Good Men*, and new musical *Big Fish*. Speaking of big fish, Tony Award winner Hugh Jackman will return to Broadway in late 2013 with *Houdini*.

park will require cutting-edge design and technology (like fiber optics to pump the underground with natural sunlight), which has locals anticipating the next big thing after that—green and sunny subway stations!

Escaping the city in summer is something locals think about way in advance of the season, making plans early in the year for housing shares in the Hamptons or Fire Island. But for those without the means, the summertime hot spot of late is Governors Island. The short ferry ride, free concerts, easy biking, and cool history make it popular with out-of-towners and locals alike.

PLANNER

When to Go

New York City weather, like its people, is a study in extremes. Much of winter brings bone-chilling winds and an occasional traffic-snarling snowfall, but you're just as likely to experience mild afternoons sandwiched by cool temperatures.

In late spring and early summer, streets fill with parades and street fairs, and Central Park has free performances. Late-August temperatures sometimes claw skyward, bringing subway station temperatures over 100°F (no wonder the Hamptons are so crowded). This is why September brings palpable excitement, with stunning yellow-and-bronze foliage complementing the dawn of a new cultural season. Between October and May, museums mount major exhibitions, most Broadway shows open, and formal opera, ballet, and concert seasons begin.

Getting Around

Without a doubt, the best way to explore New York is on foot. No matter what neighborhood you're headed to, you'll get a better sense of it by wandering around; you can check out the architecture, pop into cool-looking shops and cafés, and observe the walk-and-talk of the locals. And if you get lost, you'll find that New Yorkers are surprisingly helpful with directions.

New York's subway system is by far the most efficient and cost-effective way to get around, and it runs 24 hours a day. It can be a little intimidating at first, but other riders are generally more than happy to help you figure out your best route; they'll also help you decode loudspeaker announcements that can be difficult to understand on all but the newest trains. The subway is safe, but be smart; try to avoid riding alone—especially late at night, and avoid riding in empty cars. Speaking of empty cars, they're not an issue during rush hours, when you'll likely find that all the subway seats are taken, and you'll have to join in the particular New York sport of "strap-hanging." Train floors are sticky, stations are sweltering in summer, and platforms are grimy year-round, but this all just adds to the "charm" of riding on a system that is more than 100 years old.

If you've got a long way to go and would rather be comfy than thrifty, hail one of the ubiquitous yellow cabs that troll New York's streets around the clock. You'll be out $2.50 just for getting in, but you'll get to look at the scenery as you go. Avoid trying to hail a cab between 4 and 4:30 p.m, when drivers change shifts.

A Guide to the Grid

The map of Manhattan is, for the most part, easy to follow: north of 14th Street, streets are laid out in a numbered grid pattern. Numbered streets run east and west (crosstown), and broad avenues, most of them also numbered, run north (uptown) and south (downtown). The main exception is Broadway, which runs the entire length of Manhattan on a diagonal. Below 14th Street, street patterns get chaotic. In the West Village, West 4th Street intersects West 11th Street, Greenwich Street runs roughly parallel to Greenwich Avenue, and Leroy Street turns into St. Luke's Place for one block and then becomes Leroy again. There's an East Broadway and a West Broadway, both of which run north–south, and neither of which is an extension of Broadway, leaving even locals scratching their heads.

Street Smarts

Avoid deserted blocks in unfamiliar neighborhoods. A brisk, purposeful pace helps deter trouble wherever you go. New York City is a safe city, but it's still a city, so keep jewelry out of sight on the street; better yet, leave valuables in your hotel safe.

Of course, you want to capture every "New York minute," but instead of parading your camera—and your tourist status—consider securing it (especially if it's a pricey and bulky DSLR) in a nondescript cross-body bag.

When in bars or restaurants, never hang your purse or bag on the back of a chair or put it underneath the table. Travel light if possible so that you can wear your bag or put it on the table in front of you.

Never leave your bags unattended; they might get swiped, or worse—swooped upon by well-meaning citizens, prompted to report orphan bags thanks to the heavily promoted public-service campaign "If you see something, say something."

Expect to have yourself and your possessions inspected thoroughly in such places as airports, sports stadiums, museums, and city buildings. Police officers stationed by subway-token booths also reserve the right to check your bags before you pass through the turnstile to enter the platform.

Politely ignore panhandlers on the streets and subways, people who offer to hail you a cab, and limousine and gypsy-cab drivers who (illegally) offer rides.

Opening Hours

Subways and buses run around the clock, as do plenty of restaurants, pharmacies, and fitness clubs. Some shops and services have more extensive hours than you'll find elsewhere in the United States, so you can get groceries, or get your hair and nails done, at 11 pm. In general, though, you can safely assume that most shops are open seven days a week, from about 10 to 7 Monday–Saturday and from noon to 6 on Sunday. Bars generally close at 4 am, though some after-hours clubs are open later.

Money-Saving Tips

Consider buying a CityPass, a group of tickets to six top-notch attractions in New York: the Empire State Building, the Guggenheim Museum or Top of the Rock, the American Museum of Natural History, the Museum of Modern Art, the Metropolitan Museum of Art (including the Cloisters), and Circle Line Cruises or admission to Liberty and Ellis islands. The $89 pass, which saves you half the cost of each individual ticket, is good for nine days from first use.

Sign up for social discount shopping sites like Groupon, Gilt, Bloomspot, and LivingSocial a month before your visit to New York to score discounts on everything from trendy restaurants and clubs to beauty treatments and attractions.

WHAT'S WHERE

Numbers refer to chapters

2 Lower Manhattan. The Financial District, NY Harbor, and TriBeCa. Heavy-duty landmarks anchor the southern tip of Manhattan: Wall Street and the Financial District; the breezy waterfront parks of Battery Park City and historic South Street Seaport; ferry terminals dispatching boats out to Ellis Island and the Statue of Liberty; and the evolving construction site at Ground Zero. The tony streets of TriBeCa to the west are broader and also quieter, but it does have a busy restaurant scene.

3 SoHo, NoLIta, Little Italy, and Chinatown. The only struggling creative types in SoHo these days are sidewalk merchants hawking canvases, handmade jewelry, and T-shirts; luxe shops dominate here. To the east, NoLIta has more tiny boutiques and restaurants. And to the south, Little Italy is a shrinking zone of touristy red-sauce eateries and gelaterias. Farther south, Chinatown teems with street vendors selling knockoff handbags. Brave the crowds and explore some of the less-traveled side streets to find Chinese herb shops, exceptional noodle joints, and Hong Kong cakes.

4 The East Village and the Lower East Side. Once an edgy neighborhood of artists and punks, now filled with a combination of artists, fashionable lawyers, and students, the East Village centers around scruffy but beloved Tompkins Square Park. The neighborhood is one of the city's best for eating, both in terms of variety and quality. To the south, the once seedy, now trendy Lower East Side (bounded by the Bowery, Clinton, Houston, and Delancey streets) draws hipsters with live-music clubs, independent clothing shops, wine-and-tapas bars, and health-food joints.

5 Greenwich Village and the West Village. Happily, artists with rent-controlled apartments, out-and-proud gays, and university students are still in the Village today, but because those town houses have become so expensive, residents also include wealthy media moguls, celebrities, and socialites. From 14th Street south to Houston and from the Hudson River east to 5th Avenue, the blocks are a jumble of jazz clubs, posh restaurants, former speakeasies, and rainbow flags.

6 Chelsea and the Meatpacking District. Chelsea, like its namesake London district, has a small-town personality with big-city prices. Its leafy streets (which stretch from 14th to the upper 20s) are lined with renovated brownstones and spacious art galleries; its avenues (from 6th to the Hudson) brim with restaurants, bakeries, bodegas, and men's clothing stores. Chelsea has supplanted the Village as the center of gay life in the city. To the south, the once blue-collar Meatpacking District has evolved into a swanky clubbing and restaurant scene by night and—with the High Line and a profusion of high-end boutiques—a shopping and walking destination by day.

7 Union Square, the Flatiron District, and Gramercy Park. Bustling Union Square Park, bounded by 14th and 17th streets, Broadway, and Park Avenue, hosts the city's best greenmarket four times a week. On the 14th Street edge are broad stone steps where breakdancers and other performers busk for onlookers. North, up Broadway, is the Flatiron District, home to the Flatiron Building and Madison Square Park, beloved for its outdoor summer jazz concerts. Nearby in the East 20s, is the private and serene Gramercy Park surrounded by storied mansions and elegant town houses.

WHAT'S WHERE

8 Midtown East and Murray Hill. Midtown from 5th Avenue to the East River is the refined big sister of flashy Midtown West; you'll find grand hotels along Park Avenue, grand shopping (think Tiffany, Chanel, and Burberry), and architectural grandeur the likes of the Chrysler Building and Grand Central Terminal. Murray Hill, north of Gramercy Park, is a mix of quiet tree-and-townhouse–lined streets, high-profile attractions like the Empire State Building and the Morgan Library and Museum, and tasty enclaves like Curry Hill (aka Little India) on Lexington in the high 20s.

9 Midtown West. Head to 42nd Street to see Times Square in all its neon, scrolling tickers, and massive-TV-screen glory. Towering office buildings line Broadway up to Columbus Circle at the edge of Central Park. At Rockefeller Center are the famous ice rink and tree (in season), and nearby are swank shops like Saks, Henri Bendel, and Bergdorf Goodman. St. Patrick's Cathedral, on 5th Avenue, is a key landmark. Heading south will bring you to the stately New York Public Library and the adjacent Bryant Park.

10 The Upper East Side. North of 59th Street, between 5th and Park avenues, the Upper East Side is home to more millionaires than any other part of the city. Historic-district designation has kept the tony mansions and apartment buildings intact and largely uninterrupted by "plebeian" structures. In this area are the Museum Mile and Madison Avenue's haute boutiques.

11 Central Park. Fredrick Law Olmstead's ode to the pastoral in the heart of New York, Central Park is the place to escape the bustle of the city. The park starts at 59th Street and goes all the way to 110th at the north end; east to west, it runs from 5th to 8th avenues.

12 The Upper West Side with the Cloisters. Wide sidewalks and ornate prewar buildings set the tone, and the American Museum of Natural History and Lincoln Center are big draws. Farther north are the Columbia University campus and the grounds of the Cathedral Church of St. John the Divine, with catacombs and wandering peacocks. Farther still, is the Cloisters, a branch of the Metropolitan Museum that houses nearly 5,000 medieval works in a reconstructed monastery; it sits atop a hill in Fort Tryon Park overlooking the Hudson.

13 Harlem. A hotbed of African American and Hispanic American culture for almost a century, Harlem still sizzles today. The brownstone-lined blocks between about 110th and 145th streets are being refurbished; chic boutiques and restaurants are popping up; and music venues from the 1920s and '30s are still in full swing.

14 Brooklyn. Manhattan's largest borough counts among its stars Coney Island, Prospect Park, and the Brooklyn Botanic Gardens. Its distinct neighborhoods include the hipster haven Williamsburg, the Italian-American Carroll Gardens, the Russian and Ukranian Brighton Beach, and the Hasidic and Orthodox Jewish Borough Park.

15 Queens, the Bronx, and Staten Island. Queens is known for its ethnic communities and the Mets' Citi Field. The Bronx, north of Manhattan, may be best known for Yankee Stadium, but the New York Botanical Garden and the Bronx Zoo also score home runs. Staten Island's most compelling feature might be the ferry, but there are also reasons to stick around.

NEW YORK CITY TOP ATTRACTIONS

Metropolitan Museum of Art

(A) The largest art museum in the Western Hemisphere, the Met is a mecca for art lovers of all stripes. Treasures from all over the world and every era of human creativity make up its expansive collection. If you need a breather, you can always retire to the Temple of Dendur or the rooftop café.

Times Square

(B) Times Square is the most frenetic part of New York City: a cacophony of languages and flashing lights, outré street performers, shoulder-to-shoulder crowds, and back-to-back billboards. These days it's also a pedestrian-friendly zone, so you won't have to take your eyes off the excitement to watch where you're going.

Empire State Building

(C) It may not be the tallest building in New York anymore (the Freedom Tower reclaimed the title for the World Trade Center in May 2012), but its status as most iconic will never change. Take in the panoramic views of the city from its observatories, or just enjoy it from afar—after dark it's illuminated by colored lights that correspond to different holidays and events.

Museum of Modern Art

(D) Airy and spacious, with soaring-ceiling galleries suffused with natural light and masterpieces that include Monet's *Water Lilies* and van Gogh's *Starry Night,* this one-of-a-kind museum designed by Japanese architect Yoshio Taniguchi is as famous for its architecture as for its collections.

Brooklyn Bridge

(E) New York City's most famous bridge connects the island of Manhattan to the borough of Brooklyn, and serves thousands of pedestrians, vehicles, skaters, and bicyclists a day. Walking across is an essential New York experience.

Statue of Liberty

(F) Presented to the United States in 1886 as a gift from France, Lady Liberty is a near-universal symbol of freedom and democracy, standing 152 feet high atop an 89-foot pedestal on Liberty Island. All access to the interior of the monument is closed to the public until the end of 2012, but Liberty Island remains open, and is well worth a visit.

American Museum of Natural History

(G) The towering, spectacularly reassembled dinosaur skeletons that greet you when you enter this museum might stop you in your tracks, but there's much more to see here, including exhibits of ancient civilizations, the live Butterfly Conservatory (October–May), a hall of oceanic creatures overlooked by a 94-foot model of a blue whale, and space shows at the adjoining Rose Center for Earth and Space.

Central Park

The literal and spiritual center of Manhattan, Central Park has 843 acres of meandering paths, tranquil lakes, ponds, and open meadows. For equestrians, softball and soccer players, strollers, skaters, birdwatchers, boaters, picnickers, and outdoor performers, it's an oasis of fresh air and greenery amid the hustle of the city.

Ground Zero

The memorial at the World Trade Center site is a moving tribute to the lives lost on 9/11. After a decade of clean-up and construction, the memorial opened to the public on the 10th anniversary of the terror attacks, while construction of a museum and other parts of the site continues.

NEW YORK CITY WITH KIDS

Though much of New York revolves around the adult pursuits of making and spending money, it's also a great city for kids. Our top activities include the following:

American Museum of Natural History. The favorite could entertain most children for a week. The dinosaurs alone are worth the trip, as is the live Butterfly Conservatory (October through May). You'll also find an IMAX theater, ancient-culture displays, and wildlife dioramas with taxidermied creatures that hit the right mix of fascinating and creepy. The space shows at the Hayden Planetarium (tickets sold separately) are a big bang with kids.

Bronx Zoo. The country's largest metropolitan wildlife park is home to more than 4,000 animals, including endangered and threatened species. Plan to spend a whole day here, so your kids don't have to choose between Congo Gorilla Forest and the Siberian cats at Tiger Mountain. The World of Darkness has a black-lighted indoor exhibit of nocturnal creatures. Special tours with a docent for children can be arranged.

Central Park Zoo. Three climatic regions—Rain Forest, Temperate Territory, and Polar Circle—are represented at this small zoo. The rain-forest frogs, red pandas, and performing sea lions are all nifty—but the winner is the underwater viewing window into the polar bear pool.

Children's Museum of Manhattan. Interactive exhibits in this five-floor museum change frequently—but they're always fun. As well as visiting with TV friends like Dora the Explorer, little ones can build castles in the sand laboratory, and—in warm weather—race boats on a zigzagging outdoor watercourse.

Coney Island and the New York Aquarium. Coney Island's aquarium is home to more than 10,000 marine species, including giant sea turtles, sand-tiger sharks, and sea otters. After the seal show, the whole family can enjoy a walk along the boardwalk to take in the beach, Luna Park's amusement rides, the landmark Cyclone wooden roller coaster (54-inch height requirement), and Nathan's hotdogs.

Sony Wonder Technology Lab. The line to get into this futuristic fantasy world might be long (entry is free) but don't worry—a slightly freaky talking robot will keep kids entertained while you wait. Inside, kids can program their own robots, record their own digital music, movies, and games, and perform open-heart surgery using Haptic technology.

DUMBO. Short for Down Under the Manhattan Bridge Overpass, this former industrial neighborhood is now a cool and cultural hot spot and home to family-friendly attractions like Brooklyn Bridge Park (a picnic-perfect waterfront park with several inventive playgrounds), Jane's Carousel, Brooklyn Ice Cream Factory, a newly opened public swimming pool, and a variety of kid-centric music, arts, and kite-flying festivals.

South Street Seaport Museum. The fleet of historic square-riggers with looming masts might be the first thing to catch your children's eyes—but there's much more going on here, including weekend concerts, 16 new galleries with exhibits that include intricate replicas of ships in bottles, and special guided tours for families.

NEW YORK CITY LIKE A LOCAL

There are a few tricks to navigating this city—unspoken, hard-won bits of knowledge that help us locals get the most out of our hometown without driving ourselves crazy. And at the risk of compromising our New York credibility (after all, we consider ourselves members of an exclusive club and guard our secrets accordingly), we've decided to share those tricks here. Just don't tell anyone we told you.

Getting Around Like a Local

Hit the Ground Walking

Spend a day in a New Yorker's shoes and you'll realize why we have the reputation for being skinny: New Yorkers walk. Two feet are the preferred method of transportation so if you want to talk the talk while you're here, you'd best walk the walk, too.

The most important rule of walking here is move quickly. We're in a hurry. Unless you're holding the hand of a small child, single file is the rule; walking two or three abreast will slow busy locals down. If you need a moment to update your Facebook status or take pictures of each other, make like you're on the highway: pull over and get out of the way.

Take the Subway

When distance is involved, make like a New Yorker and take the subway. It's cheaper than a cab, and often faster, too. The subway runs 24 hours a day, 7 days a week (with reduced frequency late at night and on weekends). A single-ride subway fare is $2.50 but expect an increase in 2013. If you're planning to make extensive use of the subway while you're in town, buy a MetroCard, a magnetically encoded card that debits the fare with every swipe at the turnstile (it's cheaper than paying single fares). You can purchase MetroCards from a staffed station booth or from the vending machines located in every subway station.

Know that the most common mistake for a subway novice is to hop on a train going in the wrong direction. We've all done it. First, determine if you are going uptown or downtown. Then, figure out which train—designated by numbers or letters—stops near where you're going. Note: the signs outside some stations indicate "Uptown Only" or "Downtown Only," so pay attention on your way in. Even seasoned New Yorkers ask for/confirm directions, so don't be shy; if anything, locals like to show off their knowledge of the system. Alternately, if you're traveling with a Smartphone, the website HopStop will help you figure out the best route.

Trains can run "local" (stopping at all stops on the line) or "express," so if you're uncertain just stick with a local train; better to delay your journey by a few stops than to miss your stop altogether!

All Hail the Taxi Cab

There is no shortage of yellow cabs in Manhattan; there's just a shortage of *available* cabs—especially when it's raining or you're in a hurry. You can tell whether a taxi is available by checking its rooftop light: if the center panel is lighted and the side panels are dark, the driver is looking for passengers (so stick out your arm!); taxis whose roof lights are lighted only at the edges—not the center—are off-duty.

Once you're in a cab, know your passenger rights. Although your driver will likely careen at high speeds while simultaneously cursing, leaning on his horn, and chattering into his cell-phone headset, you're entitled to ask him to slow down. You're also allowed to ask him to turn off his phone or blaring car radio, and if he doesn't comply, refrain from tipping him. Cabbies make almost nothing aside from tips, so tack 15% to 20% onto your fare after a satisfactory ride; all cabs are now required to take credit cards, too.

Speaking of fares, you'll be charged $2.50 for just getting into the cab. After that, the cost is 40 cents for every 1/5 mile (or every 60 seconds in stalled/slow traffic). You'll have to cover any bridge or tunnel tolls, and while you're at it, a surcharge of $1 between 4 and 8 p.m.

Last, know where you're going before you get into a cab. A quick map check or call to your destination will give you the cross streets and ensure a direct route.

Dining Like a Local
Breakfast

The first rule of New York eating is, forget the heavy breakfast—at least on weekdays. Although weekend brunch is popular—as the lines in front of restaurants on Saturday and Sunday attest—when the rest of the city is on the clock, it's better to get up and go. Grab coffee and a bagel from a café, a deli, or one of the ubiquitous sidewalk carts (they're passably good), and walk while you eat.

Lunch

On TV it seems New Yorkers only eat pizza, or dine at diners or chichi restaurants, when in reality, instead of chasing stereotypes or trends, you'll find most locals chasing trucks. The food-truck phenomenon is nothing new for New York, but rather than fizzle out, food truck dining has become a competitive sport with Twitter feeds and blogs dedicated to helping New Yorkers track and find trucks and then one-up coworkers with their lunch loot, be it a Turkish Taco or an Apple Pie Melt. Work up a healthy appetite like a local and find nearby food trucks with EdibleCity.com.

Dinner

Don't skip lunch whatever you do, because if you want to experience the real New York dinner scene, you'll need to dine late. Most New York restaurants are empty around 6 pm and don't fill up until at least 7:30 or 8, so if you eat early, you'll have your pick of tables but little company. Prime-time dinner reservations—between 8 and 10 pm—are the hardest to score, but will ensure that you're surrounded by dining companions.

Of course, if you can't get a good reservation, you can always do what many savvy locals do: eat at the bar. You'll get the same great food and people-watching, plus you'll get to feel like an insider while other folks are still waiting for a table.

Coffee

It's the city that never sleeps so you know the coffee's good and plentiful. Skip the generic coffee chains posted on every other corner and caffeinate like a discerning local with a cup from an artisanal roaster, served by an enthusiastic barista, often with free Wi-Fi on the side. Some local faves include: Joe The Art of Coffee in the West Village; 9th Street Espresso with two locations in Alphabet City, and one in Chelsea Market; Abraco in the East Village; and Gimme! Coffee in NoLIta. Portland's Stumptown Coffee Roasters and San Francisco's Blue Bottle Coffee have locations in Manhattan. Find your fuel by name, neighborhood, or location at NYCMugged.com.

SITTING IN A TV AUDIENCE

Tickets to tapings of TV shows are free, but can be hard to get on short notice. Most shows accept advance requests by email, phone, or online—but for the most popular shows, like *The Daily Show with Jon Stewart*, the backlog is so deep, you might have to wait a few months. Same-day standby tickets are often available—but be prepared to wait in line for several hours, sometimes starting at 5 or 6 am, depending on how hot the show is, or the wattage of that day's celebrity guests, and we hate to tell you this, but standby tickets do not guarantee a seat in the audience. You can also follow your favorite shows on Twitter for updates on last-minute ticket availability.

The Shows

The Colbert Report. Stephen Colbert leads his "nation" through shows Monday through Thursday. Check the website for dates with open tickets. Sign-up for standby tickets happens in front of the studio at 4 pm the day of the show. ⊠ *513 W. 54th St., between 10th and 11th Aves., Midtown West* ⊕ *www.colbertnation.com* Ⓜ *C, E to 50th St.*

The Daily Show with Jon Stewart. The amiable and incisive Jon Stewart pokes fun at news headlines on this half-hour cable show. The program tapes Monday through Thursday; you can request advance tickets on the website. For standby tickets, show up well before the 5:45 pm doors-open time. Audience members must be 18 or older. ⊠ *733 11th Ave., between W. 51st and W. 52nd Sts., Midtown West* ⊕ *www. thedailyshow.com* m*C, E to 50th St..*

Good Morning America. Robin Roberts and George Stephanopoulos host this early-morning news and entertainment standby. *GMA* airs live, weekdays from 7 to 9 am, and ticket requests (online only) should be

sent four to six months in advance. ⊠ *7 Times Sq., at W. 44th St. and Broadway, Midtown West* ⊕ *www.abcnews.go.com* Ⓜ *1, 2, 3, 7, N, Q, R, S to 42nd St./Times Sq.*

Late Night with Jimmy Fallon. Musician, singer, actor, and comedian Jimmy Fallon has solidified his place in late-night TV, thanks to his house band the Roots and a steady rotation of in-demand guests. Call the Ticket Information Line for a maximum of four tickets, about one month in advance. Single standby tickets are available on taping days—Monday through Friday—at the West 49th Street side of 30 Rockefeller Plaza; arrive before 9 am. You must be 17 or older. ⊠ *30 Rockefeller Plaza, Midtown West* ☎ *212/664– 3056 ticket information line* ⊕ *www. latenightwithjimmyfallon.com* Ⓜ *B, D, F, M to 47th–50th Rockefeller Center.*

The Late Show with David Letterman. Letterman's famously offbeat humor has had fans giggling for more than three decades. For advance tickets (two maximum), you can submit a request online or fill out an application in person at the theater. For standby tickets, call 212/247–6497 starting at 11 am on tape days—Monday through Thursday. Be prepared: you may be asked to answer Letterman-related trivia to secure your ticket. You must be 18 or older to sit in the audience. ⊠ *Ed Sullivan Theater, 1697 Broadway, between W. 53rd and W. 54th Sts., Midtown West* ☎ *212/975–5853* ⊕ *www. lateshowaudience.com* Ⓜ *1, C, E to 50th St.; B, D, E to 7th Ave.*

Live! with Kelly. The sparks fly on this morning program, which books an eclectic roster of cohosts and guests. Tickets are available online about a month in advance, or by mail up to a year in advance. Standby tickets become available weekdays at 7 am at the **ABC Studios** (✉ *7 Lincoln Sq., corner of W. 67th St. and Columbus Ave., Upper West Side*). Children under 10 aren't allowed in the audience. ☎ *212/456–3054* ⊕ *www.dadt. com/live* Ⓜ *1 to 66th St./Lincoln Center.*

Martha Stewart Living Omnimedia. Master baker, crafts maker, and champion of all "good things," Martha Stewart hosts her show with a live studio audience and various celebrity guests. The program tapes weekdays at 10 am and 2 pm. You can request tickets only through the Martha Stewart website. Often, producers are recruiting for groups of people (like nurses, new moms, or brides-to-be); if you fit that category, your chances of scoring tickets increase. Occasionally standby tickets are given out two hours before showtime. Audience members must be at least 10 years old. ✉ *221 W. 26th St., between 7th and 8th Aves., Chelsea* ⊕ *www.marthastewart.com/get-tickets* Ⓜ *C or 1 to 23rd St.*

Saturday Night Live. *SNL* continues to captivate audiences. Standby tickets—one per person—are distributed at 7 am on the day of the show at the West 49th Street entrance to 30 Rockefeller Plaza. You may ask for a ticket for either the dress rehearsal (8 pm) or the live show (11:30 pm). Requests for advance tickets (two per applicant) must be submitted by email only in August to ✍ *snltickets@ nbcuni.com*; recipients are determined by lottery. You must be 16 or older to sit in the audience. ✉ *NBC Studios, Saturday Night Live, 30 Rockefeller Plaza, between W. 49th and W. 50th Sts., Midtown West* ☎ *212/664–3056* ⊕ *www.nbc. com/saturday-night-live* Ⓜ *B, D, F, M to 47th–50th Sts./Rockefeller Center.*

Today. The *Today* show doesn't have a studio audience but if you get to the corner of Rockefeller Center and 49th Street before dawn, with poster board and markers (clever signs always get camera time), comfortable shoes, and a fun attitude you might get on camera. America's first morning talk–news show airs weekdays from 7 to 10 am in the glass-enclosed, ground-level NBC studio across from its original home at 30 Rockefeller Plaza. You may be spotted on TV by friends back home while you're standing behind anchors Ann Curry, Al Roker, and Matt Lauer. ✉ *Rockefeller Plaza at W. 49th St., Midtown West* ⊕ *www.today.msnbc.msn. com* Ⓜ *B, D, F, M to 47th–50th Sts./Rockefeller Center.*

NEW YORK CITY FOR FREE

If you think everything in New York costs too much, well, you're right—almost. In fact, the city has tons of free attractions and activities; you just need to know where to look for them.

Outdoor Fun

Walk across the Brooklyn Bridge for spectacular views of the Financial District, Brooklyn, the seaport, and Manhattan.

Ride the Staten Island Ferry to see the Statue of Liberty, Ellis Island, and the southern tip of Manhattan from the water. A one-way trip takes 30 minutes and offers magnificent views—and inexpensive beer and snacks. Note that you have to disembark at St. George Terminal. Ⓜ *1 to South Ferry; 4, 5 to Bowling Green.*

Catch a free movie screening in Bryant Park in summertime. A tradition since 1992, watching films alfresco surrounded by tall Midtown buildings is a summertime rite of passage for New Yorkers. Bring a blanket and a picnic basket, and be prepared to stake out a good spot on the lawn well in advance. Movie schedules are posted at ⊕ *www.bryantpark.org* Ⓜ *B, D, F, M to 42nd St.*

Wander Battery Park City's waterfront promenade. The breeze and passing boats will make you forget you're in the gritty city, though the view of the Statue of Liberty will remind you that you couldn't be anywhere but New York. Ⓜ *4, 5 to Bowling Green; 1 to South Ferry.*

Let botany grow on you with free visits to New York Botanical Garden (free all day Wed. and Sat. 10–11 a.m.), Brooklyn Botanic Garden (free all day Tues. and Sat. 10 am–noon), and Queens Botanical Garden (free Wed. 3–6 pm and Sun. 4–6 pm). ⊕ *www.nybg.org* ⊕ *www.bbg.org* ⊕ *www.queensbotanical.org*

Head to Governor's Island, a 172-acre island oasis in the heart of New York Harbor, just a seven-minute ferry ride from Lower Manhattan. You can visit the former military base turned sculpture park and public playground late May to late September to bike, picnic, wander forts, bask in views of the New York City skyline, and enjoy a variety of cultural offerings and festivals. ⊕ *www.govisland.com for a schedule of events and ferry information* Ⓜ *1 to South Ferry; 4, 5 to Bowling Green; R to Whitehall.*

Taste the goods at the Union Square greenmarket (on Monday, Wednesday, Friday, and Saturday), where farmers offer samples of their organically grown produce, artisanal cheeses, and fresh bread. Ⓜ *4, 5, 6 to Union Sq.*

Stroll the Coney Island boardwalk for some old-school kitsch (before it's redeveloped into swanky condos). There are also plenty of free annual events, including the outrageous Mermaid Parade and the Fourth of July hot-dog-eating contest. Ⓜ *B, F, N, Q to Stillwell Ave.*

Discover Central Park with a free, volunteer-led guided tour from the Central Park Conservancy. Explore the park's history, design, and ecology with one- to two-hour tours that focus on different areas of the park from its woodlands, romantic vistas, Conservatory garden, and Seneca Village to secret corners and off-the-beaten path walks of the park. Tours meet at different points in the park so check the website for details. ⊕ *www.centralparknyc.org*

Music, Theater, and Dance

Watch tango dancers and jazz musicians *outside* Lincoln Center at the annual month-long Out of Doors festival, held in August. It includes more than 100 performances of spoken word, beatboxing, and bigwigs like Dave Brubeck and Arlo Guthrie. *1 to 66th St./Lincoln Center.*

Hit Central Park Summerstage for big-name performers like Afrobeat bandleader Seun Kuti and Columbia's own Vampire Weekend. There's also a second series of concerts in Brooklyn.

Catch rising stars in classical music, drama, and dance at the Juilliard School's free student concerts (check ⊕ *www.juilliard.edu* for a calendar of events). Free tickets are available at the Juilliard box office for theater performances; there's also a line for standby an hour before the show. ✉ *144 W. 65th St. 1 to 66th St./Lincoln Center.*

Entertain thyself at Shakespeare in the Park, one of New York City's most beloved events—80,000 watch each year. It's been going strong since 1962, and shows usually feature celebrities earning their olde English acting chops. Get in line early at the Public Theater for a shot at tickets, or head to the Delacorte Theater in Central Park. ✉ *425 Lafayette St.* Ⓜ *6 to Astor Pl.*

Get gratis giggles at the Upright Citizens Brigade Theatre's comedy shows. Professional comedians, including UCB cofounder and *Saturday Night Live* alumna Amy Poehler, are sprinkled in with amateurs during the shows. Check the schedule for free shows. ✉ *307 W. 26th St.* ⊕ *www.ucbtheatre.com* Ⓜ *A, C, E to 23rd St.*

Art and Literature

Visit the Metropolitan Museum of Art. The $25 entry fee is actually a suggested donation. You can pay as much, or as little, as you wish. Smaller donations may get some eye-rolling from the cashier, but it's a small price to pay for access to world-famous works. ✉ *1000 5th Ave. at 80th St.* ⊕ *www.metmuseum.org* Ⓜ *6 to 86th St.*

Browse the galleries scattered throughout the city. Chelsea's full of expensive galleries with free access to superstar artists, though things get edgier the closer you get to the West Side Highway; you'll also find a trendy art scene in Williamsburg, Brooklyn.

Attend a reading at one of the city's hundreds of bookstores—bit (Barnes & Noble) and small (Housing Works Bookstore Café). You can also get your fix of free words at bars like KGB in the East Village, where budding and established authors have been reading since 1993. There's poetry on Monday, nonfiction on Tuesday, and contemporary fiction on Sunday. In Williamsburg, Pete's Candy Store has an excellent reading series on alternate Thursday nights.

MoMA is free on Friday between 4 and 8 pm, when the $25 entry fee is waived. Arrive as close to 4 as you can, and once you get your ticket (the line is long but fast), avoid the crowds by working your way down from the fifth floor. ✉ *11 W. 53rd St., between 5th and 6th Aves.* ⊕ *www.moma.org* Ⓜ *E, M to 5th Ave./53rd St.; B, D, F to 47–50th St./ Rockefeller Center.*

Learn about the American Indian at Smithsonian's National Museum of the American Indian, located in the grand Alexander Hamilton U.S. Customs House in Bowling Green. Admission is free every day to the museum's collections, public programs, music and dance performances, and films. ⊕ *www.nmai.si.edu/visit/newyork* Ⓜ *4, 5 to Bowling Green; R to Whitehall St.*

MIDTOWN ARCHITECTURE: DO LOOK UP!

Midtown is the heart of the city during the workday. From every direction, people pour into the city to give it a jolt of energy. That vibrancy is intense, but is also an unmissable aspect of city life worth exploring for the average visitor. Midtown is home to many beautiful architectural sights, so don't be embarrassed to look at them.

The East Side: From the United Nations to Grand Central

Start near the river, at New York City's first glass-curtain skyscraper, the UN Building (⊠ *760 United Nations Plaza*), completed in 1949 and designed by Le Corbusier. (Technically, it's not on New York's land, but we still count it.) The iconic structure is a monument to diplomacy, though being the city's first skyscraper isn't all glory: the air-conditioning is famously persnickety in the summer months. Continuing west, you'll pass the murals of the Daily News Building (⊠ *220 E. 42nd St.*) on the south side of the street. The lobby is home to a giant globe (from the era when the *News* had international correspondents) and murals are in the WPA-style, as the art-deco building was finished in 1929. Also a can't-miss: the Chrysler Building (⊠ *405 Lexington Ave.*), which out–art decos any other structure in New York. (Dig the wheels with wings in place of gargoyles on the exterior.) Continue walking and you'll see Grand Central Terminal (⊠ *1 E. 42nd St.*), the largest train station in the world. This Beaux-Arts structure was saved from the wrecking ball by concerned citizens in the '70s, a fate that similarly styled Penn Station didn't escape. Peek inside for a look at the constellations painted on the soaring ceiling, for a nibble at the Grand Central Oyster Bar, or a cocktail at the swanky Campbell Apartment.

Midtown: Bryant Park and the New York Public Library

By the time you hit 5th Avenue, you'll be staring at the lions that guard the New York Public Library (⊠ *455 5th Ave.*). Built in 1911, the structure is a hub of learning and hosts many lecture series throughout the year. It's abutted by Bryant Park, which offers free Wi-Fi, ice-skating in the winter, and films in the summer. The library, too, was brought back from the dead during New York's darkest days. There's also the renovated Nat Sherman store (⊠ *12 E. 42nd St.*), which even has a room for smokers to sample their wares.

The West Side: The Heart of Times Square

Keep walking west and you'll hit the razzle and dazzle of Times Square. It's better than it's ever been. No, not from Guiliani's cleanup—those seedy days are long since past, and Disney predominates—but thanks to a series of pedestrian-friendly improvements, including the closure of some seats to traffic and the addition of lawn chairs, making it easier to navigate. Be sure to note the futuristic-looking 4 Times Square, where Anna Wintour of *Vogue* dictates the world of style from on high, and the kid-friendly confines of Madame Tussaud's (⊠ *234 W. 42nd St.*). Finish off by seeing the lights of Broadway from the many theaters on this stretch between 8th and 9th avenues.

1

Where to Start:	United Nations, especially for those who are architecturally inclined
Length:	1½ mi (two hours)
Where to Stop:	Grand Central, Bryant Park
Best Time to Go:	Early afternoons; weekends
Worst Time to Go:	Weekday evenings, when the after-work crush is at its peak
Highlights:	Grand Central, Chrysler Building, New York Public Library

NYC'S WATERFRONT PARKS

If Central Park makes you think, "been there, done that" head to one of the several waterfront parks to get your greenery. Many New Yorkers are just discovering some of these green getaways, too.

The Hudson River Park

This 5-mile greenway park hugs the Hudson River from 59th Street to Battery Park. Although the park has a unified design, it's divided into seven distinct sections that reflect the different neighborhoods just across the West Side Highway. Along with refurbished piers with grass and trees, there are also attractions like the *Intrepid* Sea, Air, and Space Museum at Pier 86 across from 46th Street. A few blocks south, the Circle Line and World Yacht offer boat tours of the Hudson. At piers 96 and 40, the Downtown Boat House (⊕ *www.downtownboathouse.org*) offers free kayaking. There's a mammoth sports center, Chelsea Piers, between piers 59 and 61, and a mini golf course and beach volleyball court at Pier 25. The park also sponsors free tours and classes, including free fishing. For a calendar of events and activities, go to ⊕ *www. hudsonriverpark.org*. North of Hudson River Park is one of Manhattan's more well-known parks, **Riverside Park**. *For more information see Chapter 12: Upper West Side.*

Getting Here Hudson River Park is on the far west side of the city, adjacent to the West Side Highway. Crosstown buses at 14th, 23rd, and 42nd will get you close, but you'll still have to walk a bit. It's worth it.

Governors Island

A recent addition to the city's parks scene, this little island feels like a small town just 800 yards from the tip of Manhattan. Tourists love the unparalleled views of the harbor and Lower Manhattan, and locals love the out-of-the-city experience. The 172-acre park, built in part from landfill from subway excavations, was a base for the U.S. Army and Coast Guard for almost two centuries. Until 2003, it was off-limits to the public, which could be why the 19th-century homes here are so well preserved. The island is open to the public from May to October, with weekend programs, including art showings, concerts, and family programs. Bikers can take a bike over on the ferry or rent one on the island. For more information, including updated ferry schedules and a calendar of activities, go to ⊕ *www. govisland.org*.

Getting Here A free seven-minute ferry ride takes passengers to Governors Island from a dock at 10 South St., next to the Staten Island Ferry. Get to the ferry by subway: 1 to South Ferry Station; 4, 5 to Bowling Green; or R, W to Whitehall St. Station. By bus: M1 (weekdays only), M6, M9, and M15.

The High Line

Once an elevated railroad track that serviced the long-ago factories along the lower west side, the High Line was converted into a park (really more of a promenade) that integrates landscaping with rail-inspired design and provides a fresh perspective on the city. Vegetation here includes 210 species of plants, trees, and shrubs intended to reflect the wild plants that flourished for decades after the tracks were abandoned in 1980. The park—30 feet above street level—is open between

Gansevoort Street in the Meatpacking District to 30th Street, with another section extending up to 34th Street expected to open in spring 2012. Sweeping views of the Hudson River and an extended sight line of the Meatpacking District are the highlights. For information on tours, public programs, and a calendar of events, go to ⊕ www.*thehighline*.org or call 212/500–6035.

Getting Here The High Line is accessible at Gansevoort and every two blocks between 14th and 30th streets with elevator access at 14th, 16th, 23rd, and 30th streets (no bikes allowed). It's two blocks west of the subway station at 14th Street and 8th Avenue, served by the L/A/C/E. You can also take the C/E to 23rd Street and walk two blocks west. The 1/2/3 stops at 14th Street and 7th Avenue, three blocks away. By bus: M11 to Washington Street, M11 to 9th Avenue, M14 to 9th Avenue, M23 to 10th Avenue, M34 to 10th Avenue.

Battery Park City

Built over on landfill jutting out into the Hudson River, Battery Park City is a high-rise residential neighborhood split in two by the World Financial Center and its marina. The Hudson River Park promenade borders BPC along the West Side Highway. In South Battery Park City, you'll pass by the Museum of Jewish Heritage, at 36 Battery Place. Nearby are several reasonably priced outdoor restaurants with stunning views of the Statue of Liberty. There is some interesting public art scattered throughout BPS, too.

Getting Here By subway: South Battery Park: 1, R to Rector Place; 4, 5 to Wall Street. North Battery Park: 1, 2, 3, A, C to Chambers Street; E to World Trade Center. By bus: M9, M20, M22.

The East River State Park

Stretching along the East River in the Williamsburg neighborhood of Brooklyn, this seven-acre-park has stunning views of the Manhattan skyline. Locals come here to fly kites, picnic, take in the expansive waterfront views, shop the Brooklyn Flea next door, eat at Smorgasburg (Brooklyn's food market), and attend free and ticketed concerts. Skip the subway and arrive via the East River Ferry to really make a day of it. Check ⊕ www.nywaterway.com for schedule and stop information.

Getting Here By subway: L to Bedford Ave. and walk toward the water to Kent Avenue; East River Ferry to North Williamsburg stop.

The East River Park

This recently landscaped waterfront park, stretching from Montgomery Street to 12th Street along the East River, is one of the Lower East Side's best-kept secrets, with ball fields, bike paths, tennis courts, playgrounds, gardens, and picnic areas—along with impressive views of the Brooklyn skyline and Williamsburg Bridge. Either way, it's a cool spot to chill by the river. You have to cross a footbridge over the FDR to get to the park.

Getting Here By subway: J, M, Z to Essex St.; F to 2nd Ave.

SIGHTSEEING NEW YORK CITY

Sometimes a guided tour is a good idea, even if you prefer flying solo. They can be a great way to investigate out-of-the-way areas, or learn about interesting aspects of the city's history, inhabitants, or architecture. In addition to the listings below, these are some other highly recommended tours to keep in mind: Foraging with Steve Brill, ☎ 914/835–2153 ⊕ *www.wildmanstevebrill.com*. On Location Tours, ☎212/209–3370 ⊕ *www. screentours.com*. Ghosts of NY, ☎718/ 591–4741 ⊕ *www.ghostsofny.com*. NYC Photo Tour with Citifari, ☎262/726–1201 ⊕ *www.citifari.com*. A Slice of Brooklyn Pizza tour, ☎212/209–3370 ⊕ *www.asliceofbrooklyn.com*.

Boat Tours

Circle Line Sightseeing Cruise. A Circle Line Sightseeing Cruise around Manhattan is one of the best ways to get oriented in the city. Three-hour, $38 cruises run at least once daily; the two-hour "semi-Circle" is $34. ⊠ *Pier 83 at W. 42nd St., Midtown West* ☎212/563–3200 ⊕ *www. circleline42.com* .

Manhattan By Sail. Manhattan By Sail has an 82-foot yacht dating from the 1920s that makes daily 90-minute public sails and Sunday-brunch sails from mid-April through mid-October. There are two-hour sunset sails in June, July, and August. Fares start at $45. ⊠ *North Cove Marina at World Financial Center, Lower Manhattan* ☎212/619–0907 ⊕ *www. shearwatersailing.com*.

Bus Tours

Gray Line New York Sightseeing. Gray Line runs various "hop-on, hop-off" double-decker bus tours, including a downtown Manhattan loop, an upper Manhattan loop, a Brooklyn loop, and evening tours of the city. Packages include entrance fees to attractions. ⊠ *777 8th Ave., between 46th and 47th Sts., Midtown West* ☎800/669–0051 ⊕ *www. graylinenewyork.com*.

Walking Tours

Big Onion Walking Tours. The wisecracking, PhD candidates of Big Onion Walking Tours lead themed tours such as "Irish New York" and "Jewish Lower East Side," as well as famous multiethnic eating tours and guided walks through every neighborhood from Harlem to the Financial District and Brooklyn. Tours run daily and cost $18. ☎888/606–9266 ⊕ *www.bigonion.com*.

The Municipal Art Society of New York. The Municipal Art Society of New York conducts walking tours that emphasize the architecture and history of particular neighborhoods. The cost is $20 per person. MAS also runs a tour of Grand Central Station every Wednesday, from 12:30–2, with a $10 suggested donation. ⊠ *111 W. 57th St.* ☎212/935–3960, 212/935–3960 *recorded information* ⊕ *www.mas.org*.

New York City Cultural Walking Tours. Alfred Pommer's walking tours have covered such topics as buildings' gargoyles and the Millionaire's Mile of 5th Avenue. Two-hour public tours run some Sundays from March to December, and are $15 per person (no reservations needed. ☎212/979–2388 ⊕ *www.nycwalk.com*.

New York Food Tours. Options from the New York Food walking tours include "The Freakiest and Funniest Food" and a "Tastes of Chinatown" tour. Prices start at $49 for 2½ hours' worth of walking and noshing. ☎347/559–0111 ⊕ *www. foodtoursofny.com*.

GATEWAY TO THE NEW WORLD

A quintessential part of a visit to New York, a trip to the Statue of Liberty and Ellis Island takes up the better part of a day. It involves a ferry ride, long lines, security checks, and ultimately, the rare opportunity to stand within the single most powerful symbol of American ideals, not to mention one of the world's great monumental sculptures. It's worth the effort. It's no overstatement to say that these two sights have played defining roles in American culture.

THE STATUE OF LIBERTY

Impressive from the shore, the Statue of Liberty is even more majestic up close. For millions of immigrants, the first glimpse of America was Lady Liberty, growing from a vaguely defined figure on the horizon into a towering, stately colossus. Visitors approaching Liberty Island on the ferry from Battery Park may experience a similar sense of wonder as they approach.

What's Here

The statue itself stands atop an 89-foot pedestal designed by American Richard Morris Hunt, with Emma Lazarus's sonnet "The New Colossus" ("Give me your tired, your poor, your huddled masses yearning to breathe free . . ."). This massive pedestal section and all interiors of the statue, including the museum and crown, as well as the fort that is the foundation of the statue, were closed to the public in October 2011 for a year-long renovation to improve visitor access. Even while the statue is closed it's worth visiting Liberty Island to walk around the statue, take photos in front of it, and check out the views of lower Manhattan.

Inside the pedestal is an informative and entertaining museum. Highlights include the torch's original glass flame that was replaced because of water damage (the current flame is 24-karat gold and lit at night by floodlights), full-scale copper replicas of Lady Liberty's face and one of her feet, Bartholdi's alternative designs for the statue, and a model of Eiffel's intricate framework.

The observatory platform is a great place for a photo op; you're 16 stories high with all of Lower Manhattan spread out in front of you. You'll then descend to the promenade at the bottom of the base, where you're still four stories high. Be aware that to reach the platform you'll need to walk up 26 steps from the elevator drop-off point.

Liberty Island has a pleasant outdoor café.

Know Before You Go

You're allowed access to the museum only as part of one of the free tours of the promenade (which surrounds the base of the pedestal) or the observatory (at the pedestal's top). The tours are limited to 3,000 participants a day. To guarantee a spot on one of the tours, you must order tickets ahead of time—they can be reserved up to one year in advance, by phone or over the Internet. There are a limited amount of same-day standby tickets available at the Castle Clinton and Liberty State Park ticket offices, where you catch the ferry.

Once you reach the island, there are no tickets available. And without a ticket, there is absolutely no admittance into the museum or observatory. You can get a good look at the statue's inner structure on the observatory tour through glass viewing windows that look straight into the statue. Be sure to try the view from several different viewing spots to get the whole interior. There has been no access to the torch since 1916, however the park service now offers limited access to the statue's crown.

Liberty Highlights

■ The surreal chance to stand next to, and be dwarfed by, the original glass torch and the copper cast of Lady Liberty's foot.

■ The vistas of New York from the observatory platform.

■ The rare opportunity to look up the skirt of a national monument.

Statue Basics

☎ 212/363–3200;
877/523-9849 ticket
reservations

⊕ www.statueofliberty.org

🎫 Free; ferry $13.00
round-trip (includes Ellis
Island); crown tickets $3

🕙 Daily 9:30 AM–5:00;
extended hours in
summer.

Liberty helicopters

ALTERNATIVE VIEWS

■ The free Staten Island Ferry offers a great view of New York Harbor and of the Statue of Liberty from a distance (see Chapter 2).
■ Webcams placed around the statue's torch allow you to see what Lady Liberty sees—wide views of the New York City skyline, the Hudson River, and ships in the harbor—from your computer or phone.
■ Liberty Helicopters has sightseeing tours that fly over the crown and torch (see Chapter 1).

FAST FACT: To move the Statue of Liberty from its initial home on a Paris rooftop to its final home in the New York Harbor, the statue was broken down into 350 individual pieces and packed in 214 crates. It took four months to reassemble it.

FAST FACT: The face of Lady Liberty is actually a likeness of sculptor Frederic-Auguste Bartholdi's mother—quite a tribute.

FAST FACT: *Liberty Enlightening the World*, as the statue is officially named, was presented to the United States in 1886 as a gift from France to celebrate the centennial of the United States, a symbol of unity and friendship between the two countries. The 152-foot-tall figure was sculpted by Frederic-Auguste Bartholdi and erected around an iron skeleton engineered by Gustav Eiffel (the same Eiffel who would later create the Eiffel Tower).

Foundation of the pedestal to torch: 305'6"

Heel to top head: 111'6"

ELLIS ISLAND

Chances are you'll be with a crowd of international tourists as you disembark at Ellis Island. Close your eyes for a moment and imagine the jostling crowd 100 times larger. Now imagine that your journey has lasted weeks at sea and that your daypack contains all your worldly possessions, including all your money. You're hungry, tired, jobless, and homeless. This scenario just begins to set the stage for the story of the millions of poor immigrants who passed through Ellis Island at the turn of the 20th century. Between 1892 and 1924, approximately 12 million men, women, and children first set foot on U.S. soil at the Ellis Island federal immigration facility. By the time the facility closed in 1954, it had processed the ancestors of more than 40% of Americans living today.

WHAT'S HERE

The island's main building, now a national monument, reopened in 1990 as the Ellis Island Immigration Museum, with more than 30 galleries of artifacts, photographs, and taped oral histories. The centerpiece of the museum is the Registry Room (also known as the Great Hall). It feels dignified and cavernous today, but photographs show that it took on many configurations over the years, always packed with humanity. While you're there, look out the Registry Room's tall, arched windows and try to imagine what passed through immigrants' minds as they viewed lower Manhattan's skyline to one side and the Statue of Liberty to the other.

Along with the Registry Room, the museum includes the ground-level **Peopling of America Center**, a major expansion that explores immigration to the United States before and after Ellis Island was a portal for immigrants. Graphics and poignant audio stories give firsthand accounts of the immigrants' journeys—from making the trip and arriving in the United States to their struggle and survival here. There is also the **American Family Immigration Center**, where you can search Ellis Island's records for your own ancestors; the **American Flag of Faces**, an interactive display filled with images of immigrants submitted online (submit yours at *FlagofFaces*.org). Outside, the **American Immigrant Wall of Honor**, which has the names of more than 600,000 immigrant Americans against the Manhattan skyline.

MAKING THE MOST OF YOUR VISIT

Because there's so much to take in, it's a good idea to make use of the museum's interpretive tools. Check at the visitor desk for free film tickets, ranger tour times, and special programs.

Consider starting your visit with a viewing of the free film *Island of Hope, Island of Tears*. A park ranger starts off with a short introduction, then the 25-minute film takes you through an immigrant's journey from the troubled conditions of European life (especially true for ethnic and religious minorities), to their nervous arrival at Ellis Island, and their introduction into American cities. The film is a primer into all the exhibits and will deeply enhance your experience.

The audio tour ($8) is also worthwhile: it takes you through the exhibits, providing thorough, engaging commentary interspersed with recordings of immigrants themselves recalling their experiences.

ELLIS ISLAND HIGHLIGHTS

- Surveying the Great Hall.

- The moving film *Island of Hope, Island of Tears*.

- Exploring the Peopling of America Center to gain a deeper understanding of the history of immigration in America.

- Reading the names on the American Immigrant Wall of Honor.

- Researching your own family's history.

Ellis Island Basics

☎ 212/363–3200 Ellis
Island; 212/561–4500
Wall of Honor
information

🌐 www.ellisisland.org

🚢 Free; ferry $13.00
round-trip (includes
Liberty Island)

🕑 Daily 9:30–5:00;
extended in summer.

IMMIGRANT HISTORY TIMELINE

Starting in the 1880s, troubled conditions throughout
Europe persuaded both the
poor and the persecuted to
leave their family and homes
to embark on what were
often gruesome journeys to
come to the golden shores
of America.

1880s 5.7 million immigrants arrive in U.S.

1892 Federal immigration
station opens on Ellis
Island in January.

1901–1910 8.8 million
immigrants arrive in U.S.;
6 million processed at
Ellis Island.

1907 Highest number of
immigrants (860,000) arrives
in one year, including a
record 11,747 on April 17.

1910 75% of the residents
of New York, Chicago, De-
troit, Cleveland, and Boston are now immigrants or
children of immigrants.

1920s Federal laws set
immigration quotas based
on national origin.

1954 Ellis Island immigration station is closed.

New arrivals line up to have their eyes inspected.

FAST FACT: Some immigrants who passed through
Ellis Island later became household names. A few
include Charles Atlas (1903, Italy); Irving Berlin (1893,
Russia); Frank Capra (1903, Italy); Bob Hope (1908,
England); Knute Rockne (1893, Norway); and Baron Von
Trapp and his family (1938, Germany).

FAST FACT: In
1897, a fire destroyed
the original pine im-
migration structure on
Ellis Island, including
all immigration records
dating back to 1855.

FAST FACT: The first
test that immigrants
had to pass was known
as the "six-second
medical exam." As they
entered the Great Hall,
they were watched
by doctors; if anyone
seemed disabed, their
clothing was marked
with chalk and
they were sent for
a full exam.

Four immigrants and
their belongings, on a
dock, look out over
the water; view from
behind.

PLANNING

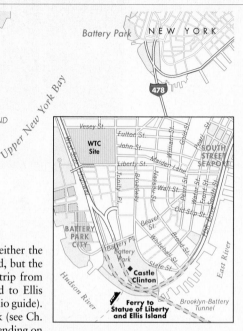

ADMISSION

There is no admission fee for either the Statue of Liberty or Ellis Island, but the ferry ride (which goes round-trip from Battery Park to Liberty Island to Ellis Island) costs $13 ($21 with audio guide). Ferries leave from Battery Park (see Ch. 2) every 30 to 40 minutes, depending on the time of year. There are often long lines, so arrive early, especially if you have a reserved-time ticket. (Oversize bags and backpacks aren't permitted on board.) Reserve tickets online—you'll still have to wait in line, both to pick up the tickets and to board the ferry, but you'll be able to pick up a Monument Pass for access to the pedestal, the museum, and the statue's interior. There is no fee for the Monument Pass, but you cannot enter the statue without it.

WHERE TO CATCH THE FERRY

Broadway and Battery Pl., Lower Manhattan Ⓜ Subway: 4, 5 to Bowling Green.

PLANNING TIPS

Buy tickets in advance. This is the only way to assure that you'll have tickets to actually enter the Statue of Liberty museum and observatory platform.

Be prepared for intense security. At the ferry security check, you will need to remove your coat; at the statue, you will need to remove your coat as well as your belt, watch, and any metal accessories. At this writing, no strollers, large umbrellas, or backpacks are allowed in the statue.

Check ferry schedules in advance. Before you go, check www.statuecruises.com.

Keep in mind that even though the last entry time for the monument is at 4:30 PM, **the last ferry to the Statue of Liberty and Ellis Island is at 3:30 PM.** You need to arrive by at least 3 PM (to allow for security checks and lines) if you want to make the last ferry of the day.

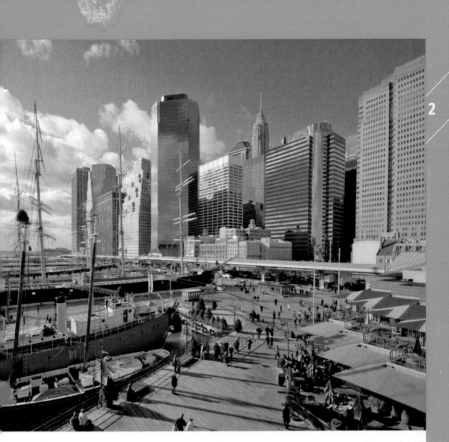

2

Lower Manhattan

WITH THE FINANCIAL DISTRICT, NEW YORK HARBOR, AND TRIBECA

WORD OF MOUTH

"The Staten Island Ferry is free and if you stand on the right side going out and the left on the return, you will have excellent views of the Statue . . . if your schedule permits you should go after dark and watch the lights of Manhattan grow as you approach."

—Aduchamp1

GETTING ORIENTED

MAKING THE MOST OF YOUR TIME

Visit the Financial District during the weekend and you might feel like a lone explorer in a canyon of buildings, and even weeknights the neighborhood largely shuts down after about 6. Weekdays, however, the sidewalks bustle so much that you can expect to be jostled if you stand still too long. End your visit by watching the sunset over the Hudson River.

The sights of the New York Harbor are some of the most quintessential of New York, but be prepared for long lines for Ellis Island and the Statue of Liberty, especially on the weekends. TriBeCa is one of the quieter neighborhoods in Manhattan, being mostly residential. There are some pleasant shops and restaurants but the neighborhood tends not to be a tourist attraction, unless the film festival is going on.

COFFEE, COCKTAILS, AND QUICK BITES

Adrienne's (⊠ *54 Stone St.*). Many say the thin-crust pizza at this sit-down restaurant is the best in the city—there are no slices.

Bean & Bean (⊠ *71 Broadway*). Stop by for excellent organic, fair trade coffee.

Brandy Library (⊠ *25 North Moore St.*). This upscale bar is an excellent spot for an after-dinner or pre-dinner cocktail.

Church Lounge (⊠ *2 6th Ave., near White St.*). Attracts a celeb crowd with 30-plus signature cocktails.

La Colombe Torrefaction (⊠ *319 Church St.*). For excellent espresso drinks and impressive latte art, check out this loft-like space just below Canal St.

TOP EXPERIENCES

Visiting Ground Zero.

Riding the Staten Island Ferry.

Touring Ellis Island and the Statue of Liberty.

Snapping a photo in front of Wall Street's bull.

Strolling along the Hudson in Hudson River Park.

BEST FOR KIDS

Castle Clinton and Battery Park

South Street Seaport Museum

GETTING HERE

Many subway lines connect to the Financial District. The Fulton Street station is serviced by eight different subway lines (A, C, J, Z, 2, 3, 4, 5) and puts you within walking distance of City Hall, South Street Seaport, and the World Trade Center site (⇨ *Ground Zero feature in this chapter*). To get to the Brooklyn Bridge, take the 4, 5, or 6 to Brooklyn Bridge City Hall.

For sights around the New York Harbor, take the 1 to South Ferry, the R to Whitehall, or the 4 or 5 to Bowling Green. The 1 subway line stops in the heart of TriBeCa (Franklin Street).

Sightseeing ★★★★★	Lower Manhattan, or in the parlance of New Yorkers emphatically giving directions to tourists, "all the way downtown," has long been where the action—and transaction—is. Originally the trading post called New Amsterdam (1626–47), it later became the focal point of immigration from all over the world.
Nightlife ★★	
Dining ★★★★	
Lodging ★★	
Shopping ★★	

FINANCIAL DISTRICT AND SOUTH STREET SEAPORT

Updated by
Arthur Bovino

Little from Manhattan's colonial era is left in lower Manhattan: apart from a precious few structures built in the 1700s, the 19th-century brick facades of South Street Seaport are about as old as it gets here. As you'll notice immediately, the Financial District has largely given way to the sometimes intimidating (and on weekends, seemingly deserted) skyscraper-lined canyons of Wall Street and lower Broadway. Bounded by the East and Hudson rivers to the east and west, respectively, and by Chambers Street and Battery Park to the north and south, the Financial District is an area you can fully and best appreciate by walking its streets.

You'll want to see what's here, but above all you'll want to see what's not, most notably in that empty but evolving gulf among skyscrapers: the World Trade Center site, known as Ground Zero.

TOP ATTRACTIONS

Battery Park. Jutting out at the southernmost point of Manhattan, tree-filled Battery Park is a respite from the narrow, winding, and (on weekdays) jam-packed streets of the Financial District. Even if you don't plan to stay for long, carve out a couple minutes of sightseeing time to sit on a bench and take in the view, which includes the Statue of Liberty and Ellis Island. On clear days you can see all the way to Port Elizabeth's cranes, which seem to mimic Lady Liberty's stance; to Governors Island, a former Coast Guard installation now managed by the National

Park Service; a hilly Staten Island in the distance; the Statue of Liberty; Ellis Island; and the old railway terminal in Liberty State Park, on the mainland in Jersey City, New Jersey. Of course, looking away from the water and toward the buildings, there's a feeling that you're at the beginning of the city, and a sense of all the possibility it possesses just a few blocks in.

The park's main structure is **Castle Clinton National Monument,** the ticket office site and takeoff point for ferries to the Statue of Liberty and Ellis Island. This monument was once 200 feet off the southern tip of the island located in what was

> ### BROOKLYN BRIDGE FACTS
>
> ■ Overall length: 6,016 feet
>
> ■ Span of twin Gothic-arch towers: 1,595½ feet
>
> ■ Distance from top of towers to East River: 272 feet
>
> ■ Distance from roadway to the water: 133 feet
>
> ■ Number of times the line "If you believe that, I've got a bridge to sell you" is used referring to the Brooklyn Bridge: Infinite

called the Southwest Battery, and was erected during the War of 1812 to defend the city. (The East Battery sits across the harbor on Governors Island.) As dirt and debris from construction were dumped into the harbor, the island expanded, eventually engulfing the landmark. Later, from 1855 to 1890, it served as America's first official immigration center (Ellis Island opened in 1892).

Inside Battery Park are several monuments and statues, including *The Sphere,* which used to stand on the plaza at the World Trade Center as a symbol of peace. It's damaged but still intact after the collapse of the towers. The southern link in a chain of parks connecting Battery Park north to Chambers Street, Robert F. Wagner Jr. Park has a tidy lawn and wide benches from which to view the harbor. A brick structure at the southeast section of Battery Parks has public bathrooms and a restaurant. ⊠ *Battery Park* ☎ *212/417–2000* ⊕ *www.batteryparkcity.org/ page/index_battery.html* Ⓜ *4, 5 to Bowling Green.*

Fodor's Choice ★ **Brooklyn Bridge.** "A drive-through cathedral" is how the journalist James Wolcott described the Brooklyn Bridge, one of New York's noblest and most recognized landmarks, perhaps outdoing Walt Whitman's comment that it was "The best, most effective medicine my soul has yet partaken." The bridge stretches over the East River, connecting Manhattan and Brooklyn. A walk across its promenade—a boardwalk elevated above a roadway, shared by pedestrians, in-line skaters, and cyclists—takes about 40 minutes and is more than worth it for the exhilarating views; if you start from downtown Manhattan, you'll end up in the heart of Brooklyn Heights. It's worth noting that on the weekends when the weather is nice, the path can get pretty congested; it's most magical, and quietest, early in the morning. ⊠ *East River Dr., Lower Manhattan* Ⓜ *4, 5, 6 to Brooklyn Bridge/City Hall; J, Z to Chambers St.; A, C to High St.–Brooklyn Bridge.*

New York Stock Exchange (NYSE). Unfortunately you can't tour it, but it's certainly worth ogling. At the intersection of Wall and Broad streets, the exchange is impossible to miss. The neoclassical building, designed by architect George B. Post, opened on April 22, 1903. It has six Corinthian columns supporting a pediment with a sculpture titled *Integrity Protecting the Works of Man,* featuring a tribute to the then-sources of American prosperity: Agriculture and Mining to the left of Integrity; Science, Industry, and Invention to the right. The Exchange was one of the world's first air-conditioned buildings. ⊠ *11 Wall St., Financial District* ☎ *866/368–3375* ⊕ *www.nyse.com/* Ⓜ *1, 4, 5, N, R to Rector; 2, 3 to Wall St.; J, Z to Broad St.*

Ground Zero. *See highlighted feature in this chapter.*

South Street Seaport Historic District. Had this charming cobblestone corner of the city not been declared a historic district in 1977, the city's largest concentration of early-19th-century commercial buildings would have been destroyed. Today, the area is largely mobbed with tourists, and if you've been to Boston's Quincy Market or Baltimore's Harborplace, you may feel a flash of déjà vu—the same company leased, restored, and adapted the existing buildings, with the result being the blend of a quasi-authentic historic district with a slightly homogenous shopping mall.

At the intersection of Fulton and Water streets, the gateway to the seaport, is the **Titanic Memorial,** a small white lighthouse that commemorates the sinking of the RMS *Titanic* in 1912. Beyond the lighthouse, Fulton Street turns into a busy pedestrian mall. On the south side of Fulton is the seaport's architectural centerpiece, **Schermerhorn Row,** a redbrick terrace of Georgian- and Federal-style warehouses and countinghouses built from 1811 to 1812. Some upper floors house gallery space, and the ground floors are occupied by shops, bars, and restaurants. Cross South Street, once known as the Street of Ships, under an elevated stretch of FDR Drive to **Pier 16,** where historic ships are docked, including the *Pioneer,* a 102-foot schooner built in 1885; the *Peking,* the second-largest sailing bark in existence; the iron-hulled *Wavertree*; and the lightship *Ambrose.* The Pier 16 ticket booth provides information and sells tickets to the museum, ships, tours, and exhibits. Pier 16 is the departure point for various seasonal cruises.

To the north is **Pier 17,** a multilevel dockside shopping mall filled mostly with national chain retailers. The weathered-wood decks at the rear of the pier are a choice spot from which to catch sight of the river, with views as far north as Midtown Manhattan and as far south as the Verrazano-Narrows Bridge. Pier 17 used to be the home of the Fulton Fish Market, which first opened in South Manhattan in 1807; starting in 1939 it was housed in the New Market Building, just north of the Seaport, but that closed in 2005 when operations were moved to a new 400,000-square-foot facility in Hunt's Point in the Bronx.

South Street Seaport Museum. At 12 Fulton Street is the main lobby of the South Street Seaport Museum, which hosts exhibits, walking tours, a fleet of eight historic vessels, and fantastic educational programs for children—all with a nautical theme. Recent shows in the museum's 16 exhibition galleries included *Timescapes,* a 22-minute history of New York, a photo exhibit of the Occupy Wall Street movement, and reflections of the former life of the South Street Seaport. ⊠ *12 Fulton*

St., between Water and South Sts., South Street Seaport ☎ *212/748–8600* ⊕ *www.southstreetseaportmuseum.org* ⊠ *$5* ☉ *Wed.–Sun. 10–6* ⊠ *South Street Seaport, South Street Seaport* ☎ *212/732–8257 events and shopping information* ⊕ *www.southstreetseaport.com* Ⓜ *2, 3, 4, 5, A, C, J, Z to Fulton St./Broadway-Nassau.*

Stone Street Historic District. Nestled amid skyscrapers and the towering New York Stock Exchange, the two-block long oasis of bars and restaurants along Stone Street feels more like a village than the center of the financial universe. In summer, the tables spill out into the cobblestone street and the mood is convivial—especially on Thursday nights. This was Manhattan's first paved street and today the cluster of historic buildings along here, with South William and Pearl streets, and Coenties Alley, make up the Stone Street Historic District. ⊠ *Financial District.*

WORTH NOTING

Bowling Green. Perhaps most recognized now as the home of Arturo Di Modica's 7,000-pound bronze *Charging Bull* (1989) statue, Bowling Green, at the foot of Broadway, became New York's first public park in 1733. Legend has it that before that, this was the sight where Peter Minuit purchased the island of Manhattan from the Native Americans, in 1626, supposedly for what amounted to 24 U.S. dollars. On July 9, 1776, a few hours after citizens learned about the signing of the Declaration of Independence, rioters toppled a statue of British king George III that had occupied the spot for 11 years; much of the statue's lead was melted down into bullets. In 1783, when the occupying British forces fled the city, they defiantly hoisted a Union Jack on a greased, uncleated flagpole so it couldn't be lowered; patriot John Van Arsdale drove his own cleats into the pole to replace the flag with the Stars and Stripes. The copper-top subway entrance here is the original one, built in 1904–05. ⊠ *Broadway at Whitehall St., Lower Manhattan* Ⓜ *4, 5 to Bowling Green.*

City Hall. Walking by, you might spot news crews jockeying on the front steps as they attempt to interview city officials, which is perhaps all you want to know about City Hall. But if the history of local politics is your thing, free tours of the hall are available. Among the highlights within are the Victorian-style **City Council Chamber;** the Rotunda where President Lincoln lay in state in 1865 under a soaring dome supported by 10 Corinthian columns; and the **Governor's Room,** which includes a writing table that George Washington used in 1789 when New York was the U.S. capital. Snap a photo of the austere columned exterior. Take a moment to enjoy the small but lovely City Hall Park, bounded by Broadway to the west and Chambers Street to the north. The layers of history buried under the city's compulsion to reinvent itself were revealed in portions of the northern part of the park in 1991, when an African burial ground was uncovered during construction of a federal office building nearby. It has since been declared a city landmark. Aside from historical interest, though, the park is also just a pleasant, underrated place to stop and take a breath. Enjoy the impressive fountain, and watch government workers and jury members taking a break from their day. ⊠ *City Hall Park, Lower Manhattan* ☎ *212/788-2656*

Continued on page 52

A GLIMPSE OF THE FUTURE WORLD TRADE CENTER

An illuminated antenna will reach to 1,776 feet to commemorate America's founding.

Tower 1
Designed by David Childs. At a height of 1,776 feet (and 105 stories) it will be the tallest building in the United States. Tentative finish: 2013.

Tower 2
Designed by Norman Foster. Ground was broken in 2010. Tentative finish: 2015.

Tower 3
Designed by Richard Rogers. Ground was broken in 2010; delays and a difficult economy may alter its finish date (currently 2015) and drastically shorten its final height (planned at 80 stories).

7 World Trade Center
Designed by David Childs. Opened in 2006. Across the street from Ground Zero.

Transportation Hub
Designed by Santiago Calatrava. Tentative finish date: 2014.

Performing Arts Center
Funding still to be worked out. To be designed by Frank Gehry.

9/11 Museum
Tentative finish: 2012. Street-level pavilion by Snøhetta; designed by Aedas.

Tower 4
Designed by Fumihiko Maki. To be 71 stories tall when it's complete in late 2013.

National September 11 Memorial
Entitled *Reflecting Absence*. Designed by Michael Arad and Peter Walker. Opened on 9/11/11.

GROUND ZERO
THE WORLD TRADE CENTER SITE

A decade after September 11, 2001, the 9/11 Memorial opened, giving Ground Zero's thousands of annual visitors a solemn place to reflect and think about that brutal day. Its accompanying underground museum, set to open in late 2012 on the same bedrock once used by the Twin Towers' foundation, will be a fitting place to display artifacts from 9/11 and its aftermath. As you plan your visit, set aside time to visit other key parts of the story, such as St. Paul's Chapel and the "Ten House" firehouse on Liberty Street.

(above) President Obama, Michelle Obama, former President George W. Bush, and Laura Bush at the National 9/11 Memorial. (below) Names on the 9/11 Memorial; (opposite) Rendition of the future WTC site.

THE TOWERS

The World Trade Towers, each 110 stories tall, were an impressive feat of engineering. Construction began in 1968, and the Twin Towers officially opened in 1973. Avoiding the typical construction used at the time, the architects gave each building an exterior skeleton made up of 244 slim steel columns and an inner "core" tube that supported the weight of the tower.

Approximately 50,000 people worked in the north tower (1 World Trade Center) and south tower (2 World Trade Center), and another 40,000 people visited the 16-acre complex every day. Beneath the towers was a multi-level mall with nearly 100 stores and restaurants.

The Twin Towers prior to 9/11

EVENTS OF THE DAY On September 11, 2001, terrorist hijackers steered two jets into the World Trade Center's Twin Towers, demolishing them and five outlying buildings.

- The first hijacked jet, American Airlines Flight 11, crashed into the north tower, 1 World Trade Center, at 8:46 AM, cutting through floors 93 to 99. The tower collapsed at 10:28 AM. Cantor Fitzgerald, a brokerage firm headquartered between the 101st and 105th floors, lost 658 of its 1,050 employees. At the Windows on the World restaurant (floors 106 and 107), 100 patrons and 72 staff members died.

- The second hijacked jet, United Airlines Flight 175, hit the south tower, 2 World Trade Center, at 9:03 AM, crashing through the 77th to 85th floors. The plane banked as it hit, so portions of the building remained undamaged on impact floors. Consequently, one stairwell initially remained passable from at least the 91st floor down. The tower collapsed at 9:58 AM.

- The attack killed 2,753 people. (Deaths are still being counted; the most recent casualty, Jerry J. Borg, died in late 2010 from pulmonary sarcoidosis, a lung disease caused by inhaling toxins from the dust cloud that formed when the towers collapsed.) The fenced-in 16-acre work site that emerged from the rubble, almost immediately dubbed Ground Zero, came to symbolize the personal, political, and historical impact of September 11.

(above) Towers burning after attack.

THE DAMAGE

Why *did* the towers fall? A three-year federal study revealed several reasons. The two airplanes used in the attack, both Boeing 767s, hit their respective towers at roughly 500 mph. They both damaged the exterior columns, destroying core supports for at least three of the north tower's floors and up to six of the south tower's floors. Ensuing fires, fed by tens of thousands of gallons of jet fuel, further weakened the buildings. The collapse of the most heavily damaged floors then triggered a domino effect, causing the towers to crumple at an estimated speed of about 125 mph.

Many other area buildings suffered collateral damage. The World Financial Center office complex, to the west of Ground Zero, has as its centerpiece the 10-story glass-domed Winter Garden. After having nearly all its glass blown out in the attacks, the atrium reopened in September 2002 after repairs that included the installation of 2,000 windows and 1.2 million pounds of stone.

The 47-story 7 World Trade Center, to the north of Ground Zero, was struck by large chunks of falling debris from the north and south towers. The building remained standing at first, but subsequent fires caused it to collapse later that afternoon. A new 52-story 7 World Trade Center opened in May 2006 with a much smaller footprint than its predecessor.

St. Paul's Chapel, across the street from Ground Zero, sustained no major dam-

age; staff there credit a huge sycamore that toppled over during the attack. Its gigantic root system, now above ground, helped to shield the building and the headstones in its attached cemetery from falling debris.

Although the New York Stock Exchange's building wasn't physically harmed during the attacks, the market remained closed for six days (including 9/11). When trading resumed on September 17, the Dow Jones industrial average dropped 684.81 points, or 7.13 percent. The American Stock Exchange (Amex), however, sustained some damage on 9/11, and for two weeks Amex stocks and exchange-traded funds were traded on the NYSE floor.

(above) A New York City fire fighter looks up at what remains of the World Trade Center after its collapse; a 9/11 memorial wreath; the "Tribute in Light" memorial on the fifth anniversary of 9/11.

A vision of the future Manhattan skyline

It may have taken longer than most observers could have imagined, but a new World Trade Center is now a reality, at least partially. Following the master plan laid down by the architect Daniel Libeskind, the footprints of the original towers have been made into pools, their rushing waterfalls part of a powerful memorial. The accompanying museum, to be seven stories underground at its deepest, is scheduled to open by the end of 2012. When all the work is finished—and there's still a great deal to do—the World Trade Center will include office buildings, a transit hub, and a performing arts center.

Future downtown skyline at dusk

NATIONAL SEPTEMBER 11 MEMORIAL

The architect Michael Arad, working in partnership with the landscape architect Peter Walker, won the international contest to design the memorial. It is entitled "Reflecting Absence," and it takes up about half of the 16-acre complex. It opened on the tenth anniversary of 9/11.

No buildings are in the space where the Twin Towers once stood. In their place are recessed waterfalls cascading thirty feet down into two subterranean reflecting pools that limn the Twin Towers' original footprints (each roughly an acre in size). The water then tumbles down into smaller square holes at the center of each pool. The effect manages to be both moving and solemn but not sentimental. In the words of Paul Goldberger, the *New Yorker's* architecture critic, "Arad figured out how to express the idea that what were once the largest solids in

Manhattan are now a void, and he made the shape of this void into something monumental."

Surrounding each waterfall on the plaza level is a low bronze wall with the names of the 2,887 victims of the 9/11 attacks (including those at the Pentagon and on flights 11, 77, 93, and 175), and the six people who died in the first World Trade Center bombing, in 1993. The names are sorted by affiliation, so that names lie etched near those of people they worked with or otherwise knew. Kiosks on the edge of the site help with finding out which panel holds a particular name or group (the information can also be found online, at *www.911memorial.org*, and through a smartphone app). Surrounding the waterfalls is a stark plaza punctuated with hundreds of swamp white-oak saplings, which some day will be 70 feet tall. Joining them is the so-called "survivor tree," a Callery pear tree that was plucked from the rubble, nursed back to

Construction as of December 2011.

Fumihiko Maki, Larry Silverstein, and Norman Foster

health elsewhere, and replanted on the site as a symbol of resilience.

Standing at an angle to the memorial's pools is the small center that will serve as the entrance to the memorial's accompanying museum, scheduled to open by the end of 2012. From here, visitors will walk down a ramp to the bedrock the towers were built on, 71 feet below. One exhibit will be the "last column," the last piece of steel to be removed from the site, which was covered with slogans and memorials from rescue crews and others.

ONE WORLD TRADE CENTER

Known for a time as the Freedom Tower, this 105-story skyscraper will have a roof that's 1,368 feet tall—identical to that of the taller of the Twin Towers. An illuminated antenna will further increase the building's height to 1,776 feet to commemorate America's founding (and make it the country's tallest building). Designed by David Childs of Skidmore, Owings & Merrill, the new 1 WTC is expected to be finished by late 2013. The three other office buildings on the site (all at various stages of construction) are each by a different prominent architect: Fumihiko Maki, Richard Rogers, and Norman Foster.

TRANSPORTATION HUB

Intended to connect New Jersey's PATH subway with 13 of New York's subway lines, this transportation hub was designed by the Spanish architect Santiago Calatrava. Inspired by the image of a child releasing a dove, the massive glass-roofed building is likely to be awe-inspiring once it's finished, but soaring costs and a complicated design mean that the tentative completion date of 2014 may be delayed.

For more information on the new structures, visit www.lowermanhattan.info and www.911memorial.org.

A GROUND ZERO WALK

Names on the 9/11 Memorial Wall.

This tour starts near the WTC Tribute Center, which runs its own well-regarded walking tours that include the memorial and other sites important to the history of 9/11. If you're just doing this walking tour, you can do it in any order.

1 One place to start your walk is at the corner of Liberty and Greenwich streets, just a short distance from where the World Trade Center's South Tower once stood. This is Ten House, a firehouse named for the number of its engine and ladder

Inspired by the giant sycamore that fell under the rubble and helped protect old headstones in St. Paul's graveyard, the *Trinity Root* sculpture, a 9/11 memorial pictured here, can be seen at Trinity Church

companies. On 9/11, the station was nearly destroyed, and six of its members lost their lives after responding to the disaster. The station's restored exterior is now covered with a 56-foot bronze bas-relief "dedicated to those who fell and to those who carry on." The Tribute WTC Visitor Center, a project of the September 11th Families' Association, is next-door. Its exhibits give a heartbreaking picture of the many lives lost on that day.

2 Head around the corner to the National 9/11 Memorial, which incorporates the footprints of the Twin Towers into two pools of water. If the 9/11 Museum has opened (it's expected to be by the end of 2012), then proceed there. Its 110,000 square feet, nearly all of them underground, take up the seven stories of space that were once occupied by the stores and parking garage under the original Twin Towers.

3 After you've finished paying your respects, head south to exit the memorial (the current exit, as of early 2012, leaves you near the corner of Albany and West streets), making a quick stop at the nearby 9/11 Memorial Visitor Center, at 90 West Street. From here, take the next left (onto Albany Street) and walk over to Trinity Place (which turns into Church Street),

The firefighters' memorial.

turn left (north) and continue until you reach the churchyard behind St. Paul's, the Episcopal chapel that became a dormitory, mess hall, and medical center in the months after 9/11. Even George Washington's pew was called back into service for the exhausted rescue workers. Across the street, at 20 Vesey Street, is the 9/11 Memorial Preview Site, which has models of what the entire World Trade Center will look like once it's completed. It also has a good selection of books and other items about 9/11 and its aftermath.

The Tribute WTC Visitor Center

VISITING THE MEMORIAL

There is airport-like security at the memorial, and no large bags are allowed, there's no bag storage, and there are no bathrooms. Entry is via free, timed tickets, available online; book ahead. Standby tickets are sometimes available at the site itself. Allow at least an hour to visit the memorial and museum, more at a busy times of the year.

VISITOR CENTERS

An **information booth** on Vesey Street, near the temporary PATH station, has maps of the area. The 9/11 Memorial Visitor Center (90 West St., 212/225-1009, www. national911memorial.org,) is open daily, 10–8:30, early Mar.–early Oct. and around Thanksgiving and Christmas; it's open 10–7 the rest of the year. The 9/11 Memorial Preview Site (20 Vesey St., 212/267-2047, free) is open daily, 10–7:30 early Mar.–early Oct. and around Thanksgiving and Christmas, and 10–7 other times. The **Tribute WTC Center** (120 Liberty St., 866/737-1184, www. tributewtc.org, $15) is open 10–6, Mon.–Sat., 10–5 on Sun.

TOURS

The Tribute WTC Center leads hour-long walking tours that include the National September 11 Memorial and nearby sites. The $20 cost ($5 if you've already paid to see the exhibits; keep your receipt) includes admission to the Tribute WTC Center exhibits. You don't need to book in advance. Booking a tour with the Tribute WTC Visitor Center saves you having to get your own timed ticket for the 9/11 memorial.

GETTING THERE

Subway: **1**, **N**, **R** to Rector St.; **2**,**3**,**4**,**5**,**A**,**C**,**J**,**Z** to Fulton St./ Broadway-Nassau; **E** to World Trade Center/Church St.

PATH: Any line to World Trade Center.

The Gangs of Five Points

In the mid-19th century the Five Points area was perhaps the city's most notorious and dangerous neighborhood. The confluence of five streets—Mulberry, Anthony (now Worth), Cross (now Park), Orange (now Baxter), and Little Water (no longer in existence)—had been built over a drainage pond that had been filled in the 1820s. When the buildings began to sink into the mosquito-filled muck, middle-class residents abandoned their homes. Buildings were chopped into tiny apartments that were rented to the poorest of the poor, who at this point were newly emancipated slaves and Irish immigrants fleeing famine.

Newspaper accounts at the time tell of robberies and other violent crimes on a daily basis. And with corrupt political leaders like William Marcy "Boss" Tweed more concerned with lining their pockets than patrolling the streets, keeping order was left to the club-wielding hooligans portrayed in *Gangs of New York*. But the neighborhood, finally razed in the 1880s to make way for Columbus Park, has left a lasting legacy. In the music halls where different ethnic groups grudgingly came together, the Irish jig and the African-American shuffle combined to form a new type of fancy footwork called tap dancing.

for tour reservations ⊕ www.nyc.gov/html/artcom/html/tours/city_hall. shtml ✉ Free ⊙ Tours available some weekdays; reserve online or by phone Ⓜ *2, 3 to Park Place; R to City Hall; 4, 5, 6 to Brooklyn Bridge/ City Hall; J, Z, A, C to Chambers St.*

Federal Reserve Bank of New York. With its imposing mix of sandstone, limestone, and ironwork, the Federal Reserve looks the way a bank ought to: strong and impregnable. The gold ingots in the subterranean vaults here are worth roughly $140 billion—reputedly a third of the world's gold reserves. Forty-five-minute-long tours (conducted six times a day and requiring reservations made at least five days in advance) include a visit to the gold vault, the trading desk, and "FedWorks," a multimedia exhibit center where you can track hypothetical trades. Visitors must show an officially issued photo ID, such as a driver's license or passport, and pass through scanning equipment to enter the building; the Fed advises showing up 20 minutes before your tour to accommodate security screening. Photography is not permitted. ⊠ *33 Liberty St., between William and Nassau Sts., Financial District* ☎ *212/720–6130* ⊕ *www.newyorkfed.org* ✉ *Free ⊙ Tour by advance reservation, weekdays 11:15–4* Ⓜ *A, C to Broadway-Nassau; J, Z, 2, 3, 4, 5 to Fulton St.*

Fraunces Tavern Museum. In his pre-presidential days as a general, George Washington celebrated the end of the Revolutionary War here in 1783, bidding an emotional farewell to his officers upon the British evacuation of New York. Today the former tavern is a museum covering two floors above a restaurant and bar. It has two fully furnished period rooms—including the Long Room, site of Washington's address—and other modest displays of 18th- and 19th-century American history. These days you'll find more tourists and Wall Street types than revolutionaries in the recently reopened tavern and restaurant these days.

✉ *54 Pearl St., at Broad St., Financial District* ☎ *212/425–1778* ⊕ *www. frauncestavernmuseum.org* 💳 *$7* 🕓 *Daily noon–5* Ⓜ *R to Whitehall St.; 4, 5 to Bowling Green; 1 to South Ferry; J, Z to Broad St.*

Museum of American Finance. Pre-9/11, a visit to the New York Stock Exchange was the ultimate high; the energy of the floor and the proximity to so much power couldn't be beat. Post-9/11 security prohibits tours of the Exchange but you can still get a feel—albeit a less exhilarating feel—for what makes the financial world go 'round (and down) by visiting this museum. Located in the grandiose former banking hall of the Bank of New York, this Smithsonian Institution affiliate is home to artifacts of the financial market's history; interactive exhibits on the financial markets, banking, entrepreneurship, and Alexander Hamilton; and well-executed temporary exhibits. As of this writing temporary gallery closures in early 2012 mean reduced admission ($5); check for updates. ✉ *48 Wall St., at William St., Financial District* ☎ *212/908– 4110* ⊕ *www.moaf.org* 💳 *$8* 🕓 *Tues.–Sat. 10–4* Ⓜ *2, 3 to Wall St.*

Museum of Jewish Heritage—A Living Memorial to the Holocaust. In a granite 85-foot hexagon at the southern end of Battery Park City, this museum pays tribute to the 6 million Jews who perished in the Holocaust. Architects Kevin Roche and John Dinkeloo built the museum in the shape of a Star of David, with three floors of exhibits demonstrating the dynamism of 20th-century Jewish culture. Visitors enter through a gallery that provides a context for the early-20th-century artifacts on the first floor: an elaborate screen hand-painted for the fall harvest festival of Sukkoth, wedding invitations, and tools used by Jewish tradesmen. Original documentary films play throughout the museum. The second floor details the rise of Nazism and anti-Semitism, and the ravages of the Holocaust. A gallery covers the doomed voyage of the SS *St. Louis,* a ship of German Jewish refugees that crossed the Atlantic twice in 1939 in search of a safe haven. Signs of hope are also on display, including a trumpet that Louis Bannet (the "Dutch Louis Armstrong") played for three years in the Auschwitz-Birkenau inmate orchestra. The third floor covers postwar Jewish life. New exhibits to be added in early 2013 explore American Jews who tried to rescue European Jews leading up to and during the Holocaust as well as the rich Jewish history of Oswiecim, the town the Germans called Auschwitz. The museum's east wing has a theater, a memorial garden, a library, more galleries, and a café. ✉ *36 Battery Pl., Battery Park City, Financial District* ☎ *646/437–4202* ⊕ *www.mjhnyc.org* 💳 *$12, free Wed. 4–10* 🕓 *Thurs. and Sun.–Tues. 10–5:45, Wed. 10–8, Fri. and eve of Jewish holidays 10–3* Ⓜ *4, 5 to Bowling Green.*

National Museum of the American Indian (Smithsonian Institution). Massive granite columns rise to a pediment topped by a double row of statues at the impressive beaux arts Alexander Hamilton U.S. Custom House (1907) building, which houses the New York branch of this Smithsonian museum (the other branch is in Washington, D.C.). Inside, the egg-shape stairwell and rotunda embellished with shipping-theme murals (completed in the 1930s) are also worth a pause. The permanent exhibit, *Infinity of Nations,* is an encyclopedic survey of Native cultures from throughout the Americas, including 700 objects from ancient times

to present day; the venue also presents changing exhibits, videos and films, and dance, music, and storytelling programs. ⊠ *1 Bowling Green, between State and Whitehall Sts., Financial District* ☎ *212/514–3700* ⊕ *www.nmai.si.edu/* ⊠ *Free* ☾ *Mon.–Wed. and Fri.–Sun. 10–5, Thurs. 10–8* Ⓜ *4, 5 to Bowling Green.*

ℭ **New York City Police Museum.** Why are police called cops? Why does a police badge have eight points? When was fingerprinting first used to solve a crime? The answers to these questions and much more can be found at this museum dedicated to New York's finest. The force's history from colonial times through the present is covered through the permanent "9/11 Remembered"—which includes a video with interviews with those who were first responders to the attack—as well as rotating exhibits. The Hall of Heroes honors police officers who have fallen in the line of duty. The Junior Officers Discovery Zone, an interactive children's exhibit, includes a model of a mobile crime lab, a police car, fingerprint labs, and other tools used for investigations. Special events include a vintage police-car show the first weekend every June. ⊠ *100 Old Slip, near South St., Financial District* ☎ *212/480–3100* ⊕ *www.nycpolicemuseum.org* ⊠ *$8* ☾ *Mon.–Sat. 10–5, Sun. noon–5* Ⓜ *2, 3 to Wall St.*

Skyscraper Museum. Why get a crick in your neck—or worse, risk looking like a tourist—while appreciating New York City's famous skyline when you can visit the Skyscraper Museum instead? At this small museum that shares a building with the Ritz Carlton in Battery Park City, you can appreciate highly detailed hand-carved miniature wood models of midtown and downtown Manhattan; explore the past, present, and future of the skyscraper—from New York City's Empire State Building to Dubai's Burj Khalifa (taller than the Empire State Building and Chicago's Sears Tower combined); and examine the history of the Twin Towers at the World Trade Center as well as the ongoing rebuilding of Ground Zero. Expect models of current or future buildings, videos, drawings, floor plans, talks, and exhibits that reveal the influence of history, real estate, and individuals on shaping city skylines. ⊠ *39 Battery Pl., across from Museum of Jewish Heritage, Financial District* ☎ *212/968–1961* ⊕ *www. skyscraper.org* ⊠ *$5* ☾ *Wed.–Sun. noon–6* Ⓜ *4, 5 to Bowling Green.*

St. Paul's Chapel. For more than a year after the World Trade Center attacks, the chapel's fence served as a shrine for visitors seeking solace. People from around the world left tokens of grief and support, or signed one of the large drop cloths that hung from the fence. After having served as a 24-hour refuge where rescue and recovery workers could eat, pray, rest, and receive counseling, the chapel, which amazingly suffered no damage, reopened to the public in fall 2002. The powerful ongoing exhibit, titled *Unwavering Spirit: Hope and Healing at Ground Zero,* honors the efforts of rescue workers in the months after September 11 with photos, drawings, banners, and other items sent to them or as memorials. Open since 1766, St. Paul's is the oldest public building in continuous use in Manhattan. ⊠ *209 Broadway, at Fulton St., Financial District* ☎ *212/233–4164* ⊕ *www.saintpaulschapel.org* ☾ *Weekdays 10–6, Sat. 10–4, Sun. 7 am–9 pm* Ⓜ *2, 3, 4, 5, A, C, J, Z to Broadway-Nassau; 4, 5 to Broadway-Nassau; E to Chambers; 6 to Brooklyn Bridge/City Hall.*

On a typical weekday, five ferries make roughly 110 trips back and forth between Staten Island and Manhattan, transporting about 60,000 passengers.

NEW YORK HARBOR

The southern tip of Manhattan has often served as a microcosm for a city that offers as many first shots as it does second chances, so it's appropriate that it's the key point of departure for the Statue of Liberty and Ellis Island. This experience should never be dismissed as too touristy. Like nothing else, the excursion will remind you that this is a city of immigrants and survivors.

TOP ATTRACTIONS

Fodor's Choice ★ **Ellis Island.** *See highlighted feature at the end of Chapter 1.*

Fodor's Choice ★ **Governors Island.** Governors Island is open to the public from May to October: get there via a short ferry ride. It's essentially a big, charming park that looks like a small New England town—it's popular with locals for its bike and running trails, festivals, art shows, concerts, and family programs. Wouter Van Twiller, a representative for Holland, supposedly purchased the island for his private use, in 1637, from Native Americans for two ax heads, a string of beads, and a handful of nails. It was confiscated by the Dutch a year later, and for the next decade its ownership switched back and forth between the Dutch and British until the Brits gained firm control of it in the 1670s. The island was officially named in 1784 for His Majesty's Governors, and was used by the American military until the 1960s, when the Coast Guard took it over. After their facilities were abandoned in 1995, the island was purchased by the public in 2002 and started welcoming visitors in 2003.

The free ferry to the island departs from the Battery Maritime Building. ⊠ *Battery Maritime Building, 10 South St., for ferry, New York Harbor* ⊕ *govisland.com* 🖃 *Free* ⊙ *June–Oct., Fri. 10–5; weekends 10–7* Ⓜ *1 to South Ferry station; 4, 5 to Bowling Green; R to Whitehall Street.*

A mix of old and new: Lower Manhattan's bright lights combine with the seaport's historic ships.

Staten Island Ferry. Every day, some 60,000 people ride the free ferry to Staten Island, one of the city's outer boroughs, and you should be one of them. Without paying a cent, you get phenomenal views of the Lower Manhattan skyline, the Statue of Liberty, and Ellis Island during the 25-minute boat ride across New York Harbor. You'll also pass tugboats, freighters, and cruise ships—a reminder that this is very much still a working harbor. The boat embarks every 15 to 30 minutes from the Whitehall Terminal at Whitehall and South streets, near the east end of Battery Park. You must disembark once you reach the opposite terminal, but you can just get back in line to board again if you don't plan to stay. ⊠ *Battery Park* ☎ *212/639–9675* ⊕ *www.siferry.com* 🖃 *Free* Ⓜ *1 to South Ferry; R to Whitehall St.; 4, 5 to Bowling Green.*

Statue of Liberty. *See highlighted feature at the end of Chapter 1.*

TRIBECA

Tucked to the west, south of Canal Street, residential TriBeCa (the triangle below Canal Street) has a quieter vibe than most other Manhattan neighborhoods. Walk the photogenic streets here, especially the stretch of Federal row houses on Harrison Street, and you'll understand why so many celebrities own apartments here. The two-block-long Staple Street, with its connecting overhead walkway, is a favorite of urban cinematographers. And although TriBeCa's money is hidden away behind grand industrial facades, you can get a taste of it at one of the posh neighborhood restaurants or when the stars turn out for the annual TriBeCa Film Festival in spring.

WORTH NOTING

🔆 **Hudson River Park.** If the chaos of New York City starts to get to you and you're craving some peace and quiet, a walk along the Hudson River can be soothing. The 5-mile path from Battery Place to 59th Street has been renovated into a landscaped park, incorporating the piers, with walking and bike paths, a seasonal mini golf course, dog runs, and skate parks. The TriBeCa portion consists of Piers 25 and 26. The area adjacent to the West Village (Piers 45 and 46) and near Chelsea (Piers 63 and 64) are particularly attractive, with lots of green spaces. ⊠ *TriBeCa* ☎ *212/627–2020* ⊕ *www.hudsonriverpark.org* Ⓜ *1 to Franklin St. for TriBeCa.*

SoHo, NoLIta, Little Italy, and Chinatown

WORD OF MOUTH

"I took the subway to SoHo and had a great breakfast at Balthazar. It was just eggs, sausage, and toast, but just the atmosphere alone made it just seem better. The waitress was very nice and sent the maitre'd over to give me directions. He had it all—he was handsome and French!"

—MichelleY

GETTING ORIENTED

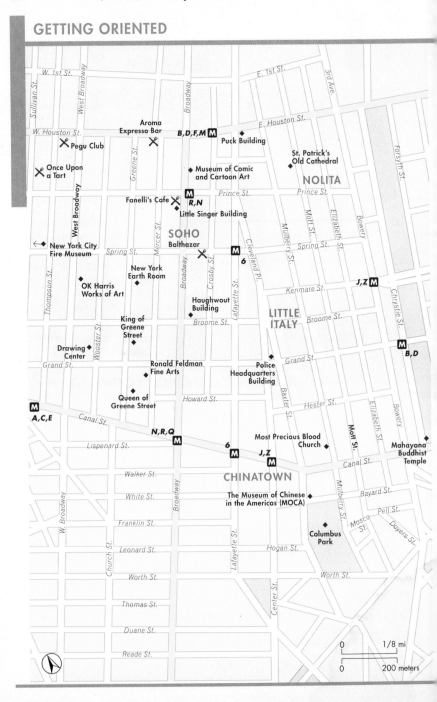

W. 1st St.

West Broadway

Sullivan St.

W. Houston St.

Broadway

E. 1st St.

E. Houston St.

3rd Ave.

Forsyth St.

Aroma
Expresso Bar

B,D,F,M M

Puck Building

X Pegu Club

Greene St.

St. Patrick's
Old Cathedral

X Once Upon
a Tart

Museum of Comic
and Cartoon Art

NOLITA

West Broadway

Fanelli's Cafe X

Prince St.

Prince St.

M
R,N

Mott St.

Elizabeth St.

Bowery

Little Singer Building

← New York City
Fire Museum

SOHO

Mercer St.

Balthazar

Spring St.

Spring St.

Mulberry St.

Spring St.

Thompson St.

OK Harris
Works of Art

New York
Earth Room

Broadway

X

M
6

Cleveland Pl.

Lafayette St.

J,Z M

Crosby St.

Kenmare St.

Chrystie St.

Haughwout
Building

LITTLE
ITALY

Broome St.

Broome St.

King of
Greene
Street

Wooster St.

Drawing
Center

Grand St.

Ronald Feldman
Fine Arts

Baxter St.

Grand St.

M
B,D

Bowery

Police
Headquarters
Building

M
A,C,E

Queen of
Greene Street

Howard St.

Hester St.

Elizabeth St.

Canal St.

Lispenard St.

N,R,Q
M

6
M

Most Precious Blood
Church

Mott St.

Mahayana
Buddhist
Temple

J,Z
M

Canal St.

Bowery

Walker St.

W. Broadway

White St.

Broadway

CHINATOWN

The Museum of Chinese
in the Americas (MOCA)

Mulberry St.

Bayard St.

Pell St.

Mosco St.

Doyers St.

Franklin St.

Leonard St.

Church St.

Lafayette St.

Columbus
Park

Hogan St.

Worth St.

Worth St.

Center St.

Thomas St.

Duane St.

Reade St.

0   1/8 mi

0   200 meters

MAKING THE MOST OF YOUR TIME

If you're coming to shop in SoHo and NoLIta, there's no need to rush out the door, because most shops don't open until 10 or 11 am; many stay open until early evening. If art is your thing, avoid Sunday, because most galleries are closed. SoHo, with national chains lining its section of Broadway, is almost always a madhouse (unless it's raining), but weekdays are somewhat less frenetic. NoLIta, with fewer chains and more boutiques, is calmer and less crowded.

Little Italy is a small area nowadays, having lost ground to a growing Chinatown. Note that food-wise, the best Italian fare is not to be found in Little Italy restaurants, where most of the checkered-tablecloth spots are touristy, with mediocre food.

If you're visiting New York in mid-September, you'll time it right for the San Gennaro festival—a huge street fair in honor of the patron saint of Naples—and you, along with thousands of others, can easily spend an entire day and night exploring the many food and souvenir booths and playing games of chance.

Chinatown bustles with local shoppers pretty much any time of day, but there are more tourists on the weekends, when it gets so busy there isn't much room on the sidewalk.

TOP EXPERIENCES

Browsing boutiques and people-watching in SoHo and NoLIta.

Ogling the out-of-the-ordinary produce and seafood in Chinatown.

Gallery hopping in SoHo.

Snacking on street food during the San Gennaro festival in Little Italy.

Eating dim sum in Chinatown.

Brunching at Balthazar.

GETTING HERE AND AROUND

SoHo (South of Houston) is roughly bounded by Houston Street, Canal Street, 6th Avenue, and Lafayette Street. To the east, NoLIta (North of Little Italy) seems to expand daily but lies pretty much bounded by Houston, the Bowery, Kenmare, and Lafayette. Plenty of subways service the area; take the 6, C, or E to Spring Street; the N or the R to Prince Street; or the B, D, F, M to Broadway-Lafayette. For Chinatown, farther south, take the J, N, Q, R, Z, or 6 to Canal Street or the B or D (Grand Street).

QUICK BITES, COFFEE, OR COCKTAILS

Aroma Espresso Bar (✉ *145 Greene St., at Houston*). Locals skip Starbucks to come here for quick service, soups, sandwiches, and pastries.

Once Upon a Tart (✉ *135 Sullivan St.*). Great name with the goods to back it up.

Fanelli's (✉ *94 Prince St.*). This divey spot is perfect for a beer at the bar or a casual lunch.

Pegu Club (✉ *77 West Houston St.*). The fine art of drinking is elevated here with fabulous, innovative cocktails.

3

Sightseeing
★★★
Nightlife
★★★
Dining
★★★
Lodging
★★★
Shopping
★★★★★

SoHo, NoLIta, Little Italy, and Chinatown all tend to be jam-packed with humanity, all the more perfect for people-watching as you shop and wander. SoHo and NoLIta are the destinations for super-trendy shopping: the shops are often overpriced but it's undeniably glamorous. Little Italy and Chinatown are more about local shopping.

SOHO

Updated by Arthur Bovino

SoHo (short for "South of Houston") was the epicenter of New York's art scene in the late 1970s, and has since evolved into a mecca of mostly chain retailers (Chelsea is more the go-to for galleries these days). Compared with other neighborhoods, you may have to look a little harder to find a local vibe, but a bit of bohemia still exists. It can be found on the cobblestone side streets where there are still a few galleries, as well as sidewalks jammed with tables full of handmade beaded jewelry, tooled leather belts, and hats and purses. There are also unique clothing boutiques, gourmet food shops, and even a few old-school divey bars thrown into the mix.

WORTH NOTING

Museum of Comic and Cartoon Art. A gem among the small museums in the city, the Museum of Comic and Cartoon Art features smartly curated artist spotlights (such as Will Eisner, Todd McFarlane, and Kim Deitch) and genre exhibits. Recent shows included a behind-the-scenes look at the creative process of turning beat poet Allen Ginsberg's *Howl* into a graphic novel, an exploration of the popularity of Batman in 1960s Japan, and a comprehensive look at the history and future of independent comics. New shows are mounted frequently, but MoCCA's website tends to list coming-very-soon shows, so don't worry if nothing seems to be happening while you're planning your trip; check the site a week or so before you arrive in the city to see what's scheduled. And stay on the lookout for MoCCA's annual art festival, a comic and cartoon bonanza typically in April. ✉ *594 Broadway, Suite 401, between W. Houston* *and Prince Sts., SoHo* ☏ *212/254–3511* ⊕ *www.moccany.org* ✉ *$6* ◷ *Tues.–Sun. noon–5* Ⓜ *B, D, F, G to Broadway–Lafayette St.; N, R to Prince St.*

New York City Fire Museum. In the former headquarters of Engine 30—a handsome beaux arts building dating from 1904—retired firefighters volunteer their time to answer visitors' questions. The collection of firefighting tools from the 18th century to the present includes hand-pulled and horse-drawn engines, speaking trumpets, pumps, and uniforms. A memorial exhibit with photos, paintings, children's artwork, and found objects relating to the September 11 attacks is also on view—a poignant reminder and tribute to the 343 firefighters who died on 9/11. The museum is two subway stops (via the E train) north of the Ground Zero site. ✉ *278 Spring St., between Hudson and Varick Sts., SoHo* ☏ *212/691–1303* ⊕ *www.nycfiremuseum.org* ✉ *$8* ◷ *Mon.–Sat. 10–5, Sun. 10–4* Ⓜ *C, E to Spring St.*

GALLERIES

Drawing Center. At this nonprofit organization the focus is only on drawings—contemporary and historical. Works often push the envelope on what's considered drawing; many projects are commissioned especially by the center. ✉ *35 Wooster St., between Broome and Grand Sts., SoHo* ☏ *212/219–2166* ⊕ *www.drawingcenter.org* ◷ *Wed. noon–6, Thurs. noon–8, Fri.–Sun. noon–6* Ⓜ *N, Q, R, J, Z, 6, A, C, E to Canal St.*

New York Earth Room. Walter De Maria's 1977 avant-garde work consists of 140 tons of gently sculpted soil (22 inches deep) filling 3,600 square feet of a second-floor gallery maintained by the Dia Art Foundation. You can't touch or walk on the dirt, nor can you take its photo. Interestingly, it's been valued at $1 million. If you like this installation, check out de Maria's *Broken Kilometer*, a few blocks away at 393 West Broadway. ✉ *141 Wooster St., between W. Houston and Prince Sts., SoHo* ☏ *212/989–5566* ⊕ *www.earthroom.org* ✉ *Free* ◷ *Wed.–Sun. noon–6 (closed 3–3:30 and mid-June–mid-Sept.)* Ⓜ *R to Prince St.; B, D, F, M to Broadway–Lafayette.*

OK Harris Works of Art. This SoHo stalwart hosts a wide range of visual arts: paintings, digitally enhanced photographs, trompe-l'oeil reliefs, and sculptures. The gallery is closed for most of July, and then through

DID YOU KNOW?

On most weekends, artists lines the sidewalks of West Broadway, below Houston, selling all sorts of handmade art. There are many paintings, as well as jewelry and other handicrafts.

CLOSE UP

SoHo and NoLIta Architecture

There are plenty of beautiful people in SoHo and NoLIta, but tilt your eyes up, beyond the turn-of-the-20th-century lampposts adorned with cast-iron curlicues, and you'll also find some of New York's most impressive architecture. SoHo has one of the world's greatest concentrations of cast-iron buildings, created in response to fires that wiped out much of Lower Manhattan in the mid-18th century. Look down and you'll see Belgian brick cobblestones lining some of the streets. Along Broadway and the neighboring streets of SoHo, you'll see lights in the sidewalk: starting in the 1850s, these vault lights were set into sidewalks to permit daylight to reach basements.

The **King of Greene Street,** at 72-76 Greene, between Grand and Canal, is a five-story Renaissance-style 1873 building with a magnificent projecting porch of Corinthian columns and pilasters. These days it's unmistakably painted in high-gloss ivory. Over at 28–30 Greene Street is the **Queen of Greene Street,** a graceful 1873, cast-iron beauty exemplified by its dormers, columns, window arches, projecting central bays, and Second Empire–style roof.

The **Haughwout Building,** at 488–492 Broadway, north of Broome, is best known for what's no longer inside—the world's first commercial passenger elevator, invented by Elisha Graves Otis. The building's exterior is worth a look, though: nicknamed the Parthenon of Cast Iron, the five-story, Venetian palazzo–style structure was built in 1857 to house department-store merchant E. V. Haughwout's china, silver, and glassware store. Each window is framed by Corinthian columns and rounded arches.

Built in 1904, the **Little Singer Building, at 561 Broadway, is a** masterpiece of cast-iron styling, its delicate facade covered with curlicues of wrought iron. The L-shape building's second facade is around the corner on Prince Street.

Charlton Street, not technically in SoHo but across 6th Avenue in the West Village, is Manhattan's longest stretch of Federal-style redbrick row houses from the 1820s and '30s. The high stoops, paneled front doors, leaded-glass windows, and narrow dormer windows are all intact. King and Vandam streets also have historic houses. Much of this was the site of a mansion called Richmond Hill, and, in the late 18th century the surrounding area was a beautiful wild meadow from where you could see the nearby "hamlet" of Greenwich Village.

Over in Little Italy/NoLIta, the magnificent old **Police Headquarters** building at 240 Center Street, between Broome and Grand, might be familiar from Martin Scorsese's *Gangs of New York.* The 1909 Edwardian baroque structure with its striking copper dome was the headquarters of the New York City Police Department until 1973. Designed to "impress both the officer and the prisoner with the majesty of the law," it was converted into luxury condos in 1988 and is known today as the Police Building Apartments.

The 1885 Romanesque Revival **Puck Building,** at 295 Lafayette Street, on the southeast corner of Houston, is a former magazine headquarters and now a busy event space—look for the statue of Puck just over the door.

The stark, simple interior of OK Harris Works of Art illustrates the typical gallery space in SoHo.

early September. ⊠ *383 West Broadway, between Spring and Broome Sts., SoHo* ☎ *212/431–3600* ⊕ *www.okharris.com* ⊗ *Tues.–Sat. 10–6* Ⓜ *C, E to Spring St.*

Ronald Feldman Fine Arts. Founded in 1971, this gallery represents more than 30 international contemporary artists; exhibits contemporary painting, sculpture, installations, drawings, and prints; and hosts performances. It has a large selection of Andy Warhol prints, paintings, and drawings. ⊠ *31 Mercer St., between Grand and Canal Sts., SoHo* ☎ *212/226–3232* ⊕ *www.feldmangallery.com* ⊗ *Tues.–Sat. 10–6* Ⓜ *N, Q, R, J, A, C, E, 6 to Canal St.*

NOLITA

Compared with SoHo, NoLIta (shorthand for "north of Little Italy") is the better place to hit for unique boutiques and quieter cafés. The area feels significantly more like a neighborhood where locals eat, shop, and live. A great place to stop for a break or picnic is DeSalvio Playground at the corner of Spring and Mulberry streets, where kids play on red, white, and green equipment (colors in honor of the Italian flag) and people play chess on stone game tables. Stores remain largely one-of-a-kind, and the indie shops featuring products from up-and-coming designers, quirky cafés, and modest eateries evoke the spirit of old SoHo.

WORTH NOTING

St. Patrick's Old Cathedral. If you've watched *The Godfather*, you've peeked inside St. Patrick's Old Cathedral—the interior shots of the infamous baptism scene were filmed here. The unadorned exterior of the cathedral gives no hint to the splendors within, which include an 1868 Henry Erben pipe organ. The enormous marble altar surrounded by hand-carved niches (*reredos*) houses an extraordinary collection of sacred statuary and other Gothic exuberance. There's a maze of mortuary vaults underneath the cathedral (older residents of Little Italy recall playing hide-and-seek in the vaults), and the outdoor cemetery is the final resting place for notable New Yorkers such as the Venerable Pierre Toussaint, an African-American who was born a slave in Haiti and made his fortune as a New York hairdresser—his many charitable works have resulted in his consideration for sainthood. ⊠ *263 Mulberry St., corner of Mott and Prince Sts., NoLIta* ☎ *212/226–8075* ⊕ *www. oldcathedral.org/* ⊘ *Hrs. may vary, usually open 8–5* Ⓜ *R to Prince St.; 6 to Bleecker St.*

LITTLE ITALY

Just east of Broadway, you'll find the remains of what once was a thriving, lively community of Italian Americans: the tangle of streets that make up Little Italy. The few nostalgic blocks surrounding Mulberry Street between NoLIta and bustling Canal Street are still a cheerful salute to all things Italian, with red-green-and-white street decorations on permanent display and specialty grocers and cannelloni makers dishing up delights. It is all a bit touristy these days, and you should look elsewhere if you're looking for a great Italian restaurant meal, but it's fun to walk around here.

Every September, Mulberry Street becomes the giant Feast of San Gennaro, a crowded 11-day festival that sizzles with the smell of sausages and onions (don't miss John Fasullo's braciole, an iconic sandwich filled with fillet of pork roasted over a coal pit and topped with peppers and onions). This is by far the city's most extensive annual street fair.

If you're looking for a current, thriving Little Italy, head up to Arthur Avenue in the Bronx (⇨ *Chapter 15)* and you'll find a cornucopia of authentic Italian goods marketed to local families rather than tourists.

WORTH NOTING

Most Precious Blood Church. The National Shrine of San Gennaro, a replica of the grotto at Lourdes, is the high point of Most Precious Blood Church's richly painted interior. The church becomes a focal point during the annual San Gennaro festival. ⊠ *109 Mulberry St., Little Italy* ☎ *212/226–6427* ⊕ *www.mostpreciousbloodchurch.net/* Ⓜ *N, Q, R, 6 to Canal St.; J, Z to Canal St.* ⊠ *Mulberry and Mott streets between Canal and Grand streets, Little Italy* ☎ *800/399–5632* ⊕ *www. littleitalynyc.com/*.

CHINATOWN

Chinatown is a living, breathing, anything-but-quiet ethnic enclave: a quarter of the city's 400,000 Chinese residents live here. The neighborhood started as a seven-block area, but now covers some 40-plus blocks above and below Canal Street (encroaching on what was once a

Some of the storefronts and signage in Chinatown are bilingual—but some are just in Chinese.

thriving Little Italy), with 200-plus restaurants serving every imaginable regional Chinese cuisine crammed into about 2 square miles. Head to **Mott Street,** south of Canal, Chinatown's main thoroughfare, where the first Chinese immigrants (mostly men) settled in tenements in the late 1880s. Today, the street is dense with restaurants, hair salons and barbershops, bakeries, tea parlors, and souvenir shops, as well as Buddhist temples, herbalists, and acupuncturists. The few blocks above Canal overflow with food shops selling vegetables and fish (some still alive and squirming). Walk carefully, as the sidewalks can be slick from the ice underneath the eels, blue crabs, snapper, and shrimp that seem to look back at you as you pass by. If you plan it right, you can create a movable feast, starting with soup dumplings, a specialty from Shanghai, and continuing with Peking duck, a yellow custard cake, and a jasmine bubble tea, each at a different place.

WORTH NOTING

Columbus Park. People-watching is the thing in this park. If you swing by in the morning, you'll see men and women practicing tai chi; the afternoons bring intense games of mah-jongg. In the mid-19th century the park was known as Five Points—the point where Mulberry Street, Anthony (now Worth) Street, Cross (now Park) Street, Orange (now Baxter) Street, and Little Water Street (no longer in existence) intersected—and was notoriously ruled by dangerous Irish gangs. In the 1880s a neighborhood-improvement campaign brought about the park's creation. ⊠ *Chinatown* ⊕ *www.nycgovparks.org/parks/M015/* Ⓜ *4, 6 J, N, Q, Z to Canal St.*

Mahayana Buddhist Temple. Visit this huge Buddhist temple in China-town and you'll be able to say you saw New York's largest Buddha; the temple is at the foot of the Manhattan Bridge Arch on the Bowery. There's an excellent gift shop on the second floor. Interestingly, before its incarnation as a place of worship in 1997, this was the Rosemary, an adult-movie theater. ⊠ *133 Canal St., at the Bowery, Chinatown* ☎ *212/343–9592* ✉ *A donation of $2 is requested.* ⊙ *Daily 8–7* Ⓜ *B, D to Grand St.*

The Museum of Chinese in America (MOCA). Founded in 1980, this museum is dedicated to preserving and presenting the history of the Chinese people and their descendants in the United States. MOCA moved in early 2009 to its new home on Centre Street, where the 14,000-square-foot gallery space increased the size of the museum more than fivefold. Designed by Maya Lin, architect of the Vietnam Veterans Memorial in Washington, D.C., MOCA features a permanent exhibit on Chinese-American history, With a Single Step: Stories in the Making of America, which includes artworks, personal and domestic artifacts, historical documentation, and films. Chinese laundry tools, a traditional general store, and antique business signs are some of the unique objects on display. Rotating shows such as America through a Chinese Lens, a contemporary photography exhibit, are on display in the second gallery. MOCA sponsors workshops, walking tours, lectures, and family events. ⊠ *215 Centre St., between Grand and Howard Sts., Chinatown* ☎ *212/619–4785* ⊕ *www.mocanyc.org* ✉ *$7* ⊙ *Thurs. 11–9, Mon. and Fri. 11–5, weekends 10–5* Ⓜ *6, J, M, N, Q, R, Z to Canal St.*

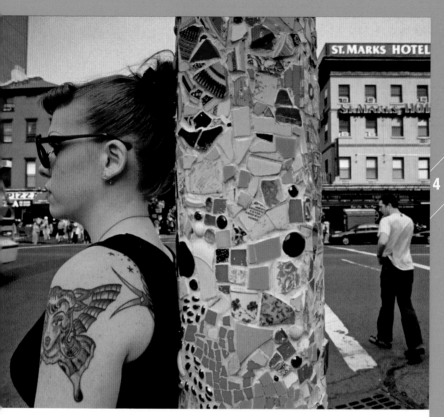

The East Village and the Lower East Side

WORD OF MOUTH

"We thought the Tenement Museum was one of the best 'museums' we've been to in a long time. The Tenement Museum, a walk around the Lower East Side, and lunch at Katz's Deli—a perfect morning/afternoon!"

—sf3707

GETTING ORIENTED

E. 14th St.

4,5,6, L,
N,Q,R

L

E. 13th St.

The Strand

E. 12th St.

Broadway

Fourth Ave.

Third Ave.

Second Ave.

First Ave.

E. 11th St.

St. Mark's
Church-in-the-Bowery

E. 10th St.

Astor Place
Subway
Station

Stuyvesant St.

E. 9th St.

PDT

Tompkins
Square Park

R

Astor Pl.

St. Mark's Place

Astor Pl.

6

Fourth Ave.

McSorley's Old Ale House

E. 7th St.   Abraço

Ave. A

Ave. B

Taras
Shevchenko
Pl.

Third Ave.

E. 6th St.

EAST VILLAGE

Merchant's
House Museum

Cooper
Square

E. 5th St.

E. 4th St.

ALPHABET
CITY

Lafayette St.

Gt. Jones St.

E. 3rd St.

E. 2nd St.

6

Bleecker St.

E. 1st St.

Il Laboratorio
del Gelato

Katz's Delicatessen

F

Russ & Daughters

B,D,F,M

E. Houston St.

Chrystie St.

Eldridge St.

Forsyth St.

Allen St.

Orchard St.

Ludlow St.

Essex St.

Norfolk St.

Suffolk St.

Mulberry St.

Mott St.

Elizabeth St.

Bowery

Stanton St.

D'Espresso

LOWER
EAST SIDE

SOHO

NOLITA

Prince St.

New
Museum

Rivington St.

Gallery
Onetwentyeight

Essex Street
Market

J,M,Z,F

6

Spring St.

Delancey St.

J,Z

Lower East Side
Tenement Museum

Broome St.

0   1/8 mile

0   200 meters

Museum at
Eldridge Street

MAKING THE MOST OF YOUR TIME

Houston Street runs east–west and neatly divides the East Village (north of Houston) and the Lower East Side (south of Houston). The eastern boundary of the East Village and Lower East Side is the East River; the western boundary is 4th Avenue and the Bowery. So many communities converge in these neighborhoods that each block seems like a new neighborhood unto itself.

The East Village lets loose on weekend nights, when nightlife seekers converge on the area, filling up the bars and spilling out onto the sidewalks. Weekday evenings are less frenetic, with more of a local vibe—although the term "local" around here always means a large number of students from New York University. Daytime is great for shopping in the local boutiques, and brunch on weekends around here generally can mean lines for hot spots like Prune and Back Forty, which fill with patrons lingering over coffee.

The Lower East Side does not tend to be an early-riser destination any day of the week. Although there's plenty to see during the day, nightfall offers a different vision: blocks that were previously empty rows of pulled-down gratings transform into clusters of throbbing bars. On the increasingly trendy streets around Rivington and Stanton, stores, bars, and cafés buzz all week but are less crowded by day.

GETTING HERE AND AROUND

For the East Village, take the N/R subway line to 8th Street, the 6 to Astor Place, or the L to 3rd Avenue. To reach Alphabet City, take the L to 1st Avenue or the F to 2nd Avenue. For the Lower East Side, head southeast from the 2nd Avenue stop on the F, or take the F/M/J/Z to the Delancey Street–Essex Street stop.

TOP EXPERIENCES

People-watching on St. Marks Place.

Shopping at boutiques and vintage clothing stores.

Visiting the Lower East Side Tenement Museum.

QUICK BITES, COFFEE, AND COCKTAILS

Abraço (✉ 86 E. 7th St.). Italian coffee, sandwiches, and sweets are the draw at this tiny spot.

D'espresso (✉ 100 Stanton St.). Italian-style coffee, plus the pastries to match.

Katz's Delicatessen (✉ 205 E. Houston St.). Sample pastrami at the counter while you're waiting. Just don't lose your ticket.

Il Laboratorio del Gelato (✉ 188 Ludlow St.). Seasonal flavors make this gelato la crème de la crème.

PDT (✉ 113 St. Marks Pl.). Short for "please don't tell," this "secret" speakeasy serves excellent cocktails. Enter through the telephone booth in Crif Dogs—though you might be turned away if it's too busy.

McSorley's Old Ale House (✉ 15 E. 7th St.). Sawdust, crowds, and beer; this is old-school New York.

4

Sightseeing
★★
Nightlife
★★★★★
Dining
★★★★★
Lodging
★★
Shopping
★★★★

American punk was born in the East Village, at the now-defunct CBGB, and the punk rock and indie scene is kept alive at the many small music venues both here and on the Lower East Side. Both neighborhoods are tamer than they once were—as the arrival of Whole Foods and several glass-and-chrome condos attests—but there's definitely still a gritty, edgy element around here. Spend some time wandering these bohemian side streets, and you'll be struck by the funky pastiche of ethnicities whose imprints are visible in the neighborhood's restaurants, shops, and, of course, people.

EAST VILLAGE

Updated by
Arthur Bovino

The concept of "La Bohème meets hipsters in vintage clothing," better known as the musical *Rent*, pegged the East Village as a community of artists, activists, and other social dissenters—and this is still the essential vibe here, although the neighborhood has become more upscale in recent years. These days, for example, St. Marks Place evokes less of the gritty, counterculture scene it once had in favor of more of a pastiche of young hipsters and Japanese expats.

East of 1st Avenue is Alphabet City, once the city's seedy drug haunt but now an ever more gentrified neighborhood. There is still a definitely young, artistic vibe in and around Tompkins Square Park.

TOP ATTRACTIONS

Alphabet City. The north-south avenues east of 1st Avenue, from Houston Street to 14th Street, are all labeled with letters, not numbers, which gives this area its nickname. While Avenues A, B, and C are mostly gentrified, Avenue D is still a bit rough around the edges. Parts of Avenues A and B run along Tompkins Square Park. The whole area has a wide variety of cafés, bars, and a steadily growing restaurant scene. A close-knit Puerto Rican community makes its home around Avenue C, also called Loisaida Avenue (a Spanglish creation meaning "Lower East Side"), which, although still filled predominantly with Latino shops and bodegas, is now also home to some happening restaurants and bars. ⊠ *East Village* Ⓜ *6 to Astor Pl.; L to 1st Ave.; F to 2nd Ave.*

St. Marks Place. The longtime hub of the edgy East Village, St. Marks Place is the name given to idiosyncratic East 8th Street between 3rd Avenue and Avenue A. During the 1950s beatniks Allen Ginsberg and Jack Kerouac lived and wrote in the area; the 1960s brought Bill Graham's Fillmore East, Andy Warhol's the Dom, the Electric Circus nightclub, and hallucinogenic drugs. The studded, pink-haired, and shaved-head punk scene followed, and there's a good chance you'll still see some pierced rockers and teenage Goths on the block, though St. Marks these days is turning into Little Japan, with several ramen and dumpling shops and lots of young Japanese students. The blocks between 2nd and 3rd avenues can feel like a shopping arcade, crammed with body-piercing and tattoo salons, and shops selling cheap jewelry, sunglasses, incense, and out-there-sloganed T-shirts. The cafés and bars along here and over to Avenue A attract customers late into the night. ⊠ *8th St., between 3rd Ave. and Ave. A, East Village* Ⓜ *6 to Astor Pl.*

☙ **Tompkins Square Park.** This leafy park fills up year-round with locals partaking in picnics and drum circles, and making use of the playground and dog run. There are movie showings and music gatherings throughout the summer, and an annual Halloween dog costume event. But it wasn't always so rosy in the park: in 1988 police followed then-mayor David Dinkins's orders to clear the many homeless who had set up makeshift homes here, and homeless rights and anti-gentrification activists fought back with sticks and bottles. The park was reclaimed and reopened in 1992 with a midnight curfew, still in effect today. ⊠ *Bordered by Aves. A and B and E. 7th and E. 10th Sts., East Village* Ⓜ *6 to Astor Pl.; L to 1st Ave.*

WORTH NOTING

Astor Place Subway Station. At the beginning of the 20th century almost all of the city's Interborough Rapid Transit (IRT) subway entrances (there were only 28 stations at the time) resembled the ornate cast-iron replica of a beaux-arts kiosk that covers this stairway leading to the uptown No. 6 train. This one, which was—and still is—the stop to get to the venerable Cooper Union college, is now on the List of Registered Historic Places in New York. Inside, plaques of beaver emblems line the tiled station walls, a reference to the fur trade that contributed to John Jacob Astor's fortune. Milton Glaser, the Cooper Union graduate who originated the "I (heart) NY" logo, designed the station's murals. ⊠ *On traffic island at E. 8th St. and 4th Ave., East Village* Ⓜ *6 to Astor Pl.*

Merchant's House Museum. Built in 1832, this redbrick house, combining Federal and Greek Revival styles, provides a glimpse into the domestic life of the period 30 years before the Civil War. Retired merchant Seabury Tredwell and his descendants lived here from 1835 until 1933. The home became a museum in 1936, with the original furnishings and architectural features preserved; family memorabilia are also on display. The fourth-floor servants' bedroom, where the Tredwell family's Irish servants slept and did some of their work, offers a rare and intimate look at the lives of Irish domestics in the mid-1800s. Self-guided tours are available without reservations. Kids under 12 are admitted free. ⊠ *29 E. 4th St., between Bowery and Lafayette St., East Village* ☎ *212/777–1089* ⊕ *www.merchantshouse.org* ▦ *$10* �é *Thurs.–Mon. noon–5* Ⓜ *6 to Astor Pl. or Bleecker St.; B, D, F, M to Broadway–Lafayette St.; R to 8th St.*

St. Mark's Church in-the-Bowery. This charming 1799 fieldstone country church stands on what was once Governor Peter Stuyvesant's *bouwerie,* or farm. It's Manhattan's oldest continually used Christian site, and both Stuyvesant and Commodore Perry are buried in vaults here. Check out the gorgeous modern stained-glass windows on the balcony, which replaced the more traditional windows (like those on the ground level) after a fire in the late '70s. Over the years St. Mark's has hosted many progressive arts events, including readings by poet Carl Sandburg and dance performances by Martha Graham and Merce Cunningham. The tradition has continued with Danspace, the Poetry Project, and the Incubator Arts Project, which give performances throughout the year. ⊠ *131 E. 10th St., at 2nd Ave., East Village* ☎ *212/674–6377* Ⓜ *6 to Astor Pl.; L to 3rd Ave.*

LOWER EAST SIDE

Often referred to as simply as LES, the Lower East Side was the historic "Gateway to America," after waves of Irish, German, Jewish, Hispanic, and Chinese immigrants pulled up stakes and moved to New York in search of a better life. Today, a cool arts and nightlife scene, several distinctively modern high-rises, and the ultracontemporary New Museum exist alongside buildings and cultural centers staunchly rooted in the past.

On Saturday night, the scene can be as raucous as in a college town, especially on Rivington and Orchard streets, but Ludlow Street, one block east of Orchard, has become the main drag for twentysomethings with attitude, its boutiques wedged in between bars and low-key restaurants.

The best time to experience the neighborhood's past is by day. The excellent Lower East Side Tenement Museum movingly captures the immigrant legacy of tough times and survival instincts. You might not find pickles being sold from barrels anymore but this is the place to nosh on typical "Jewish" food from Katz's Delicatessen or Russ & Daughters.

TOP ATTRACTIONS

★ **Gallery Onetwentyeight.** Inside the jewel-box space, artist Kazuko Miyamoto directs crisp and provocative group shows. The art space celebrated its twenty-fifth anniversary in 2012. ⊠ *128 Rivington St., between Essex and Norfolk Sts., Lower East Side* ☎ *212/674–0244* ⊕ *www. galleryonetwentyeight.org* Ⓜ *F to Delancey St.; J, M, Z to Essex St.*

☺ **Lower East Side Tenement Museum.** Step back in time and into the partially
Fodor's Choice restored 1863 tenement building at 97 Orchard Street, where you can
★ squeeze through the preserved apartments of immigrants, learn about
the struggles of past generations, and gain historical perspective on
the still contentious topic of immigration. This is America's first urban
living-history museum dedicated to the life of immigrants—and one of
the city's most underrated and overlooked institutions. The museum
itself is accessible only by guided tour: several are offered at various
times each day and limited to 15 people, so it's a good idea to buy
tickets in advance. The building tour called "Hard Times" visits the
homes of Natalie Gumpertz, a German-Jewish dressmaker (dating from
1878), and Adolph and Rosaria Baldizzi, Catholic immigrants from
Sicily (1935). "Sweatshop Workers" visits the Levines' garment shop/
apartment and the Rogarshevsky family from Eastern Europe (1918).
The "Meet the Residents" tour through the Confino family apartment is
designed for children, who are greeted by a costumed player appearing
as Victoria Confino. Her family of Sephardic Jews came from Kastoria,
Turkey, which is now part of Greece (1916). "Irish Outsiders" explores
the life of the Moores, an Irish-American family living in the building in
1869, and shows a re-created tenement backyard. A two-hour extended
experience tour with a chance for in-depth discussion is offered every
day. Walking tours of the neighborhood are also held daily. The museum's 10,000-square-foot visitor and education center has gallery space,
classrooms, a theater space screening a new original film about the
museum and the neighborhood, and an expanded gift shop. ✉ *103
Orchard St., corner of Orchard St. and Delancey St., Lower East Side*
☎ *212/982–8420* ⊕ *www.tenement.org* ✑ *$22 for a building tour; $45
for foods of the Lower East Side tour* ☉ *Daily 10–6, last tour leaves at
5* Ⓜ *B, D to Grand St.; F to Delancey St.; J, M, Z to Essex St.*

WORTH NOTING

Essex Street Market. Started in 1940 as an attempt by Mayor Fiorello
LaGuardia to establish a place for street pushcarts and vendors, the
Essex Street Market's character was defined early on by the Jewish
and Italian immigrants of the Lower East Side. These days the market
is filled with various purveyors of produce, meat, fish, and gourmet
cheeses. Standouts include Saxelby Cheesemongers, and local favorite
Shopsins, an eclectic restaurant that moved in here in 2007 after decades
in the West Village. ✉ *120 Essex St., between Rivington and Delancey
Sts., Lower East Side* ☎ *212/388–0449* ⊕ *www.essexstreetmarket.com*
☉ *Mon.–Sat. 8–7, Sun. 10–6* Ⓜ *F, V to Delancey St.; J, M, Z to Essex St.*

Museum at Eldridge Street. This was the first Orthodox synagogue erected
by the large number of Eastern European Jews who settled in the Lower
East Side in the late 19th century. The exterior is a striking mix of
Romanesque, Gothic, and Moorish motifs. Inside is an exceptional
hand-carved ark of mahogany and walnut, a sculptured wooden balcony, jewel-tone stained-glass windows, stenciled walls, and an enormous brass chandelier. The synagogue can be viewed as part of a tour,
which begins at the small museum downstairs where interactive "touch
tables" teach all ages about Eldridge Street and the Lower East Side.

4

The crowning piece of the museum's restoration of the synagogue is a stained-glass window by artist Kiki Smith and architect Deborah Gans, weighing 6,000 pounds and with more than 1,200 pieces of glass. ⊠ *12 Eldridge St., between Canal St. and Division St., Lower East Side* ☎ *212/219–0302* ⊕ *www.eldridgestreet.org* ✉ *$10* ⊘ *Sun.–Thurs. 10–5; Fri. 10–3; tours on the hr* Ⓜ *F to E. Broadway; B, D to Grand St.; N, R to Canal St.*

New Museum. This seven-story, 60,000-square-foot structure—a glimmering metal mesh-clad assemblage of off-centered squares—caused some neighborhood uproar when it was built in 2007, with some residents slow to accept the nontraditional building. Not surprisingly, given the museum's name and the building, shows are all about contemporary art: previous exhibitions have included the popular *Carsten Höller: Experience,* with a slide connecting the fourth and second floors and a sensory deprivation tank. Studio 231, the museum's adjacent, ground-floor space at 231 Bowery opened in late 2011 to allow emerging artists the opportunity to create work outside the confines of the main museum building in a studiolike space. Recent shows include *Enrico David: Head Gas,* the artist's first museum presentation in New York, and new installation and performances by London-based artist Spartacus Chetwynd. ⊠ *235 Bowery, at Prince St., Lower East Side* ☎ *212/219–1222* ⊕ *www.newmuseum.org* ✉ *$14; free Thurs. 7–9* ⊘ *Wed. and Fri.–Sun. 11–6, Thurs. 11–9* Ⓜ *6 to Spring St.; F, M to 2nd Ave.*

Greenwich Village
and the West Village

WORD OF MOUTH

"Get away from Midtown and spend time in the Village for good food and more exciting young street life."

—stokebailiey

GETTING ORIENTED

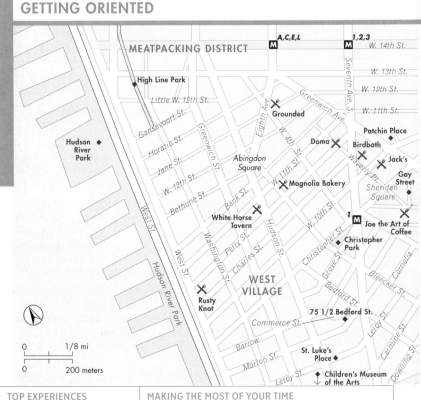

MEATPACKING DISTRICT

A,C,E,L

1,2,3

W. 14th St.

W. 13th St.

High Line Park

W. 12th St.

Little W. 12th St.

W. 11th St.

Grounded

Patchin Place

Gansevoort St.

Doma

Birdbath

Jack's

Hudson River Park

Horatio St.

Jane St.

Abingdon Square

Gay Street

W. 12th St.

Magnolia Bakery

Sheridan Square

Bethune St.

Bank St.

White Horse Tavern

Joe the Art of Coffee

Christopher Park

Charles St.

Perry St.

WEST VILLAGE

0   1/8 mi

0   200 meters

Rusty Knot

Bedford St.

75 1/2 Bedford St.

Commerce St.

Barrow

St. Luke's Place

Morton St.

Leroy St.

Children's Museum of the Arts

TOP EXPERIENCES	MAKING THE MOST OF YOUR TIME
People-watching in Washington Square Park. Strolling and window-shopping along the pretty streets of the West Village. Relaxing in one of the many cafés. Walking along Hudson River Park by the water. Eating your way along Bleecker Street.	Greenwich Village proper—around New York University and Washington Square Park—is busy any time of day with locals (especially students) and visitors. A visit to Washington Square Park is a must for people-watching and relaxing on a bench. There are lots of restaurants and shops in the neighborhood, though they do lean toward the touristy side of things. The West Village—basically from 7th Avenue and west to the Hudson River, is more residential, and tends to be pretty quiet, which makes it pleasant for strolling the pretty tree-lined streets. Upscale boutiques line Bleecker Street and Greenwich Avenue (note that there is also a Greenwich Street in this neighborhood, to confuse things). The windy streets of the West Village often seem mazelike, even to locals, because most of the streets here are named rather than numbered and they're not organized on a grid system. Assume that you're going to get a little bit lost, but don't hesitate to ask for directions.

GREENWICH VILLAGE

5

QUICK BITES, COFFEE, OR COCKTAILS

Rusty Knot (✉ *425 West St.*). This divey spot, a bit out of the way over by the West Side Highway, makes memorable cocktails that pair well with snacks like the pretzel dog.

White Horse Tavern (✉ *567 Hudson*). Dylan Thomas drank here, and so should you. The outdoor picnic tables are the place to be.

The Dove (✉ *228 Thompson St.*). This classy yet laidback bar below street level is a great stop in Greenwich Village.

Coffee options abound in this part of town: Greenwich Village has long-standing **Caffe Reggio** (✉ *119 MacDougal St.*) or relative newcomer **Joe the Art of Coffee** (✉ *141 Waverly Pl.*). Over in the West Village, you can find excellent lattes and a welcoming vibe at **Grounded** (✉ *28 Jane St.*). **Birdbath** (✉ *145 7th Ave.*) calls itself the "neighborhood green bakery" and serves to-go coffee in biodegradable cups. **Jack's** (✉ *138 W. 10th St.*) and **Doma** (✉ *17 Perry St.*) also brew excellent joe.

GETTING HERE AND AROUND

The West 4th Street–Washington Square subway stop—serviced by the A, B, C, D, E, F, and M—puts you in the center of Greenwich Village. Farther west, the 1 train has stops at West Houston Street and at Christopher Street–Sheridan Square. The A, C, E, and L trains stop at 14th Street, which is the northern boundary of the West Village.

BEST FOR KIDS

Hudson River Park

Washington Square Park

A stop at Magnolia for cupcakes

Sightseeing
★★★
Nightlife
★★★★★
Dining
★★★★★
Lodging
★★★
Shopping
★★★★

Long the home of writers, artists, bohemians, and bon vivants, the Village—subdivided here into Greenwich Village proper, surrounding Washington Square Park; and the West Village, between 7th Avenue and the Hudson River—is a magical section of the city. Greenwich Village, set as it is in prime New York University territory, has lots of young people, while the West Village is primarily residential, with lots of young upscale families and a large gay and lesbian community. Both areas also have many restaurants, cafés, and boutiques with a warm and charming neighborhood vibe.

GREENWICH VILLAGE

Updated by
Arthur Bovino

Fertile doesn't even begin to describe Greenwich Village's yield of creative genius. In the late 1940s and early 1950s, abstract expressionist painters Franz Kline, Jackson Pollock, Mark Rothko, and Willem de Kooning congregated here, as did Beat writers Jack Kerouac, Allen Ginsberg, and Lawrence Ferlinghetti. The 1960s brought folk musicians and poets, notably Bob Dylan. Its bohemian days may have faded today, but there is still a romantic allure lingering along tree-lined streets and at the back of the cafés, behind the frenetic clamor of NYU students and the professional veneer of high-rent town houses.

One of the neighborhood's top sites is Washington Square Park, where you can find just about every sort of person imaginable lounging on a summer day, from skateboarders to local moms to people who look like they've lived in the park for years, playing chess and checkers at the stone tables. The grand Washington Memorial Arch looks north to two blocks of lovingly preserved Greek Revival and Federal-style town houses known as the Row.

DID YOU KNOW?

Greenwich Village has a long bohemian history: for years it was an enclave of counter-culture, from beatniks to the antiwar movement to gay rights. Today this neighbor-hood is better known for its celebrity residents and sky-high housing costs.

Halloween in the Village

All things weird and wonderful, all creatures great and squall, all things witty and fantastical, New York City has them all—and on All Hallows' Eve they freak through the streets in New York's Halloween parade. White-sheeted ghouls feel dull compared with fishnets and leathers, sequins and feathers posing and prancing along 6th Avenue in this vibrant display of vanity and insanity.

In 1973 mask maker and puppeteer Ralph Lee paraded his puppets from house to house visiting friends and family along the winding streets of his Greenwich Village neighborhood. His merry march quickly outgrew its original, intimate route and now, decades later, it parades up 6th Avenue, from Spring Street to 21st Street, attracting 90,000 creatively costumed exhibitionists, artists, dancers, and musicians, hundreds of enormous puppets, scores of bands, and more than 2 million spectators. Anyone with a costume can join in, no advance registration required, although the enthusiastic interaction between participants and spectators makes it just as much fun to watch. It's a safe "street event" for families and singles alike, and a joyful night unlike any other.

The parade lines up on 6th Avenue between Canal and Spring streets from 6:30 pm to 8:30 pm. The walk actually starts at 7 pm, but it takes about two hours to leave the staging area. It's best to arrive from the south to avoid the crush of strollers and participants. Get there a few hours early if possible. Costumes are usually handmade, clever, and outrageous, and revelers are happy to strike a pose. The streets are crowded along the route, with the most congestion below 14th Street. Of course, the best way to truly experience the parade is to march, but if you're not feeling the face paint, it's possible to volunteer to help carry the puppets. For information visit ⊕ www.halloween-nyc.com.

—Jacinta O'Halloran

TOP ATTRACTIONS

Bleecker Street. Walking the stretch of Bleecker Street between 5th and 7th avenues provides a smattering of just about everything synonymous with Greenwich Village these days: NYU buildings, used-record stores, Italian cafés and food shops, shabby-chic eateries, takeout joints, and funky boutiques. Grab an espresso and sample some of the city's best pizza. Notable along the Greenwich Village length of the street is Our Lady of Pompeii Church, at Bleecker and Carmine, where Mother Cabrini, a naturalized Italian immigrant who became the first American saint, often prayed. Foodies love the blocks between 6th and 7th avenues for the specialty purveyors like Murray's Cheese (at 254 Bleecker Street). West of 7th Avenue, where Bleecker crosses the border into the West Village, things get more upscale, with fashion and home-furnishings boutiques featuring antiques, eyeglasses, shoes, and designer clothing. ⊠ *Bleecker St., Greenwich Village.*

🕙 **Washington Square Park.** NYU students, street musicians, skateboarders, jugglers, chess players, and those just watching the grand opera of it all generate a maelstrom of activity in this physical and spiritual heart

Fodor's Choice
★

of Greenwich Village. The partially restored 9½-acre park had inauspicious beginnings as a cemetery, principally for yellow-fever victims—an estimated 10,000–22,000 bodies lie below (a headstone was actually unearthed in 2009). At one time, plans to renovate the park called for the removal of the bodies; however, local resistance prevented this from happening. In the early 1800s the park was a parade ground and the site of public executions; bodies dangled from a conspicuous Hanging Elm that still stands at the northwest corner of the square. Today that gruesome past is all but forgotten, as playgrounds attract parents with tots in tow, dogs go leash-free inside the popular dog runs, and everyone else seems drawn toward the large central fountain.

> ### THE CUPCAKE CRAZE
>
> **Magnolia Bakery.** Magnolia Bakery, made famous in *Sex and the City,* kicked off a hunger for buttercream that still hasn't been sated. The bakeries that followed in its success (several opened by Magnolia alumni)—Buttercup Bakeshop, Billy's, Sugar Sweet Sunshine, and Butter Lane, as well as mobile vendors like the Cupcake Stop, among others—have been bringing a sugar buzz to other neighborhoods of NYC, too, and joining in the sweet success. ⊠ *401 Bleecker St., at W. 11th St., West Village* ☎ *212/462–2572* ⊕ *www.magnoliabakery.com.*

The triumphal European-style **Washington Memorial Arch** stands at the square's north end, marking the start of 5th Avenue. The original wood-and-papier-mâché arch, originally situated a half block north, was erected in 1889 to commemorate the 100th anniversary of George Washington's presidential inauguration. The arch was reproduced in Tuckahoe marble in 1892, and the statues—*Washington as General Accompanied by Fame and Valor* on the left and *Washington as Statesman Accompanied by Wisdom and Justice* on the right—were added in 1916 and 1918, respectively. ⊠ *5th Ave. between Waverly Pl. and 4th St., Greenwich Village* Ⓜ *A, B, C, D, E, F, M to W. 4th St.*

WORTH NOTING

Gay Street. A curved, one-block lane lined with small row houses, Gay Street is named after Sydney Howard Gay, managing editor of the long-defunct *New York Tribune,* who lived here during the Civil War with his wife and fellow abolitionist Lucretia Mott. In the 1930s this tiny thoroughfare and nearby Christopher Street became famous nationwide when, from No. 14, Ruth McKenney wrote the somewhat zany autobiographical stories that were published in *The New Yorker* and later in *My Sister Eileen,* based on what happened when she and her sister moved to Greenwich Village from Ohio. ⊠ *Between Christopher St. and Waverly Pl., Greenwich Village* Ⓜ *1 to Christopher St./Sheridan Sq.; A, B, C, D, E, F, M to W. 4th St.*

Patchin Place. This little cul-de-sac off West 10th Street between Greenwich and 6th avenues has 10 diminutive 1848 row houses. Around the corner on 6th Avenue is a similar dead-end street, **Milligan Place,** with five small homes completed in 1852. The houses in both quiet enclaves were originally built for waiters who worked at 5th Avenue's high-society Brevoort Hotel, long since demolished. Later Patchin

Out and On Display: George Segal's sculptures of two gay couples in Christopher Park illustrate gay pride in Greenwich Village.

Place residents included writers Theodore Dreiser, e. e. cummings, Jane Bowles, and Djuna Barnes. Milligan Place became popular among playwrights, including Eugene O'Neill. ⊠ *New York* Ⓜ *A, B, C, D, E, F, M to W. 4th St.*

The Row. Built from 1833 through 1837, this series of beautifully preserved Greek Revival row houses along Washington Square North, between University Place and MacDougal Street, once belonged to merchants and bankers, then to writers and artists such as John Dos Passos and Edward Hopper. ⊠ *1–13 and 19–26 Washington Sq. N, between University Pl. and MacDougal St., Greenwich Village* Ⓜ *A, B, C, D, E, F, M to W. 4th St./Washington Sq.*

Washington Mews. A rarity in Manhattan, this private, gated street is lined on one side with the former stables of the houses on "the Row," as it's known, on Washington Square North. You can peer in at the quaint street through the gates. ⊠ *Between 8th St. and Washington Sq. N, between 5th Ave. and University Pl., Greenwich Village* Ⓜ *A, B, C, D, E, F, M to W. 4th St.*

WEST VILLAGE

High-rises and office towers have little business among the labyrinth of small curving streets, peculiar alleys, and historic town houses here, although a new boom in distinctive apartment living by designer architects has emerged around the western edges near the Hudson River. Primarily residential, there is something unique about the tree-lined streets of the West Village, with its charming cafés, nondescript celebrities out

CLOSE UP

Bleecker Street's Little Italy

Little Italy can be besieged by slow-moving crowds, touristy shops, and restaurant hosts hollering invites as you pass to dine inside. Bleecker Street between 6th and 7th avenues, with its crowded cafés, bakeries, pizza parlors, and old-world merchants, seems more vital as a true Italian neighborhood.

For an authentic Italian bakery experience, step into **Pasticerria Rocco** (No. 243) for wonderful cannoli, cream puffs, and cookies packed up, or order an espresso and linger over the treats.

Step into the past at the old-style butcher shops, such as **Ottomanelli & Sons** (No. 285) and **Faicco's Pork Store** (No. 260), where Italian locals have gotten their pork custom cut since 1900.

The sweet (or stinky) smell of success seems nowhere more evident than at **Murray's Cheese** (No. 254), at Cornelia Street. The original shop, opened in 1940 by Murray Greenberg

(not Italian), was not much larger than the display case that stocked the stuff. Now it's a fromage fiend's emporium, with everything from imported crackers and bamboo cutting boards to a full-service sandwich counter. Samples of cheese, gelato, salami, and other goodies are frequently offered.

In a town that's fierce about its pizza, some New Yorkers swear by **John's Pizzeria** (No. 278). But be forewarned: they do whole thin-crust pies only—no individual slices. Luckily, one of the city's best slice joints is right around the corner, Joe's Pizza (7 Carmine Street). To complicate the Bleecker Street pizza situation further, newcomer **Kesté Pizza & Vino** (271 Bleecker Street) is serving up Neapolitan pies that some would argue give even Da Michele in Naples a run for its money. It is also the official location in the United States for the Associazione Pizzaiuoli Napoletani, whose mission is to protect and promote the Neapolitan pizza tradition.

5

and about, and the well-dressed children playing in the parks. Tiny as they might be, restaurants like the Little Owl and 'ino invite you to linger, as do larger restaurants with outside dining areas.

It's easy to feel like a local while shopping here. Unlike 5th Avenue or SoHo, the pace is slower, the streets are relatively quiet, and the scale is small. This is the where to come for unusual finds rather than global-brand goods. The West Village section of Bleecker Street is a particularly good place to indulge all sorts of shopping appetites; high-fashion foragers prowl the stretch between West 10th Street and 8th Avenue. Hudson Street and Greenwich Avenue are also prime boutique-browsing territory.

Christopher Street has long been the symbolic heart of New York's gay and lesbian community. On this street, among cafés, lifestyle boutiques, and clothing shops, is one of the city's most acclaimed off-Broadway theaters, the Lucille Lortel, where major off-Broadway playwrights like David Mamet, Eugene Ionesco, and Edward Albee have their own markers in the sidewalk. Nearby, at 51–53 Christopher Street, is the site of the Stonewall Inn and the historic Stonewall riots, which marked the beginning of the gay rights movement. Across the street is a green triangle named Christopher Park, where there are commemorative statues of gay and lesbian companions.

TOP ATTRACTIONS

Hudson River Park. *See the listing in the TriBeCa section of Chapter 2: Lower Manhattan.*

WORTH NOTING

75½ Bedford Street. Rising real-estate rates inspired the construction of New York City's narrowest house—just 9½ feet wide and 32 feet deep—in 1873. Built on a lot that was originally a carriage entrance of the Isaacs-Hendricks House next door, this sliver of a building was home to actor John Barrymore and poet Edna St. Vincent Millay. ⊠ *75½ Bedford St., between Commerce and Morton Sts., West Village* Ⓜ *A, B, C, D, E, F, M to W. 4th St.*

Ⓒ **Children's Museum of the Arts.** After more than a decade trying to be creative with a cramped space in SoHo, the Children's Museum of the Arts (CMA) relocated to a brand-new split-level space in the West Village in late 2011 to give children up to age 15 room to really get creative. Along with the requisite children's museum offerings like pencils, chalk, and paint, you'll find a clay bar; a media lab with a soundproof room, mounted cameras, and a recording studio; a small slide and colorful ball pond that kids can dive into; an airy exhibition space featuring rotating exhibits (and workshops inspired by exhibits); a permanent collection of children's art from more than 50 countries and dating to the 1930s, and classes in everything from ceramics and origami to animation and filmmaking. ⊠ *103 Charlton St., between Hudson and Greenwich Sts., West Village* ☎ *212/274–0986* ⊕ *www.cmany.org* ⊿ *$10* ◷ *Mon.–Wed. noon–5, Thurs. and Fri. noon–6, weekends 10–6* Ⓜ *6 to Spring St.*

Christopher Park. You may share a bench in this tiny park with George Segal's life-size sculptures of a lesbian couple. A gay male couple is also captured in mid-chat nearby. The park was a punch line in the '90s gay comedy *Jeffrey.* ⊠ *Bordered by W. 4th, Grove, and Christopher Sts., West Village* Ⓜ *1 to Christopher St./Sheridan Sq.*

St. Luke's Place. Steeped in New York City history and shaded by graceful gingko trees, this section of Leroy Street has 15 classic Italianate brownstone and brick town houses (1851–54). Novelist Theodore Dreiser wrote *An American Tragedy* at No. 16, and poet Marianne Moore resided at No. 14. Mayor Jimmy Walker (first elected in 1926) lived at No. 6; the lampposts in front are "mayor's lamps," which were sometimes placed in front of the residences of New York mayors. This block is often used as a film location: No. 12 was shown as the Huxtables' home on *The Cosby Show* (although on the show it was in Brooklyn), and No. 4 was the setting of the Audrey Hepburn movie *Wait Until Dark.* Before 1890 the playground on the south side of the street near Hudson was a graveyard where, according to legend, the dauphin of France—the lost son of Louis XVI and Marie Antoinette—is buried. ⊠ *Between Hudson St. and 7th Ave. S, West Village* Ⓜ *1 to Houston St.*

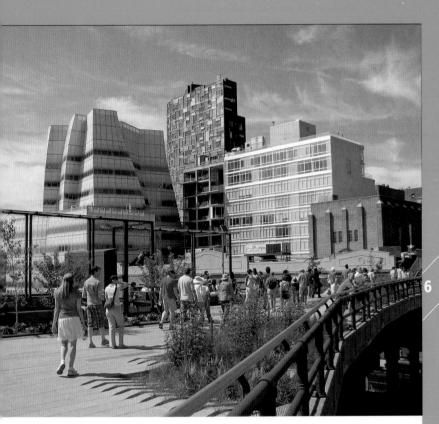

6

Chelsea and the Meatpacking District

WORD OF MOUTH

"Look into spending part of your day exploring the High Line. It's an old railroad track that they turned into New York's first elevated park. It stretches across I think about 20 blocks and it's really beautiful . . . It's really awesome."

— mstillwell820

GETTING ORIENTED

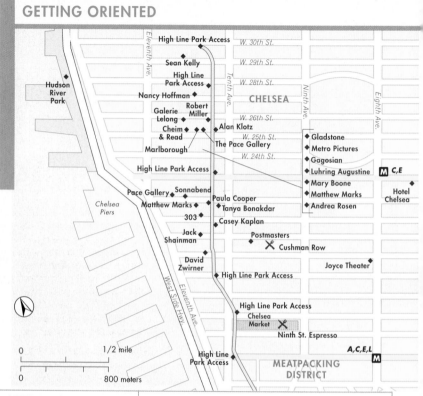

GETTING HERE AND AROUND	MAKING THE MOST OF YOUR TIME

The A, C, E, 1, 2, 3, and L trains stop at 14th Street for both the Meatpacking District and Chelsea. The latter is further served by the C, E, 1, F, and M lines at the 23rd Street stop and the 1 stop at 28th Street. 14th Street and 23rd Street are both also served by the PATH trains.

Chelsea has a dual life: Typical gallery hours are Tuesday–Saturday 10–6, but at night the neighborhood changes into a party town, with bars (gay and straight) and high-profile nightclubs that don't rev up until after 11.

To truly appreciate the Meatpacking District, make a 9 pm or later dinner reservation at a hot restaurant, then hit the bars to see where the glitterati are this week.

If shopping is your pleasure, weekdays are great; come after noon, though, or you'll find most spots shuttered.

6

QUICK BITES, COFFEE, OR COCKTAILS

The outlet of Ninth Street Espresso in Chelsea Market (9th Ave. between 15th and 16th Sts.). is popular all day. In fact, Chelsea Market has just about all of your food cravings covered—and if you want to pick up fixings for a picnic on the High Line, this is the place to go.

Donut Pub (✉ *203 W. 14th St.*). Care for an apple fritter with your coffee? Pull up a stool.

Flatiron Lounge (✉ *37 W. 19th St.*). This funky art-deco hangout offers mini-martini flights, among other inventive cocktails.

TOP EXPERIENCES

Gallery hopping in Chelsea.

Walking along the High Line.

Checking out the Meatpacking District's nightlife.

Eating your way through Chelsea Market.

Shopping at the classy shops in the Meatpacking District.

Lying on the grass in Hudson River Park, looking across the water to New Jersey.

BEST FOR KIDS

Chelsea Piers

The High Line

Hudson River Park

Sightseeing
★★★
Nightlife
★★★★★
Dining
★★★★★
Lodging
★★★
Shopping
★★★★

Chelsea long ago usurped SoHo as the epicenter of New York contemporary art galleries but the opening of the High Line above 10th Avenue created a new artery of life in this part of the city. More foot traffic means more gentrification and more restaurants. Chelsea has also replaced the West Village as the heart of the city's gay community.

Updated by
Arthur Bovino

Most of Chelsea's art galleries are found from about 20th to 27th streets, primarily between 10th and 11th avenues. The range of contemporary art on display includes almost every imaginable medium and style; if it's going on in the art world, it'll be in one of the 300 or so galleries here. Standouts include the enormous **David Zwirner Gallery** on West 19th Street, across from the amazing Frank Gehry–designed IAC office building; the **Robert Miller Gallery** on West 26th Street, whose proprietor is a titan in the New York art world and represents the estate of Diane Arbus, among others; and the galleries of **Gagosian** and **Matthew Marks**, both showing the latest in painting, photography, and sculpture. If it's performing arts that you're more interested in, the **Joyce Theater** on 8th Avenue and 19th Street showcases modern dance troupes like Pilobolus, Elisa Monte Dance, and Momix.

TOP ATTRACTIONS

Chelsea Market. This former Nabisco plant—where the first Oreos were baked in 1912—now houses more than two dozen gourmet food, wine, and flower shops, as well as one of NYC's last independent bookstores (Posman Books). Renowned specialty purveyors, including L'Arte del Gelato, Fat Witch Bakery, Amy's Bread, Jacques Torres Chocolate, Ninth Street Espresso, flank the interior walkway that stretches from 9th to 10th avenues. If it's a meal you're after, Friedman's Lunch is a standout for its excellent, well-priced food. The market's funky industrial design—a tangle of glass and metal creates the awning and art, artifacts, and a factory pipe converted into an indoor waterfall—complements the eclectic assortment of shops. There is some seating inside but if the weather's nice, take your goodies to go, and eat outside on the High Line. ⊠ *75 9th Ave., between W. 15th and W. 16th Sts., Chelsea*

☎ *212/652–2117* ⊕ *www.chelseamarket.com* ⊙ *Mon.–Sat. 7–9, Sun. 8–7* Ⓜ *A, C, E, L to 14th St.*

The High Line. Once a railroad track carrying freight trains, this elevated space has been transformed into a green retreat in the spirit of Paris's Promenade Plantée. A long "walking park" with benches, public art installations, and views of the Hudson River and the Manhattan skyline, the High Line is set above 10th Avenue in West Chelsea. Reclining chaise longues and strategically situated benches are perfect for a picnic lunch (Chelsea Market is a convenient place to pick up sandwiches). The first section of the High Line, between Gansevoort and West 20th streets opened in 2009 and was immediately the talk of the town. The second section of the park, up to West 30th Street, opened in 2011, doubling the length of the walkway. There are access points up from the street all along its length. The final section of the High Line, between West 30th and West 34th streets at the West Side Rail Yards, is privately owned and has not yet been secured for park use. ⊠ *10th Ave. from Gansevoort St. to 30th St., Chelsea* ☎ *212/206–9922* ⊕ *www. thehighline.org* Ⓜ *L to 8th Ave.; 1 to 14th St., 23rd St., or 28th St.; 2 and 3 to 14th St.; A, C, E to 14th St.; C and E to 23rd St.*

Hudson River Park. *See the listing in the TriBeCa section of Chapter 2.*

Meatpacking District. Concentrated in a few blocks of what is essentially the West Village, between the Hudson River and 9th Avenue, from Little West 12th Street to about West 17th Street, the Meatpacking District used to be the center of the wholesale meat industry for New York City. Other than beloved meat purveyor Pat LaFrieda, though, there are few meat markets left in this now rather quaint, cobblestoned area—but it's definitely a metaphorical meat market at night, when the city's trendiest frequent the equally trendy restaurants and bars here. The area is also home to some of the city's hottest retailers, with boutiques of fashion designers like Alexander McQueen and Stella McCartney. ⊠ *Chelsea.*

WORTH NOTING

Ⓒ **Chelsea Piers.** This sports-and-entertainment complex along the Hudson River between 17th and 23rd streets, a phenomenal example of adaptive reuse, is the size of four 80-story buildings if they were laid out flat. There's pretty much every kind of sports activity going on inside and out, from golf (check out the multitiered, all-weather, outdoor driving range) to ice-skating, rock climbing, soccer, bowling, gymnastics, and basketball. Plus there's a spa, elite sport-specific training, film studios, and a brewery with a restaurant. Chelsea Piers is also the jumping-off point for some of the city's varied water tours and dinner cruises. ⊠ *Piers 59–62 on Hudson River from 17th to 23rd Sts.; entrance at 23rd St., Chelsea* ☎ *212/336–6666* ⊕ *www.chelseapiers.com* Ⓜ *C, E to 23rd St.*

Cushman Row. Built in 1840, this string of homes between 9th and 10th avenues represents some of the country's most perfect examples of Greek Revival row houses. Original details include small wreath-encircled attic windows, deeply recessed doorways with brownstone frames, and striking iron balustrades and fences. Note the pineapples, a traditional symbol of welcome, on top of the black iron newels in

front of No. 416. ⊠ *406–418 W. 20th St., between 9th and 10th Aves., Chelsea* Ⓜ C, E to 23rd St.

Hotel Chelsea. The shabby aura of the hotel is part of its bohemian allure. This 12-story Queen Anne–style neighborhood landmark (1884) became a hotel in 1905, although it predominantly catered to long-term tenants. The literary roll call of live-ins is legendary: Mark Twain, Eugene O'Neill, O. Henry, Thomas Wolfe, Tennessee Williams, Vladimir Nabokov, Mary McCarthy, Arthur Miller, Dylan Thomas, William S. Burroughs,

Patti Smith, and Robert Mapplethorpe. In 1966 Andy Warhol filmed a group of fellow artists; the footage was included in *The Chelsea Girls* (1967). The hotel was also seen on-screen in *I Shot Andy Warhol* (1996) and in *Sid and Nancy* (1986), a dramatization of the real-life murder of Nancy Spungen, stabbed to death here by her Sex Pistols boyfriend Sid Vicious. Read the commemorative plaques outside, then check out the eclectic collection of art in the lobby, some rumored to have been donated in lieu of rent. The Chelsea Hotel, as it's popularly called, stopped accepting guest reservations in 2011. ⊠ *222 W. 23rd St., between 7th and 8th Aves., Chelsea* ☎ *212/243–3700* ⊕ *www. hotelchelsea.com* Ⓜ *1, 2, C, E to 23rd St.*

Rubin Museum of Art. This sleek museum spread over six floors is the largest in the Western Hemisphere dedicated to the art of the Himalayas, and the pieces here include paintings on cloth, metal sculptures, and textiles dating from the 2nd century onward. Many of the works from areas such as Tibet, Nepal, southwest China, and India are related to Buddhism, Hinduism, Bon, and other eastern religions. A pleasant café and gift shop are on the ground floor. ⊠ *150 W. 17th St., near 7th Ave., Chelsea* ☎ *212/620–5000* ⊕ *www.rmanyc.org* ⊠ *$10* ⊗ *Mon. and Thurs. 11–5, Wed. 11–7, Fri. 11–10, weekends 11–6* Ⓜ *1 to 18th St.*

GALLERIES

303 Gallery. International cutting-edge artists shown here include photographer Doug Aitken and installation artists Karen Kilimnik, and Jane and Louise Wilson. ⊠ *547 W. 21st St., between 10th and 11th Aves., Chelsea* ☎ *212/255–1121* ⊕ *www.303gallery.com* ⊗ *Tues.–Sat. 10–6; closed Aug.; closed Sun. July–Sept.* Ⓜ *C, E to 23rd St.*

Alan Klotz Gallery. Fine 19th- and 20th-century and contemporary photography is the focus of the exhibitions here. Shows range from the modern photo-realistic domestic scenes by Melissa Ann Pinney to the more playful portraits of photojournalist Jonathan Torgovnik. There are extensive collections from some of history's most important photographers, including Josef Sudek, Berenice Abbott, and Eugene de Salignac. ⊠ *511 W. 25th St., Suite 701, between 10th and 11th*

You never know what you might see in Chelsea's galleries: works by well-known artists like Alexander Calder, or pieces by up-and-coming artists.

Aves., Chelsea ☎ *212/741–4764* ⊕ *www.klotzgallery.com* ☾ *Wed.–Sat. noon–6* Ⓜ *C, E to 23rd St.*

Andrea Rosen Gallery. Artists on the cutting edge, such as sculptor Andrea Zittel, Felix Gonzalez-Torres, and painter and installation artist Matthew Ritchie, are on view here. ⊠ *525 W. 24th St., between 10th and 11th Aves., Chelsea* ☎ *212/627–6000* ⊕ *www.andrearosengallery.com* ☾ *Tues.–Sat. 10–6* Ⓜ *C, E to 23rd St.*

Casey Kaplan. Founded in 1995, the Casey Kaplan gallery represents contemporary artists from Europe and the Americas. Sophisticated exhibitions have included works by such artists as Henning Bohl, Matthew Brannon, Johannes Wohnseifer, and Julia Schmidt. ⊠ *525 W. 21st St., between 10th and 11th Aves., Chelsea* ☎ *212/645–7335* ⊕ *www. caseykaplangallery.com* ☾ *Tues.–Sat. 10-6* Ⓜ *C, E to 23rd St.*

Cheim & Read. This prestigious gallery represents artists such as Louise Bourgeois, William Eggleston, Joan Mitchell, Jenny Holzer, Donald Baechler, and Jack Pierson. ⊠ *547 W. 25th St., between 10th and 11th Aves., Chelsea* ☎ *212/242–7727* ⊕ *www.cheimread.com* ☾ *Tues.–Sat. 10–6* Ⓜ *C, E to 23rd St.*

David Zwirner. Proving his finger is on the pulse of contemporary art, Zwirner shows works in all mediums by such emerging artists as Luc Tuymans, Stan Douglas, Thomas Ruff, Diana Thater, and Yutaka Sone. ⊠ *525 W. 19th St., between 10th and 11th Aves., Chelsea* ☎ *212/727–2070* ⊕ *www.davidzwirner.com* ☾ *Tues.–Sat. 10–6* Ⓜ *C, E to 23rd St.*

Gagosian Gallery. This enterprising modern gallery has two large Chelsea branches and a third on the Upper East Side, as well as around the

CLOSE UP

Chelsea Galleries 101

Good art, bad art, edgy art, downright disturbing art—it's all here waiting to please and provoke in the contemporary art capital of the world. For the uninitiated, the concentration of nearly 300 galleries within a seven-block radius can be overwhelming, and the sometimes cool receptions on entering and deafening silence, intimidating. Art galleries are not exactly famous for their customer-service skills, but they're free, and you don't need a degree in art appreciation to stare at a canvas or an installation.

There's no required code of conduct, although most galleries are library-quiet and cell phones are seriously frowned upon. Don't worry, you won't be pressured to buy anything; staff will probably be doing their best to ignore you.

Galleries are generally open Tuesday through Saturday from 10 am to 6 pm. Gallery hop on a Saturday afternoon—the highest-traffic day—if you want company. You can usually find a binder with the artist's résumé, examples of previous work, and exhibit details (usually including prices) at the front desk. If not, ask. Also ask whether there's information you can take with you.

You can't see everything in one afternoon, so if you have specific interests, plan ahead. Find gallery information and current exhibit details by checking the listings in the *New Yorker* or the weekend section of the *New York Times*. Learn more about the galleries and the genres and artists they represent at ⊕ *www.artincontext.org*.

—Jacinta O'Halloran

world. All show works by heavy hitters such as sculptor Richard Serra, the late pop-art icon Roy Lichtenstein, Willem de Kooning, and bad boy Damien Hirst. ⊠ *555 W. 24th St., at 11th Ave., Chelsea* ☎ *212/741–1111* ⊕ *www.gagosian.com* ☉ *Tues.–Sat. 10–6* Ⓜ *C, E to 23rd St.*⊠ *522 W. 21st St., between 10th and 11th Aves., Chelsea* ☎ *212/741–1717* ☉ *Mon.–Sat. 10–6.*

Galerie Lelong. This large gallery presents challenging installations and art, as well as many Latin American artists. Look for Alfredo Jaar, Andy Goldsworthy, Cildo Meireles, Ana Mendieta, Hélio Oiticica, Sean Scully, and Petah Coyne. ⊠ *528 W. 26th St., between 10th and 11th Aves., Chelsea* ☎ *212/315–0470* ⊕ *www.galerielelong.com* ☉ *Tues.–Sat. 10–6* Ⓜ *C, E to 23rd St.*

Gladstone Gallery. The international roster of artists in this gallery's two locations includes sculptor Anish Kapoor, photographer Sharon Lockhart, and multimedia artists Matthew Barney and Richard Prince. ⊠ *515 W. 24th St., between 10th and 11th Aves., Chelsea* ☎ *212/206–9300* ⊕ *www.gladstonegallery.com* ☉ *Tues.–Sat. 10–6* Ⓜ *C, E to 23rd St.* ⊠ *530 W. 21st St., between 10th and 11th Aves., Chelsea* ☎ *212/ 206–7606* ☉ *Tues.–Sat. 10–6.*

Jack Shainman Gallery. Emerging and established artists such as Subodh Gupta, a young sculptor from India, and Kerry James Marshall, whose art deals with African-American issues, are shown here. You might find works by Phil Frost, whose imagery is derived from graffiti, or Zwelethu

Mthethwa, a South African photographer. ✉ *513 W. 20th St., between 10th and 11th Aves., Chelsea* ☎ *212/645–1701* ⊕ *www.jackshainman. com* ⊘ *Tues.–Sat. 10–6* Ⓜ *C, E to 23rd St.*

Luhring Augustine. Owners Lawrence Luhring and Roland Augustine have been working with established and emerging artists from Europe, Japan, and America, since 1985. ✉ *531 W. 24th St., between 10th and 11th Aves., Chelsea* ☎ *212/206–9100* ⊕ *www.luhringaugustine.com* Ⓜ *C, E to 23rd St.*

Marlborough. With galleries in London, Monaco, and Madrid, the Marlborough empire also operates two of the largest and most influential galleries in New York City. The Chelsea location (the other is on 57th Street) shows the latest work of modern artists, with a focus on sculptural forms, such as the large-scale work of Michele Oka Doner. Red Grooms, Richard Estes, and Fernando Botero are just a few of the 20th-century luminaries represented. ✉ *545 W. 25th St., between 10th and 11th Aves., Chelsea* ☎ *212/463–8634* ⊕ *www.marlboroughgallery. com* ⊘ *Tues.–Sat. 10–5:30* Ⓜ *C, E to 23rd St.*

Mary Boone Gallery. It was once a hot gallery in SoHo during the 1980s, but this venue now resides both in Midtown and in the newer flash point of Chelsea. Boone continues to show established artists such as Barbara Kruger and Eric Fischl, as well as newcomers. ✉ *541 West 24th St., between 10th and 11th Aves., Chelsea* ☎ *212/752–2929* ⊕ *www. maryboonegallery.com* ⊘ *Tues.–Sat. 10–6* Ⓜ *C, E to 23rd St.*

Matthew Marks Gallery. A hot venue for both the New York and international art crowd, openings at any of the four Matthew Marks galleries are always an interesting scene. Swiss artist Ugo Rondinone made his U.S. debut here, as did Andreas Gursky. Nan Goldin, Ellsworth Kelly, Brice Marden, Katharina Fritsch, and a cast of illustrious others also show here. ✉ *523 W. 24th St., between 10th and 11th Aves., Chelsea* ☎ *212/243–0200* ⊕ *www.matthewmarks.com* ⊘ *Tues.–Sat. 10–6* Ⓜ *C, E to 23rd St.* ✉ *502 West 22nd St., between 10th and 11th Aves., Chelsea* ☎ *212/243–0200* ⊕ *www.matthewmarks.com* ⊘ *Tues.–Sat. 11–6* ✉ *522 W. 22nd St., between 10th and 11th Aves., Chelsea* ☎ *212/243–0200* ⊘ *Tues.–Sat. 11–6* ✉ *526 West 22nd St., between 10th and 11th Aves., Chelsea* ☎ *212/243–0200* ⊘ *Tues.–Sat. 11–6.*

Metro Pictures. The hottest talents in contemporary art shown here include Cindy Sherman, whose provocative photographs have brought her international prominence. ✉ *519 W. 24th St., between 10th and 11th Aves., Chelsea* ☎ *212/206–7100* ⊕ *www.metropicturesgallery.com* ⊘ *Tues.–Sat. 10–6* Ⓜ *C, E to 23rd St.*

Nancy Hoffman Gallery. Contemporary painting, sculpture, drawing, photography, and video works by an impressive array of international artists are on display here. Artists range from Viola Frey, known for her heroic-scale ceramic male and female figures, to other well-established artists such as Don Eddy and Joseph Raffael, to a strong group of young artists embarking with their first solo shows. ✉ *520 W. 27th St., between 10th and 11th Aves., Chelsea* ☎ *212/966–6676* ⊕ *www. nancyhoffmangallery.com* ⊘ *Tues.–Sat. 10–6* Ⓜ *C, E to 23rd St.*

The Pace Gallery. The impressive roster of artists represented by the Pace Gallery includes a variety of upper-echelon artists, sculptors, and photographers, including Elizabeth Murray, Chuck Close, Sol LeWitt, and Robert Rauschenberg. In addition to the Midtown location, there are three spaces in Chelsea. ⊠ *534 W. 25th St., between 10th and 11th Aves., Chelsea* ☎ *212/929–7000* ⊕ *www.thepacegallery.com* ⊗ *Tues.–Sat. 10–6* Ⓜ *C, E to 23rd St.*⊠ *510 West 25th St., between 10th and 11th Aves., Chelsea* ☎ *212/255–4044* ⊗ *Tues.–Sat. 10–6*⊠ *545 W. 22nd St., between 10th and 11th Aves., Chelsea* ☎ *212/989–4258* ⊗ *Tues.–Sat. 10–6.*

Paula Cooper Gallery. SoHo pioneer Paula Cooper moved to Chelsea in 1996, and enlisted architect Richard Gluckman to transform a warehouse into a dramatic space with tall ceilings and handsome skylights. There are now two galleries that showcase the minimalist sculptures of Carl André, among other works. ⊠ *534 W. 21st St., between 10th and 11th Aves., Chelsea* ☎ *212/255–1105* ⊕ *www.paulacoopergallery. com* ⊗ *Tues.–Sat. 10–6* Ⓜ *C, E to 23rd St.*⊠ *521 West 21st St., 2nd fl., between 10th and 11th Aves., Chelsea* ☎ *212/255–1105* ⊗ *Tues.–Sat. 10–6.*

Postmasters. Postmasters shows new and established conceptual artists, with one room devoted to multimedia shows. Past exhibits have included Claude Wampler's *Pomerania*—a series of photographs, sculptures, video, and drawings examining the artist's relationship with her pet Pomeranian. ⊠ *459 W. 19th St., between 9th and 10th Aves., Chelsea* ☎ *212/727–3323* ⊕ *www.postmastersart.com* ⊗ *Tues.–Sat. 11–6* Ⓜ *C, E to 23rd St.*

Robert Miller Gallery. Miller, a titan of the New York art world, represents some of the biggest names in modern painting and photography, including Diane Arbus and the estates of Lee Krasner and Alice Neel. ⊠ *524 W. 26th St., between 10th and 11th Aves., Chelsea* ☎ *212/366–4774* ⊕ *www.robertmillergallery.com* ⊗ *Aug.–June: Tues.–Sat 10–6; July: Mon.–Fri. 10–6* Ⓜ *C, E to 23rd St.*

Sean Kelly Gallery. Drop in at this large space to see works by top contemporary American and European artists such as Marina Abramovic, Robert Mapplethorpe, Antony Gormley, Joseph Kosuth, and James Casebere. ⊠ *528 W. 29th St., between 10th and 11th Aves., Chelsea* ☎ *212/239–1181* ⊕ *www.skny.com* ⊗ *Tues.–Fri. 11–6; Sat. 10–6* Ⓜ *1 to 28th St.; C, E to 23rd St.*

Sonnabend. This pioneer of the SoHo art scene continues to show important contemporary artists in its Chelsea space, including Jeff Koons, Ashley Bickerton, and the British art duo Gilbert & George. ⊠ *536 W. 22nd St., between 10th and 11th Aves., Chelsea* ☎ *212/627–1018* ⊕ *www.sonnabendgallery.com* ⊗ *Tues.–Sat. 10–6* Ⓜ *C, E to 23rd St.*

Tanya Bonakdar Gallery. Contemporary artists such as Uta Barth, whose blurry photos challenge ideas about perception, and Ernesto Neto, a Brazilian artist who has made stunning room-size installations of large nylon sacks filled with spices, are shown here. ⊠ *521 W. 21st St., between 10th and 11th Aves., Chelsea* ☎ *212/414–4144* ⊕ *www. tanyabonakdargallery.com* ⊗ *Tues.–Sat. 10–6* Ⓜ *C, E to 23rd St.*

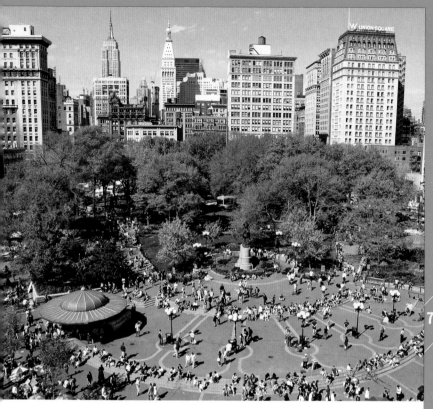

Union Square, the Flatiron District, and Gramercy Park

WORD OF MOUTH

"Union Square is very lively and very busy . . . on any given day there is a protest or a commercial filming or a news crew grabbing 'man on the street' interviews . . . and 2 blocks south is one of the best bookstores in the United States—the Strand."   —mp

GETTING ORIENTED

MAKING THE MOST OF YOUR TIME

Union Square seems like it's busy at just about every time of day and night, with commuters and people hanging out on the steps to eat lunch or just hang out, but market days—Monday, Wednesday, Friday, and Saturday—are even busier. Early weekday mornings are quietest, before the market is set up, though without all the people, the area loses its allure.

This is definitely an area for strolling, shopping, and eating, so plan your visit around a meal—or several.

If you're planning to eat at the Shake Shack in Madison Square Park, come at noon if you can; the lines here can get pretty long.

GETTING HERE AND AROUND

Union Square/14th Street is a major subway hub, with the L, N, Q, R, 4, 5, and 6 lines all converging here. For Madison Square Park, take the local R to 23rd Street. The 6 also stops at 23rd and 28th streets.

TOP EXPERIENCES

Strolling in Union Square Park and checking out the produce and other goodies at the greenmarket.

Browsing the miles of books in the Strand bookstore.

Picnicking in Madison Square Park.

QUICK BITES, COFFEE, OR COCKTAILS

Coffee & Tea Bar (⊠ *71 Irving Pl.*). The owners here roast their own beans—always a good sign.

OralFix Aphrodisiac Cafe (⊠ *233 5th Ave.*). Bored with that latte? Experiment with 3,000-year-old aphrodisiacs and elixirs instead!

City Bakery (⊠ *3 W. 18th St.*). "Pretzel croissants," chocolate-chip cookies, and super-thick hot chocolate are just some of the signature snacks here.

Eataly (⊠ *200 5th Ave. at 23rd St.*). For everything gourmet Italian.

Shake Shack (⊠ *Madison Square Park*). A true contender for New York's best burger.

Ace Hotel (⊠ *20 W. 29th St.*). It's an ultracool hot spot for visiting and local hipsters.

Pete's Tavern (⊠ *129 E. 18th St.*). An iconic bar with a neighborhood feel, and a good beer selection.

7

Sightseeing
★★★★

Nightlife
★

Dining
★★★

Lodging
★★★

Shopping
★★★★

Union Square is a hub of seemingly never-ending activity and people-watching that anchors the quieter neighborhoods of Gramercy and the Flatiron District. When that certain brand of New Yorkers say they don't like to travel above 14th Street, they're usually thinking about Union Square as the cut-off.

UNION SQUARE

Updated
by Jacinta
O'Halloran

The energy of Union Square reaches its peak during its greenmarket days (Monday, Wednesday, Friday, and Saturday), when more than 25 farms and food purveyors set up shop on the square's north and west sides to peddle everything from produce to meat and fresh fish to baked goods. The market is a great place to rub elbows with—and get elbowed by—local shoppers and chefs and a great source for tasty souvenirs (locally produced honeys, jams, and cheeses) as well as lunch. Find a bench in the park to savor your goodies and take in the scene. Sometimes political rallies happen here, too.

Even if it's a nonmarket day, though, Union Square regularly has vendors of all kinds, selling everything from art to jewelry to T-shirts. New York University students, nannies with their charges, visitors, and locals alike all gather in this open space that can at times feel more like an outdoor version of Grand Central Station than a park. Just south of Union Square, on Broadway at 12th Street, is the Strand, the giant bookstore that attracts book lovers like a magnet.

It was in Union Square, on September 5, 1882, that Labor Day was born, when more than 10,000 New York City union workers took an unpaid day off to march from City Hall to Union Square.

TOP ATTRACTIONS

Union Square Park and Greenmarket. A park, farmers' market, meeting place, and site of rallies and demonstrations, this pocket of green space sits in the center of a bustling residential and commercial neighborhood. The name Union originally signified that two main roads—Broadway

and 4th Avenue—crossed here, but it took on a different meaning in the late 19th and early 20th centuries, when the square became a rallying spot for labor protests; many unions, as well as fringe political parties, moved their headquarters nearby.

Union Square is at its best on Monday, Wednesday, Friday, and Saturday (8–6), when the largest of the city's greenmarkets brings farmers and food purveyors from the tri-state area. Browse the stands of fruit and vegetables, flowers, plants, fresh-baked pies and breads, cheeses, cider, New York State wines, fish, and meat. Between Thanksgiving and Christmas, there is a gift market where artisans sell gift items in candy-cane-stripe booths at the square's southwest end.

> **TIME OUT!**
>
> Union Square's most love-it-or-hate-it feature is the *Metronome* sculpture with its bank of cascading numbers. Half art installation, half timepiece, it sits above Nordstrom Rack, and is actually a clock that counts both time elapsed and time remaining in the day. At noon and midnight huge bursts of steam emerge, turning into trickles throughout the day.

New York University dormitories, theaters, and cavernous commercial spaces occupy the handsomely restored 19th-century commercial buildings that surround the park, along with chain coffee shops and restaurants. The run of diverse architectural styles on the Decker Building at 33 Union Square West is as imaginative as its former contents: this was once home to Andy Warhol's studio. The building at 17th Street and Union Square East, now housing the New York Film Academy and the Union Square Theater, was the final home of Tammany Hall, an organization famous in its day as a corrupt and powerful political machine. Statues in the park include those of George Washington, Abraham Lincoln, Mahatma Gandhi (often wreathed in flowers), and the Marquis de Lafayette sculpted by Frederic Auguste Bartholdi, creator of the Statue of Liberty. Plaques in the sidewalk on the southeast and southwest sides chronicle the park's history from the 1600s to 1800s. ⊠ *E. 14th to E. 17th Sts., between Broadway and Park Ave. S, Flatiron District* Ⓜ *L, N, Q, R, 4, 5, 6 to Union Sq./14th St.*

FLATIRON DISTRICT

The Flatiron District—anchored by Madison Square Park on the north and Union Square to the south—is one of the city's busiest neighborhoods, particularly along 5th Avenue and Park Avenue South. In some ways it should still be called Ladies' Mile: the area is a favorite for spotting models because of the number of agencies and photography studios here. Lovely Madison Square Park, a pleasant green space hemmed in by the neighborhood's notable architecture—from the triangular Flatiron to the dazzling, gold-pyramid-topped New York Life Building and the Metropolitan Life Tower, with its elegant clock face—is the best place to savor the view. Sit and admire the scene with a burger and shake from the park's always busy Shake Shack, or takeout from the new foodie favorite, Eataly, across the street from the west side of the park.

The wedge-shaped Flatiron Building got its nickname because of its resemblance to the shape of a clothes iron; its original name is the Fuller Building.

TOP ATTRACTIONS

Flatiron Building. When completed in 1902, the Fuller Building, as it was originally known, caused a sensation. Architect Daniel Burnham made ingenious use of the triangular wedge of land at 23rd Street, 5th Avenue, and Broadway, employing a revolutionary steel frame that allowed for the building's 22-story, 286-foot height. Covered with a limestone and white terra-cotta facade in the Italian Renaissance style, the building's shape resembled a clothing iron, hence its nickname. When it became apparent that the building generated strong winds, gawkers would loiter at 23rd Street hoping to catch sight of ladies' billowing skirts. Local traffic cops had to shoo away the male peepers—one purported origin of the phrase "23 skidoo." There is a small display of historic building and area photos in the lobby, but otherwise you will have to settle for appreciating this building from the outside . . . at least for now; the building may be converted to a luxury hotel when current occupant leases expire in 2013. ⊠ *175 5th Ave., bordered by E. 22nd and E. 23rd Sts., 5th Ave., and Broadway, Flatiron District* Ⓜ *R, W to 23rd St.*

Madison Square Park. The benches of this elegant tree-filled park afford great views of some of the city's oldest and most charming skyscrapers (the Flatiron Building, the Metropolitan Life Insurance Tower, the New York Life Insurance Building, and the Empire State Building) and serve as a perfect vantage point for people-, pigeon-, dog-, or squirrel-watching. Add free Wi-Fi, the Shake Shack, temporary art exhibits, and a summer music series, and you'll realize that a bench here is definitely the place to be. New York City's first baseball games were played in this 7-acre park in 1845 (though New Jerseyans are quick to point out

Lounging on the grass in Madison Square Park.

that the game was actually invented across the Hudson in Hoboken, New Jersey). On the north end of the park, an imposing 1881 statue by Augustus Saint-Gaudens memorializes Civil War naval hero Admiral David Farragut. An 1876 statue of Secretary of State William Henry Seward (the Seward of the term from "Seward's Folly," coined when the United States purchased Alaska from the Russian Empire in 1867) sits in the park's southwest corner, though it's rumored that the sculptor placed a reproduction of the statesman's head on a statue of Abraham Lincoln's body. ⊠ *E. 23rd to E. 26th Sts., between 5th and Madison Aves., Flatiron District* ☎ *212/538–1884* ⊕ *www.madisonsquarepark. org/* Ⓜ *R to 23rd St.*

WORTH NOTING

Appellate Division Courthouse. Sculpted by Frederick Ruckstuhl, figures representing Wisdom and Force flank the main portal of this imposing Beaux-Arts courthouse, built in 1899. Melding the structure's purpose with artistic symbolism, statues of great lawmakers line the roof balustrade, including Moses, Justinian, and Confucius. In total, sculptures by 16 artists adorn the ornate building, a showcase of themes relating to the law. This is one of the most important appellate courts in the country: it hears more than 3,000 appeals and 6,000 motions a year, and also admits approximately 3,000 new attorneys to the bar each year. Inside the courtroom is a stunning stained-glass dome set into a gilt ceiling. All sessions, which are generally held Tuesday to Friday afternoons, are open to the public. (Visitors can call the main number ahead of time to be sure court is in session.) ⊠ *27 Madison Ave., entrance on E. 25th St.,*

Flatiron District ☎ *212/340–0400* ⊕ *www.courts.state.ny.us/courts/ ad1/* ⊙ *Weekdays 9–5* Ⓜ *N, R, 6 to 23rd St.*

Metropolitan Life Insurance Company Tower. When it was added to the original building on this site, in 1909, the 700-foot tower resembling the campanile of St. Mark's in Venice made this 1893 building the world's tallest; it was surpassed in height a few years later (by the Woolworth Building). It was stripped of much of its classical details during renovations in the early 1960s but it remains a prominent feature of the Midtown skyline today. The clock's four faces are each three stories high, and their minute hands weigh half a ton each. ✉ *1 Madison Ave., between E. 23rd and E. 24th Sts., Flatiron District* Ⓜ *R, 6 to 23rd St.*

Museum of Sex. You can ponder the profound history and cultural significance of sex here while you stare at vintage pornographic photos, S&M paraphernalia, anti-masturbation devices from the 1800s, vintage condom tins, and silent movies. Exhibits probe topics such as Japanese pornographic art from the 1700s or classic American pinup art. The subject matter is given serious curatorial treatment, though the gift shop is full of fun sexual kitsch. Evenings bring readings by cutting-edge authors and performance artists. No one under 18 is admitted. ✉ *233 5th Ave., entrance on 27th St., Flatiron District* ☎ *212/689–6337* ⊕ *www.museumofsex.com* 🎟 *$17.50* ⊙ *Sun.–Thurs. 10–8, weekends 10–9* Ⓜ *R to 28th St.*

GRAMERCY PARK

The haste and hullabaloo of the city calms considerably once you reach the more residential neighborhoods of Gramercy Park to the east. Dignified Gramercy Park, named for its 1831 gated garden square ringed by historic buildings and private clubs, is an early example of the city's best creative urban planning. Even though you can't unpack your picnic in the exclusive residents-only park, pick a spot on the sidewalk in front of the cast-iron gate and gaze upward to take in the beautiful Greek Revival, Italianate, Gothic Revival, and Victorian Gothic buildings—including the **Players Club** and the **National Arts Club,** both established to indulge and encourage a passion for the arts—that flank the sides of the park.

Just north of the park is Ian Schrager's cooler-than-cool reincarnation of the Gramercy Park Hotel on Lexington Avenue, with one of the city's best rooftop bars. Indeed, as gorgeous as Gramercy views may be during the day, its nighttime skyline is doubly spectacular. And south of the park, running north–south from 14th is **Irving Place**, a short street honoring Washington Irving, that feels calm, green, and exclusive, and has a combination of old and new eateries, stores, and architecture. **Pete's Tavern** (⇨ *Nightlife Chapter 17*) on Irving Place since 1864, maintains its claim as the oldest original bar in the city and its reputation as a neighborhood hangout. Two famous writers, O. Henry (*Gift of the Magi*) and Ludwig Bemelmans (*Madeline*), were "inspired" here, probably from the amazing eggnog or Pete's House Ale.

TOP ATTRACTIONS

Gramercy Park. You may not be able to enter this private park, but a look through the bars in the wrought-iron fence that encloses it is well worth your time, as is a stroll around its perimeter. The beautifully planted 2-acre park, designed by developer Samuel B. Ruggles, dates from 1831, and is flanked by grand examples of early-19th-century architecture and permeated with the character of its many celebrated occupants.

When Ruggles bought the property, it was known as Krom Moerasje ("little crooked swamp"), named by the Dutch settlers. He drained the swamp and set aside 42 lots for a park to be accessible exclusively to those who bought the surrounding lots in his planned London-style residential square. The park is still owned by residents of buildings in the surrounding square, although neighbors from the area can now buy visiting privileges. ■ TIP→ Guests of the Gramercy Park Hotel (⇨ Chapter 17) can enjoy coveted access to this private park. In 1966 the New York City Landmarks Preservation Commission designated Gramercy Park a historic district. Notable buildings: No. 15 was once home to Samuel Tilden, governor of New York. It was designed by Calvert Vaux in Gothic Revival brownstone with black granite trim and included a secret passageway to 19th Street so Tilden could escape his political enemies. It is now home to the 100-year-old National Arts Club. Next door at No. 16 Gramercy Park South lived the actor Edwin Booth, perhaps most famous for being the brother of Lincoln's assassin. In 1888 he turned his Gothic-trim home into the Players Club, a clubhouse for actors and theatrical types who were not welcome in regular society. A bronze statue of Edwin Booth as Hamlet has pride of place inside the park. ✉ *Lexington Ave. and E. 21st St., Gramercy Park* Ⓜ *L, N, Q, R, 4, 5, 6 to Union Sq./14th St.*

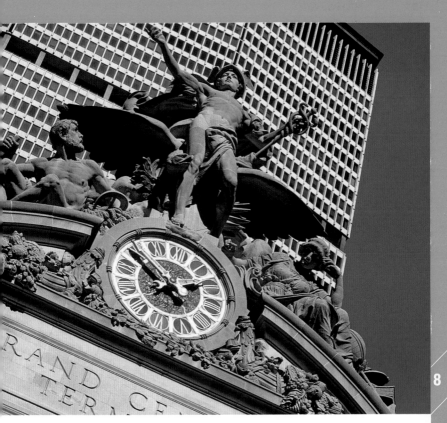

Midtown East

WITH MURRAY HILL

WORD OF MOUTH

"Empire State Building for sure! It's a true NYC experience . . . The lobby is beautiful, and they have some cool exhibits, like the construction of the building, to look at while you wait in line. Plus it has better downtown views, and you can see the Statue of Liberty . . . I went first thing in the morning and barely had a wait."

—World_Wanderer

GETTING ORIENTED

MAKING THE MOST OF YOUR TIME

The east side of Midtown is somewhat more laid back than the west side, but there's still lots to keep you busy. Wherever you're headed, try to make sure you at least pass through Grand Central—it'll be a madhouse on weekday mornings or right after work, and extremely quiet on the weekends, so you might want to visit on a weekday afternoon.

If you're planning to visit the Empire State Building, try to do so either early or late in the day—morning is the least crowded time, and late at night the city lights are dazzling. Allow at least two hours for your visit if you plan to visit the observation deck.

It's also worth making time for a visit to the United Nations for a tour of the building.

TOP EXPERIENCES

Standing in the center of Grand Central Terminal's main concourse.

Strolling down 5th Avenue.

Viewing the rare manuscripts at the Morgan Library.

Dining with locals in Koreatown.

GETTING HERE

To get to the east side of Midtown, take the 4, 5, 6, or the 7 to Grand Central. The S or Shuttle travels back and forth between Grand Central and Times Square.

You can reach the Empire State Building via the B, D, F, N, Q, R, or M line to 34th Street or the 6 to 33rd Street. The 6 also stops at 23rd, 28th, and 33rd streets.

QUICK BITES, COFFEE, OR COCKTAILS

Grand Central Market. The concourse on the lower level of Grand Central Terminal is a cornucopia of gourmet snack options, including Eli Zabar's, Ciao Bella Gelateria, Joe the Art of Coffee, and even an outpost of Junior's, the famed Brooklyn restaurant known for their classic cheesecake.

Crumbs (✉ *501 Madison Ave. at 52nd St.*). If you need a cupcake fix, check out Crumbs for the decadent flavors (there are many locations around the city).

King Cole Bar (✉ *2 E. 55th St.*). A swank and storied watering hole at the St. Regis Hotel.

P. J. Clarke's (✉ *915 3rd Ave.*). New York's most famous Irish bar, and for good reason.

8

Fifth Avenue is Manhattan's dividing line, marking the divergence of east side and west side, but the avenue itself seems to connote so much of what the city's East Side is all about. The east side of mid-Manhattan is where some of the city's most iconic buildings are found, including the Empire State Building, which is technically in the Murray Hill neighborhood.

MIDTOWN EAST

Updated by
Robert Brenner

In terms of architecture, Midtown East has some of the city's most notable gems, including the stately Chrysler Building, considered an art-deco triumph and the bustling Beaux Arts masterpiece Grand Central Terminal. At night the streets around here are relatively quiet, but the restaurants are filled with expense-account diners celebrating their successes. Some of the most formal dining rooms and most expensive meals in town can be found here, at restaurants like the posh landmarks the Four Seasons and L'Atelier de Joel Robuchon. The lower section of 5th Avenue is also a shopper's paradise, home to megabrand flagships such as Louis Vuitton, Yves Saint Laurent, and Chanel, and some of the world's most famous jewelry stores, including Tiffany, Van Cleef & Arpels, and Harry Winston. Upscale department stores like Bloomingdales and Saks Fifth Avenue are also around here.

TOP ATTRACTIONS

Chrysler Building. A monument to modern times and the mighty automotive industry, the former Chrysler headquarters wins many a New Yorker's vote for the city's most iconic and beloved skyscraper (the world's tallest for 40 days until the Empire State Building stole the honor). Architect William Van Alen, who designed this 1930 art-deco masterpiece, incorporated car details into its form: American eagle gargoyles made of chromium nickel sprout from the 61st floor, resembling car-hood ornaments used on 1920s Chryslers; winged urns festooning the 31st floor reference the car's radiator caps. Most breathtaking is the pinnacle, with tiered crescents and spiked windows that radiate out like a magnificent steel sunburst. View it at sunset to catch the light gleaming off the tip. Even better, observe it at night, when its peak illuminates the sky. The inside is off-limits apart from the amazing time-capsule lobby replete with chrome "grillwork," intricately patterned wood elevator doors, marble walls and floors, and an enormous ceiling mural saluting transportation and the human endeavor. ⊠ *405 Lexington Ave., at E. 42nd St., Midtown East* Ⓜ *4, 5, 6, 7, S to 42nd St./Grand Central.*

Fodor'sChoice
★

Grand Central Terminal. Grand Central is not only the world's largest (76 acres) and the nation's busiest (nearly 700,000 commuters and subway riders use it daily) railway station, but also one of the world's most magnificent, majestic public spaces. Past the glimmering chandeliers of the waiting room is the jaw-dropping **main concourse,** 200 feet long, 120 feet wide, and 120 feet (roughly 12 stories) high, modeled after an ancient Roman public bath. In spite of it being completely cavernous, Grand Central manages to evoke a certain sense of warmth rarely found in buildings its size. Overhead, a twinkling fiber-optic map of the constellations covers the robin's egg–blue ceiling. To admire it all with some sense of peace, avoid visiting at rush hour, or brave the chaos at peak travel times and be swept into the tides and eddies of human traffic swirling around the central information kiosk, the room's crown jewel with its polished marble counter and backlit, multifaced clock beaming the time in four directions.

To escape the crowds, head up one of the sweeping staircases at either end, where three upscale restaurants occupy the balcony space. Any would make an enjoyable perch from which to survey the concourse, but for a real taste of the station's early years, head beyond the western staircase to the **Campbell Apartment,** a clubby cocktail lounge housed in the restored private offices and salon of 1920s tycoon John W. Campbell. Located around and below the main concourse are fantastic shops and eateries (this is, of course, home to the eponymous Grand Central Oyster Bar), making this one of the best—if somewhat labyrinthine— "malls" in the city.

To best admire Grand Central's exquisite Beaux Arts architecture, start from its ornate south face on East 42nd Street, modeled after a Roman triumphal arch. Crowning the facade's Corinthian columns and 75-foot-high arched windows, a graceful clock keeps time for hurried commuters. In the central window stands an 1869 bronze statue of Cornelius Vanderbilt, who built the station to house his railroad empire. Also noteworthy is the 1½-ton, cast-iron bald eagle displaying its 13-foot wingspan atop a ball near the corner of 42nd Street and Vanderbilt Avenue.

Grand Central still functions primarily as a railroad station, and might resemble its artless cross-town counterpart, Penn Station, were it not for Jackie Kennedy Onassis's public information campaign to save it as a landmark. Underground, more than 60 ingeniously integrated railroad tracks carry trains upstate and to Connecticut via Metro-North Commuter Rail. The subway connects here as well. A massive four-year renovation completed in October 1998 restored the 1913 landmark to its original splendor—and then some.

8

Irish pride takes to the streets and sweeps up 5th Avenue in the annual St. Patrick's Day Parade.

The **Municipal Art Society** (☎ 212/935–3960 ⊕ *www.mas.org*) leads architectural tours of the terminal that begin here every Wednesday from 12:30 to 2. Reservations are not required, and a $10 donation is suggested. Meet at the information booth, Main Concourse. ⊠ *Main entrance, E. 42nd St. at Park Ave., Midtown East* ☎ 212/935–3960 ⊕ *www.grandcentralterminal.com* Ⓜ *4, 5, 6, 7, S to 42nd St./Grand Central.*

St. Patrick's Cathedral. This Gothic edifice—the largest Catholic cathedral in the United States, seating approximately 2,400 people—is among Manhattan's most striking churches, with its double spires topping out at 330 feet. St. Pat's, as locals call it, holds a special place in the hearts of many New Yorkers and Catholics around the country and indeed the world, receiving more than 3 million visitors annually. Its widely broadcast midnight Mass at Christmas has become somewhat of a social event for politicians and celebrities, yet tickets are always made available to the general public months in advance.

The church dates back to 1858–79. Among the statues in the alcoves around the nave is a modern depiction of the first American-born saint, Mother Elizabeth Ann Seton, and its pietà is three times larger than the pietà in St. Peter's in Rome. Its rose window by Charles Connick is considered to be the stained-glass artist's greatest work. The 5th Avenue steps are a convenient, scenic rendezvous spot. Sunday Mass can overflow with tourists; off-hours are significantly more peaceful. Many of the funerals for fallen New York City police and firefighters after 9/11 were held here. ⊠ *5th Ave. between E. 50th and E. 51st Sts.,*

Midtown East ☎ *212/753–2261 rectory* ⊕ *www.saintpatrickscathedral. org* ⊙ *Daily 6:30 am–8:45 pm* Ⓜ *E, M to 5th Ave./53rd St.*

★ **United Nations Headquarters.** Officially an "international zone" and not part of the United States, the U.N. Headquarters is a working symbol of global cooperation. Built between 1947 and 1961, the headquarters sits on a lushly landscaped, 18-acre tract on the East River, fronted by flags of member nations. The main reason to visit is the 45-minute guided tour (given in 20 languages; reservations can be made through the website), which includes the **General Assembly** and major council chambers, though some rooms may be closed on any given day. The tour includes displays on war, peacekeeping, nuclear nonproliferation, human rights, and refugees, and passes corridors overflowing with imaginatively diverse artwork. Free tickets to assemblies are sometimes available on a first-come, first-served basis before sessions begin; pick them up in the General Assembly lobby. If you just want to wander around, the grounds include a beautiful riverside promenade, a rose garden with 1,400 specimens, and sculptures donated by member nations. The complex's buildings (the slim, 505-foot-tall green-glass **Secretariat Building**; the much smaller, domed **General Assembly Building**; and the **Dag Hammarskjöld Library**) evoke the influential French modernist Le Corbusier (who was on the team of architects that designed the complex), and the surrounding park and plaza remain visionary. The public concourse, beneath the visitor entrance, has a coffee shop, gift shops, a bookstore, and a post office where you can mail letters with U.N. stamps. Make sure you take proper ID as you'll have to go through a security check to enter the grounds. ⊠ *Visitor entrance, 1st Ave. at E. 46th St., Midtown East* ☎ *212/963–8687* ⊕ *www.un.org* ▢ *Tour $16 (plus $2 service charge for online ticketing)* ⊙ *Tours weekdays 9:45–4:45; tours in English leave visitors lobby every 30 mins; for other languages, call 212/963–7539 on the day of your visit* Ⓜ *4, 5, 6, 7, S to 42nd St./Grand Central* ☞ *Children under 5 not admitted.*

WORTH NOTING

Daily News Building. The lobby of this art-deco tower contains an illuminated 12-foot globe that revolves beneath a black glass dome. Around it, spreading across the floor like a giant compass and literally positioning New York at the center of the world, bronze lines indicate mileage to various international destinations. *The Daily News,* however, hasn't called this building home since the mid-1990s, 15 years after it played the offices of the fictional newspaper the Daily Planet in the original *Superman* movie. ⊠ *220 E. 42nd St., between 2nd and 3rd Aves., Midtown East* ☎ *212/210–2100* Ⓜ *4, 5, 6, 7, S to 42nd St./Grand Central.*

Helmsley Building. This Warren & Wetmore–designed 1929 landmark was intended to match neighboring Grand Central Station in bearing, and it succeeded, with a gold-and-copper roof topped with an enormous lantern (originally housing a 6,000-watt light) and distinctive dual archways for traffic on Park Avenue. The building's history gets quirky, however: when the millionaire real estate investor Harry Helmsley purchased the building in 1977, he changed its name from the New York Central Building to the New York General Building in order to save money by replacing only two letters in the facade (only later did he rename it after himself). During a renovation the following year, however, he actually gilded the building, applying gold paint even to limestone and bronze—it was removed by a succeeding owner. In 2010, after a $100 million renovation, the Helmsley Building became the first prewar office tower to receive LEED Gold certification for energy efficiency. Despite being blocked from view from the south by the MetLife Building (originally, the Pan Am Building), the Helmsley Building remains a defining—and now "green," as opposed to gold—feature of one of the world's most lavish avenues. ⊠ *230 Park Ave., between 45th and 46th Sts., Midtown East* Ⓜ *4, 5, 6, 7, S to 42nd St./ Grand Central.*

Japan Society. The stylish, serene lobby of the Japan Society has interior bamboo gardens linked by a second-floor waterfall. Works by well-known Japanese artists are exhibited in the second-floor gallery—past shows have included the first-ever retrospective of Yoko Ono's works, a display of artwork created by children from Tohoku after Japan's 2011 earthquake, and *Deco Japan: Shaping Art and Culture, 1920– 1945.* ⊠ *333 E. 47th St., between 1st and 2nd Aves., Midtown East* ☎ *212/832–1155* ⊕ *www.japansociety.org* ⊉ *$12* ◷ *Building weekdays 9:30–5:30; gallery Tues.–Thurs. 11–6, Fri. 11–9, weekends 11–5* Ⓜ *6 to 51st St./Lexington Ave.; E, M to Lexington–3rd Aves./53rd St.*

Koreatown. Despite sitting in the shade of the Empire State Building, and within steps of Herald Square, Koreatown, or K-Town as it's locally known, is not a tourist destination. In fact, it feels decidedly off-the-beaten track and insulated, as though locals wryly planted their own place to eat, drink, be merry, and get a massage, right under the noses of millions of tourists. Technically, Koreatown runs from 31st to 36th streets and between Fifth and Sixth avenues, though the main drag is 32nd Street between Fifth and Broadway. Known as Korea Way, this strip is home to 24/7 Korean barbecue joints, karaoke bars, and spas, all piled on top of each other. Fill up on kimchi (spicy pickled cabbage), kimbap (seaweed rice), and red bean doughnuts (delicious), try some authentic Asian karaoke, and then top off your Koreatown experience with a step into a sauna shaped like a jade igloo (at Juvenex Spa, 25 West 32nd St.). Expect bang for your buck, to rub elbows with locals, and bragging rights over visitors who followed the crowds to Chinatown. ⊠ *Bordered by 31st and 36th Sts., 5th and 6th Aves., Murray Hill* Ⓜ *B, D, F, N, Q, R, M to 34th St./Herald Sq.; 6 to 33rd St.*

Seagram Building. Ludwig Mies van der Rohe, a pioneer of modern architecture, built this boxlike bronze-and-glass tower in 1958. The austere facade belies its wit: I-beams, used to hold buildings up, here are merely attached to the surface, representing the *idea* of support. The Seagram Building's innovative ground-level plaza, extending out to the sidewalk, has since become a common element in urban skyscraper design. ⊠ *375 Park Ave., between E. 52nd and E. 53rd Sts., Midtown East* Ⓜ *6 to 51st St./Lexington Ave.; E, M to Lexington–3rd Aves./53rd St.*

Sony Wonder Technology Lab. Have kids in tow? The free Sony Wonder Technology Lab in the Sony Building lets them program robots, create

The restoration and cleaning of Grand Central in the late 1990s uncovered the elaborate astronomical design on the ceiling of the main concourse.

movie trailers, perform virtual heart surgery, and work as a team to produce a high-definition news broadcast. The lab also shows classic and contemporary films for both young and adult audiences in its 73-seat HD theater. Admission is free but reservations are strongly recommended; they can be made a minimum of 7 days and up to 3 months from the time of visit. A limited number of same-day tickets are available. ⊠ *Sony Plaza, 550 Madison Ave., at 56th St* ☎ *212/833–8100, 212/833–7875 for week-of screening reservations* ⊕ *www.sonywondertechlab.com* ⊙ *Tues.–Sat. 9:30–5:30* ⊠ *550 Madison Ave., between E. 55th and E. 56th Sts., Midtown East* ⊙ *Daily 7 am–11 pm* Ⓜ *E, M to 5th Ave./53rd St.*

Trump Tower. The tallest all-glass building in Manhattan when it was completed in 1983, this skyscraper's ostentatious atrium flaunts that decade's unbridled luxury, with expensive boutiques and gaudy brass everywhere. You'll half expect the pleasant-sounding waterfall streaming down to the lower-level food court to flow with champagne. ⊠ *725 5th Ave., at E. 56th St., Midtown East* ☎ *212/832–2000* ⊕ *www.trump.com* Ⓜ *N, R to 5th Ave./59th St.*

Tudor City. Before Donald Trump, there was Fred F. French. In 1925 the prominent real-estate developer became one of the first to buy up a large number of buildings—more than 100, in fact, most of them tenements—and join their properties into a single new development. He designed a collection of nine apartment buildings and two parks in the "garden city" mode, which placed a building's green space not in an enclosed courtyard but in the foreground. French also elevated the entire development 70 feet (40 stone steps) above the river and built a

39-by-50-foot "Tudor City" sign atop one of the 22-story buildings. The development's residential towers opened between 1927 and 1930, borrowing a marketable air of sophistication from Tudor-style stonework, stained-glass windows, and lobby design flourishes. An official city landmark, Tudor City has featured in numerous films, including all three *Spider-Man* movies, and its gardens remain a popular lunch spot among office workers. ⊠ *Between 41st and 43rd Sts. and 1st and 2nd Aves., Midtown East* Ⓜ *4, 5, 6, 7, S to 42nd St./Grand Central.*

GALLERIES

Edwynn Houk. The impressive stable of 20th-century photographers shown here includes Sally Mann, Robert Polidori, and Elliott Erwitt. The gallery also has prints by masters Edward Weston and Alfred Stieglitz. ⊠ *745 5th Ave., between E. 57th and E. 58th Sts., 4th fl., Midtown East* ☎ *212/750–7070* ⊕ *www.houkgallery.com* ◷ *Tues.–Sat. 11–6* Ⓜ *N, R to 5th Ave.*

The Pace Gallery. The giant gallery—now with several outposts in Chelsea as well—focuses on such modern and contemporary painters as Julian Schnabel, Mark Rothko, and New York School painter Ad Reinhardt. ⊠ *32 E. 57th St., between Park and Madison Aves., 2nd fl., Midtown East* ☎ *212/421–3292* ⊕ *www.thepacegallery.com* ◷ *Tues.–Fri. 9:30–6; Sat. 10–6* Ⓜ *N, R to 5th Ave.*

Spanierman. This venerable gallery deals in 19th- and early-20th-century American painting and sculpture. Their inventory list and scholarship is amazing, and they frequently sell to museums looking to broaden their own collections. Just down the block at 53 East 58th St., Spanierman Modern (⊕ *www.spaniermanmodern.com*) represents such contemporary artists as Dan Christensen and Frank Bowling. ⊠ *45 E. 58th St., between Park and Madison Aves., Midtown East* ☎ *212/832–0208* ⊕ *www.spanierman.com* ◷ *Tues.–Sat. 9:30–5:30* Ⓜ *N, R to 5th Ave.*

MURRAY HILL

Murray Hill stretches roughly from about 30th to 40th streets between 5th and 3rd avenues and is a mix of high-rises, restaurants, and bars filled mostly with a postcollege crowd, and the small but solid enclave of Little India (also known as Curry Hill), primarily around Lexington and 28th Street, where you can sample authentic cuisine and shop for traditional clothing and other goods in a handful of boutiques. Farther north a few side streets are tree-lined and townhouse-filled with some high-profile haunts, including the Morgan Library and Museum with its vast book stacks and rare manuscripts. But perhaps the biggest reason to visit this neighborhood is to see New York's biggest skyscraper, the Empire State Building.

TOP ATTRACTIONS

Ⓒ **Empire State Building.** The pencil-slim silhouette of the Empire State
Fodor's Choice Building, recognizable virtually worldwide, is an art-deco monument
★ to progress, a symbol for New York City, and a star in some great romantic scenes, on- and off-screen. Its cinematic résumé—the building has appeared in more than 200 movies—means that it remains a

The view from Midtown over the East River and into Queens.

fixture of popular imagination, and many visitors come to relive favorite movie scenes. You might just find yourself at the top of the building with *Sleepless in Seattle* look-alikes or even the building's own *King Kong* impersonator.

Built in 1931 at the peak of the skyscraper craze, this 103-story limestone giant opened after a mere 13 months of construction. The framework rose at an astonishing rate of 4½ stories per week, making the Empire State Building the fastest-rising skyscraper ever built. Unfortunately, your rise to the observation deck might not be quite so record breaking.

There are three lines to get to the top of the Empire State Building; a line for tickets, a line for security, and a line for the elevators. ■ TIP→ Save time and skip one of the lines by purchasing your tickets in advance (⊕ esb-nyc.com). You can't skip the security line, but you can skip to the front of both this line and the line for elevators by purchasing an Express Pass for an extra $45—if time is tight, it guarantees you'll get to the observation deck in 20 minutes. If you don't want to pony up for express service, do yourself a favor and skip that last elevator line at the 80th floor by taking the stairs.

If this is your first visit, keep yourself entertained during your ascent by renting a headset with an audio tour by Tony, a fictional but "authentic" native New Yorker, available in eight languages.

The 86th-floor observatory (1,050 feet high) has both a glass-enclosed area (heated in winter and cooled in summer) and an outdoor deck spanning the building's circumference. Don't be shy about going outside into the wind (even in winter) or you'll miss half the experience. Also, don't be deterred by crowds; there's an unspoken etiquette when

The Lights of the Empire State Building

At night the Empire State Building lights up the Manhattan skyline with a colorful view as awe-inspiring from a distance as the view from the top. The colors at the top of the building are changed regularly to reflect seasons, events, and holidays, so New Yorkers and visitors from around the world always have a reason to look at this icon in a new light.

The building's first light show was in November 1932, when a simple searchlight was used to spread the news that New York–born Franklin Delano Roosevelt had been elected president of the United States. Douglas Leigh, sign designer and mastermind of Times Square's kinetic billboard ads, tried to brighten up prospects at the "Empty State Building" after the Depression by negotiating with the Coca-Cola Company to occupy the top floors. He proposed that Coca-Cola could change the lights of the building to serve as a weather forecast and then publish a small guide on its bottles to decipher the colors. Coca-Cola loved this idea, but the deal fell through because of the bombing at Pearl Harbor, when the U.S. government needed office space in the building.

In 1956 the revolving "freedom lights" were installed to welcome people to America; then in 1964 the top 30 floors of the building were illuminated to mark the New York World's Fair. Douglas Leigh revisited the lights of the ESB in 1976, when he was made chairman of City Decor to welcome the Democratic Convention. He introduced the idea of color lighting, and so the building's tower was ablaze in red, white, and blue to welcome the convention and to mark the celebration of the American Bicentennial. The

color lights were a huge success, and they remained red, white, and blue for the rest of the year.

Leigh's next suggestion of tying the lights to different holidays, a variation on his weather theme for Coca-Cola, is the basic scheme still used today. In 1977 the lighting system was updated to comply with energy conservation programs and to allow for a wider range of colors. Leigh further improved this new system in 1984 by designing an automated color-changing system so vertical fluorescents in the mast could be changed. For a full lighting schedule, visit ⊕ *www.esbnyc.com.*

—Jacinta O'Halloran

it comes to sharing the views and backdrop, and there's plenty of city to go around. Bring quarters for the high-powered binoculars—on clear days you can see up to 80 mi—or bring binoculars of your own so you can get a good look at some of the city's rooftop gardens. If it rains, the deck will be less crowded and you can view the city between the clouds or watch the rain travel sideways around the building from the shelter of the enclosed walkway. The views of the city from the 86th-floor deck are spectacular, but the views from 16 stories up on the 102nd-floor observatory are even more so—and yet, fewer visitors make it this far. Instead of rushing back to elevator lines, ask yourself when you'll be back again and then head up to the enclosed 102nd floor. It will cost you an extra $15 (at the 86th-floor kiosk), but you will be rewarded with peaceful, bird's-eye views of the entire city. Also, there are fewer visitors angling for photo ops, so you can linger a while and really soak in the city and experience.

■ TIP→ Even if you skip the view from up top, be sure to step into the lobby and take in the ceiling, beautifully restored in 2009. The gilded gears and sweeping art-deco lines, long hidden under a drop ceiling and decades of paint, are a romantic tribute to the machine age and part of the original vision for the building.

NY SKYRIDE. Although some parents blanch when they discover both how much it costs and how it lurches, the second-floor NY SKY-RIDE, New York's only aerial virtual tour simulator, is a favorite of the seven- and eight-year-old set, and it's cheaper than an actual aerial tour of New York. Narrated by actor Kevin Bacon, the ride takes the viewer on a 30-minute virtual tour of New York, soaring by the Brooklyn Bridge, the Statue of Liberty, Central Park, Times Square, Yankee Stadium, and other top attractions along the way. There's also a brief but poignant trip back in time to visit the World Trade Center's Twin Towers—a sight sure to drive you straight into the arms of the first I [Heart] NY T-shirt vendor you see when you leave the building. It's a fun way to get a sense of the city's highlights, though teenagers may find the technology a little dated, and baseball buffs may gripe that the footage has not been updated to reflect the new Yankee Stadium. ■ TIP→ When you purchase a Skyride–Empire State Building combo ticket, you'll visit the Skyride first and then join the line for the observation deck at the elevators, skipping up to half the wait. ⊠ *Empire State Building, entrance on 33rd St.* ☎ *212/279–9777, 888/759–7433* ⊕ *www.nyskyride.com* 🎟 *$42; $54 combo Skyride and observatory (significant discounts are available on the website)* ◔ *Daily 8 am–10 pm* ⊠ *350 5th Ave., at E. 34th St., Murray Hill* ☎ *212/736–3100, 877/692–8439* ⊕ *www.esbnyc.com* 🎟 *$22* ◔ *Daily 8 am–2 am; last elevator up leaves at 1:15 am* Ⓜ *B, D, F, N, Q, R, M to 34th St./Herald Sq.; 6 to 33rd St.*

★ **Morgan Library and Museum.** The treasures inside this museum, gathered by John Pierpont Morgan (1837–1913), one of New York's wealthiest financiers, are exceptional: medieval and Renaissance illuminated manuscripts, old master drawings and prints, rare books, and autographed literary and musical manuscripts. Architect Renzo Piano's redesign of the museum was unveiled in April 2006. The original Renaissance-style building (1906) by Charles McKim of McKim, Mead & White has been preserved, but now there's twice the gallery space, an enlarged auditorium, a dining room, and a café. Crowning achievements produced on paper, from the Middle Ages to the 20th century, are on view here: letters penned by John Keats and Thomas Jefferson; a summary of the theory of relativity in Einstein's own elegant handwriting; three Gutenberg Bibles; drawings by Dürer, Leonardo da Vinci, Rubens, Blake, and Rembrandt; the only known manuscript fragment of Milton's *Paradise Lost;* Thoreau's journals; and original manuscripts and letters by Charlotte Brontë, Jane Austen, Thomas Pynchon, and many others.

In 2010 the Morgan completed the dynamic transformation begun with its expansion in 2006 by restoring the interior of the McKim building—once the private study and library of Mr. Morgan—to its original grandeur. A new lighting system was installed to illuminate the extraordinary murals and decor of the four historic rooms; newly designed display cases were added to exhibit some of the Morgan's most valued objects; marble surfaces were cleaned, period furniture was reupholstered, and original fixtures were restored and reinstalled; and the North Room was opened to visitors for the first time.

The library shop is within an 1852 Italianate brownstone, once the home of Morgan's son, J. P. Morgan Jr. Outside on East 36th Street, the sphinx in the right-hand sculptured panel of the original library's facade was rumored to wear the face of architect Charles McKim. ⊠ *225 Madison Ave., at 36th St., Murray Hill* ☎ *212/685–0008* ⊕ *www.themorgan. org* ⊠ *$15* ⊗ *Tues.–Thurs. 10:30–5, Fri. 10:30–9, Sat. 10–6, Sun. 11–6* Ⓜ *B, D, F, N, Q, R, V to 34th St./Herald Sq.; 6 to 33rd St.*

WORTH NOTING

🕙 **B. Altman Building/New York Public Library–Science, Industry, and Business Library (SIBL).** In 1906 department-store magnate Benjamin Altman gambled that his fashionable patrons would follow him uptown from his popular store in the area now known as the Ladies' Mile Historic District. His new store, one of the first of the grand department stores on 5th Avenue, was designed to blend with the mansions nearby. Note in particular the beautiful entrance on 5th Avenue. In 1996 the New York Public Library set up a high-tech library here. A 33-foot-high atrium unites the building's two floors, the lending library off the lobby and the research collections below. Downstairs a wall of electronic ticker tapes and TVs tuned to business-news stations beams information and instructions to patrons. Free tours are offered Thursday at 2. ⊠ *188 Madison Ave., between E. 34th and E. 35th Sts., Murray Hill* ☎ *212/592–7000* ⊕ *www.nypl.org* ⊗ *Mon., Fri., and Sat. 11–6, Tues.–Thurs. 10–8* Ⓜ *6 to 33rd St.*

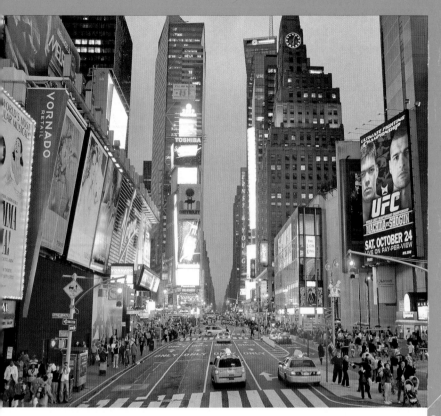

Midtown West

WITH TIMES SQUARE AND ROCKEFELLER CENTER

WORD OF MOUTH

"The lights of Times Square will be much more impressive after the Broadway show when it's dark out. Right before curtain time, it's just nuts with people running to make it to the theater in time, plus all the people leaving work from all the huge office buildings in the area."

—nyer

GETTING ORIENTED

Central Park

Mandarin Oriental Bar

Columbus Circle

Central Park South

N,Q,R

M A,B,C,D,1

AQ Kafé

Fika

Hirschl & Adler

W. 58th St.

Marian Goodman Gallery

N,Q,R

M

W. 57th St.

F

Carnegie Hall

Marlborough

Greenberg Van Doren

Broadway

Eighth Ave.

W. 56th St.

Tibor de Nagy Gallery

David Findlay Jr. Gallery

Zibetto

W. 55th St.

University Club

W. 54th St.

B,D,E

M

W. 53rd St.

MoMA

Avenue of the Americas

E,M

M

NYC Visitors Center

Seventh Ave.

W. 52nd St.

The Paley Center for Media

W. 51st St.

Radio City Music Hall

C,E

M

1

M

W. 50th St.

G.E. Building/Top of the Rock/ NBC Studios

HELL'S KITCHEN

M

W. 49th St.

Rockefeller Center

Lower Plaza/ Prometheus

N,Q,R

W. 48th St.

M

B,D,F,M

Christie's

Fifth Ave.

W. 47th St.

Times Square Visitor Center

W. 46th St.

Restaurant Row

Intrepid Sea, Air and Space Museum

W. 45th St.

TIMES SQUARE

TKTS booth

W. 44th St.

International Center of Photography (ICP)

W. 43rd St.

A,C,E

M

Madame Tussaud's New York

Times Square

B,D,F,M

M

W. 42nd St.

M

7

M

N,Q,R,S 1,2,3,7

Port Authority Terminal

W. 41st St.

Bryant Park

New York Public Library (NYPL) Main Branch: Stephen A. Schwartzman Building

New York Times Building

W. 40th St.

W. 39th St.

Broadway

W. 38th St.

0   1/4 mi

W. 37th St.

0   1/4 km

MAKING THE MOST OF YOUR TIME

Most people think of Midtown as Times Square, but there's a lot else going on here. The Museum of Modern Art is one of the big blockbusters here, and you might also want to make time for the *Intrepid* Sea, Air & Space Museum and maybe a stroll through Bryant Park.

Times Square is almost always a frenetic mass of people, staring up at the lights and the giant televisions. If you're in a hurry to get somewhere, try to avoid walking—or cabbing—through here. If you want to experience the thrill of thousands of racing workaday suits, though, visit Rockefeller Center at rush hour on a weekday. If you're staying in Midtown, you can take advantage of the prime location and rise early to be first in line at landmarks, museums, or the TKTS booth for discount day-of theater tickets (⇨ *Chapter 16: Performing Arts*).

QUICK BITES, COFFEE, AND COCKTAILS

Fika (✉ *41 W. 58th St.*). Take a coffee break with a Swedish twist.

Zibetto (✉ *1385 6th Ave.*). No seats, but arguably the best espresso drinks in New York.

AQ Kafé (✉ *1800 Broadway*). Classic and Scandinavian-influenced sandwiches and fresh breads, and excellent coffee.

Mandarin Oriental Bar (✉ *80 Columbus Circle at 60th St.*). For top-notch (and pricey) cocktails, with stunning views, you can't beat the bar on the 35th floor of this luxury hotel; it's a good splurge.

TOP EXPERIENCES

Elbowing your way through Times Square.

Lounging in the grass in Bryant Park.

Skating at Rockefeller Center.

Checking out the views from the Top of the Rock; opinions vary on whether the better views are from here or from the Empire State Building. Either way, if you go at night, the city spreads out below in a mesmerizing blanket of lights.

Fighting the crowds along 5th Avenue.

GETTING HERE

You can get to Midtown via (almost) all the subways; many make numerous stops throughout the area. For Midtown West, the 1, 2, 3, 7, A, C, E, N, Q, and R serve Times Square and West 42nd Street. The S or Shuttle travels back and forth between Times Square and Grand Central (if you're going to the east side). The B, D, F, and M trains serve Rockefeller Center.

9

Sightseeing
★★★★★

Nightlife
★★★

Dining
★★★★★

Lodging
★★★★★

Shopping
★★★★★

Big is the buzz in Times Square, where neon-lighted billboards, ginormous television screens, towering skyscrapers, and Broadway theaters play starring roles alongside megastores like the Disney Store and Hershey's. Love it or hate it, Times Square throbs New York—but remember that there's also a lot more to see and experience in this side of Midtown.

Updated by
Robert Brenner

Luckily, you needn't go far from Times Square to get away from the hustle and bustle. Head over to 9th Avenue—also known as Hell's Kitchen—and the calmer side streets, home to mixed bag of locals, many who work in the theater industry. There are lots of ethnic restaurants, pretheater options, and cute boutiques for shopping.

You can score good seats to some of the hottest Broadway and Off Broadway shows for half the going rate at the TKTS booth in Duffy Square at 47th Street and Broadway (⇨ *Chapter 20, Performing Arts*). Although people think of Broadway as the heart of the theater scene, few theaters actually line the thoroughfare. For some of the grandes dames, head west on 45th Street. There are several Broadway beauties here, including the **Booth,** the **Schoenfeld,** the **Jacobs,** the **Music Box,** and the **Imperial.** On the southern side of 45th Street there's the pedestrians-only **Shubert Alley,** distinguished by colorful posters advertising the latest hit plays and musicals, and the **Shubert Theatre,** one of Broadway's most lustrous gems. Head west along 44th Street to see its neighbors, the **Helen Hayes,** the **Broadhurst,** the **Majestic,** and the **St. James.**

TOP ATTRACTIONS

Bryant Park. This lovely green space nestled among landmarks and skyscrapers is one of Manhattan's most popular parks. Tall London plane trees line the perimeter of the sunny central lawn, overlooking stone terraces, formal flower beds, gravel pathways, and a smattering of kiosks selling everything from sandwiches to egg creams (in season). The garden tables scattered about fill with lunching office workers and folks enjoying the park's free Wi-Fi (signs show you how to log on).

In summer you can check out free live jazz and "Broadway in Bryant Park" musical-theater performances, and author readings. Most popular of all is the Summer Film Festival: locals leave work early to snag a spot on the lawn for the outdoor screenings each Monday at dusk. At the east side of the park, near a squatting bronze cast of Gertrude Stein, is the stylish Bryant Park Grill, which has a rooftop garden, and the adjacent open-air Bryant Park Café, open seasonally. On the south side of the park is an old-fashioned **carousel** (📽 *$2*) where kids can ride fanciful rabbits and frogs instead of horses, and attend storytellings and magic shows. Come late October the park rolls out the artificial frozen "**pond**" (🕙 *Nov.–Feb., Sun–Wed. 8 am–10 pm, Fri. and Sat. 8 am–midnight; skate rental $14*) for ice skating. Surrounding the ice rink are the Christmas market–like stalls of the **Holiday Shops**, selling handcrafted goods. ✉ *6th Ave. between W. 40th and W. 42nd Sts., Midtown West* ☎ *212/768–4242* ⊕ *www.bryantpark.org* 🕙 *Hrs vary by month. See website for exact times.* Ⓜ *B, D, F, M to 42nd St.; 7 to 5th Ave.*

🔄 **Intrepid Sea, Air & Space Museum.** The centerpiece of the *Intrepid* Sea, Air & Space Museum complex is the 900-foot *Intrepid* aircraft carrier, making it Manhattan's only floating museum. The carrier's most trying moment of service, the day it was attacked in World War II by kamikaze pilots, is recounted in a multimedia presentation. Aircraft on deck include an A-12 Blackbird spy plane, a Concorde, helicopters, and 30 other aircraft. Docked alongside, and also part of the museum, is the *Growler,* a strategic-missile submarine. The interactive Exploreum contains 18 hands-on exhibits. You can experience a flight simulator, transmit messages in Morse code, and see what it was like to live aboard the massive carrier. The space shuttle *Enterprise* is set to be moved here in the summer of 2012 but as of this writing it was unclear how the museum will incorporate it. Check the website for further details. ■TIP➔ **There are frequent ticket discounts if you purchase through the museum website.** ✉ *Pier 86, W 46th St. and 12th Ave., Midtown West* ☎ *212/245–0072, 877/957–7447* ⊕ *www.intrepidmuseum.org* ✉ *$24* 🕙 *Apr.–Oct., Mon.–Fri. 10–5, Sat.–Sun. 10–6; Nov.–Mar., Tues.–Sun. 10–5; last admission 1 hr before closing* Ⓜ *A, C, E to 42nd St.; M42 bus to pier.*

Radio City Music Hall. *See the listing in Chapter 20: Performing Arts.*

★ **Rockefeller Center.** If Times Square is New York's crossroads, Rockefeller Center is its communal gathering place, where the entire world converges to snap pictures, skate on the ice rink, peek in on a taping of the *Today* show (or—with luck—NBC's *30 Rock*), shop, eat, and take in the monumental art-deco structures and public sculptures from the past century. Totaling more than 75 shops and 40 eateries (1.4 million square feet in all), the complex runs from 47th to 52nd streets between 5th and 7th avenues. Special events and huge pieces of art dominate the central plazas in summer. In December an enormous twinkling tree towers above the ice-skating rink, causing huge crowds of visitors from across the country and the globe to shuffle through with necks craned and cameras flashing. The first official tree-lighting ceremony was held in 1933.

9

Keeping It Real in Times Square

How to act like a local in Times Square? Look as if you want to leave. The local art of walking in Times Square involves zigzagging around the slow crowds that gather like obstacles. Avoid looking overtly at the billboards, and whatever you do, don't snap pictures. Display an ironic detachment: you're just passing through.

Why the snide comments? Consider the noise and billboards from a New Yorker's perspective. The chains that dominate here from Applebee's to M&M's World to Toys "R" Us with its Ferris wheel make some locals mourn the old "naughty, bawdy, gaudy" Times Square portrayed in the musical *42nd Street*.

In truth, a visit to Times Square can be great fun when the lights stand out at nighttime, especially if you're with kids (whose hands you must *never* release because of the undertow-like crowds)—just try to focus on the flashing walls of neon colors and not the overwhelming corporate advertising.

Although nobody's really nostalgic (no matter what they may say) for the derelict Times Square of the '70s and '80s, at least that Times Square reflected (however grotesquely) the challenges all the city's residents were facing. New Yorkers pride themselves on their survivor's ability to tough out the harshness of city living. For decades Times Square embodied that toughness ("if I can make it here, I can make it anywhere"). Out in the open, underneath the bright-lighted billboards, it was clear as day what New York City had to offer newcomers, take it or leave it.

The Times Square of today—in which each building is required to give off a minimum amount of light between the ground and 65 feet up—is a family-friendly, open-air promenade of familiar brand names in theme park–like settings, including the world's largest McDonald's. But not all change is bad; we also have the stadium seating behind TKTS, and, along Broadway, pedestrian-friendly spaces closed to traffic, including tables and chairs. And, of course, we never lost the rich theater scene itself, which locals frequent along with visitors.

The world's most famous **ice-skating rink** occupies Rockefeller Center's sunken lower plaza October through April (it's a café in summer). Skaters swoop or stumble across the ice while crowds gather at street level to watch the spins and spills. The gold-leaf statue of the fire-stealing Greek hero **Prometheus**—Rockefeller Center's most famous sculpture—hovers above, forming the backdrop to zillions of photos. Carved into the wall behind it, a quotation from Aeschylus reads "Prometheus, teacher in every art, brought the fire that hath proved to mortals a means to mighty ends." The lower plaza also provides access to the marble-lined corridors underneath Rockefeller Center, which house restaurants, a post office, and clean public restrooms—a rarity in Midtown.

Rising up on the Lower Plaza's west side is the 70-story (850-foot-tall) art-deco **GE Building**, a testament to modern urban development. Here Rockefeller commissioned and then destroyed a mural by Diego Rivera upon learning that it featured Vladimir Lenin. He replaced it

The iconic marquee at Radio City Music Hall

with the monumental *American Progress* by José María Sert, still on view in the lobby, flanked by additional murals by Sert and English artist Frank Brangwyn. While in the lobby, pick up a free "Rockefeller Center Visitor's Guide" at the **information desk**. Up on the 65th floor sits the now-shuttered Rainbow Room, a glittering big-band ballroom from 1934 through 2009. ⊠ *Between 5th and 6th Aves. and W. 49th and W. 50th Sts., Midtown West* ☎ *212/332–7654 for the rink* Ⓜ *B, D, F, M to 47th–50th Sts./Rockefeller Center* ⊠ *30 Rockefeller Plaza* ⊕ *www.rockefellercenter.com/.*

Times Square. Hands down, this is the most frenetic part of New York City, a cacophony of flashing lights and shoulder-to-shoulder crowds that many New Yorkers studiously avoid. Originally named after the *New York Times* (whose headquarters has relocated nearby), the area has seen many changes since the first subway line, which included a 42nd Street station, opened in 1904. You won't find speakeasies and unsavory clubs around here nowadays, it's more of a vibrant, family-friendly destination, with a pedestrianized stretch of Broadway and stadium seating behind discount-theater-ticket-seller TKTS, all under the glare of brand names like MTV and M&Ms. If you like sensory overload, the chaotic mix of huge underwear billboards, flashing digital displays, on-location television broadcasts, and street performers will give you your fix. The focus of the entertainment may have shifted over the years, but showtime is still the heart of New York's theater scene and there are 40 Broadway theaters nearby. ⊠ *Broadway between 42nd and 44th streets, Midtown West* ☎ *212/768–1560* ⊕ *www.timessquarenyc.org* Ⓜ *1, 2, 3, 7, N, Q, R, S to Times Square–42 St.*

Ice-skating under the sculpture of Prometheus, at Rockefeller Center, is a winter ritual for many local and visiting families.

Times Square Visitor Center. After its $1.8 million renovation, this visitor center is a savvy place to take shelter and get your bearings when the crowds start to overwhelm you. On display are a past New Year's Eve ball and a New Year's Eve "Wishing Wall," where you can write on confetti that will become one of the actual pieces to flutter down at midnight on January 1. You can also watch a video on Times Square's unsavory past in a mock-peep booth. Stop by for multilingual kiosks, MetroCards, a peek in the gift shop, sightseeing and theater tickets, and (most important!) free restrooms. ⊠ *1560 Broadway, entrance on 7th Ave., between 46th and 47 Sts., Midtown West* ☎ *212/768–1560* ⊕ *www.timessquarenyc.org* ✉ *Times Square Expose tour, free* ☉ *daily 8–8. Tours leave Fri. at noon from the Visitor Center* Ⓜ *1, 2, 3, 7, N, Q, R, S to 42nd St./Times Sq.*

Fodor'sChoice
★

Top of the Rock. Rockefeller Center's multifloor observation deck, the Top of the Rock, on the 69th–70th floors of the building provides views that rival those from the Empire State Building—some would say they're even better because the views include the Empire State Building. Arriving just before sunset affords a view of the city that morphs before your eyes into a dazzling wash of colors, with a bird's-eye view of the tops of the Empire State Building, the Citicorp Building, and the Chrysler Building, and sweeping views northward to Central Park and south to the Statue of Liberty. Reserved-time ticketing eliminates long lines. Indoor exhibits include films of Rockefeller Center's history and a model of the building. Especially interesting is a Plexiglas screen on the floor with footage showing Rock Center construction workers dangling on beams high above the streets; the brave can even "walk"

Art in Rockefeller Center

The mosaics, murals, and sculptures that grace Rockefeller Center—many of them considered art-deco masterpieces—were all part of John D. Rockefeller Jr.'s plans. In 1932, as the steel girders on the first of the buildings were heading heavenward, Rockefeller put together a team of advisers to find artists who could make the project "as beautiful as possible." More than 50 artists were commissioned for 200 individual works.

Some artists scoffed at the idea of decorating an office building: Picasso declined to meet with Rockefeller, and Matisse replied that busy businessmen wouldn't be in the "quiet and reflective state of mind" needed to appreciate his art. Those who agreed to contribute, including muralists Diego Rivera and José María Sert, were relatively unknown, though a group of American artists protested Rockefeller's decision to hire "alien" artists.

As Rockefeller Center neared completion in 1932, Rockefeller still needed a mural for the lobby of the main building and he wanted the subject of the 63-by-17-foot mural to be grandiose: "human intelligence in control of the forces of nature." He hired Rivera.

With its depiction of massive machinery moving mankind forward, Rivera's *Man at the Crossroads* seemed exactly what Rockefeller wanted—until it was realized that a portrait of Soviet Premier Vladimir Lenin surrounded by red-kerchiefed workers occupied a space in the center. Rockefeller, who was building what was essentially a monument to capitalism, was less than thrilled. When Rivera was accused of propagandizing, he famously replied, "All art is propaganda."

Rivera refused to remove the offending portrait and, in early 1934, as Rivera was working, representatives for Rockefeller informed him that his services were no longer required. Within a half hour, tar paper had been hung over the mural. Despite negotiations to move it to the Museum of Modern Art, Rockefeller was determined to get rid of the mural once and for all. Not content to have it painted over, he ordered ax-wielding workers to chip away the entire wall.

Rockefeller ordered the mural replaced by a less offensive one by Sert. Rivera did have the last word: he re-created the mural in the Palacio de Bellas Artes in Mexico City, adding a portrait of Rockefeller among the champagne-swilling swells ignoring the plight of the workers.

The largest of the original artworks that remained is Lee Lawrie's 2-ton sculpture, *Atlas.* Its building also stirred controversy, as it was said to resemble Italy's fascist dictator, Benito Mussolini. The sculpture, depicting a muscle-bound man holding up the world, drew protests in 1936. Some even derided Paul Manship's golden *Prometheus,* which soars over the ice-skating rink, when it was unveiled the same year. Both are now considered to be among the best public artworks of the 20th century.

Lawrie's sculpture *Wisdom,* perched over the main entrance of 20 Rockefeller Plaza, is another gem. Also look for Isamu Noguchi's stainless-steel plaque *News* over the entrance of the Bank of America Building at 50 Rockefeller Plaza and Attilio Piccirilli's 2-ton glass-block panel called *Youth Leading Industry* over the entrance of the International Building.

9

across a beam to get a sense of what it might have been like to erect this skyscraper. ⊠ *Entrance on 50th St., between 5th and 6th Aves., 30 Rockefeller Plaza, Midtown West* ☎ *212/698–2000, 212/698–2000* ⊕ *www.topoftherocknyc.com* 🎟 *$25 adult; children under 6 not admitted* ⊙ *Daily 8–midnight; last elevator at 11 pm* Ⓜ *B, D, F, M to 47th–50th Sts./Rockefeller Center.*

WORTH NOTING

Christie's. One of the first items to be auctioned at the New York outpost of this infamous auction house, when it opened in 2000, was the "Happy Birthday" dress worn by Marilyn Monroe when she sang to President Kennedy (it sold for more than $1.2 million, in case you were wondering). Lucian Freud's "Benefits Supervisor Sleeping" sold for $33,641,000 here in 2008, setting a world auction record for any living artist. Yes, the auction house has come a long way since James Christie launched his business in England by selling two chamber pots, among other household goods, in 1766. The salesroom offers a free look at properties destined for the block in the days leading up to an auction; check the website for upcoming viewings. The lobby's specially commissioned abstract Sol Lewitt mural makes it worth visiting the 310,000-square-foot space, but you can also participate in Christie's auctions via live online video should you prefer to bid from atop the mattress stuffed with your Picasso money. ⊠ *20 Rockefeller Plaza, on 49th St. between 5th and 6th Aves., Midtown West* ☎ *212/492–5485* ⊕ *www.christies.com* Ⓜ *B, D, F, M to 47th–50th Sts./Rockefeller Center.*

International Center of Photography. Founded in 1974 by photojournalist Cornell Capa (photographer Robert Capa's brother), this top-notch photography museum and school has a permanent collection focused on American and European documentary photography of the 1930s to the 1990s. Changing exhibits display work by famous and should-be-famous photographers, while themed group shows focus on topics such as ecology, health, religion, science, war, and candid street shots. The gift shop has amazing imagery on postcards, posters, and prints, and outstanding photography books. ⊠ *1133 Ave. of the Americas, at 43rd Street, Midtown West* ☎ *212/857–0000* ⊕ *www.icp.org* 🎟 *$12* ⊙ *Tues.–Wed., Sat. and Sun. 10–6, Thurs.–Fri. 10–8* Ⓜ *B, D, F, M to 42nd St.*

Madame Tussaud's New York. Sit in the Oval Office with President Obama, sing along with an American Idol, pose with your favorite heartthrob—be it Justin Bieber or Robert Pattinson, or forecast tomorrow's weather with Al Roker. Much of the fun here comes from the photo opportunities—you're encouraged to pose with and touch the nearly 200 realistic replicas of the famous and infamous (disposable cameras are for sale). But there's more to do here than just pal around with the waxworks. Interactive options include a karaoke café, a celebrity walk down the red carpet, and a haunted town, the latter populated with both wax figures and real people. ⊠ *234 W. 42nd St., between 7th and 8th Aves., Midtown West* ☎ *866/841–3505* ⊕ *www.madame-tussauds.com* 🎟 *$36* ⊙ *Sun.–Thurs. 10–8; Sat. and Sun. 10–10* Ⓜ *1, 2, 3, 7, A, C, E, N, Q, R, S to 42nd St.*

NBC Studios. The GE Building also houses NBC Studios, whose news tapings, visible at street level, attract gawking crowds. Studio tours are available every day of the week and last about 70 minutes; you can reserve online. Tours start at the NBC Experience Store (49th Street between 5th and 6th avenues). ✉ *30 Rockefeller Plaza, between 5th and 6th Aves. at 49th St., Midtown West* ☎ *212/664–3700* ⏺ *www. nbcstudiotour.com* ✉ *NBC Studio Tour $24* ⊙ *Tours depart every 15 mins Mon.–Thurs. 8:30–5:30, Fri. and Sat. 8:30–6:30, Sun. 9:15–4:30* Ⓜ *B, D, F, M to 47th–50th Sts./Rockefeller Center* ✆ *Children under 6 not permitted.*

New York Public Library (NYPL) Main Branch: Stephen A. Schwarzman Building. In 2011 the "Library with the Lions" celebrated its centennial as a masterpiece of Beaux Arts design and one of the great research institutions in the world, with more than 6 million books, 12 million manuscripts, and 3 million pictures. You don't have to crack a book to make it worth visiting, though: an hour or so at this National Historic Landmark is a peaceful (and free!) escape from Midtown's bustle, along with some incredible architecture, especially when combined with a stroll through the adjacent **Bryant Park.** The marble staircase at the library's grand 5th Avenue entrance is an excellent perch for people-watching, before or after you explore the opulent interior.

The library's bronze front doors open into **Astor Hall,** which leads to several special exhibit galleries and, to the left, a stunning periodicals room with wall paintings of New York publishing houses. Ascend the sweeping double staircase to a second-floor balconied corridor overlooking the hall, with panels highlighting the library's development. Make sure to continue up to the magisterial **Rose Main Reading Room**—297 feet long (almost two full north–south city blocks), 78 feet wide, and just over 51 feet high; walk through to best appreciate the rows of oak tables and the extraordinary ceiling. Several additional third-floor galleries show rotating exhibits on print and photography (past exhibits have included old New York restaurant menus and a 1455 Gutenberg Bible). Free one-hour tours leave Monday–Saturday at 11 and 2 and Sunday at 2 from Astor Hall. Women's bathrooms are on the ground floor and third floor, and there's a men's bathroom on the third floor. ✉ *5th Ave. between E. 40th and E. 42nd Sts., Midtown West* ☎ *212/930–0800 for exhibit information* ⏺ *www.nypl.org* ⊙ *Mon. and Thurs.–Sat. 10–6, Sun. 1–5, Tues. and Wed. 10–8; exhibitions until 6* Ⓜ *B, D, F, M to 42nd St.; 7 to 5th Ave.*

The New York Times Building. This 52-story building with its distinctive, ladderlike ceramic rods is a testament to clean-lined modernism. The architect, Renzo Piano, extended the ceramic rods beyond the top of the building so that it would give the impression of dissolving into the sky. One of the skyscraper's best features—and the one that's open to the public—is the building's lobby atrium, which includes an open-air moss garden with 50-foot paper birch trees and a wooden footbridge, a 560-screen media art installation titled *Moveable Type* streaming a mix of the newspaper's near-real time and archival content, and a flagship store by minimalist home-goods designer Muji. Plus, you never know which famous journalists you'll spy. Unfortunately, tours are not

THE MUSEUM OF MODERN ART (MOMA)

✉ 11 W. 53rd St., between 5th and 6th Aves., Midtown East ☎ 212/708-9400 🌐 www.moma.org 💲 $25 🕗 Sat.-Mon., Wed., and Thurs. 10:30-5:30, Fri. 10:30-8. Closed Tues. Ⓜ E, M to 5th Ave./53rd St.; B, D, F, M to 47th-50th Sts./Rockefeller Center.

TIPS

■ Tickets are available online (moma.org) at a reduced price.

■ Entrance between 4 and 8 pm on Friday is free, but lines are long.

■ Free Wi-Fi service allows you to listen to audio tours as you wander the museum (log on to www.moma.org/wifi with your HTML browser-enabled device).

■ With so much art on display, it's hard to remember that MoMA has three movie theaters. Film passes to the day's screenings are included in your admission.

■ Tickets to MoMA also include free admission to its affiliated PS1 in Queens. Save your ticket and you can go in for free any time within 30 days of your original purchase.

■ Grab a quick bite at one of MoMA's two cafes—Cafe 2 and Terrace 5, or dine leisurely at the upscale Modern. In summer there is gelato in the Sculpture Garden.

Art enthusiasts and novices alike are often awestruck by the masterpieces before them here, including Monet's *Water Lilies*, Picasso's *Les Demoiselles d'Avignon*, and Van Gogh's *Starry Night*. In 2004, the museum's $425 million face-lift by Yoshio Taniguchi increased exhibition space by nearly 50%, including space to accommodate large-scale contemporary installations. The museum continues to collect: most recently it obtained important works by Martha Rosler, Valie Export, Christian Marclay, David Wojnarowicz, and Kara Walker. One of the top research facilities in modern and contemporary art is housed inside the museum's eight-story Education and Research building.

HIGHLIGHTS

In addition to the artwork, one of the main draws of MoMA is the building itself. A maze of glass walkways permits art viewing from many angles.

The 110-foot atrium entrance (accessed from the museum's lobby on either 53rd or 54th streets) leads to the movie theaters and the main-floor restaurant, The Modern, with Alsatian-inspired cuisine.

A favorite resting spot is the Abby Aldrich Rockefeller Sculpture Garden. Designed by Philip Johnson, it features Barnett Newman's *Broken Obelisk* (1962–69). The glass wall lets visitors look directly into the surrounding galleries from the garden, where there's also a reflecting pool and trees.

Contemporary art (1970 to the present) from the museum's seven curatorial departments shares the second floor of the six-story building, and the skylighted top floor showcases an impressive lineup of changing exhibits.

offered. ✉ *620 8th Ave., between 40th and 41st Sts., Midtown West* ☎ *212/984–8128* ⊕ *www.newyorktimesbuilding.com* Ⓜ *A, C, E to 42nd St.; 1, 2, 3, 7, N, Q, R, S to 42nd St./Times Sq.*

The Paley Center for Media. Three galleries of photographs and artifacts document the history of broadcasting in this 1989 limestone building, but the main draw here is the computerized catalog of more than 150,000 television and radio programs. If you want to see a performance of "Turkey Lurkey Time" from the 1969 Tony Awards, for example, type the name of the song, show, or performer into a computer terminal, then proceed to one of the semiprivate screening areas to watch your selection. People nearby might be watching classic comedies from the '50s, miniseries from the '70s, or news broadcasts from the '90s. Possibly the most entertaining part of these TV shows from yesteryear is the fact that the original commercials are still embedded in many of the programs; if ads are your thing you can also skip the programming altogether and watch compilations of classic commercials. ✉ *25 W. 52nd St., between 5th and 6th Aves., Midtown West* ☎ *212/621–6800* ⊕ *www.paleycenter.org* ✉ *$10* ⊕ *Wed., Fri., Sat., and Sun. noon–6, Thurs. noon–8* Ⓜ *E, M to 5th Ave./53rd St.; B, D, F, V to 47th–50th Sts./Rockefeller Center.*

University Club. Among the best surviving works of McKim, Mead & White, New York's leading turn-of-the-20th-century architects, this 1899 pink Milford granite palace was built for an exclusive club of degree-holding men. Note the crests of various prestigious universities engraved into the facade above its windows. The club's popularity declined as individual universities built their own clubs and as gentlemen's clubs became less important to the New York social scene. Still, the nine-story Italian High Renaissance Revival building (the facade looks as though it's three stories) stands out, grand as ever, among the shiny 5th Avenue shops. ✉ *1 W. 54th St., at 5th Ave., Midtown West* ☎ *212/247–2100* ⊕ *www.universityclubny.org* Ⓜ *E, M to 5th Ave./53rd St.*

GALLERIES

David Findlay Jr. Gallery. This well-established gallery concentrates on contemporary and 20th-century American artists from Whistler to Herman Cherry, Byron Brown, and David Aronson, and specializes in the New York School. ✉ *724 Fifth Ave., 8th fl., Midtown West* ☎ *212/486–7660* ⊕ *www.davidfindlayjr.com* ⊕ *Mon.–Sat. 10–5:30* Ⓜ *N, R to 5th Ave.*

Greenberg Van Doren Gallery. Solo and group shows of postwar artists as well as emerging young artists can be found here. ✉ *730 5th Ave., at*

9

W. 57th St., 7th fl., Midtown West ☎ *212/445–0444* ⊕ *www.gvdgallery. com* ⊗ *Tues.–Sat. 10–6* Ⓜ *N, R to 5th Ave.*

Hirschl & Adler. Although this gallery has a selection of European works, it's best known for American paintings, prints, and decorative arts. The celebrated 19th- and 20th-century artists whose works are featured include Stuart Davis, Childe Hassam, Camille Pissarro, and John Singleton Copley. ✉ *730 5th Ave., at W. 57th St., 4th fl., Midtown West* ☎ *212/535–8810* ⊕ *www.hirschlandadler.com* ⊗ *Tues.–Fri. 9:30–5:15, Sat. 9:30–4:45* Ⓜ *N, R to 5th Ave. St./Hunter College.*

Marian Goodman Gallery. The excellent contemporary art here includes Jeff Wall's staged photographs presented on light boxes, South African artist William Kentridge's video animations, and Gerhard Richter's paintings. ✉ *24 W. 57th St., between 5th and 6th Aves., Midtown West* ☎ *212/977–7160* ⊕ *www.mariangoodman.com* ⊗ *Mon.–Sat. 10–6* Ⓜ *F to 57th St.*

Marlborough. The Marlborough gallery has an international reputation, representing modern artists such as Claudio Bravo, Magdalena Abakanowicz, Red Grooms, and photorealist Richard Estes. Look for sculptures by Tom Otterness—his whimsical bronzes are found in several subway stations. There is also a branch in Chelsea. ✉ *40 W. 57th St., between 5th and 6th Aves., Midtown West* ☎ *212/463–8634* ⊕ *www.marlboroughgallery.com* ⊗ *Tues.–Sat. 10–5:30* Ⓜ *F to 57th St.*

Tibor de Nagy. Founded in 1950, this gallery shows work by 20th-century artists such as Biala, Nell Blaine, Jane Freilicher, and Shirley Jaffee. Instrumental in bringing many of America's finest abstract expressionist artists to public attention in the mid-20th century, the gallery now shows abstract and realistic work. ✉ *724 5th Ave., 12th fl., between W. 56th and W. 57th Sts., Midtown West* ☎ *212/262–5050* ⊕ *www.tibordenagy.com* ⊗ *Tues.–Sat. 10–5:30* Ⓜ *N, R to 5th Ave.*

The Upper East Side

WORD OF MOUTH

"If you are an art buff, the Frick is a magnificent home and gallery. Mr. Frick had an eye for art, and the fortune to make the best of it!"
—Johnnyman7

GETTING ORIENTED

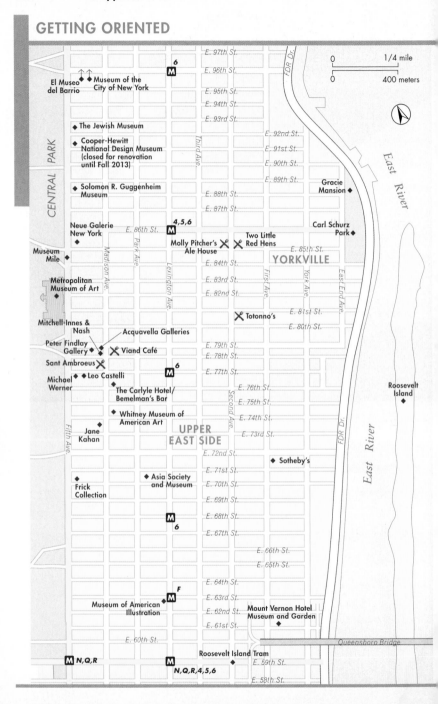

E. 97th St.

E. 96th St.

6

El Museo del Barrio ◆ ↑↑ ◆ Museum of the City of New York

E. 95th St.

E. 94th St.

E. 93rd St.

◆ The Jewish Museum

E. 92nd St.

◆ Cooper-Hewitt National Design Museum (closed for renovation until Fall 2013)

E. 91st St.

E. 90th St.

E. 89th St.

◆ Solomon R. Guggenheim Museum

E. 88th St.

Gracie Mansion ◆

E. 87th St.

Neue Galerie New York ◆

E. 86th St.

4,5,6

Carl Schurz Park ◆

Museum Mile ◆

Molly Pitcher's ✕ ✕ Two Little Ale House   Red Hens

E. 85th St.

YORKVILLE

E. 84th St.

Metropolitan Museum of Art ◆

E. 83rd St.

E. 82nd St.

Mitchell-Innes & Nash ◆

✕ Totonno's

E. 81st St.

E. 80th St.

◆ Acquavella Galleries

Peter Findlay Gallery ◆ ✕ Viand Café

E. 79th St.

E. 78th St.

Sant Ambroeus ✕

E. 77th St.

6

Michael ◆ ◆ Leo Castelli
Werner

The Carlyle Hotel / Bemelman's Bar

E. 76th St.

E. 75th St.

◆ Whitney Museum of American Art

E. 74th St.

UPPER EAST SIDE

E. 73rd St.

Jane Kahan ◆

E. 72nd St.

E. 71st St.

◆ Sotheby's

◆ Asia Society and Museum

E. 70th St.

Frick Collection ◆

E. 69th St.

E. 68th St.

6

E. 67th St.

E. 66th St.

E. 65th St.

E. 64th St.

E. 63rd St.

F

Museum of American Illustration ◆

E. 62nd St.

Mount Vernon Hotel Museum and Garden ◆

E. 61st St.

E. 60th St.

Queensboro Bridge

N,Q,R

Roosevelt Island Tram ◆

E. 59th St.

N,Q,R,4,5,6

E. 58th St.

CENTRAL PARK

Third Ave.

Park Ave.

Madison Ave.

Lexington Ave.

First Ave.

York Ave.

East End Ave.

Second Ave.

Fifth Ave.

FDR Dr.

East River

Roosevelt Island

East River

0   1/4 mile
0   400 meters

MAKING THE MOST OF YOUR TIME

The Upper East Side lends itself to a surprising variety of simple but distinct itineraries: exploring the landmarks on Museum Mile; languorous gallery grazing; window shopping on Madison Avenue; or bar hopping for just-out-of-college kids on 2nd Avenue. If it's the museums you're after, make sure to plan at least a few hours per museum—with some snack/coffee breaks. There's a lot to see, so we'd advise not more than one museum a day.

The Upper East Side's town houses, boutiques, consignment stores, and hidden gardens are easy to miss unless you take some time to wander. If all that walking wears you out, you can always hit one of the nail salons and indulge in a neighborhood stereotype of the pampered Upper East Sider. A well-deserved post–Museum Mile foot rub and mani/pedi are surprisingly reasonably priced.

GETTING HERE

Take the Lexington Avenue 4 or 5 express trains to 59th or 86th Street. The 6 local train also stops at 59th, 68th, 77th, 86th, and 96th streets. If you're coming from Midtown, the F train will let you out at Lexington Avenue at 63rd Street, where you can transfer to the 4, 5, and 6 after a short walk (and without paying subway fare again). From the Upper West Side, take one of the crosstown buses, the M66, M72, M79, M86, and M96. You can also take the N or R train to 59th Street and Lexington Avenue.

TOP EXPERIENCES

Exploration any of the world-class museums up here—permanent exhibits or temporary shows may guide your interest; make sure to plan a relaxing, restorative lunch, too.

Window shopping on Madison Avenue.

Strolling in Central Park (⇨ *see Chapter 11*).

COFFEE, COCKTAILS, AND QUICK BITES

Sant Ambroeus (✉ *1000 Madison Ave., at 77th St.*). This bustling café is great for cappuccino and even better for people-watching.

Two Little Red Hens (✉ *1652 2nd Ave., by 86th St.*). First-rate joe and the cupcakes to match.

Viand Cafe (✉ *1011 Madison Ave., by 78th St.*). Classic New York diner.

Totonno's (✉ *1544 2nd Ave., by 80th St.*). No slices, but the best white pizza you'll ever eat.

Bemelmans Bar (✉ *35 E. 76th St., by Madison Ave.*). Classy (and pricey) but unpretentious.

Molly Pitcher's Ale House (✉ *1641 2nd Ave., by 85th St.*). A sports bar with 16 beers on tap.

10

Sightseeing
★★★
Nightlife
★
Dining
★★
Lodging
★★
Shopping
★★★★

To many New Yorkers the Upper East Side connotes old money and high society—alongside Central Park, between 5th and Lexington avenues, up to East 96th Street, the trappings of wealth are everywhere apparent: posh buildings, Madison Avenue's flagship boutiques, and doormen in braided livery. It's also a key destination for visitors because some of the most fantastic museums in the country are here.

Updated by
John Rambow

Although a glance up and down the manicured grass meridian of Park Avenue may conjure scenes from *Bonfire of the Vanities* or *Gossip Girl*, there are more than palatial apartments, elite private schools, and highfalutin clubs up here—starting with fantastic museums. The **Metropolitan Museum of Art,** the **Solomon R. Guggenheim Museum,** the **Whitney Museum,** and many others lie on and around "Museum Mile," as do a number of worthy art galleries. For a local taste of the luxe life, hit up the platinum-card corridor that is Madison Avenue for its lavish boutiques—between East 60th and East 82nd Street is like stepping into the pages of a glossy magazine and many fashion houses have their flagships here and showcase their lush threads in equally exquisite settings. Compared with the megastores of Midtown, Madison Avenue feels quieter; it's significantly less crowded and more conducive to leisurely shopping (window or otherwise). Beyond clothing, the boutiques here carry baubles to satisfy anyone's champagne wishes, whether it's a box of truffles at **La Maison du Chocolat** or an intriguing read at **Crawford Doyle Booksellers.**

Venture east of Lexington Avenue and you encounter a less wealthy—and more diverse—Upper East Side, one inhabited by couples seeking some of the last (relatively) affordable places to raise a family south of 100th Street, and recent college grads getting a foothold in the city (on weekend nights 2nd Avenue resembles a miles-long fraternity and sorority reunion). One neighborhood particularly worth exploring is northeast-lying Yorkville, especially between 78th and 86th streets east of 2nd Avenue. Once a remote hamlet with a large German population, its several remaining ethnic food shops, 19th-century row houses, and, one of the city's best-kept secrets, **Carl Schurz Park,** make for a good half-day's exploration, as does touring the most striking residence there, **Gracie Mansion.**

If art galleries are your thing, there are some classy places to visit on the Upper East Side. In keeping with the tony surroundings, the emphasis here is on works by established masters rather than up-and-coming (or even still-living) artists. Their locations are eminent as well: large town houses and upper stories in and around Madison and 5th avenues. Note that galleries often have limited hours, so make sure to check times in advance.

TOP ATTRACTIONS

Asia Society and Museum. The Asian art collection of Mr. and Mrs. John D. Rockefeller III forms the core of this museum's holdings, which include South Asian stone and bronze sculptures; art from India, Nepal, Pakistan, and Afghanistan; bronze vessels, ceramics, sculpture, and paintings from China; Korean ceramics; and paintings, wooden sculptures, and ceramics from Japan. Founded in 1956, the society has a regular program of lectures, films, and performances, in addition to changing exhibitions of traditional and contemporary art. Trees grow in the glass-enclosed Garden Court Café, which serves an eclectic Asian menu for lunch and dinner. ■ TIP→ Admission is free on Fridays from 6 to 9. ⊠ *725 Park Ave., at 70th St., Upper East Side* ☎ *212/288–6400* ⊕ *asiasociety.org* ✉ *$10* ⊙ *Tues.–Sun. 11–6, open until 9 on Fri. from the day after Labor Day to July 1* Ⓜ *6 to 68th St./Hunter College.*

El Museo del Barrio. *El barrio* is Spanish for "the neighborhood" and the nickname for East Harlem, a largely Spanish-speaking Puerto Rican and Dominican community. El Museo del Barrio, on the edge of this neighborhood, focuses on Latin American and Caribbean art, with some 10% of its collection concentrated on works by self-taught artists from New York, Puerto Rico, the Caribbean, and Latin America. The more than 6,500-object permanent collection includes over 400 pre-Columbian artifacts, sculpture, photography, film and video, and traditional art from all over Latin America. The collection of 360 *santos,* carved wooden folk-art figures from Puerto Rico, is popular. ⊠ *1230 5th Ave., between E. 104th and E. 105th Sts., Upper East Side* ☎ *212/831–7272* ⊕ *www.elmuseo.org* ✉ *$9* ⊙ *Tues.–Sat. 11–6, Sun. 1–5* Ⓜ *6 to 103rd St.*

Fodor's Choice
★ **Frick Collection.** Henry Clay Frick made his fortune amid the soot and smoke of Pittsburgh, where he was a coke (a coal fuel derivative) and steel baron, but this lovely museum, once Frick's private New York residence, is decidedly removed from soot. Édouard Manet's *The Bullfight* (1864) hangs in the East Gallery, which also exhibits a Chinard portrait bust (1809; bought in 2004). Two of the Frick's three Vermeers—*Officer and Laughing Girl* (circa 1658) and *Girl Interrupted at Her Music* (1660–61)—hang by the front staircase. Nearly 50 additional paintings, as well as sculpture, decorative arts, and furniture, are in the West and East galleries. Three Rembrandts, including *The Polish Rider* (circa 1655) and *Self-Portrait* (1658), as well as a third Vermeer, *Mistress and Maid* (circa 1665–70), hang in the former; paintings by El Greco, Goya, Millet, Greuze, and Hogarth in the latter. In late 2011, the museum

unveiled a new 665-square-foot gallery, the Portico Gallery, created by enclosing the portico along the building's Fifth Avenue garden. The addition—the museum's first in 35 years—completes Frick's original vision to build an addition for his growing collection of sculpture. An audio guide, available in several languages, is included with admission, as are the year-round temporary exhibits. The tranquil indoor garden court is a magical spot for a rest. Children under 10 are not admitted, and those ages 10–16 with adult only. ⊠ *1 E. 70th St., at 5th Ave., Upper East Side* 🕾 *212/288–0700* ⊕ *www.frick.org* 🖾 *$18* ⊗ *Tues.–Sat. 10–6, Sun. 11–5* Ⓜ *6 to 68th St./Hunter College.*

Gracie Mansion. The official mayor's residence, Gracie Mansion was built in 1799 by shipping merchant Archibald Gracie, and enlarged in 1966. Tours of the impressive interior—which must be scheduled in advance and take place under limited hours—take you through the building's history and its colorful rooms furnished over centuries and packed with American objets d'art. Nine mayors have lived here since it became the official residence in 1942, but New York City's current mayor, Michael Bloomberg, broke with tradition and chose to stay in his own 79th Street town house. He does use Gracie Mansion, however, for meetings and functions. ⊠ *Carl Schurz Park, East End Ave. at 88th St., Upper East Side* 🕾 *212/570–4751* 🖾 *$7* ⊗ *45-min guided tours Wed. 10–2* Ⓜ *4, 5, 6 to 86th St.*

The Jewish Museum. In a Gothic-style 1908 mansion, the Jewish Museum draws on a large collection of art and ceremonial objects to explore Jewish identity and culture spanning more than 4,000 years. The two-floor permanent exhibition *Culture and Continuity: The Jewish Journey* displays nearly 800 objects complemented by interactive media. The wide-ranging collection includes a 3rd-century Roman burial plaque, 20th-century sculpture by Elie Nadelman, and contemporary art from artists such as Marc Chagall and Man Ray. ■TIP➔ Admission to the museum is free on Saturday. ⊠ *1109 5th Ave., at E. 92nd St., Upper East Side* 🕾 *212/423–3200* ⊕ *www.jewishmuseum.org* 🖾 *$12* ⊗ *Fri.–Tues. 11–5:45, Thurs. 11–8; closed Fri. mid-Mar.–Oct.* Ⓜ *6 to 96th St.*

Fodor'sChoice
★
Metropolitan Museum of Art. *See highlighted listing in this chapter.*

★ **Museum of the City of New York.** In a Colonial Revival building designed for the museum in the 1930s, the city's history and many quirks are revealed through engaging exhibits here. The building is currently undergoing renovations to the permanent galleries that will continue into early 2013, but rotating exhibits on subjects such as architecture, fashion, history, and politics are still on display. Don't miss *Timescapes*, a 25-minute media projection that innovatively illustrates New York's physical expansion and population changes. The museum hosts New York–centric lectures, films, and walking tours. ■TIP➔ When you're finished touring the museum, cross the street and stroll through the Vanderbilt Gates to enter the Conservatory Garden, one of Central Park's hidden gems. ⊠ *1220 5th Ave., at E. 103rd St., Upper East Side* 🕾 *212/534–1672* ⊕ *www.mcny.org* 🖾 *$10 suggested donation* ⊗ *Daily 10–6* Ⓜ *6 to 103rd St.*

SOLOMON R. GUGGENHEIM MUSEUM

✉ *1071 5th Ave., between E. 88th and E. 89th Sts., Upper East Side* ☎ *212/423–3840* ⊕ *www.guggenheim.org* 💲 *$18* ☉ *Sun.–Wed. 10–5:45, Fri. 10–5:45, Sat. 10–7:45. Closed Thurs.* Ⓜ *4, 5, 6 to 86th St.*

TIPS

■ Gallery talks provide richer understanding of the master-pieces in front of you. Tours are included in your admission fee, so be sure to take advantage.

■ Take it from the top: Escape the crowded lobby and keep your legs fresh for the rest of the museum by taking the elevator to the top and work-ing your way down the spiral.

■ The museum is pay-what-you-wish on Saturday from 5:45 to 7:45. Lines can be long, so arrive early. The last tickets are handed out at 7:15.

■ Eat before you visit; res-taurants on Lexington Avenue offer more varied fare than the museum's small Café 3 espresso and snack bar on the third floor.

Frank Lloyd Wright's landmark nautiluslike museum building is renowned as much for its famous architec-ture as for its superlative collection of art and well-curated shows. Opened in 1959, shortly after Wright's death, the Guggenheim is acclaimed as one of the greatest buildings of the 20th century. Inside, under a 92-foot-high glass dome, a ramp spirals down past the artworks of the current exhibits (the ramp is just over a quarter mile long, if you're wondering). The museum has strong holdings of Wassily Kandinsky, Paul Klee, Marc Chagall, Pablo Picasso, and Robert Mapplethorpe.

HIGHLIGHTS

Wright's design was criticized by some who believed that the distinctive building detracted from the art within, but the interior nautilus design allows artworks to be viewed from several different angles and distances. Be sure to notice not only what's in front of you but also what's across the spiral from you.

Even if you aren't planning to eat, stop at the museum's modern American restaurant, the Wright, for its stun-ning design created by Andre Kikosk.

On permanent display, the museum's Thannhauser Collection is made up primarily of works by French impressionists and postimpressionists van Gogh, Toulouse-Lautrec, Cézanne, and Matisse. Perhaps more than any other 20th-century painter, Wassily Kandin-sky, one of the first "pure" abstract artists, has been closely linked to the museum's history: beginning with the acquisition of his masterpiece *Composition 8* (1923) in 1930, the collection has grown to encompass more than 150 works.

10

WHITNEY MUSEUM OF AMERICAN ART

✉ *945 Madison Ave., at E. 75th St., Upper East Side*
☎ *212/570-3600 8639*
⊕ *www.whitney.org* 🎟 *$18*
🕐 *Wed., Thurs., weekends 11–6, Fri. 1–9* Ⓜ *6 to 77th St.*

TIPS

■ After 6 pm on Friday the price of admission is pay-what-you-wish. On some of those nights the Whitney Live series presents new artists and reinterpretations of American classics. Be fore-warned that this may result in long lines.

■ Catch it while you can: In 2015, the Whitney will head downtown to an exciting new space, designed by Renzo Piano Building Workshop in partnership with Cooper, Robertson & Partners. The new museum will feature more than 50,000 square feet of gallery space, as well as outdoor exhibition areas overlooking the High Line (New York's beloved elevated park), a multiuse theater, and an education center for family events.

■ The Untitled restaurant in the basement (by Danny Meyer of the Union Square Café, serves updated diner classics; it's open for breakfast and lunch, Tuesday through Saturday, and for dinner Thursday through Saturday.

With its bold collection of 20th- and 21st-century and contemporary American art, the Whitney presents an eclectic mix drawn from more than 19,000 works in its permanent collection. The museum was originally a gallery in the studio of sculptor and collector Gertrude Vanderbilt Whitney, whose talent and taste were accompanied by the money of two wealthy families. In 1930, after the Met turned down Whitney's offer to donate her collection of 20th-century American art, she established an independent museum in Greenwich Village. The museum moved uptown in 1996, into this minimalist gray-granite building designed by Marcel Breuer and Hamilton Smith.

HIGHLIGHTS

Start your visit on the fifth floor, where the galleries house rotating exhibitions of postwar and contemporary works from the permanent collection by artists such as Jackson Pollock, Jim Dine, Jasper Johns, Mark Rothko, Chuck Close, Cindy Sherman, and Roy Lichtenstein.

Although the collection on display constantly changes, notable pieces often on view include Hopper's *Early Sunday Morning* (1930), Bellows's *Dempsey and Firpo* (1924), Alexander Calder's beloved *Circus*, and several of Georgia O'Keeffe's dazzling flower paintings.

The lower floors feature exhibitions of contemporary artists such as Kara Walker and Gordon Matta-Clark, as well as retrospective exhibitions that focus on movements and themes in American art.

The often-controversial Whitney Biennial, which showcases the most important developments in American art over the previous two years, takes place in the spring of even-numbered years.

★ **Neue Galerie New York.** Early-20th-century German and Austrian art and design are the focus here, with works by Gustav Klimt, Wassily Kandinsky, Paul Klee, Egon Schiele, Josef Hoffman, and other designers from the Wiener Werkstätte taking center stage. The Neue Galerie was founded by the late art dealer Serge Sabarsky and cosmetics heir and art collector Ronald S. Lauder, in a 1914 wood- and marble-floored mansion designed by Carrère and Hastings, which was once home to Mrs. Cornelius Vanderbilt III. An audio guide is included with admission. Note that children under 12 are not admitted, and teens 12–16 must be accompanied by an adult. **Café Sabarsky**, in an elegant, high-ceiling space below the Neue Galerie, is a destination in its own right, for their Viennese coffee, cakes, strudels, and Sacher tortes (Monday and Wednesday 9–6, Thursday–Sunday 9–9). If you seek something more than a sugar fix, the savory menu includes trout crepes and Hungarian goulash. Café Fledermaus, on the lower level of the museum, offers the same menu as Café Sabarsky. ⊠ *1048 5th Ave., at E. 86th St., Upper East Side* ☎ *212/628–6200* ⊕ *www.neuegalerie. org* ☞ *$20* ⊘ *Thurs.–Mon. 11–6* Ⓜ *4, 5, 6 to 86th St.* ☞ *Children under 12 not admitted.*

Cooper-Hewitt, National Design Museum, Smithsonian Institution. The Cooper-Hewitt National Design Museum is closed while undergoing renovations that will increase the Cooper-Hewitt's exhibition space by 60% (from approximately 10,000 square feet to 16,000 square feet). It is scheduled to reopen in fall 2013. In the meantime the museum is staging exhibitions around the city; check the website for more information. Hours and admission prices are yet to be determined at this writing. ⊠ *2 E. 91st St., at 5th Ave., Upper East Side* ☎ *212/849–1549* ⊕ *www. cooperhewitt.org* Ⓜ *4, 5, 6 to 86th St.*

WORTH NOTING

☾ **Carl Schurz Park.** Facing the East River, this park, named for a German immigrant who was a prominent newspaper editor in the 19th century, is so tranquil you'd never guess you're directly above FDR Drive. Walk along the promenade, where you can take in views of the river and the Roosevelt Island Lighthouse across the way. To the north are Randall's and Wards islands and recently renamed Robert F. Kennedy Bridge (aka the Triborough Bridge)—as well as the more immediate sight of locals pushing strollers, riding bikes, or walking their dogs. If you enter the park at its 86th Street entrance or you're exiting there, you'll find yourself approaching the grounds of a Federal-style wood-frame house that belies the grandeur of its name—Gracie Mansion.

■ TIP→ If you exit the park at 86th Street, cross East End Avenue for a stroll through Henderson Place, a miniature historic district of 24 connected Queen Anne–style houses in a dead end. The small redbrick houses, built in 1881 "for persons of moderate means," have turrets marking the corner of each block and symmetrical roof gables, pediments, parapets, chimneys, and dormer windows. ⊠ *Carl Schurz Park spans East End Ave. to the East River, E. 84th to E. 90th Sts., Upper East Side* ☎ *212/459–4455* ⊕ *www.carlschurzparknyc.org* Ⓜ *4, 5, 6 to 86th St.*

10

Continued on page 155

Mesmerizing carvings in the ancient Egyptian Temple of Dendur.

THE METROPOLITAN MUSEUM OF ART

If the city held no other museum than the colossal Metropolitan Museum of Art, you could still occupy yourself for days roaming its labyrinthine corridors. Because the Metropolitan Museum has more than 2 million works of art representing 5,000 years of history, you're going to have to make tough choices. Looking at everything here could take a week.

Before you begin exploring the museum, check the museum's floor plan, available at all entrances, for location of the major wings and collections. Pick up the "Today's Events" flier at the desk where you buy your ticket. The museum offers gallery talks on a range of subjects; taking a tour with a staff curator can show you some of the collection's hidden secrets.

The posted adult admission, though only a suggestion, is one that's strongly encouraged. Whatever you choose to pay, admission includes all special exhibits and same-day entrance to the Cloisters (see Chapter 12). The Met's audio guide costs an additional $7, and if you intend to stay more than an hour or so, it's worth it. The generally perceptive commentary covers museum highlights and directors' picks, with separate commentary tracks directed at kids.

If you want to avoid the crowds, visit weekday mornings. Also good are Friday and Saturday evenings, when live classical music plays from the Great Hall balcony. If the Great Hall (the main entrance) is mobbed, avoid the chaos by heading to the street-level entrance to the left of the main stairs, near 81st Street. Ticket lines and coat checks are much less ferocious here.

What to see? Check out the museum highlights on the following pages.

- ✉ 5th Ave. at 82nd St., Upper East Side
- Ⓜ Subway: 4, 5, 6 to 86th St.
- ☎ 212/535-7710
- 🌐 www.metmuseum.org
- 💵 $25 suggested donation
- 🕑 Tues.–Thurs. and Sun. 9:30–5:30, Fri. and Sat. 9:30–9

10

Left, Great Hall

MUSEUM HIGHLIGHTS

Egyptian Art

A major star is the **Temple of Dendur** (circa 15 BC), in a huge atrium to itself and with a moatlike pool of water to represent its original location near the Nile. The temple was commissioned by the Roman emperor Augustus to honor the goddess Isis and the sons of a Nubian chieftain. Look for the scratched-in graffiti from 19th-century Western explorers on the inside. Egypt gave the temple as a gift to the U.S. in 1965; it would have been submerged after the construction of the Aswan High Dam.

Temple of Dendur

The Egyptian collection as a whole covers 4,000 years of history, with papyrus pages from the Egyptian Book of the Dead, stone sarcophagi inscribed with hieroglyphics, and tombs. The galleries should be walked through counterclockwise from the Ancient Kingdom (2650–2150 BC), to the period under Roman rule (30 BC–400 AD). In the latter, keep an eye out for the enormous, bulbous **Sarcophagus of Horkhebil**, sculpted from basalt.

Greek and Roman Art

Today's tabloids have nothing on ancient Greece and Rome. They had it all—sex, cults, drugs, unrelenting violence, and, of course, stunning art. The recently redone Greek and Roman galleries encompass 6,000 works of art that reveal aspects of everyday life in these influential cultures.

The urnlike terracotta kraters were used by the Greeks for mixing wine and water at parties and other events. Given that, it's not surprising that most depict slightly racy scenes. Some of the most impressive can be found in the gallery covering 5th century BC.

Engelhard Court

On the mezzanine of the Roman galleries, the Etruscan bronze chariot from 650 BC depicts scenes from the life of Achilles. Notice how the simplistic Etruscan style in combination with the Greek influence evolved into the naturalistic Roman statues below.

The frescoes from a bedroom in the Villa of P. Fannius Synistor preserved by the explosion of Mt. Vesuvius in 79 AD give us a glimpse into the stylistic achievement of perspective in Roman painting.

An artifact from ancient Greece.

Modern Art

Special
Exhibitions

European
Painting

The American
Wing

19th-Century
European
Painting and
Sculpture

Access Route

Greek and
Roman Art

Modern and
Contemporary Art

Balcony Café

Art of
the Arab Lands

Asian
Galleries

Astor Court

SECOND AND THIRD FLOORS

MEZZANINES

Petrie Court
Café

The Cafeteria
(on ground floor)

The American
Wing

Modern Art

Elevator to
Roof Garden

European Sculpture
and Decorative Arts

Arms and
Armor

Art of Africa,
Oceania &
Americas

Equestrian
Court

Temple of
Dendur

Shop

Greek and
Roman Art

Access Route

Great Hall

Egyptian Art

FIRST FLOOR

5th Avenue

The American Wing of the Metropolitan Museum of Art.

American Wing

After years of extensive renovations, the Met's revitalized **New American Wing Galleries for Paintings, Sculpture, and Decorative Arts** reopened in 2012 with 30,000 square feet of skylit space to showcase one of the best and largest collections of American art in the country.

There's much to see, from Colonial furniture to the works of the great masters, including John Singleton Copley, Gilbert Stuart, Thomas Cole, Frederic Edwin Church, Winslow Homer, and Thomas Eakins, among others. The highlight of the new installation is Emanuel Gottlieb Leutze's magnificent 1851 painting, *Washington Crossing the Delaware*. Hung in an immense gilded frame (recreated from an 1864 photograph of the painting), Leutze's iconic work is displayed just as it was at a fundraiser for Union soldiers in 1864—flanked by Frederic Church's *Heart of the Andes* and Albert Bierstadt's *Rocky Mountains*.

Also not to be missed are John Singer Sargent's *Madame X*, a once-scandalous portrait of a Parisian socialite; the recreation of the entrance hall of the 18th Century Van Rensselaer Manor House in Albany, New York; and the collection of portrait miniatures—detailed watercolors to be carried or gifted as tokens of love.

TIME TO EAT?
INSIDE THE MUSEUM

The **Petrie Café**, at the back of the 1st-floor European Sculpture Court, has waiter service. Prices range from $12 for a sandwich to $21 for organic chicken salad. Tea, sweets, and savories are served from 2:30 PM to 4:30 PM during the week.

The **Great Hall Balcony Bar** is located on the second floor belcony overlooking the Great Hall. On Fridays and Saturdays, 4 PM TO 8:30 PM waiters serve appetizers and cocktails accompanied by live classical music.

The **cafeteria** on the ground floor has stations for pasta, main courses, antipasti, and sandwiches.

Looking for one of the best views in town? The **Roof Garden** (open May–Oct.) exhibits contemporary sculpture, but most people take the elevator here to have a drink or snack while checking out Central Park and the skyline.

Tiffany

Arms and Armor

The **Equestrian Court**, where the knights are mounted on armored models of horses, is one of the most dramatic rooms in the museum. For a bird's-eye view, check it out again from the balconies in the Musical Instruments collection on the second floor.

European Sculpture and Decorative Arts

Among the many sculptures in the sun-filled Petrie Court, *Ugolino and His Sons* still stands out for the despairing poses of its subjects. Ugolino, a nobleman whose family's tragic story is told in Dante's *Inferno*, was punished for treason by being left to starve to death with his grandsons and sons in a locked tower. (It's not clear if putting such a sculpture so near the Petrie Court's café is some curator's idea of a joke or not.) By the way, the redbrick and granite wall on the court's north side is the museum's original entrance.

The newly renovated Wrightsman Galleries for French Decorative Arts on the first floor displays the opulence that caused Louis the XVI to lose his head. The blindingly golden Boiserie from the Hotel de Cabris, a remnant of French 18th century Neo-classical interiors, represents the finest collection of French decorative arts in the country.

Modern Art

The museum's most famous Picasso is probably his 1906 portrait *Gertrude Stein* in which the writer's face is stern and masklike. The portrait was bequeathed to the museum by Stein herself.

Of the Georgia O'Keeffes on view, 1931's *Red, White, and Blue* painting of a cow skull is a standout. The color, composition, and natural motif work together to create a work with religious as well as nationalist overtones.

European Paintings

On the second floor, the 13th- to 18th-century paintings are grouped at the top of the Great Hall's stairs.

Recently, the Met spent about $45 million to buy Duccio di Buoninsegna's *Madonna and Child,* painted circa 1300. The last remaining Duccio in private hands, this painting, the size of a piece of typewriter paper, is unimpressive at first glance. The work, though rigid, represents a revolution in Byzantine art. The humanity reflected in the baby Jesus grabbing his mother's veil changed European painting.

TIME TO EAT?
OUTSIDE THE MUSEUM

Because museum admission is good all day, you can always leave for lunch and come back later. The deli-style **City Market Café** (1100 Madison Ave., between. 82nd and 83rd Sts., 212/535-2070) with 10 small tables, serves pizzas, sandwiches, and make-your-own salad. At the fairly inexpensive sit-down eatery **Le Pain Quotidien** (1131 Madison Ave., at 84th St., 212/327-4900), the hungry dine at long communal tables for sandwiches (around $9), salads, and pastries high in both calories and quality. If you'd rather try for a typical New York diner, head for the **Amity Restaurant** (1134 Madison Ave, between 84th and 85th Sts., 212/861-3255). A burger with fries costs under $10.

IN FOCUS THE METROPOLITAN MUSEUM OF ART

10

Equestrian Court (1930)

Rembrandt's masterful *Aristotle with a Bust of Homer* (1653) shows a philosopher contemplating worldly gains versus values through its play of light and use of symbols. Around Aristotle is a gold medal of Alexander the Great, one of the philosopher's students.

In the room dedicated to **Monet** you can get to all his greatest hits—poplar trees, haystacks, water lilies, and the Rouen Cathedral. The muted tones of Pissaro are followed by a room full of bright and garish colors announcing works by Gauguin, Matisse, and Van Gogh.

Vincent van Gogh,
Wheatfield with Cypresses

Islamic Galleries

In late 2011, after an eight-year renovation, the Met reopened its Islamic galleries, a suite of 15 galleries housing one of the world's premier collections of Islamic art. Now known as the "Art of the Arab Lands, Turkey, Iran, Central Asia, and Later South Asia," the collection comprises more than 12,000 works of art and traces the course of Islamic Civilization over a span of 13 centuries. Highlights include an 11-foot-high 14th century mihrab, or prayer niche, decorated with glazed ceramic tiles; the recently restored Emperor's Carpet—a 16th century Persian carpet that was presented to the Hapsburg Emperor Leopold I by Peter the Great of Russia; the Damascus Room—a Syrian Ottoman reception room decorated with poetic verses; and glass, ceramics, and metalwork from Egypt, Syria, Iraq, and Iran.

Asian Galleries

The serene **Astor Court**, which has its own skylight and pond of real-life koi (goldfish), is a model of a scholar's court garden in Soochow, China.

The Han dynasty (206 BC–220 AD) introduced the practice of sending the dead on to the afterlife with small objects to help them there. Keep an eye out for these **small clay figures**, which include farm animals (enclosed in barnyards) and dancing entertainers.

On display in a glass case in the center of an early-Chinese gallery is a complete set of 14 **bronze altar vessels.** Dating 1100 BC—800 AD, these green and slightly crusty pieces were used for worshipping ancestors. The Met displays some of its finest **Asian stoneware and porcelain** along the balcony overlooking the Great Hall.

The teak dome and minature balconies from a **Jain meeting hall** in western India were carved in the 16th century. Just about the entire surface is covered with musicians, animals, gods, and servants.

WHAT'S TO COME

The front steps of the Met are one of Manhattan's iconic meeting places but plans to remodel the front and the four-block long stretch of 5th Avenue into a more pleasing, accessible, and environmentally friendly space. Stay tuned.

Standing eight-armed
Avalokiteshvara

↻ **Mount Vernon Hotel Museum and Garden.** Built in 1799, this former carriage house (i.e., stable) became a day hotel (a sort of country club) in 1826. Now restored and owned by the Colonial Dames of America, it provides a glimpse of the days when the city ended at 14th Street and this area was a country escape for New Yorkers. A 45-minute tour passes through the eight rooms that display furniture and artifacts of the Federal and Empire periods. Many rooms have real artifacts such as clothes, hats, and fans that children can handle. There is a lovely adjoining garden, designed in an 18th-century style. ⊠ *421 E. 61st St., between York and 1st Aves., Upper East Side* ☎ *212/838–6878* ⊕ *www.mvhm.org* ✉ *$8* ⊙ *Tues.–Sun. 11–4* Ⓜ *4, 5, 6, F, N, R to 59th St./Lexington Ave.*

Museum of American Illustration. Founded in 1901, the museum of the Society of Illustrators presents its annual "Oscars," a juried, international competition, from January to March. The best in children's book illustrations is featured October through November. In between are eclectic exhibitions on science fiction, fashion, political, and historical illustration. ⊠ *128 E. 63rd St., between Lexington and Park Aves., Upper East Side* ☎ *212/838–2560* ⊕ *www.societyillustrators.org* ✉ *Free* ⊙ *Tues. 10–8, Wed.–Fri. 10–5, Sat. noon–4* Ⓜ *F to 63rd St.; 4, 5, 6, N, R to 59th St./Lexington Ave.*

↻ **Roosevelt Island.** The 2-mi-long East River slice of land that parallels Manhattan from East 48th to East 85th streets is now a quasi-suburb of 10,000 people, and the vestiges of its infamous asylums, hospitals, and prisons make this an offbeat trip for the historically curious. At the south tip are the eerie ruins of a **Smallpox Hospital,** built in 1854 in a Gothic Revival style by the prominent architect James Renwick Jr. (Among many other works, Renwick also designed St. Patrick's and the Smithsonian's Castle.) On a small park at the island's north tip is a lighthouse built in 1872 by island convicts. Most of what's in between (new as well as 1970s-era condominiums and a modern-day hospital) is fairly banal, but riverside esplanades provide nice panoramas of Manhattan. You can get here by subway, but it's more fun to take the five-minute ride on the **Roosevelt Island Tramway,** the only commuter cable car in North America, which lifts you 250 feet in the air, with impressive views of Queens and Manhattan. A visitor center, made from an old trolley kiosk, stands to your left as you exit the tram. Red buses service the island for 25¢ a ride. ⊠ *Tramway entrance at 2nd Ave. and either 59th St. or 60th St., Upper East Side* ☎ *212/832–4540* ⊕ *www. rioc.com* ✉ *$2.25 (subway Metrocard accepted)* ⊙ *Tram Sun.–Thurs. 6 am–2 am, Fri. and Sat. 6 am–3:30 am; leaves approximately every 15 min* Ⓜ *F to Roosevelt Island.*

10

GALLERIES

Acquavella Galleries. The 19th- and 20th-century art shown inside this five-story marble-floored mansion tends to be by the big names, from Impressionists through Pop artists, including Picasso, Lucian Freud, and James Rosenquist. ⊠ *18 E. 79th St., between 5th and Madison Aves., Upper East Side* ☎ *212/734–6300* ⊕ *www.acquavellagalleries. com* ⊙ *Mon.–Sat. 10–5* Ⓜ *6 to 77th St.*

Jane Kahan. This welcoming gallery represents some lofty works. In addition to tapestries by modern masters like Pablo Picasso, Joan Miró, and Alexander Calder—one of this gallery's specialties—you'll see works by late-19th- and early-20th-century modern artists such as Fernand Léger and Marc Chagall. ⊠ *922 Madison Ave., 2nd fl., between E. 73rd and E. 74th Sts., Upper East Side* ☎ *212/744–1490* ⊕ *www. janekahan.com* ☉ *Mon.–Sat. 10–6 except Memorial Day–Labor Day: weekdays 11–5* Ⓜ *6 to 77th St.*

★ **Leo Castelli.** Castelli was one of the most influential dealers of the 20th century. He helped foster the careers of many important artists, including one of his first discoveries, Jasper Johns. The gallery continues to show works by Roy Lichtenstein, Ed Ruscha, Jackson Pollock, Robert Morris, and other heavies. ⊠ *18 E. 77th St., between 5th and Madison Aves., Upper East Side* ☎ *212/249–4470* ⊕ *www.castelligallery.com* ☉ *Tues.—Sat. 10–6* Ⓜ *6 to 77th St.*

Michael Werner. This branch of a well-established German gallery specializes in American and European paintings. Works by Sigmar Polke, Peter Doig, and Francis Picabia have all been displayed in the east side town house. ⊠ *4 E. 77th St., between 5th and Madison Aves., Upper East Side* ☎ *212/988–1623* ⊕ *www.michaelwerner.com* ☉ *Mon.–Sat. 10–6* Ⓜ *6 to 77th St.*

Mitchell-Innes & Nash. This sleek spot represents the estates of Roy Lichtenstein and Jack Tworkov as well as other Impressionist, modern, and contemporary masters. ⊠ *1018 Madison Ave., between 78th and 79th Sts., Upper East Side* ☎ *212/744–7400* ⊕ *www.miandn.com* ☉ *Mon.–Fri. 10–5* Ⓜ *6 to 77th St.*

★ **Sotheby's.** Occupying its own 10-story building, this branch of the storied U.K. auction house puts on display many of the items it will be auctioning. A sizable portion of these are extremely high profile: a copy of the Magna Carta, Fabergé eggs, rare Tiffany lamps, and Norman Rockwell's 1943 painting *Rosie the Riveter* have all been sold through this Sotheby's. ⊠ *1334 York Ave., at E. 72nd St., Upper East Side* ☎ *212/606–7000* ⊕ *www.sothebys.com* Ⓜ *6 to 77th St.*

Peter Findlay Gallery. Covering 19th- and 20th-century works by European artists, this gallery shows pieces by Mary Cassatt, Paul Klee, and Alberto Giacometti. ⊠ *16 E. 79th St., 2nd fl., Upper East Side* ☎ *212/644–4433* ⊕ *www.findlay.com* ☉ *Mon.–Fri. 1:30–5* Ⓜ *N, R to 5th Ave.*

11

Central Park

WORD OF MOUTH

"Central Park was fabulous! I love that this busy, bustling city has such a huge expanse of peaceful parkland."

— cathies

OUR BACKYARD

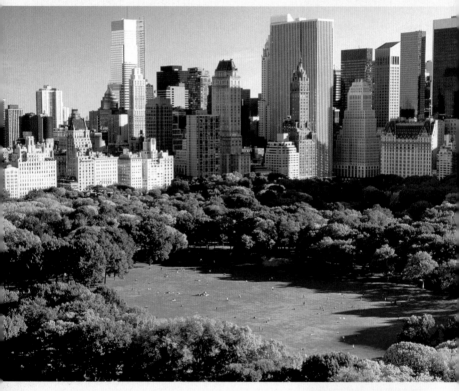

HOW A SWAMP BECAME AN OASIS

1855 Using the power of eminent domain, New York City acquires 843 acres of undeveloped swamp for the then-obscene sum of $5 million, displacing 1,600 people living there.

1857 The landscape architect Frederick Law Olmsted becomes superintendent of a park that does not yet exist. He spends days clearing dirt and evicting squatters and evenings working with architect Calvert Vaux on what will become the Greensward plan. The plan is the winning entry in the city's competition to develop a design for the park.

While the Panic of 1857 creates widespread unemployment, thousands of workers begin moving five million cubic yards of dirt and planting more than five million trees and plants. Beleaguered by bureaucrats, Olmsted and Vaux unsuccessfully submit resignations several times.

1873 The Greensward plan is completed. It has been the basic blueprint for Central Park ever since.

More than thirty-five million people visit Central Park each year; on an average summer weekend day, a quarter of a million children and adults flood these precincts, frolicking in the 21 playgrounds, bellying up to the 150 drinking fountains (water not guaranteed), and collapsing on more than 9,000 benches, which would span seven miles if you lined them up. There are more than 50 monuments and sculptures in the park, and countless ways to have fun.

⟨30⟩ THINGS WE LOVE TO DO IN CENTRAL PARK

1 Take a rowboat out on the lake

2 Watch the sea lions play at feeding time at the zoo

3 Walk around the Reservoir

4 Ice-skate at Wollman Rink

5 Watch rollerbladers show off

6 Go bird-watching at the Ramble

7 Lie in the grass at Sheep Meadow

8 Rent a bike at the Boathouse

9 Sit on the hill behind the Met Museum

10 See a free concert or play

11 Catch a softball game

12 Clap for the jugglers

13 Remember John Lennon at Strawberry Fields

14 Run through a playground sprinkler

15 Rent a gondola and a gondolier

16 Cross the park on the bridle path

17 Stand under the 72nd Street Wisteria Pergola

18 Hear the Delacorte Clock's musical chimes

19 Crunch the snow before anyone else

20 Pilot a model boat at Conservatory Water

21 Stroll through Shakespeare Garden

22 Fish at Harlem Meer

23 Watch dogs play

24 Smell the Conservatory Garden tulips

25 Shoot photos from Bow Bridge

26 Ride the Carousel; wave at everyone

27 People-watch at Bethesda Fountain

28 Picnic on the Great Lawn

29 Pet the bronze Balto statue

30 Climb to the top of Belvedere Castle

(top left) Monarch butterfly pollinates at Conservatory Garden (top center) Bethesda Fountain (top right) Chrysanthemums near Sheep Meadow (center) The skyline with some of the park's 26,000 trees (bottom) Park skaters in the 1860s.

PARK BASICS

Several entrances lead into the park. You can enter from the east, west, south, and north by paved pedestrian walkways, just off Fifth Avenue, Central Park North (110th St.), Central Park West, and Central Park South (59th St.).

Four roads, or transverses, cut through the park from east to west—66th, 79th, 86th, and 96th streets. The East and West drives are both along the north–south axis; Center Drive enters the south edge of the park at Sixth Avenue and connects with East Drive around 66th Street.

There are five Visitor Centers—the Dairy (just south of the 66th St. transverse), Belvedere Castle (just north of the 79th Street transverse), the Chess & Checkers House (mid-park at 64th St.), and the Charles A. Dana Discovery Center (at the top of the park at Central Park North)—that have directions, park maps, event calendars, and volunteers who can guide you. Until a new restaurant opens in its place, the former Tavern on the Green (west side near 66th St.) is also serving as a visitor center, with food vendors as well.

TOURS

The **Central Park Conservancy** gives several different free walking tours of the park based on the season. Most tours are 60 to 90 minutes, and custom tours are also available. If you'd rather go it alone, the Conservancy also offers an audio guide you can follow on your cell phone. Each description is read by a different celebrity or NYC VIP. Dial 646/862-0997, then the extension that corresponds to each landmark and hit the pound sign. For more information, see *centralparknyc.org*.

WHERE AM I?

Along the main loop and some smaller paths, lampposts are marked with location codes. Posts bear a letter—always "E" (for east) or "W" (for west)—followed by four numbers. The first two numbers tell you the nearest cross street. The second two tell you how far you are from either 5th Avenue or Central Park West (depending on whether it's an "E" or "W" post). So E7803 means you're near 78th Street, three posts in from 5th Avenue. For street numbers above 99, the initial "1" is omitted, for example, E0401 (near 104th Street, one post in from 5th Avenue).

PERFORMERS AND THE PARK: SOULMATES

It was inevitable that Central Park, conceived to give so much and ask little in return, would attract artists and art lovers who feel the same way.

Be they superstars like Paul Simon, Diana Ross, or Barbra Streisand or one of the amateur musicians, animal handlers, or jugglers who delight passersby, they all share the urge to entertain and give back to the city, the park, and its visitors.

Information on scheduled events is provided, but if you can't catch one, don't fret: you'll be rewarded by the serendipitous, particularly on summer and autumn days. Just keep your ears peeled for the music, applause, and laughter. The Central Park Conservancy, in cooperation with other arts patrons, organizes a series of free events, including the Harlem Meer Performance Festival and the Great Lawn performances by the Metropolitan Opera and New York Philharmonic. SummerStage has yielded a cornucopia of international performers.

Perhaps the brass ring of park performances is Shakespeare in the Park, which celebrated its 50th year in 2012. Every summer's performances of works by the Bard (and others) wow as many as 90,000 New Yorkers and visitors. Free tickets (two per person) are given out starting at 1 PM for the performance that evening, but you need to line up by midmorning or earlier, depending on the show. Tickets are also distributed via online lottery on the show day at www. shakespeareinthepark.org. Either way, the trouble is worth it, as casts are often studded with stars like Meryl Streep, Philip Seymour Hoffman, Natalie Portman, Morgan Freeman, Denzel Washington, and Kevin Kline.

GOINGS ON

Central Park Conservancy Film Festival: Five nights at end of summer; Rumsey Playfield, near E. 72nd St. entrance.

Harlem Meer Performance Festival: Late June–early Sept., Sun.; at Dana Discovery Center, near Lenox Ave. entrance.

New York Grand Opera: Performances July.–Aug.; Naumburg Bandshell; mid-park near 72nd St.

New York Philharmonic: Two performances in the summer; Great Lawn.

Shakespeare in the Park: June–early Aug., Tues.– Sun. evenings.

Storytelling: June–Sept., Sat. 11 AM; Hans Christian Andersen Statue at 72nd St. and 5th Ave.

SummerStage: Late May or June–early Sept.; Rumsey Playfield. Big-name musicians perform here, sometimes for free.

Swedish Cottage Marionette Theatre: Since 1947, puppeteers have entertained in this 1876 Swedish schoolhouse. $8 adults/$5 kids. Daily hours vary; reservations required; visit www. cityparksfoundation.org.

(center) N.Y. Philharmonic associate conductor Xian Zhang (right) Shakespeare's *Much Ado About Nothing*

FROM 59TH TO 72ND ST.

The busy southern section of Central Park is where most visitors get their first impression; it's also where most of the park's child-friendly attractions are centered. Artists line the entrances off Central Park South, and horse carriages await passengers. But no matter how many people gather here, you can always find a spot to picnic, ponder, or just take in the beauty, especially on a sunny day.

At the southeast corner of the park, you will come upon one of its prettiest areas, the **Pond.** Swans and ducks cruise on its calm waters, and if you follow the shore line to Gapstow Bridge and look southward, you'll see much of New York City's skyline: to the left (east) are the peak-roofed Sherry-Netherland Hotel, the black-and-white GM Building, the Chippendale-style top of the Sony Building, and the black-glass Trump Tower. In front of you is the château-style Plaza Hotel.

Opening in late October, **Trump Wollman Skating Rink** sits inside the park against a backdrop of Central Park South skyscrapers. You can rent skates, buy snacks, and have a perfect city-type outing. There's a

lively feeling here with lots of great music playing and a terrace so you can watch if you're not into skating.

The **Friedsam Memorial Carousel,** also known as the Central Park Carousel, was built in 1908. It has 58 nearly life-size hand-carved horses and remains a favorite among young and old. Its original Wurlitzer organ plays calliope waltzes, polkas, and standards. Even if you don't need visitor infomation, the **Dairy** is worth a stop for its Swiss-chalet exterior.

If you saw the film *Madagascar,* you may recognize the **Central Park Zoo.** Here, the polar bears play at the Polar Circle, monkeys frolic in the open-air Temperate Territory, and the Rain Forest showcases flora and fauna that you wouldn't expect to see in Manhattan. An unusual exhibit is the ant colony—even New York City's zoo has a sense of humor. Stick around to see the sea lion feedings (call for times) and to watch the animal statues dance to a variety of nursery rhymes at the **Delacorte Musical Clock** just outside, on the hour and half-hour from 8 AM to 5 PM.

Wedged between the zoo and the clock is **The Arsenal,** the second-oldest building in the park. Inside are rotating

exhibits that often cover park history and landscape art.

North of the clock is **Tisch Children's Zoo,** where kids can pet and feed sheep, goats, rabbits, cows, and pigs. Enter through the trunk of a make-believe tree and arrive at The Enchanted Forest, filled with huge "acorns,"

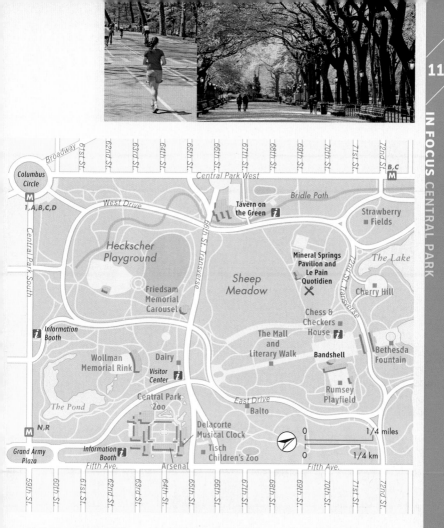

a climbable "spider web," and hoppable "lily pads."

Perhaps more pettable than any of the zoo's occupants is a decidedly more inert creature, perched on a rockpile at East 67th Street: **Balto**. Shiny in places from constant touching, this bronze statue commemorates a real-life sled dog who led a team of huskies that carried medicine for 674 mi across perilous

ice to Nome, Alaska, during a 1925 diphtheria epidemic.

The Mall, at the intersection of Central Drive and East Drive, is arguably the most elegant area of Central Park. In the beginning of the 20th century, it was the place to see and be seen. Today, these formal walkways are still a wonderful place to stroll, meander, or sit and take in the "parade" under a canopy of the largest col-

lection of American elms in North America. The mall's southern end, known as **Literary Walk**, is lined with statues of authors and artists such as Robert Burns and William Shakespeare.

(from left to right) Riding on the outside track (recommended) of the Carousel; Getting in a workout on a park drive loop; The Mall, where Dustin Hoffman's character famously teaches his son to ride a bike in *Kramer vs. Kramer*.

The large expanse to the west of the Mall is known as the **Sheep Meadow**, the only "beach" that some native New Yorkers have ever known. Join in on a Frisbee or football game, admire the tenacity of kite flyers, or indulge simultaneously in the three simplest meadow pleasures of them all—picnicking, sunbathing, and languorously reading a book or magazine.

There's a reason why the ornate **Bethesda Fountain**, off the 72nd Street transverse, shows up in so many movies set in New York City: the view from the staircase above is one of the most romantic in the city. The statue in the center of the fountain, **The Angel of the Waters**, designed by Emma Stebbins, is surrounded by four figures symbolizing Temperance, Purity,

Health, and Peace. There's a good amount of New York–style street entertainment here, too, with break dancers, acrobats, and singers all vying for your spare change. It's also a great place to meet, sit, and admire the beautiful lake with its swans. For a glimpse of the West Side skyline, walk slightly west to **Cherry Hill**. Originally a watering area for horses, this circular plaza has a small wrought-iron-and-gilt fountain. It's particularly beautiful in the spring when the cherry trees are in full pink-and-white bloom. Farther west are the Oak Bridge and the lovely Ladies Pavilion, emblematic of the park's past.

Across from the Dakota apartment building on Central Park West is **Strawberry Fields**, named for

the Beatles' 1967 classic, "Strawberry Fields Forever." Sometimes called the "international garden of peace," this spot draws fans who come to reflect among its shrubs, trees, and flower beds, and lay flowers on the black-and-white "Imagine" mosaic. On December 8, hundreds of Beatles fans mark the anniversary of Lennon's death by gathering here.

(top from left to right) Horse-drawn carriages; Artist painting the oft-rendered Gapstow bridge, which spans the northeast end of the Pond; Cutting through the park is a classic midday timesaver and post-work respite; Seals at the Central Park Zoo (center left); Nighttime at Wollman Rink serves up twinkling skyscrapers and skaters of all abilities (center right); The late John Lennon and his widow, Yoko Ono, often visited the site of what would become Strawberry Fields.

FROM 72ND ST. TO THE RESERVOIR

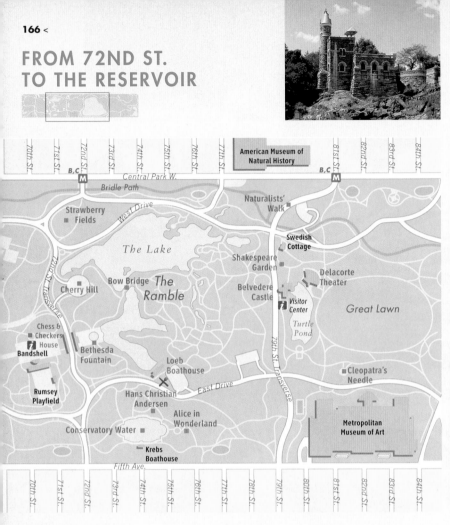

Playgrounds, lawns, jogging and biking paths, and striking buildings populate the midsection of the park. You can soak up the sun, have a picnic, or even play in a pick-up basketball or baseball game by the Great Lawn; get your cultural fix at the Metropolitan Museum of Art; or train for the next New York City Marathon along the Reservoir.

A block from Fifth Avenue, just north of the 72nd Street entrance, is a peaceful section of the park where you'll find the **Conservatory Water**, named for a conservatory that was never built. Generations of New Yorkers have grown up racing radio-controlled model sailboats here. It's a tradition that happens each Saturday at 10 AM from April through Oct. During those months smaller boats are available for rent

daily. At the north end is the **Alice in Wonderland** statue; on the west side of the pond, a bronze statue of **Hans Christian Andersen**, the Ugly Duckling at his feet, is the site of Saturday storytelling hours during summer.

At the neo-Victorian **Loeb Boathouse** on the park's 18-acre Lake, you can rent a rowboat, kayak, bike, or ride in an authentic Venetian gondola. The attached café is a worthy pit stop.

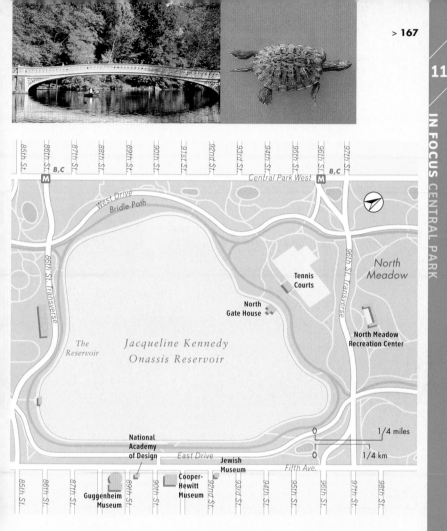

Designed to resemble upstate New York's Adirondack Mountain region, the **Ramble** covers 38 acres and is laced with twisting, climbing paths. This is prime bird-watching territory, since it's a rest stop along a major migratory route and a shelter for many of the more than 230 species of birds that have been sighted in the park; bring your binoculars. Because the Ramble is so dense and isolated, however, don't wander here alone, or after dark. Head south through the Ramble and you'll come to the beautiful cast-iron **Bow Bridge**, spanning part of the Lake between the Ramble and Bethesda Fountain. From the center of the bridge, you can get a sweeping view of the park as well as of the apartment buildings on both the East Side and the West Side.

North of the Ramble atop Vista Rock, **Belvedere Castle** is the second-highest natural point in the park. If you can't get tickets for Delacorte Theater, you can climb to one of the castle's

(from left to right) Belvedere means "beautiful view" in Italian, a clue to why we climb to the top of Belvedere Castle; Birders, photographers, and couples of all ages are drawn to Bow Bridge; Red-eared slider turtles frolic in Turtle Pond, at the base of Belvedere Castle.

three terraces and look down on the stage. You'll also get a fantastic view of the Great Lawn—it's particularly beautiful during the fall foliage months—and of the park's myriad bird visitors. Since 1919 the castle has served as a U.S. Weather Bureau station, and meteorological instruments are set on top of the tower. If you enter the Castle from the lower level, you can visit the Henry Luce Nature Observatory, which has nature exhibits, children's workshops, and educational programs.

Somewhat hidden behind Belvedere Castle, **Shakespeare Garden** is an informal jumble of flowers, trees, and pathways, inspired by the flora mentioned in Shakespeare's plays and poetry. Bronze plaques throughout the garden bear the bard's lines mentioning the plants.

The Great Lawn hums with action on weekends, on warm days, and on most summer evenings, when its baseball fields and picnic grounds fill with city folks and visitors alike. Its 13 acres have endured millions of footsteps, thousands of ball games, hundreds of downpours, dozens of concerts, fireworks displays, and even a papal mass. On a beautiful day, everyone seems to be here.

Chancing upon the 70-ft-tall **Cleopatra's Needle** always feels a bit serendipitous and delightfully jarring, even to the most cynical New Yorkers. This weathered hieroglyphic-covered obelisk began life in Heliopolis, Egypt, around 1500 BC, but has only a little to do with Cleopatra—it's just New York's nickname for the work. It was eventually carted off to Alexandria by the Romans in 12 BC, and

it landed here on January 22, 1881, when the khedive of Egypt made it a gift to the city.

At the southwest corner of the Great Lawn is the fan-shaped **Delacorte Theater**, home to the summer Shakespeare in the Park festival.

If you want to take in several sites in a single brisk jaunt, consider walking the **Naturalists' Walk**. On this path you can wind your way

toward the Swedish Cottage, the Shakespeare Garden, and Belvedere Castle on a landscaped nature

(top, from left to right) A female Canada goose and goslings on Turtle Pond; Cyclists make good use of the bike paths; Bikers as well as joggers boost their egos by outpacing the hansom carriages; Racing boats at Conservatory Water (center) In the 1930s, a flock of sheep was evicted from what would later be known as the Sheep Meadow.

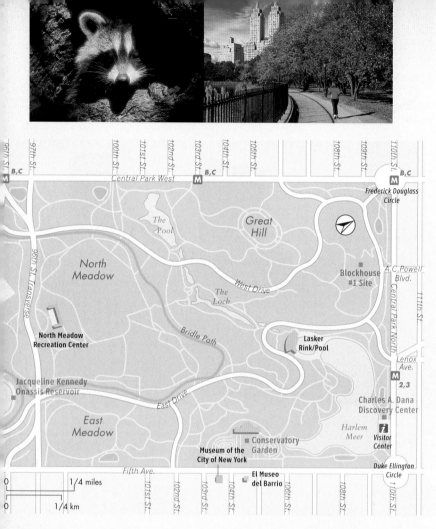

walk with spectacular rock outcrops, a stream that attracts bird life, a woodland area with various native trees, stepping-stone trails, and, thankfully, benches.

North of the Great Lawn and the 86th Street transverse is a popular gathering place for New Yorkers and visitors alike, the **Jacqueline Kennedy Onassis Reservoir**. Rain or shine, you'll see runners of all ages and paces heading counterclockwise around the 1.58-mi dirt path that encircles the water. The path in turn is surrounded by hundreds of trees that burst into color in the spring and fall. The 106-acre reservoir, finished in 1862, was a source of fresh water for Manhattanites. It holds more than a billion gallons, but it's no longer used for drinking water; the city's main reservoirs are upstate. From the top of the stairs at 90th Street just off 5th Avenue you have a 360-degree panorama of the city's exciting skyscrapers and often-brilliant sunsets. On the south side, there are benches so you can rest and recharge.

FROM THE RESERVOIR TO 110TH ST.

 More locals than tourists know about the wilder-looking, less-crowded northern part of Central Park, and there are hidden gems lurking here that enable even the most tightly wound among us to decompress, at least for a short while.

Walking along Fifth Avenue to 105th Street, you'll see a magnificent wrought-iron gate—once part of the 5th Avenue mansion of Cornelius Vanderbilt II—that marks the entrance to the **Conservatory Garden**. As you walk through it, you enter a different world, a quiet place that's positively idyllic for reading and slowing down. The Italian-style **Central Garden** is a beauty, with an expansive lawn, a strikingly simple fountain, and a wisteria-draped pergola that just oozes romance.

The French-inspired **North Garden** is a colorful place with plants placed into elaborate patterns. Springtime is magical—thousands of tulips come to life in a circle around the garden's striking Untermyer Fountain and its three bronze dancers; in the fall, chrysanthemums take their place. The English-style **South Garden** conjures up images from the classic children's book *The Secret Garden*. The garden is a beautiful hodgepodge of trees, bushes, and flowers that bloom year-round. A free tour is conducted on Saturday at 11 AM, from April through October.

At **Harlem Meer**, the third-largest body of water in Central Park, you can borrow fishing poles (identification required) from mid-April through October and try your hand at catching (and releasing) the largemouth bass, catfish, golden shiners, and bluegills that are stocked in the water's 11 acres. You can also learn about the upper park's geography, ecology, and history at the Victorian-style **Charles A. Dana Discovery Center**.

Although only a shell of this stone building remains, **Blockhouse #1** serves as a historical marker: the structure was built in 1814 as a cliffside fortification against the British. The area is deserted and dense with trees, so go as a group here, and avoid it at night.

(left) A pensive raccoon in the park's northern reaches; (center) A jogger makes her counterclockwise progress along the reservoir; (right) Inside the Central Park Conservancy Garden.

CONTACT INFORMATION

Central Park Conservancy
☎ 212/310–6600
🌐 www.centralparknyc.org

Central Park SummerStage
☎ 212/360–2756
🌐 www.summerstage.org

Central Park Wildlife Center (Central Park Zoo)
☎ 212/439–6500
🌐 www.centralparkzoo.org

Central Park Visitor Centers
☎ 212/794–6564 (Dairy)
🌐 www.nycgovparks.org

Charles A. Dana Discovery Center
☎ 212/860–1370

Loeb Boathouse, Boathouse Restaurant
☎ 212/517–2233
🌐 www.thecentral parkboathouse.com

Shakespeare in the Park
☎ 212/539–8500 (Public Theater)
🌐 www.shakespeareinthe park.org

Swedish Cottage Marionette Theatre
☎ 212/988–9093
🌐 www.cityparks foundation.org/swedish_ cottage.html

Wollman Memorial Rink
☎ 212/439–6900
🌐 www.wollmanskating rink.com

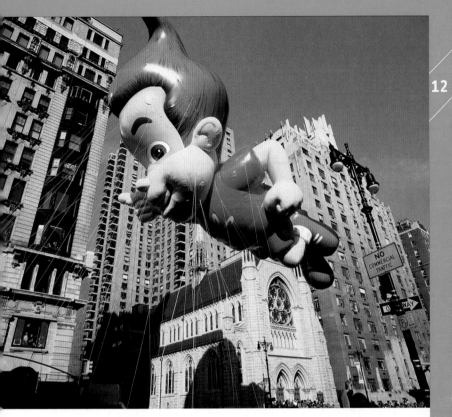

12

The Upper West Side

WITH THE CLOISTERS

WORD OF MOUTH

"The Upper West Side is more residential . . . there are of course a few stops that you might want to see and my best suggestions would be: NY Historical Society, Museum of Natural History, the Cloisters, St. John the Divine, Columbia University, and LOTS of good shopping on Broadway from 72nd to 90th Sts."

—travelbuff

GETTING ORIENTED

105th–123rd St.

59th–85th St.

Grant's Tomb

The Cloisters Museum and Gardens

W.123rd St.
W.121st St.
W.120th St.
W.119th St.
W.118th St.
W.117th St.

Barnard College

Columbia University

Broadway

Amsterdam Ave.

Morningside Dr.

Morningside Park

W.116th St.

1

B,C

W.115th St.
W.114th St.
W.113rd St.

MORNINGSIDE HEIGHTS

W.115th St.
W.114th St.
W.113rd St.

St. Nicholas Ave.

W.112nd St.
W.111st St.

Cathedral Church of St. John the Divine

Hungarian Pastry Shop

Cathedral Pkwy.

1

B,C

Central Park N.

W.109th St.
W.108th St.

W.107th St.
W.106th St.
W.105th St.

Riverside Park

Henry Hudson Parkway

Broadway

Central Park

105th–123rd St.

W. 85th St.

59th–85th St.

Riverside Park

Children's Museum of Manhattan

W. 84th St.
W. 83rd St.

Great Lawn

W. 82nd St.
W. 81st St.

B,C

Belvedere Castle

Zabar's Café

1

79th St. Boat Basin

Amsterdam Ave.

Columbus Ave.

W. 80th St.
W. 79th St.
W. 78th St.
W. 77th St.

American Museum of Natural History

UPPER WEST SIDE

Broadway

W. 76th St.

New-York Historical Society

The Lake

Promenade

Fairway

W. 75th St.
W. 74th St.

Riverside Drive

W. 73rd St.

Verdi Square

W. 72nd St.

Gray's Papaya

B,C

Statue of Eleanor Roosevelt

1,2,3

W. 71st St.
W. 70th St.

Emerald Inn

Sheep Meadow

W. 69th St.
W. 68th St.
W. 67th St.

West End Ave.

Central Park West

Hudson River

West Side Highway

W. 66th St.
W. 65th St.

American Folk Art Museum

W. 64th St.

W. 63rd St.

Lincoln Center for the Performing Arts

W. 62nd St.

W. 61st St.
W. 60th St.

Bouchon Bakery

Time Warner Center

A,B,C,D,1

Central Park South

Columbus Circle

0   1/4 mile

0   400 meters

W. 59th St.

Museum of Arts and Design

MAKING THE MOST OF YOUR TIME

Broadway is one of the most walkable and interesting thoroughfares on the Upper West Side, because of its broad sidewalks and aggressive mix of retail stores, restaurants, and apartment buildings. If you head north from the Lincoln Center area (around 65th Street) to about 81st Street (about 1 mile), you'll get a feel for the neighborhood's local color, particularly above 72nd Street. Up here you'll encounter residents of every conceivable age and ethnicity either shambling or sprinting, street vendors hawking used and newish books, and such beloved landmarks as the 72nd Street subway station, the Beacon Theater, the produce mecca Fairway (the cause of perhaps the most perpetually congested block), and Zabar's, a food spot that launches a memorable assault on all five of your senses—and your wallet. The Upper West Side's other two main avenues—Columbus and Amsterdam—are more residential but also have myriad restaurants and shops.

If you're intrigued by having the city's only Ivy League school close at hand, hop the 1 train to 116th Street and emerge on the east side of the street, which puts you smack in front of Columbia University and its Graduate School of Journalism. Pass through the gates and up the walk for a look at a cluster of buildings so elegant you'll understand why it's an iconic NYC setting.

GETTING HERE

The A, B, C, D, and 1 subway lines will take you to Columbus Circle. From there, the B and C lines run along Central Park, stopping at 72nd, 81st, 86th, 96th, 103rd, and 110th streets. The 1 train runs up Broadway, making local stops at 66th, 72nd, 79th, 86th, 96th, 103rd, 110th, 116th, and 125th streets. The 2 and 3 trains, the express trains that also go along Broadway, stop at 72nd and 96th.

TOP EXPERIENCES

Walking along Broadway—for the shopping, people-watching, and snacking.

Grazing at Zabar's.

Strolling through Riverside Park past the boat basin.

Strolling in Central Park. (*See Chapter 11*)

Standing below the gigantic blue whale at the Museum of Natural History.

Watching performers and students rushing to rehearsals and classes at Lincoln Center.

QUICK BITES, COFFEE, AND COCKTAILS

Hungarian Pastry Shop (E*1030 Amsterdam Ave.*). Linger over a Danish with the Columbia kids. If there's room.

Zabar's Café (⊠ *2245 Broadway, at 80th St.*). Brewed with the beans from their store next door.

Bouchon Bakery (⊠ *10 Columbus Circle, Time Warner Center, 3rd fl.*). Excellent coffee, sandwiches, and pastries at premium prices.

Gray's Papaya (⊠ *2090 Broadway, at 72nd St.*). Hot-dog gods. Go to the counter and say, "Two with everything, medium papaya."

Emerald Inn (⊠ *205 Columbus Ave., at 69th St.*). A longtime neighborhood Irish bar near Lincoln Center.

Sightseeing
★★★
Nightlife
★★
Dining
★★
Lodging
★
Shopping
★★★★

The Upper West Side is one of the city's quieter, more family-oriented neighborhoods, with wide sidewalks, a relatively slower pace, and more of a residential feel than you'll find in many other parts of New York City. On weekends, stroller-pushing parents cram sidewalks, shuttling their kids to soccer practice and birthday parties. Shoppers jam gourmet food emporiums such as Zabar's and Fairway, and other specialty stores along Broadway and Columbus Avenue.

Updated by
John Rambow

The tree-lined side streets of the Upper West Side are lovely, with high stoops leading up to stately brownstones. Central Park, of course, is one of the main attractions here, no matter the season or time of day, though residents know that Riverside Park, along the Hudson River can be even more appealing, with smaller crowds—you could almost say that these parks are the neighborhood's communal backyards.

The Upper West Side also has its share of cultural institutions, from the cultural bastion building in the 16-acre **Lincoln Center** complex, to the impressive collection at the **New-York Historical Society** to Columbus Circle's **Museum of Arts and Design** end the much-loved **American Museum of Natural History.**

Most people think the area north of 106th Street and south of 125th Street on the West Side is just an extension of the Upper West Side. But technically it's called Morningside Heights, and it's largely dominated by Columbia University, along with a cluster of academic, religious, and medical institutions—Barnard College, and the **Cathedral Church of St. John the Divine,** to name a few. Within the gates of the Columbia or Barnard campuses or inside the hushed St. John the Divine, New York City takes on a different character. This is an *uptown* student neighborhood—less hip than the Village, but friendly, fun, and intellectual. Even farther uptown, and not technically part of the Upper West Side, are the **Cloisters Museum and Gardens,** with the Metropolitan Museum's medieval collection.

TOP ATTRACTIONS

Fodor's Choice ★ **American Museum of Natural History.** *See highlighted feature in this chapter.*

★ **Cathedral Church of St. John the Divine.** The largest Gothic-style cathedral in the world, even with its towers and transepts still unfinished, this divine behemoth comfortably asserts its bulk in the country's most vertical city. The seat of the Episcopal diocese in New York, it acts as a sanctuary for all, giving special services that include a celebration of New York's gay and lesbian community as well as the annual Blessing of the Bikes, when cyclists of all faiths bring their wheels for a holy-water benediction. The cathedral hosts **musical performances** (⊕ *www. stjohndivine.org*) and has held funerals and memorial services for such artists as Duke Ellington, Jim Henson, George Balanchine, James Baldwin, and Alvin Ailey. Reopened at the end of 2008 after a 2001 fire left it damaged, the church now looks newly scrubbed and magnificent.

Built in two long spurts starting in 1892, the cathedral remains only two-thirds complete. What began as a Romanesque-Byzantine structure under the original architects George Heins and Christopher Grant Lafarge shifted (upon Heins's death in 1911) to French Gothic under the direction of Gothic Revival purist Ralph Adams Cram. You can spot the juxtaposition of the two medieval styles by comparing the finished Gothic arches, which are pointed, with the still-uncovered arches, which are rounded in the Byzantine style.

To get the full effect of the cathedral's size, approach from Broadway on West 112th Street. Above the 3-ton central bronze doors is the intricately carved **Portal of Paradise,** which depicts St. John witnessing the Transfiguration of Jesus, and 32 biblical characters. The cavernous nave holds some 5,000 worshippers. Turn around to see the **Great Rose Window,** made from more than 10,000 pieces of colored glass, the largest stained-glass window in the United States. At the end of the nave, surrounding the altar, are seven chapels expressing the cathedral's interfaith tradition and international mission—with menorahs, Shinto vases, and dedications to various ethnic groups. The **Saint Saviour Chapel** contains a three-panel bronze altar in white-gold leaf with religious scenes by artist Keith Haring (his last work before he died in 1990).

Outside in the cathedral's south grounds, the **Peace Fountain** depicts the struggle of good and evil in the form of the archangel Michael decapitating Satan, whose head hangs from one side. Encircling it are whimsical animals cast in bronze from pieces sculpted by children.

On the first Sunday of October , in honor of St. Francis of Assisi, the patron saint of animals, the church holds Sunday service with a twist: the service is attended by men, women, children, dogs, cats, rabbits, hamsters, and the occasional horse, sheep, or ant farm. In past years upward of 3,500 New Yorkers have shown up to have their pets blessed. A procession is led by such guest animals as elephants, camels, llamas, and golden eagles. Regular Sunday services are at 8, 9, 11, 1, and 4. "Highlight Tours" and "Vertical Tours" are offered throughout the week: check the website for details and to reserve space. ⊠ *1047 Amsterdam Ave., at W. 112th St., Upper West Side* ☎ *212/316–7540*

Continued on page 186

INSECTS AND MYRIAPODS

SEGMENTED WO

AMERICAN MUSEUM
OF NATURAL HISTORY

Theodore Roosevelt
Memorial Hall

The largest natural history museum in the world is also one of the most impressive sights in New York. Four city blocks make up its 45 exhibition halls, which hold more than 30 million artifacts and wonders from the land, the sea, and outer space. With all those wonders, you won't be able to see everything on a single visit, but you can easily hit the highlights in half a day.

Before you begin, plan a route before setting out. Be sure to pick up a map when you pay your admission. The museum's four floors (and lower level) are mazelike.

To get the most from the museum's stunning riches, try to allow enough time to slow down and take advantage of the computer stations and the volunteer "Explainers," who are knowledgeable and able to point out their own favorite exhibits.

Getting into the museum can be time consuming. For the shortest lines, use the below-street-level entrance connected to the 81st Street subway station (look for the subway entrance to the left of the museum's steps). This entrance gives you quick access to bathrooms and the food court. The entrance on Central Park West, where the vast steps lead up into the impressive, barrel-ceilinged Theodore Roosevelt Rotunda, is the most impressive and memorable entrance at the museum. Its central location makes a good starting place for exploring.

The Rose Center for Earth and Space, a must-visit, is attached to the museum. Enter from West 81st Street, where a path slopes down to the entrance, after which elevators and stairs descend to the ticket line on the lower level.

What to see? Check out the museum highlights on the following pages.

> ✉ Central Park West at W. 79th St., Upper West Side
>
> Ⓜ Subway: B, C to 81st St.
>
> ☎ 212/769-5100
>
> ⊕ www.amnh.org
>
> 💵 $19 suggested donation, includes admission to Rose Center for Earth and Space
>
> ◷ Daily 10–5:45.

MUSEUM HIGHLIGHTS

Left, Woolly Mammoth
Above, Tyrannosaurus rex

Dinosaurs and Mammals

An amazing assembly of dinosaur and mammal fossils covers the entire fourth floor. The organization can be hard to grasp at first, so head to the **Wallace Orientation Center,** where a short film explains how each of the Fossil Halls lead into each other. You'll want to spend at least an hour here—the highlights include a *T. rex*, an *Apatosaurus* (formerly called a Brontosaurus), and the *Buettneria*, which resembles a modern-day crocodile.

The specimens are not in chronological order; they're put together based on their shared characteristics. Key branching-off points—a watertight egg, a grasping hand—are highlighted in the center of rooms and surrounded by related fossil groups. Check out the touch screens here; they make a complex topic more comprehensible.

Reptiles and Amphibians

Head for the Reptiles and Amphibians Hall on the third floor to check out the Komodo Dragon lizards and a 23-foot-long python skeleton. The weirdest display is the enlarged model of the Suriname toad *Pipa pipa*, whose young hatch from the female's back. The Primates Hall carries brief but interesting comparisons between apes, monkeys, and humans. Also on the third floor is the upper gallery of the famed Akeley Hall of African Mammals.

SPECIAL SHOWS AND NEW EXHIBITS

Special exhibits, the IMAX theater, and the Space Show cost extra. The timed tickets are available in advance at the museum's Web site and are sold same day at the door. Between October and May, don't miss the warm, plant-filled Butterfly Conservatory, where blue morphos, monarchs, and other butterflies flit and feed. Ten minutes is probably enough time to enjoy it.

THIRD FLOOR

Wallach Orientation Center

Café on 4

Vertebrate Origins

Milstein Hall of Advanced Mammals

Saurischian Dinosaurs

Astor Turret

Primitive Mammals

Ornithischian Dinosaurs

FOURTH FLOOR

Akeley Hall of African Mammals

Hayden Planetarium Space Theater

Reptiles and Amphibians Hall

Rose Center for Earth and Space

Ross Hall of Meteorites

FIRST FLOOR

Guggenheim Hall of Minerals

Columbus Ave. Entrance

Entrance (open seasonally)

Rose Center for Earth and Space

Spitzer Hall of Human Origins

Morgan Memorial Hall of Gems

Akeley Hall of African Mammals

Big Bang

Café on 1

Entrance

Exit only

Lefrak IMSX Theater

Entrance

Heilbrunn Cosmic Pathway

Milstein Hall of Ocean Life

Heilbrunn Cosmic Pathway

Information, Group Tickets, and Will Call

81st St. Entrance

Main Entrance

SECOND FLOOR

Hall of Biodiversity

Gottesman Hall of Planet Earth

Rose Center for Earth and Space

Entrance

Theodore Roosevelt Memorial Hall

Akeley Hall of African Mammals

Opened in 1936, this hall on the third floor is one of the most beloved parts of the museum. Its 28 dramatically lighted dioramas may seem merely kitschy at first glance, but take a little time to let their beauty and technical brilliance shine through.

The hall was the life's work of the explorer Carl Akeley, who came up with the idea for the hall, raised the funds for the expeditions, gathered specimens, and sketched landscape studies for what would become the stunning backgrounds. (The backgrounds themselves were painted by James Perry Wilson, whose works can be found throughout the museum.)

Akeley died a decade before the hall opened on an expedition in what's now Rwanda. His grave site is near the landscape portrayed in the gorilla diorama, completed after his death as a memorial to him and his work. The dioramas make irresistible photo ops. If you want to snap one yourself, it's best to turn off your flash to prevent reflections off the glass.

Hall of Human Origins

The Spitzer Hall of Human Origins on the first floor is a comprehensive exhibit that allows visitors to draw their own conclusions about human evolution by presenting both the scientific methods and the material evidence that goes into evolutionary theory. Visitors gain insight into the techniques and thinking of scientists and anthropologists.

The exhibit then traces the evolution of our species over six million years of fossil record and spells out our ancestors' physical and intellectual advancements. Highlights include casts of our famous hairy relative "Lucy," who walked the plains of Africa over 1.8 million years ago.

Hall of Biodiversity

The small **Hall of Biodiversity** on the first floor includes a shady replica of a Central African Republic rain forest. Within a few yards are 160 species of flora and fauna—and also evidence of the forest's destruction. Nearby, the **Spectrum of Life Wall** showcases 1,500 specimens and models, helping show just how weird life can get. The wall opens into the gaping Milstein Hall of Ocean Life, designed to give it an underwater glow and to show off the 94-foot model of a **blue whale** that's suspended from the ceiling. The hall focuses on the vast array of life in the ocean that covers our planet.

AMNH ON FILM

Does the inside of AMNH look familiar? It should. The museum is a popular location for movies filming in New York. Here are a few of its recent close ups:

Spider-Man 2: Peter Parker (Tobey Maguire) has yet another bad day wrestling with his secret identity while in the Rose Center.

Night at the Museum: Larry (Ben Stiller) is chased through the halls by a T. Rex and outsmarts a monkey in the Hall of African Mammals while working as a night security guard.

Blue Whale

The Squid & the Whale: Walt Berkman (Jesse Eisenberg) comes to a revelation that he is the squid and his father is the whale in front of the Hall of Ocean Life's famous diorama.

The Devil Wears Prada: Andrea (Anne Hathaway) wins over Miranda (Meryl Streep) by remembering the names of high society guests while attending a benefit here.

ROSE CENTER FOR EARTH AND SPACE

The vast expanses of space and time involved in the creation of the universe can be hard to grasp even with the guiding hand of a museum, so you may want to visit the center when you're at your sharpest. The stunning glass building's centerpiece is the aluminum-clad Hayden Sphere, 87 feet in diameter. Enclosed within are the planetarium, called the Space Theater, and an audiovisual Big Bang presentation consisting of four minutes of narration by Maya Angelou, indistinct washes of color, and frightening bursts of sound. The rock-filled **Hall of Planet Earth** is particularly timely given the earthquakes and other natural disasters of recent years: one section uses a working earthquake monitor to help explain just what causes such seismic violence.

The Space Theater

At the Space Theater, the stage is the dome above you and the actors, heavenly projections. One of the world's largest virtual reality simulators, the theater uses surround sound and slight vibrations in the seats, to immerse you in scenes of planets, star clusters, and galaxies. *Journey to the Stars*, narrated by actress Whoopi Goldberg, launches viewers through space and time; you'll never see the night sky in the same way again.

TIME TO EAT?

Inside the museum: The main food court on the lower level serves sandwiches for about $7.95; hamburgers cost $5.50. The animal- and planet-shaped cookies are draws for kids; adults should check out the barbecue station.

The small Café on 4, in a turret next to the fossil halls, sells pre-made sandwiches and salads, and yogurt and desserts, but nothing warm.

The über-white Café on 1, tucked away beside the Hall of Human Origins, sells warm sandwiches, soup, salads, beer and wine at New York prices.

Nights at the museum aren't just for kids! Bust out your moonwalk and enjoy a few *cosmic*politans at the Rose Center's monthly One Step Beyond series, featuring live bands, DJs, VJs, cocktails, and dynamic visuals. Get tickets at amnh.org/rose/specials.

AMNH TALKS TO FODOR'S

Rose Center for Earth and Space

Interview with Ellen V. Futter, President of the American Museum of Natural History, conducted by Michelle Delio.

If You Only Have an Hour: The American Museum of Natural History has the world's finest collection of dinosaur fossils, so a visit to the fourth-floor's Fossil Halls, where more than 600 specimens are on display, is a must. An extraordinarily high percentage of the specimens on view—85%—are real fossilized bones as opposed to casts. At most museums those percentages are reversed, so here visitors have the chance to see the real thing including T. rex, velociraptor, and triceratops.

What to Hit Next? The museum also is renowned for its habitat dioramas, which are considered among the finest examples in the world. Visits to the Akeley Hall of African Mammals, the Hall of North American Mammals, and the Sanford Hall of North American Birds provide an overview of the diorama arts—pioneered and advanced at the museum—while allowing visitors to come face-to-face with some glorious and beautiful animals depicted in their natural habitats—habitats which in many cases no longer exist in such pristine conditions.

If You're Looking to Be Starstruck: Even if you don't have time to take in a space show in the Hayden Planetarium, the Rose Center for Earth and Space has lots of fascinating exhibits describing the vast range of sizes in the cosmos; the 13-billion-year history of the universe; the nature of galaxies, stars, and planets; and the dynamic features of our own unique planet Earth—all enclosed in a facility with spectacular award-winning architecture.

Hidden gems

The museum consists of 45 exhibition halls in 25 interconnected buildings so there are gems around every corner. Some lesser-known treasures include:

Star of India: The 563-carat Star of India, the largest and most famous star sapphire in the world, is displayed in the Morgan Memorial Hall of Gems.

WHERE'S PLUTO?

With all the controversy about what constitutes a planet, some visitors enjoy hunting for Pluto in the Cullman Hall of the Universe in the Rose Center for Earth and Space. We'll give you a hint: it's not with the other planets.

Black Smokers: These sulfide chimneys—collected during groundbreaking museum expeditions to the Pacific Ocean—are the only such specimens exhibited anywhere. Black smokers form around hot springs on the deep ocean floor and support a microbial community that does not live off sunlight but instead on the chemical energy of the Earth. Some of these microbes are considered the most ancient forms of life on Earth and may offer clues to the development of life here and the possibility of life elsewhere. See them in the Gottesman Hall of Planet Earth.

Spectrum of Life: The Hall of Biodiversity aims to showcase the glorious diversity of life on Earth resulting from 3.5 billion years of evolution. The impressive "Spectrum of Life" display is a 100-foot-long installation of more than 1,500 specimens and models—microorganisms and mammals, bacteria and beetles, fungi and fish. Use the computer workstations to learn more about the species depicted in each area.

Dodo: One of the museum's rarest treasures is the skeleton of a dodo bird, displayed along with other endangered or extinct species in the "Endangered Case" in the Hall of Biodiversity.

Small Dioramas: Tucked along the sides of the Hall of North American Mammals are two easy-to-miss corridors displaying a number of exquisitely rendered dioramas. In these jewel-box-like displays, some a mere 3 feet deep, you will see the smaller animals such as wolves galloping through a snowy night, a Canada lynx stalking a snowshoe hare, and a spotted skunk standing on its hands, preparing to spray a cacomistle, to name just a few of the evocative scenes.

Dinosaur Eggs: In 1993 museum scientists working in the Gobi Desert of Mongolia were the first to unearth fossilized embryos in dinosaur eggs, as well as the fossil of an adult oviraptor in a brooding posture over its nest. This discovery provided invaluable information about dinosaur gestation and revolutionized thinking about dinosaur behavior. Look for the display in the museum's Fossil Halls on the fourth floor.

Ross Terrace: In warmer months the Ross Terrace, with its fountains and cosmic theme, offers a wonderful outdoor spot for resting and reflecting, while providing a spectacular view of the Rose Center for Earth and Space.

Star of India

A diorama featuring a Komodo Dragon, the largest and most powerful lizard in the world.

MOST INTERESTING OBJECT?

What's most interesting about the American Museum of Natural History is not any single object on exhibit, but the sheer range and scope of what you can experience here. Think of it is a field guide to the natural world, the universe, and the cultures of humanity—all under one roof. The experience of visiting the museum is ultimately about awakening a sense of discovery, wonder, awe, and stewardship of this Earth we call home.

⊕ *www.stjohndivine.org* ✉ *Tours $6* ⊘ *Mon.–Sat. 7–6, Sun. 7–7; tours Tues.–Sat. at 11 and 1, Sun. at 2* Ⓜ *1 to 110th St./Cathedral Pkwy.*

Fodor's Choice
★
♻

Central Park. *See Chapter 11.*

Lincoln Center for the Performing Arts. *See the listing in Chapter 16, Performing Arts.*

★ **New-York Historical Society.** Manhattan's oldest museum, founded in 1804, has one of the city's finest research libraries and a collection of 6 million pieces of art, literature, and memorabilia. Special exhibitions shed light on New York's—and America's—history, art, and architecture. Major exhibits have included Hudson River School landscapes and an examination of New York City's role in the slavery debate and the Civil War. Unlike other museums that keep much of their collections in storage, virtually all of the museum's huge and eclectic permanent collection—ranging from 19th-century cockroach traps to the armchair that George Washington sat in during his inaugural ceremony—are displayed in glass shelves in the museum's Henry Luce III Center for the Study of American Culture. It's a bit of a jumble, but you're bound to stumble across many wonderful things.

The recently completed $65-million renovation snatched the museum from the purview of history buffs and placed it center stage for everyone interested in New York City. The already spectacular block-long neoclassical building now offers a more contemporary experience on a par with its large cousins across Central Park. Visitors now enter through the Great Hall, where kiosks and interactive exhibits explain original objects tied to key themes of American history, such as commerce and immigration. Special exhibits, like the recent "Revolution," are well-curated to show off the museum's collection. Caffé Storico, the light-filled new Stephen Starr (of Buddakan and Morimoto) restaurant on the first floor (with a separate entrance) serves upscale Italian food at lunch and dinner, and is open for brunch on the weekends. ⊠ *170 Central Park West, Upper West Side* ☎ *212/873–3400* ⊕ *www.nyhistory.org* ✉ *$15* ⊘ *Tues.–Thurs. and Sat. 10–6, Fri. 10–8, Sun. 11–5* Ⓜ *B, C to 81st St.*

OFF THE
BEATEN
PATH

The Cloisters Museum and Gardens. Perched on a wooded hill in Fort Tryon Park, near Manhattan's northwestern tip, the Cloisters Museum and Gardens, which shelters the medieval collection of the Metropolitan Museum of Art, is a scenic destination in its own right. Colonnaded walks connect authentic French and Spanish monastic cloisters, a French Romanesque chapel, a 12th-century chapter house, and a Romanesque apse. One room is devoted to the 15th- and 16th-century Unicorn Tapestries from around 1500—a must-see masterpiece of medieval mythology. The tomb effigies are another highlight. Two of the three enclosed gardens shelter more than 250 species of plants similar to those grown during the Middle Ages, including flowers, herbs, and medicinals; the third is an ornamental garden planted with both modern and medieval plants, providing color and fragrance from early spring until late fall. Concerts of medieval music are held here regularly (concert tickets include same-day admission to the museum). The outdoor Trie Café is open 10 am to 4:15 daily except Monday, from April through October, and serves sandwiches, coffee, and snacks. ■TIP→ Fee includes same-day admission to the Metropolitan Museum of Art's main building on East 82nd Street. ✉ *99 Margaret Corbin Dr., Fort Tryon Park, Upper West Side* ☎ *212/923–3700* ⊕ *www.metmuseum.org* 💲 *$25 suggested donation* ⊗ *Mar.–Oct., Tues.–Sun. 9:30–5:15; Nov.–Feb., Tues.–Sun. 9:30–4:45* Ⓜ *A to 190th St.*

WORTH NOTING

American Folk Art Museum. After a near death, or rather, near *debt* experience the American Folk Art Museum left its home of 10 years on 53rd Street, adjacent to the MoMA, in late 2011 and returned to its humble rental near Lincoln Center. Here, minus the distractions of an artsy facade and celebrity neighbor, the focus returns to its incredible collection of contemporary self-taught artists of the 20th and 21st centuries, including the single largest collection of reclusive Chicago artist Henry Darger, known for his painstakingly detailed collage-paintings of fantasy worlds. The museum's gift shop has an impressive collection of handcrafted items. ✉ *2 Lincoln Sq., Columbus Ave. at 66th St., Upper West Side* ☎ *212/595–9533* ⊕ *www.folkartmuseum.org* 💲 *free* ⊗ *Tues.–Sat. noon–7:30, Sun. noon–6* Ⓜ *1 to 66th St./Lincoln Center; A, B, C, D to 59th St./Columbus Circle.*

ⓒ ★ **Children's Museum of Manhattan.** In this five-story exploratorium children ages one to seven are invited to paint their own masterpieces, float boats down a "stream" (weather permitting), join forces with a mischievous Chinese monkey, and walk through giant interactive organs to explore the connections between food, sleep, and play. Art workshops, science programs, and storytelling sessions are held daily. ✉ *212 W. 83rd St., between Broadway and Amsterdam Ave., Upper West Side* ☎ *212/721–1223* ⊕ *www.cmom.org* 💲 *$11* ⊗ *Tues.–Sun. 10–5, Sat. 10–7* Ⓜ *1 to 79th St. or 86th St.*

Columbus Circle. This busy traffic circle at Central Park's southwest corner anchors the Upper West Side and makes a good starting place for exploring the neighborhood if you're coming from south of 59th Street. The central 700-ton granite monument (capped by a marble statue of Christopher Columbus) serves as a popular meeting place. To some people, Columbus Circle is synonomous with the **Time Warner Center** building (☎ *212/823–6300* ⊕ *www.shopsatcolumbuscircle.com*) and its several floors of shops and restaurants—including takeout-friendly Bouchon Bakery and Whole Foods, both perfect places to pick up picnic fixings to take to Central Park. ✉ *Broadway at 57th St. to 59th St.* Ⓜ *A, B, C, D, 1 to 59 St./Columbus Circle.*

Grant's Tomb. Walk through upper Riverside Park and you're sure to notice this towering granite mausoleum (1897), the final resting place of Civil War general and two-term president Ulysses S. Grant and his wife, Julia Dent Grant. As the old joke goes, who's buried here? Nobody—they're *entombed* in a crypt beneath a domed rotunda, surrounded by photographs and Grant memorabilia. Once a more popular sight than the Statue of Liberty, this pillared Classical Revival edifice feels more like a relic of yesteryear, but it remains a moving tribute. The words engraved on the tomb, "Let Us Have Peace," recall Grant's speech to the Republican convention upon his presidential nomination. Surrounding the memorial are the so-called rolling benches, covered with colorful mosaic tiles that bring to mind the works of architect Antonio Gaudí's Parc Güell, in Barcelona. Made in the 1970s as a public art project, they are now as beloved as they are incongruous with the grand memorial they surround. ⊠ *Riverside Dr. at W. 122nd St., Upper West Side* 🕾 *212/666–1640* ⊕ *www.nps.gov/gegr* 🖾 *Free* ⊙ *Daily 9–5; tours at 10, noon, 2, and 4* Ⓜ *1 to 116th St.*

Museum of Arts and Design. In a funky-looking white building right across the street from the Time-Warner Center, the Museum of Arts and Design celebrates joyful quirkiness and personal, sometimes even obsessive, artistic visions. The art is human-scale here, much of it neatly housed in display cases rather than on the walls, with a strong focus on contemporary jewelry, glass, ceramic, fiber, wood, and mixed-media works. Recent exhibits included *Swept Away: Dust, Ashes, and Dirt in Contemporary Art and Design,* which showcased contemporary artworks made from dust, ashes, smog, and sand, and *Korean Eye: Energy and Matter,* which focused on contemporary Korean artists. Thursday evening is a good time to drop by; the admission is pay-what-you-wish. ⊠ *2 Columbus Circle, 59th St. at 8th Ave., Upper West Side* 🕾 *212/299–7777* ⊕ *www.madmuseum.org* 🖾 *$15* ⊙ *Tues., Wed., weekends 11–6, Thurs. and Fri. 11–9* Ⓜ *A, B, C, D, 1 to Columbus Circle/59th St.; N, Q, R to 57th St./7th Ave.; F to 57th St./6th Ave.*

Ⓒ **Riverside Park.** Surrounded by concrete and skyscrapers all day, you might not realize that there is an expansive green space running along the water just blocks away. Riverside Park—which, runs along the Hudson from 58th to 156th streets—dishes out a dose of tranquility. The original sections of Riverside Park, designed by Frederick Law Olmsted Law and Calvert Vaux of Central Park fame and laid out between 1873 and 1888, are outshone by Olmsted's "other" park—Central Park—but with its waterfront bike and walking paths, this green space more than holds its own.

There are several access points to the park, including one at West 72nd Street and Riverside Drive (look for the **statue of Eleanor Roosevelt**) where you'll reach the waterfront path after heading through an underpass beneath the West Side Highway. You can then head north along the Hudson River, past the **79th Street Boat Basin,** where you can watch a flotilla of houseboats bobbing in the water. Above it, a ramp leads to the Rotunda, home in summer to the **Boat Basin Café,** a dog-friendly open-air café that's open for lunch and dinner in the warmer months (from about March through October). The **91st Street Garden,** planted by community gardeners, explodes with flowers in most seasons and is a level up from the water: leave the waterside path near 92nd Street by taking another underpass and then heading up the path on the right. To the south, cresting a hill along Riverside Drive at West 89th Street, stands the Civil War **Soldiers' and Sailors' Monument** (1902), an imposing 96-foot-high circle of white-marble columns designed by Paul M. Duboy, who also designed the Ansonia Hotel. ⊠ *W. 58th St. to W. 156th St. between Riverside Dr. and Hudson River, Upper West Side* ⊕ *www. nycgovparks.org* Ⓜ *1, 2, 3 to 72nd St.*

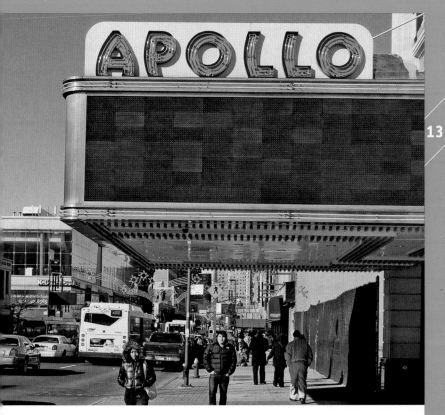

Harlem

WORD OF MOUTH

"Dress for church and plan to attend the entire service. You will be welcome. People in Harlem dress for Sunday services. It's embarrassing when tourists in jeans, T-shirts, and flip-flops on my bus think they are going to church. . . . You are doing your homework and you will be welcome wherever you go."

—Sue NYC

GETTING ORIENTED

MAKING THE MOST OF YOUR TIME

One enduring, simple pleasure in Harlem is its terrific architecture: take a little time to walk the areas around Strivers' Row, Hamilton Heights, and 116th Street to see some impressive and often fanciful brownstones. While you're at it, visit the Studio Museum in Harlem, which showcases contemporary works of Harlem's artist community (note that the museum is open only Thurs.—Sun.), or the Morris-Jumel Mansion, for a trip back to colonial New York.

GETTING HERE AND AROUND

The 2 and 3 subway lines stop on Lenox Avenue; the 1 goes along Broadway, to the west; and the A, B, C, and D trains travel along St. Nicholas and 8th avenues. And yes, as the song goes, the A train is still usually "the quickest way to Harlem."

The city's north–south avenues take on different names in Harlem: 6th Avenue is called both Malcolm X Boulevard and Lenox Avenue; 7th Avenue is Adam Clayton Powell Jr. Boulevard (it's named for the influential minister and congressman); and 8th Avenue is Frederick Douglass Boulevard. West 125th Street, the major east–west street and Harlem's commercial center, is sometimes called Dr. Martin Luther King Jr. Boulevard.

SAFETY

In the past two decades Harlem's crime rate has decreased far below the heights it reached in the 1980s. Like everywhere else in New York, however, you should still use common sense. Stay close to main commercial areas like 125th Street and Lenox Avenue if you visit at night.

TOP EXPERIENCES

Check out some jazz at Lenox Lounge.

Attend a gospel service.

Walk along 125th Street.

13

Indulge in a soul-food lunch or dinner—fried chicken and waffles . . . mmm!

QUICK BITES, COFFEE, AND COCKTAILS

Hue-Man Bookstore & Cafe (⊠ *2319 Frederick Douglass Blvd., near 125th St.*) Stop by for a cup of joe at this landmark bookstore.

Levain Bakery (⊠ *2167 Frederick Douglass Blvd.*) The giant cookies here are to die for.

Make My Cake (⊠ *121 St. Nicholas Ave., at 116th St.*) Especially made for red-velvet cake lovers.

Harlem Tavern (⊠ *2153 Frederick Douglass Blvd.*). There's something for everyone here: jazz, cocktails, and more than 20 kinds of beer on tap.

Nectar Wine Bar (⊠ *2235 Frederick Douglass Blvd.*). Restorative cocktails are the key here.

Lenox Lounge (⊠ *288 Lenox Ave., near 125th St.*) Quintessential Harlem jazz spot.

Sightseeing ★★	Harlem is known throughout the world as a center of Afri-can-American culture, music, and life. Today many reno-vated and new buildings join such historic jewels as the Apollo Theater, architecturally splendid churches, and cultural magnets like the Studio Museum in Harlem and the Schomburg Center for Research in Black Culture.
Nightlife ★★★★	
Dining ★★★	
Lodging ★★	
Shopping ★★	

Updated by
John Rambow

As overcrowded apartments and expensive rents downtown make Harlem a more and more attractive area, professionals and young families are restoring many of Harlem's classic brownstone and limestone buildings. This new growth has brought life and commerce to the community, but it has also priced out some longtime residents.

Back in 2001, former president Bill Clinton's selection of 55 West 125th Street as the site of his New York office was an inspiration to businesses considering a move to Harlem; now the busy thoroughfare sprouts outposts of Starbucks, Old Navy, MAC Cosmetics, and H&M side by side with local restaurants and clothing stores, including a smattering of boutiques. Outside, the sidewalk is a continuous traffic jam of people, offering a concentrated glimpse of neighborhood life. Pedestrians compete with street-side hawkers selling bootleg DVDs, books, and homemade essential oils in nondescript bottles.

Some of Harlem's most interesting religious buildings—especially its Baptist churches—stand on 116th Street, particularly between St. Nicholas Avenue and Lenox (Malcolm X) Boulevard. Admire the ornate theatrical facade of the giant **First Corinthian Baptist Church** or fill your soul with the mellifluous gospel music of the **Canaan Baptist Church of Christ's** choir during a Sunday service. Take a hint from the parishioners and follow up with the smothered chicken and waffles at **Amy Ruth's,** at 113 W. 116th. After lunch, walk by the green-domed **Masjid Malcolm Shabazz**—a mosque attended primarily by West Africans and African-Americans. Finish at **Malcolm Shabazz Harlem Market** to stock up on African jewelry, masks, crafts, and caftans at good prices. On Saturday, the jazz players jam at the market from 1:30 to 3.

Many of Harlem's historic jazz venues (found mostly on 125th Street) are still active, so you can pay respect to legends like Duke Ellington and Louis Armstrong, then listen to one of their musical heirs. A giant digital marquee announces the **Apollo Theater,** where jazz and funk godfather James Brown debuted in 1956 and was laid out in splendor after his death in 2006. (Following this tradition, king of pop Michael Jackson was also given a final farewell here in 2009.) Around the corner, the **Lenox Lounge** (✉ *288 Lenox Ave., at W. 125th St.*) is a trip back in time. Continue the pilgrimage at **Minton's Playhouse** (✉ *206 W. 118th St.*), the birthplace of bebop, where Thelonious Monk was house pianist in the 1940s. It reopened in 2006 after being closed since 1974. If you're here on Thursday or Friday, when exhibits are open until 9 pm, check out the contemporary African-American–oriented artworks at the **Studio Museum in Harlem.**

13

TOP ATTRACTIONS

Abyssinian Baptist Church. This 1923 Gothic-style church holds one of Harlem's richest legacies, dating to 1808 when a group of parishioners defected from the segregated First Baptist Church of New York City and established the first African-American Baptist church in New York State. Among its legendary pastors was Adam Clayton Powell Jr., a powerful orator and civil rights leader and the first black U.S. congressman. Today sermons by pastor Calvin Butts III are fiery, and the seven choirs are excellent. Because of its services' popularity, the church maintains separate lines for parishioners and tourists at its 11 am service. Dress your best, remember not to take pictures or videos, and get there early—at least two hours ahead of time. ✉ *132 Odell Clark Pl., W. 138th St., between Adam Clayton Powell Jr. Blvd., 7th Ave., and Malcolm X Blvd., Lenox Ave./6th Ave.* ☎ *212/862–7474* ⊕ *www. abyssinian.org* ☉ *Sun. services for visitors at 11; no visitors services on major holidays* Ⓜ *2, 3 to 135th St.*

Apollo Theater. *See the listing in Chapter 16 Performing Arts.*

Canaan Baptist Church of Christ. One of the most ornate structures in Harlem, the Canaan Baptist Church of Christ kicked off its life in 1913 as the Regent Theatre, one of the country's early movie palaces that replaced the nickelodeons. Its elaborately columned and arched facade loosely resembles the Doges' Palace in Venice. The Regent was sold to the church in 1964. To attend, arrive at least an hour ahead of time. ✉ *132 W. 116th St., between Malcolm X Blvd., Lenox Ave./6th Ave., and Adam Clayton Powell Jr. Blvd., 7th Ave.* ☎ *212/866–0301* ⊕ *www. cbccnyc.org* ☉ *Services Sun. at 8 and 11 am* Ⓜ *2, 3 to 116th St.*

Hamilton Heights. To taste this neighborhood's Harlem Renaissance days, walk down tree-lined Convent Avenue, detouring onto adjacent **Hamilton Terrace,** and see a time capsule of elegant stone row houses in mint condition. (Until 2008 Hamilton Grange, founding father Alexander Hamilton's Federal-style mansion, stood at 287 Convent Avenue. The clapboard structure, owned by the National Park Service, has been moved around the corner to Saint Nicholas Park. At this writing it's closed for refurbishment and scheduled to reopen for tours in summer

D.I.Y. Harlem Gospel Tours

For the past decade, the popularity of gospel tours, conducted by bus, has surged, so if you're thinking of doing it, here are some tips. A bus tour is generally a speedy and not so authentic way to experience Harlem: some tours include only a 20-minute stop at a church to hear some of the sermon and the gospel music, then you're off to another sight or to a soul-food brunch. Prices may be as high as $99. One tour company based in the neighborhood that does get high marks for its gospel tours is **Harlem Heritage Tours** (☎ 212/280–7888 ⊕ www.harlemheritage.com).

Tours garner mixed reactions from the community. Some see it as an opportunity to broaden horizons and encourage diversity. But others find tours disruptive and complain that tourists take seats away from regular parishioners (churches regularly fill to capacity). If you decide to go on one of these tours or to visit a church on your own, plan ahead. Most churches have services at 11, but you may need to arrive as much as two hours early to actually get in. Most important, remember that parishioners do not consider the service, or themselves, to be tourist attractions

or entertainment. Dress nicely—no shorts, sneakers, or jeans. Harlem churchgoers take the term "Sunday best" to heart. Be as quiet as possible, and do not take photos or videos or use your cell phone.

The following are some of the uptown churches with gospel choirs:

Abyssinian Baptist Church is one of the few churches that does not allow tour groups. Services for visitors are at 11. Arrive at least two hours ahead of time for this service. **Canaan Baptist Church of Christ** has services at 8 and 11. **Convent Avenue Baptist Church** (✉ 420 W. 145th St., between Convent and St. Nicholas Aves., Harlem ☎ 212/234–6767 ⊕ www.conventchurch.org) has services at 8, 11, and 5. **First Corinthian Baptist Church** has services at 8 and 11.

Greater Refuge Temple (✉ 2081 Adam Clayton Powell Jr. Blvd., at 124th St., Harlem ☎ 212/866–1700 ⊕ www.greaterrefugetemple.org) has services at 11, 4, and 7:30. **Memorial Baptist Church** (✉ 141 W. 115th St., between Adam Clayton Powell Jr. and Malcolm X Blvds., Harlem ☎ 212/663–8830 ⊕ www.mbcvisionharlem.org) has services at 8 and 11.

2011: visit ⊕ *www.nps.gov/hagr* for updates). Continue down Convent Avenue and see the looming Gothic spires (1905) of **City College.** The stately Oxford-inspired buildings here are New York to the core: they are clad with the schist rock unearthed when the city was building what is now the 1 subway line. When you're ready to move on, head east through Saint Nicholas Park, which will bring you to Strivers' Row. ✉ *Convent Ave. between 138th and 150th Sts.* Ⓜ *A, B, C, D to 145th St.*

Morris-Jumel Mansion. During the Revolutionary War, General Washington used this wooden, pillared 8,500-square-foot house (1765) as his headquarters, and when he visited as president in 1790, he brought along John Quincy Adams, Jefferson, and Hamilton. Inside are rooms furnished with period decorations—upstairs, keep an eye out for the hand-painted wallpaper (original to the house) and a "commode chair,"

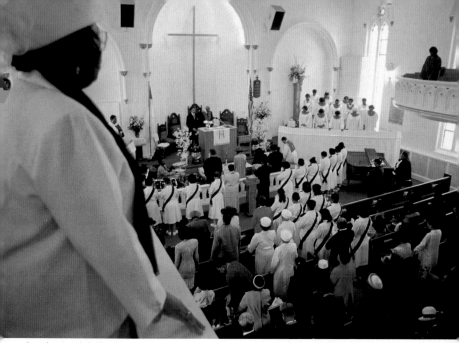
Gospel at St. Luke's Church

stuck in a corner. Outside, behind the house, is a Colonial-era marker that says it's 11 miles to New York: a reminder of what a small sliver of Manhattan the city was at that time. East of the house is the block-long Sylvan Terrace, a row of crisp two-story clapboard houses built in the 1880s. ⊠ *65 Jumel Terr., north of W. 160th St.; between St. Nicholas Ave. and Edgecome Ave.* ☎ *212/923–8008* ⊕ *www.morrisjumel. org* ⊠ *$5; guided tours $6* ☿ *Wed.–Sun. 10–4; guided tours Sat. noon.*

Strivers' Row. This block of gorgeous 1890s Georgian and neo-Italian homes earned its nickname in the 1920s from less affluent Harlemites who felt its residents were "striving" to become well-to-do. Some of the few remaining private service alleys, used when deliveries arrived via horse and cart, lie behind these houses and are visible through iron gates. Note the gatepost between No. 251 and 253 on West 138th Street that says, "Private Road. Walk Your Horses." When the houses failed to sell to whites, the properties on these blocks were sold to African-American doctors, lawyers, and other professionals; the composers and musicians W. C. Handy and Eubie Blake were also among the residents. If you have the time, detour a block north to see the palazzo-style group of houses designed by Stanford White, on the north side of West 139th Street. ⊠ *W. 138th and W. 139th Sts. between Adam Clayton Powell Jr. and Frederick Douglass Blvds.* Ⓜ *B, C to 135th St.*

★ **Studio Museum in Harlem.** Contemporary art by African-American, Caribbean, and African artists is the focus of this small museum with a light-filled sculpture garden. Its changing exhibits included *The Bearden Project,* a year-long tribute to artist Romare Bearden featuring the works of one hundred artists inspired or influenced by Bearden. Three artists in residence present their works each year. The gift shop has some interesting items. ⊠ *144 W. 125th St., between Lenox Ave. and Adam Clayton Powell Jr. Blvd.* ☎ *212/864–4500* ⊕ *www.studiomuseum.org* ≊ *$7 suggested donation* ⊘ *Thurs. and Fri. noon–9, Sat. 10–6, Sun. noon–6* Ⓜ *2, 3 to 125th St.*

WORTH NOTING

First Corinthian Baptist Church. One of the most ornate structures in Harlem, this church kicked off its life in 1913 as the Regent Theatre, one of the country's early movie palaces that replaced the nickelodeons. Its elaborately columned and arched facade loosely resembles the Doges' Palace in Venice. The Regent was sold to the church in 1964. To attend services, arrive at least an hour ahead of time. ⊠ *1912 Adam Clayton Powell Jr. Blvd., at 7th Ave.* ☎ *212/864–5976* ⊕ *www.fcbcsermons. com/* ⊘ *Services Sun. at 8 and 11* Ⓜ *2, 3 to 116th St.*

The Hispanic Society of America Museum and Library. This is the best collection of Spanish art outside the Prado in Madrid, with (primarily 15th- and 16th-century) paintings, sculptures, textiles, and decorative arts from Spain, Portugal, Italy, and South America. There are notable pieces by Goya, El Greco, and Velázquez. An entire room is filled with a collection of antique brass knockers. ⊠ *613 West 155th St., Audubon Terr., Broadway, between W. 155th and W. 156th Sts., entrance up steps to left* ☎ *212/926–2234* ⊕ *www.hispanicsociety.org* ≊ *Free* ⊘ *Sept.–July, Tues.–Sat. 10–4:30, Sun. 1–4* Ⓜ *1 to 157th St.*

Masjid Malcolm Shabazz (*Mosque*). Talk about religious conversions. In the mid-'60s the Lenox Casino was transformed into this house of worship and cultural center, and given bright yellow arches and a huge green onion dome that proclaims its presence in a neighborhood of churches. Once functioning as Temple No. 7 under the Nation of Islam with a message of pro-black racism, the mosque was bombed after the assassination of Malcolm X, who had preached here. It was then rebuilt and renamed for the name Malcolm took at the end of his life, El-Hajj Malik Shabazz; its philosophy now is one of inclusion. These days the Sunni congregation has a large proportion of immigrants from Senegal, many of whom live in and around 116th Street. ⊠ *102 W. 116th St., at Malcolm X Blvd., Lenox Ave./6th Ave.* ☎ *212/662–2200* Ⓜ *2, 3 to 116th St.*

Sugar Hill. Standing on the bluff of Sugar Hill overlooking Jackie Robinson Park, outside the slightly run-down **409 Edgecombe Ave.** you'd never guess that here resided such influential African-Americans as NAACP founder W.E.B. DuBois and Supreme Court Justice Thurgood Marshall, or that farther north at **555 Edgecombe**, known as the "Triple Nickel," writers Langston Hughes and Zora Neale Hurston and jazz musicians Duke Ellington, Count Basie, and others lived and played. And it's also here that for more than a decade musician Marjorie Eliot has been hosting jazz concerts in her apartment, 3F, from 4 to 6:30 every Sunday for the last decade. ⊠ *Bounded by 145th and 155th Sts. and Edgecombe and St. Nicholas Aves.* Ⓜ *A, B, C, D to 145th St.*

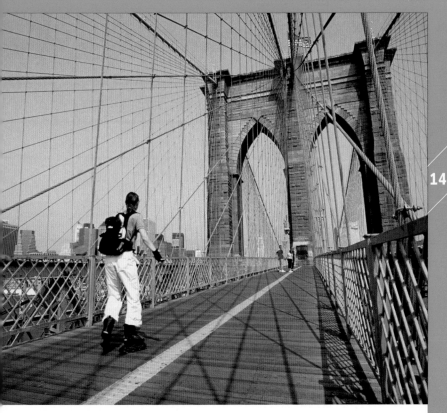

Brooklyn

WORD OF MOUTH

"Walking over the Brooklyn Bridge was a really neat experience; I liked being elevated above the bridge deck, with the traffic below us on both sides. . . . A word of caution . . . be sure to stay out of the bike lane, as the cyclists come whipping past you like they're being chased by the law."

—artstuff

GETTING ORIENTED

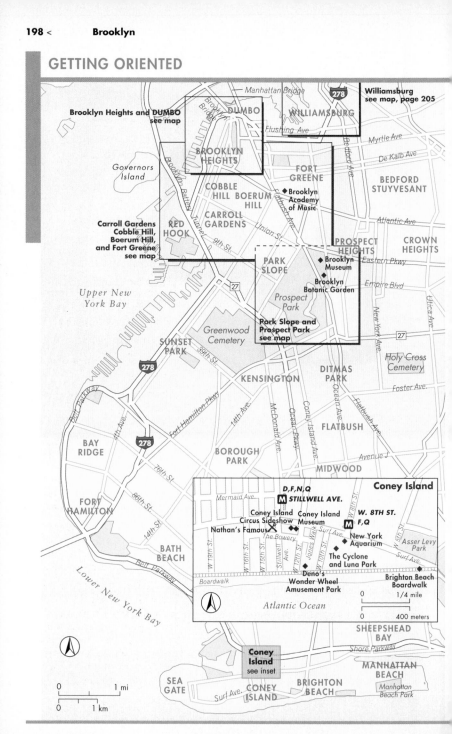

Manhattan Bridge

278

Williamsburg
see map, page 205

Brooklyn Heights and DUMBO
see map

DUMBO

WILLIAMSBURG

Flushing Ave.

Myrtle Ave.

De Kalb Ave.

BROOKLYN
HEIGHTS

FORT
GREENE

BEDFORD
STUYVESANT

Governors
Island

COBBLE
HILL BOERUM
HILL

Brooklyn Academy
of Music

Atlantic Ave.

Carroll Gardens
Cobble Hill,
Boerum Hill,
and Fort Greene
see map

CARROLL
GARDENS

Union St.

PROSPECT
HEIGHTS

CROWN
HEIGHTS

RED
HOOK

9th St.

PARK
SLOPE

Brooklyn
Museum

Eastern Pkwy.

Upper New
York Bay

27

Brooklyn
Botanic Garden

Empire Blvd.

Utica Ave.

Prospect
Park

Park Slope and
Prospect Park
see map

27

Greenwood
Cemetery

Holy Cross
Cemetery

SUNSET
PARK

39th St.

278

KENSINGTON

DITMAS
PARK

Foster Ave.

FLATBUSH

BAY
RIDGE

278

4th Ave.

Fort Hamilton Pkwy.

14th Ave.

McDonald Ave.

Ocean Ave.

Coney Island Ave.

Flatbush Ave.

Avenue J

76th St.

BOROUGH
PARK

MIDWOOD

FORT
HAMILTON

86th St.

14th Ave.

Coney Island

BATH
BEACH

Belt Parkway

Mermaid Ave.

D,F,N,Q
M STILLWELL AVE.

W. 8TH ST.
M F,Q

Coney Island
Circus Sideshow

Coney Island
Museum

Nathan's Famous

The Bowery

Surf Ave.

New York
Aquarium

Asser Levy
Park

W. 19th St.

W. 16th St.

W. 15th St.

Stillwell Ave.

Jones Walk

W. 12th St.

W. 10th St.

W. 8th St.

Surf Ave.

The Cyclone
and Luna Park

Boardwalk

Deno's
Wonder Wheel
Amusement Park

Brighton Beach
Boardwalk

Lower New York Bay

Atlantic Ocean

0   1/4 mile

0   400 meters

SHEEPSHEAD
BAY

Shore Parkway

Coney
Island
see inset

MANHATTAN
BEACH

Manhattan
Beach Park

SEA
GATE

Surf Ave.

CONEY
ISLAND

BRIGHTON
BEACH

0   1 mi

0   1 km

MAKING THE MOST OF YOUR TIME

The best way to get to Brooklyn is by its most majestic bridge. Walking along the wooden pedestrian path of the Brooklyn Bridge—a classic New York experience—takes about 30 minutes, all worth it for the panoramic views of the skylines and the harbor. Note that on summer weekends the path is crowded, unless you go early in the morning. Exit the bridge onto Cadman Plaza on the Brooklyn side, then walk southwest to get to Brooklyn Heights, a charming neighborhood of posh 19th-century brownstone homes, or walk north into the hip neighborhood of DUMBO to check out its adorable shops and stunning waterfront parks. Another option is just to walk half way across the bridge and then turn around.

GETTING HERE

To get to Williamsburg, take the L train from any 14th Street station in Manhattan to Bedford Avenue, the first stop in Brooklyn. You can reach Brooklyn Heights by the 2 or 3 train to Clark Street, the R to Court Street, or the 4 or 5 to Borough Hall. To get to DUMBO, take the F train to York Street or walk from Brooklyn Heights. The F to 7th Avenue will take you to the center of Park Slope. From there, walk uphill to reach Prospect Park or walk north on 7th Avenue to sample the shops. The hipper boutiques and eateries are two long blocks west, on 5th Avenue, best accessed by the R train to Union Street. To reach the Brooklyn Museum, Brooklyn Botanic Garden, and Prospect Park take the 2 or 3 train to Eastern Parkway/Brooklyn Museum. Coney Island is the last stop on the D, F, N, and Q trains, and the Q or B will take you to Brighton Beach. Allow a good part of the day for these trips, since it takes about an hour to reach the ocean from Manhattan.

TOP EXPERIENCES

Late-night music or bar-hopping in Williamsburg.

Screaming at the top of the Cyclone roller coaster.

Smelling the roses, and everything else, at the Brooklyn Botanic Garden.

Catching a show at BAM.

Pizza at Grimaldi's after a walk across the Brooklyn Bridge.

14

BEST FOR KIDS

Brooklyn Children's Museum

Brooklyn Ice Cream Factory

Brooklyn Superhero Supply Co.

New York Aquarium in Coney Island

Transit Museum

QUICK BITES, COFFEE, OR COCKTAILS

Coffee in Park Slope: Gorilla Coffee (✉ *97 5th Ave.*). Grab a fair-trade Brooklyn-roasted shot. Red Horse Café (✉ *497 6th Ave.*). Sip some micro-roast.

Sweets Near the Bridge: Brooklyn Ice Cream Factory (✉ *1 Water St.*). Superlative flavors and hot fudge sauce, too.

Cocktails in Carroll Gardens: Clover Club (✉ *210 Smith St.*). For swanky modern cocktails in a cozy atmosphere. The Jake Walk (✉ *282 Smith St.*). Fifty wines, 130 whiskeys, and 40 artisanal cheeses; how can you go wrong?

Sightseeing
★★★

Nightlife
★★★★

Dining
★★★★

Lodging
★

Shopping
★★★

Updated by
Anja Mutić

To put it mildly, Brooklyn is exploding, and it has been for a while. Hardly Manhattan's wimpy sidekick, this is the largest and most populous of all the boroughs, with more than 2.5 million residents, and a ton of cool places to eat, drink, shop, and explore.

Brooklyn was a city itself until the end of the 19th century, with its own widely circulated newspaper, the *Brooklyn Eagle,* its own expansive park (Prospect Park), and its own baseball team that would eventually be called the Brooklyn Dodgers. And in 1883, it got its own bridge: the Brooklyn Bridge, which drew the attention of the entire country.

Aside from Brooklyn's mellow, family-friendly vibe in areas such as **Brooklyn Heights, Cobble Hill, Carroll Gardens,** and **Boerum Hill,** the borough is also home to the hipster, for lack of a better term. And if you're looking for the hipster hangouts, head to **Williamsburg,** where young artists started infiltrating the residential neighborhood back in the late 1990s. The area soon became known for its galleries, and then for the funky bars, restaurants, and music venues.

Downtown Brooklyn encompasses multiple brownstone-filled neighborhoods, from **Fort Greene** to family-friendly **Park Slope,** and **Prospect Heights,** on the edge of Prospect Park, that are a joy to explore on foot. Indeed, with the exception of art exhibits at the Brooklyn Museum, the lush grounds of the Brooklyn Botanic Garden, and cutting-edge performances at the Brooklyn Academy of Music, so-called "sights" are thin on the ground here. Instead, the neighborhoods' real draws are their residential vibe, proudly local restaurants, and down-home shops and bars.

BROOKLYN HEIGHTS

Brooklyn's toniest neighborhood offers residents something wealthy Manhattanites will never have: a stunning view of the Manhattan skyline from the **Brooklyn Heights Promenade.** First developed in the mid-1800s as the business center of the then-independent city of Brooklyn,

Hanging out in Brooklyn Bridge Park, with a view of the iconic bridge rising in the background.

Brooklyn Heights showcases historic cobblestone streets of pristine brownstones.

The majestic Brooklyn Bridge has one foot in Brooklyn Heights, and a walk across it either to or from Lower Manhattan is one of the quintessential New York experiences. Don't miss a stroll around the leafy Pier 1, the newly expanded section of Brooklyn Bridge Park, accessible from Old Fulton Street.

There is a lot of history in Brooklyn Heights itself. In the early to mid-20th century the Heights was a bohemian haven, home to writers like Arthur Miller, Truman Capote, Alfred Kazin, Marianne Moore, Norman Mailer, and W. E. B. Du Bois. In the '80s a new generation of gentrifiers moved in, and—even with a softening real estate market—homes here are still as pricey as their Manhattan counterparts.

Much of Brooklyn Heights's early architecture has been preserved, thanks to its designation as New York's first historic district in the 1960s. Some 600 buildings built in the 19th century represent a wide range of American building styles. Many of the best line **Columbia Heights,** a residential street that runs parallel to the promenade, but any of its adjoining streets are also worth strolling. On **Willow Street** be sure to note No. 22, Henry Ward Beecher's prim Greek Revival brownstone, and Nos. 155–159. These three brick Federal row houses are said to have been stops on the Underground Railroad. The skylight in the pavement by the gate to No. 157 provided the light for an underground tunnel leading to an 1880 carriage house.

Brooklyn Heights and DUMBO

TOP ATTRACTIONS

Fodor's Choice ★ **Brooklyn Bridge.** (⇨ Chapter 2) Ⓜ 4, 5, 6 to Brooklyn Bridge/City Hall; J, Z to Chambers St.; A, C to High St.–Brooklyn Bridge.

☺ Fodor's Choice ★ **Brooklyn Heights Promenade.** Stretching from Orange Street to Remsen Street, the Brooklyn Heights esplanade provides enthralling views of Manhattan, especially in the evening when the lights of the city twinkle across the East River. Find a bench and take in the skyline, the Statue of Liberty, and the Brooklyn Bridge—an impressive 1883 steel suspension bridge designed by John Augustus Roebling. Below the promenade is the Brooklyn–Queens Expressway and an industrial waterfront of warehouses, piers, and parking lots. Ⓜ 2, 3 to Clark St.; A, C to High St.

☺ **New York Transit Museum.** Step down into a 1930s subway station, where you'll find more than 60,000 square feet devoted to the history of public transportation. Visitors can wander around the collection of vintage trains and turnstiles and sit behind the wheel of city buses. The old subway advertisements and signs are amusing. The gift store is a great place for NYC-theme souvenirs (there's also a shop at Grand Central). ✉ Boerum Pl., at Schermerhorn St. ☎ 718/694–1600 ⊕ www.mta.info/museum/ 💲 $7 ⏰ Tues.–Fri. 10–4, weekends noon–5 Ⓜ 2, 3, 4, 5 to Borough Hall; A, C, F to Jay St.; M, R to Court St.

WORTH NOTING

Brooklyn Borough Hall. Built in 1848 as Brooklyn's City Hall, this Greek Revival landmark is one of Brooklyn's handsomest buildings. Adorned with Tuckahoe marble, it features a hammered square rotunda and a two-story Beaux-Arts courtroom. Today the building serves as the office of Brooklyn's borough president and the home of the **Brooklyn Tourism & Visitors Center** (☎ 718/802–3846 ⊕ www.visitbrooklyn.org), which has historical exhibits, a gift shop, and helpful information. It's open weekdays 10–6. Each Tuesday and Saturday as well as Thursday from April through December a greenmarket sets up on the flagstone plaza in front. ⊠ *209 Joralemon St., between Court and Adams Sts.* ☎ *718/802–3700* ⊕ *www.brooklyn-usa.org/* ⬚ *Free* Ⓜ *2, 3, 4, 5 to Borough Hall; M, R to Court St; A, C, F to Jay St.*

Brooklyn Historical Society. Housed in an 1881 Queen Anne–style National Landmark building (one of the gems of the neighborhood), the Brooklyn Historical Society displays memorabilia, artifacts, art, and interactive exhibitions. Upstairs, an impressive library—which contains an original copy of the Emancipation Proclamation—is invaluable to researchers. ⊠ *128 Pierrepont St., at Clinton St.* ☎ *718/222–4111* ⊕ *www.brooklynhistory.org* ⬚ *$6* ⊘ *Wed.–Fri. and Sun. noon–5, Sat. 10–5* Ⓜ *2, 3, 4, 5 to Borough Hall; A, C, F to Jay St.; M, R to Court St.*

DUMBO

Walk downhill from Brooklyn Heights, toward the water, and you'll reach the area called DUMBO (*Down Under the Manhattan Bridge Overpass*). It was once known as Fulton Landing, after the inventor and engineer Robert Fulton, who introduced steamboat ferry service from Brooklyn to Manhattan in 1814. Factories and dry-goods warehouses thrived here until the Manhattan Bridge was completed in 1909. DUMBO then fell on hard times, but since the 1970s artists have been drawn by the historic warehouses for use as spacious studios. Today the area is full of luxury condos, art galleries, and small businesses.

The **Fulton Ferry Landing**'s view of Manhattan and the Brooklyn Bridge makes it a favorite site for wedding photos; the New York Water Taxi stops here as well. When all that sightseeing makes you hungry, walk uphill to the always excellent, always crowded, **Grimaldi's Pizzeria** and the **Brooklyn Ice Cream Factory.** Wander the empty, old cobblestone streets for photo ops (try to frame the Empire State Building within the anchorage of the Manhattan Bridge), and visit the art galleries and boutiques.

TOP ATTRACTIONS

Ⓒ **Brooklyn Bridge Park.** On the waterfront between the Brooklyn Bridge and the Manhattan Bridge, this vast park is a great place for a riverside picnic or to just enjoy the view. There are several sections of the park, including Pier 1, Pier 6, the Main Street Lot (with DUMBO's free Wi-Fi network), and the newly renovated Empire-Fulton Ferry. The large playground at Pier 1 has a replica of a boat for make-believe voyages across the East River. In the Empire-Fulton Ferry part of the park is one of the park's new highlights: the fabulously restored **Jane Carousel,** originally

built in 1922 and now housed in a pavilion designed by renowned French architect Jean Nouvel. The carousel runs all year but is closed on Tuesday; rides are $2, or you can buy 12 tickets for $20. From April to October the park is home to a wide range of arts performances, and on Thursday nights in July and August, Movies with a View projects New York classic films on an outdoor screen with no cover charge. ⊠ *New Dock St. at Water St.* ☎ *718/858–4708* ⊕ *www.brooklynbridgepark.org* ◻ *Free* ☉ *Daily dawn–dusk* Ⓜ *A, C to High St.; F to York St.*

GALLERIES

No trip to DUMBO would be complete without some gallery hopping—most are open afternoons Wednesday or Thursday through Sunday.

DUMBO Arts Center (*DAC*). This 3,000-square-foot gallery draws visitors for the contemporary art exhibits, workshops, and lectures. The annual DUMBO Arts Festival (⊕ *dumboartsfestival.com*) in September is three fabulous art- and music-packed days in the area's galleries, open studios, warehouses, parks, and streets. ⊠ *30 Washington St., between Water and Plymouth Sts.* ☎ *718/694–0831* ⊕ *www.dumboartscenter. org* ◻ *$2* Ⓜ *A or C to High St.*

Smack Mellon. Inside a 6,000-square-foot restored boiler building, Smack Mellon exhibits work by up-and-coming artists, and nurtures them with studio space and other support. ⊠ *92 Plymouth St., at Washington St.* ☎ *718/834–8761* ⊕ *www.smackmellon.org* Ⓜ *A or C to High St.*

Spring. At exhibition space and design shop Spring, you can view contemporary art, then satisfy your shopping urges with quirky home goods. ⊠ *126a Front St.* ☎ *718/222–1054* ⊕ *www.spring3d.net* Ⓜ *A or C to High St.*

SHOPPING

Blueberi. Striking window displays will lure you into this sleek boutique where the vintage and contemporary designer wear, shoes, and accessories hail from the five boroughs as well as the faraway corners of the world. ⊠ *143 Front St.* ☎ *718/422–7724* ⊕ *www.blueberi.net* Ⓜ *A or C to High St.*

Jacques Torres Chocolate. You'll feel like Charlie getting a peek at the Oompa Loompas as you peer into the small chocolate factory while munching on an unusually flavored chocolate bonbon or sipping a cup of thick, rich hot chocolate. (For the latter, try the "wicked" flavor, spiked with chipotle peppers and cinnamon.) The adjacent ice-cream shop serves scoops, sundaes, and ice-cream sandwiches, with flavors from mango sorbet to caramel-rum vanilla. ⊠ *66 Water St.* ☎ *718/875–1269* ⊕ *www.mrchocolate.com* Ⓜ *A or C to High St.*

The powerHouse Arena. This stunning 5,000-square-foot space with soaring 24-foot ceilings, glass frontage, and amphitheater-style seating does multiple duty as gallery, boutique, bookstore, and performance space. It's a must-stop for culture hawks and bookworms. ⊠ *37 Main St.* ☎ *718/666–3049* ⊕ *www.powerhousearena.com* Ⓜ *A or C to High St.*

WILLIAMSBURG

For much of the 20th century this industrial area on the East River was home to a mix of Latin Americans, Poles, Hasidic Jews, and factories. Then, as Manhattan rents rose in the 1990s, artists, misfits, and indie rockers migrated across on the L train to transform the neighborhood into a creative bohemian center. Not surprisingly, rents soon started to rise here, too.

Today Williamsburg's main drag of Bedford Avenue is a veritable catwalk of fabulously dressed starving artists and wealthy hipsters on their way from the L train to a range of stylish bars and clubs, artists' studios, vintage stores, and costly boutiques. Meanwhile, the area's young families and migrating Manhattanites head to one of the many posh restaurants near the Williamsburg Bridge. Note that the shops and attractions listed here are spread out, so be prepared to walk a few blocks on generally safe (though sometimes graffitied and abandoned) blocks filled with former factories.

GALLERIES

Williamsburg's 70-plus galleries are distributed randomly, with no single main drag. Plan your trip ahead of time using the online **Brooklyn Art Guide** at ⊕ *www.wagmag.org*. (You can also pick up a copy at neighborhood galleries and some cafés.) Hours vary widely, but almost all are open weekends. Call ahead. Although serendipitous poking is the best way to sample the art, two longtime galleries are must-sees.

Pierogi Gallery. Nope, it's not a restaurant, it's a hip art gallery. Check out the famous "Flat Files," an online collection of the portfolios of more than 700 young contemporary artists. The Boiler, a larger space nearby (⊠ *191 North 14th Street* ☎ *718/599–2144* Ⓜ *G to Nassau Ave, L to Bedford Ave.*), has somewhat more limited hours. ⊠ *177 N. 9th St., between Bedford and Driggs Aves.* ☎ *718/599–2144* ⊕ *www. pierogi2000.com* Ⓜ *L to Bedford Ave.*

Sideshow Gallery. The focus is on local Williamsburg artists at this pioneering gallery, but there are traveling exhibits as well, and sometimes readings and concerts. ⊠ *319 Bedford Ave.* ☎ *718/486–8180* ⊕ *www. sideshowgallery.com* Ⓜ *L to Bedford Ave.*

SHOPPING

Although the boutiques on Bedford Avenue are best for people-watching, you'll also find stores along Grand Street, and on many side streets, especially North 6th.

A&G Merch. Contemporary, stylish, and affordable home accessories, from large to small, are what you'll find at this Brooklyn shop. ⊠ *111 N. 6th St.* ☎ *718/388–1779* ⊕ *www.aandgmerch.com* Ⓜ *L to Bedford Ave.*

Beacon's Closet. Local fashionistas and out-of-towners alike flock to Beacon's Closet for its huge selection of used and vintage clothing and accessories where real deals can be scored if you devote some time to browsing. ⊠ *88 N. 11th St.* ☎ *718/486–0816* ⊕ *www.beaconscloset. com* Ⓜ *L to Bedford Ave.*

Bedford Cheese Shop. The small size of the Bedford Cheese Shop belies the fact that this is one of the city's best cheese stores, packed with an encyclopedic assortment of artisan cheeses as well as small-producer cured meats, gourmet imported oils, chocolates, and dry goods. The quirky and occasionally salacious descriptions of the cheeses ("looks like dirty scrimshaw but tastes like a peat-covered goat teat") add entertainment to your shopping experience. ⊠ *229 Bedford Ave., at N. 4th St.* ☎ *718/599–7588* ⊕ *www.bedfordcheeseshop.com* Ⓜ *L to Bedford Ave.*

Catbird. One of the standout boutiques on Bedford, Catbird is a dollhouse-size shop with shelves filled with handmade jewelry, home accessories, and whimsical hats. ⊠ *219 Bedford Ave., near N. 5th St.* ☎ *718/599–3457* ⊕ *www.catbirdnyc.com* Ⓜ *L to Bedford Ave.*

The Future Perfect. Brooklyn's thriving home-design scene is often credited to the Future Perfect, which has since opened a Manhattan branch. Even if you're not planning on shipping home a Bone Chair made entirely of cow ribs, it's fun to browse the playful and often ironic furnishings from local Brooklyn and international designers. ⊠ *115 N. 6th St., at Berry St.* ☎ *718/599–6278* ⊕ *www.thefutureperfect.com* Ⓜ *L to Bedford Ave.*

Realform Girdle Building. The Realform Girdle Building is the closest thing Williamsburg has to a mall; it houses a small café, a new/used record store, several achingly hip boutiques, and an art bookstore. ✉ *218 Bedford Ave.* Ⓜ *L to Bedford Ave.*

Love Brigade Clothing. With local design labels like Social Rebel and international collections in the vein of London's Laura Dawson, Love Brigade + Friends showcases a unique mix of fashion and accessories: from pencil skirts to soft cotton tees with vibrant typography. The retail outlet, adjacent to the creative studio, employs some of the friendliest staff in Williamsburg. ✉ *230 Grand St., ground fl., Williamsburg* ☎ *718/715–0430* ⊕ *www.lovebrigade.com* ⊗ *Wed.–Fri. 1–8, Sat. noon–8, Sun. 2–8* Ⓜ *L to Bedford Ave.*

CONEY ISLAND

14

Coney Island is almost practically synonymous with the sounds, smells, and sights of a New York City summer: hot dogs and ice cream, suntan lotion, excited crowds, and weathered old men fishing.

Named Konijn Eiland (Rabbit Island) by the Dutch for its wild rabbit population, the Coney Island peninsula has a boardwalk, a 2.5-mi-long beach, amusement parks, and the **New York Aquarium.** Eating a Nathan's Famous hot dog (✉ *1310 Surf Ave., Coney Island*) and strolling seaside has been a classic New York experience since 1916.

Among the other entertainments out here are the freakish attractions at **Coney Island Circus Sideshow** and the **Coney Island Museum,** the heart-stopping plunge of the granddaddy of all roller coasters—the **Cyclone.** The minor-league baseball team, the Cyclones, plays at MCU park, where music concerts are held in summer. The area's banner day is the raucous Mermaid Parade, held in June. A fireworks display lights up the sky Friday nights from late June through Labor Day.

TOP ATTRACTIONS

Ⓒ **The Cyclone and Luna Park.** The highlight of Coney Island's amusement park will always be the Cyclone, one of the oldest roller coasters still operating—the world-famous, wood-and-steel colossus first roared around the tracks in 1927 and is still making riders scream. Luna Park is the amusement grounds that grew up in place of Astroland; it's fun if you keep your expectations in check: the rides are mostly for kids. ✉ *834 Surf Ave., at W. 10th St.* ☎ *718/265–2100* ✍ *Cyclone: $8 for first ride, $5 for additional rides* ⊗ *Luna Park: May–Oct., noon–midnight; Cyclone: Memorial Day–Labor Day, daily noon–8; weekends only, Apr.–mid-May and Labor Day–Oct.* Ⓜ *B, F, N, Q to Coney Island–Stillwell Ave.*

Ⓒ **New York Aquarium.** Home to more than 8,000 creatures of the ocean, New York City's only aquarium is also the nation's oldest. Tropical fish, sea horses, and jellyfish luxuriate in large tanks; otters, walruses, penguins, and seals lounge on a replicated Pacific coast; and a 90,000-gallon tank is home to several different types of sharks. ✉ *502 Surf Ave., at W. 8th St.* ☎ *718/265–3474* ⊕ *www.nyaquarium.com* ✍ *$14.95* ⊗ *Apr.–Memorial Day and Labor Day–Nov., weekdays 10–5, weekends 10–5:30; Memorial Day–Labor Day, weekdays 10–6, weekends 10–7;*

Strolling on the boardwalk at Coney Island.

Nov.–early Apr., daily 10–4:30; last ticket sold 45 mins before closing Ⓜ *F, Q to W. 8th St.; N, D to Coney Island–Stillwell Ave.*

WORTH NOTING

Coney Island Circus Sideshow. Step right up for lively circus-sideshow entertainment, complete with a fire-eater, sword swallower, snake charmer, and contortionist. Upstairs, the small museum has Coney Island memorabilia and lots of tourist information. ✉ *1208 Surf Ave., at W. 12th St.* ☎ *718/372–5159* ⊕ *www.coneyisland.com/sideshow.shtml* ✉ *Sideshow $10, museum $5* ⊙ *Sideshows: Memorial Day–Labor Day, daily shows; Sept.–May, some weekends. Museum: weekends noon–6.* Ⓜ *D, F, N, Q to Coney Island–Stillwell Ave.*

🔄 **Deno's Wonder Wheel Amusement Park.** You'll get a wide perspective from atop the 150-foot-tall Wonder Wheel at Deno's Amusement Park. The Wonder Wheel was built in 1920 and although it appears tame, the swinging cars will quicken your heart rate. There are plenty of rides here to amuse the kids. ✉ *3059 Denos Vourderis Pl., at W. 12th St.* ☎ *718/372–2592* ⊕ *www.wonderwheel.com* ✉ *$6 per ride, 5 rides for $25* ⊙ *Memorial Day–Labor Day, daily 11 am–midnight; Apr., May, Sept., and Oct., weekends noon–9* Ⓜ *D, F, N, Q to Coney Island–Stillwell Ave.*

BRIGHTON BEACH

A pleasant stroll down the boardwalk from Coney Island is Brighton Beach, named after Britain's beach resort. In the early 1900s Brighton Beach was a resort in its own right, with seaside hotels that catered to

CLOSE UP

Brooklyn Flea

Brooklyn Flea. Quirky, inclusive, and full of unclaimed treasures—that's Brooklyn in a nutshell, and it also aptly describes the Brooklyn Flea. This little market that could is now one of Brooklyn's most popular shopping attractions, luring locals and bargain hunters from afar with vintage finds, hip crafts, and crazy-delicious eats.

The Flea is a hybrid of traditional flea market, garage sale, and crafts fair, a tumble of the expensive, the cheap, and the strange. Some vendors hawk high-end items like antique doors refashioned into tables, rescued fixtures from prewar houses, or midcentury lamps identical to those in Mad Men. The most "Brooklyn-y" component is the local artisans, and buying their one-of-a-kind handmade wares gives shoppers the altruistic feeling of supporting arts and crafts, whether that's silk-screen T-shirts of giant squid, tongue-in-cheek charm bracelets with little daggers, or hand-stitched stuffed elephants. You'll also find a number of oddly specialized booths like the vendor who sells nothing but oil paintings of bicycles. Why not? Finally, there is plenty of bric-a-brac to sift through: great stuff that may not be practical (mink stoles, nonfunctional alarm clocks, Star Wars collectibles), but that makes for fun browsing.

When you've exhausted the shopping side of things, the Flea boasts some fantastic food options. You'll find fat pretzels from Sigmund Pretzel Shop, funny franks from Asia Dogs, cold cuts and sandwiches from Mile End delicatessen, organic ice cream from Blue Marble, family-farmed coffee from Crop to Cup, and all sorts of pickled produce from popular McClure's Pickles.

The Flea takes place in two locations every weekend from mid-March to late November: the parking lot of a local school on Saturday and the stunning interior of the landmark Williamsburgh Savings Bank (now an event space known as Skylight One Hanson) on Sunday. During the colder months the Flea takes place at its indoor location on weekends. ✉ *Mid-Mar.–late Nov., Sat.: Bishop Laughlin Memorial High School, 176 Lafayette Ave., between Clermont and Vanderbilt Ave., Fort Greene; Sun.: One Hanson Pl., Fort Greene* ✉ *Winter: One Hanson Pl., Fort Greene* ✉ *Fort Greene* ⊕ *www. brooklynflea.com* 📧 *Free* 🕐 *Weekends 10–5* Ⓜ *A, C to Lafayette Ave. for outdoor location; 2, 3, 4, 5, B, Q to Atlantic Ave.; D, N, R to Atlantic Ave.– Pacific St. for indoor location.*

14

rich Manhattan families visiting for the summer. Since the 1970s and '80s Brighton Beach has been known for its 100,000 Soviet émigrés.

To get to the heart of "Little Odessa" from Coney Island, walk about a mile east along the boardwalk to Brighton 1st Place, then head up to Brighton Beach Avenue. To get here from Manhattan directly, take the B or Q train to the Brighton Beach stop; the trip takes about an hour.

TOP ATTRACTIONS

Brighton Beach boardwalk. The Brighton Beach section of the boardwalk, especially between Brighton 3rd and 6th streets, bustles with restaurants serving traditional Russian dishes. The beach tends to be slightly less crowded in summer than at Coney Island, filled with local sunbathers and Manhattanites who've come out for the day. Brighton Beach is about a mile from Coney Island. ⊠ *Between Ocean Pkwy. and Coney Island Ave., Brighton Beach* 🚇 Ⓜ *B or Q to Coney Island.*

Brighton Beach Avenue. The shops, bakeries, markets, and restaurants along Brighton Beach Avenue, the neighborhood's main artery, cater primarily to the neighborhood's Russian community, but shopping along here is a primary reason to visit. This is the place to find knishes with every filling imaginable, borscht, *blinis* (small crepes or pancakes), fruit and veggies, Russian liquor, and cups of dark-roast coffee, plus caviar at prices that can put Manhattan purveyors to shame. ⊠ *Brighton Beach Ave. from Brighton 1st St. to Brighton 6th St.* Ⓜ *Q to Brighton Beach.*

FORT GREENE

Thriving Fort Greene is one of the latest hot Brooklyn 'hoods. It can be a trek to get to from Manhattan, but the rewards are many, including some of the best restaurants in Brooklyn, lovely tree-lined streets, and beautiful Fort Greene park. Fort Greene, as with many other areas of Brooklyn, has long been a home to famous writers and musicians, and fittingly it's also the locale of one of the city's top performing arts powerhouses, the Brooklyn Academy of Music, known as BAM (⇨ *Chapter 16 Performing Arts).*

CARROLL GARDENS, COBBLE HILL, AND BOERUM HILL

On Atlantic Avenue's south side, the three adjacent neighborhoods of Carroll Gardens, Cobble Hill, and Boerum Hill form a quiet residential area of leafy streets lined with 19th-century town houses. The action swirls around Smith Street, a restaurant row augmented by fresh, fashionable boutiques, as well as Court Street's restaurants, bookstores, and old-fashioned bakeries. Nearby on Atlantic Avenue between Court and Clinton is a rapidly gentrifying Middle Eastern enclave, which includes the emporium Sahadi's (⊠ *187 Atlantic Ave.*), great for purchasing a veritable bazaar of olives, baklava, and other treats. Get to this neighborhood by taking the F train to Bergen Street or Carroll Street.

PARK SLOPE AND PROSPECT HEIGHTS

The neighborhood that literally slopes down from Prospect Park, **Park Slope** is known affectionately as "Stroller Land." This family-friendly neighborhood is full of academics, writers, and late-blooming couples pushing Bugaboo strollers to its cafés and designer boutiques. One of Brooklyn's most comfortable places to live, Park Slope has row after row of immaculate brownstones that date from its turn-of-the-20th-century heyday, when it had the nation's highest per-capita income. To see some of the neighborhood's most beautiful houses, walk between

Carroll Gardens, Cobble Hill, Boerum Hill, and Fort Greene

7th Avenue and Prospect Park along any of the streets between Sterling Place and 4th Street.

You can follow dog walkers and bicyclists to idyllic 585-acre **Prospect Park** nearby, designed by Olmsted and Vaux of Central Park fame. Along with rolling meadows, shady forests, and a series of lakes, there are concerts and kids' programs. Adjacent to the park are two of Brooklyn's main attractions: the **Brooklyn Botanic Garden,** a must-see during its springtime Cherry Blossom Festival, and the **Brooklyn Museum,** known for its Egyptian and feminist art collections. At the northeast corner of Prospect Park is the neighborhood of **Prospect Heights**, with its elegant high-rises overlooking the Brooklyn Museum and Botanic Garden.

TOP ATTRACTIONS

Brooklyn Botanic Garden. The 52 acres of this beloved Brooklyn retreat, one of the finest botanic gardens in the country, are a must-see, especially in spring and summer. A major attraction is the beguiling Japanese Hill-and-Pond Garden—complete with a pond, blazing red *torii* gate, and Shinto shrine. Nearby, the Japanese cherry arbor turns into a breathtaking cloud of pink every spring; the Sakura Matsuri, a two-day cherry-blossom festival, is a hugely popular event.

Also be sure to wander through the Cranford Rose Garden (5,000 plants, 1,200 varieties); the Fragrance Garden, designed especially for

Park Slope and Prospect Heights

the blind; and the Shakespeare Garden, featuring more than 80 plants immortalized by the Bard. At the Steinhardt Conservatory, desert, tropical, temperate, and aquatic vegetation thrives. Don't miss the extraordinary C. V. Starr Bonsai Museum for close to 100 miniature Japanese specimens, some more than a century old. Near the conservatory are a café and a gift shop, with bulbs, plants, and gardening books as well as jewelry.

Entrances to the garden are on Eastern Parkway, next to the subway station; on Washington Avenue, behind the Brooklyn Museum; and on Flatbush Avenue at Empire Boulevard. Free garden tours meet at the front gate every weekend at 1 pm. ⊠ *900 Washington Ave., between Crown and Carroll Sts.* ☎ *718/623–7200* ⊕ *www.bbg.org* ☑ *$10; free all day Tues., Sat. before noon, and weekdays from mid-Nov. to mid-Mar. Combo ticket with Brooklyn Museum $18* ☉ *Mid-Mar.–late Oct.: grounds Tues.–Fri. 8–6, weekends 10–6; conservatory daily 10–5:30. Nov.–mid-Mar.: grounds Tues.–Fri. 8–4:30, weekends 10–4:30; conservatory daily 10–4. Closed Mon. except holidays* Ⓜ *2, 3 to Eastern Pkwy.; B, Q to Prospect Park.*

☾ **Prospect Park.** Brooklyn residents are fiercely passionate about Prospect Park. Designed by Frederick Law Olmsted and Calvert Vaux, the park was completed in the late 1880s. Olmsted once said that he was prouder of it than of any of his other works—including Manhattan's Central Park.

A good way to experience the park is to walk along its 3½-mi circular drive and make detours off it as you wish. The drive is closed to cars at all times except weekday rush hours. Families with children should head straight for the eastern side, where most kids' attractions are clustered.

The park's north entrance is at **Grand Army Plaza**, where the Soldiers' and Sailors' Memorial Arch honors Civil War veterans. (Look familiar? It's patterned after the Arc de Triomphe in Paris.) Three heroic sculptural groupings adorn the arch: atop, a dynamic four-horse chariot; to either side, the victorious Union Army and Navy of the Civil War. The inner arch has bas-reliefs of presidents Abraham Lincoln and Ulysses S. Grant, sculpted by Thomas Eakins and William O'Donovan, respectively. To the northwest of the arch, Neptune and a passel of debauched Tritons leer over the edges of the **Bailey Fountain**. On Saturdays year-round a greenmarket at the plaza sells produce, flowers and plants, cheese, and baked goods to throngs of locals. Other days, you can find a few vendors selling snacks here and at the 9th Street entrance.

Lefferts Historic House. Lefferts Historic House is a Dutch Colonial farmhouse built in 1783 and moved to Prospect Park in 1918. Rooms of the historic house-museum are furnished with antiques and reproductions from the 1820s, when the house was last redecorated. The museum hosts all kinds of activities for kids; call for information. ☎ 718/789–2822 ✉ *Free* ☺ *Apr. and May, Sat. and Sun. noon–5; June and Sept., Thurs.–Sun. noon–5; July and Aug., Thurs.–Sun. noon–6; Oct., Thurs.–Sun. noon–4; Nov. and Dec., and Feb. and Mar., Sat. and Sun. noon–4.*

Litchfield Villa. If you walk down the park's west drive from Grand Army Plaza, you'll first encounter Litchfield Villa, an Italianate hilltop mansion built in 1857 for a prominent railroad magnate. It has housed the park's headquarters since 1883; visitors are welcome to step inside and view the domed octagonal rotunda. ☎ *718/965–8951* ✉ *Free* ☺ *Weekdays 9–5.*

Prospect Park Audubon Center and Visitor Center at the Boathouse. Styled after Sansovino's 16th-century Library at St. Mark's in Venice, the Prospect Park Audubon Center and Visitor Center at the Boathouse, built in 1904, sits opposite the Lullwater Bridge, creating an idyllic spot for watching pedal boats and wildlife, or just taking a break at the café. Interactive exhibits, park tours, and educational programs for kids make this a fun place to learn about nature. On a nice day, take a ride on the electric boat to tour the Lullwater and Prospect Lake. You can also sign up for a bird-watching tour to see some of the 200 species spotted here. ✉ *Just inside the Lincoln Road/Ocean Ave. entrance, Prospect Park* ☎ *718/287–3400* ⊕ *www.prospectpark.org/audubon* ✉ *Audubon Center free; electric-boat tours $8* ☺ *Audubon Center: Apr.–Sept., Thurs.–Sun. noon–5; Oct.–Mar., weekends noon–4; closed in Jan.; call for program and tour times. Electric-boat tours: May–Aug., Thurs.–Sun. noon–4:30; Sept.–mid-Oct., weekends noon–3:30, every 30 mins.*

Fodor's Choice **Prospect Park Band Shell.** The Prospect Park Band Shell is the home of
★ the annual Celebrate Brooklyn Festival, which from early June through
mid-August sponsors free films and concerts that have included Afro-
Caribbean jazz, flamenco dance troupes from Spain, David Byrne, and
the Brooklyn Philharmonic. ☎ *718/855–7882 for the Celebrate Brooklyn Festival* ⊕ *www.bricartsmedia.org.*

Prospect Park Carousel. Climb aboard a giraffe or sit inside a dragon-
pulled chariot at the immaculately restored Prospect Park Carousel,
handcrafted in 1912 by master carver Charles Carmel. ☎ *718/282–
7789* 🖃 *$2 per ride* ◎ *Apr.–June, Sept., and Oct., Thurs.–Sun. noon–5;
July–Labor Day, Thurs.–Sun. noon–6.*

Prospect Park Zoo. Of the 400 inhabitants and 125 species at the
small, friendly Prospect Park Zoo, kids seem especially fond of the
sea lions and the red pandas. An outdoor discovery trail has a simu-
lated prairie-dog burrow, a duck pond, and kangaroos and wallabies
in habitat. Be aware that there are no cafés, only vending machines.
✉ *450 Flatbush Ave.* ☎ *718/399–7339* ⊕ *www.prospectparkzoo.com*
🖃 *$8* ◎ *Apr.–Oct., weekdays 10–5, weekends 10–5:30; Nov.–Mar.,
daily 10–4:30; last ticket 30 mins before closing* Ⓜ *2, 3 to Eastern
Pkwy.; B, Q to Prospect Park* ✉ *450 Flatbush Ave.* ☎ *718/965–8951*
⊕ *www.prospectpark.org/.*

WORTH NOTING

☾ **Brooklyn Children's Museum.** A mile east of Grand Army Plaza is the old-
est children's museum in the world, now housed in a sparkling Rafael
Viñoly–designed "green" building. Kids will have a blast, trekking
through natural habitats found in the city, running a bakery, creating
African-patterned fabric, and even becoming DJs, mixing the rhythms
of the outdoors to make music. ✉ *145 Brooklyn Ave., at St. Marks Ave.,
Crown Heights* ☎ *718/735–4400* ⊕ *www.brooklynkids.org* 🖃 *$7.50*
◎ *Tues.–Sun. 10–5* Ⓜ *C to Kingston–Throop Aves.; 3 to Kingston Ave.,
A, C to Nostrand Ave.*

★ **Brooklyn Museum.** Although it may be overshadowed by the big name
museums in Manhattan, the Brooklyn Museum, with more than 1
million pieces in its permanent collection—from Rodin sculptures to
Andean textiles and Assyrian wall reliefs—and a roster of consistently
popular shows and neighborhood events, is a worthwhile and relatively
peaceful museum-going experience.

Along with changing exhibitions, highlights include one of the best collections of Egyptian art in the world and impressive collections of African, pre-Columbian, and Native American art. It's also worth seeking
out the museum's works by Georgia O'Keeffe, Winslow Homer, John
Singer Sargent, George Bellows, Thomas Eakins, and Milton Avery—all
stunners. The Elizabeth A. Sackler Center for Feminist Art hosts traveling exhibits in addition to serving as the permanent home to Judy Chicago's installation *The Dinner Party* (1974–79). On the first Saturday
of each month (except September) the museum throws an extremely
popular free evening of art, music, dancing, film screenings, and readings, from 5 to 11 pm. There are several cash bars. ✉ *200 Eastern*

A view of the pond at the Brooklyn Botanic Garden, seen through the blossoming cherry trees.

Pkwy., at Washington Ave. ☎ 718/638–5000 ⊕ www.brooklynmuseum. org ✉ $12 suggested donation. Combo ticket with Brooklyn Botanic Garden $20 ⊙ Wed., Fri., Sat., 11–6, Thurs. 11–10; 1st Sat. of month 11–11 Ⓜ 2, 3 to Eastern Pkwy./Brooklyn Museum.

Central Library. Across Grand Army Plaza from the entrance to Prospect Park stands this sleek, modern temple of learning—the central location of the Brooklyn Public Library. The building resembles an open book, with the entrance at the book's spine; on the facade, gold-leaf figures celebrate art and science. Bright limestone walls and perfect proportions make this an impressive 20th-century New York building. Inside, more than 1.5 million books, public programs, and exhibitions in the lobby will keep you busy for at least a few hours. ✉ *10 Grand Army Plaza* ☎ *718/230–2100* ⊕ *www.brooklynpubliclibrary.org* ⊙ *Mon.–Thurs. 9–9, Fri. and Sat. 10–6, Sun. 1–5* Ⓜ *2, 3 to Grand Army Plaza; Q to 7th Ave.*

SHOPPING

Seventh Avenue is Park Slope's main shopping street, with long-established restaurants, bookstores, shops, cafés, bakeries, churches, and real-estate agents (one favorite neighborhood pastime is window-shopping for new apartments). More fun, however, are the newer restaurants and cute boutiques along 5th Avenue.

Bierkraft. Yes, this gourmet food store is all about the beer—there are nearly 1,000 craft beers available by the bottle—but there is also an impressive section of artisanal cheeses, boutique chocolates, olives, and other edible goodies, including deliciously prepared sandwiches to order. Beer tastings are Tuesday at 7 pm. ⊠ *191 5th Ave., near Union St., Park Slope* ☏ *718/230–7600* ⊕ *www.bierkraft.com* Ⓜ *R to Union St.; B and Q to 7th Ave.*

Bird. An extremely well-curated selection of designers—think Martin Margiela and 3.1 Phillip Lim—makes Bird one of the best of the many excellent women's clothing stores dotting the area. There are two other Brooklyn locations (in Cobble Hill ⊠ *220 Smith Street* ☏ *718/797–3775*, and in Williamsburg ⊠ *203 Grand Street* ☏ *718/388–1656*). ⊠ *316 5th Ave., between 2nd and 3rd Sts., Park Slope* ☏ *718/797–3776* ⊕ *www.shopbird.com* Ⓜ *F and G to Bergen St.*

☺ **Brooklyn Superhero Supply Co.** Where else can young superheroes purchase capes, grappling hooks, secret identity kits, and more from staff who never drop the game of pretend? Proceeds benefit the free drop-in tutoring center (run by nonprofit organization 826NYC) in a "secret lair" behind a swinging bookcase. ⊠ *372 5th Ave., at 7th St., Park Slope* ☏ *718/499–9884* ⊕ *www.superherosupplies.com* Ⓜ *R to 4th Ave.; F and G to Smith/9th Sts.*

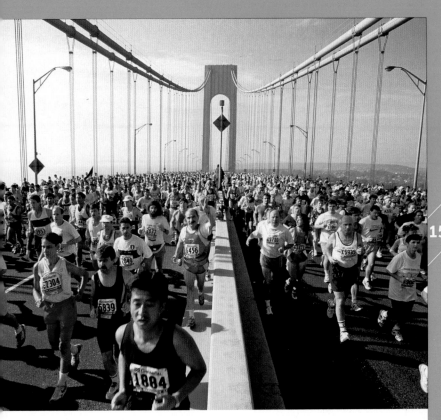

Queens, the Bronx, and Staten Island

WORD OF MOUTH

"[Combine] a visit to Arthur Avenue with a visit to the New York Botanical Garden which is located just north of the Belmont section. Take a MetroNorth train from Grand Central to the Botanical Garden stop. Walk across the street and enter the gardens. There are many acres of outdoor exhibits."

—ellenem

GETTING ORIENTED

MAKING THE MOST OF YOUR TIME

Queens is rich with superb museums. An afternoon in Long Island City and Astoria will enable you to take in the PS1 Contemporary Art Center, the Museum of the Moving Image, and the Noguchi Museum. After that, jump on the 7 train and have dinner in Jackson Heights or Flushing at one of the borough's excellent restaurants.

It is easy to spend a full day at either of the Bronx's treasures: the New York Botanical Garden or the Bronx Zoo. To visit both, start early and plan on a late lunch or early dinner in the Arthur Avenue area. The garden and the zoo are less crowded on weekdays during the school year.

Many tourists' only sight of Staten Island is during a round-trip ride on the ferry, but the borough also holds unexpected offerings in its small museums and historic villages. Set aside the better part of a day for Historic Richmond Town, and add on a couple of hours for the Museum of Tibetan Art.

GETTING HERE

Queens is served by many subway lines. To get to Astoria, take the N train. For Long Island City, take the E, M, or 7 train. To get to Jackson Heights, take the 7 subway train to the 74th Street–Broadway stop. You can also take the E, F, R, or M train to Roosevelt Avenue.

The Bronx is serviced by the 2, 4, 5, 6, B, and D subway trains. The attractions in the Bronx are spread out across the borough, so you'll need to take different lines to get where you want to go, and it's not necessarily convenient to make connections across town. The B, D, and 4 trains all go to Yankee Stadium, and the B and D continue uptown to take you to Arthur Avenue from the west. The 2 and 5 trains take you to the Bronx Zoo and to Arthur Avenue.

From the scenic and free Staten Island Ferry you can catch a local bus to attractions. Tell the driver where you're going, and ask about the return schedule.

TOP EXPERIENCES

Ethnic eats in Queens.

Catching a game at the new Yankee Stadium or Citi Field.

Taking a free ride on the Staten Island Ferry.

NEARBY MUSEUMS

Jacques Marchais Museum of Tibetan Art

MoMA PS1

Museum of the Moving Image

New York Hall of Science

The Noguchi Museum

Queens Museum of Art

COFFEE, COCKTAILS, AND QUICK BITES

Drinks in Queens: Dutch Kills (✉ *27-24 Jackson Ave.*). Swank cocktails at Queens prices. Bohemian Hall & Beer Garden (✉ *29-19 24th Ave.*). Perfect on a summer night.

Snacks in the Bronx: Zero Otto Nove (✉ *2357 Arthur Ave.*). Serious Neapolitan pizza. Mike's Deli (✉ *2344 Arthur Ave.*). For sandwiches as big as your head.

Good Eats in Staten Island: Adobe Blues (✉ *63 Lafayette Ave.*). Southwestern food and more than 200 beers. Café Botanica (✉ *Snug Harbor Cultural Center, Cottage Row*). Come for American classics, like fresh biscuits with whipped butter.

15

Sightseeing
★★★

Nightlife
★★★

Dining
★★★★

Lodging
★

Shopping
★★★★

Many tourists miss out on Queens, the Bronx, and Staten Island—the three boroughs of New York City other than the biggies, Manhattan and Brooklyn—and that's a shame. There are some noteworthy restaurants, museums, and attractions, and the subway's handful of express trains means that they're closer than you might think.

QUEENS

Updated by
Alexander
Basek

Just for the museums and restaurants alone, a short 15-minute trip on the 7 train from Grand Central or Times Square to **Long Island City** and **Astoria** is truly worth it. In Long Island City, major must-sees are **MoMA PS1** and the **Noguchi Museum.** No trip to Astoria, nicknamed "Little Athens" would be complete without sampling Greek cuisine and stopping at newly renovated **Museum of the Moving Image.**

Jackson Heights is home to the city's largest Indian population. It's a wonderful place to spend an afternoon browsing its shops and dining in one of the many authentic restaurants.

Top reasons to trek out to **Flushing** and **Corona** include seeing the New York Mets new stadium, **Citi Field,** spending time at the expansive **Flushing Meadows–Corona Park**—especially if traveling with kids—and enjoying Italian ices from the **Lemon Ice King of Corona,** a neighborhood institution.

LONG ISLAND CITY AND ASTORIA

Long Island City (LIC for short) is the outer-borough art capital, with **MoMA PS1,** which presents experimental and formally innovative work; the **Noguchi Museum,** showcasing the work of Japanese-American sculptor Isamu Noguchi in a large, peaceful garden and galleries; and **Socrates Sculpture Park.**

Nearby Astoria, nicknamed Little Athens, was the center of Greek immigrant life in New York City for more than 60 years. An increase

TIPS FOR QUEENS ADDRESSES

Addresses in Queens can seem confusing at first. Not only are there 30th Street and 30th Avenue, but there are also 30th Place and 30th Road, all next to one another. Then there are those hyphenated building numbers. But the system is actually much more logical than you might think. Sequentially numbered avenues run east-to-west, and sequentially numbered streets run north-to-south. If there are any smaller roads between avenues, they have the same number as the nearest avenue, and are called roads or drives. Similarly, smaller side roads between streets are called places or lanes. Thus, 30th Place is one block east of 30th Street. Most buildings have two pairs of numbers, separated by a hyphen. The first pair indicates the nearest cross street, and the second gives the location on the block. So 47-10 30th Place is 10 houses away from the corner of 47th Avenue and 30th Place. Logical, right? If this all still seems confusing to you, there's good news: locals are used to giving directions to visitors.

15

in Greek affluence has meant that many have left the borough, but they still return for authentic restaurants, grocery stores, and churches. Here you can buy kalamata olives and salty sheep's-milk feta from storeowners who can tell you where to go for the best spinach pie. Today substantial numbers of Asian, Eastern European, Irish, and Latino immigrants also live in Astoria. The heart of what remains of the Greek community is on Broadway, between 31st and Steinway streets. Thirtieth Avenue is another busy thoroughfare, with almost every kind of food store imaginable. Astoria is also home to the nation's only museum devoted to the art, technology, and history of film, TV, and digital media. The newly redone **Museum of the Moving Image** has countless hands-on exhibits that allow visitors to edit, direct, and step into favorite movies and television shows.

TOP ATTRACTIONS

Fodor'sChoice **MoMA PS1.** A pioneer in the "alternative-space" movement, PS1 rose
★ from the ruins of an abandoned school in 1976 as a sort of community arts center for the future. MoMA PS1 focuses on the work of currently active experimental and innovative artists. Long-term installations include work by Sol LeWitt and Pipilotti Rist. Every available corner of the enormous 100-room building is used; discover art not only in galleries but also on the rooftop, in the boiler room, and even in some bathrooms. On summer Saturdays from 3 to 9 pm outdoor dance parties attract a hip art-school crowd. ⊠ *22-25 Jackson Ave., at 46th Ave., Long Island City* ☎ *718/784–2084* ⊕ *ps1.org/* ⊠ *$10 suggested donation, free with MoMA entrance ticket* ☉ *Thurs.–Mon. noon–6* Ⓜ *7 to 45th Rd.–Courthouse Sq.; E, M to 23rd St.–Ely Ave.; G to 21st St.*

Museum of the Moving Image. Like switching to a widescreen television, the newly renovated Museum of the Moving Image is twice as nice as before. The new Thomas Lesser design includes a three-story addition and a panoramic entrance to this museum full of Hollywood and television memorabilia. Exhibitions range from *Behind the Screen*, which

CLOSE UP

Filmmaking in Astoria

Hollywood may be the king of moviemaking now, but in the early days of sound, Queens was where it was at. In the 1920s such stars as Gloria Swanson, Rudolph Valentino, and Claudette Colbert all acted in one of the more than 100 films made at Astoria Studios. Opened in 1920 by the film company that would become Paramount, "the Big House" was the largest and most important filmmaking studio in the country.

Though Astoria's ideal location provided easy access to Broadway and vaudeville stars, Hollywood's weather soon lured away most studios. Astoria was able to hold its own for a while longer, creating such films as the Marx Brothers classics *The Cocoanuts* and *Animal Crackers*. But in 1942 the studio was sold to the U.S. Army.

It became the Signal Corps Photographic Center, producing training films and documentaries, including Frank's Capra's classic seven-film series *Why We Fight*. The army retained the studio until 1970.

In 1980 the city leased the studio to real-estate developer George S. Kaufman, in partnership with Alan King and Johnny Carson. Kaufman-Astoria Studios, with six stages, is a thriving operation once again, used for television series (*Sesame Street, Law & Order*) as well as movies (*The Wiz, Hair,* and *The Pink Panther*). Although the studio is not open to the public, movie buffs can hope to spot stars at the Studio Café and learn more about the craft next door at the fantastic Museum of the Moving Image.

demonstrates how movies are produced and shot to watching the live editing of Mets baseball games as they happen on SNY. Classic family films are shown as matinees on Saturdays and Sundays, while the museum also has a section devoted to video artists for visitors looking for some culture. Film buffs will love the film retrospectives, lectures, and other special programs. ⊠ *3601 35th Ave., at 37th St., Astoria* 🕾 *718/777–6888* ⊕ *www.movingimage.us* 🎫 *$10; free after 4 on Fri.* ☉ *Wed. and Thurs. 10:30–5, Fri. 11–8, weekends 10:30–7* Ⓜ *R, M to Steinway St.; N to 36th Ave.*

The Noguchi Museum. In 1985 the Japanese-American sculptor Isamu Noguchi (1904–88) transformed this former photo-engraving plant into a place to display his modernist and earlier works. A peaceful central garden is surrounded by gallery buildings, providing room to show more than 250 pieces done in stone, metal, clay, and other materials. Temporary exhibits have featured his collaborations with others, such as industrial designer Isamu Kenmochi. The museum is about a mile from subway stops; check the website for complete directions. On Sunday a shuttle bus leaves from the northeast corner of Park Avenue and 70th Street in Manhattan (in front of the Asia Society) hourly, beginning at 12:30; the round-trip costs $10. ⊠ *9-01 33rd Rd., Long Island City* 🕾 *718/204–7088* ⊕ *www.noguchi.org* 🎫 *$10; 1st Fri. of month, pay what you wish* ☉ *Wed.–Fri. 10–5, weekends 11–6* Ⓜ *N or Q to Broadway.*

Long Island City
and Astoria

WORTH NOTING

SculptureCenter. Founded by artists in 1928 to exhibit innovative contemporary work, SculptureCenter now occupies a former trolley repair shop renovated by artist Maya Lin and architect David Hotson, not far from MoMA PS1. Their indoor and outdoor exhibition spaces sometimes close between shows; call ahead before visiting. ⊠ *4419 Purves St., at Jackson Ave., Long Island City* ☎ *718/361–1750* ⊕ *www. sculpture-center.org* ⊠ *$5 suggested donation* ☉ *Thurs.–Mon. 11–6* Ⓜ *7 to 45th Rd.—Courthouse Sq.; E, M to 23rd St.–Ely Ave.; G to Court Sq.*

☺ **Socrates Sculpture Park.** In 1986 local artist Mark di Suvero and other residents rallied to transform what had been an abandoned landfill and illegal dump site into this 4.5-acre waterfront park devoted to public art. Today a superb view of the river and Manhattan frames changing exhibitions of contemporary sculptures and multimedia installations. Free public programs include art workshops and an annual outdoor film series (July and August, Wednesday evenings). ⊠ *32-01 Vernon Blvd., at Broadway, Long Island City* ☎ *718/956–1819* ⊕ *www. socratessculpturepark.org* ⊠ *Free* ☉ *Daily 10–sunset* Ⓜ *N to Broadway, then walk 8 blocks west or take Q104 bus along Broadway to Vernon Blvd.*

Flushing and Corona

EAST FLUSHING

678

Northern Blvd.

7 M FLUSHING-MAIN ST.

Bowne St.
Robinson St.
Union St.

WILLETS POINT

Spicy and Tasty

Main St.

Kissena Blvd.

FLUSHING

Colden St.

Flushing Bay

25A

Roosevelt Ave.

College Point Blvd.

Queens Botanical Garden

Kissena Corridor Park

678

Booth Memorial Ave.

58th Ave.

Citi Field

7 M METS-WILLETS POINT

Main St.

60th Ave.

25A

Flushing Meadows-Corona Park

495

111th St.

USTA Billie Jean King National Tennis Center

Grand Central Pkwy.

Arthur Ashe Stadium

63rd Ave.

Main St.

Louis Armstrong House Museum

Roosevelt Ave.

World's Fair Unisphere

108th St.

New York Hall of Science

Queens Museum of Art

104th St.

103rd St.

Van Wyck Expwy.

7 M 103RD ST.-CORONA PLAZA

Queens Zoo

Cedar Grove Cemetery

99th St.

National St.

Corona Ave.

Lemon Ice King of Corona

111th St.

Meadow Lake

CORONA

106th St.

678

495

Jewel Ave.

0   1/2 mi

0   1/2 km

JACKSON HEIGHTS

Even in the diverse borough of Queens, Jackson Heights stands out for being a true polycultural neighborhood. In just a few blocks surrounding the three-way intersection of Roosevelt Avenue, 74th Street, and Broadway, you can find shops and restaurants catering to the area's strong Indian, Bangladeshi, Colombian, Mexican, and Ecuadorian communities. Built as a planned "garden community" in the late 1910s, the area boasts many prewar apartments with elaborate block-long interior gardens as well as English-style homes. Celebs who grew up in the area include Lucy Liu and Gene Simmons. It's also the birthplace of the board game Scrabble.

SHOPPING

Patel Brothers. At Patel Brothers let your nose lead your way through the aisles of this Indian grocery store minichain, inhaling the heady scents of rich spices, rare Kesar mangoes, and other exotic produce. Then follow your curiosity through dozens of varieties of lentils and an entire aisle devoted to rice before stocking up on spicy fried snacks and cheap souvenirs for the folks back home. ⊠ *37-27 74th St., near 37th Ave.* ☎ *718/898–3445* M *7 to 74th St.-Broadway.*

Sahil Sari Palace. For special keepsakes, head to Sahil Sari Palace, filled with bolts of colorful silks and ready-to-wear sequined saris. ⊠ *37-39 74th St., between Roosevelt and 37th Aves.* ☎ *718/426–9526* Ⓜ *7 to 74th St.-Broadway.*

FLUSHING AND CORONA

Before it became a part of New York City, Queens was once many small independent townships. So it makes sense that the historic town of Flushing is today a microcosm of a larger city, including a bustling downtown area, fantastic restaurants, and bucolic suburbanlike streets nearby.

Flushing may seem like a strange name for a town, but it's an English adaptation of the original (and hard-to-pronounce) Dutch name Vlissingen. The Dutch named it for a favorite port city in the Netherlands.

Next door, quiet Corona could easily be overlooked, but that would be a mistake. Here are two huge legacies: the music of Satchmo and the cooling simplicity of an Italian ice.

15

TOP ATTRACTIONS

Fodor's Choice
★ **Citi Field.** The Mets are justly proud of their brand-new stadium, designed to hark back to Ebbets Field (where the Dodgers played in Brooklyn) with a brick exterior and plenty of bells and whistles, from a batting cage and wiffle-ball field to the original giant apple taken from the team's old residence, Shea Stadium. The Mets unfortunately christened the stadium in 2009 with a terrible season, but even those who aren't Mets fans and simply love baseball should come to see the Jackie Robinson Rotunda, a soaring multistory entrance and history exhibit dedicated to the Dodgers player who shattered baseball's color barrier. While here, don't miss making a stop at the more-than-fabulous food court behind center field, Shake Shack burgers, surprisingly inexpensive beers such as Czechvar and Leffe, and even lobster rolls and tacos. Though it seats fewer people than Shea by about 10,000, tickets are not hard to come by, especially later in the season. Still feeling nostalgic for the old Shea? Pay your respects at the plaque in the parking lot. ⊠ *Roosevelt Ave. off Grand Central Pkwy.* ☎ *718/507–8499* ⊕ *www. mets.com* Ⓜ *7 to Mets/Willets Point.*

☺ **Flushing Meadows–Corona Park.** Standing in the lush grass of this park, you'd never imagine that it was once a swamp and a dumping ground. But the gleaming Unisphere (an enormous 140-foot-high steel globe) might tip you off that this 1,255-acre park was also the site of two World's Fairs. Take advantage of the park's barbecue pits and sports fields, but also don't forget that there's an art museum, a petting zoo, golf and minigolf, and even a model-plane field. There's way too much to see here to pack into a day, so aim to hit a few primary spots, noting that while several are clustered together on the northwest side of the park, visitors should be prepared for long peaceful walks in between. The flat grounds are ideal for family biking; rent bikes near the park entrance or Meadow Lake from March to October. ■ TIP→ **Although the park is great in daytime, avoid visiting once it gets dark; there has been some crime in this area.** ⊠ *Between 111th St./Grand Central Pkwy. and Van Wyck Expressway at 44th Ave.* Ⓜ *7 to 111th St. or Willets Point.*

New York Hall of Science. At the northwestern edge of Flushing Meadows–Corona Park, the New York Hall of Science has more than 400 hands-on exhibits that make science a playground for inquisitive minds of all ages. Climb aboard a replica of John Glenn's space capsule, throw a fastball and investigate its speed, or explore Charles and Ray Eames's classic Mathematica exhibition. ⊠ *Between 111th St./Grand Central Pkwy. and Van Wyck Expressway at 44th Ave., 47-01 111th St.* ☎ *718/699–0005* ⊕ *www.nysci.org* ✎ *$11; free Fri. 2–5 and Sun. 10–11 Sept.–June* ☉ *Sept.–June, Mon.–Thurs. 9:30–2, Fri. 9:30–5, weekends 10–6; July and Aug., weekdays 9:30–5, weekends 10–6* Ⓜ *7 to 111th St.; walk 3 blocks south.*

Queens Museum of Art. Between the zoo and the Unisphere in Flushing Meadows–Corona Park, you'll find the Queens Museum of Art. Don't miss the astonishing Panorama, a nearly 900,000-building model of NYC made for the 1964 World's Fair. Many unsuspecting park visitors looking for a bathroom instead find themselves spending hours checking out the intricate structures that replicate every block in the city. There are also rotating exhibitions of contemporary art and a permanent collection of Louis Comfort Tiffany stained glass. ⊠ *Between 111th St./Grand Central Pkwy. and Van Wyck Expressway at 44th Ave.* ☎ *718/592–9700* ⊕ *www.queensmuseum.org* ✎ *$5 suggested donation* ☉ *Sept.–June, Wed.–Sun. noon–6; call for extended hrs in July and Aug.* Ⓜ *7 to 111th St. or Willets Point.*

Queens Zoo. Behind the Hall of Science in Flushing Meadows–Corona Park lies the intimate Queens Zoo, whose small scale is especially well suited to easily tired young visitors. In only 11 acres you'll find North American animals such as bears, mountain lions, bald eagles, and pudu—the world's smallest deer. Buckminster Fuller's geodesic dome from the 1964 World's Fair is now the aviary. Across the street is a petting zoo. ⊠ *Between 111th St./Grand Central Pkwy. and Van Wyck Expressway at 44th Ave.* ☎ *718/271–1500* ⊕ *www.queenszoo.com* ✎ *$8* ☉ *Early Apr.–late Oct., weekdays 10–5, weekends 10–5:30; late Oct.–early Apr., daily 10–4:30; last ticket sold 30 mins before closing* Ⓜ *7 to 111th St. or Willets Point.*

USTA Billie Jean King National Tennis Center. Each August, 700,000 fans come here for the U.S. Open, which claims the title of highest-attended annual sporting event in the world. The rest of the year the 45 courts (33 outdoor and 12 indoor, all Deco Turf II) are open to the public for $20–$60 hourly. Make reservations up to two days in advance. ⊠ *Flushing Meadows–Corona Park* ☎ *718/760–6200* ⊕ *www.usta.com* Ⓜ *7 to Willets Point.*

WORTH NOTING

Louis Armstrong House Museum. For the last 28 years of his life the famed jazz musician lived in this modest three-story house in Corona with his wife, Lucille. Take a guided 40-minute tour and note the difference between the rooms vividly decorated by Lucille in charming midcentury style and Louis's dark den, cluttered with phonographs and reel-to-reel tape recorders. Although photographs and family mementos throughout the house impart knowledge about Satchmo's life, it's in

The jungle habitat at the Bronx Zoo will make you forget the surrounding urban jungle.

his den that you'll really understand his spirit. ⊠ *34-56 107th St., at 37th Ave., Corona* ☎ *718/478–8274* ⊕ *www.louisarmstronghouse.org* ⊠ *$8* ⊘ *Tours hourly Tues.–Fri. 10–5, weekends noon–5* Ⓜ *7 to 103rd St.–Corona Plaza.*

NEED A BREAK?
Lemon Ice King of Corona. If you're looking for authentic Queens experiences, there are few as true as eating an Italian ice from the Lemon Ice King of Corona while strolling by a nearby bocce court on a hot summer day. There are no seats and the service can often be gruff at this neighborhood institution of more than 60 years, but none of that will matter after your first taste. And yes, there are plenty of other flavors other than lemon. ⊠ *52-02 108th St., at 52nd St., Queens, Corona* ☎ *718/699–5133* ⊕ *thelemonicekingofcorona.com* Ⓜ *7 to 103rd St.–Corona Plaza.*

THE BRONX

The Bronx is the city's most maligned and misunderstood borough. Its reputation as a gritty, down-and-out place is a little outdated, and there's lots of beauty to be found, if you know where to look. There is more parkland in the Bronx than any other borough, as well as one of the world's finest botanical collections, the largest metropolitan zoo in the country, and, of course, Yankee Stadium, The Bronx does cover a large area, though, so the attractions are spread out. Whether you're relaxing at a ball game or scoping out exotic species at the zoo, there's plenty of fun to be had here.

TOP ATTRACTIONS

The Bronx Zoo. When it opened its gates in 1899, the Bronx Zoo had only 843 animals. But today, with 265 acres and more than 4,000 animals (of more than 600 species), it's the largest metropolitan zoo in the United States. Get up close and personal with exotic creatures in outdoor settings that re-create natural habitats; you're often separated from them by no more than a moat or wall of glass. Don't miss the **Congo Gorilla Forest** (✉ $5) a 6½-acre re-creation of a lush African rain forest with two troops of lowland gorillas, as well as white-bearded DeBrazza's monkeys, okapis, and red river hogs. At **Tiger Mountain** an open viewing shelter lets you get incredibly close to Siberian tigers, who frolic in a pool, lounge outside (even in cold weather), and enjoy daily "enrichment sessions" with keepers. As the big cats are often napping at midday, aim to visit in the morning or evening. In the new $62 million exhibit **Madagascar!**, the formality of the old Lion House has been replaced with a verdant re-creation of one of the most threatened natural habitats in the world. Here you'll see adorable lemurs and far-from-adorable hissing cockroaches.

Go on a minisafari via the **Wild Asia Monorail** (✉ $4), open May–October, weather permitting. As you wend your way through the forest, see Asian elephants, Indo-Chinese tigers, Indian rhinoceroses, gaur (the world's largest cattle), Mongolian wild horses, and several deer and antelope species. ■TIP→ Try to visit the most popular exhibits, such as Congo Gorilla Forest, early to avoid lines later in the day. In winter the outdoor exhibitions have fewer animals on view, but there are also fewer crowds, and plenty of indoor exhibits to savor. From mid-November to January 1 the zoo is decorated with holiday lights and open until 9 pm. ✉ *2300 Southern Blvd., Fordham* ☎ *718/367–1010* ⊕ *www.bronxzoo.com* ✉ *$16; extra charge for some exhibits; free Wed., donation suggested; parking $13* ☼ *Apr.–Oct., weekdays 10–5, weekends 10–5:30; Nov.–Mar., daily 10–4:30; last ticket sold 30 mins before closing* Ⓜ *2, 5 to E. Tremont/West Farms, then walk 2 blocks up Boston Rd. to zoo's Asia entrance; Bx11 express bus to Bronx River entrance.*

The New York Botanical Garden. Considered one of the leading botany centers of the world, this 250-acre garden is one of the best reasons to make a trip to the Bronx. Built around the dramatic gorge of the Bronx River, the Garden offers lush indoor and outdoor gardens, and acres of natural forest, as well as classes, concerts, and special exhibits. Be astounded by the captivating fragrance of the Peggy Rockefeller Rose Garden's 2,700 plants of more than 250 varieties; see intricate orchids that look like the stuff of science fiction; relax in the quiet of the forest or the calm of the Conservatory; or take a jaunt through the Everett Children's Adventure Garden: a 12-acre, indoor-outdoor museum with a boulder maze, giant animal topiaries, and a plant discovery center.

The Garden's roses bloom in June and September, but there's plenty to see year-round. The Victorian-style **Enid A. Haupt Conservatory** (✉ *$20, part of the Combination Ticket*) houses re-creations of misty tropical rain forests and arid African and North American deserts as well as exhibitions, such as the annual Holiday Train Show and the Orchid Show. The **Combination Ticket** (✉ *$20*) gives you access to the

The New York
Botanical Garden
and Bronx Zoo

Conservatory, Rock Garden, Native Plant Garden, Tram Tour, Everett
Children's Adventure Garden, and exhibits in the library.

The most direct way to the Garden is via **Metro-North Railroad**
(⊕ *www.mta.info/mnr*) from Grand Central Terminal (Harlem Local
Line, Botanical Garden stop). Round-trip tickets are $10.50 to $14,
depending on time of day. A cheaper alternative is to take the D or
4 train to Bedford Park Boulevard, then walk east. ⊠ *2900 Southern
Blvd., Bedford Park* ☎ *718/817–8700* ⊕ *www.nybg.org* ✉ *Grounds
only $6, free Sat. 10–noon and all day Wed.; All-Garden Pass $20;
parking $12* ⊙ *Tues.–Sun. 10–6* Ⓜ *B, D, 4 to Bedford Park Blvd.,
then walk 8 blocks downhill to the garden; Metro-North to Botanical Garden.*

Fodor's Choice **Yankee Stadium.** Fans are still mourning the original, legendary Yankee
★ Stadium, which saw its last season in 2008. Though the team is still
breaking it in, the new Yankee Stadium—right next to the House that
Ruth Built—has gotten off to a good start, with the Yankees winning
the World Series in its inaugural year. Tickets can be ridiculously expensive, but the experience is like watching baseball in Las Vegas's Bellagio
hotel. Meaning, it's incredibly opulent and over-the-top: traditional
white frieze adorns the stadium's top; inside, limestone-and-marble
hallways are lined with photos of past Yankee greats; lower-level seats

have cushions, cup holders, and a boffo meatery, NYY Steak. Like the team, all the amenities don't come cheap. But the spirit of the original still remains. History buffs and hard-core fans should be sure to visit Monument Park, with plaques of past team members, by Center Field—it survived from the old stadium. Aside from the subway, you can also get here by Metro-North, to the Yankees–153rd Street Station. ✉ *River Ave. at 161st St., South Bronx* 🕾 *718/293–6000* ⊕ *www.yankees.com* Ⓜ *B (weekdays only), D, or 4 to 161st St.–Yankee Stadium.*

WORTH NOTING

OFF THE
BEATEN
PATH

Wave Hill. Drawn by stunning views of the Hudson River and New Jersey's dramatic cliffs, 19th-century Manhattan millionaires built summer homes in the Bronx suburb of Riverdale. One of the most magnificent, Wave Hill, is now a 28-acre public garden and cultural center that attracts green thumbs from all over the world. Along with exquisite gardens, grand beech and oak trees adorn wide lawns, an elegant pergola overlooks the majestic river view, and benches on curving pathways provide quiet respite. Wave Hill House (1843) and Glyndor House (1927) now house art exhibitions, Sunday concerts, and gardening workshops. Even England's queen stayed here during a visit. It's worth the schlep. ✉ *Independence Ave. at W. 249th St., Riverdale* 🕾 *718/549–3200* ⊕ *www.wavehill.org* 💲*$6; free Tues. and Sat. mornings* ⊙ *Mid-Apr.–mid-Oct., Tues.–Sun. 9–5:30; mid-Oct.–mid-Apr., Tues.–Sun. 9–4:30; closed Mon. except holidays. Free garden tours Sun. at 2* Ⓜ *1 to 231st St., then Bx7 or Bx10 bus to 252nd St. and Riverdale Ave. or free van service hourly from W. 242nd St. station between 9:10 am and 4:10 pm.*

ARTHUR AVENUE (BELMONT)

Arthur Avenue (Belmont). Manhattan's Little Italy is sadly overrun with mediocre restaurants aimed at tourists, but Belmont, the Little Italy of the Bronx, is a real, thriving Italian-American community. Unless you have family in the area, the main reason to come here is for the food: eating it, buying it, looking at it fondly through windows. A secondary, but just as important, reason is chatting with shopkeepers so you can steal their recipes.

Nearly a century after pushcarts on Arthur Avenue catered to Italian-American workers constructing the zoo and Botanical Garden, the area teems with meat markets, bakeries, and cheese makers. There are long debates about which store or restaurant is the "best," but thanks to generations of Italian grandmothers, vendors here wouldn't dare offer anything less than superfresh, handmade foods.

Although the area is no longer solely Italian—many Latinos and Albanians share this neighborhood now—Italians dominate the food scene. Regulars mostly shop on Saturday afternoon; you'll find many stores shuttered on Sunday and after 6 pm. ✉ *Arthur Ave. between Crescent Ave./E. 184th St. and E. 188th Sts., and 187th St. from Lorillard Pl. to Hughes Ave.* ⊕ *www.arthuravenuebronx.com/* Ⓜ *B, D, 4 to Fordham Rd., then Bx12 east; 2, 5 to Pelham Pkwy., then Bx12 west.*

SHOPPING

Arthur Avenue Retail Market. The covered Arthur Avenue Retail Market, which houses more than a dozen vendors, was opened by Mayor Fiorello LaGuardia in an effort to get the pushcarts off the crowded streets. Inside, you'll find great sandwiches and pizza, barrels of olives, a butcher specializing in offal, and lots of fresh pastas. Cigars are rolled by hand right at the building's entrance, alongside Italian gifts and kitchenware. It's open Monday through Saturday 6–6. ✉ *2344 Arthur Ave., at E. 187th St.* ☎ *718/367–5686* ⊕ *www.arthuravenuebronx.com/* Ⓜ *B, D, 4 to Fordham Rd., then 15-min walk or Bx12 east.*

Borgatti's Ravioli & Egg Noodles. Let an Italian nonna (grandmother) sell you homemade fresh pastas of every kind, shape, and flavor at Borgatti's Ravioli & Egg Noodles. It's closed all day Monday and Sunday afternoon, and frequently has shorter hours in summer. ✉ *632 E. 187th St., between Belmont and Hughes Aves.* ☎ *718/367–3799* ⊕ *borgattis. com/ravioli/index.php.*

Calabria Pork Store. Don't miss the porcine spectacle of Calabria Pork Store, where a forest of house-aged salamis dangles thickly from the rafters. ✉ *2338 Arthur Ave., between 186th St. and Crescent Ave.* ☎ *718/367–5145.*

Calandra Cheese. At Calandra Cheese bulbous spheres of freshly made cheese hang from the ceiling. Go for the *cacciocavallo*—a dry, salty mozzarella—or the clean-tasting ricotta. ✉ *2314 Arthur Ave., between 186th St. and Crescent Ave.* ☎ *718/365–7572.*

Madonia Brothers Bakery. The brick ovens at Madonia Brothers Bakery have been turning out golden-brown loaves since 1918, but the true stars are fresh, crispy cannoli, filled only when you order, with not-too-sweet ricotta cream. ✉ *2348 Arthur Ave., at 187th St.* ☎ *718/295–5573.*

Teitel Brothers. At Teitel Brothers, grab a number and stand elbow-to-elbow with locals buying pungent olives, hulking hunks of hard cheeses, pounds of dried beans, and gallons of olive oil. ✉ *2372 Arthur Ave., at E. 186th St.* ☎ *718/733–9400* ⊕ *teitelbros.com/.*

15

STATEN ISLAND

Legally part of New York City, Staten Island is in many ways a world apart. The "Forgotten Borough," as some locals refer to it, is geographically more separate, less populous, politically more conservative, and ethnically more homogeneous than the rest of the city.

Still, it's full of surprises. Along with suburban sprawl, there are wonderful small museums, including a premier collection of Tibetan art, to walkable woodlands, and a historic village replicating New York's rural past. And for a view of the skyline and the Statue of Liberty, nothing beats the 25-minute free ferry trip to Staten Island. To explore the borough, take the Staten Island Ferry from the southern tip of Manhattan. After you disembark, grab an S40 bus to the **Snug Harbor Cultural Center** (about 10 minutes) or take the S74 and combine visits to the **Tibetan Museum** and **Historic Richmond Town.**

TOP ATTRACTIONS

Historic Richmond Town. Think of Virginia's Colonial Williamsburg (the
Fodor'sChoice polar opposite of Brooklyn's scene-y Williamsburg), and you'll under-
★ stand the appeal of Richmond Town. This 100-acre village, constructed
from 1695 to the 19th century, was the site of Staten Island's original
county seat. Fifteen of the site's 27 historic buildings are open to the
public. Highlights include the Gothic Revival **Courthouse,** the one-room
General Store, and the **Voorlezer's House,** one of the oldest buildings on
the site. It served as a residence, a place of worship, and an elementary
school. Also on-site is the **Staten Island Historical Society Museum,**
built in 1848 as the second county clerk's and surrogate's office, which
now houses Staten Island artifacts plus changing exhibits about the
island. Audio tours are free with admission.

You may see staff in period dress demonstrate Early American crafts
and trades such as tinsmithing or basket making, though the general
era meant to be re-created is 1820–1860. December brings a monthlong
Christmas celebration. Take the S74–Richmond Road bus (30 minutes)
or a car service (about $15) from the ferry terminal. ⊠ *441 Clarke Ave.,
Richmondtown* ☎ *718/351–1611* ⊕ *www.historicrichmondtown.org*
🎟 *$8* ☉ *July and Aug., Wed.–Sun. 11–5; Sept.–June, Wed.–Sun. 1–5*
Ⓜ *S74 bus to St. Patrick's Pl.*

LIFE RING BUOY
WITH LINE

Jacques Marchais Museum of Tibetan Art. At the top of a hill sits this replica of a Tibetan monastery containing one of the largest collections of Tibetan and Himalayan sculpture, paintings, and artifacts outside Tibet. Meditate with visiting Buddhist monks, or just enjoy the peaceful views from the terraced garden. ⊠ *338 Lighthouse Ave., Richmondtown* ☎ *718/987–3500* ⊕ *www.tibetanmuseum.org* 🖃 *$6* ☉ *Thurs.–Sun. 1–5* Ⓜ *S74 bus to Lighthouse Ave. and walk uphill 15 mins.*

WORTH NOTING

★ **Snug Harbor Cultural Center and Botanical Garden.** Once part of a sprawling farm, this 83-acre community is now a popular spot to see maritime art, frolic in the **Children's Museum**, or take a stroll through lush gardens.

Made up of 26 mostly restored historic buildings, Snug Harbor's center is a row of mid-19th-century Greek Revival temples. Main Hall—the oldest building on the property—is home to the **Eleanor Proske Visitors Center** (🖃 *$3, including Newhouse Center*), which has exhibits on art and Snug Harbor's history. The adjacent **Newhouse Center for Contemporary Art** (☎ 718/425–3524 🖃 *$3, including visitor center*) shows multidisciplinary videos, mixed media, and performances. Next door at the **Noble Maritime Collection** (☎ 718/447–6490 ⊕ *www. noblemaritime.org* 🖃 *$5*) an old seamen's dormitory is now a museum of ocean-inspired artwork.

From the Staten Island Ferry terminal, take the S40 bus 2 mi (about seven minutes) to the Snug Harbor Road stop. Or grab a car service at the ferry terminal. (The ride should cost you about $5.)

Staten Island Children's Museum. The Staten Island Children's Museum has five galleries with hands-on exhibits introducing such topics as insects, great explorations, and storytelling. Portia's Playhouse, an interactive children's theater, invites youngsters to step up to the stage and try on costumes. Ladder 11 is a thrill for firefighter fans. ☎ *718/273–2060* ⊕ *www.statenislandkids.org* 🖃 *$6* ☉ *School year, Tues.–Fri. noon–5, weekends 10–5; in summer until 8 on Thurs.*

Staten Island Botanical Garden. Spread over the cultural center grounds is the Staten Island Botanical Garden, which includes an orchid collection, 9/11 memorial, 20-acre wetland, Chinese Scholar's Garden, and a sensory garden with fragrant, touchable flowers and a tinkling waterfall. Children love the Connie Gretz Secret Garden with its castle and maze among the flowers. ☎ *718/448–2500* ⊕ *www.snug-harbor. org* 🖃 *Free; $5 for Chinese Garden and Secret Garden* ☉ *Daily dawn–dusk; Chinese Garden and Secret Garden Apr.–Sept., Tues.–Sun. 10–5; Oct.–Mar., Tues.–Sun. noon–4* ⊠ *1000 Richmond Terr., between Snug Harbor Rd. and Tyson Ave., Livingston* ☎ *718/448–2500* ⊕ *www.snug-harbor.org* 🖃 *$3; gardens and galleries combined $6; Cultural Center grounds free* ☉ *Tues.–Sun. 10–5; Noble Maritime Thurs.–Sun. 10–5; grounds dawn–dusk every day except major holidays.*

The Performing Arts

WORD OF MOUTH

"Seating is personal preference and does depend on the theater.
I like aisle seats best and will always opt for one if it's available.
For a musical, often first few rows of the mezzanine is better than
back of the orchestra but try to get as close to the center of the
theater as possible (not on extreme sides)."

—mclaurie

Updated by
Lynne Arany

"Where do you wait tables?" is the not-so-ironic question New York performers get when they say they're in the arts. But even more telling is that most of these toughened artists won't miss a beat when they respond with the restaurant's name. Fact is, if you're an aspiring performer here, you'd better be tough and competitive. There is a constant influx of artists from around the globe, and all these actors, singers, dancers, and musicians striving for their big break infuse the city with a crackling creative energy.

Just as tough are the audiences, many out-of-towners, many discerning local patrons, who help drive the arts scene as they thrive on keeping up with the latest—flocking to a concert hall to hear a world-class soprano deliver a flawless performance, then crowding into a cramped café to support young writers floundering through their own prose.

New York has somewhere between 200 and 250 legitimate theaters (meaning those with theatrical performances, not movies or strip shows), and many more ad hoc venues—parks, churches, lofts, galleries, rooftops, even parking lots. The city is also a revolving door of special events: summer jazz, one-act-play marathons, film festivals, and music and dance celebrations from the classical to the avant-garde, to name just a few. It's this unrivaled wealth of culture and art that many New Yorkers cite as the reason why they're here, and the reason why many millions more say they're visiting here.

BUYING TICKETS AT FULL PRICE

What do tickets sell for, anyway? Not counting the limited "premium seat" category (or discount deals), the top ticket price for Broadway musicals is now hovering at $136; the low end for musicals is in the $50 range. Nonmusical comedies and dramas start at about $70 and top out at about $120. Off Broadway show tickets average $50–$90, and off off Broadway shows can run as low as $15–$25. Tickets to an opera start at about $25 for nosebleed seats and can soar close to $400 for prime locations. Classical music concerts go for $25 to $100 or more, depending on the venue. Dance performances are usually in the $15 to $60 range, but expect seats for the ballet in choice spots to cost more.

Scoring tickets is fairly easy, especially if you have some flexibility. But if timing or cost is critical, the only way to ensure you'll get the seats you want is to make your purchase in advance—and that might be months ahead for a hit show. In general, tickets for Saturday evening and for weekend matinees are the toughest to secure.

For opera, classical music, and dance performances, go to the box office or order tickets through the venue's website.

For smaller performing-arts companies, and especially for Off Broadway shows, try **Ticket Central** (✉ *416 W. 42nd St., between 9th and 10th Aves., Midtown West* ☎ *212/279–4200* ⊕ *www.ticketcentral.com* ☉ *Daily noon–8* Ⓜ *A, C, E to 42nd St.*), which is right in the center of Theater Row; service charges are nominal here. **SmartTix** (☎ *212/868–4444* ⊕ *www.smarttix.com*) is a reliable resource for (usually) smaller performing-arts companies, including dance and music; their service charges are nominal as well.

Inside the Times Square Information Center is the **Broadway Concierge and Ticket Center** (✉ *1560 Broadway, between W. 46th and W. 47th Sts., Midtown West* ☎ *888/broadway* ⊕ *www.livebroadway.com* ☉ *Tickets: Mon.–Sat. 9–7, Sun. 10–6* Ⓜ *1, 2, 3, 7, N, Q, R, S to 42nd St./Times Sq.; N, R to 49th St.*), where you can purchase full- and premium-price tickets for most Broadway (and some Off Broadway) shows.

Sure bets for Broadway (and some other big-hall events) are the box office or either **Telecharge** (☎ *212/239–6200, 800/432–7250 outside NYC* ⊕ *www.telecharge.com*) or **Ticketmaster** (☎ *212/307–4100, 866/448–7849 automated service, 212/220–0500 premium tickets* ⊕ *www.ticketmaster.com*). Virtually all larger shows are listed with one service or the other, but never both; specifying "premium" will help you get elusive—and expensive (upward of $200–$350)—seats. A broker or your hotel concierge should be able to procure last-minute tickets, but prices may even exceed "premium" rates. Be prepared to pay steep add-on fees (per ticket *and* per order) for all ticketing services.

■ **TIP →** Although most online ticket services provide seating maps to help you choose, the advantage of going to the box office is twofold: there are no add-on service fees, and a ticket seller can personally advise you about sight lines—and knee room—for the seat location you are considering. Broadway box offices do not usually have direct phone lines; their walk-in hours are generally 10 am until curtain.

BUYING DISCOUNT TICKETS

The cheapest—though chanciest—ticket opportunities are found at participating theater box offices on the day of the performance. These rush tickets, usually about $25, may be distributed by lottery and are usually for front-row (possibly neck-craning) seats. Check the comprehensive planner on ⊕ *www.nytix.com* or go to the box office of the show you are interested in to discover whether they have such an offer and how to pursue it. Obstructed-view seats or those in the very rear balcony

16

Best Tips for Broadway

Whether you're handing over a hundred bucks for a top ticket or shoestringing it in a nosebleed seat, seeing one show or seven, you'll have better Broadway experiences to brag about if you take our advice.

Do your homework. Remember— your friends' "must-see" may not be yours. If you're new to theater, or not a regular, try to discover Broadway for yourself. Subscribe to online services ahead of your trip; you'll get access to show synopses, special ticket offers, and more. If it's a classic play, like Shakespeare, you might enjoy it more if you read it before you go.

Reserve ahead. The TKTS booth is great if you're up for what the fates make available, but for must-sees, book early. While you're at it, ask whether the regular cast is expected. (An in-person stop at the box office is the most reliable way to score this information, but don't hold them to it unless it's the day of performance. If there is a change then—and the replacement cast is not acceptable to you—you may get a refund.) For musicals, live music will always add a special zing; confirm when ticketing to avoid surprises on the rare occasion when recorded music is used.

Check theater seating charts. Front mezzanine is a great option; with seats that overhang the stage, they can be better (though not always less expensive) than many orchestra locations. Always book with a seating chart at hand (available online and at the box office); although even the priciest seats might be tight, it is always worth splurging for the best sight lines. Check accessibility, especially at older theaters with multiple flights of stairs and scarce elevators.

Know when to go. Surprisingly, Friday evening is a good option; Saturday night and weekday matinees are the most difficult. Do as the locals do and go on weeknights. Tuesday is especially promising, and typically an earlier curtain—7 or 7:30 instead of the usual 8 pm—helps ensure that you'll get a good night's sleep for your next day of touring.

Dress right. You can easily throw on jeans to go to the theater these days, but personally we feel Bermuda shorts have no place on Broadway. Bring binoculars if your seats are up high, leave behind the heavy coat (coat checks are *not* the norm), and drop packages off at your hotel room in advance.

Travel smart. Trying to get to the show in time? Unless you don't mind watching the meter run up while you're stuck in traffic, avoid cabs into or out of Times Square. The pre- and post-theater crush will render Broadway virtually unwalkable, but that said, walk, especially if you're within 10 blocks of the theater. Otherwise, take the subway.

Dine off Broadway. Dining well on a budget and doing Broadway right are not mutually exclusive notions. Key is avoiding the temptation to eat in Times Square proper—even the national chains are overpriced. Consider instead supping in whatever neighborhood you're touring that day. Or, if you're already in Midtown, head west of the district to 9th Avenue. That's where many actors and other theater folk actually live, and you never know who you'll see on the street or at the next table. Prix-fixe deals and ethnic eateries are plentiful.

are sometimes available for advance purchase; the price point on these is usually in the $35–$40 range.

But for advanced discount purchases, the best seating is likely available by using a discount "code"—procure these codes, good for 20% to 50% off, online. (You will need to register on each website.) The excellent no-subscription-required ⊕ *www.broadwaybox.com* site is comprehensive and posts all discount codes currently available for Broadway shows. As with all discount codes offered through online subscriber services—**TheaterMania** (⊕ *www.theatermania.com*), **Playbill** (⊕ *www.playbill.com*), and **Best of Off Broadway** (⊕ *bestofoffbroadway. com*) among them—to avoid service charges, you must bring a printout of the offer to the box office, and make your purchase there.

For seats at 25%–50% off the usual price, go to one of the **TKTS booths** (⊠ *Father Duffy Sq., W. 47th St. and Broadway, Midtown West* Ⓜ *1, 2, 3, 7, N, Q, R, S, W to 42nd St./Times Sq.; N, R, W to 49th St.; 1 to 50th St.* ⊠ *South St. Seaport, Front and John Sts., Lower Manhattan* Ⓜ *2, 3, 4, 5, A, C, E, J, M, Z to Fulton St./Broadway–Nassau* ⊠ *Downtown Brooklyn, at the Myrtle St. Promenade and Jay St., Brooklyn* Ⓜ *A, C, F to Jay St.–Borough Hall; R, 2, 3, 4, 5 to Court St.–Borough Hall* ⊕ *www.tdf.org*). Although they do tack on a $4-per-ticket service charge, and not all shows are predictably available, the broad choices and ease of selection—and of course, the solid discount—make TKTS the go-to source for the flexible theatergoer. Check the electronic listings board near the ticket windows to mull over your options while you're in line. At the spiffed-up Duffy Square location (look for the red glass staircase), there is a separate *"Play Express"* window (for nonmusical events) to further simplify—and speed—things. Duffy hours are Monday and Wednesday–Saturday 3–8, and Tuesday 2–8 (for evening performances); for Wednesday and Saturday matinees 10–2; for Sunday matinees 11–3; Sunday evening shows, from 3 until a half hour before curtain. Seaport hours are Monday–Saturday 11–6, Sunday 11–4. Brooklyn hours are Tuesday–Saturday 11–6. With the exception of matinee tickets at the Seaport and Brooklyn locations, which sell these for next-day performances only, all shows offered are for that same day. Credit cards, cash, or traveler's checks are accepted *at all locations.*

■ TIP→ Planning ahead? The TKTS website lists what was available at the booths in the previous week to give you an idea of what shows you'll find. Note: Ticket-booth hours may vary over holiday periods.

LOWER MANHATTAN

FINANCIAL DISTRICT
MUSIC
WFC Winter Garden. Count on the WFC Winter Garden for an inspired array of musical events from gospel to site-specific sonic installations—and a little theater, dance, and film as well—all presented within its spectacular crystal-encased atrium or on its outdoor plaza. It's all free, and all befitting the incomparable setting overlooking the Hudson. ⊠ *World Financial Center, West St., between Vesey and Liberty Sts., Financial*

District ☎ *212/945–0505* ⊕ *www.artsworldfinancialcenter.com* Ⓜ *E to World Trade Center; 1 to Rector St.*

READINGS AND LECTURES

Poets House. Having settled into a new home hard by the Hudson in 2009, Poets House finally has a setting that rises to its theme: it is an open resource for all ages, one that offers a huge library and readings and events that exalt the art of poetry. ✉ *10 River Terr., at Murray St., Battery Park City, Financial District* ☎ *212/431–7920* ⊕ *www. poetshouse.org* Ⓜ *E to World Trade Center; 1, 2, 3 to Chambers St.*

TRIBECA

MUSIC

☺ **Tribeca Performing Arts Center.** The Tribeca Performing Arts Center celebrates theater (with a clever children's series) and dance, but more so, jazz in all its forms. Highlights in Jazz and Lost Jazz Shrines are two of its special series. ✉ *199 Chambers St., at Greewich St., TriBeCa* ☎ *212/ 220–1459* ⊕ *www.tribecapac.org* Ⓜ *1, 2, 3 to Chambers St.*

PERFORMANCE CENTER

92YTribeca. The film and reading programs at 92YTribeca, a branch of the 92nd Street Y, are intended to appeal to a 20- to 30-ish set, but visitors of all ages will find something to their liking in the extensive daytime and evening lineups. Film series emphasize participation, with directors often on hand for post-film Q&A, and strive for fresh concepts, with the likes of Closely Watched Films (classics revisited) and a late-night sing-along series. Readings and talks can be equally eclectic, with topics like American Media & the Green Movement to JewBu: Exploring Jewish Dharma, and themes from the arts, food, and technology. ✉ *200 Hudson St., at Canal St., TriBeCa* ☎ *212/601–1000* ⊕ *www.92y.org/92yTribeca* Ⓜ *1, E to Canal St.*

READINGS AND LECTURES

The Jerome L. Greene Performance Space (the Greene Space). Local favorite WNYC Radio invites the public into its intimate (125 seats), technologically forward-thinking digs, the Jerome L. Greene Performance Space (the Greene Space). Live shows—music, audio theater, interviews—match its renowned, and equally forward-thinking, on-air programming. ✉ *44 Charlton St., at Varick St., TriBeCa* ☎ *646/829–4000* ⊕ *www.thegreenespace.org* Ⓜ *C, E to Spring St.; 1 to Houston St. or Canal St.*

SOHO

FILM

Angelika Film Center. Foreign, independent, and, some mainstream films are screened at the Angelika Film Center. Despite its (six) tunnel-like theaters, small screens, and the occasionally audible subway rumble below, it's usually packed; get a snack at their café while you wait for your movie to be called. ✉ *18 W. Houston St., at Mercer St., Greenwich Village* ☎ *212/995–2570* ⊕ *www.angelikafilmcenter.com* Ⓜ *B, D, F, M to Broadway–Lafayette St.; 6 to Bleecker St.*

The Tribeca Film Festival brings celebrities out to the red carpet but plenty of "regular" people get tickets, too.

READINGS AND LECTURES

Housing Works Used Book Café. Amid its collection of 45,000 titles for sale, the Housing Works Used Book Café sponsors readings—often by breakout local authors or from books on social issues—and a monthly acoustic music series. Events at this cozy nonprofit benefit homeless people with HIV/AIDS. ✉ *126 Crosby St., between E. Houston and Prince Sts., SoHo* ☎ *212/334–3324* ⊕ *www.housingworksbookstore. com/* Ⓜ *R, W to Prince St.; B, D, F, M to Broadway–Lafayette St.; 6 to Bleecker St.*

THEATER

HERE Arts Center. The HERE Arts Center, the original home of Eve Ensler's 1997 Obie winner *The Vagina Monologues*, 2007's lauded *Removable Parts*, and all manner of genre-bending productions, also has an art gallery and café. ✉ *145 6th Ave., between Spring and Broome Sts., SoHo* ☎ *212/352–3101 tickets* ⊕ *www.here.org* Ⓜ *C, E to Spring St.*

EAST VILLAGE AND LOWER EAST SIDE

EAST VILLAGE
FILM
Anthology Film Archives. Dedicated to preserving and exhibiting independent and avant-garde film, Anthology Film Archives comprises a film repository and two gemlike screening rooms in a renovated redbrick courthouse. Committed cinephiles make their way here for hard-to-find films and videos. The Essential Cinema series delves into the works of filmmakers from Stan Brakhage and Charles Ludlam to Robert

Bresson and Jean Cocteau. ⊠ *32 2nd Ave., at E. 2nd St., East Village* ☎ *212/505–5181* ⊕ *anthologyfilmarchives.org* Ⓜ *F, V to 2nd Ave.*

Village East Cinema. The Village East Cinema, with programming more on the indie side than that of its SoHo sister the Angelika, is housed in a former Yiddish theater that was restored and converted to a six-screen multiplex. Catch a film that's screening in the original theater space upstairs (you can call ahead to find out); its Moorish Revival–style decor, domed ceiling, and grand chandelier are best appreciated from the balcony. ⊠ *181–189 2nd Ave., at E. 12th St., East Village* ☎ *212/529–6799* ⊕ *www.villageeastcinema.com* Ⓜ *6 to Astor Pl.; L to 1st Ave.*

READINGS AND LECTURES

Nuyorican Poets Café. The reigning arbiter of poetry slams, the Nuyorican Poets Café schedules open-mike events, most often on Wednesday night, and hosts the influential granddaddy (b. 1989) of the current spoken-word scene, the Friday Night Poetry Slam. ⊠ *236 E. 3rd St., between Aves. B and C, East Village* ☎ *212/780–9386* ⊕ *www.nuyorican.org* Ⓜ *F, M to 2nd Ave.*

The Poetry Project. The Poetry Project had its start in 1966, and has been a source of sustenance for poets (and their audiences) ever since. This is where Allen Ginsberg, Amiri Baraka, and Sam Shepard first found their voices, and where you're likely to find folks of the same caliber today. Prime times: Monday, Wednesday, and Friday. ⊠ *St. Mark's Church in-the-Bowery, 131 E. 10th St., at 2nd Ave., East Village* ☎ *212/674–0910* ⊕ *poetryproject.org* Ⓜ *6 to Astor Pl.*

THEATER

Classic Stage Company. At the cozy 178-seat theater belonging to the Classic Stage Company you can see excellent literary revivals—such as Chekhov's *Three Sisters* or Shakespeare's *The Tempest*—perhaps with a modern spin, and often with reigning theatrical stars. ⊠ *136 E. 13th St., between 3rd and 4th Aves., East Village* ☎ *212/677–4210, 212/352–3101, 866/811–4111 tickets* ⊕ *www.classicstage.org* Ⓜ *4, 5, 6, L, N, Q, R to Union Sq.*

La MaMa E.T.C. Ellen Stewart, also known as La Mama, founded La MaMa E.T.C. in a small basement space in 1961. It's grown now, and her influential Experimental Theater Club continues to support new works that cross cultures and performance disciplines. ⊠ *74A E. 4th St., between Bowery and 2nd Ave., East Village* ☎ *212/475–7710* ⊕ *lamama.org* Ⓜ *F to 2nd Ave.; B, D, F, M to Broadway–Lafayette St.; 6 to Bleecker St.*

New York Theater Workshop (NYTW). The New York Theater Workshop (NYTW) produces work by new and established playwrights. Jonathan Larson's *Rent* got its pre-Broadway start here, and current works by Tony Kushner (*Homebody/Kabul*), Caryl Churchill, and Paul Rudnick are staged. Hit the box office for Sunday night CheapTix; those seats are $20—in cash, in advance only—as available. ⊠ *79 E. 4th St., between Bowery and 2nd Ave., East Village* ☎ *212/460–5475, 212/780–9037 tickets* ⊕ *www.nytw.org* Ⓜ *F, M to 2nd Ave.; B, D, F, M to Broadway–Lafayette St.; 6 to Bleecker St.*

★ **Performance Space 122 (P.S. 122).** Performance Space 122 (P.S. 122) became a launching pad for now well-recognized talent like Karen Finley, Spalding Gray, Ann Magnuson, and Eric Bogosian back in the day, and continues to offer a dazzling repertoire of performance from the fringe. Their Avant-Garde-Arama! festival has drawn crowds since the nonprofit's founding in 1980. ⊠ *150 1st Ave., at E. 9th St., East Village* ☎ *212/477–5829 tickets* ⊕ *www.ps122.org* Ⓜ *6 to Astor Pl.*

The Public Theater. The Public Theater presents fresh theater such as the 2010 six-hour F. Scott Fitzgerald marathon, *Gatz*, a 2008 Stephen Sondheim debut, *and* the latest work of Suzan-Lori Parks. Many noted productions that began here (*Hair, A Chorus Line*) went on to Broadway. Go to the Public's box office one hour before curtain to snag limited-availability $20 rush standby tickets (two tickets max; cash only). In summer you won't want to miss their incomparable—and free—Shakespeare in the Park performances, which are held at the Delacorte Theatre in Central Park. Although you can stand in line for hours—and still not get a ticket voucher—the easiest way to score these scarce tickets is to register online with their "virtual line" after midnight on the night before the performance you would like to attend; an email response confirms (or denies) success. ⊠ *425 Lafayette St., south of Astor Pl., East Village* ☎ *212/539–8500, 212/967–7555 tickets* ⊕ *www.publictheater. org* Ⓜ *6 to Astor Pl.; R to 8th St.*

Theater for the New City. A four-theater cultural complex, Theater for the New City stages short runs of shows by new and emerging American playwrights. Favorite longtime troupers and presenters of seriously giant puppets (upward of 12 feet is typical), the 1960s NYC-rooted, and still seriously political, Bread & Puppet Theater put in an annual appearance as well. ⊠ *155 1st Ave., between E. 9th and E. 10th Sts., East Village* ☎ *212/254–1109* ⊕ *www.theaterforthenewcity.net* Ⓜ *6 to Astor Pl.*

LOWER EAST SIDE

FILM

Sunshine Cinema. With vestiges of its life as a vaudeville theater all but gone, the Sunshine Cinema, with its five decent-size screens, is the neighborhood go-to for a mix of art-house and smaller-release mainstream films. ⊠ *143 E. Houston St., between 1st and 2nd Aves., Lower East Side* ☎ *212/330–8182* ⊕ *www.landmarktheatres.com* Ⓜ *F, M to 2nd Ave.*

READINGS AND LECTURES

Fodor's Choice
★

The Bowery Poetry Club. "Poetry Czar" Bob Holman's The Bowery Poetry Club serves up coffee and comestibles along with its ingenious poetry events. Expect slams and every other permutation of the spoken word—as well as art and music. ⊠ *308 Bowery, at Bleecker St., East Village* ☎ *212/614–0505* ⊕ *www.bowerypoetry.com* Ⓜ *B, D, F, M to Broadway–Lafayette St.; 6 to Bleecker St.*

16

GREENWICH VILLAGE AND WEST VILLAGE

GREENWICH VILLAGE

FILM

Cinema Village. Cinema Village has three tiny screening rooms (with surprisingly good sight lines) that show a smart selection of hard-to-find (some might say obscure) first-run domestic and foreign films. ⊠ *22 E. 12th St., between University Pl. and 5th Ave., Greenwich Village* ☎ *212/924–3363* ⊕ *www.cinemavillage.com* Ⓜ *4, 5, 6, L, N, Q, R to 14th St./Union Sq.*

Quad Cinema. Movie lovers are quite attached to the Quad Cinema despite the patina of its early 1970s vintage—probably because the four teacup-size theaters feel so much like their own private screening rooms. A finely balanced selection of first-run art documentaries and foreign films is the fare here. ⊠ *34 W. 13th St., between 5th and 6th Aves., Greenwich Village* ☎ *212/255–2243* ⊕ *www.quadcinema.com* Ⓜ *1, 2, 3, F, M to 14th St.; L to 6th Ave.*

READINGS AND LECTURES

Center for Architecture. The Center for Architecture, a contemporary glass-faced gallery, hosts lively discussions (which may be accompanied by films or other visuals) on topics like radical architecture in Mexico City or visionary American architects of the 1930s. ⊠ *536 LaGuardia Pl., between W. 3rd and Bleecker Sts., Greenwich Village* ☎ *212/683–0023* ⊕ *www.aiany.org* Ⓜ *A, B, C, D, E, F, M to W. 4th St./Washington Sq.*

The New School. At The New School topical panels predominate (Women Writers of the Diaspora) but are complemented with poetry (An Evening with John Ashbery) and film; expect incisive and thought-provoking results, whether the subject is philosophy, economics, or design. Jazz and chamber music performances are also part of New School's low-priced lineup ($5 is typical for panel events; free–$20 for music). ⊠ *66 W. 12th St., between 5th and 6th Aves., Greenwich Village* ☎ *212/229–5600* ⊕ *www.newschool.edu/events* Ⓜ *1, 2, 3, F, M to 14th St.*

New York Studio School. The venerable New York Studio School hosts two—usually free, almost always on Tuesday and Wednesday—evening lecture series on contemporary issues in art. Hear from both emerging and established artists, and from some of the biggest names in art history and criticism. ⊠ *8 W. 8th St., between 5th and 6th Aves., Greenwich Village* ☎ *212/673–6466* ⊕ *www.nyss.org* Ⓜ *A, B, C, D, E, F, M to W. 4th St./Washington Sq.*

THEATER

Skirball Center for the Performing Arts. A pristine wood-lined theater, the 866-seat Skirball Center for the Performing Arts, supports emerging artists, with a growing repertoire of interesting dance, music, and theater events, often in collaboration with other esteemed companies—including its Village neighbor, the Public. The Skirball was built in 2003 and designed by Kevin Roche. This contemporary venue on the New York University campus provides a rare larger-scale anchor for the arts in this part of town. ⊠ *566 LaGuardia Pl., at Washington Sq. S, Greenwich*

Village ☎ *212/992–8484 tickets* ⊕ *www.skirballcenter.nyu.edu* Ⓜ *A, B, C, D, E, F, M to W. 4th St./Washington Sq.*

WEST VILLAGE

FILM

Fodor's Choice ★ **Film Forum.** In addition to premiering new releases, the Film Forum, a very special nonprofit theater with three small screening rooms, hosts movies by directors from Hitchcock to Bertolucci, genre series with themes from pre-Code to Fritz Lang's Hollywood, and newly restored prints of classic works. The café in the sleek little Euro-style lobby serves tasty cakes and fresh-popped popcorn. ⊠ *209 W. Houston St., between 6th Ave. and Varick St., West Village* ☎ *212/727–8110* ⊕ *www.filmforum.org* Ⓜ *1 to Houston St.*

READINGS AND LECTURES

★ **Cornelia Street Café.** The Cornelia Street Café is a good bet for original poetry—the Pink Pony West open-mike series takes place downstairs here—as do fiction and nonfiction readings, live jazz, and the superb monthly Entertaining Science evenings hosted by the Nobel laureate chemist Roald Hoffmann. Upstairs, you can tuck into a good meal of steak frites or black sesame–crusted salmon, or simply share a bottle of merlot at a street-side table on this quiet West Village lane. ⊠ *29 Cornelia St., between W. 4th and Bleecker Sts., West Village* ☎ *212/989–9319* ⊕ *www.corneliastreetcafe.com* Ⓜ *A, B, C, D, E, F, M to W. 4th St./Washington Sq.*

Lesbian, Gay, Bisexual & Transgender Community Center. The Lesbian, Gay, Bisexual & Transgender Community Center sponsors Second Tuesdays, Center Voices, and other series of engaging and topical talks (and occasional films, dance, or theatrical events), with themes ranging from out lawyers to Elaine Stritch. ⊠ *208 W. 13th St., between 7th and 8th Aves., West Village* ☎ *212/620–7310* ⊕ *www.gaycenter.org* Ⓜ *1, 2, 3, A, C, E, F, M to 14th St.; L to 8th Ave.*

THEATER

Lucille Lortel Theatre. A venerable neighborhood survivor, the Lucille Lortel Theatre has its roots in the 1950s Brechtian traditions championed by its namesake owner of the time and became known for its influential interpretations of works by Brecht and Dos Passos. Previously called the Theatre De Lys, this 299-seater has forged on to become the home to 21st-century productions of the MCC Theater company (known for Neil LaBute's challenging plays in the century's first decade), the Atlantic Theater company, and free summer shows that appeal to both children and adults by Theatreworks/USA. ⊠ *121 Christopher St., between Hudson and Bleecker Sts., West Village* ☎ *212/924–2817 tickets* ⊕ *www.lucillelorteltheatre.com* Ⓜ *1 to Christopher St.*

CHELSEA

DANCE

☼ ★ **Dance Theater Workshop.** Dance Theater Workshop, an important venue for the dance world since its founding in 1965, serves as a laboratory for new choreographers; performances are often accompanied by

16

enlightening post-show talks with the dance makers themselves. DTW is also known for its multimedia and kid-friendly Family Matters series. ✉ *219 W. 19th St., between 7th and 8th Aves., Chelsea* ☎ *212/691–6500* ⊕ *www.dancetheaterworkshop.org* Ⓜ *1 to 18th St.; A, C, E, L to 14th St.–8th Ave.*

Fodor'sChoice ★ **Joyce Theater.** In a former Art Deco movie house in Chelsea, the 472-seat Joyce Theater has superb sight lines and presents a full spectrum of contemporary dance. **Garth Fagan Dance** (⊕ *garthfagandance.org*), **Ballet Hispanico** (⊕ *www.ballethispanico.org*), and taut and athletic **Parsons Dance** (⊕ *www.parsonsdance.org*) are regulars on the Joyce's always rewarding lineup. ✉ *175 8th Ave., at W. 19th St., Chelsea* ☎ *212/691–9740, 212/242–0800 tickets* ⊕ *www.joyce.org.*

Joyce SoHo. The Joyce SoHo, their satellite location, is a 74-seat theater that shows smaller-scale, experimental work. Both offer $10 tickets for some performances. ✉ *155 Mercer St., between Houston and Prince Sts., SoHo* ☎ *212/691–9740, 212/242–0800 tickets* ⊕ *www.joyce.org* Ⓜ *R to Prince St.; B, D, F, M to Broadway–Lafayette St.* Ⓜ *A, C, E to 14th St.; L to 8th Ave.*

THEATER

The Kitchen. The Kitchen is *the* place for multimedia performance art, and has been a crucible for artists on the experimental edge—think Charles Atlas, Kiki Smith, Elizabeth Streb—since 1971. Literary events are often free; most others can be seen for as little as $10–$15. ✉ *512 W. 19th St., between 10th and 11th Aves., Chelsea* ☎ *212/255–5793* ⊕ *www.thekitchen.org* Ⓜ *C, E to 23rd St.*

16

MIDTOWN WEST

DANCE

Baryshnikov Arts Center (BAC). The 299-seat Jerome Robbins Theater opened in 2010, and with it, the first full season of the Baryshnikov Arts Center (BAC). Mikhail Baryshnikov's longtime vision has come to fruition in this modern venue for contemporary performance dedicated to movement, which can be as much about theater as it is about dance. The seminal Wooster Group (⊕ *www.thewoostergroup.org*) is now in residence, and their productions, along with those of a roster of boundary-breaking international choreographers (George Stamos, Donna Uchizono, and Emmanuèle Phuon), co-productions with The Kitchen, and BAC Flicks (*Mondays with Merce* and more), are all part of the vibrant—and very well-priced—programming here. ✉ *37 Arts, 450 W. 37th St., between 9th and 10th Aves., Midtown* ☎ *646/731–3200* ⊕ *www.bacnyc.org* Ⓜ *A, C, E, to 34th St./Penn Station.*

FILM

Museum of Modern Art (MoMA). The Museum of Modern Art (MoMA) has some of the most engaging international repertory you'll find anywhere; it's shown in the state-of-the-art Roy and Niuta Titus Theaters 1 and 2. Movie tickets are available at the museum for same-day screenings (a limited number are released up to one week in advance for an extra fee); they're free if you have purchased museum admission. ✉ *11 W. 53rd St., between 5th and 6th Aves., Midtown West* ☎ *212/708–9400*

⊕ *www.moma.org* ✉ *$25* Ⓜ *E, M to 5th Ave./53rd St.; B, D, F, M to 47th–50th Sts./Rockefeller Center.*

The Paris. Adjacent to the Plaza Hotel sits the The Paris—a rare stately remnant of the single-screen era. Opened in 1948, it retains its wide screen (and its balcony) and is a fine showcase for new movies, often foreign and with a limited release. ✉ *4 W. 58th St., between 5th and 6th Aves., Midtown West* ☎ *212/688–3800* ⊕ *www.theparistheatre.com* Ⓜ *N, R to 5th Ave./59th St.; F to 57th St.*

★ **Ziegfeld Theatre.** Its vintage is late 1960s, but the Ziegfeld Theatre is as close as you'll come to a movie-palace experience in New York today. Its chandeliers and crimson decor, raised balcony, wide screen, some 1,200 seats, good sight lines, and solid sound system make the Ziegfeld a special place to view anything it serves up. Grand-opening red-carpet galas often take place here as well. ✉ *141 W. 54th St., between 6th and 7th Aves., Midtown West* ☎ *212/307–1862* ⊕ *www.clearviewcinemas. com/ziegfeld/ziegfeld-home.html* Ⓜ *F to 57th St./6th Ave.; N, Q, R to 57th St./7th Ave.*

MUSIC

Town Hall. Historic Town Hall is where Garrison Keillor's *A Prairie Home Companion* radio show broadcasts from in December. It also hosts programs of jazz, cabaret, and rock, the Peoples Symphony Concert series, and a variety of international music, theater, and dance events. ✉ *123 W. 43rd St., between 6th and 7th Aves., Midtown West* ☎ *212/840–2824* ⊕ *www.the-townhall-nyc.org* Ⓜ *1, 2, 3, 7, N, Q, R, S to 42nd St./Times Sq.*

☾ **Carnegie Hall.** Carnegie Hall is, of course, one of the world's most
Fodor's Choice famous concert halls. Its incomparable acoustics make it one of the
★ best venues—anywhere—to hear classical music, but its presentations of jazz, pop, cabaret, and folk music are superlative as well. Since Tchaikovsky conducted the opening-night concert on May 5, 1891, virtually every important musician the world has known has performed in this Italian Renaissance–style building, often at the peak of his or her creative powers. Leonard Bernstein had his debut here; Vladimir Horowitz made his historic return to the concert stage here. The world's top orchestras perform in the grand and fabulously steep 2,804-seat **Isaac Stern Auditorium**, the 268-seat **Weill Recital Hall** often features young talents making their New York debuts, and the subterranean 644-seat **Judy and Arthur Zankel Hall** attracts big-name artists such as the Kronos Quartet, Milton Nascimento, and Ravi Shankar to its modern and stylish space. A noted roster of family concerts is also part of Carnegie's programming. ■TIP→ The Carnegie box office offers $10 rush tickets on the day of performance, or you may buy partial-view seating in advance at 50% off the full ticket price. ✉ *881 7th Ave., at W. 57th St., Midtown West* ☎ *212/247–7800* ⊕ *www.carnegiehall.org* Ⓜ *N, Q, R to 57th St.; B, D, E to 7th Ave.*

OPERA

Gotham Chamber Opera. The Gotham Chamber Opera presents less-known chamber works from the baroque era to the present in inspired productions. Catching a broader audience's attention, shows include

Moisés Kaufman's acclaimed rendition of the 1947 *El Gato Con Botas* by Xavier Montsalvatge (staged at the New Victory Theater); Handel's *Arianna in Creta;* a collaboration with choreographer Karole Armitage, *Ariadne Unhinged;* and a joint venture with the Hayden Planetarium of Haydn's *Il Mondo della Luna,* or *The World on the Moon.* ⊠ *410 W. 42nd St., between 9th and 10th Aves., Midtown West* ☎ *212/868–4460* ⊕ *www.gothamchamberopera.org* Ⓜ *A, C, E to 42nd St./Port Authority.*

PERFORMANCE CENTERS

★ **New York City Center.** New York City Center has a neo-Moorish look, built in 1923 for the Ancient and Accepted Order of the Mystic Shrine. Pause as you enter to admire the beautifully ornate tile work that plasters the lobby; a painstaking 2011 renovation makes the freshly refurbished detail hard to miss. The 2,200-seat main stage is perfectly suited for its role as a showplace for dance and special theatrical events. **Alvin Ailey American Dance Theater** (⊕ *www.alvinailey.org*) and **Paul Taylor Dance Company** (⊕ *www.ptdc.org*) present their primary New York seasons here. City Center's annual Fall for Dance festival is a must; all tickets are $10, the performances sell out very quickly. Another seasonal highlight—usually throughout January—is the lively productions of the **New York Gilbert & Sullivan Players** (☎ *212/769–1000* ⊕ *www.nygasp.org*), which feature such G&S favorites as *The Pirates of Penzance* and *The Mikado,* plus rarities like Sullivan's last completed work, *The Rose of Persia.* The popular Encores! musicals-in-concert series is staged here, as are—on the smaller **City Center Stages I** and **II**—a number of productions and programs of the Manhattan Theatre Club and the Pearl Theatre Company. ⊠ *131 W. 55th St., between 6th and 7th Aves., Midtown West* ☎ *212/581–1212 CityTix* ⊕ *www. nycitycenter.org* Ⓜ *N, Q, R to 57th St./7th Ave.; F to 57th St./6th Ave.*

Radio City Music Hall. This icon of New York City was built to enchant everyone who stepped inside its doors. Shortly after the stock market crash of 1929, John D. Rockefeller wanted to create a symbol of hope in what was a sad, broke city. He selected a piece of real estate in an area of Manhattan then known as "the speakeasy belt," and partnered with the Radio Corporation of America to build a grand theater, a place where everyday people could see the finest entertainment at sensible prices. Every inch of the interior was designed to be extraordinary. RCA head David Sarnoff named the creation Radio City Music Hall. When it opened, some said it was so grand that there was no need for performances, because people would get more than their money's worth simply by sitting there and enjoying the space. Despite being the largest indoor theater in the world with its city-block-long marquee, it feels warm and intimate. One-hour "Stage Door" walking tours run year-round, but avoid taking the tour during show times, as access is limited. Day-of tour tickets are sold at the Radio City Avenue Store on a first-come, first-served basis; advanced tickets are available by phone or through the website (☎ *212/247–4777* ⊠ *$19.25* ⊙ *Tours: daily 11–3*).

Although there are performances and media events here year-round, more than a million visitors every year come to see the Radio City Christmas Spectacular, starring the iconic Rockettes. Make reservations as early as possible, especially if you want to attend near the

Christmas holidays or on weekends. The shows tend to sell out, but you can usually find tickets until mid-October. Happily, there are no bad seats at Radio City Music Hall, so if you are booking late, grab what you can get. Tickets—$45–$105 per person for the 90-minute show—can be purchased at Radio City Music Hall; on the Web (⊕ *www. radiocitychristmas.com*); by phone on the Christmas Spectacular hotline (☎ 866/858–0007); or through Ticketmaster. ⊠ *1260 6th Ave., between W. 50th and W. 51st Sts., Midtown West* ☎ *212/247–4777* ⊕ *www.radiocity.com* Ⓜ *B, D, F to 47th–50th/Rockefeller Center; N, R to 49th St.*

READINGS AND LECTURES

Fodor's Choice
★

Municipal Art Society (MAS). The nonprofit Municipal Art Society (MAS) is a committed advocate for smart urban planning and the architectural treasures that define this metropolis. Count on their walking tours—on weekends mostly, plus a downtown series that sets out at midday on Tuesday—to offer a fresh perspective and feature the rarely seen, from Dawn Powell's Greenwich Village to a rolling tour of Grand Central Station to a visit to Little Syria in Manhattan's lower west side. Their resource library has the corner on NYC arcana. ⊠ *111 W. 57th St., between 6th and 7th Aves., Midtown West* ☎ *212/935–3960, 212/935–3960 Tour Hotline* ⊕ *www.mas.org* Ⓜ *F to 57th St.; D, E to 7th Ave./53rd St.*

New York Public Library. The New York Public Library presents LIVE from the NYPL, a rich program of lectures and reading events at the famous main library and its branches elsewhere in the city. ⊠ *Celeste Bartos Forum, W. 42nd St. at 5th Ave., Midtown West* ☎ *212/930–0855, 888/718–4253* ⊕ *www.nypl.org/* Ⓜ *B, D, F, M to 42nd St.*

THEATER

American Airlines Theatre. The onetime Selwyn—the venerable home to the works of Coward, Kaufman, and Porter in their heyday—is now known as the American Airlines Theatre. After incarnations as a burlesque hall and pornographic movie house, this splendidly restored 1918 Venetian-style playhouse is now home to the not-for-profit Roundabout Theatre Company, which is acclaimed for its revivals of classic musicals and plays, such as a Doug Hughes–directed production of *A Man for All Seasons*. ⊠ *227 W. 42nd St., between 7th and 8th Aves., Midtown West* ☎ *212/719–1300 tickets* ⊕ *www.roundabouttheatre.org* Ⓜ *1, 2, 3, 7, N, Q, R, S to 42nd St./Times Sq.; A, C, E to 42nd St./Port Authority.*

New Amsterdam Theater. In 1997 Disney refurbished the elaborate 1903 Art Nouveau New Amsterdam Theater, where Eddie Cantor, Will Rogers, Fanny Brice, and the Ziegfeld Follies once drew crowds. *The Lion King* ruled here for the first nine years of its run; *Mary Poppins* has prevailed ever since. ⊠ *214 W. 42nd St., between 7th and 8th Aves., Midtown West* ☎ *212/282–2907* ⊕ *newamsterdam.newyorkcitytheatre. com* Ⓜ *1, 2, 3, 7, N, Q, R, S to 42nd St./Times Sq.; A, C, E to 42nd St./Port Authority.*

☺
Fodor's Choice
★

The New Victory Theater. In a magnificently restored century-old performance space, The New Victory Theater presents an international roster of supremely kid-pleasing plays, music, and dance performances. Be dazzled by the likes of Canada's Circus INcognitus; Mabou Mines's Peter & Wendy—featuring Bunraku puppets and Celtic music; Mischief, a brilliant U.K.-based introduction to dance—with the inspired help of giant foam noodles; and Australian puppet madness, in The Tragical Life of Cheeseboy. Count on reasonable ticket prices ($17 is the average), high-energy and high-class productions, and the opportunity for kids to chat with the artists after many performances. ✉ *209 W. 42nd St., between 7th and 8th Aves., Midtown West* ☎ *646/223–3010* ⊕ *www.newvictory.org* Ⓜ *1, 2, 3, 7, A, C, E, N, Q, R, S to 42nd St./ Times Sq.*

Playwrights Horizons. Playwrights Horizons is known for its support of new work by American playwrights. The first home for eventual Broadway hits such as *Grey Gardens* and Wendy Wasserstein's *Heidi Chronicles*, this is where you will find the latest work from Craig Lucas, Doug Wright, and Edward Albee. ✉ *416 W. 42nd St., between 9th and 10th Aves., Midtown West* ☎ *212/564–1235, 212/279–4200 tickets* ⊕ *www.playwrightshorizons.org* Ⓜ *A, C, E to 42nd St./Port Authority.*

Signature Theatre Company. The Signature Theatre Company's brand-new, Frank Gehry–designed Pershing Square Signature Center has three theater spaces—all the better to present their roster of playwrights-in-residence (Edward Albee, Horton Foote, August Wilson, Sam Shepard, and Tony Kushner among them). The new space makes it possible to explore the work of several playwrights at once, and all tickets are $25 for a show's first run. A central space with a café and bookstore connects the theaters, so come early or stay late for a bite to eat; the café is open until midnight Tuesday through Sunday. ✉ *Pershing Square Signature Center, 480 W. 42nd St., between 8th and 9th Aves., Midtown West* ☎ *212/967–1913 info and tickets* ⊕ *www.signaturetheatre.org* Ⓜ *A, C, E to 42nd St./Port Authority.*

St. James. Moorish Revival in style, the St. James went up in 1927, and has been running legit at least since the late 1930s. Home of Mel Brooks's juggernaut *The Producers* in its heyday, and where a Tony-laden revival of *Gypsy* held sway late in the first decade of the 21st century, the St. James is where Lauren Bacall was an usherette in the '40s, and where a little show called *Oklahoma!* premiered, with a rousing score and choreography to match, and changed the musical forever. ✉ *246 W. 44th St., between Broadway and 8th Ave., Midtown West* ☎ *212/239–6200 tickets* ⊕ *www.jujamcyn.com* Ⓜ *1, 2, 3, 7, N, Q, R, S to 42nd St./Times Sq.; A, C, E to 42nd St./Port Authority.*

16

UPPER EAST SIDE

OPERA

☾ **Dicapo Opera Theatre.** Dicapo Opera Theatre may be in a church basement (albeit that of the distinctively French Provincial St. Jean Baptiste), but the 204-seater's boffo reputation—and its thoroughly modern facility—belie its humble-sounding setting. Productions range from Puccini to Tobias Picker's *Emmeline*. Their complementary children's programming, Opera for Kids, offers—at nominal seat prices—one-hour renditions of the classics on weekends. ✉ *184 E. 76th St., between Lexington* *and 3rd Aves., Upper East Side* ☎ *212/288–9438, 212/868–4444 tickets* ⊕ *www.dicapo.com* Ⓜ *6 to 77th St.*

PERFORMANCE CENTER

☾ **92nd Street Y.** Well-known soloists, jazz musicians, show-tune stylists, and chamber music groups perform in the 92nd Street Y 905-seat **Kaufmann Concert Hall.** But the Y's programming is hardly limited to music—purchase tickets early for their popular lectures-and-readings series featuring big-name authors, poets, playwrights, political pundits, and media bigwigs. Also worth the Upper East Side trek here are the Harkness Dance Festival, film programs, and all manner of family-friendly events. ✉ *1395 Lexington Ave., at E. 92nd St., Upper East Side* ☎ *212/415–5440, 212/415–5500 tickets* ⊕ *www.92y.org* Ⓜ *6 to 96th St.*

READINGS AND LECTURES

★ **Works & Process.** Insight into the creative process is what the superb Works & Process program is all about. Often drawing on dance and theater works-in-progress, live performances are complemented with illuminating discussions with their (always top-notch) choreographers, playwrights, and directors. ✉ *Guggenheim Museum, 1071 5th Ave., at E. 89th St., Upper East Side* ☎ *212/423–3587* ⊕ *www.worksandprocess.org* Ⓜ *4, 5, 6 to 86th St.*

UPPER WEST SIDE

MUSIC

The Cathedral Church of St. John the Divine. Anything you come to hear at the The Cathedral Church of St. John the Divine will likely be an unforgettable experience, but the seasonal programming of the **Early Music New York** (☎ *212/749–6600, 212/280–0330 tickets* ⊕ *www.earlymusicny.org*) ensemble is essential. ✉ *1047 Amsterdam Ave., at W. 112th St., Upper West Side* ☎ *212/316–7540 performance line* ⊕ *www.stjohndivine.org* Ⓜ *1, B, C to 110th St./Cathedral Pkwy.*

Jazz at Lincoln Center. This Columbus Square jazz mecca a few blocks south of Lincoln Center's main campus was dedicated to Jazz at Lincoln Center in 2004. Stages in Rafael Viñoly's crisply modern **Frederick P. Rose Hall** feature the 1,100-seat **Rose Theater** (where a worthy Jazz for Young People series joins the buoyant adult programming a few times each year). Also here is the **Allen Room,** an elegant and intimate 460-seater, and the even more intimate 140-seat Dizzy's Club Coca-Cola, known for its late-night After Hours concerts. ✉ *Time Warner Center, 33 West 60 St., Floor 11, Upper West Side* ☎ *212/258–9800* ⊕ *www.jalc.org* Ⓜ *1, A, B, C, D to 59th St./Columbus Circle.*

★ **Miller Theatre.** Adventurous programming of jazz, classical, early and modern music, and dance continues at the Miller Theatre. A well-designed 688-seater, this is a hall that rewards serious listeners. ✉ *Columbia University, 2960 Broadway, at W. 116th St., Morningside Heights* ☎ *212/854–1633, 212/854–1633 box office* ⊕ *www.millertheatre.com* Ⓜ *1 to 116th St.*

The fountain in front of Lincoln Center is particularly lovely in the evening.

PERFORMANCE CENTERS

Fodor'sChoice ★ **Lincoln Center for the Performing Arts.** This massive white travertine-clad complex contains Alice Tully Hall, the Metropolitan Opera House, Avery Fisher Hall, the Juilliard School, the New York City Ballet, and the Film Center of Lincoln Center, making it one of the most concentrated places for the performing arts in the nation. Its 16-acre campus was built over the course of several years from 1962 to 1969, on the once gritty urban ground that set the scene for the musical *West Side Story*. Renovations that were done to celebrate Lincoln Center's 50th anniversary, which coincided with the 2009–2010 season, included remodeling the centerpiece of the plaza, the Revson Fountain, as well as Alice Tully Hall , which has won accolades from critics for its design. In August, Lincoln Center's longest-running classical series, the Mostly Mozart Festival (☎ *212/875–5399*), captures the crowds. You can purchase tickets to performances online, by phone, or at the various box offices.

■TIP→ Discounted day-of-show tickets for most Lincoln Center venues may be purchased in person at the David Rubenstein Atrium on Broadway between West 62nd and West 63rd streets; there is a limit of four tickets per customer, and the amount of discount depends on the performance. Although the box office there is closed on Monday, they sell any available tickets for Monday performances on Sunday. Box office hours: Tuesday–Saturday noon–7:45; Sunday noon–5:45.

Alice Tully Hall (✉ *1941 Broadway, at W. 65th St.* ☎ *212/671–4050*) is considered to be as acoustically perfect as a concert hall can get; the hall's primary resident is the Chamber Music Society of Lincoln Center

(✉ *212/875–5788* ⊕ *www.chambermusicsociety.org*). **Avery Fisher Hall** is home to the New York Philharmonic (☎ *212/875–5656* ⊕ *nyphil. org*); the season is late September to early June. Orchestra rehearsals at 9:45 am are open to the public on selected weekday mornings (usually Wednesday or Thursday). A popular Young People's Concert series is offered on Saturday afternoon, four times throughout the season.

The largest hall, the **Metropolitan Opera House** (✉ *30 Lincoln Center Plaza, Columbus Ave., between W. 62nd and W. 65th Sts.* ☎ *212/362–6000*), is notable for its dramatic arched entrance as well as its lobby's immense chandeliers and Marc Chagall paintings, both of which can be seen from outside. The titan of American opera companies and an institution since its founding in 1883, the **Metropolitan Opera** (☎ *212/362–6000* ⊕ *www.metfamilyopera.org*) brings the world's leading singers to the vast stage here from October to April. An extra perk is that all performances, including those sung in English, are unobtrusively subtitled on small screens on the back of the seat in front of you. Also resident at the Met is the **American Ballet Theatre** (ABT) (☎ *212/477–3030* ⊕ *www.abt.org*), renowned for its gorgeous full-program renditions of the 19th-century classics (*Swan Lake, Giselle, The Sleeping Beauty*) with choreography reenvisioned by 20th-century masters. ABT has two New York seasons: eight weeks of performances begin in May here at the Met, and starting with the 2010 holiday season, their *Nutcracker* is staged at the Brooklyn Academy of Music (BAM) (⇨ *see full listing*).

The **David H. Koch Theater** (✉ *Columbus Ave., at W. 62nd St.* ☎ *212/870–5570*) may not be as famous as the Met next door, but the **New York City Opera** (☎ *212/870–5570* ⊕ *www.nycopera.com*) has its own vibrant personality. Founded in 1943, the company is known for its diverse repertory and its soft spot for American composers. City Opera performs October to November and March to April. Supertitles—the opera's libretto, line-by-line—are displayed above the stage. Sharing the Koch is the formidable **New York City Ballet** (NYCB, ☎ *212/870–5570* ⊕ *www.nycballet.com*), with its unmatched repertoire of 20th-century works, predominantly by George Balanchine, Jerome Robbins, and Peter Martins. The company particularly excels at short-form programs. Its fall season goes from September to early October, then returns in late November through December for the beloved annual production of Balanchine's *The Nutcracker*. Its winter repertory program runs in January and February, and a spring season runs from May into June.

The **Lincoln Center Theater** complex, home to a rich tradition of plays and musicals, houses the **Vivian Beaumont Theater,** the intimate **Mitzi E. Newhouse Theater**, and, as of 2012, the new rooftop **Claire Tow Theater**, which has 131 seats and a small grassy terrace for attendees.

The auditorium of the **Walter Reade Theater** (✉ *165 W. 65th St., between Broadway and Amsterdam Ave.* ☎ *212/875–5600* ⊕ *www. filmlinc.com*) shows film series devoted to "the best in world cinema" that run the gamut from silents (with occasional live organ accompaniment) and documentaries to retrospectives and recent releases, often on the same theme or from the same country. There are also HD screenings on periodic Saturdays of *The Met: Live*.

The **Elinor Bunin-Monroe Film Center** (⊠ *W. 65th St., between Broadway and Amsterdam Ave.* ⊕ *www.filmlinc.com*), which opened in 2011, has two small screening rooms, a café, and an archive that encourages further immersion into NYC's film arts.

■ TIP→ The David Rubinstein Atrium, on Broadway between 62nd and 63rd streets, is open seven days, 9 am–10 pm and has free Wi-Fi, tables and lounge nooks, a branch of Tom Colicchios's 'wichcraft café, and that rarest of NYC commodities, a public restroom. ⊠ *W. 62nd to W. 66th Sts. from Broadway/Columbus Ave. to Amsterdam Ave., Upper West Side* ☎ *212/875–5456 customer service daily 9–9, 212/721–6500 CenterCharge, 212/875–5456 for accessibility information* ⊕ *www. lincolncenter.org* Ⓜ *1 to 66th St./Lincoln Center.*

☺
★ **Symphony Space.** Symphony Space presents an energetic roster of music (including its famed Wall to Wall composer programs), from world to classical. On the literary front, its two halls—the **Peter Jay Sharpe Theatre** and the **Leonard Nimoy Thalia** Thalia of yore)—host a celebrated roster of literary events, including Bloomsday and the well-known Selected Shorts series of stories read by prominent actors and broadcast live on National Public Radio. Opera on film and Thalia Film Sundays (usually a true-to-its-roots art-house screening) round out the adult programming. For the family, turn to their hugely popular **Just Kidding** lineup for a nonstop parade of zany plays, sing-alongs, midday Saturday (and sometimes Sunday) movies, and animations, like the Gustafer Yellowgold Show. ⊠ *2537 Broadway, at 95th Street, Upper West Side* ☎ *212/864–5400* ⊕ *www.symphonyspace.org* Ⓜ *1, 2, 3 to 96th St.*

16

HARLEM

MUSIC
Apollo Theater. If the Apollo's famed Amateur Night doesn't get you off the couch, keep in mind its more intimate Apollo Music Café events on Friday, Saturday, and Monday nights, featuring some of the finest artists in jazz and other music traditions—and some right on the edge of fame. The Apollo's notable weeklong Harlem Jazz Shrines festival in May is held in venerable nearby venues Lenox Lounge, Minton's Playhouse, and Showman's Café. ⊠ *253 W. 125th St., at 8th Ave./Frederick Douglass Blvd., Harlem* ☎ *212/531–5300, 800/745–3000 tickets (Ticketmaster)* ⊕ *www.apollotheater.org* Ⓜ *A, B, C, 2, 3, 4, 5, 6 to 125th St.*

BROOKLYN

BROOKLYN HEIGHTS
MUSIC
Bargemusic. In Brooklyn, Bargemusic keeps chamber music groups busy year-round on a re-outfitted harbor barge with a fabulous view of the Manhattan skyline. ⊠ *Fulton Ferry Landing, Old Fulton and Furman Sts., Brooklyn Heights* ☎ *718/624–2083* ⊕ *www.bargemusic.org* Ⓜ *A, C to High St.; 2, 3 to Clark St.*

DOWNTOWN BROOKLYN
PERFORMANCE CENTERS

Fodor's Choice **Brooklyn Academy of Music (BAM).** America's oldest performing arts cen-
★ ter, the Brooklyn Academy of Music (BAM), presented its first show in
1861. Today it has a much-deserved reputation for the unusual and the
unexpected, presented in grand-scale stagings. The most contemporary
dance, music, opera, and cross-media productions mingle here with an
array of classics. A restored Renaissance Revival palace built in 1908—
the 2,100-seat **Howard Gilman Opera House**—and the 874-seat **Harvey
Theater,** an updated 1904 theater a block away at 651 Fulton Street, are
BAM's primary performance spaces. Every fall the Next Wave Festival
fills the house with crackling energy and events that highlight a global
mix of remarkable artists. The holidays bring a run of American Ballet Theatre's 2010-debuted Nutcracker, and with springtime comes a
top-notch roster of international theater companies (such as Ireland's
renowned Abbey) in repertory. Year-round you can catch a movie at
the four-screen **BAM Rose Cinemas,** which offers BAMcinématek, an
eclectic repertory series (from Kurosawa's Samurai films to Hungarians
in Hollywood), as well as first-run indies, documentaries, and foreign-
language films. Or, hit the industrial-glam **BAMcafé** (☎ *718/623–7811
reservations*) for Between the Lines, a synapse-sparking lecture series
on Thursday night; it becomes a cabaret venue on Friday and Saturday
nights. ■TIP→ BAM gets kudos for its down-to-earth range of ticket prices;
$25 to $60 is typical. ✉ *Peter Jay Sharp Bldg., 30 Lafayette Ave., between
Ashland Pl. and St. Felix St., Fort Greene* ☎ *718/636–4100* ⊕ *www.
bam.org* Ⓜ *C to Lafayette Ave.; 2, 3, 4, 5, B, Q to Atlantic Ave.; D, N,
R to Atlantic Ave.–Pacific St.*

THEATER

☟ **Puppetworks.** Finely detailed wooden marionettes and hand puppets are
on the bill at Puppetworks. Familiar childhood tales like *Little Red
Riding Hood* and *Peter and the Wolf* come to life most weekends in
this 75-seat neighborhood theater. ✉ *338 6th Ave., at 4th St., Park
Slope* ☎ *718/965–3391 Reservations essential* ⊕ *www.puppetworks.
org* Ⓜ *F to 7th Ave.*

DUMBO
THEATER

Fodor's Choice **St. Ann's Warehouse.** St. Ann's Warehouse has hosted everything from
★ the boundary-stretching 2009 opera *La Didone* to award-winning performances from the famous Edinburgh Fringe Festival, all in a onetime
spice-milling factory. ✉ *38 Water St., between Main and Dock Sts.,
DUMBO* ☎ *718/254–8779, 866/911–4111 tickets* ⊕ *stannswarehouse.
org* Ⓜ *A, C to High St.; F to York St.*

QUEENS

FILM

☟ **Museum of the Moving Image: film programs.** The Museum of the Moving Image presents special film programming to go along with the
museum's radical face-lift and relaunch in 2011. Video art, digital
screenings, live musical collaborations, and in-person appearances by

New York's Film Festivals

New York's extreme diversity is also what makes it a cinephile's heaven: dozens of festivals for both niche interests and for those just wanting to be at the front end of what's out there. New releases and premieres dominate the festival scene, but the city has its share of retrospective events, especially in summer.

The city's preeminent film event is the annual **New York Film Festival** (⊕ *www.filmlinc.com*); sponsored by the **Film Society of Lincoln Center,** annually from late September into October. Screenings are announced more than a month in advance to often rapid sellout. Film venues are usually Lincoln Center's Alice Tully Hall and Walter Reade Theater. In January, the Film Society joins forces with the Jewish Museum to produce the **New York Jewish Film Festival,** in March it joins with MoMA to present **New Directors/New Films,** and June brings its collaboration with the **Human Rights Watch Film Festival.**

The **Tribeca Film Festival** (⊕ *www. tribecafilmfestival.org*) takes place in mostly downtown venues for about two weeks starting in late April, and features mainstream premieres along with indie treasures, as well as a **Family Festival,** which attracts big crowds for its street fair and movies for ages eight and up.

Fans also flock to other noteworthy annuals like the **Asian American International Film Festival** (⊕ *www. asiancinevision.org*) in July (usually at the Clearview Chelsea Cinemas); the **New York International Latino Film Festival** (⊕ *www.nylatinofilm. com*) later that same month and also screening at the Clearview Chelsea Cinemas; the **New York Korean Film**

Festival (⊕ *koreanfilmfestival.org*) in late September at MoMA and BAM; the Paley Center for Media's **DocFest** (⊕ *paleycenter.org*) in October; and in November at the American Museum of Natural History, the **Margaret Mead Film & Video Festival** (⊕ *www. amnh.org/programs/mead/*), which presents a rich roster of international documentaries.

And for kids, the year-round programs of the **New York International Children's Film Festival (NYICFF)** (⊕ *www.gkids.com*) peak in late February with a two-week extravaganza of about 100 new films and videos for ages 3–18.

Summer in New York sees a bonanza of alfresco film; screenings are usually free (but arrive early to secure a space; screenings begin at dusk). The **HBO Bryant Park Summer Film Festival** (☎ *212/512–5700* ⊕ *www. bryantpark.org*) has classic films on Monday nights, June–August. The Hudson River Park (⊕ *www. hudsonriverpark.org*) **RiverFlicks** series in July and August has movies for grown-ups on Wednesday evening on Pier 54; RiverFlicks for kids are at Pier 46, on Fridays. The Upper West Side has Summer on the Hudson (⊕ *www.nycgovparks.org*) with Wednesday-night screenings on Pier 1. **Rooftop Films'** (⊕ *www. rooftopfilms.com*) Underground Movies Outdoors is NYC's most eclectic film series, with shows outdoors in summer on rooftops in all five boroughs. Check their schedule for off-season screenings as well.

Summer Thursday nights, check out **Movies with a View** in Brooklyn Bridge Park (⊕ *www. brooklynbridgepark.org*).

16

SERIES AND REVIVALS

Although many of the screens listed here also show first-run releases, old favorites and rarities are the heart of their programming. These gems—which include every genre from noir to the most au courant experimental work—frequently screen at museums, cultural societies, and other public spaces, such as the **French Institute** (☎ 212/355–6100 ⊕ www.fiaf.org), **Scandinavia House** (☎ 212/879–9779 ⊕ www.scandinaviahouse.org), **Instituto Cervantes** (☎ 212/308–7720 ⊕ www.cervantes.org), and even branches of the **New York Public Library** (⊕ www.nypl.org). Harlem's **Maysles Cinema** (⊕ www.mayslesinstitute.org), under the aegis of legendary documentary film-maker Albert Maysles, is, no surprise, the place for doc screenings, old and new. Silent films (⊕ www.silentclowns.com) are the fare at Lincoln Center's **Library for the Performing Arts**. And a reliably creative range of repertory screenings can always be found at **Anthology Film Archives** (☎ 212/505–5181 ⊕ www.anthologyfilmarchives.org), **Film Forum** (☎ 212/727–8110 ⊕ www.filmforum.org), the **Museum of Modern Art (MoMA)** (☎ 212/708–9400 ⊕ www.moma.org), the **Museum of the Moving Image** (☎ 718/784–0077 ⊕ www.movingimage.us), **BAM Rose Cinemas/BAMcinématek** (☎ 718/636–4100 ⊕ www.bam.org), and **Walter Reade Theater** (☎ 212/875–5600 ⊕ www.filmlinc.com).

moviemaker luminaries are regular features, as are the sort of retrospectives and themed repertory they programmed previously, like an Alain Resnais series, Recovered Treasures (from world archives), or Avant-Garde Masters. It's also a great choice for kids: weekend Family Film matinees take place in Tut's Fever Movie Palace, the fab Red Grooms and Lysiane Luong–designed installation that's a holdover from this 1920 Astoria Studio building's first incarnation as a museum in the late 1980s. ✉ 3601 35th Ave., at 37th St., Astoria ☎ 718/784–0077 ⊕ www.movingimage.us Ⓜ R, M to Steinway St.; N to 36th Ave.

Nightlife

WORD OF MOUTH

"Have you been to a jazz club? There are the standards (like Blue Note [pictured above]), but I also like Smoke on the Upper West Side. Decent food (not fabulous, but better than average for a jazz club) and not touristy."

—frogoutofwater

Updated by
Alexander
Basek

New York is fond of the "work hard, play hard" maxim, but the truth is that Gothamites don't need much of an excuse to gather together. Monday is the new Thursday, which replaced Friday and Saturday, but it doesn't matter: the bottom line is that there's always plenty to do in this 24-hour city, and visitors will quickly see that whether it's going to a divey 1930s saloon, a gay sports bar, or a swanky rooftop lounge, it isn't hard to get a piece of the action.

The nightlife scene still resides largely downtown—in dives in the East Village and Lower East Side, classic jazz joints in the West Village, and the Meatpacking District's and Chelsea's see-and-be-seen clubs. Midtown, especially around Hell's Kitchen, has developed a vibrant scene, too, and plenty of preppy hangouts dot the Upper East and Upper West sides. Brooklyn, especially in Williamsburg, is the destination for hipsters.

Keep in mind that *when* you go is just as important as *where* you go. A spot sizzles only when it's hopping—a club that is packed at 11 might empty out by midnight, and a bar that raged last night may be completely empty tonight. *Paper* magazine has a good list of the roving parties. You can check their online nightlife guide, *PM* (NYC), via their website ⊕ *www.papermag.com*. Another streetwise mag, *The L Magazine* (⊕ *www.thelmagazine.com*), lists what's happening at many of the city's lounges and clubs, as well as dance and comedy performances. Scour industry-centric websites, too, like Eater and Grub Street, which catalog the comings and goings of many a nightlife impresario. The *New York Times* has listings of cabaret and jazz shows, most comprehensively in their Friday and Sunday Arts section. Bear in mind that a venue's life span is often measured in months, not years. Phone ahead to make sure your target hasn't closed or turned into a polka hall (although you never know—that could be fun, too).

LOWER MANHATTAN

TRIBECA

BARS

B-flat. The decor is red-on-red here, and the Asian-style cocktails are particularly groovy (literally—one, with citrusy Japanese yuzu juice and vodka, is dubbed the Groovy) at this Japan-meets-'50s America lounge. Get some fine Japanese food treats and check out the upstairs area with amazing wall and ceiling murals of the Tokyo Bar. ✉ *277 Church St., between Franklin and White Sts., TriBeCa* ☎ *212/219–2970* ⊕ *www.bflat.info* Ⓜ *1 to Franklin St.*

★ **Brandy Library.** Alas, the only wish book in this exquisite, wood-paneled room is the leather-bound menu listing hundreds of brandies and single-malt scotches. The bottles are on gorgeous backlighted "bookshelves," though, and you can learn what makes each of them special by chatting with the spirit sommelier—or by attending the twice-weekly Spirit School tastings. ✉ *25 N. Moore St., between Varick and Hudson Sts., TriBeCa* ☎ *212/226–5545* ⊕ *www.brandylibrary.com* Ⓜ *1 to Franklin St.*

Canal Room. Polished wood floors, potted palms, and stylish chairs give this intimate club an air of glamour. Musicians perform here several times a month, but they also come just to enjoy themselves. The owners' record-business connections, a spectacular sound system, celeb sightings, and DJs with reputations as big as their turntables (size does matter) keep the crowds moving. ✉ *285 West Broadway, at Canal St., TriBeCa* ☎ *212/941–8100* ⊕ *www.canalroom.com* Ⓜ *A, C, E to Canal St.*

M1-5. For the more bohemian of TriBeCa pub goers, this lipstick-red, high-ceiling spot is a vast playground (as in pool and darts). A reggae jukebox helps keep it real, as do discounts for local artists on the diverse cocktail menu. Extra points, too, for the bar's name, which cites TriBeCa's warehouse zoning law. ✉ *52 Walker St., between Broadway and Church St., TriBeCa* ☎ *212/965–1701* ⊕ *www.m1-5.com* Ⓜ *J, M, Z, N, Q, R, 6 to Canal St.*

Smith and Mills. Attractive scenesters frolic giddily at this tiny gem of a gin mill, where mixologists who resemble Daniel Day-Lewis dispense elixirs (and caviar) from a bar hung with pots and pans. There are cozy table-nooks for couples, and an elevator-toilet (yes, you read that correctly) for anyone who feels "nature's call" while heeding "the call of the wild." ✉ *71 N. Moore St., between Hudson and Greenwich Sts., TriBeCa* ☎ *212/219–8568* ⊕ *www.smithandmills.com* Ⓜ *1 to Franklin St.*

DANCE CLUBS AND DJ VENUES

Santos Party House. "Now *this* is what I call a dance club," says Arthur Baker, the legendary DJ (and legendary record producer), about this glorious downtown dance club, where the velvet ropes part for everyone. Co-owned by the rocker Andrew W. K., the bi-level Santos ain't fancy, but that's the point, and the customers are as eclectic (everybody from punks to Upper East Siders) as the DJs, including Mr. Baker, who flies in regularly from London. Hence the musical vibe—underground dance, mostly—is simply kaleidoscopic. ✉ *96 Lafayette St., between White and*

17

Walker Sts., TriBeCa ☎ *212/584–5492* ⊕ *www.santospartyhouse.com* Ⓜ *J, M, Z, N, Q, R, 6 to Canal St.*

SOHO AND NOLITA

NOLITA
BARS

Sweet and Vicious. The name of this unpretentious butterfly-logo'ed lounge doesn't signify the looks (sweet) and attitude (vicious) of certain downtown pretty things that frequent the bars on this LES stretch. So what makes this bar in particular so sweet? A lovely back garden perfect for rendezvous more private than the sceney bars they might otherwise hit in Soho and NoLiTa. ✉ *5 Spring St., between the Bowery and Elizabeth St., NoLIta* ☎ *212/334–7915* ⊕ *www.sweetandviciousnyc.com/* Ⓜ *6 to Spring St.; J, M to Bowery.*

SOHO
BARS

Broome Street Bar. A local hangout since 1972, the casual yet essential Broome still feels like the old SoHo, before trendy boutiques replaced artists' lofts. There's an impressive selection of draft beers and a full menu of hefty burgers and other sturdy pub fare. ✉ *363 West Broadway, at Broome St., SoHo* ☎ *212/925–2086* ⊕ *broomestreetbar.ypguides.net* Ⓜ *C, E to Spring St.*

Don Hill's. An attempt by nightlife impresarios Paul Sevigny and Nur Khan (Beatrice Inn) to bring a punk ethos to downtown nightlife, the reborn Don Hill's is downtown's hottest spot (for now). Near the river in the sleepy area of Hudson Square, the nondescript building hides a raunchy interior stuffed with graffiti, explicit photographs, and oodles of boldface names, from Iggy Pop to the Olsen twins. Skip the cocktails in favor of a visit to the Jaegermeister machine. ✉ *511 Greenwich St., at Spring St., SoHo* ☎ *212/219–2850* ⊕ *www.donhills.com* Ⓜ *C, E to Spring St.*

★ **Fanelli's.** Linger over the *New York Times* at this terrific neighborhood bar and restaurant, which is pretty down-to-earth for a SoHo landmark that's been serving drinks (and amazing cuisine—dig those burgers!) since 1847. Check out the hilarious old-timey photos on the walls, too. ✉ *94 Prince St., at Mercer St., SoHo* ☎ *212/226–9412* Ⓜ *R to Prince St.*

Jimmy. Way up on the top floor of the new James Hotel, Jimmy is the second project from the team behind the West Village's Hotel Griffou. Here their take on the rooftop hotel bar is better than it has to be, given the stellar views; sit in a corner nook to gaze at the Empire State Building, or head toward the outdoor pool area to survey the bridges over the East River. Cocktails are a highlight, featuring seasonal ingredients and innovations like ice cubes made from cinnamon water. ✉ *15 Thompson St., at Grand St., SoHo* ☎ *212/465–2000* ⊕ *www.jameshotels.com* Ⓜ *C, E to Spring St.*

★ **Lani Kai.** Julie Reiner, the brains behind the beloved Flatiron Lounge and Clover Club, has expanded her portfolio with a tiki bar. It sounds out of place in SoHo, but it works—and it's authentic, or as authentic as a tiki bar gets, thanks to Reiner's upbringing in Hawaii. Tropical plants, shells, and even a "fire pit" make it feel like a luau. Many of the cocktails are rum based, and the punches seem to include everything but the kitchen sink. Pupu, it's not. ✉ *525 Broome St., between Sullivan and Thompson Sts., SoHo* ☎ *646/596–8778* ⊕ *www.lanikainy. com* Ⓜ *1, 2 to Canal St.*

MercBar. This neighborhood staple keeps packing in the crowds. Eleven different martinis, 9 bourbons, and 13 single-malt scotches are just the beginning of the extensive drink menu. ✉ *151 Mercer St., between Prince and W. Houston Sts., SoHo* ☎ *212/966–2727* ⊕ *www.mercbar. com* Ⓜ *B, D, F, M to Bradway–Lafayette St.; N, R to Prince St.*

Pegu Club. Modeled after an officers' club in what's now Myanmar, the Pegu manages to feel expansive and calm even when packed. The well dressed and flirtatious come here partly for the exotically lovely surroundings, but primarily for the cocktails, which are innovative, prepared with superlative ingredients, and predictably pricey. ✉ *77 W. Houston St., 2nd fl., between West Broadway and Wooster St., SoHo* ☎ *212/473–7348* ⊕ *www.peguclub.com* Ⓜ *B, D, F, M to Broadway– Lafayette St.; 6 to Bleecker St.*

Pravda. This Russian retreat has more than 70 brands of vodka, including 10 house-infused flavored vodkas, which means your choice of martinis is nearly endless. And teetotalers need not feel left out, because just about anywhere will serve New York's favorite nonalcoholic cocktail, the Lippy, which is simply a mix of every fruit juice that the bartender has on hand. Trust us—it's every bit as delicious aş the harder stuff. ✉ *281 Lafayette St., between Prince and W. Houston Sts., SoHo* ☎ *212/226–4944* Ⓜ *B, D, F, M to Broadway–Lafayette St.*

LIVE MUSIC VENUES

★ **SOB's.** The initials stand for "Sounds Of Brazil" (no, not what you—and everybody else—might think), and this is *the* place for reggae, African, and Latin music, with some jazz gigs like Marcus Miller sprinkled in. The late, great Cuban sensation Cachao used to hold court here, as does calypso's Mighty Sparrow when he's up north. Don't miss the monthly Southeast Asian party Basement Bhangra, the Haitian dance parties, or the bossa nova brunches. Dinner is served as well. ✉ *204 Varick St., SoHo* ☎ *212/243–4940* ⊕ *www.sobs.com* Ⓜ *1 to Houston St.*

EAST VILLAGE AND LOWER EAST SIDE

EAST VILLAGE
BARS
Beauty Bar. Grab a seat in a barber chair or under a dryer at this made-over hair salon where, during happy hour, the manicurist will do your nails for a fee that includes a drink. (How's that for multitasking?) The DJ spins everything from Britpop to rock—a great soundtrack for primping. ✉ *231 E. 14th St., between 2nd and 3rd Aves., East Village* ☎ *212/539–1389* ⊕ *www.thebeautybar.com* Ⓜ *4, 5, 6, L, N, Q, R to 14th St./Union Sq.*

CLOSE UP

Kickin' Karaoke

If you're looking for a venue other than the shower to bust out your rendition of Queen's "Somebody to Love," you're in good company. Otherwise jaded New Yorkers have become hooked on the goofy, addictive pleasure of karaoke. The K-word means "empty orchestra" in Japanese, and seems to tickle both downtown hipsters (who dig the irony of kitsch) and uptown financiers (who need a good rebel yell after the end of a workday), and everybody in between who loves to flex the golden pipes after a few drinks.

There are three ways of getting your lead-vocalist groove on: doing it in public, at a barwide Karaoke Night; reserving a private space at a bar ("karaoke boxes," they're called), where only your friends can hear you scream—er, sing; and bounding up onstage in front of a live band.

The hardcore karaoke places tend to be either grungy or glitzy, with as many as 15 available boxes for rent by the hour or full night (each box including music machine, microphones, and bar service), as well as up to 80,000 songs on tap for you to warble. (Don't worry, that figure includes stuff by Journey, REO Speedwagon, Britney Spears, and other grotesquely catchy Top 20 music.) The most popular of this lot include Chinatown's scruffy **Winnie's** (⊠ *104 Bayard St., at Baxter St.* ☎ *212/732–2384*), the East Village's **Sing-Sing** (⊠ *9 St. Marks Place* ☎ *212/387–7800*), the triple-serving-of-cheesiness at Midtown's **Pulse** (⊠ *135 W. 41st St., between Broadway and 6th Ave.* ☎ *646/461–7717*), and just about anywhere else in the unofficial Koreatown that sprawls around Herald Square. Try **Karaoke Duet 35** (⊠ *53 W. 35th St., 2nd fl., between 5th and 6th Aves.* ☎ *646/233–2685*).

For live-band karaoke, head to the Lower East Side's hottest sing-fest: Monday-night rock-n-roll karaoke at **Arlene's Grocery** (⊠ *95 Stanton St.* ☎ *212/995–1652*).

Fodor's Choice
★

The Bourgeois Pig. What do you get when you serve all kinds of different fondue concoctions as well as all kinds of inventively delicious cocktails in a velvety yet chilled-out French bordello setting that's smack dab in the middle of the East Village? This keeper of a lounge, that's what. ⊠ *111 E. 7th St., between 1st Ave. and Ave. A, East Village* ☎ *212/475–2246* ⊕ *bourgeoispigny.com/about.php* Ⓜ *F to Lower East Side/2nd Ave.; 6 to Astor Pl.*

★   **The Bowery Hotel.** Combining old-world hunting-lodge elegance with the height of comfort, the Bowery sets a standard for what all hotel lobbies should feature: sofas you can get lost in, a grand fireplace, a beautiful garden, an unusually friendly staff, and enough good vibes to compensate for the loss of CBGB down the block. ⊠ *335 Bowery, between 2nd and 3rd Aves., East Village* ☎ *212/505–9100* ⊕ *www.theboweryhotel. com* Ⓜ *F to Lower East Side/2nd Ave.; 6 to Astor Pl.*

Death + Company. It's all about "speakeasy chic" at this sister lounge to the equally imaginative and classy nearby bars Mayahuel and Bourgeois Pig. A hilarious wall mural toward the rear sets the tone for the tongue-and-cheek satanic vibe here, but in the end, it's all about the outlandishly delicious cocktails. ✉ *433 E. 6th St., between 1st Ave. and Ave. A, East Village* ☎ *212/388–0882* ⊕ *www.deathandcompany.com* Ⓜ *F to Lower East Side/2nd Ave.; 6 to Astor Pl.*

★ **Mayahuel.** This is the newest kid on the downtown, designer-bar block, and what a kid: all manner of Aztec spirits (raspberry tea–infused tequilas! pineapple-infused mescal!) make for the fiendishly rococo cocktails here, courtesy of master mixologist Philip Ward. Equally good are snacks such as popcorn with lime, cheese, and chili. The bi-level setting conjures a sort of demonic south-of-the-border bordello. As for the name, it derives from an Aztec legend (the fun menu fills you in). ✉ *304 E. 6th St., between 1st and 2nd Aves., East Village* ☎ *212/253–5888* ⊕ *mayahuelny.com/* Ⓜ *F to Lower East Side/2nd Ave.; 6 to Astor Pl., R, W to 8th St.–Broadway.*

McSorley's Old Ale House. One of New York's oldest saloons (it claims to have opened in 1854) and immortalized by *New Yorker* writer Joseph Mitchell, McSorley's is a must-visit for beer lovers, even if only two kinds of brew are served: McSorley's Light and McSorley's Dark. It's also essential for blarney lovers, and much friendlier to women than it was before the '80s. (The motto here once was "Good ale, raw onions, and no ladies.") Go early to avoid the down-the-block lines on Friday and Saturday night. ✉ *15 E. 7th St., between 2nd and 3rd Aves., East Village* ☎ *212/474–9148* ⊕ *www.mcsorleysnewyork.com* Ⓜ *6 to Astor Pl.*

Otto's Shrunken Head Tiki Bar & Lounge. Who says NYC doesn't appeal to all tastes? Should you get a sudden urge to visit a tiki bar while in the East Village—and who doesn't sometimes?—the ultrapopular Otto's is your ticket. You'll find more than just a bamboo bar here: namely fish lamps, a tattooed, punk-rock crowd, cute little banquettes, drinking mugs in the form of shrunken heads, beef jerky for sale, and DJs prone to spinning anything from '50s rock to "Soul Gidget" surf music. ✉ *538 E. 14th St., between Aves. A and B, East Village* ☎ *212/228–2240* ⊕ *www.ottosshrunkenhead.com* Ⓜ *L to 1st Ave.*

PDT. Those who crave their cocktails with a little cloak-and-dagger will flip over PDT (which stands for "Please Don't Tell"). Housed below the unassuming hot-dog joint Crif Dogs, this pseudo-speakeasy can be reached only through a phone booth on the main floor. Patrons with phoned-in reservations are escorted through the phone booth's false back into the building's underbelly, which is decorated with warm wooden beams and tongue-in-cheek taxidermy. ✉ *113 St. Marks Pl., between 1st Ave. and Ave. A, East Village* ☎ *212/614–0386* ⊕ *www. pdtnyc.com* Ⓜ *6 to Astor Pl.*

Summit Bar. Manhattan's easternmost cocktail bar, Summit Bar serves up high-end sips in a low-key environment. Still, much thought and care is put into the drinks, right down to the herbs that come from the Summit's rooftop garden. The menu aims to please, and splits between "classic" and more ambitious "alchemist" sections, the latter boasting drinks with caraway-infused agave and shiso leaf. There's a snug outdoor patio as well, ideal come summer for sampling the Summit's surprising take on a margarita. ✉ *133 Ave. C, between 8th and 9th Sts., East Village* ☎ *No phone* ⊕ *www.thesummitbar.net* Ⓜ *L to 1st Ave.*

17

Temple Bar. Unmarked and famous for its classic cocktails and romantic atmosphere, the Temple is prime first-date territory, especially once you drift past the sleekly wonderful bar to the back, where, swathed in almost complete darkness, you can lounge on a comfy banquette, order an old-fashioned, and do what people on first dates do. ✉ *12 East Essex St., East Village* ☎ *212/925–4242* ⊕ *www.templebarnyc.com* Ⓜ *B, D, F, M to Broadway–Lafayette St.; 6 to Bleecker St.*

CABARET AND PIANO BARS

Joe's Pub. Wood paneling, red-velvet walls, and comfy sofas make a lush setting for top-notch performers and the A-list celebrities who love them, or pretend to. Named for the Public Theater's near-mythic impresario Joe Papp, and located inside the Public, Joe's doesn't have a bad seat—but if you want to occupy one, buy tickets beforehand and/or arrive at least half an hour early for the Italian-inspired dinner menu. ✉ *425 Lafayette St., between E. 4th St. and Astor Pl., East Village* ☎ *212/967–7555* ⊕ *www.joespub.com* Ⓜ *6 to Astor Pl.*

GAY NIGHTLIFE

Fodor's Choice ★

Beige. Gay men in fashion and advertising predominate at this long-running Tuesday get-together at the B-Bar. An occasional celebrity or two keeps it lively, and with the right weather, the garden doubles or even triples the populace. Dress up, or look so freaking hot that you don't have to. ✉ *40 E. 4th St., at the Bowery, East Village* ☎ *212/475–2220* Ⓜ *6 to Astor Pl.*

Urge. A bi-level bastion of East Village boy action, Urge has two levels of muscly hipsters, go-go boys, drag acts on Sunday, Bingo Monday, and a contest on Wednesday whose name we can't print here. Best of all, it's cheek by jowl with several other fun East Village gay bars like the new **DTOX.** ✉ *33 2nd Ave., at 2nd St., East Village* ☎ *212/645–8613* Ⓜ *F to Lower East Side/2nd Ave.*

ROCK CLUB

Fodor's Choice ★

Lit Lounge. With a rock roster that's included musical forces as diverse as Devendra Banhart and the Hold Steady, Lit is a wonderfully grungy East Village classic. The raucous arty crowd hits not only shows but its charming art gallery Fuse and its theme parties, which cater to fans of specific bands (the White Stripes, Devo, and the Buzzcocks, to name just three). ✉ *93 2nd Ave., Grand Central Station, East Village* ☎ *212/777–7987* ⊕ *www.litloungenyc.com* Ⓜ *F to Lower East Side/2nd Ave., 6 to Astor Pl.*

LOWER EAST SIDE

BARS

Fodor's Choice ★

Back Room. The Prohibition-era atmospheric touches here include tin ceilings, chandeliers, velvet wallpaper, mirrored bars, an amply sized fireplace, and a "hidden" outdoor entrance (which you'll find easily enough, though the back-alley walk to the second, indoor entrance puts you in the speakeasy spirit). The music consists of rock CDs rather than a live spinmeister, and the drinks come in old-fashioned teacups or wrapped in paper bags. These, and other prize quirks, attract a slightly older clientele than many of its rowdy "boho" (aka bohemian)

The crowd at SOB's can get pretty lively.

neighbors do. ✉ *102 Norfolk St., between Delancey and Rivington Sts., Lower East Side* ☎ *212/228–5098* Ⓜ *F to Delancey St.; J, M, Z to Essex St.*

Max Fish. One of the Lower East Side's most iconic bars, Max Fish has been the scene of many a shenanigan since it opened back in 1989. It has one of the most eclectic jukeboxes in town, a pool table in back, and a constant stream of rock-and-rollers and those who rock (and sometimes roll) with them. It's open till 4 am daily. ✉ *178 Ludlow St., between E. Houston and Stanton Sts., Lower East Side* ☎ *212/529–3959* ⊕ *www. maxfish.com* Ⓜ *F to Essex/Delancey.*

★ **The Pink Pony.** Maintaining a defiantly boho feel on trendy Ludlow Street, this shabby-chic bar-café draws young writers, filmmakers, and designers who come to escape the cacophony from nearby music venues and make conversation over bottles of cheap wine and cup after cup (after cup) of coffee. ✉ *176 Ludlow St., between E. Houston and Stanton Sts., Lower East Side* ☎ *212/253–1922* ⊕ *www.pinkponynyc. com* Ⓜ *F to 2nd Ave.*

Spitzer's Corner. No, you won't rub shoulders with disgraced ex-governor Eliot Spitzer here, but you will find 40 types of beer on tap plus a selection of the bottled variety, good food, floor-to-ceiling windows that pop open in fine weather, and wooden walls supposedly taken from pickle barrels. (Fortunately, the air is free of any scents from the barrel's former contents.) ✉ *101 Rivington St., at Ludlow St., Lower East Side* ☎ *212/228–0027* ⊕ *www.spitzerscorner.com* Ⓜ *F to Delancey St.; J, M, Z to Essex St.*

White Star. Master mixologist Sasha Petraske won kudos for his innovative cocktails at Milk and Honey, but the hassles associated with that bar (reservations, membership, and so on) mean that White Star, its elegantly less-is-more sister bar, is a better choice. Named for the Moroccan lamps that hang above the bar (and front door), the Star features nattily dressed barkeeps, a scintillating drinks menu, and a tiny sunken back room that is one of NYC's best sites for a double date. ☒ *21 Essex St., between Canal and Hester Sts., Lower East Side* ☎ *212/995–5464* Ⓜ *F to East Broadway.*

LIVE MUSIC VENUES

Arlene's Grocery. On Monday nights crowds pack into this converted convenience store for rock-n-roll karaoke, where they live out their rock-star dreams by singing favorite punk anthems onstage with a live band. The other six nights of the week are for local bands, and are accordingly hit-or-miss. ☒ *95 Stanton St., between Ludlow and Orchard Sts., Lower East Side* ☎ *212/358–1633* ⊕ *www.arlenesgrocery. net* Ⓜ *F to 2nd Ave.*

Fodor's Choice
★
Bowery Ballroom. This theater with art-deco accents is probably the city's top midsize concert venue. Packing in the crowds here is a rite of passage for musicians on the cusp of stardom, including the Gossip, Manic Street Preachers, and the exuberant Go! Team. Grab one of the tables on the balcony (if you can), stand (and thus get sandwiched) on the main floor, or retreat to the comfortable bar in the basement, which really fills up after each show. ☒ *6 Delancey St., between the Bowery and Chrystie St., Lower East Side* ☎ *212/533–2111* ⊕ *www.boweryballroom.com* Ⓜ *J, M, Z to Bowery St.*

Fodor's Choice
★
Living Room. Terre Roche, Connie Acher, and other ace singer-songwriters—some solo, some with their bands—are found at this unpretentiously delightful club. Craving a more intimate experience? Head upstairs to Googie's Lounge, their humbler acoustic space with just a piano. (Or else sashay next door to **Cakeshop,** which has music and boozin' in a shabby-chic setting.) ☒ *154 Ludlow St., between Stanton and Rivington Sts., Lower East Side* ☎ *212/533–7327* ⊕ *www. livingroomny.com* Ⓜ *F to 2nd Ave.*

★
Mercury Lounge. You'll have to squeeze past all the sardine-packed hipsters in the front bar to reach the stage, but it's worth it. Not only does this top-quality venue, a "little sister to the Bowery Bar," specialize in cool bands on the indie scene (Holly Golightly, Echo and the Bunnymen, and the Apostle of Hustle, anyone?), but it was where the late great Jeff Buckley used to stop by to do spontaneous solo shows. ☒ *217 E. Houston St., at Ave. A, Lower East Side* ☎ *212/260–4700* ⊕ *mercuryloungenyc.com* Ⓜ *F to 2nd Ave.*

Piano's. With two music venues for live music and DJs—the Showroom downstairs and Lounge upstairs—as well as a full bar that serves food downstairs, there's something for everyone at this Lower East Side staple. It's a blast late nights. ☒ *158 Ludlow St. , just south of Stanton St., Lower East Side* ☎ *212/505–3733* ⊕ *www.pianosnyc.com* Ⓜ *F to Delancey St.*

GREENWICH VILLAGE AND WEST VILLAGE

GREENWICH VILLAGE

BARS

The Dove Parlour. On a colorful block that evokes the Greenwich Village of yore—cigar store, vegetarian cafés, a bootleg music shop, and not one but two stores specializing in chess—is this wonderful bar whose elegant atmosphere (red-velvet wallpaper, white-wood paneling) is belied by the revelry of the very sexy young customers. ⊠ *228 Thompson St., between W. 3rd and Bleecker Sts., Greenwich Village* ☎ *212/254–1435* ⊕ *www. thedoveparlour.com* Ⓜ *E to Spring St.*

Vol de Nuit. Tucked away from the street, the "Belgian Beer Bar" (as everybody calls it) features a European-style, enclosed outdoor courtyard and a cozy interior, all red light and shadows. NYU grad-student types come for the mammoth selection of beers on tap as well as for the fries, which are served with a Belgian flair, in a paper cone with an array of sauces on the side. ⊠ *148 W. 4th St., at 6th Ave., Greenwich Village* ☎ *212/982–3388* ⊕ *www.voldenuitbar.com* Ⓜ *A, B, C, D, E, F, M to W. 4th St./Washington Sq.*

JAZZ VENUES

Fodor's Choice ★ **Blue Note.** Considered by many (not least its current owners) to be "the jazz capital of the world," the Blue Note was once the stomping ground for such legends as Dizzy Gillespie, and still hosts a varied repertoire from Chris Botti to the Count Basie Orchestra to Boz Scaggs. Expect a steep cover charge except for late shows on weekends, when the music goes from less jazzy to more funky. ⊠ *131 W. 3rd St., near 6th Ave., Greenwich Village* ☎ *212/475–8592* ⊕ *www.bluenotejazz.com* Ⓜ *A, B, C, D, E, F, M to W. 4th St.*

Knickerbocker Bar and Grill. Jazz acts are on the menu on Friday and Saturday nights at this old-fashioned steak house, a longtime staple of the city's more intimate music scene. ⊠ *33 University Pl., at E. 9th St., Greenwich Village* ☎ *212/228–8490* ⊕ *www.knickerbockerbarandgrill. com* Ⓜ *R to 8th St.*

LIVE MUSIC VENUES

★ **(Le) Poisson Rouge.** Underneath the site of the late, lamented Village Gate jazz emporium is this cutting-edge jewel of a place, whose name means "the Red Fish" and whose parentheses around Le remain a sacred mystery. Blending just the right mix of posh notes (the lush decor, the fine dining) and brave music programming (jazz, classical, electronic, cabaret, rock, folk—even, with the splendiferous Ralph's World, children's music), the Poisson is quite simply an essential NYC fixture. ⊠ *158 Bleecker St., at Thompson St., Greenwich Village* ☎ *212/505–3474* ⊕ *www.lepoissonrouge.com* Ⓜ *A, B, C, D, E, F, M to W. 4th St.*

WEST VILLAGE

BARS

Corner Bistro. Opened in 1961, this neighborhood saloon serves what many think are the best hamburgers in town. Once you actually get a seat, the space feels nice and cozy, but until then, be prepared to drink a beer amid loud and hungry patrons. ⊠ *331 W. 4th St., at 8th Ave.,*

17

West Village ☎ *212/242–9502* ⊕ *cornerbistrony.com* Ⓜ *A, C, E to 14th St.; L to 8th Ave.*

Employees Only. The dapper, white-coated bartenders (many of them impressively mustachioed) at this Prohibition era–style bar mix delicious, well-thought-out cocktails with debonair aplomb and freshly squeezed mixers. Sip one in the dimly lit, unpretentious bar area and you just might feel like you've stepped back in time—if it weren't for the crush of trendy West Village locals and visitors in the know at your back. Look for the green awning that says EO and the neon "Psychic" sign out front. Dinner is served in the restaurant at the back: it's quality, but pricey. ⊠ *510 Hudson St., West Village* ☎ *212/242–3021* ⊕ *www. employeesonlynyc.com* Ⓜ *1 to Christopher St.; A, B, C, D, E, F, M to W. 4th St.*

★ **Hudson Bar and Books.** Along with its sister branches—Beekman Bar and Books on Beekman Place and Lexington Bar and Books on, yep, Lexington—the Hudson reflects a literary bent on its cocktails with names like the Dewey Decimal, the Cervantes Spritzer, and Alphabet Absinthe (topped off with floating letter-shape sugar cubes). Despite that, it's hardly a hushed library where well-read butlers serve you; no—the atmosphere here is more about book decor than serious literature. It's seriously clubby, with wood paneling and leather banquettes, and it's one of the few places you can still smoke. ⊠ *636 Hudson St., at Horatio St., West Village* ☎ *212/229–2642* ⊕ *www.barandbooks.cz* Ⓜ *A, C, E to 14th St.; L to 8th Ave.*

Fodor's Choice
★ **Little Branch.** The owners of the secretive, hard-to-access lounge Milk & Honey (now closed) created this open-to-everyone cousin, the site of N.Y.'s legendary '80s Milk Bar, with the same simple yet high-quality cocktails. The dim lighting and snug booths make it the ideal spot for you to hide from creditors or share a romantic first kiss in equal measure. ⊠ *20 7th Ave., at Leroy St., West Village* ☎ *212/929–4360* Ⓜ *1 to Houston St.*

Otheroom. Ever wish that the bar you're drinking in had something more interesting on its walls than Budweiser signs? At this art gallery by day, upscale drinking spot by night, the walls are as visually arresting as you'd hope. The menu is pretty creative, too, with dozens of microbeers as well as American wines available by the glass. ⊠ *143 Perry St., between W. Greenwich and Washington Sts., West Village* ☎ *212/645–9758* ⊕ *www.theotheroom.com* Ⓜ *1 to Sheridan Sq.–Christopher St.*

★ **White Horse Tavern.** According to New York legend, Dylan Thomas drank himself to death in this historic and quintessential West Village tavern founded in 1880. The Horse remains perpetually popular with literary types, but thankfully it's lacking more death-by-alcohol-poisoning cases of late. When the weather's nice, try to snag a seat at one of the sidewalk tables for prime—and, given the neighborhood, we do mean prime—people-watching. ⊠ *567 Hudson St., at W. 11th St., West Village* ☎ *212/989–3956* ⊕ *whitehorsetavern.us* Ⓜ *1 to Christopher St./Sheridan Sq.*

CABARET AND PIANO BARS

The Duplex. No matter who's performing, the largely gay audience hoots and hollers in support of the often kitschy performers at this music-scene staple on busy Sheridan Square since 1951. Singers and comedians hold court in the cabaret theater, while those itching to take a shot at open mike head downstairs to the lively piano bar. ⊠ *61 Christopher St., at 7th Ave. S, West Village* ☎ *212/255–5438* ⊕ *www.theduplex. com* Ⓜ *1 to Christopher St.*

GAY NIGHTLIFE

Cubbyhole. Early in the evening the crowd is mixed at this neighborhood institution, where the DJs, the unpretentious decor, and the inexpensive margaritas are popular. Later on, the women take charge—and how. ⊠ *281 W. 12th St., at W. 4th St., West Village* ☎ *212/243–9041* ⊕ *www. cubbyholebar.com* Ⓜ *A, C, E to 14th St.; L to 8th Ave.*

Fodor's Choice
★

Henrietta Hudson. The nightly parties at this laid-back West Village HQ for the Sapphic set attract young professional women, out-of-towners, and longtime regulars. Because the DJ and the pool table quickly create a crowd, though, stake your claim to a spot early, especially on—yup, you guessed it—weekends. ⊠ *438 Hudson St., at Morton St., West Village* ☎ *212/924–3347* ⊕ *www.henriettahudson.com* Ⓜ *1 to Christopher St./Sheridan Sq.*

JAZZ VENUES

Garage Restaurant & Café. Good news for you budget-minded jazzers: there's no cover *and* no minimum at this West Village hot spot, where two jazz groups jam seven nights a week and a fireplace sets the mood upstairs. ⊠ *99 7th Ave. S, between Bleecker and Christopher Sts., West Village* ☎ *212/645–0600* ⊕ *www.garagerest.com* Ⓜ *1 to Christopher St./Sheridan Sq.*

Fodor's Choice
★

Village Vanguard. This prototypical jazz club, tucked into a cellar in Greenwich Village since the 1940s, has been the haunt of legends like Thelonious Monk and Barbra Streisand (who recently came back for a one-night-only gig). Today you can hear jams from the jazz-star likes of Bill Charlap and Ravi Coltrane, and on Monday night the sizable resident Vanguard Jazz Orchestra blows its collective heart out. ⊠ *178 7th Ave. S, between W. 11th and Perry Sts., West Village* ☎ *212/255–4037* ⊕ *www.villagevanguard.com* Ⓜ *1, 2, 3 to 14th St.*

17

CHELSEA AND THE MEATPACKING DISTRICT

CHELSEA

BARS

★ **Half King.** Writer Sebastian Junger (*The Perfect Storm*) is one of the owners of this would-be literary mecca. We say "would-be" because the ambience can be more publike than writerly—but that's fine, since the King draws such a friendly crowd (media types, mostly). We like it best for its frequent readings, gallery exhibits, and Irish-American menu. ⊠ *505 W. 23rd St., between 10th and 11th Aves., Chelsea* ☎ *212/ 462–4300* ⊕ *www.thehalfking.com* Ⓜ *C, E to 23rd St.*

Indie band Beirut blows away the Bowery Ballroom.

★ **Tillman's.** Nothing in Chelsea is quite like this glorious "Old Harlem" lounge, resplendent as it is with fireplace, banquettes, good eats, even better cocktails, inventive decor, jazz and blues sounds on the soundtrack, and tastefully uniformed servers complete with a cigarette girl. ✉ *165 W. 26th St., between 6th and 7th Aves., Chelsea* ☎ *212/627–8320* ⊕ *www.tillmansnyc.com* Ⓜ *F, M, 1 to 28th St.*

COMMEDY CLUBS

Fodor's Choice
★ **Upright Citizens Brigade Theatre.** Raucous sketch comedy, audience-initiated improv, and classic stand-up take turns onstage here at the city's absolute capital for alternative comedy. There are even classes available; the Upright Citizens bill their program as the world's largest improv school, where you can catch indie comic darlings like *SNL*'s Amy Poehler or *Human Giant*'s Rob Huebel. ✉ *307 W. 26th St., between 8th and 9th Aves., Chelsea* ☎ *212/366–9176* ⊕ *www.uprightcitizens. org* Ⓜ *C, E to 23rd St.*

GAY NIGHTLIFE

Big Apple Ranch. Taking *Brokeback Mountain* style to the dance floor, the Ranch lets you unleash your inner "cowboy dancer" every Saturday night, with half-hour two-step lessons at 8 pm, line dancing at 8:30 pm, and then a down-home country-and-western dance party. Make sure the DJ plays some Hank Williams, just to keep things honest (and remember these immortal words from Hank: "I don't need nobody standing by me in a barfight 'cept for my mama with a broken bottle in her hand"). ✉ *Dance Manhattan, 39 W. 19th St., 5th Floor, Chelsea* ☎ *212/358–5752* ⊕ *www.bigappleranch.com* Ⓜ *F, R, M to 23rd St.; 1 to 18th St.*

Gym Sports Bar. At New York's first gay sports bar, the plentiful flat-screen TVs and cheap Budweisers draw athletic enthusiasts of every stripe, from athlete to armchair. Nobly enough, the bar sponsors—and frequently hosts parties for—a number of local gay sports teams. The only problem: couldn't they have thought up a more savory name for the place? ⊠ *167 8th Ave., at W. 18th St., Chelsea* ☎ *212/337–2439* ⊕ *www.gymsportsbar.com* Ⓜ *A, C, E to 14th St.; L to 8th Ave.*

Fodor's Choice ★ **Splash.** At this large, perennially crowded Chelsea bar–club, beefy go-go boys vie for attention with equally buff bartenders who, for some reason (can't the management afford uniforms?) don't have on much more than underwear. The daily happy hour, with campy music videos on three huge screens, is a hit. Our only caveat: late-night covers can be high. ⊠ *50 W. 17th St., between 5th and 6th Aves., Chelsea* ☎ *212/691–0073* ⊕ *www.splashbar.com* Ⓜ *6 to Astor Pl.*

THE MEATPACKING DISTRICT

BARS

675 Bar. How can you not love a spot where the bouncer greets you with a grin instead of a scowl, board games abound, a giant black-lacquered horse stands guard next to the pool table, the drinks get amply poured, and each small room along the subterranean stone corridor is decorated in a different creative way? As an ideal spot for both dates (plenty of dark corners) and raucous merriment (bright, big central space), the 675 scores highest for having less attitude than the rest of this supremely haughty nightlife neighborhood. ⊠ *675 Hudson St., between Hudson St. and 9th Ave. (enter on 13th St.), Meatpacking District* ☎ *212/699–2410* ⊕ *www.675bar.com* Ⓜ *A, C, E to 14th St.; L to 8th Ave.*

Hogs & Heifers. This raucous place is all about the saucy barkeeps using megaphones to berate male customers and bait the females to get up on the bar and dance (and add their bras to the collection on the wall). Celebrities of the *Us Weekly* variety still drop in from time to time to get their names in the gossip columns. ⊠ *859 Washington St., at W. 13th St., Meatpacking District* ☎ *212/929–0655* ⊕ *www.hogsandheifers.com* Ⓜ *A, C, E to 14th St.; L to 8th Ave.*

Plunge. The Gansevoort Hotel's slick rooftop bar would be worth visiting even without its mouthwatering views, though that helps. The adjectives sleek and glossy could easily be illustrated by Plunge, where the lighting is soft, the furnishings are cool and comfy (at least to a degree), the music isn't too loud, servers of both sexes are sexy, and the ample space—indoor as well as outdoor—make it practically iconic. ⊠ *18 9th Ave., at W. 13th St., Meatpacking District* ☎ *212/660–6766* ⊕ *www.hotelgansevoort.com* Ⓜ *A, C, E to 14th St.; L to 8th Ave.*

Spice Market. The posh come here to gorge on Asian street fare served with upscale twists and the equally exotic cocktails. Ginger margaritas, anyone? Or a kumquat *mojito* (when in season)? And if you're looking for tranquility, the multilevel open space has slowly rotating fans, intricately carved woodwork, and flowing curtains that create a palpable aura of calm. ⊠ *403 W. 13th St., at 9th Ave., Meatpacking District* ☎ *212/675–2322* ⊕ *spicemarketnewyork.com* Ⓜ *A, C, E to 14th St.; L to 8th Ave.*

17

★ **The Standard Hotel Biergarten, Grill, and Living Room.** Practically the official bar of the High Line park, the Standard is a lush diversion. The media was quick to pick up on the riotous behavior of hotel guests here who displayed themselves to High Line visitors, leaving their shades wide open during salacious activities. But the real story is in the sprawling and already riotous beer garden, grill bar, and very cool indoor Living Room lounge. As for the chic hot spot on the top floor, unofficially called the Boom Boom Room, it's currently the hardest "door" in town ("hardest," that is, to get through), but given the quality of the accessible fun down below, we'll forgive their snobbery. ⊠ *848 Washington St., at W. 13th St., Meatpacking District* ☎ *212/645–4646* ⊕ *www. standardhotels.com* Ⓜ *A, C, E, L to 14th St.*

DANCE CLUBS AND DJ VENUES

Cielo. Relatively mature dance-club goers (if the word mature can ever be applied to such a crowd) gravitate to this small but sturdy Meatpacking District "music-head" mecca to toss back cocktails, dig the high-quality sound system, groove to top-flight DJs spinning soulful Latin beats and techno, boogie on the sunken dance floor, and smoke in the no-frills garden outside. On Monday nights are the award-winning Deep Space parties, where resident DJ François K. (as well as guest spinmeisters like Dmitri from Paris) rev up the faithful with everything from dubstep to Stravinsky. ⊠ *18 Little W. 12th St., between 9th Ave. and Washington St., Meatpacking District* ☎ *212/645–5700* ⊕ *www. cieloclub.com* Ⓜ *A, C, E to 14th St.; L to 8th Ave.*

Fodor'sChoice ★ **Kiss & Fly.** One of New York's most discerning nightlife experts, the dance-music artist Sir Ivan, swears by Kiss And Fly, and it's obvious why: this modest-size dance club has sensational music (pumped as loud as can be, of course), a beautiful interior design (dig all the butterfly motifs), and creative lighting that actually lets you see who you're dancing/speaking/kissing/sipping with. It's pricey, tough to get into, and a bit snooty, but now that you've been duly warned, have a ball. ⊠ *409 W. 13th St., between 9th Ave. and Washington St., Meatpacking District* ☎ *212/255–1933* ⊕ *www.kissandflyclub.com* Ⓜ *A, C, E to 14th St.; L to 8th Ave.*

UNION SQUARE, GRAMERCY, AND THE FLATIRON DISTRICT

GRAMERCY

BARS

★ **Old Town Bar.** The proudly unpretentious bi-level Old Town is redolent of old New York, and why not—it's been around since 1892. Tavern-style grub, mahogany everywhere, and atmosphere, atmosphere, atmosphere make this a fun stop on any pub crawl. Men, don't miss the giant, person-size urinals. ⊠ *45 E. 18th St., between Broadway and Park Ave. S, Gramercy* ☎ *212/529–6732* ⊕ *www.oldtownbar.com* Ⓜ *4, 5, 6, L, N, Q, R to 14th St./Union Sq.*

Pete's Tavern. Allegedly the place where that great transplanted New Yorker O. Henry wrote his sweet tale *The Gift of the Magi* (in the booth up front), Pete's has charm to spare even today, when it's crowded with locals enjoying a beer or a (fantastic) burger. ⊠ *129 E. 18th St., at Irving*

Pl., Gramercy ☎ *212/473–7676* ⊕ *www.petestavern.com* Ⓜ *4, 5, 6, L, N, Q, R to 14th St./Union Sq.*

JAZZ VENUES

Fodor'sChoice **Jazz Standard.** The Standard's sizable underground room draws the
★ top names in the business. As a part of Danny Meyer's Southern-food restaurant Blue Smoke, it's one of the few spots where you can get dry-rubbed ribs to go with your bebop. Bring the kids for the Jazz Standard Youth Orchestra concerts every Sunday afternoon. ⊠ *116 E. 27th St., between Park and Lexington Aves., Gramercy* ☎ *212/576–2232* ⊕ *www.jazzstandard.net* Ⓜ *6 to 28th St.*

LIVE MUSIC VENUES

Fodor'sChoice **Irving Plaza.** This two-story venue is known for its solid rock perfor-
★ mances, both indie (DJ Shadow and Sleater-Kinney) and more mainstream (Lenny Kravitz, Blues Traveller)—even if they can get a little pricey. Red walls and chandeliers add a Gothic touch. And if the main floor gets too cramped, seek sanctuary in the form of the chill upstairs bar. ⊠ *17 Irving Pl., at E. 15th St., Gramercy* ☎ *212/777–6800* ⊕ *www. irvingplaza.com* Ⓜ *4, 5, 6, L, N, Q, R to 14th St./Union Sq.*

FLATIRON DISTRICT

BARS

★ **The Ace Hotel.** A hot spot for the digital set, the lobby and adjoining restaurant spaces—the Breslin and the John Dory—have been packed since they've opened at this Pacific Northwest import. If your bearded hipster friend came into some cash, it would look like the lobby here, with reclaimed wood tables, beer signs, and beautiful folks in oversize eyeglasses. ⊠ *20 W. 29th St., between Broadway and 5th Ave., Gramercy* ☎ *212/679–2222* ⊕ *www.acehotel.com* Ⓜ *R to 28th St.*

Flatiron Lounge. Here, resident mixologists rely on the freshest (and sometimes most exotic) ingredients available. The cocktail menu changes often, but if you're stumped, tell the bartenders what you like and they'll happily invent a new concoction on the spot. ⊠ *37 W. 19th St., between 5th and 6th Aves., Flatiron* ☎ *212/727–7741* ⊕ *www.flatironlounge. com* Ⓜ *F, M, N, R to 23rd St.*

UNION SQUARE

BARS

Rye House. A welcoming bar with slick cocktails and clever takes on comfort food, the Rye House beckons just steps from the chain store overload of Union Square. From boiled peanuts and fried pickles to their own take on a Sazerac, the space is a welcome respite from the hustle and bustle outside. ⊠ *11 W. 17th St., between Broadway and 5th Ave., Union Square* ☎ *212/255–7260* ⊕ *www.ryehousenyc.com* Ⓜ *4, 5, 6, L, N, Q, R to 14th St./Union Sq.*

MIDTOWN EAST

BARS

The Bar Downstairs. The bar without a name in the basement of the newly opened Andaz Fifth Avenue may lack a moniker, but it certainly has a pedigree. Alchemy Consulting, a joint venture from Chicago's

17

Violet Hour and New York's Death and Co., designed the cocktails here; look for spins on the Negroni and Manhattan in the sleek subterranean space. The food menu is similarly up-market, with a variety of nebulously Spanish small plates on offer. ⊠ *485 5th Ave., at 41st St., Midtown East* ☎ *212/601–1234* Ⓜ *6 to 42nd St.*

Fodor's Choice
★
Campbell Apartment. Commuting professionals pack into this Grand Central Terminal bar on their way to catch trains home during the evening rush, but don't let the crush of humanity scare you away—you can have a deeply romantic time here in one of Manhattan's more beautiful rooms. The restored space dates to the 1920s, when it was the private office of an executive named John W. Campbell, and as the exquisite decor suggests, old JWC knew how to live. Sample the good life as you knock back a well-built cocktail from an overstuffed chair. Just try to avoid that evening rush. ⊠ *15 Vanderbilt Ave. entrance, Grand Central Station, Midtown East* ☎ *212/953–0409* ⊕ *www.hospitalityholdings. com* Ⓜ *4, 5, 6, 7, S to 42nd St./Grand Central.*

Fodor's Choice
★
Galway Hooker. The name actually refers to a kind of Irish fishing boat (but then, you knew that already, right?). It's sought out as one of Midtown's most authentic, and best, Irish pubs. Even on a block with a high number of fine drinking establishments, the Hooker stands out thanks to its gorgeous circular bar, intriguing orange lighting, spirited after-work crowd, and bartenders, some of whom might just actually hail from the Emerald Isle. Snag one of their business cards, too—on the back are words of wisdom from the best Irish writers. ⊠ *7 E. 36th St., between 5th Ave. and Madison Murray Hill, Midtown East* ☎ *212/725–2353* ⊕ *www.galwayhookernyc.com* Ⓜ *6 to 34th St.*

King Cole Bar. A justly beloved Maxfield Parrish mural of "Old King Cole" himself, as well as his psychedelic court, adds to the already considerable elegance at this romantic and essential Midtown meeting place. Try a Bloody Mary—this is where the drink was introduced to Americans. ⊠ *St. Regis Hotel, 2 E. 55th St., between 5th and Madison Aves., Midtown East* ☎ *212/753–4500* ⊕ *www.starwoodhotels.com* Ⓜ *E, M to 5th Ave./53rd St.*

Pine Tree Lodge. Who says that the zaniest places are all below 14th Street? This insane theme bar offers serious competition. Think "summer camp on psychedelics"—we're talking mounted wildlife, rafts, and other outdoorsy-kitsch decor. Don't overlook the very spacious backyard or the racy raccoon picture in the comfy side room—you'll never view those critters the same way again. ⊠ *591 1st Ave. at 34th St., Midtown East* ☎ *212/481–5490* ⊕ *www.pinetreelodgeny.com/* Ⓜ *6 to 34th St.*

★
P. J. Clarke's. Mirrors and polished wood and other old-time flair adorn New York's most famous Irish bar, a redbrick brawler of a joint. Steeped in Hollywood lore—Steve McQueen was once a regular, and scenes from the 1945 movie *Lost Weekend* were shot here—Clarke's draws in the after-work crowd that appreciates drinking beer and eating exceptionally juicy burgers around a sense of history. ⊠ *915 Third Ave., 55th St., Midtown East* ☎ *212/317–1616* ⊕ *www.pjclarkes.com* Ⓜ *4, 5, 6, N, R to 59th St.–Lexington Ave.*

Rodeo Bar. If the honky-tonk music, the bison over the front bar, and the peanut shells littering the floor at this neighborhood institution don't clue you in, the rockin' vibe and friendly service will: this is the go-to spot for good times and free live music every night of the week. The Tex Mex food is good (try the Cowboy kisses: shrimp and jalapeños wrapped in bacon), but the real draw is the music. Local bands and touring pros play blues, bluegrass, country, alt-country, rockabilly, and rock and roll. The margaritas are legendary, and the selection of beer includes hard to find quaffs like Shiner Bock from Texas. ⊠ *375 3rd Ave., at 27th St., Midtown East* ☎ *212/683–6500* ⊕ *www.rodeobar. com* Ⓜ *6 to 28th St.*

Top of the Tower. There are lounges at higher altitudes, but this one on the 26th floor wins wide acclaim for its atmosphere of subdued elegance and East Side location, within spitting distance of the United Nations. (But no spitting on the diplomats, please—it's not diplomatic.) There's live piano music Wednesday–Sunday nights. ⊠ *Beekman Tower Hotel, 3 Mitchell Pl., near 1st Ave. at E. 49th St., Midtown East* ☎ *866/298–4606* ⊕ *www.thebeekmanhotel.com* Ⓜ *6 to 51st St./Lexington Ave.; E, M to Lexington Ave./53rd St.*

Fodor'sChoice
★
The Volstead. Named for the Volstead Act, which instituted Prohibition back in the '20s, this new subterranean bastion of cool is simply indispensable. In a gorgeous though tasteful setting that features just the right mix of mirrors, chandeliers, polished wood, and velvet wallpaper, a friendly staff and an ace barkeep serve up specialties like jalapeño margaritas and strawberry *caipiroskas*. ⊠ *125 E. 54th St., between Park and Lexington Aves., Midtown East* ☎ *212/583–0411* ⊕ *www. thevolstead.com* Ⓜ *E, M to 53rd St.*

GAY NIGHTLIFE

Evolve Bar and Lounge. Rising from the ashes of a popular gay club on the same site, this glossy, raucous Chelsea-style bar–club gets the Upper East Side rocking, with its sexy-yet-genial staff and its theme nights like Pop-off Thursday, Bulge Friday, and Disco Balls Sunday. ⊠ *221 East 58th St., between 2nd and 3rd Aves., Midtown East* ☎ *212/355–3395* ⊕ *www.evolvebarandloungenyc.com* Ⓜ *4, 5, 6, N, R to 59th St./Lexington Ave.*

Townhouse Bar. It's the elegant yin to the rowdy yang of **Evolve**, which is just across the block at East 58th Street. Distinguished mature men from the Upper East Side meet younger would-be versions of themselves at this "gentlemen's club," which looks like the home of a blueblood with superb taste. As always the attire is "uptown casual," if not fancier. ⊠ *236 E. 58th St., between 2nd and 3rd Aves., Midtown East* ☎ *212/754–4649* ⊕ *www.townhouseny.com* Ⓜ *4, 5, 6, N, R to 59th St.–Lexington Ave.*

MIDTOWN WEST

BARS

Cellar Bar. Underneath the Bryant Park Hotel—and a tiled, arched ceiling—is one of the more spectacular spaces in Midtown. As a DJ with a taste for classic R&B spins the night away, a fashion-industry crowd gets up to dance—and spills its collective drink. ✉ *40 W. 40th St., between 5th and 6th Aves., Midtown West* ☎ *212/869–0100* ⊕ *www. bryantparkhotel.com/* Ⓜ *B, D, F, M to 42nd St.; 7 to 5th Ave.*

Joe Allen. Everybody's en route either to or from a show at this "old reliable" on the boisterous Restaurant Row, celebrated in the musical version of *All About Eve.* Chances are you'll even spot a Broadway star at the bar or in the dining room. Still, our favorite thing about Joe's is not the fun show crowd but the hilarious "flop wall," adorned with posters from musicals that bombed, sometimes spectacularly. (Check out the ones for *Paradox Lust, Got To Go Disco,* and *Dude,* which was the unfortunate sequel to *Hair.*) ✉ *326 W. 46th St., between 8th and 9th Aves., Midtown West* ☎ *212/581–6464* ⊕ *www.joeallenrestaurant. com* Ⓜ *A, C, E to 42nd St.*

The Oak Room. One of the great classic cabaret venues, the Algonquin's Oak Room is formal (jackets are mandatory; ties are the norm) and decorated sumptuously. You might find the hopelessly romantic singer Andrea Marcovicci, among other top-notch performers, crooning here. ✉ *Algonquin Hotel, 59 W. 44th St., between 5th and 6th Aves., Midtown West* ☎ *212/758–7777* ⊕ *www.oakroomny.com/* Ⓜ *B, D, F, M to 42nd St.; 7 to 5th Ave.*

Russian Vodka Room. Forget **Russian Samovar** across the block—here's where the serious vodka drinking goes down, along with (almost) everything that goes along with serious vodka drinking. The Vodka Room features a glowing, sophisticated front room with nightly piano player (and the superlative Dmitri Kolesnik Jazz Trio on Monday, free of charge), a more sumptuous back room, a generous Attitude Adjustment Hour (that's Russki for "Happy Hour"), and more exotically infused vodkas (horseradish! ginger! pepper!) than you can shake a babushka at. For those who crave variety, a vodka tasting menu is available, as are culinary standards like borscht. ✉ *265 W. 52nd St., between Broadway and 8th Ave., Midtown West* ☎ *212/307–5835* ⊕ *www. russianvodkaroom.com* Ⓜ *C, E, 1 to 50th St.*

Salon de Ning. Take a break from 5th Avenue shopping at this glass-lined penthouse bar on the 23rd floor of the über-ritzy Peninsula Hotel. Drinks are pricey, of course, but what isn't in this neighborhood? Plus, the views are inarguably worth it, especially from the rooftop terraces. ✉ *Peninsula Hotel, 700 5th Ave., at W. 55th St., Midtown West* ☎ *212/956–2888* ⊕ *www.salondening.com/* Ⓜ *E, M to 5th Ave./53rd St.*

COMEDY CLUBS

Caroline's on Broadway. This high-gloss club presents established names as well as comedians on the edge of stardom. Janeane Garofalo, Colin Quinn, and Gilbert Gottfried have headlined. ✉ *1626 Broadway, between W. 49th and W. 50th Sts., Midtown West* ☎ *212/757–4100* ⊕ *www.carolines.com* Ⓜ *N, R to 49th St.; 1 to 50th St.*

Chicago City Limits. This crew touts itself as performing in the longest-running improv show in the city. The shows, heavy on audience participation, take place Wednesday through Saturday and seldom fail to whip visitors into what the comics might call a "phun phrenzy." ✉ *318 W.*

53rd St., between 8th and 9th Aves., Midtown West ☎ *212/888–5233* ⊕ *www.chicagocitylimits.com* Ⓜ *C, E to 50th St.*

DANCE CLUBS AND DJ VENUES

Pacha. Maybe you've been to the exclusive Pacha clubs in Buenos Aires, Ibiza, and London. Congratulations. But the jewel in the crown of the Pacha empire may well be here. Assuming you pass muster to enter, you'll find four stories' worth of high-tech fittings (blinding lights, go-go girls, humungous sound), plus celeb DJs, celeb customers, even celeb bathroom attendants. (OK, maybe not that last part.) ✉ *618 W. 46th St., between 11th and 12th Aves., Midtown West* ☎ *212/209–7500* ⊕ *www.pachanyc.com* Ⓜ *C, E to 50th St.*

GAY NIGHTLIFE

Posh. Lest you think that Hell's Kitchen has no fine gay lounges, Posh has walls covered in fine canvases by local artists, trophies over the bar, ample room for kibitzing and dancing, plenty of neon decor, and hours that are "4 pm to 4 am GUARANTEED." Who says nothing is certain anymore in these confusing times? ✉ *405 West 51th St., at 9th Ave., Midtown West* ☎ *212/957–2222* ⊕ *www.poshbarnyc.com* Ⓜ *C, E to 50th St.*

JAZZ VENUES

Birdland. This place gets its name from bebop saxophone great Charlie "Yardbird" (or just "Bird") Parker, so expect serious musicians such as John Pizzarelli, the Dave Holland Sextet, and Chico O'Farrill's Afro-Cuban Jazz Orchestra (on Sunday night). The dining room serves moderately priced American fare with a Cajun accent. If you sit at the bar, your cover charge includes a drink. ✉ *315 W. 44th St., between 8th and 9th Aves., Midtown West* ☎ *212/581–3080* ⊕ *www.birdlandjazz.com* Ⓜ *A, C, E to 42nd St./Port Authority.*

Iridium. This cozy, top-drawer club is a sure bet for big-name talent like the David Murray Black Saint Quartet and Michael Wolff. The sight lines are good, and the sound system was designed with the help of Les Paul, the inventor of the solid-body electric guitar, who used to play here every Monday night. The rest of the week sees a mix of artists like Chuck Mangione and the Eddie Daniels Band. ✉ *1650 Broadway, at W. 51st St., Midtown West* ☎ *212/582–2121* ⊕ *theiridium.com/* Ⓜ *1 to 50th St.; N, R to 49th St.*

LIVE MUSIC VENUES

B. B. King Blues Club & Grill. This lavish Times Square club is vast and shiny and host to a range of musicians, from the Harlem Gospel Choir to George Clinton and the P-Funk All-Stars. It's also where surviving rock legends like Little Richard, Chuck Berry, and, yes, the still-relentlessly-touring owner plays as well. (If you happen to meet Mr. King here, give our regards to Lucille, his guitar.) ✉ *237 W. 42nd St., between 7th and 8th Aves., Midtown West* ☎ *212/997–4144* ⊕ *www.bbkingblues.com* Ⓜ *1, 2, 3, 7, A, C, E, N, Q, R, S to 42nd St./Port Authority.*

17

UPPER EAST SIDE

BARS

American Trash. You might tell from the name that this isn't exactly your granddad's UES drinking establishment. Bicycle tires, golf clubs, and other castoffs cover the walls and ceiling, ensuring that the 20-year-old Trash, a sanctum of sleaze, merits its descriptive name. Eight plasma TVs, three video games, a defiantly rock-and-roll jukebox, and a pool table keep the neighborhood crowd (as well as stray bikers who hate them) busy. Some nights local bands play classic rock. ⊠ *1471 1st Ave., between E. 76th and E. 77th Sts., Upper East Side* ☎ *212/988–9008* ⊕ *www.americantrashnyc.com* Ⓜ *6 to 77th St.*

Fodor's Choice
★ **Auction House.** This Victorian lounge brings a touch of downtown chic to the sometimes suburban-feeling Upper East Side with its candle-lighted tables, high tin ceilings, and velvet couches. Rap and hip-hop fans should look elsewhere (the only tunes coming out of this joint are alternative and rock), and baseball caps and sneakers are strictly forbidden here, as are—at the other end of the spectrum—fur coats. ⊠ *300 E. 89th St., between 1st and 2nd Aves., Upper East Side* ☎ *212/427–4458* Ⓜ *4, 5, 6 to 86th St.*

Bar Pleiades. The cocktail bar companion to Café Boulud, also in the Surrey Hotel, Bar Pleiades is a livelier alternative to the more staid atmosphere at the Carlyle's Bemelmans. The decor is classic to a fault, employing a black-and-white theme that's positively Audrey Hepburn–esque. Drinks rotate seasonally, and there are nibbles from the café kitchen to create a base layer. Though it doesn't have the same drink menu, the rooftop bar is a cozy aerie good for people- (and skyscraper-) watching. ⊠ *20 E. 76th St., between 5th and Madison Aves., Upper East Side* ☎ *212/905–1477* Ⓜ *4, 5, 6 to 77th St.*

★ **Opia.** The motto for this upscale-yet-unpretentious bar–restaurant—"If you like us, tell your friends, and if you don't, tell your enemies!"—isn't necessary, given its manifold charms: a drop-dead-gorgeous design, plenty of space for canoodling and cavorting, a romantic balcony (though 57th Street isn't exactly a scenic beach), plus no cover or minimum for the live jazz on Monday night. Opia is ideal for couples in full-on infatuation or spouses hoping to remember the wine-and-roses days before the kids. ⊠ *130 E. 57th St., between Lexington and 3rd Aves., Upper East Side* ☎ *212/688–3939* ⊕ *www.opiarestaurant. com* Ⓜ *N, R, 6, to 59th St.*

CABARET AND PIANO BARS

Fodor's Choice
★ **The Carlyle.** The hotel's discreetly sophisticated Café Carlyle hosts such top cabaret and jazz performers as Christine Ebersole, John Pizzarelli, and Steve Tyrell. Stop by on a Monday night and take in Woody Allen, who swings on the clarinet with the Eddy Davis New Orleans Jazz Band. The less fancy-schmancy (though still pricey) **Bemelmans Bar**, with a mural by the author of the *Madeline* books, features a rotating cast of pianist-singers. ⊠ *35 E. 76th St., between Madison and Park Aves., Upper East Side* ☎ *212/744–1600* ⊕ *www.thecarlyle.com* Ⓜ *6 to 77th St.*

Feinstein's at Loews Regency. That the world-touring Michael Feinstein performs a residency here only once a year (usually in winter) and still gets the venue named after him speaks volumes about the charismatic cabaret star. This tastefully appointed space in Loews Regency Hotel presents Broadway babe and *30 Rock* regular Jane Krakowski and other top names in the business—plus, when we're lucky, Tony Danza. ✉ *540 Park Ave., at E. 61st St., Upper East Side* ☎ *212/339–4095* ⊕ *feinsteinsattheregency.com* Ⓜ *4, 5, 6, N, R to 59th St.–Lexington Ave.*

GAY NIGHTLIFE

Fodor'sChoice
★

Brandy's Piano Bar. A singing waitstaff warms up the mixed crowd at this delightful and intimate Upper East Side lounge, getting everyone in the mood to belt out their favorite tunes. In fact, the Brandy's scene is so cheerful that some patrons have used this as a musical Prozac, keeping depression at bay. ✉ *235 E. 84th St., between 2nd and 3rd Aves., Upper East Side* ☎ *212/744–4949* ⊕ *www.brandysnyc.com* Ⓜ *4, 5, 6 to 86th St.*

UPPER WEST SIDE

BARS

Ding Dong Lounge. "Gabba gabba hey," kids—the CBGB's punk ethos is most alive and well not downtown but way up near Columbia University, at this out-and-out rock-and-roll bar. All manner of music posters (along with punk chanteuse Patti Smith's actual birth certificate) adorn the walls; the bathrooms are wallpapered entirely with do-it-yourself concert fliers. An exuberant young student crowd swills the many beers on tap, and candles at every table do little to dispel the near-total darkness. Just wear night-vision goggles—and maybe a crash helmet, given how often the DJs really shake up the joint. ✉ *929 Columbus Ave., between W. 105th and W. 106th Sts., Upper West Side* ☎ *212/663–2600* ⊕ *www.dingdonglounge.com* Ⓜ *B, C to 103rd St.*

The Empire Hotel Rooftop Bar. The only thing better than hanging out in Lincoln Center on a lovely night is hanging out a dozen stories above Lincoln Center. Thanks to the refurbished Empire Hotel's sprawling rooftop bar, you can enjoy that pleasure even on nights that are less than lovely. We're talking thousands of square feet here, most of it outdoors, and heated in winter. ✉ *44 W. 63rd St., between Broadway and Columbus Ave., Upper West Side* ☎ *212/265–7400* ⊕ *www.empirehotelnyc.com/* Ⓜ *1 to 66th St./Lincoln Center.*

JAZZ VENUES

Smoke. If you can't wait until sunset to get your riffs on, head uptown to this lounge near Columbia University, where the music starts as early as 6 pm. Performers include some of the top names in the business, including turban-wearing organist Dr. Lonnie Smith and the drummer Jimmy Cobb (who laid down the beat on Miles Davis's seminal album *Kind of Blue*). ✉ *2751 Broadway, between W. 105th and W. 106th Sts., Upper West Side* ☎ *212/864–6662* ⊕ *www.smokejazz.com* Ⓜ *1 to 103rd St.*

17

HARLEM

JAZZ VENUES

Lenox Lounge. This impeccably detailed art-deco lounge opened in the 1930s, and hosts jazz ensembles, blues acts, and jam sessions in the Zebra Room. The restaurant in back serves great food to go with the soulful music. ✉ *288 Lenox Ave., between W. 124th and W. 125th Sts., Harlem* ☎ *212/427–0253* ⊕ *www.lenoxlounge.com* Ⓜ *2, 3 to 125th St.*

BROOKLYN

DUMBO

BARS

reBar. Occupying several rooms inside a former factory, this cavernous industrial space does multiple duty as bar, lounge, indie movie theater, gastropub, and supper club. Sample one of the many beers and enjoy the dungeony vibe under terra-cotta ceilings and antique chandeliers. ✉ *147 Front St., DUMBO, Brooklyn* ☎ *718/766–9110* ⊕ *www.rebarnyc.com* Ⓜ *F to York St.; A, C to High St.*

Superfine. The huge orange pool table is a focal point (it's free) at the front of this sprawling restaurant and bar at the base of the Manhattan Bridge. Rotating artwork, exposed-brick walls lined with tall windows, sunken secondhand chairs, and mellow music (including a bluegrass brunch on Sunday) make this a fun, neighborhoody place to hang out. ✉ *126 Front St., between Jay and Pearl Sts., DUMBO, Brooklyn* ☎ *718/243–9005* ⊘ *Closed Mon.* Ⓜ *F to York St.*

PERFORMANCE SPACE

Galapagos Art Space. Performances here almost take a backseat to the unique architecture of supper-club red banquettes floating above a huge lagoon of water (hold on to your purse!). Thankfully, the theater, music, and performance art is dynamic enough to keep your attention. ✉ *16 Main St., DUMBO, Brooklyn* ☎ *718/222–8500* ⊕ *www. galapagosartspace.com* ⊟ *Ticket prices vary* ⊘ *Opening times vary* Ⓜ *F to York St.; A, C to High St.*

WILLIAMSBURG

BARS

Barcade. Like Chuck E. Cheese for grown-up hipsters, Barcade invites you to stop reminiscing about your arcade-loving youth and start playing the more than 30 vintage arcade games. You'll find everything from familiar favorites like Ms. Pacman to rarities like Rampage. And it's not just about the games; there's also a full menu of small-label beers to choose from. ✉ *388 Union Ave., near Ainslie, Williamsburg, Brooklyn* ☎ *718/302–6464* ⊕ *www.barcadebrooklyn.com* Ⓜ *L to Lorimer St.*

Bembe. This steamy two-level lounge is Williamsburg's answer to Miami clubbing, except it's constructed of found items from all over New York, including the old redwood front door from a winery. The crowd is as eclectic as the DJ-spun beats, from reggae to Brazilian, often accompanied by live drumming. The tropical bar menu gives it proper Latin cred. ✉ *81 South 6th St., at Berry St., Williamsburg, Brooklyn* ☎ *718/387–*

5389 ⊕ *www.bembe.us* ☉ *Mon.–Thurs. 7:30–4; Fri.–Sun. 7–4* Ⓜ *L to Bedford Ave.; J, M, Z to Marcy Ave.*

Brooklyn Bowl. This former ironworks foundry packs in 16 bowling lanes, a cocktail bar, a music stage, and a restaurant—the food is conjured up by the team behind Blue Ribbon and includes Louisiana-style Southern specialties like po' boy sandwiches, Cajun catfish, and excellent signature fried chicken. Hipster crowds congregate over local brews on tap. Weekends means crowds so it can take a while to get a bowling lane but you'll have a blast while you wait. ✉ *61 Wythe Ave., at N. 11th St., Williamsburg, Brooklyn* ☎ *718/963–3369* ⊕ *www.brooklynbowl. com* 🖃 *$20 per lane for 30 min* ☉ *Weekdays 6 pm–2 am; weekends noon–2 am* Ⓜ *L to Bedford Ave.*

Brooklyn Brewery. Brooklyn was once known as America's brewing capital: at the turn of the 20th century Williamsburg alone was home to nearly 60 breweries. The originals are mostly gone, but this relative newcomer has been bringing the hops back to the 'hood since it opened in 1996. Friday-evening happy hour means $4 beers—the Brooklyn Lager is popular, as is the Belgian-inspired Local 1, and there are usually seasonal brews, too. Beer buffs can join a free guided tour on Saturday or Sunday afternoon; other tours are by reservation only. ✉ *79 N. 11th St., between Berry St. and Wythe Ave., Williamsburg, Brooklyn* ☎ *718/486–7422* ⊕ *www.brooklynbrewery.com* ☉ *Fri. 6–11 pm, Sat. and Sun. noon–6 pm* Ⓜ *L to Bedford Ave.*

Pete's Candy Store. A retro feel, friendly crowd, and cheerful bartenders make this a perennial favorite, slightly off the Willamsburg beaten path. The back room, smaller than a subway car, hosts intimate music performances nightly. Hipsters come out for spelling bees, bingo, and the infamous quiz-off contest every Wednesday night. There's a short menu of sandwiches and cocktails, but no actual candy here. Pete's is also home to one of Brooklyn's preeminent reading series, held on alternate Thursday nights. ✉ *709 Lorimer St., between Frost and Richardson Sts., Williamsburg, Brooklyn* ☎ *718/302–3770* ⊕ *www. petescandystore.com* Ⓜ *L to Lorimer St.*

Radegast Hall & Biergarten. The perfect alternative if you don't want to trek out to Queens for alfresco Slavic beers, Radegast Hall & Biergarten serves Central European suds and hearty eats under a retractable roof. Schnitzel, goulash, and pretzels are authentic complements to the beer, along with live music on some nights. ✉ *113 N. 3rd St., Williamsburg, Brooklyn* ☎ *718/963–3973* ⊕ *radegasthall.com* Ⓜ *L to Bedford Ave.*

Spuyten Duyvil. Only the geekiest of beer geeks will recognize the names of the more than 100 imported microbrews available here. Fortunately for the rest of us, the friendly connoisseurs behind the bar are more than happy to offer detailed descriptions. ✉ *359 Metropolitan Ave., near Havermeyer St., Williamsburg, Brooklyn* ☎ *718/963–4140* ⊕ *www. spuytenduyvilnyc.com* Ⓜ *L to Lorimer St.*

Union Pool. This former pool-supply store is a funky warehouselike venue complete with a corrugated-tin-backed bar, a photo booth, a small stage for live music, and cheap PBR. The back patio has a taco truck and a fire pit, all part of the hipster-paradise package. ✉ *484*

17

Union Ave., near Meeker Ave., Williamsburg, Brooklyn ☎ *718/609–0484* ⊕ *www.unionpool.blogspot.com* ☉ *Weekdays 5–4; weekends 1 pm–4 am* Ⓜ *L to Lorimer St.*

LIVE MUSIC VENUES

Knitting Factory. This concert venue for rock, indie, and underground hip hop does double duty as a neighborhood watering hole, with a dimly lit bar up front and a small stage behind a glass wall. There's a happy hour daily (5–7 pm) and 10 beers on tap, including Brooklyn Brewery's Pennant Ale. ⊠ *361 Metropolitan Ave., at Havemeyer St., Williamsburg, Brooklyn* ☎ *347/529–6696* ⊕ *www.knittingfactory.com* 🎫 *Admission $8–$35* ☉ *Bar daily 5–4* Ⓜ *L to Bedford Ave.*

Music Hall of Williamsburg. This former mayonnaise factory is Brooklyn's answer to the Bowery Ballroom and, indeed, it's run by the bookers for Bowery Presents. The three-level venue with balcony seating has rounded ceilings and walls, which makes for excellent acoustics; no surprise that it draws die-hard live-music hawks. ⊠ *66 N. 6th St., near Wythe Ave., Williamsburg, Brooklyn* ☎ *718/486–5400* ⊕ *www. musichallofwilliamsburg.com* 🎫 *$10–$20* Ⓜ *L to Bedford Ave.*

PARK SLOPE

BARS

Barbès. It's not *quite* like stepping into the funky Parisian neighborhood of the same name, but this cozy bar does have French-accented bartenders, pressed-tin ceilings, and a red-tinted back room. Diverse events range from the energetic Slavic Soul Party performance on Tuesday to classical music concerts. ⊠ *376 9th St., at 6th Ave., Park Slope, Brooklyn* ☎ *347/422–0248* ⊕ *www.barbesbrooklyn.com* Ⓜ *F to 7th Ave.*

Union Hall. Comfortably hip is the name of the game at this Brooklyn hangout. Grab a beer in the "library" area up front, cozy up around the fireplace in winter, or if you're up for a little sport, join the friendly locals in a game of bocce ball. In the basement, check out some rising indie rock stars on stage. ⊠ *702 Union St., at 5th Ave., Park Slope, Brooklyn* ☎ *718/638–4400* ⊕ *www.unionhallny.com* Ⓜ *R to Union St.*

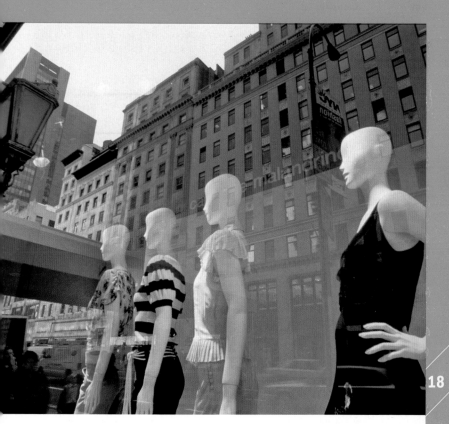

Shopping

WORD OF MOUTH

"At Century 21, I've purchased beautiful ties for $16; a first-quality Polo Ralph Lauren wool suit for $200, and all-cotton queen-size sheet sets for $30."

—Anthony

Updated
by Christina
Valhouli

The Big Apple is one of the best shopping destinations in the world, rivaled perhaps only by London, Paris, and Tokyo. Its compact size, convenient subway system, and plentiful cabs (unless it's raining) make it easy to navigate with plenty of bags in tow. But what it really comes down to is the staggering number and variety of stores. If you can't find it in New York, it probably doesn't exist.

If you like elegant flagships and money is no object, head to Midtown, where you'll find international megabrands like Louis Vuitton, Yves Saint Laurent, and Gucci, as well as famed department stores Bergdorf Goodman and Barneys. Nearby Madison Avenue offers couture from Carolina Herrera and Vera Wang, and 5th Avenue is lined with famous jewelry stores like Tiffany, Van Cleef & Arpels, and Harry Winston. This is also the neighborhood to indulge in bespoke goods, such as ordering handmade shoes from John Lobb or designing a custom yacht at OC Concept Store. If you like designer pieces but can't afford them, don't despair—there are plenty of upscale consignment shops dotted around the city where you can find last season's Chanel suit or a vintage YSL jacket.

The small, independent shops that once lined SoHo have largely been swallowed up by J. Crew and Uniqlo, but if you want to hit the chains, this is a great place to do it, since SoHo also provides high-quality people-watching and superb lunches. If you're craving some of SoHo's artistic spirit, don't discount the street vendors' stalls, which sell handmade jewelry and simple cotton dresses. You never know—you might buy something from a soon-to-be-famous designer.

The East Village and Lower East Side are hotbeds of creativity and quirky coolness, with little boutiques selling everything from retro furniture to industrial-inspired jewelry tucked among bars and tenement apartments. The Meatpacking District is another great shopping destination, where you'll find chic stores like Diane Von Furstenberg and Catherine Malandrino.

BEST BETS FOR NYC SHOPPING

With thousands of shops to choose from, how will you decide where to go? Below you'll find some of Fodor's writers and editors favorites to help you get started. You can also search by category within each neighborhood for noteworthy shops, and peruse the spotlights about specific neighborhoods.

Fodor's Choice ★

ABC Carpet & Home, p. 328

Agent Provocateur, p. 296

Alexis Bittar, p. 305

Bloomingdales, p. 332

Diane von Furstenberg, p. 325

FAO Schwarz Fifth Avenue, p. 337

Fishs Eddy, p. 329

Flight 001, p. 322

Intermix, pp. 300, 352

Jacques Torres Chocolates, p. 303

Kidrobot, p. 306

La Petite Coquette, p. 318

McNally Jackson, p. 307

Mxyplyzyk, p. 322

Partners & Crime Mystery Booksellers, p. 319

The Strand, p. 330

Tani, p. 352

Tiffany & Co. , p. 333

BEST CHILDREN'S CLOTHING

A Time for Children, p. 352

Bonpoint, p. 343

Bu and the Duck, p. 293

Bundle, p. 295

Giggle, p. 296

Les Petits Chapelais, p. 296

Shoofly, p. 293

BEST DENIM

3X1, p. 296

7 for all Mankind, p. 296

Earnest Sewn, p. 327

Madewell, p. 300

Seven New York, p. 302

BEST DEPARTMENT STORES

Barneys, p. 348

Bergdorf Goodman, p. 338

Bloomingdales, p. 332

Macy's, p. 339

Saks Fifth Avenue, p. 332

BEST HANDBAGS

Anya Hindmarch, p. 306

Devi Kroell, p. 350

Fendi, p. 336

Furla, p. 336

Hermès, p. 350

High Way, p. 311

Judith Leiber, p. 351

Kate Spade, p. 306

Longchamp, p. 306

Louis Vuitton, p. 336

Lulu Guiness, p. 322

Token, p. 311

Stuart Weitzman, p. 337

BEST LINGERIE

Agent Provocateur, p. 296

Bra Smyth, p. 343

Kiki di Montparnasse, p. 300

La Petite Coquette, p. 318

BEST MEN'S BOUTIQUES

Duncan Quinn, p. 307

Dunhill, p. 332

Jay Kos, p. 310

John Varvatos, p. 313

Paul Smith, p. 301

Reiss, p. 302

BEST SHOES

Belle by Sigerson Morrison, p. 311

Camper, p. 306

Christian Louboutin, p. 350

Jimmy Choo, p. 350

John Fluevog Shoes, p. 311

John Lobb, p. 350

Leffot, p. 322

Tod's, p. 351

BEST TOY STORES

American Girl Place, p. 337

Dinosaur Hill, p. 315

FAO Schwarz, p. 337

Kidrobot, p. 306

BEST VINTAGE SHOPS

Edith Machinist, p. 317

INA, p. 307

Frock, p. 307

New York Vintage, p. 324

Resurrection, p. 310

What Goes Around Comes Around, p. 303

18

Deals and Steals

Everyone loves a bargain—including a temporary New Yorker. Scoring a good deal is a rite of passage, and the city offers everything from low-cost department stores like Century 21 to hawkers of pseudo-Rolex watches and Kate Spade bags stationed at street corners and in Canal Street stalls. And then there are the sample sales.

If a seasonal sale makes New Yorkers' eyes gleam, a sample sale throws shoppers into a frenzy. With so many designer flagships and corporate headquarters in town, merchandise fallout periodically leads to tremendous deals. Although technically the term sample sale refers to stock that's a sample design, a show model, a leftover, or is already discounted, the term is now also used for sales of current-season goods. Location adds a bit of an illicit thrill to the event: sales are held in hotels, warehouses, offices, or loft spaces, where items both incredible and unfortunate jam a motley assortment of racks, tables, and bins. Generally, there is a makeshift communal dressing room, but mirrors are scarce, so veteran sample-sale shoppers come prepared for wriggling in the aisles; some wear tank tops with tights or leggings for modest quick changes. Two rules of thumb: grab first and inspect later, and call in advance to find out what methods of payment are accepted. One of the ultimate experiences is the Barneys Warehouse Sale, held in February and August in Chelsea. Other luscious sales range from the Vera Wang bridal-gown sale (early winter) to Dwell Studio (spring and late fall).

How to find out about these events? The level of publicity and regularity of sales vary. The print and online versions of *New York* magazine are always worth checking for sample sale tip-offs, as are regular bulletins on Racked (⊕ *racked.com*) and Daily Candy (⊕ *www.dailycandy.com*). If you're interested in specific designers, call their shops and inquire—you may get lucky.

LOWER MANHATTAN AND TRIBECA

FINANCIAL DISTRICT
BARGAIN SHOPPING

Fodor'sChoice
★
Century 21. For many New Yorkers this downtown fixture—right across the street from the former World Trade Center site—remains the mother lode of discount shopping. Four floors are crammed with everything from Marc Jacobs shoes and half-price cashmere sweaters to Donna Karan sheets, though you'll have to sift through racks and fight the crowds to find the gems. Best bets for men are shoes and designer briefs; the full floor of designer women's wear can yield some dazzling finds, such as a Calvin Klein leather trench coat for less than $600. Don't miss the children's section, either, for brands like Ralph Lauren and Ed Hardy. There's also a branch on the Upper West Side, at Broadway and 66th Street. ■TIP→ Since lines for the communal dressing rooms can be prohibitively long, do what the locals do: wear leggings and change discreetly in the aisles. ⊠ *22 Cortlandt St., between Broadway and Church St.,*

Lower Manhattan ☎*212/227–9092* ⊕*www.c21stores.com/* Ⓜ*R to Cortlandt St.*

CAMERAS AND ELECTRONICS

J&R. Just south of City Hall, J&R has emerged as the city's most competitively priced one-stop electronics outlet, with an enormous selection of video equipment, cameras, computers, and stereos. The hands-on staff is super-knowledgeable; many of them are A/V wizards who've

worked here since the early 1990s. Home-office supplies are at No. 1, computers at No. 15, small appliances at No. 27. ⊠*23 Park Row, between Beekman and Ann Sts., Lower Manhattan* ☎*212/238–9000* Ⓜ*4, 5, 6 to Brooklyn Bridge/City Hall.*

CHILDREN'S CLOTHING

Aminah et Les Amis. Trendy downtown moms flock to this shop for stylish American and European fashion for newborns up to age 12. Brands stocked include Petite Bateau, Lola et Moi, and Glug Baby. ⊠*72 Warren St., TriBeCa* ☎*212/227–0117* Ⓜ*1,2, 3, A, C to Chambers St.*

CLOTHING

Abercrombie & Fitch. This brand is known for its casual preppy clothes for men, women, and kids. ⊠*199 Water St.* ☎*212/809–9000* ⊕*abercrombie.com* Ⓜ*2, 3 to Wall St.* ⊠*720 Fifth Ave., Midtown West* ☎*212/306–0936* Ⓜ*N, Q, R to 5th Ave./59th St.*

TRIBECA

CHILDREN'S CLOTHING

Bu and the Duck. Vintage-inspired children's clothing, shoes, and toys distinguish this shop. The Italian-made spectator boots might make you wish your own feet were tiny again. ⊠*106 Franklin St., between West Broadway and Church St., TriBeCa* ☎*212/431–9226* ⊕*buandtheduck.com/* Ⓜ*1 to Franklin St.*

Shoofly. Children's shoes and accessories imported from all over the world are the name of the game here. Choose from Mary Janes, trendy sneakers, and motorcycle boots along with pom-pom hats, brightly patterned socks, eclectic toys, and jewelry. ⊠*42 Hudson St., between Thomas and Duane Sts., TriBeCa* ☎*212/406–3270* ⊕*www.shooflynyc.com* Ⓜ*1 to Franklin St.*

CLOTHING

Issey Miyake. This flagship, designed by Frank Gehry, attracts a non-fashion crowd who come just to gawp at his undulating 25-foot high titanium sculpture, *The Tornado.* Miyake's signature style offers clothes that are sleek and slim-fitting, and made from polyester or ultrahigh-tech textiles. This flagship carries the entire runway collection, as well as Pleats Please and Issey Miyake Fête. ⊠*119 Hudson St., at N. Moore St., TriBeCa* ☎*212/226–0100* ⊕*www.tribecaisseymiyake.com/* Ⓜ*1 to Franklin St.*

18

Street Vendor Shopping

If you're looking for original or reproduced artwork, the two areas to visit for street vendors are the stretch of 5th Avenue in front of the Metropolitan Museum of Art (roughly between 81st and 82nd streets) and the SoHo area of West Broadway, between Houston and Broome streets. In both areas you'll find dozens of artists selling original paintings, drawings, and photographs (some lovely, some lurid), as well as photo reproductions of famous New York scenes (the Chrysler building, South Street Seaport). Prices can start as low as $10, but be sure to haggle.

The east–west streets in SoHo are an excellent place to look for handmade crafts: Spring and Prince streets, especially, are jammed with tables full of beaded jewelry, tooled leather belts, cotton sundresses, and homemade hats and purses. These streets are also great places to find deals on art books; several vendors have titles featuring the work of artists from Diego Rivera to Annie Leibovitz, all for about 20% less than you'd pay at a chain.

It's best to know which books you want ahead of time, though; street vendors wrap theirs in clear plastic, and can get testy if you unwrap them but don't wind up buying.

Faux-designer handbags, sunglasses, wallets, and watches are some of the most popular street buys in town—but crackdowns on knockoffs have made them harder to find. The hub used to be Canal Street, roughly between Greene and Lafayette streets, but many vendors there have swept their booths clean of fake Vuitton, Prada, Gucci, and Fendi merchandise. You might have better luck finding a Faux-lex near Herald Square or Madison Square Garden, and good old-fashioned fake handbags are still sold by isolated vendors around such shopping areas as Rockefeller Center and the stretch of lower 5th near Union Square. If you're looking for cheap luggage, skip Canal Street, as the bags there might not last beyond the flight home, and instead pick up a bargain at Marshalls, TJ Maxx, or Loehmann's.

J.Crew Men's Shop at the Liquor Store. It would be easy to walk right past this place and think it's a bar rather than an outpost of J.Crew for men, because it's filled with manly knickknacks like old Jack Kerouac books and vintage photographs. Some of the best finds are the limited-edition suits and cashmere sweaters, as well as non–J.Crew items like Barbour jackets and classic Alden shoes. ⊠ *235 West Broadway, at White St., TriBeCa* ☎ *212/226–5476* ⊕ *www.jcrew.com* Ⓜ *1 to Franklin St.*

SOHO AND NOLITA

SOHO

ANTIQUES AND COLLECTIBLES

Jacques Carcanagues Gallery. Crammed with goods from Japan to India, this SoHo gallery offers an eclectic array of objects, from pillboxes to 18th-century Burmese Buddhas and teak tables. ⊠ *21 Greene St., between Grand and Canal Sts., SoHo* ☎ *212/925–8110* ⊕ *www. jacquescarcanagues.com* Ⓜ *4, 5, 6, R to Canal St.*

BARGAIN SHOPPING

★ **Pearl River Mart.** Whether you're looking for a decorative birdcage or a massive bag of jasmine rice, this mega–department store has everything Asian under one roof—at bargain prices. Browse through housewares like bamboo rice steamers and ceramic tea sets, or decorate your apartment with paper lanterns and porcelain stools. On the main floor, under a ceiling festooned with dragon kites and rice-paper parasols, you can buy kimono-style robes, pajamas, and embroidered satin slippers for the whole family. There's also a dry-goods section, where you can load up on ginger candy, jasmine tea, and cellophane noodles. ✉ *477 Broadway, between Broome and Grand Sts., SoHo* ☎ *212/431–4770* ⊕ *pearlriver. com* Ⓜ *N, R, Q to Canal St.*

BEAUTY

MiN. If the selection of grooming products at Duane Reade doesn't cut it for you, head to MiN. This wood-paneled shop is decidedly male-friendly, with leather couches and exposed brick walls. Shop for unusual scents from Santa Maria Novella and L'Artisan Parfumeur, shaving products from Old Bond Street, or quirky items like mustache wax. ✉ *117 Crosby St., between Prince and Houston Sts., SoHo* ☎ *212/206– 6366* Ⓜ *N, R to Prince St.*

BOOKS AND STATIONERY

Scholastic Store. Kids and the young at heart will be delighted by the whimsical design here, including an 11-foot orange dinosaur, a life-size Magic School Bus, and a massive Harry Potter. In addition to the thousands of books, kids can amuse themselves with games, toys, DVDs, computers, and arts-and-crafts workshops. It is so kid-friendly that parents will find a separate entrance just for strollers (at 130 Mercer St.). ✉ *557 Broadway, at Prince St., SoHo* ☎ *212/343–6166* ⊕ *www. scholastic.com/sohostore/* Ⓜ *R to Prince St.*

18

CAMERAS AND ELECTRONICS

★ **Apple Store.** Located in a former SoHo post office, this sleek space sells everything Apple related. The Genius Bar can help with any tech problems, and there's also a small area for those doing business as well as a space dedicated just for iPods. Climb the glass staircase for the children's section and accessories like printers. There are also stores on the Upper East Side, Upper West Side, and in the Meatpacking District. ■TIP➔ In-store events include hour-long tutorials on topics like getting to know your iPhone and navigating new Mac software. ✉ *103 Prince St., at Greene St., SoHo* ☎ *212/226–3126* ⊕ *apple.com* Ⓜ *R to Prince St.* ✉ *1981 Broadway, Upper West Side* ☎ *212/209–3400* ✉ *401 W. 14th St., Meatpacking District* ☎ *212/444–3400* Ⓜ *A, C, E to 14th St.*

CHILDREN'S CLOTHING

Bundle. This SoHo boutique goes above and beyond selling fashionable onesies by offering a concierge service. If you can't make it to the store to choose a gift, just email them and they'll reply with suggestions. Visit and choose adorable clothes from brands including Kissy Kissy, Baby CZ, and Tea. ✉ *128 Thompson St., between Prince and Houston Sts., SoHo* ☎ *212/982–9465* ⊕ *bundlenyc.com* Ⓜ *C, E to Spring St.*

Giggle. This high-end baby store is often crammed with stroller grid-lock, but it stocks nearly everything a stylish parent (and baby) could ever need. The Giggles flagship carries all the gear and accessories to build a chic nursery, including Dwell bedding, plush toys, and funky kids' clothing. Even the basic gear, like strollers and high chairs, are sold. The staff is often extra helpful and attentive. ⊠ *120 Wooster St., between Spring and Prince Sts., SoHo* ☎ *312/829–4222* ⊕ *www.giggle. com* Ⓜ *N, R to Prince St.*

Les Petits Chapelais. Designed and made in France, these kids' clothes (from newborn up to age 12) are cute and stylish but also practical. Corduroy outfits have details like embroidered flowers and contrasting cuffs, and soft, fleecy jackets are reversible. There's also a line of sailor-inspired clothes. ⊠ *86 Thompson St., between Spring and Prince Sts., SoHo* ☎ *212/625–1023* Ⓜ *C, E to Spring St.*

CLOTHING

3X1. In this huge denim shop, which doubles as a factory, customers can watch their bespoke jeans being made. The walls of the pristine white space are lined with more than 100 bolts of denim. After you select the perfect fabric, jeans are hand cut and sewn by the in-house seamstresses, who work in a glass-enclosed space. Shoppers can also buy off-the-rack jeans; unfinished hems are tailored on the spot (starting at $295). ⊠ *15 Mercer St., SoHo* ☎ *212/391–6969* Ⓜ *N,R,4,6 to Canal St.*

7 for All Mankind. Whether you're hunting for super skinny, high-waisted, or boot-cut jeans in a dark or distressed finish, this temple to denim offers it all. The jeans are a firm celebrity favorite (Cameron Diaz is a fan), but be warned: although they are guaranteed to make your derri-ere look good, they don't come cheap. You'll also find stylish and sexy dresses here, plus sweaters and jackets for men and women. ⊠ *394 West Broadway, between Broome and Spring Sts., SoHo* ☎ *212/226–8615* Ⓜ *A,C, E to Spring St.*

A Bathing Ape. Known simply as BAPE to devotees, this exclusive label has a cult following in its native Tokyo. At first it may be hard to see what the fuss is about. A small selection of camouflage gear and limited-edition T-shirts is placed throughout the minimalist space; the real scene stealers are the flashy retro-style sneakers in neon colors. ⊠ *91 Greene St., between Prince and Spring Sts., SoHo* ☎ *212/925–0222* Ⓜ *R to Prince St.*

Fodor's Choice **Agent Provocateur.** If Victoria's Secret is too tame for you, try this British
★ lingerie shop, which has a naughty twist. Showpieces include boned cor-sets, lace sets with contrast-color trim, bottoms tied with satin ribbons, and a few fetish-type leather ensembles. A great selection of stockings is complemented by the garter belts to secure them. ⊠ *133 Mercer St., between Prince and Spring Sts., SoHo* ☎ *212/965–0229* Ⓜ *R to Prince St.*

Alexander Wang. *Vogue* darling Alexander Wang has finally opened his first retail outlet. The vibe of the clothes—as well as the store—is unfussy–cool but also luxurious. Shoppers can take a break on a fur hammock in between browsing for perfectly slouchy tank tops, sheath dresses, or edgy ankle boots. ⊠ *103 Grand St., between Greene and Mercer Sts., SoHo* ☎ *212/977–9683* Ⓜ *6 to Spring St.*

Allan & Suzi. The duo behind Allan & Suzi have been selling their pristine vintage clothing to celebrities for years—and have also outfitted the cast of *Sex and the City*. Their new downtown store offers a mix of new and vintage finds, ranging from the elegant to the wacky. Dig and you may find a Gaultier gown or a Pauline Trigere dress, along with crazy disco gear. ⊠ *237 Centre St, between Grand and Broome Sts., SoHo* ☎ *212/724–7445* Ⓜ *N, R, 4, 6 to Canal St.*

Anna Sui. The violet-and-black salon, with its Victorian rock-chick vibe, is the ideal setting for Sui's bohemian and rocker-influenced designs and colorful beauty products. ⊠ *113 Greene St., between Prince and Spring Sts., SoHo* ☎ *212/941–8406* Ⓜ *R to Prince St.*

A.P.C. This hip French boutique sells deceptively simple clothes in an equally understated setting. Watch your step on the uneven wooden floorboards while choosing narrow gabardine and corduroy suits or dark denim jeans and jackets. For women, best bets include striped sweaters and skinny jeans. ⊠ *131 Mercer St., between Prince and Spring Sts., SoHo* ☎ *212/966–9685* Ⓜ *6 to Spring St.; R to Prince St.*

Betsey Johnson. The SoHo store departs from the traditional (if such a word can be applied) hot-pink interior; instead its walls are whitewashed with painted roses, and there's a bordello-red lounge area in back. Most of her dresses, coats, and accessories have slightly kooky patterns; the calmest items are the little black dresses. This is not the place for natural fibers—it's ruled by rayon, stretch, and the occasional faux fur. ⊠ *138 Wooster St., between Prince and W. Houston Sts., SoHo* ☎ *212/995–5048* Ⓜ *R to Prince St.*

Christopher Fischer. Featherweight cashmere sweaters, wraps, and throws in every hue from Easter-egg pastels to rich jewel tones have made Fischer the darling of the preppy set. His shop also carries leather accessories and such home wares as throw pillows and baby clothes. ⊠ *80 Wooster St., between Spring and Broome Sts., SoHo* ☎ *212/965–9009* ⊕ *www.christopherfischer.com* Ⓜ *R, W to Prince St.*

18

Comptoir des Cotonniers. The "cotton counter" angles for multigenerational shopping, lining up stylish, comfortable basics for babies, twentysomethings, ladies of a certain age, and everyone in between. There's a subtle Parisian vibe to the understated tunics, dresses, and separates; colors tend to be earthy. The brand's first U.S. branch has a nature-friendly minimalist look, with pale-wood floors and lots of natural light. ⊠ *155 Spring St., at West Broadway, SoHo* ☎ *212/274–0830* ⊕ *www.comptoirdescotonniers.com* Ⓜ *C, E to Spring St.*

Costume National. Everything about this boutique is sexy and minimalist, with an edge. The clothes—and lighting—are dark. Shoppers will find sharply tailored wool pants for men and silky tops for women in muted shades of black, gray, and charcoal, along with motorcycle boots and leather gloves. ⊠ *160 Mercer St., between Prince and W. Houston Sts., SoHo* ☎ *212/431–1530* Ⓜ *C, E to Spring St.*

Emporio Armani. At this middle child of the Armani trio, the clothes are dressy without quite being formal, and are frequently offered in cream, muted blues, and ever-cool shades of taupe. ⊠ *410 West Broadway, at Spring St., SoHo* ☎ *646/613–8099* Ⓜ *C, E to Spring St.*

SOHO

Somehow, everything looks a bit more beautiful here. Maybe it's because of the way sunlight filters down the cast-iron facades, glinting off the shop windows. Maybe it's because the uneven cobblestone streets prompt you to slow down, giving you time to notice details.

Jaded locals call this neighborhood a touristy outdoor mall. True, you'll see plenty of familiar company names, and several common, less expensive chains, like Banana Republic and Sephora, have made land grabs on Broadway. There's also a certain amount of luxury one-upmanship, as stores like Prada, Chanel, and Louis Vuitton have planted themselves here for downtown cred. But you can still hit a few clothing and housewares boutiques you won't find elsewhere in this country. The hottest shopping area runs west from Broadway over to 6th Avenue, between West Houston and Grand streets. Don't overlook a couple of streets east of Broadway: Crosby and Lafayette each have a handful of intriguing shops.

BEST TIME TO GO

Wednesday through Friday afternoons, when all the stores are open and the people-watching is prime but the streets aren't hideously crowded. On weekends, Broadway and Prince Street can feel like a cattle drive.

BEST SOUVENIR FOR YOUR IN-LAWS

If they're caffeine fiends, consider the house-blend coffees and teas at **Dean & Deluca** (✉ *560 Broadway, at Prince St.*), which you can pair with sophisticated snacks in a D&D tote or metal lunch box.

W. Houston St. E. Houston St.

0   1/8 mile
0   200 meters

◆ Versani

Prince St.   Prada ◆   **N,R** Ⓜ ◆
◆ Fragments   Dean & DeLuca

◆ Kirna Zabête

Spring St.   Balthazar ✗   **6** Ⓜ

Cleveland Pl.

Sullivan St.   Thompson St.   W. Broadway   Wooster St.   Greene St.   Mercer St.   Broadway   Crosby St.   Lafayette St.

Kate Spade ◆

Broome St.

KEY
Ⓜ Subway stops

Grand St.

Ⓜ **A,C,E**

3x1 ◆
Howard St.   ◆ De Vera

Canal St.   Ⓜ **J,N,Q,R,Z,6**

REFUELING

Balthazar Restaurant. For something on the fly, drop by Balthazar Restaurant for a scone, *canelé*, or sticky bun with a potent cup of coffee. If you'd rather have a seat, make your way to the tearoom hidden in the back of Marie Belle for a cup of their excellent hot chocolate. ⊠ *80 Spring St., between Broadway and Crosby St.* ☎ *212/965–1414* ⊕ *www. balthazarny.com.*

BEST FOR

ACCESSORIES
Fragments: Scoop up innovative jewelry from emerging or established designers.

Versani: If you believe that bigger and bolder is better, you'll love the jewelry here.

HOUSEWARES
De Vera: Eclectic selection of antiques and new objets d'art, from Murano glass to Japanese lacquer.

WHAT TO WEAR
3X1: Watch your custom jeans be hand-cut and sewn in-store.

Kate Spade: The mother lode for clever handbags, plus retro-ish shoes and a few baubles.

Kirna Zabête: Uncommon, sought-after women's clothing in a cheerful, unpretentious space.

Prada: The high-concept, Rem Koolhaas–designed store steals the spotlight from the clothes.

18

French Connection. This British-owned company stocks an impressive collection of on-trend clothing for men and women at reasonable prices. Some of the best bets are the sharply tailored trench coats and jeans, as well as dresses. For men, try the cashmere sweaters and skinny trousers. ✉ *435 W. Broadway, SoHo* ☎ *212/219–1197* ⊕ *www. frenchconnection.com* Ⓜ *C, E to Spring St.* ✉ *700 Broadway, East Village* ☎ *212/473–4486.*

Fodor's Choice
★ **Intermix.** This boutique is stocked with a healthy mid- to high-range lineup of established and emerging designers—think Chloé, Stella McCartney, and La Rok. You'll find everything from denim to silk frocks, along with stylish outerwear. ✉ *98 Prince St., between Greene and Mercer Sts., SoHo* ☎ *212/249–7858* ⊕ *www.intermixonline.com* Ⓜ *R to Prince St.*

Isabel Marant. The cool, slouchy clothes this Parisian designer is known for have made their mark in the U.S. market, as she recently opened her first store here. The tailored jackets, shorts, and flirty dresses are eclectic and sophisticated, with their textured, deeply hued fabrics. ✉ *469 Broome St., at Greene St., SoHo* ☎ *212/219–2284* Ⓜ *R to Prince St.*

Kiki de Montparnasse. Named for Man Ray's mistress and muse from the 1940s, this upscale lingerie store showcases decadent styles in a seductive but artistic setting. Shoppers will find exquisitely made corsets and bra and underwear sets, but a large portion of the store is used as a rotating art gallery for erotic art. ✉ *79 Greene St., at Spring St., SoHo* ☎ *212/965–8150* Ⓜ *R to Prince St.*

★ **Kirna Zabête.** A heavy-hitting lineup of prestigious designers—Balenciaga, Alexander Wang, Lanvin, Proenza Schouler—is managed with an exceptionally cheerful flair. Step downstairs for dog apparel, coffee-table books, and hip infant gear from Kit and Lili. ✉ *96 Greene St., between Spring and Prince Sts., SoHo* ☎ *212/941–9656* Ⓜ *R to Prince St.*

Madewell. Come here for casual men's and women's staples like jeans, T-shirts, and sweaters. ✉ *486 Broadway, SoHo* ☎ *212/226–6954* ⊕ *www.madewell.com* Ⓜ *6 to Spring St.*

Marc Jacobs. Marc Jacobs is steadily populating the West Village with his various boutiques. This location, housed in a former garage, is filled with ladylike designs made with luxurious fabrics: silk, cashmere, wool bouclé, and tweeds ranging from the demure to the flamboyant. The details, though—oversize buttons, circular patch pockets, and military-style grommet belts—add a sartorial wink. ✉ *163 Mercer St., between W. Houston and Prince Sts., SoHo* ☎ *212/343–1490* Ⓜ *R to Prince St.*

Marni. If you're a fan of the boho-chic look, stock up on Consuelo Castiglioni's bright-colored, happy clothes here. Silk dresses are printed in bold fabrics, and trousers are sharply tailored. Jackets and accessories are also eye-popping. ✉ *161 Mercer St., between W. Houston and Prince Sts., SoHo* ☎ *212/343–3912* Ⓜ *R to Prince St.*

Miu Miu. Prada front woman Miuccia Prada established a secondary line (bearing her childhood nickname, Miu Miu) to showcase her more experimental ideas. Look for Prada-esque styles in more daring colors and cuts, such as high-waist skirts with scalloped edges, Peter

Pan–collar dresses in trippy patterns, and patent-leather pumps. ✉ *100 Prince St., between Mercer and Greene Sts., SoHo* ☎ *212/334–5156* ⊕ *www.miumiu.com* Ⓜ *R to Prince St.*

Moncler. Many New York women swear by Moncler coats to keep them warm but still looking stylish throughout the brutal winters. This store is the Italian brand's first foray into New York, and is the largest Moncler store in the world. The knee-length puffer is a firm favorite, but there are also shorter ski jackets and accessories, along with pieces created in collaboration with designers like Giambattista Valli. ✉ *90 Prince St., between Mercer St. and Broadway, SoHo* ☎ *646/350–3620* ⊕ *www.moncler.com* Ⓜ *R to Prince St.*

Opening Ceremony. Just like Colette in Paris, Opening Ceremony bills itself as a concept store, which means you never know what you will find. The owners are constantly globetrotting to soak up the style and designers in a foreign country, and bring back the best clothing, products, and vintage items to showcase in their store. Hong Kong, Japan, Brazil, and the United Kingdom have all been represented. There's also a gallery space here. ✉ *35 Howard St., between Broadway and Lafayette St., SoHo* ☎ *212/219–2688* ⊕ *www.openingceremony.us* Ⓜ *N, R to Canal St.*

Paul Smith. Fans love Paul Smith for his classic-with-a-twist clothes, and his 5,000-square-foot flagship is a temple to his design ethos and inspirations. Victorian mahogany cases complement the dandyish British styles they hold. Embroidered vests; brightly striped socks, scarves, and shirts; and tongue-in-cheek cuff links leaven the classic, double-back-vent suits for men. Women head for the tailored suits and separates, classic outerwear, and dresses. Plus, you'll find furniture and a selection of photography books and ephemera. ✉ *142 Greene St., between Prince and W. Houston Sts., SoHo* ☎ *646/613–3060* ⊕ *www.paulsmith. co.uk* Ⓜ *R to Prince St.*

Philosophy di Alberta Ferretti. The designer's eye for delicate detailing and soft, feminine design is evident in the perforated hemlines, embroidered stitching, and sprinkling of beads across gauzy fabrics and knits. ✉ *452 West Broadway, between W. Houston and Prince Sts., SoHo* ☎ *212/460–5500* Ⓜ *B, D, F, M to Broadway–Lafayette St.*

Prada. This ultramodern space, designed by Rem Koolhaas, incorporates so many technological innovations that it was written up in *Popular Science*. The dressing-room gadgets alone include liquid crystal displays, changeable lighting, and scanners that link you to the store's database. ✉ *575 Broadway, at Prince St., SoHo* ☎ *212/334–8888* ⊕ *www.prada. com* Ⓜ *R to Prince St.*

R by 45rpm. Shopping at this Japanese clothing store is a Zen-like experience, thanks to a stone pathway, limestone dressing rooms, and denim dangling from wooden trees. Although it's pricey, fans love the label for its attention to detail, like hand-dyed denim that has been woven on antique looms. The T-shirts are particularly funky. ✉ *169 Mercer St., between W. Houston and Prince Sts., SoHo* ☎ *917/237–0045* ⊕ *rby45rpm.com* Ⓜ *R to Prince St.*

18

★ **Reiss.** Think of Reiss as the Banana Republic of Britain—a go-to place for casual-but-tailored clothes at a relatively gentle price. Kate Middleton is a loyal customer. Standouts for women include cowl-neck sweater dresses and A-line skirts. Men's wool combat trousers are complemented by shrunken blazers, military-inspired peacoats, and trim leather jackets. ⊠ *387 West Broadway, between Spring and Broome Sts., SoHo* ☎ *212/925–5707* ⊕ *www.reissonline.com* Ⓜ *R, W to Prince St.*

Sean. Not to be confused with Sean John, this French-owned shop carries low-key, well-priced, and comfortable menswear imported from Europe. Linen and cordoruy painter's coats are best sellers, along with V-neck sweaters and a respectable collection of suits and dress shirts. ⊠ *199 Prince St., between Sullivan and MacDougal Sts., SoHo* ☎ *212/598–5980* ⊕ *www.seanstore.com* Ⓜ *R, W to Prince St.*

Seize sur Vingt. In bringing a contemporary sensibility to custom tailoring, this store realized an ideal fusion. Brighten a suit or cotton moleskin flat-front pants with a checked or striped shirt; all can be made to order. Women are also the beneficiaries of the store's crisp button-downs and single-pleat trousers. ⊠ *78 Greene St., between Spring and Broome Sts., SoHo* ☎ *212/625–1620* ⊕ *16sur20.com* Ⓜ *R, W to Prince St.*

Seven New York. This massive store is a temple to all things denim and in every wash and cut. Want them straight, skinny, boot cut, or pleated? No problem. Not content with dressing just customers' lower halves, 7 for All Mankind also sells trendy tops, sweaters, and jackets to complete the look. There are also nondenim dresses and trousers. ⊠ *110 Mercer St., between Prince and Spring Sts., SoHo* ☎ *646/654–0156* ⊕ *sevennewyork.com* Ⓜ *N, R to Prince St.*

Tess Giberson. This former creative director of cashmere company TSE, known for her fluid designs in muted colors, recently opened her first store. The boutique has an airy, minimalist feel, with whitewashed walls and rotating art exhibits. The best bets are floaty silk dresses and lean blazers. ⊠ *97 Crosby St., between Prince and Spring Sts., SoHo* ☎ *212/226–1932* Ⓜ *N, R to Prince St.*

Topshop. British cult favorite Topshop, which has only two U.S. locations, is a master at pumping out of-the-minute-fashion at reasonable prices. It can be a madhouse, and items sell quickly, but it's worth fighting the crowds. Slinky dresses are around $130, and jeans and jumpsuits are about $90. Coats and shoes are also standouts. Male stylists can browse through the ground-level Topman. ⊠ *480 Broadway, at Broome St., SoHo* ☎ *212/966–9555* Ⓜ *6 to Spring St.; R to Prince St.*

★ **UNIQLO.** The SoHo location is the brand's global flagship, and shoppers will find items here they can't find anywhere else. Seasonal staples like cashmere sweaters and tees in a rainbow of colors are stacked up to the ceiling. The tri-level space bursts with affordable, well-tailored basics. Cashmere crew- and V-necks (most under $100), slim-fit denims, and casual coats share space with edgier tees designed by Japanese graphic artists. Most of the clothing has been tweaked or made specifically for the American market. There are several outlets throughout the city.

■TIP→ Weekday mornings are the best time to avoid long lines for the dressing rooms. ✉ *546 Broadway, between Prince and Spring Sts., SoHo* ☎ *917/237–8800* ⊕ *www.uniqlo.com* Ⓜ *R to Prince St.*

Vera Wang. Not content designing just wedding dresses, Wang is also a star at evening wear and casual-but-chic daywear. Her entire ready-to-wear collection is showcased here in this gleaming, all-white store. Choose from clothes ranging from sexy one-shouldered satin gowns and cashmere sweaters to wool pencil skirts. ✉ *158 Mercer St., between Prince and W. Houston Sts., SoHo* ☎ *212/382–2184* ⊕ *www.verawang. com* Ⓜ *N, R to Prince St.*

Vivienne Tam. Tam is known for her playful "China chic" take on familiar Asian images. Cold-weather creations in jewel-color silk are embroidered; the warm-weather clothes are floaty and romantic. ✉ *40 Mercer St., at Grand St., SoHo* ☎ *212/966–2398* ⊕ *www.viviennetam.com* Ⓜ *R to Prince St.*

What Goes Around Comes Around. Professional stylists flock here to dig up vintage items like Levi's and Azzedine Alaïa dresses, as well as one-of-a-kind rock-concert T-shirts. WGACA also sells its own line of vintage-inspired clothing, from dresses to coats and tops. The vintage rock tees (think Black Sabbath, Mötley Crüe) are great finds but can set you back an eye-watering $300–$600. ✉ *351 West Broadway, between Grand and Broome Sts., SoHo* ☎ *212/343–1225* ⊕ *www.whatgoesaroundnyc. com* Ⓜ *J, M, N, Q, R, Z, 6 to Canal St.*

Zara. This European women's clothing brand offers on-trend styles at bargain prices. ✉ *580 Broadway* ☎ *212/343–1725* ⊕ *www.zara.com* Ⓜ *B, D, F, M to Broadway–Lafayette St..*

FOOD AND TREATS

Harney & Sons. Fancy a cuppa? Harney & Sons is famous for producing more than 250 varieties of loose tea, which can be sampled at its store and tea salon in SoHo. The design is sleek and dramatic, with a 24-foot-long tasting bar and floor-to-ceiling shelves stocked with tea. Shoppers will find classic brews like English Breakfast and Oolong, along with interesting herbals (ginger and liquorice, or mint verbena). And no cup of tea would be complete without a scone or two, available at the tea salon. ✉ *433 Broome St., between Broadway and Crosby St., SoHo* ☎ *212/933–4853* ⊕ *harneysoho.blogspot.com* Ⓜ *4, 6 to Spring St.*

Fodor's Choice
★
Jacques Torres Chocolates. Visit the café and shop here and you'll literally be surrounded by chocolate. The glass-walled downtown space also houses Torres's chocolate factory, so you can watch the goodies being made while you sip a richly spiced cocoa or nibble on a Java Junkie bar. ■TIP→ Signature taste: the "wicked" chocolate, laced with cinnamon and chili pepper. ✉ *350 Hudson St., at King St., SoHo* ☎ *212/414–2462* ⊕ *www.mrchocolate.com* Ⓜ *1 to Houston St.*

Kee's Chocolates. Owner Kee Ling Tong whips up delicious truffles and macaroons with unusual, Asian-inspired flavors. Try the ginger peach and rosewater lychee macaroons, or truffles flavored with lemongrass mint and tamarind. ✉ *80 Thompson St., between Spring and Broome Sts., SoHo* ☎ *212/334–3284* ⊕ *www.keeschocolates.com* Ⓜ *A, C to Spring St.*

18

MarieBelle. The handmade chocolates here are nothing less than works of art. Square truffles and bonbons—which come in such flavors as Earl Grey, cappuccino, passion fruit, and saffron—are painted with edible dyes (cocoa butter dyed with natural coloring) so each resembles a miniature painting. Relax in the Cacao Bar and Tea Salon while sipping an Aztec hot chocolate, which is made from rich cacao, rather than cocoa powder. ⊠ *484 Broome St., between West Broadway and Wooster St., SoHo* ☎ *212/925–6999* ⊕ *www.mariebelle.com* Ⓜ *R, W to Prince St.*

Vosges Haut Chocolat. This chandeliered salon lined with apothecary shelves takes a global approach to chocolate. Many of the creations are travel-inspired: the Budapest bonbons combine dark chocolate and Hungarian paprika, and the Black Pearls contain wasabi, but the most unexpected treat might be the chocolate bacon bars. ⊠ *132 Spring St., SoHo* ☎ *212/625–2929* ⊕ *www.vosgeschocolate.com* Ⓜ *R, W to Prince St.*

HOME DECOR

Armani Casa. In keeping with the Armani aesthetic, the minimalist furniture and homewares have a subdued color scheme (gold, grays, cream, and black). Big-ticket items include luxuriously upholstered sofas and sleek coffee tables. The desk accessories and throw pillows are equally understated. ⊠ *Decoration & Design Building, 979 3rd Ave., Suite 1424, between East 58th and 59th, Midtown East* ☎ *212/334–1271* Ⓜ *4, 5, 6 or Q, N, R to 59th St.*

de Vera. Owner Federico de Vera crisscrosses the globe searching for unique decorative products, so shoppers will never know what they might find here. Venetian glass vases, Thai Buddhas, and antique rose–cut diamond rings are typical finds. ⊠ *1 Crosby St., at Howard St., SoHo* ☎ *212/625–0838* ⊕ *www.deveraobjects.com* Ⓜ *N, Q, R, 6 to Canal St.*

Kiosk. Is it a gallery or a boutique? Duck under the neon arrow sign, head up the stairway, and you'll come upon this novelty shop–cum–art installation. The owners travel the globe in search of locally unique, interestingly designed or packaged items, then sell their gleanings at this outpost. A new destination is highlighted every few months. You might find pipe tobacco from Massachusetts or a sled from Sweden. ⊠ *95 Spring St., 2nd Floor, SoHo* ☎ *212/226–8601* ⊕ *kioskkiosk.com* Ⓜ *R to Prince St.*

Matter. This beautifully curated store will appeal to fans of sleek, modern furniture—if money is no object. How about bar stools designed by Zaha Hadid, a $20,000 brass chandelier, or a green lacquered dining table for $5,000? Even if your budget is limited, Matter is worth a drool for inspiration. ⊠ *405 Broome St., between Centre and Lafayette Sts., SoHo* ☎ *212/343–2600* Ⓜ *4, 6 to Spring St.*

Pylones. It's hard to beat Pylones for crazily cheerful products. Utilitarian products like toasters and thermoses have been given makeovers of stripes or flowers, hairbrushes have pictures of frogs or ladybugs on their backs, and pepper mills are turned into pirates. There are several branches around the city. ■TIP➔ There are plenty of fun gifts for less than $20, such as old-fashioned robot toys and candy-color boxes. ⊠ *69*

Spring St., between Crosby and Lafayette Sts., SoHo ☎ *718/387–7484* ⊕ *www.pylones-usa.com* Ⓜ *6 to Spring St.*

Room & Board. Fans of streamlined, midcentury modern furniture will be in heaven here. This location is stocked with sleek sofas, beds, and other pieces of furniture that look like they could have been designed by the Eames Brothers. Instead, it is all new and comes with a relatively affordable price tag. Design aficionados can also choose from designer classics like seating cubes from Frank Gehry and Eames molded plywood chairs. ⊠ *105 Wooster St., between Spring and Prince Sts., SoHo* ☎ *212/334–4343* ⊕ *www.roomandboard.com* Ⓜ *N, R to Prince St.*

JEWELRY AND ACCESSORIES

Fodor's Choice

★

Alexis Bittar. Bittar began selling his first jewelry line, made from Depression-era glass, on a corner in SoHo. Now the Brooklyn-born designer counts A-list celebs and fashion editors among his fans. He makes clean-line, big-statement jewelry from vermeil, colored Lucite, pearls, and vintage glass. The stores mirror this aesthetic with a mix of old and new, like antiqued-white Victorian-era lion's-claw tables and Plexiglas walls. ⊠ *465 Broome St., between Mercer and Greene Sts., SoHo* ☎ *212/625–8340* ⊕ *www.alexisbittar.com* Ⓜ *R to Prince St.*

★ **Fragments.** This spot glitters with pieces by emerging designers, many of them local, as well as established ones. Most use semiprecious stones—you could try on turquoise-bead shoulder-duster earrings, an oversize opal ring, or a tourmaline pendant—but a few bust out the bling. ⊠ *116 Prince St., between Greene and Wooster Sts., SoHo* ☎ *212/334–9588* ⊕ *www.fragments.com* Ⓜ *R to Prince St.*

Robert Lee Morris. If you buy into the mantra that bigger is better, make a stop here. Morris designs big, chunky jewelry that is anything but understated. Gold and silver cuffs have a serious weight to them, and necklaces and earrings have dangling hammered disks for a "wind chime" effect. Some pieces incorporate diamonds; others have semiprecious stones like turquoise or citrine. ⊠ *400 West Broadway, between Broome and Spring Sts., SoHo* ☎ *212/431–9405* Ⓜ *C, E to Spring St.*

Stuart Moore. Everything about this boutique is minimalist, from the architecture to the jewelry. Most of the designs (from Heinrich + Denzel to Beatrice Mueller) have a streamlined, almost industrial look: diamonds are set in brushed platinum, and gold bangles are impossibly delicate. ⊠ *411 West Broadway, at Spring St., SoHo* ☎ *212/941–1023* ⊕ *www.stuartmoore.com* Ⓜ *A, C, E to Spring St.*

Swarovski Crystallized. A shrine to all things sparkly, this crystal superstore is a combination boutique and café, and allows shoppers to customize their purchases. Shoppers mix and match pieces from the striking "library of light" to create designs. If you're lacking ideas, there's always ready-made jewelry. Look out for pieces created by top designers like Catherine Malandrino and Prabal Gurung. ⊠ *499 Broadway, between Spring and Broome Sts., SoHo* ☎ *212/966–3322* Ⓜ *R to Prince St.; 6 to Spring St.*

Versani. Most of the jewelry here is big, bold, and unisex—and more than a little quirky. Silver teams up with all kinds of materials: leather,

18

denim, and snakeskin, as well as semiprecious stones. There's a good selection of silver rings and pendants under $50. ⊠ *152 Mercer St., between Prince and W. Houston Sts., SoHo* ☎ *212/941–7770* ⊕ *www. versani.com* Ⓜ *R, W to Prince St.*

SHOES, HANDBAGS, AND LEATHER GOODS

Anya Hindmarch. Although Anya Hindmarch is arguably most famous for her "I'm Not a Plastic Bag" tote, her real standouts are buttery leather shoulder bags and hobos, which are decidely understated. Hindmarch's designs run the gamut from cheeky to ladylike. ⊠ *29 E. 60th St., between Madison and Park Aves., Upper East Side* ☎ *212/750–3974* Ⓜ *4, 5, 6 to 59th St.*

★ **Camper.** These Euro-fave walking shoes, with their sturdy leather uppers and nubby rubber soles, have also proved popular on the cobblestone streets of SoHo. Comfort is a priority; all the slip-ons and lace-ups here have generously rounded toes and a springy feel. ⊠ *125 Prince St., at Wooster St., SoHo* ☎ *212/358–1841* Ⓜ *R to Prince St.*

Frye Boots. This 6,000-square-foot mecca to boots has a Western feel, thanks to the exposed brick walls and reclaimed barn doors. Boots can be tattooed—or hot stamped—with your initials while you wait in the lounge. In addition to Frye's famed boots, shoppers can also pick from flats, oxfords, clogs, and mules. ⊠ *113 Spring St., between Mercer and Greene Sts., SoHo* ☎ *212/226–3793* Ⓜ *N, R to Prince St.*

★ **Kate Spade.** Spade's runaway success with classic kicky, retro-style tote bags has blossomed into a full-fledged lifestyle company. The flagship looks—and feels—like an elegant living room. The totes are still for sale, along with leather handbags, kitten heels, and accessories like eyeglasses and paper. Even the diaper bags are ridiculously stylish. Around the corner you'll find **Jack Spade,** filled with bags, dopp kits, and other men's accessories in a nostalgic setting. ⊠ *454 Broome St., between Mercer and Greene Sts., SoHo* ☎ *212/274–1991* Ⓜ *C, E to Spring St.*

Longchamp. Its Le Pliage foldable nylon bags have become an Upper East Side and Hamptons staple, but don't think this label is stuffy. Kate Moss designs a line for Longchamp that includes wallets, satchels, and hobos. The store carries the entire line of luggage, leather handbags, and totes in a rainbow of colors. ⊠ *132 Spring St., at Elizabeth St., SoHo* ☎ *212/343–7444* ⊕ *www.longchamp.com* Ⓜ *N, R to Prince St.*

TOYS

Ⓒ
★
Kidrobot. This shop will appeal to kids, nerds, and the young at heart, who all flock here to stock up on the latest toys from Asian designers. This is a far cry from Mattel—the shelves are stocked with Dunny bunnies, Tokidokis, and Devilrobots. There's also a selection of cool silk-screened T-shirts and hoodies. ⊠ *118 Prince St., between Greene and Wooster Sts., SoHo* ☎ *212/966–6688* ⊕ *www.kidrobot.com* Ⓜ *N, R to Prince St.*

NOLITA

BEAUTY

★ **Lafco New York.** A heavy, iron-barred door leads to a hushed, scented inner sanctum of beauty products. This location is the official retailer of the 600-year-old Santa Maria Novella products from Italy, which include intriguingly archaic colognes, creams, and soaps such as Tooth Cleansing Water and pomegranate soap. Everything is packaged in bottles and jars with antique-style apothecary labels. ✉ *285 Lafayette St., between E. Houston and Prince Sts., NoLIta* ☎ *212/925–0001* ⊕ *www.lafcony.com* Ⓜ *N, R to Prince St.*

BOOKS AND STATIONERY

Fodor's Choice
★

McNally Jackson. This cozy, independent bookstore manages to be comprehensive without overwhelming visitors. Check the tables up front for hot-off-the-press novels, nonfiction, and manifestos. The staff is clearly literary minded, so ask for recommendations if you're browsing. Literature extends beyond the packed shelves here—just grab a coffee from what owner Sarah McNally calls the "booksiest bookstore café" to see for yourself—even the menu has literary references. ✉ *52 Prince St., between Lafayette and Mulberry Sts., NoLIta* ☎ *212/274–1160* ⊕ *mcnallyjackson.com* Ⓜ *R to Prince St.*

CLOTHING

Creatures of Comfort. Owner Jade Lai has brought her popular L.A. outpost to New York. The open, airy boutique offers cool clothes from emerging designers alongside products sourced from around the world. Most of the colors are muted, and brands carried include Acne, MM6, and the house label, Creatures of Comfort. There's a small selection of shoes, plus you never know what you might find for sale on a side table, such as candy and lip gloss from Asia. ✉ *205 Mulberry St., between Spring and Kenmare Sts., NoLIta* ☎ *212/925–1005* ⊕ *www. creaturesofcomfort.us* Ⓜ *6 to Spring St.*

Duncan Quinn. Shooting for nothing less than sartorial splendor, this designer provides everything from chalk-stripe suits to cuff links and croquet shirts, all in a shop not much bigger than its silk pocket squares. Only a few of each style of shirt are made, so the odds are slim that you will see someone else in your blue, violet, or orange button-down with contrast-color undercuffs. Bespoke customers can choose from thousands of fabrics, but there are plenty of off-the-rack options as well. ✉ *8 Spring St., between Elizabeth and Bowery Sts., NoLIta* ☎ *212/226–7030* ⊕ *duncanquinn.com* Ⓜ *6 to Spring St.*

Frock. Models and stylists frequent this tiny shop for vintage women's wear from the 1960s through the early '90s. The store carries pieces from Oscar de la Renta, Galanos and Missoni, as well as Valentino, Alaïa, and Chanel. ✉ *170 Elizabeth St., between Spring and Kenmare Sts., NoLIta* ☎ *212/594–5380* ⊕ *frocknyc.com* Ⓜ *B, D, F, M to Broadway–Lafayette St.*

INA. The clothing at this couture consignment store harks back only one or two seasons, and in some cases, the item has never been worn.

18

NOLITA

The Nabokovian nickname NoLITa, shorthand for "North of Little Italy," covers a neighborhood that has taken the commercial baton from SoHo and run with it.

Like SoHo, NoLIta has gone from a locals-only, understated area to a crowded weekend magnet, as much about people-watching as it is about shopping. Still, unlike those of its SoHo neighbor, these stores remain largely one-of-a-kind. Running along the parallel north–south spines of Elizabeth, Mott, and Mulberry streets, between East Houston and Kenmare streets, NoLIta's boutiques tend to be small and, as real estate dictates, somewhat pricey.

BEST TIME TO GO

Wednesday through Friday afternoons if you're keen to shop without too many distractions, weekends for more people to scope out. Shops stay open latest (usually until 8 pm) Thursday through Saturday.

BEST SOUVENIR FOR YOUR BABYSITTER

Beautifully packaged candles exclusive to **Red Flower** (✉ *13 Prince St., at Elizabeth St.* ☎ *212/966–5301*) in dreamy scents like Italian blood orange and Japanese peony. Or perhaps some calming chamomile or lavender bath products from the ancient Italian perfumer-pharmacist **Lafco/Santa Maria Novella.**

Map labels:
0 — 1/8 mile
0 — 200 meters
E. Houston St.
Calypso
Tory Burch
Bowery St.
Chrystie St.
B,D,F,M,6 M
Me&Ro
Café Habana to Go
Café Gitane
Red Flower
N,R M
Prince St.
Belle by Sigerson Morrison
Resurrection
Duncan Quinn
6 M
Spring St.
Mulberry St.
Mott St.
Elizabeth St.
Creatures of Comfort
Kenmare St.
Broadway
Crosby St.
Lafayette St.
J,Z M
Calypso Outlet
Calypso Home
Broome St.
Calypso
Cleveland Pl.
Centre St.
Grand St.

KEY

M Subway stops

REFUELING

Café Gitane. Hit the takeout window of Café Gitane for an espresso, or head inside for Moroccan French dishes like avocado toast or couscous. ✉ *242 Mott St., at Prince St.* ☎ *212/334–9552.*

Café Habana to Go. If you don't mind getting your fingers messy, stop by Café Habana to Go for an addictive grilled ear of corn, topped with chili powder, cheese, and a splash of lime. ✉ *17 Prince St., at Elizabeth St.* ☎ *212/625–2002.*

BEST FOR

FOXY SHOES
Belle by Sigerson Morrison: Choose between sexy knee-high boots, gladiator sandals, and flats.

... AND OTHER ACCESSORIES
Me&Ro: Indian-inspired gold and silver jewelry, from shoulder-duster earrings to tiny lotus-petal pendants.

TOO-COOL-FOR-SCHOOL CLOTHES
Calypso: Browse the multiple locations in NoLIta for softly exotic clothes and housewares.

Creatures of Comfort: The funky separates here are in pale, muted colors.

Duncan Quinn: Whether customized or off the rack, these button-downs and suits are perfectly cut.

Resurrection: Mint-condition vintage Pucci and Courrèges make this a stylist's gold mine.

Tory Burch: Score a pair of her signature ballet flats or bohemian chic tunics and skinny cords in eye-popping colors.

18

Browse through the racks to spot gems from Lanvin, Chanel, and Alexander McQueen. Although there are multiple locations around the city, this flagship also carries menswear. ✉ *15 Bleecker St., at Elizabeth St., NoLIta* ☎ *212/228–8511* ⊕ *www.inanyc.com* Ⓜ *6 to Bleecker St.*

Jay Kos. There aren't too many boutiques where the owner sometimes whips up a snack for customers in the boutique's custom kitchen, but this designer—famous for dressing Diddy and Johnny Depp—wanted his new boutique to have a homey feel. The clothes veer toward the fabulous: suede shoes, linen suits, and cashmere sweaters, which are displayed in armoires. ✉ *293 Mott St., at E. Houston St., NoLIta* ☎ *212/319–2770* Ⓜ *B, D, F, M to Broadway-Lafayette St.*

Malia Mills. Fit fanatics have met their match here—especially those gals who are different sizes on top and bottom (bikini tops go up to a size D). Bikini tops and bottoms are sold separately: halters, bandeaus, and triangle tops, plus boy-cut, side-tie, and low-ride bottoms. There's a collection of one-pieces as well, which are sold by bra size. ✉ *199 Mulberry St., between Spring and Kenmare Sts., NoLIta* ☎ *212/625–2311* Ⓜ *6 to Spring St.*

Nanette Lepore. "Girly" may well be the description that comes to mind as you browse through this cheerful shop; skirts are pleated and adorned with bows, jackets are enhanced by embroidery and floral appliqués, fur shrugs have tiny sleeves. ✉ *423 Broome St., between Lafayette and Crosby Sts., NoLIta* ☎ *212/219–8265* ⊕ *www.nanettelepore.com* Ⓜ *6 to Spring St.*

Paul Frank. The store's mascot, the cheeky Julius monkey, is plastered everywhere here—on flannel PJs, skateboards, and, of course, T-shirts. Also look for tees evoking such formative elements of '80s youth as corn dogs and break dancing. A selection of monkey-free accessories, including perfect weekender bags, is more stylish than sassy. ✉ *195 Mulberry St., at Kenmare St., NoLIta* ☎ *212/965–5079* Ⓜ *6 to Spring St.*

★ **Resurrection.** This small but tidy crimson shop is a treasure trove of vintage clothing. Stocked with Chanels, Puccis, and Yves Saint Laurent, it's a retro-chic gold mine—but be prepared to pay dearly. Designers like Marc Jacobs and Anna Sui have sought inspiration among the racks, and the store returns the love by presenting occasional in-store designer exhibits, often with pieces from an honoree's personal collection. ✉ *217 Mott St., between Prince and Spring Sts., NoLIta* ☎ *212/625–1374* Ⓜ *6 to Spring St.*

Tory Burch. Bright-orange lacquer zings through this space, which has the same boho-luxe feel as the clothing. Orange joins navy, flamingo pink, and mossy green on embellished tunics, printed dresses, and superskinny cords. The medallion flats are one of Burch's best sellers. ✉ *257 Elizabeth St., between E. Houston and Prince Sts., NoLIta* ☎ *212/334–3000* ⊕ *www.toryburch.com* Ⓜ *R to Prince St.*

JEWELRY AND ACCESSORIES

Condor. Owner Loriann Smoak is the consummate world traveler, and she has stocked her serene, white-marbled clothing boutique with plenty of international designers, as well as local ones. Everything from coffee-table books to dangly earrings and scarves is available here. ✉ *259 Elizabeth St., between E. Houston and Prince Sts., NoLIta* ☎ *212/966–4280.*

Dinosaur Designs. Translucent and colorful, this antipodean work uses an untraditional medium: resin. Some resins look like semiprecious stone, such as onyx or jade. The rest delve into stronger colors like

aqua or crimson. Cruise the stacks of chunky bangles and cuffs or rows of rings; prices start at $50. There's some striking tableware, too. ✉ *211 Elizabeth St., between Prince and E. Houston Sts., NoLIta* ☎ *212/680–3523* Ⓜ *R to Prince St.*

Erica Weiner. This eponymous designer specializes in vintage-inspired jewelry as well as antiques: delicate art-deco earrings, vintage lockets, and necklaces fashioned from antique compasses. The boutique's tile floor and wooden display cabinets reflect Weiner's aesthetic. Prices are surprisingly reasonable. ✉ *173 Elizabeth St., between Kenmare and Spring Sts., NoLIta* ☎ *212/334–6383* Ⓜ *4, 6 to Spring St.*

Me&Ro. Minimalist, Eastern styling has gained these designers a cult following. The Indian-inspired, hand-finished gold bangles, earrings, and necklaces are covered with tiny dangling rubies, sapphires, or brown diamonds. Although the fine jewelry is expensive, small sterling silver earrings start at around $120. ✉ *241 Elizabeth St., between Prince and E. Houston Sts., NoLIta* ☎ *917/237–9215* Ⓜ *R to Prince St.*

SHOES, HANDBAGS, AND LEATHER GOODS

★ **Belle by Sigerson Morrison.** The company's secondary shoe line will appeal to those with high taste but a (relatively) lower budget—a pair of flats will still set you back around $300. Choose from knee-high boots, gladiator sandals, or chunky wedges. ✉ *28 Prince St., between Mott and Elizabeth Sts., SoHo* ☎ *212/941–5404* Ⓜ *N, R to Prince St.*

High Way. The bags here marry form and function. Totes and messenger bags come in durable leather and nylon, and some handbags open to disclose a wealth of inner pockets. ✉ *238 Mott St., between Prince and Spring Sts., NoLIta* ☎ *212/966–4388* Ⓜ *6 to Bleecker St.*

★ **John Fluevog Shoes.** The inventor of the Angelic sole (protects against water, acid, "and Satan"), Fluevog designs chunky, funky shoes and boots for men and women. ✉ *250 Mulberry St., at Prince St., NoLIta* ☎ *212/431–4484* ⊕ *www.fluevog.com* Ⓜ *R to Prince St.*

Kathryn Amberleigh. This designer, an FIT grad, has perfected the sexy-but-edgy look in her hand-crafted shoes. There are simple flats and wedges along with peep-toe ankle boots and sky-high heels. Most designs hover around the $250 mark. ✉ *219 Mott St., between Prince and Spring Sts, NoLIta* ☎ *212/625–3933* Ⓜ *4, 6 to Spring St.*

Token. Although messenger bags are now ubiquitous, pay homage to the store that started it all. Super-durable messenger bags come in waxed canvas as well as nylon, and the line has expanded to include totes, duffels, and travel bags, all in unadorned, simple styles. ✉ *258 Elizabeth St.,*

18

Cool Spots for Souvenirs

What to get from the city that has everything? Major tourist attractions keep their gift shops well stocked with all the standard souvenirs, and dozens of gift shops dot the Times Square area. If you're looking for grungier souvenirs of downtown (T-shirts with salty messages, tattoos), troll St. Marks Place between 2nd and 3rd avenues in the East Village. *But for more unique mementos of the city, see this chapter's neighborhood spotlights for ideas and try the sources below.*

City Store. The official store of NYC sells anything and everything having to do with the city, from books and pamphlets to fun gift ideas. Pick up NYPD T-shirts, taxicab medallions, garbage truck toys, and dishtowels silk-screened with the skyline. The store shuts at 5 pm on weekdays and is closed weekends. ✉ *1 Centre St., at Chambers St., Lower Manhattan* ☎ *212/669–8246* Ⓜ *4, 5, 6 to City Hall/Brooklyn Bridge.*

Eleni's. Take a bite out of the Big Apple—in cookie form—with these perfectly decorated treats. The "New York, New York" tin includes sugar cookies that mimic local icons like yellow cabs, the Wall Street sign, and the Statue of Liberty. ✉ *Chelsea Market, 75 9th Ave., between W. 15th and W. 16th Sts., Chelsea* ☎ *212/255–6804* ⊕ *elenis.com* Ⓜ *A, C, E to 14th St.; L to 8th Ave.*

New York City Transit Museum Gift Shop. In the symbolic heart of New York City's transit system, all the store's merchandise is somehow linked to the MTA, from straphanger ties to earrings made from old subway tokens. ✉ *Grand Central Terminal, Vanderbilt Pl. and E. 42nd St., Midtown East* ☎ *866/289–6986* ⊕ *www. transitmuseumstore.com* Ⓜ *4, 5, 6, 7 to 42nd St./Grand Central Terminal.*

Zabar's. When it comes to authentic New York food, it's hard to beat rugelach, bagels, or lox from this favorite emporium. ✉ *2245 Broadway, at 80th St., Upper West Side* ☎ *212/787–2000* Ⓜ *1 to 79th St.*

between E. Houston and Prince Sts., NoLIta ☎ *212/226–9655* ⊕ *www. tokenbags.com* Ⓜ *R to Prince St.*

EAST VILLAGE AND LOWER EAST SIDE

EAST VILLAGE
ANTIQUES AND COLLECTIBLES

Lost City Arts. This sprawling shop is one of the best places to shop for 20th-century-design furniture, lighting, and accessories. Lost City can help you relive the Machine Age with an in-house, retro-modern line of furniture. ✉ *18 Cooper Sq., at E. 5th St., East Village* ☎ *212/375–0500* ⊕ *www2.lostcityarts.com/* Ⓜ *6 to Astor Pl.*

Partners & Spade. Owners Andy Spade and Anthony Perduti have lined this small space with all kinds of carefully curated knickknacks, ranging from the silly to the sublime. You might find a surfboard fin or custom-painted bicycle. The shop's own line of books is wonderfully quirky, covering everything from girls on bikes to the benefits of looking up in

Manhattan. The shop is open by-appointment-only midweek but open to the public on weekends. ✉ *40 Great Jones St., between Lafayette and Bowery Sts., East Village* ☎ *646/861–2827* ⊕ *partnersandspade. com* Ⓜ *4, 6 to Bleecker St.*

BEAUTY

Bond No. 9. Created by the same fragrance team as Creed, this line of scents is intended to evoke the New York City experience, with a scent for every neighborhood: Central Park, a men's fragrance, is woodsy and "green," and Park Avenue is discreet but not too sweet. The shop, with its airy space and wood-panel Tea Library, is a lovely place to linger. ✉ *9 Bond St., between Lafayette St. and Broadway, East Village* ☎ *212/228–1732* ⊕ *www.bondno9.com/* Ⓜ *6 to Bleecker St.*

Kiehl's Since 1851. At this favored haunt of top models and stylists, white-smocked assistants can help you choose between the lotions and potions, all of which are packaged in simple-looking bottles and jars. Some of the products, such as the Ultra Facial Cream, Silk Groom hairstyling aid, and superrich Creme de Corps, have attained near-cult status among beautyphiles. ■TIP➡ **Kiehl's is known for being generous with samples, so be sure to ask for your own bag of take-home testers.** ✉ *109 3rd Ave., at E. 13th St., East Village* ☎ *212/677–3171* Ⓜ *4, 5, 6, L, N, Q, R, W to 14th St./Union Sq.*

BOOKS AND STATIONERY

St. Mark's Bookshop. Downtown residents, NYU students, and intellectuals in general love this store, spending hours poking through popular and oddball fiction and nonfiction. You'll find a truly eclectic, attitudinal collection of books here, not unlike the salespeople. On the main floor, books on critical theory are right up front, across from new fiction titles—this is perhaps the only place where you can find Jacques Derrida facing off against T. C. Boyle. Cultural and art books are up front as well; literature and literary journals fill the back of the store. ■TIP➡ **It's open daily until midnight.** ✉ *31 3rd Ave., between 8th and 9th Sts., East Village* ☎ *212/260–7853* ⊕ *www.stmarksbookshop.com* Ⓜ *6 to Astor Pl.*

CLOTHING

John Varvatos. Varvatos has long been inspired by rock and roll. His ad campaigns have starred Franz Ferdinand and Green Day, so it is only fitting that he transformed the former CBGB club into his New York flagship. The space is dotted with vintage pianos and guitars, as well as old vinyl records. And the clothes? The jeans, leather pants, and suede shoes will give you rock-star cred, but there are also classic, understated styles for the corporate set. ✉ *315 Bowery, between E. 1st and E. 2nd Sts., East Village* ☎ *212/358–0315* ⊕ *www.johnvarvatos. com* Ⓜ *4, 6 to Bleeker St.*

Pas de Deux. Fashion editors love this little boutique—which looks like it was imported straight from Paris—thanks to the marble checkerboard floor, chandeliers, and fine woodwork. The well-edited selection includes dresses, trench coats, and denim from Rag & Bone, Philip Lim, and Vena Cava. There are also lots of lovely little accessories, like eyeglasses, cardholders, and delicate necklaces. ✉ *328 E. 11th St.,*

18

between 1st and 2nd Aves., East Village ☎ *212/475–0075* ⊕ *pasdedeuxny.com* Ⓜ *4, 6 to Astor Pl.*

Patricia Field. If you loved Carrie Bradshaw's wild outfits on *Sex and the City*, this is the place for you. As well as designing costumes for the show, Field has been a long-time purveyor of flamboyant and

campy club-kid gear. Her 4,000-square-foot East Village emporium is chockablock with teeny kilts, lamé, marabou, pleather, and vinyl, as well as wigs in every color and stiletto heels in some very large sizes. ⊠ *302 Bowery, between Bleecker and E. Houston Sts., East Village* ☎ *212/966–4066* ⊕ *www.patriciafield.com* Ⓜ *6 to Bleecker St.*

Screaming Mimi's. Browse through racks bulging with vintage finds from the 1950s through '80s. Retro wear includes everything from dresses to soccer shirts and prom dresses. Although most of the non-designer finds are affordable, Screaming Mimi's also carries vintage designer duds from Valentino, Chloe, and Gaultier. ⊠ *382 Lafayette St., between 4th and Great Jones Sts., East Village* ☎ *212/677–6464* ⊕ *www.screamingmimis.com* Ⓜ *B, D, F, M to Broadway–Lafayette St.*

Tokio 7. Even fashion designers like Alexander Wang have been known to pop into this high-end consignment store to browse. Racks are loaded with goodies from A-list designers such as Gucci, Stella McCartney, DVF, and Philip Lim. ⊠ *83 E. 7th St., between 1st and 2nd Aves., East Village* ☎ *212/353–8443* ⊕ *tokio7.net* Ⓜ *4, 6 to Astor Pl.–8th St.*

Trash and Vaudeville. This punk mecca is famous for dressing stars like Debbie Harry and the Ramones back in the '70s, and its rock-and-roll vibe lives on. Goths, punks, and pro wrestlers shop here for bondage-inspired pants and skirts, as well as vinyl corsets and mini-kilts. ⊠ *4 St. Marks Pl., between 2nd and 3rd Aves., East Village* ☎ *212/982–3590* ⊕ *www.trashandvaudeville.com* Ⓜ *6 to Astor Pl.*

FOOD AND TREATS

Max Brenner: Chocolate by the Bald Man. This Aussie arrival is all about a Wonka-ish sense of entertainment. The cafés encourage the messy enjoyment of gooey creations like chocolate fondues and chocolate burgers for kids. Take-away treats include caramelized pralines and tins of hot-chocolate powder. ⊠ *841 Broadway, between E. 13th and E. 14th Sts., East Village* ☎ *212/388–0030* ⊕ *www.maxbrenner.com* Ⓜ *L, N, Q, R, 4, 5, 6 to 14th St./Union Sq.*

HOME DECOR

White Trash. Looking for a midcentury modern Danish desk? This is your place. Owner Stuart Zamsky crams his store with surprisingly affordable pieces that are mostly from the '40s through '70s, including tables, lamps, and chairs. Some pieces you might find include paper mobiles from the '70s, old fondue sets, and antique medical-office cabinets. ⊠ *304 E. 5th St., between 1st and 2nd Aves., East Village* ☎ *212/598–5956* ⊕ *www.whitetrashnyc.com* Ⓜ *4, 6 to Astor Pl./8th St.*

MUSIC STORES

Other Music. DJs and musicians flock to this antidote to music megastores for hard-to-find genres on CD and vinyl, from Japanese electronica and Krautrock to acid folk and Americana. You can buy concert tickets at the in-house box office. ■TIP→ There's also a great selection of used CDs, including seminal punk classics from the Clash and the Stooges. ⊠ *15 E. 4th St., between Lafayette St. and Broadway, East Village* ☎*212/477–8150* Ⓜ *6 to Astor Pl.*

TOYS

Dinosaur Hill. Forget about Elmo. This little shop stocks quirky gifts for kids like hand puppets and marionettes from Asia, mini-bongos, and wooden rattles. A small selection of children's clothing is also for sale. ⊠ *306 E. 9th St., between 1st and 2nd Aves., East Village* ☎*212/473–5850* ⊕ *dinosaurhill.com* Ⓜ *R to 8th St.; 6 to Astor Pl.*

WINE

Astor Wines & Spirits. Stock up on wine, spirits, and sake at this beautiful shop. For unwinding, and learning more about food and wine, there's also a wine library and kitchen for cooking classes. ⊠ *399 Lafayette St., at E. 4th St., East Village* ☎*212/674–7500* ⊕ *www.astorwines. com* Ⓜ *6 to Astor Pl.*

Union Square Wine & Spirits. Tastings are easy at this well-stocked store, thanks to Enomatic machines. These card-operated contraptions let you sample dozens of wines. If machines don't do it for you, generous tastings are held most Fridays and Saturdays. ⊠ *140 4th Ave., at 13th St., East Village* ☎*212/675–8100* ⊕ *www.unionsquarewines.com* Ⓜ *L, N, Q, R, 4, 5, 6 to 14th St./Union Sq.*

LOWER EAST SIDE

ANTIQUES AND COLLECTIBLES

Las Venus. Step into this kitsch palace and you may feel as though a time machine has zapped you back to the '50s, '60s, or groovy '70s. Look for bubble lamps, lots of brocade, and Knoll knockoffs. Midcentury modern Danish credenzas are also big here. ⊠ *163 Ludlow St., between E. Houston and Stanton Sts., Lower East Side* ☎*212/982–0608* ⊕ *www. lasvenus.com* Ⓜ *F to 2nd Ave.*

CLOTHING

Gargyle. This boutique serves up country-club attire with a nudge and a wink. The floor is covered in astroturf, and the clothes reference classically preppy sports such as golf and tennis, but always in a fashionable way. Choose from argyle sweaters and miniskirts from top labels including Karen Walker, Lover, Shipley & Halmos, and Opening Ceremony. ⊠ *16 Orchard St., between Canal and Hester Sts., Lower East Side* ☎*917/470–9367* ⊕ *www.gargyle.com* Ⓜ *F to Broadway.*

TG-170. Named for owner Terry Gillis, this shop showcases up-and-coming as well as established designers. Cotton dresses from Rachel Mara and jumpsuits from San & Sonni are perfectly on trend. Complete your designer look with fierce heels and a huge cocktail ring from Netti. ⊠ *77 Ludlow St., between Ludlow and Broome Sts., Lower East Side* ☎*212/995–8660* ⊕ *www.tg170.com/* Ⓜ *F, J, M, Z to Delancey St./Essex St.*

18

LOWER EAST SIDE

Once home to multitudes of Jewish immigrants from Russia and Eastern Europe, the Lower East Side has traditionally been New Yorkers' bargain beat. The center of it all is Orchard Street, where vendors still holler, "Lady, have I got a deal for you!"

Here tiny, no-nonsense clothing stores and scrappy stalls hang on to the past while funky local designers gradually claim more turf. A few cool vintage clothing and furniture spots bridge the two camps. Ludlow Street, one block east of Orchard, has become the main drag for twentysomethings with attitude, its boutiques wedged in between bars and low-key restaurants. Anything too polished is looked on with suspicion—and that goes for you, too. For the full scope of this area, prowl from Allen to Essex streets, south of East Houston Street down to Broome Street.

BEST TIME TO GO

Come on a Sunday afternoon, when Orchard Street between East Houston and Delancey streets becomes a vehicle-free pedestrian zone. On Saturday the old-school stores close for the Jewish Sabbath.

BEST SOUVENIR FOR YOUR FAVE KITCHEN AIDE

Raid the **Lower East Side Tenement Museum** gift shop (✉ *108 Orchard St., between Delancey and Broome Sts.* ☎ *212/982-8420*) for a cheery reproduction 1950 Empire State souvenir kitchen towel or a ceramic version of the Greek key coffee cup.

BEST FOR

CLOTHES WITH BITE

Foley & Corinna: Mixes vintage-y new clothes with the truly vintage.

J.D. Fisk: Classic but cool menswear like distressed boots, vintage T-shirts, and denim jackets.

OLD-WORLD FOOD

The Pickle Guys. Move beyond the half-sours to the zingy full-sour and horseradish pickle spears. ✉ *49 Essex St.* ☎ *212/656–9739* ⊕ *pickleguys.com.*

Russ & Daughters. Smoked salmon, pickled herring, and babka, oh my. ✉ *179 E. Houston St., at 1st Ave.* ☎ *212/475–4880* ⊕ *russanddaughters.com.*

VINTAGE

Edith Machinist: Big names from the 1970s and '80s, whopping shoulder pads, and often hefty price tags.

Las Venus: Danish modern furniture, princess phones, boomerang ashtrays in punchy colors.

18

REFUELING

il laboratorio del gelato. Get your calcium with a stop at il laboratorio del gelato for creamy scoops of ice cream and sorbet in unusual flavors like chestnut, lemon verbena, and fresh fig. ✉ *188 Ludlow St., at Houston St., Lower East Side* ☎ *212/343–9922* ⊕ *www.laboratoriodelgelato.com.*

Sugar Sweet Sunshine. Cake with your gelato? Zip to Sugar Sweet Sunshine, a homey little bakery where you can nibble on a cupcake with chocolate-almond frosting or a slice of red-velvet cake. ✉ *126 Rivington St., between Essex and Norfolk Sts.* ☎ *212/995–1960* ⊕ *www.sugarsweetsunshine.com.*

SHOES, HANDBAGS, AND LEATHER GOODS

Altman Luggage. Having trouble bringing all your purchases home? Altman sells top-of-the-line luggage from Samsonite, Delsey, and Tumi at discount prices. A wide selection of pens is also for sale. ⊠ *135 Orchard St., between Delancey and Rivington Sts., Lower East Side* ☎ *212/254–7275* ⊕ *www.altmanluggage.com* Ⓜ *F, J, M, Z to Delancey St./Essex St.*

J. D. Fisk. Although the shoes are the main attraction, think of J. D. Fisk as a one-stop shop for men. The footwear has a rugged American classic look, although some are punk inspired. There's also a small selection of clothing, such as denim jackets and vintage-inspired T-shirts. ⊠ *159½ Ludlow St., between Rivington and Stanton Sts., Lower East Side* ☎ *212/475–0565* ⊕ *www.jdfisk.com* Ⓜ *F, J, M, Z to Delancey St./Essex St.*

GREENWICH VILLAGE AND WEST VILLAGE

GREENWICH VILLAGE

BEAUTY

★ **C. O. Bigelow.** If you find shopping at Duane Reade and CVS a little boring and impersonal, try this old-fashioned pharmacy. Founded in 1838, it is the oldest apothecary-pharmacy in the United States; Mark Twain used to fill prescriptions here. They still fill prescriptions, but the real reason to come is for the hard-to-find-brands like Klorane shampoo and Elgydium toothpaste. Bigelow also has its own line of products, including green-tea lip balm and quince hand lotion. ⊠ *414 6th Ave., between W. 9th and W. 10th, Greenwich Village* ☎ *212/473-7324* ⊕ *www.bigelowchemists.com* Ⓜ *B, D, F, M to W. 4th St.*

CLOTHING

Fodor'sChoice **La Petite Coquette.** Everything at this lingerie store is unabashedly sexy, ★ and the helpful staff can find the perfect fit. The store's own line of silk slips, camisoles, and other underpinnings comes in a range of colors. ⊠ *51 University Pl., between E. 9th and E. 10th Sts., Greenwich Village* ☎ *212/473-2478* ⊕ *www.thelittleflirt.com* Ⓜ *R to 8th St.*

WEST VILLAGE

ANTIQUES AND COLLECTIBLES

Kaas Glassworks. From the outside, this shop is cuter than cute, with its old-fashioned sign and ivy-covered brick facade. The specialty here is decoupage that has been turned into quirky coasters and trays. Owner Carol Kaas uses vintage postcards, maps, and botanical prints in her works. ⊠ *117 Perry St., between Greenwich and Hudson Sts., West Village* ☎ *212/366-0322* ⊕ *www.kaas.com* Ⓜ *1 to Christopher St./ Sheridan Sq.*

BEAUTY

★ **Aedes De Venustas.** Arguably the best place to buy fragrance in town, the super-knowledgeable staff here will help shoppers find the perfect scent. High-end brands like Anick Goutal and Lubin are stocked here, along with luxurious skin-care products and pricey candles from Diptyque and L'Artisan Parfumeur. Their signature gift wrap is as beautiful as what's inside the box. ⊠ *9 Christopher St., between 6th and 7th Aves.,*

West Village ☎ *212/206–8674* ⊕ *www.aedes.com* Ⓜ *1 to Christopher St./Sheridan Sq.*

BOOKS AND STATIONERY

bookbook. Published diaries, letters, biographies, and autobiographies fill this neighborly store. There's also a thoughtful assortment of general nonfiction, fiction, guidebooks, and children's books. But the real focus here is the carefully selected sale tables that spill out onto the sidewalk—they have deals on everything from Graham Greene to Chuck Palahniuk. ⊠ *266 Bleecker St., between 6th and 7th Aves., West Village* ☎ *212/807–8655* ⊕ *www.bookbooknyc.com* Ⓜ *1 to Christopher St./Sheridan Sq.*

Fodor's Choice
★

Partners & Crime Mystery Booksellers. Signed first editions, helpful staff, a rental library, and whodunits galore—new and out of print—make this a must-browse for fans. Books are organized by fun categories, including "Hardboiled," "Softboiled," and "Espionage–non 007." ⊠ *44 Greenwich Ave., between 6th and 7th Aves., West Village* ☎ *212/243–0440* ⊕ *www.crimepays.com* Ⓜ *F, M, 1, 2, 3 to 14th St.*

Three Lives & Company. Three Lives has one of the city's best book selections. The display tables and counters highlight the latest literary fiction and serious nonfiction, classics, quirky gift books, and gorgeously illustrated tomes. The staff members' literary knowledge is formidable, so don't be afraid to ask them for their own picks. ⊠ *154 W. 10th St., at Waverly Pl., West Village* ☎ *212/741–2069* ⊕ *threelives.com* Ⓜ *1 to Christopher St./Sheridan Sq.*

CLOTHING

Castor & Pollux. The store's interior signals a finely tuned balance of high taste (vintage Bergdorf Goodman display cases) and quirkiness (grass-cloth wall coverings and small horse sculptures). Hard-to-find brands like Hache are mixed with better-known names like Acne and 3.1 Philip Lim. There's also an eye-catching in-house line of jewelry, clutches, and sweaters. ⊠ *238 W. 10th St., at Hudson St., West Village* ☎ *212/645–6572* Ⓜ *1 to Christopher St./Sheridan Sq.*

Cynthia Rowley. Rowley delivers flirty, whimsical dresses that are perfect for cocktail parties. To complete the look, throw on some of her colorful pumps and sharply tailored coats. The handbags with small inset mirrors are ideal for checking your lipstick. ⊠ *376 Bleecker St., between Charles and Perry Sts., West Village* ☎ *212/242–3803* ⊕ *cynthiarowley.com* Ⓜ *1 to Christopher St./Sheridan Sq.*

Hotoveli. This unprepossessing nook with its squeaky plank floors and dressmaker's dummies is home to some of the most elegant designers in the city. Besides carrying a good selection of Vivienne Westwood, the store stockpiles whisper-light cashmere by Kristesen du Nord and gauzy separates from Ilaria Nistri. ⊠ *378 Bleecker St., between Charles and Perry Sts., West Village* ☎ *212/206–7475* Ⓜ *A, C, E, F, M to W. 4th St./Washington Sq.*

Ludivine. Ignore the tacky surroundings and make a beeline for this store if you love French designers. Owner Ludivine Grégoire showcases of-the-moment Gallic (and a few Italian) designers like Vanessa Bruno, Jerome Dreyfuss, and Carvin. ⊠ *172 W. 4th St., between Jones*

18

WEST VILLAGE

BEST TIME TO GO

It's easy to feel like a local, not a tourist, while shopping in the West Village. Unlike 5th Avenue or SoHo, the pace is slower, the streets are relatively quiet, and the scale is small. This is the place to come for unusual finds rather than global-brand goods (well, if you don't count Marc Jacobs).

Tuesday through Friday afternoon for a focused shopping stint, Saturday afternoon if you get a buzz from people-watching or the competitive aspect of busier boutiques. (Keep in mind that most stores here are small, so even a half dozen fellow browsers can make a shop feel crowded.) On Sunday the area's a bit bogged down by brunchers, and stores have shorter hours.

Bleecker Street is a particularly good place to indulge all sorts of shopping appetites. Foodies love the blocks between 6th and 7th avenues for the specialty purveyors like Murray's Cheese (254 Bleecker Street). Fashion foragers prowl the stretch between West 10th Street and 8th Avenue, and avid readers lose themselves in the bookbook bookshop. Hudson Street and Greenwich Avenue are also prime boutique-browsing territory. Christopher Street, true to its connection with the lesbian and gay community, has a handful of rainbow-flag stops. High rents mean there are fewer student-oriented shops around NYU than you might expect.

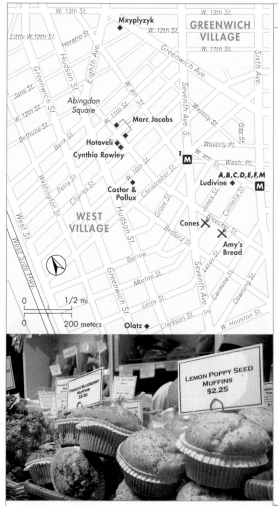

BEST FOR

NONCHALANT-CHIC CLOTHES

Castor & Pollux: Feminine pieces that feel simultaneously vintage and modern.

Cynthia Rowley: Party-friendly outfits for when a girl needs a halter top or a filmy dress.

Motoveli: The place to pair cult jeans, motorcycle boots, and a revealing top.

Ludivine: A direct feed to the Parisian femme's fashion scene.

Marc Jacobs: The casual (but not cheap) line with seemingly unstoppable downtown street cred.

HOME DECOR

Mxyplyzyk: Household necessities and accessories get a jolt of saucy humor.

Olatz: Divine bedding and pajamas in a Havana-inspired setting.

REFUELING

Skip Magnolia Bakery; there's always a line, and besides, there are so many other great spots for a pick-me-up in this neighborhood.

Amy's Bread. The house-made sweets at Amy's Bread, like the layer-cake slices and "kitchen sink" cookies, are both homey and delicious. ⊠ *250 Bleecker St., at Leroy St.* ☎ *212/675–7802* ⊕ *www.amysbread.com.*

Cones. At Cones, you can lap up a rich ginger or pistachio ice cream. ⊠ *272 Bleecker St., between Morton and Jones Sts.* ☎ *212/414–1795.*

and Cornelia Sts., West Village ☎646/336–6576 Ⓜ *1 to Christopher St./Sheridan Sq.*

FOOD AND TREATS

Chocolate Bar. What sets this chocolate emporium apart is its midcentury modern design, which is also evident in the groovy packaging.

Scoop up some retro chocolate bars, whose flavors include salty pretzel, coconut cream pie, and key lime. Or try a salted caramel bonbon and a steaming cup of spicy hot chocolate. ⊠ *19 8th Ave., between Jane and W. 12th Sts., West Village* ☎212/366–1541 ⊕ *www.chocolatebarnyc. com* Ⓜ *A, C, E, to 14th St.*

Li-Lac Chocolates. They've been feeding the Village's sweet tooth since 1923. Indulge with almond bark and coconut clusters as well as such specialty items as chocolate-molded Statues of Liberty. ⊠ *40 8th Ave., at Jane St., West Village* ☎212/924–2280 ⊕ *www.li-lacchocolates.com* Ⓜ *A, C, E to 14th St.*

HOME DECOR

Fodor'sChoice ★

Mxyplyzyk. Named after a character from Superman, this shop is hard to pronounce (*mixy-pliz-ick*) and equally hard to resist. The specialty is creative riffs on household standbys such as measuring cups fashioned from Russian dolls and a squirrel-shape nutcracker. More serious items include Lucite chairs and George Nelson clocks. ⊠ *125 Greenwich Ave., at W. 13th St., West Village* ☎212/989–4300 ⊕ *mxyplyzyk.com* Ⓜ *A, C, E, L to 14th St./8th Ave.*

Olatz. Olatz Schnabel modeled her linen shop on a historic Havana pharmacy after a visit to Cuba. The black-and-white checkerboard floors and mint-green walls breathe a sort of lazy, faded elegance, a spot-on backdrop to her collection of luxurious sheets, blankets, and pajama sets, all of which have sky-high thread counts and are bordered with bold stripes or intricate damask embroidery. ⊠ *43 Clarkson St., between Hudson and Greenwich Sts., West Village* ☎212/255–8627 ⊕ *olatz.com* Ⓜ *1 to Houston St.*

SHOES, HANDBAGS, AND LEATHER GOODS

Fodor'sChoice ★

Flight 001. Frequent flyers can one-stop-shop at this travel-theme store that puts a creative spin on everyday accessories. Shop for bright luggage tags, passport holders, satin sleep masks, and even paper soap. ⊠ *96 Greenwich Ave., between W. 12th and Jane Sts., West Village* ☎212/989–0001 ⊕ *www.flight001.com/* Ⓜ *A, C, E to 14th St.*

Leffot. This simple, understated store focuses on one thing: selling top-quality men's shoes. Owner Steven Taffel, who previously worked at Prada, has stocked his shop with selections from Church's, Basil Racuk, and Artioli. These shoes are meant to last a lifetime, and many have a price tag to match. Bespoke footware is also available. ⊠ *10 Christopher St., at Gay St., West Village* ☎212/989–4577 Ⓜ *1, 2 to Christopher St.*

Lulu Guinness. Hit this black-and-white-stripe salon for cheerfully eccentric accessories such as handbags (some lip shaped) adorned with appliqué, beads, and bows; polka-dot scarves; and umbrellas patterned with poodles. ⊠ *394 Bleecker St., between W. 11th and Perry Sts., West Village* ☎ *212/367–2120* ⊕ *www.luluguinness.com* Ⓜ *1 to Christopher St./Sheridan Sq.*

CHELSEA AND THE MEATPACKING DISTRICT

CHELSEA

BARGAIN SHOPPING

Fisch for the Hip. The racks at this high-end consignment store are evenly split between men's and women's clothes, with a well-edited selection throughout. You may find 7 for All Mankind jeans, Gucci suits, and Marni dresses. Hermès bags are a specialty. ⊠ *153 W. 18th St., between 6th and 7th Aves., Chelsea* ☎ *212/633–9053* Ⓜ *F, M, 1, 2, 3 to 14th St.*

Loehmann's. This discount store doesn't attract the hordes of tourists like Century 21, but you'll still have to dig through crammed racks to unearth bargains. Label searchers can find DVF wrap dresses for $100 and Betsey Johnson coats for around $200, and men can find Juicy Couture T-shirts and Versace ties. The "back room" has the best women's designers. ⊠ *101 7th Ave., at W. 16th St., Chelsea* ☎ *212/352–0856* Ⓜ *1, 2, 3 to 14th St.*

BOOKS AND STATIONERY

★ **Books of Wonder.** Readers young and old will delight in Manhattan's oldest and largest independent children's bookstore. The friendly, knowledgeable staff can help select gifts for all reading levels. Don't miss the extensive Oz section as well as the collection of old, rare, and collectible children's books and original children's book art. An outpost of the Cupcake Café gives little browsers a second wind. ⊠ *18 W. 18th St., between 5th and 6th Aves., Chelsea* ☎ *212/989–3270* ⊕ *www. booksofwonder.com* Ⓜ *F, M to 14th St.*

Rob Warren Bookseller. Come to this plant-filled shop for out-of-print books in all categories, a large Beat Generation selection, literary first editions, and books on photography and art. ⊠ *51 W. 28th St., between Broadway and 6th Ave., Chelsea* ☎ *212/759–5463* Ⓜ *N, R to 28th St.*

CLOTHING

Balenciaga. Creative director Nicolas Ghesquière continues to wow the fashion world with his avant-garde looks. In this cavelike boutique, you might luck onto a reissue from the (Cristobal) Balenciaga archives, made up in modern fabrics. The stash of more accessible handbags and shoes is worth a browse. ⊠ *542 W. 22nd St., between 10th and 11th Aves., Chelsea* ☎ *212/206–0872* ⊕ *www.balenciaga.com* Ⓜ *C, E to 23rd St.*

Comme des Garçons. The designs in this stark, white, swoopy space consistently push the fashion envelope with brash patterns, unlikely juxtapositions (tulle and neoprene), and cuts that are meant to be thought-provoking, not flattering. Architecture students come just for the interior design. ⊠ *520 W. 22nd St., between 10th and 11th Aves., Chelsea* ☎ *212/604–9200* Ⓜ *C, E to 23rd St.*

18

Limelight Marketplace. Housed in a former nightclub (which used to be a church), this massive space is now a bustling marketplace for clothing, accessories, and gourmet food. Browse through the various boutiques, selling everything from organic oils and Hunter wellies to handcrafted jewelry. Refuel at Baci Gelato or the Butterfly Bakeshop, or save your appetite for brick-oven pizza from Grimaldi's. ⊠ *47 W. 20th St., at 6th Ave., Chelsea* ☏ *212/359–5600* Ⓜ *F, V to 23rd St.*

New York Vintage. Stylists to the stars, TV costumers, and the odd princess descend upon this boutique to browse racks of prime vintage clothing. Everything is high-end, so don't expect any bargains. If money is no object, take your pick from Yves Saint Laurent, Madame Grès, and Thierry Mugler pieces. There's a good selection of handbags and pumps, too. ⊠ *117 W. 25th St., between 6th and 7th Aves., Chelsea* ☏ *212/647–1107* ⊕ *newyorkvintage.com* Ⓜ *1 to 28th St.*

MUSIC STORES AND MEDIA

Jazz Record Center. If you're seeking rare or out-of-print jazz recordings, this is your one-stop shop. Long-lost Ellingtons and other rare pressings come to light here; the jazz-record specialist also stocks collectibles, DVDs, videos, posters, CDs, and LPs. ⊠ *236 W. 26th St., between 7th and 8th Aves., 8th fl., Chelsea* ☏ *212/675–4480* Ⓜ *1 to 28th St.*

Movie Star News. As you flip through images from blockbusters, cult faves, and memorable bombs, it's hard to doubt their claim that they have the world's largest variety of movie photos and posters. Behind the counter are signed photos of many of the stars seen on the posters. ■TIP➔ A poster of a New York film such as *Manhattan, The Royal Tenenbaums,* or *Taxi Driver* makes a good souvenir for less than $20. ⊠ *134 W. 18th St., between 6th and 7th Aves., Chelsea* ☏ *212/620–8160* Ⓜ *1, 2, 3 to 14th St.*

WINE

★ **Bottlerocket Wine & Spirit.** Fun and approachable, this shop puts a new spin on wine shopping. Vintages are organized by quirky factors like their compatibility with Chinese takeout and whom they'd best suit as gifts (ranging from "Someone You Barely Know" to "The Boss"). A reference library, kids' play nook, and doggie area make the space extra welcoming. ⊠ *5 W. 19th St., between 5th and 6th Aves., Chelsea* ☏ *212/929–2323* ⊕ *bottlerocketwine.com* Ⓜ *N, R, Q, 4, 5, 6 to 14th St.*

MEATPACKING DISTRICT

CLOTHING

Alexander McQueen. The late designer's New York flagship is a futuristic, podlike space—an ideal setting for the avant-garde clothing. Now under the helm of Sarah Burton, the designs are still theatrical with exquisite tailoring and a touch of softness. ⊠ *417 W. 14th St., between 9th and 10th Aves., Meatpacking District* ☏ *212/645–1797* Ⓜ *A, C, E to 14th St.*

Catherine Malandrino. Celebs like Halle Berry love this French-born designer for her sexy-without-trying-too-hard looks. Shop for silk V-neck gowns or one-shouldered ruched wool dresses. ⊠ *652 Hudson St., at W. 13th St., Meatpacking District* ☏ *212/929–8710* ⊕ *www. catherinemalandrino.com* Ⓜ *A, C, E to 14th St.*

Charles Nolan. Despite the downtown location, the vibe here is decidedly uptown. Formerly an exclusive designer for Saks, Nolan offers impeccable craftsmanship: wool shirtdresses, sequined A-line skirts, and billowy white blouses. Don't overlook the front-of-store gift selection, including chunky glass candlesticks and cashmere scrunch scarves. ⊠ *30 Gansevoort St., at Hudson St., Meatpacking District* ☎ *212/924–4888* ⊕ *www.charlesnolan.com* Ⓜ *A, C, E to 14th St.*

Fodor's Choice ★ **Diane von Furstenberg.** Browse for a classic DVF wrap dress or a long, gauzy blouse here. The gleaming white space has just a hint of disco, with mirrored discs sparkling on the ceiling. ⊠ *874 Washington St., at 14th St., Meatpacking District* ☎ *646/486–4800* ⊕ *www.dvf.com* Ⓜ *A, C, E to 14th St.*

Iris. As the Italian shoe manufacturers for stylish brands like John Galliano, Marc Jacobs, Veronique Branquinho, and Chloé, Iris's sole U.S. store is able to carry every style from those lines, including pieces not previously available on our shores. ⊠ *827 Washington St., at Little W. 12th St., Meatpacking District* ☎ *212/645–0950* ⊕ *www.irisnation. com/newyork* Ⓜ *A, C, E, L to 14th St.*

Jeffrey. The Meatpacking District really arrived when this Atlanta-based mini-Barneys opened its doors. You can find an incredible array of designer shoes—Valentino, Lanvin, and red-soled Christian Louboutin are some of the best sellers—plus überlabels like Marni, Prada, and Gucci. ⊠ *449 W. 14th St., between 9th and 10th Aves., Meatpacking District* ☎ *212/206–1272* ⊕ *www.jeffreynewyork.com* Ⓜ *A, C, E, L to 14th St./8th Ave.*

Rebecca Taylor. Taylor is known for her soft, feminine designs, which run the gamut from sexy to understated, all with a slightly vintage flair. Her new flagship is a serene, spacious environment for browsing racks of silky shirtdresses, embroidered tunics, and ruffled overcoats. Also look out for her collaborations with Citizens of Humanity denim and Porselli shoes. ⊠ *34 Gansevoort St., between Greenwich and Hudson Sts., Meatpacking District* ☎ *212/243–2600* ⊕ *www.rebeccataylor.com* Ⓜ *A, C, E to 14 St.*

Stella McCartney. McCartney's new flagship store has a luxe look, thanks to parquet flooring and touches of gold found in the art-deco sculptures and clothing racks. Her main collection, done mostly in gauzy, muted colors, is on the top floor, while children's, Adidas by Stella McCartney, and lingerie are on the lower level. In keeping with McCartney's vegetarianism, fur and leather are verboten. ⊠ *112 Greene St., between Spring and Prince Sts., SoHo* ☎ *212/255–1556* ⊕ *www.stellamccartney. com/default/stores/New-York* Ⓜ *N, R to Prince St.*

Tracy Reese. Unabashedly girly but wearable garb is Reese's specialty, as she plays with lush fabrics (silk chiffon is a favorite), quirky color combos, and notice-me embellishments like rhinestones and ruffles. The cuts flatter all sorts of figures, often emphasizing the waist. This flagship carries both the ladylike Tracy Reese line and the funkier, lower-price Plenty label. ⊠ *641 Hudson St., between Horatio and Gansevoort Sts., Meatpacking District* ☎ *212/807–0505* ⊕ *tracyreese.com* Ⓜ *A, C, E to 14th St.*

18

THE MEATPACKING DISTRICT

For nearly a century, this industrial western edge of downtown Manhattan was defined by slaughterhouses and meatpacking plants, blood-splattered cobblestone streets, and men lugging carcasses into warehouses way before dawn.

But in the late 1990s the area bounded by West 14th Street, Gansevoort Street, Hudson Street, and 11th Avenue speedily transformed into another kind of meat market. Many of the old warehouses now house ultrachic shops, nightclubs, and restaurants packed with angular fashionistas. Jeffrey, a pint-size department store, was an early arrival, followed by edgy but established brands like Alexander McQueen and a few lofty furniture stores. Despite the influx of a few chains—albeit stylish ones like Scoop—eclectic boutiques keep popping up. The one thing it's hard to find here is a bargain.

BEST TIME TO GO

Wednesday through Friday afternoon. Most stores are open daily, but a few are closed Monday and Tuesday. On weekends some stores stay open until 7 or 8 pm, overlapping with the overeager nightlife crowd.

BEST SOUVENIR FOR YOUR GIRLFRIEND (OR BOHO AUNT)

Jewelry from **Ten Thousand Things** or a sweet treat from **Jacques Torres Chocolate**, such as a Brûlée Crunch bar.

W. 16th St.

0   1/8 mile

0   200 meters

Tenth Avenue

Jacques Torres
Chocolate

Ninth Avenue

W. 15th St.

Pop Burger

Ten Thousand
Things

La Perla

Apple Store

Jeffrey

Alexander
McQueen

W. 14th St.

W. 13th St.

Pastis

Catherine
Malandrino

Little W. 12th St.

Earnest
Sewn

Hudson St.

Eleventh Avenue

Gansevoort St.

Greenwich St.

Christian
Louboutin

West Side Highway

Washington St.

Horatio St.

Jane St.

W. 12th St.

REFUELING

Pastis. Hit the buzzing bistro Pastis for a croque monsieur, a bracing coffee, or a cocktail with the namesake hooch. ⊠ *9 9th Ave., at Little W. 12th St.* ☎ *212/929–4844* ⊕ *www.pastisny.com.*

Pop Burger. For a quick stop, follow the smell of grilled meat to Pop Burger. The mini-burgers are tempting, but locals swear by the sides: crispy fries and onion rings, and thick-as-cement milk shakes. ⊠ *58–60 9th Ave., between 14th and 15th Sts.* ☎ *212/414–8686* ⊕ *www.popburger.com.*

BEST FOR

DENIM
Earnest Sewn (⊠ *821 Washington St.* ☎ *212/242–3414*): Customize the cut, buttons, and pockets of your cult jeans.

FABULOUS FROCKS
Alexander McQueen: Impeccably tailored, take-no-prisoners style.

Catherine Malandrino: Romantic chiffon and swingy layers, at more-reasonable prices.

Jeffrey: Culls the coolest outfits from high-end labels.

KILLER ACCESSORIES
Christian Louboutin: Vampy heels with telltale crimson soles.

La Perla: The most minxy outpost for this brand's lace lingerie.

18

JEWELRY AND ACCESSORIES

Ten Thousand Things. You might find yourself wishing for 10,000 things from the showcases in this elegant boutique. Designs run from delicate gold and silver chains to long Peruvian opal earrings. Many shapes are abstract reflections of natural forms, like twigs or seedpods. Unusual stones beckon from the glass cases, such as the pendants of purple rubies or labradorite. ✉ *423 W. 14th St., between 9th and 10th Aves., Meatpacking District* ☎ *212/352–1333* Ⓜ *A, C, E to 14th St.*

UNION SQUARE AND THE FLATIRON DISTRICT

FLATIRON DISTRICT

BOOKS AND STATIONERY

Idlewild Books. Named for the pre-1960s JFK Airport, this travel-inspired bookstore groups its goods by destination. It has much more than guidebooks, though; novels, histories, cookbooks, and children's books share each segment, giving you a fascinating look at any given locale. If those chairs look familiar, it may be because you spent a layover in one of them once upon a time in the American Airlines terminal. ✉ *12 W. 19th St., 2nd fl., at 5th Ave., Flatiron District* ☎ *212/414–8888* ⊕ *www. idlewildbooks.com* Ⓜ *4, 5, 6, L, Q, R to 14th St./Union Sq.*

CHILDREN'S CLOTHING

Space Kiddets. The funky (Elvis-print rompers, CBGB onesies) mixes with the old-school (retro cowboy-print pants, brightly colored clogs, Bruce Lee T-shirts) and the high-end (Lilli Gaufrette, Kenzo, Boo Foo Woo from Japan) at this casual, trendsetting store that is a favorite of Julianne Moore. ✉ *26 E. 22nd St., between Broadway and Park Ave., Flatiron District* ☎ *212/420–9878* Ⓜ *6 to 23rd St.*

CLOTHING

Anthropologie. Bohemian-chic is the aesthetic of this popular women's clothing and home accessories chain. ✉ *85 Fifth Ave.* ☎ *212/627–5885* ⊕ *www.anthropologie.com* ✉ *Chelsea Market, 75 9th Ave., Chelsea* ☎ *212/620–3116* ✉ *375 West Broadway, SoHo* ☎ *212/343–7070* ✉ *50 Rockefeller Center, Midtown West* ☎ *212/246–0386* .

HOME DECOR

Fodor's Choice ★ **ABC Carpet & Home.** If you love eclectic goods from around the world, then this is your place. Spread over 10 floors is a superb selection of rugs, antiques, textiles, furniture, and bedding. Shoppers can find sleek sofas or Balinese daybeds. The ground floor is a wonderland of silk pillows and jewelry. To refuel, there's an in-house restaurant from Jean-Georges Vongerichten. More rugs and carpets are unrolled across the street at 881 Broadway. ✉ *888 Broadway, at E. 19th St., Flatiron District* ☎ *212/473–3000* ⊕ *www.abchome.com* Ⓜ *L, N, Q, R, 4, 5, 6 to 14th St./Union Sq.*

The Conran Shop. This British stylemonger sells a sleek, understated lifestyle out of this outlet tucked in the basement of ABC Carpet and Home. Everything from kitchen and garden implements, fabrics, furniture, and glassware is for sale. Even the shower curtains are cool. ✉ *Lower Level, 888 Broadway, at E. 19th St., Flatiron District* ☎ *866/755–9079* ⊕ *www.conranusa.com* Ⓜ *L, N, Q, R, 4, 5, 6 to 14th St./Union Sq.*

CLOSE UP

Holiday Markets

Between Thanksgiving and Christmas, holiday markets—rows of wooden stalls, many with red-and-white-stripe awnings—spring up around town. The gifts and goods vary from year to year, but there are some perennial offerings: colorful handmade knitwear and jewelry; sweet-smelling soaps, candles, and lotions with hand-lettered labels; glittery Christmas ornaments of every stripe; and New York–theme gift items (a group called Gritty City offers T-shirts, coin purses, and undies printed with pictures of taxicabs and manhole covers).

Though the holiday market in **Grand Central Terminal's Vanderbilt Hall** is indoors, most vendors set up outside. There's one every year at **Columbus Circle,** near the southwest entrance to Central Park, and another at **Bryant Park,** behind the New York City Public Library. The largest and most popular, however, is at the south end of **Union Square,** where you can go from the greenmarket to the stalls like the downtowners who meet in the afternoon or after work to look for unique or last-minute gifts.

Fodor'sChoice
★

Fishs Eddy. The dishes, china, and glassware for resale come from all walks of crockery life, from corporate dining rooms to failed restaurants and ocean liners. Fishs Eddy also sells its own line of dishes, which have a classic look. ⊠ *889 Broadway, at E. 19th St., Flatiron District* ☎ *212/420–9020* ⊕ *www.fishseddy.com* Ⓜ *L, N, Q, R, 4, 5, 6 to 14th St./Union Sq.*

Marimekko. If you love bright, cheerful patterns, make a beeline to the new Marimekko flagship. This 4,000-square-foot store is designed primarily in white, so the colorful merchandise pops. Everything from pot holders and shower curtains to coats and dresses is available here in the signature Marimekko bold prints. If you're feeling crafty, pick up a few yards of fabric to whip up your own creations. ⊠ *200 5th Ave, between 23rd and 24th Sts., Flatiron* ☎ *212/843–9121* Ⓜ *F, M to 23rd St.*

JEWELRY AND ACCESSORIES

Beads of Paradise. Not your ordinary bead store, the baubles here are sourced from around the world. Shoppers can choose silver from Bali and Mexico and ancient glass beads from China, along with semiprecious stones. Sign up for a class to learn how to put it all together. ⊠ *16 E. 17th St., between 5th Ave. and Broadway, Flatiron District* ☎ *212/620–0642* ⊕ *www.beadsofparadisenyc.com* Ⓜ *4, 5, 6, N, Q, R to 14th St./Union Sq.*

TOYS

Kidding Around. This independent shop is piled high with old-fashioned wooden toys, sturdy musical instruments, and plenty of arts-and-crafts materials. The costume racks are rich with dress-up potential. ⊠ *60 W. 15th St., between 5th and 6th Aves., Flatiron District* ☎ *212/645–6337* ⊕ *www.kiddingaround.us* Ⓜ *L, N, Q, R, 4, 5, 6 to 14th St./Union Sq.*

18

UNION SQUARE

BOOKS AND STATIONERY

Fodor'sChoice ★ **The Strand.** Opened in 1927, and still run by the same family, this monstrous book emporium—home to 2 million volumes and "18 Miles of Books"—is a symbol of a bygone era, a mecca for serious bibliophiles, and a local institution. The store has survived the Great Depression, World War II, competition from Barnes & Noble, and the tremendous shift in how readers are consuming literature. The stock includes both new and secondhand books, plus thousands of collector's items. A separate rare-book room is on the third floor and closes at 6:20 daily. The basement has discounted, barely touched reviewers' copies of new books, organized by author. ■TIP➔ If you're looking for souvenirs, visit the New York section of the bookstore; you'll find New York–centric literature, poetry, history, photography, and cookbooks, as well as T-shirts, gadgets, and totes. ✉ *828 Broadway, at E. 12th St., Union Square* ☎ *212/473–1452* ⊕ *www.strandbooks.com/* ⊗ *Mon.–Sat. 9:30 am–10:30 pm, Sun. 11–10:30* Ⓜ *L, N, Q, R, 4, 5, 6 to Union Sq./ 14th St.*

MIDTOWN EAST

ANTIQUES AND COLLECTIBLES

The Chinese Porcelain Company. Though the name of this prestigious shop indicates one of its specialties, its stock covers more ground, ranging from lacquerware to Khmer sculpture as well as European decorative arts. ✉ *475 Park Ave., at E. 58th St., Midtown East* ☎ *212/838–7744* ⊕ *www.chineseporcelainco.com* Ⓜ *N, R to 5th Ave.*

Flying Cranes Antiques. At this world leader in Japanese antiques, shoppers will find a collection of rare, museum-quality pieces from the Meiji period, the time known as Japan's Golden Age. Items include ceramics, cloisonné, metalwork, baskets, and samurai swords and fittings. ✉ *Manhattan Art and Antiques Center, 1050 2nd Ave., between E. 55th and E. 56th Sts., Midtown East* ☎ *212/223–4600* ⊕ *www. flyingcranesantiques.com* Ⓜ *N, R, 4, 5, 6 to 59th St./Lexington Ave.*

Leo Kaplan Ltd. The impeccable items here include art Nouveau glass and pottery, porcelain from 18th-century England, antique and modern paperweights, and Russian artwork. ✉ *114 E. 57th St., between Park and Lexington Aves., Midtown East* ☎ *212/355–7212* ⊕ *leokaplan.com* Ⓜ *N, R, 4, 5, 6 to 59th St./Lexington Ave.*

Newel Art Galleries. Housed in a six-story building, this huge collection spans the Renaissance through the 20th century. The nonfurniture finds, from figureheads to bell jars, make for prime conversation pieces. Newel is also a major supplier of antiques for Broadway shows, television, and film. ✉ *425 E. 53rd St., between 1st Ave. and Sutton Pl., Midtown East* ☎ *212/758–1970* ⊕ *newel.com* Ⓜ *6 to 51st St./Lexington Ave.; E, M to Lexington–3rd Aves./53rd St.*

BOOKS AND STATIONERY

Argosy Bookstore. Family owned since 1925, Argosy keeps a scholarly stock of rare books and autographs. It's also a great place to look for low-price maps and prints that make ideal gifts. ✉ *116 E. 59th St.,* *between Park and Lexington Aves., Midtown East* ☎ *212/753–4455* ⊕ *www.argosybooks.com* Ⓜ *N, R, 4, 5, 6 to 59th St./Lexington Ave.*

The Complete Traveller Antiquarian Bookstore. Founded in the '80s by two former travel writers, this store specializes in rare and antique voyage-related books, and holds the largest selection of out-of-print Baedeker travel guides. They stock surprisingly affordable vintage maps, unusual tomes with New York City themes, and a full spectrum of books—from history and geography to poetry and fiction— that emphasize travel. ✉ *199 Madison Ave., at 35th St., Midtown East* ☎ *212/685–9007* ⊕ *www.ctrarebooks.com* Ⓜ *6 to 33rd St.*

Posman Books. One of the last independent book stores in New York City, Posman Books has an outstanding selection of cheeky and serious high-quality greeting cards, as well as a great range of contemporary and classic books across genres. ✉ *9 Grand Central Terminal, at Vanderbilt Ave. and 42nd St., Midtown East* ☎ *212/983–1111* ⊕ *www.posmanbooks.com* ✉ *30 Rockefeller Plaza, Concourse Level, Midtown West* ☎ *212/489–9100* ✉ *75 9th Ave., Chelsea Market, Chelsea* ☎ *212/627–0304.*

CAMERAS AND ELECTRONICS

Apple Store. Apple's New York flagship is topped by a giant translucent cube and is open 24 hours a day, every day, to satisfy those wee-hours computer cravings. At all stores you'll have to elbow through a crowd, but they're the best places to check out the latest equipment, software, demos, and troubleshooting Genius Bars. ✉ *767 5th Ave., between E. 58th and E. 59th Sts., Midtown East* ☎ *212/336–1440* ⊕ *apple.com* Ⓜ *N, Q, R to 5th Ave./59th St.*

SONY Style. Located on the ground floor of the Sony Building, this sunny space is a wonderland of electronics. You'll find all the latest stereo and entertainment systems, digital cameras, high-def TVs, and MP3 players on the shelves. ✉ *550 Madison Ave., at E. 55th St., Midtown East* ☎ *212/833–8800* ⊕ *store.sony.com* Ⓜ *E, M, 6 to 51st St./Lexington Ave.*

CLOTHING

Brooks Brothers. The clothes at this classic American haberdasher are, as ever, traditional, comfortable, and fairly priced. Summer seersucker, navy-blue blazers, and the peerless oxford shirts have been staples for generations. The women's and boys' selections have variations thereof. ■ TIP→ Get scanned by a digital tailor for precisely measured custom shirts or suits; appointments are recommended. ✉ *346 Madison Ave., at E. 44th St., Midtown East* ☎ *212/682–8800* ⊕ *www.brooksbrothers.com* Ⓜ *4, 5, 6, 7, S to 42nd St./Grand Central.*

Burberry. This six-story glass-and-stone flagship is a temple to all things plaid and British. The iconic trench coat can be made-to-measure here, and the signature plaid can be found on bikinis, scarves, and wallets. For children, there are mini-versions of quilted jackets and cozy sweaters. ✉ *9 E. 57th St., between 5th and Madison Aves., Midtown East* ☎ *212/407–7100* ⊕ *www.burberry.com* Ⓜ *N, R, W to 5th Ave./59th St.*

Chanel. The Midtown flagship has often been compared to a Chanel suit—slim, elegant, and timeless, and decorated in the signature

18

black-and-white colors. Inside wait the famed suits themselves, along with other pillars of Chanel style: chic little black dresses and evening gowns, chain-handled bags, and yards of pearls. There's also a small cosmetics area where you can stock up on the famed scents and nail polish. ⊠ *15 E. 57th St., between 5th and Madison Aves., Midtown East* ☏ *212/355–5050* Ⓜ *N, R to 5th Ave./59th St.*

Christian Dior. This very white, very glossy space offers a serene background to showcase the luxe ready-to-wear collection along with handbags and accessories. If you're not in the market for an investment gown or fine jewelry, peruse the latest status bag. The Dior menswear boutique is next door; the rocking cigarette-thin suits are often pilfered by women. ⊠ *21 E. 57th St., at Madison Ave., Midtown East* ☏ *212/931–2950* Ⓜ *E, V to 5th Ave./53rd St.*

Dunhill. If you're stumped on what to buy the man in your life, head to Dunhill. The menswear is exquisitely tailored; the accessories like wallets and cuff links are slightly more affordable. The walk-in humidor stores top-quality tobacco and cigars. ⊠ *545 Madison Ave., at E. 55th St., Midtown East* ☏ *800/776–4053* ⊕ *www.dunhill.com* Ⓜ *F to 57th St.*

Gucci. Located in the Trump Building, this 46,000-square-foot flagship with floor-to-ceiling glass windows is the largest Gucci store in the world. Shoppers will find a special "heritage" department, plus goods exclusive to the store. The clothing is less aggressively sexy than it was in the Tom Ford era, but still edgy. Skintight pants might be paired with a luxe leather jacket; silk tops leave a little more to the imagination. The accessories, like wraparound shades or snakeskin shoes, many with signature horsebit detailing, continue to spark consumer frenzies. ⊠ *725 5th Ave., at 56th St., Midtown East* ☏ *206/682–7467* ⊕ *www. gucci.com/us/worldofgucci/articles/new-york-flagship* Ⓜ *N, R to 5th Ave./59th St.*

Yves Saint Laurent. Tom Ford's successor, Stephano Pilati, is lightening up the fabled French house. Think seduction instead of sexpot, with white trench coats, Grecian column dresses, and ruffled silk blouses. ⊠ *3 E. 57th St., between 5th and Madison Aves., Midtown East* ☏ *212/980–2970* ⊕ *www.ysl.com* Ⓜ *N, R to 5th Ave./59th St.*

DEPARTMENT STORES

FodorśChoice
★
Bloomingdale's. Only a few stores in New York occupy an entire city block; the uptown branch of this New York institution is one of them. The main floor is a crazy, glittery maze of mirrored cosmetic counters and perfume-spraying salespeople. Once you get past this dizzying scene, you can find good buys on designer clothes, bedding, and housewares. ⊠ *1000 3rd Ave., main entrance at E. 59th St. and Lexington Ave., Midtown East* ☏ *212/705–2000* ⊕ *bloomingdales.com* Ⓜ *N, R, 4, 5, 6 to 59th St./Lexington Ave.*

Saks Fifth Avenue. Saks sells an astonishing array of clothing. The choice of American and European designers is impressive without being esoteric—the women's selection includes Gucci, Narciso Rodriguez, and Marc Jacobs, plus devastating ball gowns galore. The footwear collections are gratifyingly broad, from Ferragamo to Juicy. In the men's department, sportswear stars such as John Varvatos counterbalance formal wear and current trends. The ground-floor beauty department stocks everything from the classic (Sisley, Lancôme, La Prairie) to the fun and edgy (Nars, M.A.C). ⊠ *611 5th Ave., between E. 49th and E. 50th Sts., Midtown East* ☎ *212/753–4000* ⊕ *saksfifthavenue.com* Ⓜ *E, M to 5th Ave./53rd St.*

JEWELRY AND ACCESSORIES

A La Vieille Russie. Antiques dealers since 1851, this shop specializes in European and Russian decorative arts, jewelry, and paintings. Behold bibelots by Fabergé and others, enameled or encrusted with jewels. If money is no object, there are also antique diamond necklaces and pieces of china once owned by Russian nobility. ⊠ *781 5th Ave., at E. 59th St., Midtown East* ☎ *212/752–1727* ⊕ *www.alvr.com* Ⓜ *N, R to 5th Ave./59th St.*

Cartier. Pierre Cartier allegedly won the 5th Avenue mansion location by trading two strands of perfectly matched natural pearls with Mrs. Morton Plant. The jewelry is still incredibly persuasive, from such established favorites as the Trinity ring and Tank watches to exquisite cuff links for men. ⊠ *653 5th Ave., at E. 52nd St., Midtown East* ☎ *800/227–8437* ⊕ *www.cartier.com* Ⓜ *E, M to 5th Ave./53rd St.*

H. Stern. Sleek designs pose in an equally modern 5th Avenue setting; smooth cabochon-cut stones, most from South America, glow in pale wooden display cases. The designers make notable use of semiprecious stones such as citrine, tourmaline, and topaz. ⊠ *645 5th Ave., between E. 51st and E. 52nd Sts., Midtown East* ☎ *212/655–3910* ⊕ *hstern.net* Ⓜ *E, M to 5th Ave./53rd St.*

Fodor's Choice ★ **Tiffany & Co.** The display windows can be soigné, funny, or just plain breathtaking. Alongside the $80,000 platinum-and-diamond bracelets, much here is affordable on a whim (check out the sterling-silver floor)—and everything comes wrapped in that unmistakable Tiffany blue box. ⊠ *727 5th Ave., at E. 57th St., Midtown East* ☎ *212/755–8000* ⊕ *www.tiffany.com* Ⓜ *N, R to 5th Ave./59th St.*

Van Cleef & Arpels. This French jewelry company is considerably more low-key than many of its blingy neighbors, in both the designs and marketing ethos (you won't see them opening a store in a suburban mall). Their best-known design is the cloverleaf Alhambra, which can be found on rings, necklaces, and earrings. Other designs are just as understated. ⊠ *744 5th Ave., between E. 57th St. and E. 58th Sts., Midtown East* ☎ *212/644–9500* ⊕ *www.vancleef-arpels.com* Ⓜ *N, R to 5th Ave./59th St.*

SHOES, HANDBAGS, AND LEATHER GOODS

Bally. A few curveballs, like olive-green or canary-yellow pumps, liven up the mainly conservative selection. Carry-ons and clothing, such as deerskin or lamb jackets, join the shoe leather. ⊠ *628 Madison Ave., at E. 59th St., Midtown East* ☎ *212/446–3930* ⊕ *www.bally.com* Ⓜ *N, R, 4, 5, 6 to 59th St./Lexington Ave.*

Bottega Veneta. The signature crosshatch weave graces leather handbags, slouchy satchels, and shoes; the especially satisfying brown shades extend from fawn to deep chocolate. The stylish men's and women's ready-to-wear collection is also sold here. ⊠ *699 5th Ave.,*

FIFTH AVENUE AND 57TH STREET

Fifth Avenue from Rockefeller Center to Central Park South pogos among landmark department stores, glossy international designer boutiques, and casual national chains. What they all have in common: massive flagship spaces.

The intersection of 5th Avenue with 57th Street distills this mix of old and new, exclusive and accessible. From these corners you'll see blue-chip New York classics (jeweler Tiffany & Co., the Bergdorf Goodman department stores), luxury giants (Gucci and the glass box of Louis Vuitton), a high-tech wonderland (another glass box for Apple), and show-off digs for informal brands (NikeTown, Abercrombie & Fitch). Capping this shopping stretch at East 58th Street is the colossal, exceptional toy store FAO Schwarz. If you're keen to shop the high end or to see the impressive flagships, it's worth coming to this neighborhood—but if large-scale doesn't do it for you, you're better off heading downtown.

BEST TIME TO GO

Wednesday through Friday if you're trying to avoid crowds. Weekends before the winter holidays get extremely hectic and can spark "sidewalk rage" in even the most patient shopper—try to come earlier in the week, especially if you want to see the fantastic department-store window displays.

BEST SOUVENIR FOR KIDS

An incredibly lifelike stuffed animal from **FAO Schwarz**. They've got exclusive Steiff "purebred" dogs, for instance, that come with authenticity certificates from the American Kennel Club.

REFUELING

Fika. Soothe frazzled nerves with a stop at Fika, a calm, friendly Swedish café. Settle in for a meatball sandwich, a bracing cup of coffee, and a chocolate truffle. ⊠ *41 W. 58th St., between 5th and 6th Aves.* ☏ *212/832–0022* ⊕ *www.fikanyc.com.*

Primeburger. If you'd like to stay in the energetic current of 5th Avenue, nab a table, or a seat with a fold-down tray, at the stuck-in-the-'60s Primeburger. Go for a diner classic like an all-day omelet or a burger. ⊠ *5 E. 51st St., between 5th and Madison Aves.* ☏ *212/759–4730* ⊕ *www.primeburger.com.*

BEST FOR

DEPARTMENT STORES

Bergdorf Goodman: These partner stores (one for women, the other for men; guess which has the housewares) are both genteelly tasteful.

Saks Fifth Avenue: Fashion and nothing but.

FLAGSHIP STORES

Apple: All sorts of chip-driven devices, 24 hours a day.

Chanel: All the hallmarks, from little black dresses to double-C jewelry.

Gucci: Check out classic designs and goodies exclusive to this store.

Louis Vuitton: Every permutation of the signature handbags and leather goods, plus the jet-set clothing line upstairs.

SERIOUS JEWELRY

Cartier: Both classic and slinky new designs glitter in a turn-of-the-20th-century mansion.

Harry Winston: The ultimate for diamonds (just ask Marilyn Monroe).

Tiffany & Co.: Hum "Moon River," check out the dazzling gems and pearls, then head upstairs for all sorts of silver ornaments.

Van Cleef & Arpels: The jewels may be big, but the logos and styles are understated.

18

Department Store Discounts

If you don't have one of these stores in the state where you live, take advantage of special discounts available by showing a state ID card.

Bloomingdale's: Go to the visitor center on the balcony level between the ground and second floors for a 10% discount on all purchases bought that day.

Lord & Taylor: Hit the ground-floor information desk to pick up a coupon for 15% off that day's purchases.

Macy's: Stop by the visitor center on the balcony level between the ground and second floors for a 10% discount voucher. The coupon is valid for five days for U.S. visitors and one month for international visitors.

---

between E. 54th and E. 55th Sts., Midtown East ☎ *212/371–5511* Ⓜ *N, R, 4, 5, 6 to 59th St./Lexington Ave.*

Fendi. Once known for its furs, Fendi is now synonymous with decadent handbags. The purses are beaded, embroidered, and fantastically embellished within an inch of their lives, resulting in prices well over $1,000. Fancy leathers, ladylike evening dresses, coats, and other accessories are also available. ✉ *677 5th Ave., between E. 53rd and E. 54th Sts., Midtown East* ☎ *212/759–4646* ⊕ *www.fendi.com/* Ⓜ *E, F to 5th Ave./53rd St.*

Fratelli Rossetti. Don't come here expecting sexy, skyscraper stilettos. This Italian leather goods company excels at beautiful, classic shoes. Their riding boots are among the most popular items, but there are also pumps, loafers, and slouchy ankle boots. Men can choose from oxfords and boots. There's also a line of leather handbags. ✉ *625 Madison Ave., between E. 58th and E. 59th Sts., Midtown East* ☎ *212/888–5107* ⊕ *www.fratellirossetti.com* Ⓜ *N, R, 4, 5, 6 to 59th St.*

Furla. Shoulder bags, oblong clutches, and roomy totes can be quite proper or attention-getting, from a cocoa-brown, croc-embossed zipper-top to a patent leather, cherry-red purse. ✉ *598 Madison Ave., at E. 57th St., Midtown East* ☎ *212/980–3208* Ⓜ *N, R, 4, 5, 6 to 59th St.*

Louis Vuitton. In the mammoth 57th Street store vintage examples of Vuitton's famous monogrammed trunks float above the fray on the ground floor, where shoppers angle for the latest accessories. Joining the initials are the Damier check pattern and colorful striated leathers, plus devastatingly chic clothes and shoes designed by Marc Jacobs. ✉ *1 E. 57th St., at 5th Ave., Midtown East* ☎ *212/758–8877* ⊕ *www. louisvuitton.com* Ⓜ *E, V to 5th Ave./53rd St.*

Salvatore Ferragamo. Elegance and restraint typify these designs, from black-tie patent to weekender ankle boots. The company reworks some of their women's styles from previous decades, like the girlish Audrey (as in Hepburn) ballet flat, released seasonally for limited runs. Don't miss the silk ties for men. ✉ *655 5th Ave., at E. 52nd St., Midtown East* ☎ *212/759–3822* ⊕ *www.ferragamo.com* Ⓜ *E, M to 53rd St.*

Stuart Weitzman. The broad range of styles, from wing tips to strappy sandals, is enhanced by an even wider range of sizes and widths. Bridal shoes are hugely popular, if pricey. ✉ *625 Madison Ave., between E. 58th and E. 59th Sts., Midtown East* ☎ *212/750–2555* ⊕ *www. stuartweitzman.com* Ⓜ *N, R, 4, 5, 6 to 59th St./Lexington Ave.*

TOYS

American Girl Place. No pink toy convertibles here; instead, the namesake dolls are historically themed, from Felicity of colonial Virginia to Kit of Depression-era Cincinnati. Each character has her own affiliated books, furniture, clothes, and accessories. There's a doll hairdressing station, a café, and a Dress Like Your Doll shop. ✉ *609 5th Ave., at E. 49th St., Midtown East* ☎ *877/247–5223* ⊕ *www.americangirl.com/stores/ location_ny.php* Ⓜ *B, D, F, M to 47th–50th Sts./Rockefeller Center.*

Fodor'sChoice ★ **FAO Schwarz Fifth Avenue.** A New York classic that's better than ever, this children's paradise more than lives up to the hype. The ground floor is a zoo of extraordinary stuffed animals, from cuddly $20 teddies to towering, life-size elephants and giraffes (with larger-than-life prices to match). FAO Schwartz stocks M&Ms in every color of the rainbow. Upstairs, you can dance on the giant musical floor keyboard, browse through Barbies wearing Armani and Juicy Couture, and design your own Muppet puppet. ✉ *767 5th Ave., at E. 58th St., Midtown East* ☎ *212/644–9400* Ⓜ *4, 5, 6 to E. 59th St.*

MIDTOWN WEST

18

CAMERAS AND ELECTRONICS

★ **B&H Photo Video and Pro Audio.** As baskets of purchases trundle along on tracks overhead, you can plunge into the excellent selection of imaging, audio, video, and lighting equipment. The staff is generous with advice, and will happily compare merchandise. Low prices, good customer service, and a liberal returns policy make this a favorite with pros and amateurs alike. ■TIP→ Be sure to leave a few extra minutes for the checkout procedure; also, keep in mind that the store is closed Saturday. ✉ *420 9th Ave., between W. 33rd and W. 34th Sts., Midtown West* ☎ *212/444–6615* ⊕ *www.bhphotovideo.com* Ⓜ *N, Q, R to 5th Ave./59th St.*

CLOTHING

Cheap Jack's. Jack's two-floor space may be 12,000 square feet, but it's still jammed with interesting duds—although they are not as cheap as the name would suggest. There's almost everything you could wish for: track suits, bomber jackets, early 1980s madras shirts, old prom dresses, and vintage concert T-shirts with the eau-de-mothball stamp of authenticity. ✉ *303 5th Ave., at 31st St., Midtown West* ☎ *212/777–9564* ⊕ *www.cheapjacks.com* Ⓜ *N, Q, R to 34th St./Herald Sq.*

Club Monaco. Stylish cuts and intricate details separate this men's and women's clothing brand from the mass-market pack. There are branches all over town. ✉ *6 West 57th St.* ☎ *212/459–9863* ⊕ *www. clubmonaco.com* ✉ *2376 Broadway, Upper West Side* ☎ *212/ 579–2587* ✉ *211 Columbus Ave., Upper West Side* ☎ *212/724–4076* ✉ *160 Fifth Ave., Flatiron District* ☎ *212/352–0936* ✉ *121 Prince St., SoHo* ☎ *212/533–8930* ✉ *520 Broadway, SoHo* ☎ *212/941–1511.*

Forever 21. The pounding music, plethora of jeggings, and graffiti-covered N.Y.C. taxicab parked inside will appeal to tween shoppers. But even if you are older than 21, you'll still find a reason to shop here. This location, clocking in at a whopping 90,000 square feet, is the biggest Forever 21 on the East Coast. Come for supertrendy clothes that won't break the bank, such as slouchy sweaters, shirtdresses, and pouffy skirts. Menswear and children's clothes are also sold here, and the jewelry is surprisingly well done. There are several locations in Manhattan. ✉ *303 5th Ave., at 31st St., Midtown West* ☎ *212/777–9564* ⊕ *www. forever21.com* Ⓜ *B, D, F, M to 47th - 50th St./Rockefeller Ctr.* ✉ *Herald Towers, 50 W. 34th St., Midtown West* ☎ *212/564–2346* ✉ *40 E. 14th St., Union Square* ☎ *212/228–0598* ✉ *568 Broadway, SoHo* ☎ *212/941–5949* ✉ *693 Fifth Ave., Upper East Side* ☎ *212/588–8949* ✉ *1540 Broadway, Midtown West* ☎ *212/302–0594.*

H&M. Of-the-moment trends are captured for the mass market at this affordable European clothing chain with several stores in Manhattan. ✉ *640 5th Ave.* ☎ *212/489–0390* ⊕ *www.hm.com* ✉ *435 7th Ave., at 34th St., Chelsea* ☎ *212/643–6955* ✉ *125 W. 125th St., Harlem* ☎ *212/665–8300* ✉ *731 Lexington Ave., at 59th St., Upper East Side* ☎ *212/935–6781* ✉ *150 E. 86th St., Upper East Side* ☎ *212/289–1724* ✉ *558 Broadway, SoHo* ☎ *212/343–2722* ✉ *505 Fifth Ave., at 42nd St., Midtown East* ☎ *212/661–7012* ✉ *1328 Broadway, at 34th St., Midtown West* ☎ *646/473–1165* ✉ *111 5th Ave., at 18th St., Flatiron District* ☎ *212/539–1741.*

Norma Kamali. A fashion fixture from the 1980s has a newly modern, though still '80s-influenced, line. Her luminously white store carries bold black-and-white-pattern bathing suits, Grecian-style draped dresses, and her signature poofy "sleeping-bag coats." The in-house Wellness Café sells olive oil–based beauty products and healthful snacks like kale chips. ✉ *11 W. 56th St., between 5th and 6th Aves., Midtown West* ☎ *212/957–9797* Ⓜ *N, Q, R 5th Ave./59th St.*

DEPARTMENT STORES

★ **Bergdorf Goodman.** Good taste reigns here in an elegant and sophisticated setting. Bergdorf's carries some brilliant lines, such as Marchesa, Narciso Rodriguez, and Balenciaga. In the basement Level of Beauty, find a seat in the manicure—pedicure lounge or go for Bergdorf Blonde highlights at the in-house John Barrett salon. The home department has rooms full of magnificent linens, tableware, and gifts. To fully be a lady who lunches, grab a bite at the seventh-floor BG Restaurant, with

Central Park views. ⊠ *754 5th Ave., between W. 57th and W. 58th Sts., Midtown West* ☎ *212/753–7300* ⊕ *www.bergdorfgoodman.com* Ⓜ *N, R to 5th Ave.*

Henri Bendel. Behind the graceful Lalique windows you'll discover a mecca of niche boutiques stocking beauty products, accessories, and gifts (but no clothing). Bendel's dedication to the unusual begins in the ground-floor cosmetics area and percolates through the floors of women's lingerie and jewelry, scarves, and sunglasses. The in-house lines are displayed throughout. ⊠ *712 5th Ave., between W. 55th and W. 56th Sts., Midtown West* ☎ *212/247–1100* ⊕ *www.henribendel.com* Ⓜ *E, M to 5th Ave./53rd St.*

Lord & Taylor. This is not your mother's Lord & Taylor. The department store has been working hard to attract a younger, hipper crowd. Thanks to a recent makeover, the clothing departments are easier to navigate and shoppers will find classic brands like Coach, Donna Karan, and Ralph Lauren. The ground-floor beauty department also got a face-lift, with store exclusives like Lancôme's first mascara bar. ⊠ *424 5th Ave., between W. 38th and W. 39th Sts., Midtown West* ☎ *212/391–3344* ⊕ *www.lordandtaylor.com* Ⓜ *B, D, F, N, Q, R, M to 34th St./Herald Sq.*

★ **Macy's.** Macy's headquarters has more than 1 million square feet of retail space, so expect to lose your bearings at least once. Fashion-wise, there's a concentration on the mainstream rather than on the luxe. One strong suit is denim, with everything from Hilfiger and Calvin Klein to Earl Jeans and Paper Denim & Cloth. There's also a reliably good selection of American designs from Ralph Lauren, DKNY, and Sean John. For cooking gear and housewares, the Cellar nearly outdoes Zabar's. ⊠ *Herald Sq., 151 W. 34th St., between 6th and 7th Aves., Midtown West* ☎ *212/695–4400* Ⓜ *B, D, F, N, Q, R, M to 34th St./Herald Sq.*

HOME DECOR

Muji. If you're into simple, chic, cheap style, Muji will be your tri-fecta. The name of this Japanese import translates to "no brand," and indeed, you won't find a logo plastered on the housewares or clothes. Instead, their hallmark is streamlined, often monochromatic design. The whole range of goods, from milky porcelain teapots to wooden toys, is invariably user-friendly. At this branch, you can glimpse the lobby of the *New York Times*. ⊠ *620 8th Ave., at W. 40th St., Midtown West* ☎ *212/382–2300* ⊕ *www.muji.us* Ⓜ *A, C, E to 42nd St./Port Authority* ⊠ *455 Broadway, SoHo* ☎ *212/334–2002* ⊠ *MoMa Design Store, 81 Spring St., SoHo* ☎ *646/613–1367* ⊠ *MoMa Design Store, 11 W. 53rd St., Midtown West* ☎ *212/414–9024* ⊠ *16 W. 19th St., Chelsea* ☎ *212/414–9024.*

JEWELRY AND ACCESSORIES

Bulgari. This Italian company is certainly not shy about its name, which encircles gems, watch faces, and an ever-growing accessories line. There are beautiful, weighty rings, pieces mixing gold with stainless steel or porcelain, and the brand's signature cabochon multicolored sapphires. Wedding and engagement rings are slightly more subdued. ⊠ *730 5th Ave., at W. 57th St., Midtown West* ☎ *212/315–9000* Ⓜ *N, R to 5th Ave.*

18

Harry Winston. These jewels regularly adorn celebs at the Oscars, and you'll need an A-list bank account to shop here. The ice-clear diamonds are of impeccable quality, and are set in everything from emerald-cut solitaire rings to wreath necklaces resembling strings of flowers. No wonder the jeweler was immortalized in the song "Diamonds Are a Girl's Best Friend." ⊠ *718 5th Ave., at W. 56th St., Midtown West* ☎ *212/245–2000* ⊕ *www.harrywinston.com* Ⓜ *F to 57th St.*

Mikimoto. The Japanese originator of the cultured pearl, Mikimoto presents a glowing display of high-luster pearls. Besides the creamy strands from their own pearl farms, check out diamond-and-pearl earrings, bracelets, and rings. ⊠ *730 5th Ave., between W. 56th and W. 57th Sts., Midtown West* ☎ *212/457–4600* ⊕ *www.mikimotoamerica.com* Ⓜ *F to 57th St.*

MUSEUM STORES

Museum of Arts and Design. In this museum's new home, the gift shop stocks crafts such as beautiful handmade tableware, unusual jewelry, and rugs, often tied in to ongoing exhibits. ⊠ *2 Columbus Circle, at 8th Ave., Midtown West* ☎ *212/299–7777* ⊕ *www.madmuseum.org* Ⓜ *1, A, B, C, D to 59th St./Columbus Circle.*

★ **Museum of Modern Art Design and Book Store.** The redesigned MoMA expanded its in-house shop with a huge selection of art posters and a gorgeous selection of coffee-table books on painting, sculpture, film, and photography. Across the street is the **MoMA Design Store,** where you can find Charles and Ray Eames furniture reproductions, vases designed by Alvar Aalto, and lots of clever trinkets. ⊠ *11 W. 53rd St., between 5th and 6th Aves., Midtown West* ☎ *212/708–9400* ⊕ *www. moma.org/visit/plan/stores* Ⓜ *E, M to 5th Ave./53rd St.*

MUSIC STORES

Colony Music Center. Siphoning energy from Times Square, this place keeps its neon blinking until 1 am Monday through Saturday, and midnight on Sunday. Inspired by the Broadway musical or concert you've just seen? Snap up the sheet music, CD, or karaoke set here. ⊠ *1619 Broadway, at W. 49th St., Midtown West* ☎ *212/265–2050* ⊕ *www. colonymusic.com* Ⓜ *R to 49th St.*

PERFORMING ARTS MEMORABILIA

Drama Book Shop. If you're looking for a script, be it a lesser-known Russian translation or a Broadway hit, chances are you can find it here. The range of books spans film, music, dance, TV, and biographies. The shop also hosts Q&As with leading playwrights. ⊠ *250 W. 40th St., between 7th and 8th Aves., Midtown West* ☎ *212/944–0595* ⊕ *www. dramabookshop.com* Ⓜ *A, C, E to 42nd St./Port Authority.*

One Shubert Alley. This was the first store to sell Broadway merchandise outside of a theater. Today souvenir posters, tees, and other knick-knacks memorializing past and present Broadway hits still reign at this Theater District shop. ⊠ *1 Shubert Alley, between W. 44th and W. 45th Sts., Midtown West* ☎ *212/944–4133* Ⓜ *N, Q, R, S, 1, 2, 3 to 42nd St./Times Sq.*

Triton Gallery. Theatrical posters large and small are available, and the selection is democratic, with everything from Marlene Dietrich's *Blue*

Angel to recent Broadway shows represented. ✉ *630 9th Ave., between W. 44th and W. 45th Sts., Suite 808, Midtown West* ☎ *212/765–2472* ⊕ *www.tritongallery.com* Ⓜ *A, E to 42nd St./Port Authority.*

SHOES, HANDBAGS, AND LEATHER GOODS

Cole-Haan. This once-conservative brand now shines with shoes made in exotic skins like python and crocodile; for warm weather, check out the orange suede thongs for men and metallic gladiator sandals for women. If comfort is key, many shoes have Nike Air cushioning in the heels. ✉ *620 5th Ave., at Rockefeller Center, Midtown West* ☎ *212/765–9747* Ⓜ *E, M to 5th Ave./53rd St.*

Manolo Blahnik. These sexy status shoes are some of the most expensive on the market. The signature look is a pointy toe with a high, delicate heel, but there are also ballet flats, gladiator sandals, and over-the-knee dominatrix boots that cost nearly $2,000. Pray for a sale. ✉ *31 W. 54th St., between 5th and 6th Aves., Midtown West* ☎ *212/582–3007* Ⓜ *E, M to 5th Ave./53rd St.*

Smythson of Bond Street. Although Smythson still sells stationery fit for a queen - check out the royal warrant from England's HRH - its newly expanded line of leather goods include on-trend handbags and wallets. The hues range from sedate brown and black to eye-popping tangerine. The softbound leather diaries, address books, and travel accessories make ideal gifts. ✉ *4 W. 57th St., between 5th and 6th Aves., Midtown West* ☎ *212/265–4573* Ⓜ *F to 57th St.*

TOYS

Toys "R" Us. The Times Square megastore is so big that a three-story Ferris wheel—complete with 14 individually themed cars—revolves inside. With all the movie tie-in merchandise, video games, yo-yos, stuffed animals, and what seems to be the entire Mattel oeuvre, good luck extracting your kids from here. ✉ *1514 Broadway, at W. 44th St., Midtown West* ☎ *646/366* Ⓜ *1, N, Q, R to 42nd St./Times Sq.*

18

THE UPPER EAST SIDE

ANTIQUES AND COLLECTIBLES

Florian Papp. Established in 1900, this store has an unassailed reputation among knowledgeable collectors. Expect to find American and European antiques and paintings from the 18th to 20th century. Gilt mirrors and mahogany tables abound. ✉ *962 Madison Ave., between E. 75th and E. 76th Sts., Upper East Side* ☎ *212/288–6770* ⊕ *florianpapp.com* Ⓜ *6 to 77th St.*

Keno Auctions. Leigh Keno of *Antique Roadshow* fame presides over this auction house, which specializes in Americana. As expected, he has a good eye and an interesting inventory; he's sold silver sauceboats from Paul Revere, paintings, and Chippendale furniture. ✉ *127 E. 69th St., between Park and Lexington Aves., Upper East Side* ☎ *212/734–2381* ⊕ *www.kenoauctions.com* Ⓜ *6 to 68th St./Hunter College.*

L'Antiquaire & The Connoisseur, Inc. Proprietor Helen Fioratti has written a guide to French antiques, but she's equally knowledgeable about her Italian and Spanish furniture and decorative objects from the

Cool Local Chains

New Yorkers in the know hit these fabulous local chains for unique frocks and the best of the city's one-stop-shopping.

Calypso. Catch an instant island-vacation vibe from Calypso's colorful silk women's wear, dangly jewelry, and boho housewares at the brand's New York flagship, which has a suitably beachy vibe (check out the shell chandeliers). There are multiple branches throughout the city with different themes, as well as an outlet on Broome Street. ☒ *900 Madison Ave., between E. 72nd and E. 73rd Sts., Upper East Side* ☎ *212/535–4100.*

Ricky's. Loud and fun, these drug-stores sprinkled around the city attract an eclectic, mostly young crowd who come just as often for the crazy-color wigs or false eyelashes as they do for Dove body wash and Neutro-gena soap. Every fall the stores turn into Halloween Central, with a huge assortment of feather boas, masks, and trendy costumes referencing

everything from Avatar to Jersey Shore. The flagship store is located in TriBeCa. ☒ *375 Broadway, TriBeCa* ☎ *212/925–5490* ⊕ *www.rickysnyc. com.*

Scoop. These clothes help you fit in with the too-cool-to-dress-up crowd. They have lots of jeans (Levi's, Citizens of Humanity), slinky tops, vintage-looking tees, and cozy knits from designers like Stella McCartney, Theory, and Halston Heritage. Other locations in the city feature menswear. ☒ *473–475 Broadway, between Broome and Grand Sts., SoHo* ☎ *212/925–3539* ⊕ *www.scoopnyc.com.*

Searle. Mostly strung along the east side, these stores have a devoted following for their coats—especially sleek designs from Moncler and Postcard. There are plenty of other designer items to layer, from cowl-neck sweaters to fitted tees. ☒ *635 Madison Ave., between E. 59th and E. 60th Sts., Midtown East* ☎ *212/750–5153* ⊕ *www.searlenyc.com.*

15th through the 18th centuries, as well as about the medieval arts. ☒ *36 E. 73rd St., between Madison and Park Aves., Upper East Side* ☎ *212/517–9176* ⊕ *www.lantiquaire.us* Ⓜ *6 to 77th St.*

BEAUTY

Fresh. Long a beauty favorite, with ingredients that are good enough to eat (think brown sugar, soy, and black tea), Fresh recently revamped its New York flagship. The boutique has an apothecary-inspired look, with beautifully packaged soaps displayed like pastries in a glass case and a Sensorial Bar, featuring discontinued perfumes on tap. Pull up at a seat at the communal Kitchen Table to try out a new product. ☒ *872 Broadway, between 18th and 19th Sts., Union Square* ☎ *212/477–1100* ⊕ *www.fresh.com* Ⓜ *N,Q,R,4,5,6 to 14th St./Union Sq.*

Jo Malone. Tangy scents such as lime blossom and mandarin, and pome-granate noir can be worn alone or layered for the Malone style. Since Malone uses colognes, not perfumes, it's not overpowering. You can also stop by for a quick fragrance-combining consultation or a hand-and-arm massage from one of the store's stylists. ☒ *946 Madison Ave.,* *between E. 74th and E. 75th Sts., Upper East Side* ☎ 212/472–0074 Ⓜ *6 to 77th St.*

BOOKS AND STATIONERY

Crawford Doyle Booksellers. You're as likely to see an old edition of Wodehouse as a best seller in the window of this shop. Bibliophiles will find a high-quality selection of fiction, nonfiction, and biographies, plus some rare books on the balcony. Salespeople offer their opinions *and* ask for yours. ✉ *1082 Madison Ave., between E. 81st and E. 82nd Sts., Upper East Side* ☎ 212/288–6300 Ⓜ *4, 5, 6 to 86th St.*

★ **Shakespeare & Co. Booksellers.** The stock here represents what's happening in just about every field of publishing today: students can grab a last-minute Gertrude Stein for class, then rummage through the homages to cult pop-culture figures. ✉ *939 Lexington Ave., between E. 68th and E. 69th Sts., Upper East Side* ☎ 212/570–0201 Ⓜ *6 to 68th St./Hunter College.*

CHILDREN'S CLOTHING

★ **Bonpoint.** The sophistication here lies in the beautiful designs and impeccable workmanship— pony-hair baby booties and hand-embroidered jumpers and blouses. Older kids can rock Liberty print dresses and peacoats. ✉ *1269 Madison Ave., at E. 91st St., Upper East Side* ☎ 212/722–7720 ⊕ *www.bonpoint.com* Ⓜ *4, 5, 6 to 86th St.*

Infinity. Prep-school girls and their mothers giggle and gossip over the preteen slinky clothes (with more than a few moms picking up T-shirts and jeans for themselves) with Les Tout Petits dresses, Juicy Couture jeans, and slogan tees. ✉ *1116 Madison Ave., at E. 83rd St., Upper East Side* ☎ 212/734–0077 Ⓜ *4, 5, 6 to 86th St.*

CLOTHING

Barbour. The signature look here is the company's waxed cotton jacket, available for men and women. The quilted jackets, tweeds, moleskin pants, lamb's-wool sweaters, and tattersall shirts invariably call up images of country rambles. ✉ *1047 Madison Ave., at E. 80th St., Upper East Side* ☎ 212/570–2600 ⊕ *www.barbour.com* Ⓜ *6 to 77th St.*

BCBG Max Azria. If flirtation's your sport, you'll find your sportswear here: fluttering skirts, beaded camisoles, chiffon dresses, and leather pants fill the racks. There are several locations throughout the city. ✉ *770 Madison Ave., at E. 66th St., Upper East Side* ☎ 212/717–4225 ⊕ *www.bcbg.com* Ⓜ *6 to 68th St./Hunter College.*

Bra Smyth. Chic and sweetly sexy French and Canadian underthings in soft cottons and silks line the shelves of this uptown staple. In addition to the selection of bridal-ready white bustiers and custom-fit swimsuits (made, cleverly, in bra-cup sizes), the store is best known for its knowledgeable staff, many of whom can offer tips on proper fit and size you up on sight. Cup sizes run from AA to J. There is also a shop on the Upper West Side. ✉ *905 Madison Ave., at 73rd St., Upper East Side* ☎ 212/772–9400 ⊕ *www.brasmyth.com* Ⓜ *6 to 68th St./Hunter College.*

Calvin Klein. Though the namesake designer has bowed out, the label keeps channeling his particular style. This stark flagship store emphasizes the luxe end of the clothing line. Men's suits tend to be soft around

18

MADISON AVENUE

GIORGIO ARMANI

If you're craving a couture fix, cab it straight to Madison Avenue between East 57th and East 79th streets. Here the greatest Italian, French, and American fashion houses form a platinum-card corridor for ladies who lunch. (If you're going to be pointedly overlooked by a salesperson, odds are it will happen here.)

Most occupy large, glass-facade spaces, but there are some exceptions, from intimate boutiques in old brownstones to the pair of mansions that are home to Ralph Lauren. Barneys, a full-fledged if very select department store, fits right in with the avenue's recherché roll call. But Madison isn't just a fashion funnel. A couple of marvelous booksellers and several outstanding antiques dealers and art galleries share this address as well.

BEST TIME TO GO

Saturday is the busiest day and thus better for people-watching. Perhaps because of the European influence, the pace is calmer here, especially on weekdays. Avoid coming on a Sunday, because several stores close, especially in summer when they figure their main clientele is out in the Hamptons.

BEST SOUVENIR FOR AN EX-MANHATTANITE

Take a whiff of the Manhattan-inspired perfumes like Chelsea Flowers and Park Avenue at **Bond No. 9.** Can't decide? Snap up the sampler box with travel-size spray scents wrapped like bonbons.

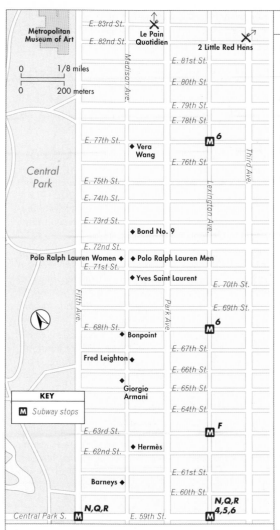

Métropolitan Museum of Art

E. 83rd St.

E. 82nd St. — Le Pain Quotidien

2 Little Red Hens

E. 81st St.

E. 80th St.

E. 79th St.

E. 78th St.

0 — 1/8 miles

0 — 200 meters

E. 77th St.

◆ Vera Wang

M 6

Madison Ave.

Third Ave.

Lexington Ave.

E. 76th St.

Central Park

E. 75th St.

E. 74th St.

E. 73rd St.

◆ Bond No. 9

E. 72nd St.

Polo Ralph Lauren Women ◆

◆ Polo Ralph Lauren Men

E. 71st St.

◆ Yves Saint Laurent

E. 70th St.

Park Ave.

E. 69th St.

Fifth Ave.

E. 68th St. — ◆ Bonpoint

M 6

E. 67th St.

Fred Leighton ◆

E. 66th St.

◆ Giorgio Armani

E. 65th St.

KEY

M Subway stops

E. 64th St.

E. 63rd St.

M F

◆ Hermès

E. 62nd St.

E. 61st St.

Barneys ◆

E. 60th St.

N,Q,R M

N,Q,R 4,5,6 M

Central Park S.

E. 59th St.

BEST FOR

BLING
Fred Leighton: If you believe diamonds are a girl's best friend, check out the vintage jewelry here.

FANCY CHILDREN'S CLOTHES
Bonpoint: Precious European designs with hand embroidering, velvet ribbons—you get the picture.

INTERNATIONAL MEGA-DESIGNERS
Barneys: Dozens of the most cutting-edge names.

Giorgio Armani: A sleek setting for perfectly cut suits and dramatic evening wear.

Hermès: Those divine silk scarves and handbags are waiting....

Polo Ralph Lauren: Haute-WASP style in two beautiful mansions.

Vera Wang: The classic bridal gown.

Yves Saint Laurent: Left Bank chic, *fabuleux* accessories.

18

REFUELING

Le Pain Quotidien. Join the Upper East Side moms and their trilingual children here for a fruit tart, ham-and-Gruyere tartine, or bowl of cocoa. ✉ *1131 Madison Ave., between E. 84th and E. 85th Sts.* ☎ *212/327–4900* ⊕ *www.lepainquotidien.com.*

Two Little Red Hens. If you're willing to pull yourself away from Madison Avenue, the front room of this American-style bakeshop has some small tables where you can eat latticed pie or a walnut-pear tart. ✉ *1652 2nd Ave., between E. 85th and E. 86th Sts.* ☎ *212/452–0476* ⊕ *www.twolittleredhens.com.*

the edges; women's evening gowns are often a fluid pouring of silk. There are also shoes, accessories, housewares, and makeup. ✉ *654 Madison Ave., at E. 60th St., Upper East Side* ☎ *212/292–9000* Ⓜ *N, R, 4, 5, 6 to 59th St./Lexington Ave.*

Carolina Herrera. A favorite of the society set (and Renee Zellweger), Herrera's designs are ladylike and elegant. On her suits, gowns, and cocktail dresses, expect anything from demure, shimmering bands of decoration to knockout swaths of beaded lace. ✉ *954 Madison Ave., at E. 75th St., Upper East Side* ☎ *212/249–6552* Ⓜ *6 to 77th St.*

DKNY. The signature style here is casual sophistication—in other words, a very New York look. Slinky wrap dresses, chunky-knit sweaters, and dark denim are some of the best bets here. If hunger strikes, head to the second floor for a wrap or a salad at Blanche's Organic Café. ✉ *655 Madison Ave., at E. 60th St., Upper East Side* ☎ *212/223–3569* ⊕ *www.dkny.donnakaran.com* Ⓜ *N, R, W, 4, 5, 6 to 59th St./Lexington Ave.* ✉ *420 West Broadway, SoHo* ☎ *646/613–1100* ⊕ *www.dkny. donnakaran.com* Ⓜ *B, D, F, M to Broadway–Lafayette St.*

Dolce & Gabbana. It's easy to feel like an Italian movie star amid these exuberant (in every sense) clothes. Pinstripes are a favorite; for women, they could be paired with something sheer, furred, or leopard-print, and for men they elongate the sharp suits. ✉ *825 Madison Ave., between E. 68th and E. 69th Sts., Upper East Side* ☎ *212/249–4100* Ⓜ *6 to 68th St./Hunter College.*

Etro. Trademark paisleys and bold patterns sprawl over richly covered suits, dresses, and lustrous pillows at this Italian designer's boutique, while juicy colors and rich detailing and embroidery keep things modern. ✉ *720 Madison Ave., between E. 63rd and E. 64th Sts., Upper East Side* ☎ *212/317–9096* Ⓜ *6 to 68th St./Hunter College.*

Lanvin. This French label has been around since 1889, and is the oldest French fashion house still in existence. After a period of hibernation, Lanvin reemerged on the fashion radar in 2001, when designer Alber Elbaz took over the reins. The signature look is fluid and sexy; think one-shouldered cocktail dresses, cigarette pants, and ruffled blouses. This elegant town house is the first U.S. outpost. The interior design itself is a showstopper; the three-story space oozes old money and glamour with its art-deco chandeliers and soothing gray walls. And the clothes? Just as slinky. ✉ *815 Madison Ave., between E. 68th and E. 69th Sts., Upper East Side* ☎ *646/439–0381* ⊕ *www.lanvin.com* Ⓜ *6 to 68th St./Hunter College.*

La Perla. If money is no object, shop here for some of the sexiest underthings around. Choose from items ranging from sheer lace sets and corsets to bathing suits and racy nightgowns. ✉ *803 Madison Ave., between E. 67th and E. 68th Sts., Upper East Side* ☎ *212/570–0050* ⊕ *www.laperla.com* Ⓜ *6 to 68th St./Hunter College.*

Marina Rinaldi. If you are a curvy size 10–22 and want to celebrate your figure rather than hide it, shop here. Marina Rinaldi sells form-flattering knit dresses, wool trousers, and coats that are tasteful and luxurious. ✉ *13 E. 69th St., between Madison and 5th Aves., Upper East Side* ☎ *212/734–4333* Ⓜ *6 to 68th St./Hunter College.*

stupor. ⊠ *1018 Madison Ave., between E. 78th and 79th Sts., Upper East Side* ☎ *212/744–7117* ⊕ *www.lamaisonduchocolat.com* Ⓜ *6 to 77th St.*

JEWELRY AND ACCESSORIES

Asprey. Asprey's claim to fame is jewelry; its own eponymous diamond cut has A-shape facets. Its net spreads to cater to all kinds of luxury tastes, though, from leather goods and rare books to polo equipment and cashmere sweaters. ⊠ *853 Madison Ave., between 70th and 71st Sts., Upper East Side* ☎ *212/688–1811* ⊕ *www.asprey.com* Ⓜ *6 to 68th St./Hunter College.*

Fred Leighton. If you're in the market for vintage diamonds, this is the place, whether your taste is for tiaras, art-deco settings, or sparklers once worn by a Vanderbilt. The skinny, stackable diamond eternity bands are hugely popular. ⊠ *773 Madison Ave., at E. 66th St., Upper East Side* ☎ *212/288–1872* ⊕ *www.fredleighton.com* Ⓜ *6 to 68th St./Hunter College.*

Ivanka Trump. The Donald's daughter would like to see you dripping with her diamonds. The new Soho location has an art-deco look, with black-and-white furniture and plenty of glittering chandeliers. But the real bling is the jewelry—drop earrings, tassel lariats, and bold cocktail rings. There's also a new bridal salon and couture gallery. ⊠ *109 Mercer St., between Prince and Spring Sts., SoHo* ☎ *212/756–9912* ⊕ *www. ivankatrumpcollection.com/* Ⓜ *N, R to Prince St.*

OC Concept Store. This boutique, founded by jeweler Orianne Collins (ex-wife of singer Phil), sells high-end jewelry from Chopard, Jacob & Co., and Audemars Piguet as well as her own designs. Shoppers can browse for one-of-a-kind art, but many of the gifts are aimed at the person who has everything and might enjoy a Lucite foosball table or crocodile-embossed dumbbells. There are also interactive screens so customers can build their own yacht. To make shopping even more enjoyable, there's also a fully stocked champagne and caviar bar. ⊠ *655 Madison Ave., between E. 60th and E. 61st Sts., Upper East Side* ☎ *212/759–9220* ⊕ *occonceptstore.com* Ⓜ *N, R, 4, 5, 6 to 59th St./Lexington Ave.*

18

MUSEUM STORES

Cooper-Hewitt, National Design Museum. Prowl the shelves here for intriguing urban oddments and ornaments, like sculptural tableware, rare design books, colorful Band-Aids from Cynthia Rowley, and ceramic versions of iconic New York deli coffee cups. ⊠ *2 E. 91st St., at 5th Ave., Upper East Side* ☎ *212/849–8400* ⊕ *www.cooperhewitt.org* Ⓜ *4, 5, 6 to 86th St.*

Metropolitan Museum of Art Shop. This sprawling shop offers a phenomenal book selection, as well as posters, art videos, and computer programs. Reproductions of statuettes and other *objets* fill the gleaming cases in every branch. Don't miss the jewelry selection, with its Byzantine- and Egyptian-inspired baubles. ⊠ *1000 5th Ave., at E. 82nd St., Upper East Side* ☎ *212/570–3894* Ⓜ *4, 5, 6 to 86th St.*

Museum of the City of New York. Satisfy your curiosity about New York City's past, present, or future with the terrific selection of books, cards, toys, and photography posters. ⊠ *1220 5th Ave., at E. 103rd St., Upper East Side* ☎ *212/534–1672* ⊕ *www.mcny.org* Ⓜ *6 to 103rd St.*

Neue Galerie. Like the museum, this bookshop focuses on German, Austrian, and Central European art. The solid selection includes catalogs, literature, and decorative items, including lovely wrapping papers. Many designs found in the collection have been reproduced as part of the museum's own Neue Haus line. ✉ *1048 5th Ave., between E. 85th and E. 86th Sts., Upper East Side* ☎ *212/628–6200* ⊕ *www.neuegalerie. org* Ⓜ *4, 5, 6 to 86th St.*

SHOES, HANDBAGS, AND LEATHER GOODS

★ **Christian Louboutin.** Lipstick-red soles are the signature of Louboutin's delicately sexy couture slippers and stilettos, and his latest, larger downtown store has carpeting to match. The pointy-toe creations come trimmed with brocade, tassels, buttons, or satin ribbons. ✉ *965 Madison Ave., between E. 75th and E. 76th Sts., Upper East Side* ☎ *212/396–1884* ⊕ *www.christianlouboutin.com* Ⓜ *6 to 77th St.*

Church's English Shoes. Beloved by bankers and lawyers, these shoes are indisputably of quality. You could choose something highly polished for an embassy dinner, a loafer or crepe-sole suede ankle boot for a weekend, or even a black-and-white spectator style worthy of Fred Astaire. ✉ *689 Madison Ave., at E. 62nd St., Upper East Side* ☎ *212/758–5200* Ⓜ *N, R, 4, 5, 6 to 59th St.*

Devi Kroell. You may have spotted her snakeskin hobo on celebs such as Halle Berry and Ashley Olsen. This serene space is a perfect backdrop for the designer's luxury handbags and shoes, which are crafted from premium leather. Roomy shoulder bags come in python and calf leather, and evening bags have a touch of sparkle. There's also a selection of jewelry and scarves. ✉ *717 Madison Ave., between E. 63rd and E. 64th Sts., Upper East Side* ☎ *212/644–4499* ⊕ *www.devikroell.com* Ⓜ *N, R, 4, 5, 6 to 59th St.*

Hermès. This legendary French retailer is best known for its iconic handbags, the Kelly and the Birkin, named for Grace Kelly and Jane Birkin, as well as its silk scarves and neckties. True to its roots, Hermès still stocks saddles and other equestrian items in addition to a line of beautifully simple separates. ✉ *691 Madison Ave., at E. 62nd St., Upper East Side* ☎ *212/751–3181* Ⓜ *N, R, 4, 5, 6 to 59th St./Lexington Ave.*

Jimmy Choo. Pointy toes, low vamps, narrow heels, ankle-wrapping straps—these British-made shoes are undeniably vampy, and sometimes more comfortable than they look. ✉ *716 Madison Ave., between E. 63rd and E. 64th Sts., Upper East Side* ☎ *212/759–7078* Ⓜ *M to 68th St./Hunter College.*

Jack Rogers. This brand, beloved by prepsters everywhere, is most famous for its Navajo sandal, which was worn by Jackie Onassis. You can still buy the Navajo at the Jack Rogers flagship store, as well as other footwear like ballet pumps, boots, and wedges. ✉ *1198 Madison Ave., between 87th and 88th Sts., Upper East Side* ☎ *212/259–0588* Ⓜ *4, 5, 6 to 86th St.*

John Lobb. If you truly want to be well heeled, pick up a pair of these luxury shoes, whose prices start at around $1,100. Owned by Hermès, John Lobb offers classic styles such as oxfords, loafers, boots, and slippers. ⊠ *680 Madison Ave., between E. 61st and E. 62nd Sts., Upper East Side* ☎ *212/888–9797* Ⓜ *N, R, 4, 5, 6 to 59th St.*

Judith Leiber. A door handle twinkling with Swarovski crystals signals the entrance to the Kingdom of Sparkle. Instantly recognizable handbags are completely frosted in crystals, from simple, colorful boxes to minaudières shaped like pigs or stars. Crystals also spangle the heels of satin pumps and the bows of oversize (to cut the glare?) sunglasses. ⊠ *680 Madison Ave., at E. 61st St., Upper East Side* ☎ *212/223–2999* ⊕ *www.judithleiber.com* Ⓜ *4, 5, 6 to E. 59th St.*

Robert Clergerie. Although best known for its chunky, comfy wedges, this French brand is not without its sense of fun. The sandal selection includes beaded starfish shapes, and for winter the ankle boots have killer heels but the soles are padded. ⊠ *19 E. 62nd St., between 5th and Madison Aves., Upper East Side* ☎ *212/207–8600* Ⓜ *R to 5th Ave.*

Tod's. Diego Della Valle's coveted driving moccasins, casual loafers, and boots are the top choice for jet-setters who prefer low-key, logo-free luxury goods. Though most of the women's selection is made up of low-heel or flat styles, an increasing number of high heels are bent on driving sales, rather than cars. The handbags and satchels have the same fine craftsmanship. ⊠ *650 Madison Ave., near E. 60th St., Upper East Side* ☎ *212/644–5945* Ⓜ *N, R to 5th Ave./59th St.*

HOME DECOR

Jonathan Adler. Everything at this flagship is fun, groovy, and happy. Adler funks up midcentury modern designs with his striped, striated, or curvy handmade pottery (ranging from a $30 vase to a chunky $400 lamp) as well as the hand-loomed wool pillow covers, rugs, and throws with blunt graphics (stripes, crosses, circles). There are also locations on the Upper West Side and Greenwich Village. ⊠ *1097 Madison Ave., at 83rd St., Upper East Side* ☎ *212/772–2410* ⊕ *www.jonathanadler. com* Ⓜ *4, 5, 6 to 86th St.*

Ankasa. Owners Sachin and Babi Ahluwalia used to source textiles for luxury designers like Oscar de la Renta. Now they are using that same design sensibility to produce a gorgeous line of housewares and accessories that are globally inspired. The bedding is done in muted colors such as slate and duck-egg blue. They've also launched a ready-to-wear collection for women that has a downtown, edgy look. ⊠ *135 E. 65th, between Park and Lexington Aves., Upper East Side* ☎ *212/861–6800* Ⓜ *4, 6 to E. 68th St./Hunter College.*

THE UPPER WEST SIDE

BOOKS AND STATIONERY

Westsider Books & Westsider Records. This wonderfully crammed space is a lifesaver on the otherwise sparse Upper West Side. Squeeze in among the stacks of art books and fiction; clamber up the steep stairway and you'll find all sorts of rare books. ⊠ *2246 Broadway, between W. 80th and W. 81st Sts., Upper West Side* ☎ *212/362–0706* ⊕ *westsiderbooks. com* Ⓜ *1 to 79th St.*

18

CHILDREN'S CLOTHING

A Time for Children. When you shop at this funky boutique, you'll also be doing some good, as 100% of the profits go to the Children's Aid Society. Choose from toys, books, and clothing, which include classics such as Petit Bateau as well as cool vintage-inspired onesies. ⊠ *506 Amsterdam Ave., between W. 84th and W. 85th Sts., Upper West Side* 🕾 *212/580–8202* Ⓜ *1, 2 to 86th St.*

CLOTHING

BOC. Who needs to go downtown for cutting-edge designers? Short for Boutique on Columbus, this store has an industrial chic look, and the labels are just as sleek. Separates from Rebecca Taylor, Vivienne Westwood, and Alexander Wang all line the shelves. There's also a small selection of candles and cosmetics. ⊠ *491 Coumbus Ave., between W. 83th and W. 84th Sts., Upper West Side* 🕾 *212/362–5405* Ⓜ *1, 2 to 86th St.*

Fodor'sChoice
★

Intermix. Whether you're looking for the perfect daytime dress, pair of J Brand jeans, or a puffer coat that won't make you look like the Michelin man, Intermix offers a well-edited mix of emerging and established designers. Expect to see designs from DVF, Chloe, and Missoni. ⊠ *210 Columbus Ave., between W. 69th and W. 70th Sts., Upper West Side* 🕾 *212/769–9116* ⊕ *www.intermixonline.com* Ⓜ *1, 2, 3 to 72nd St.*

★

Mint. Trendy dresses that won't break the bank are what Mint is all about. The collection includes BB Dakota, Susana Monaco, and Joe's Jeans. The walls are painted, of course, in mint. ⊠ *448 Columbus Ave., between W. 81st and W. 82nd Sts., Upper West Side* 🕾 *212/644–8888* ⊕ *mintny.com/* Ⓜ *1 to 79th St.*

SHOES, HANDBAGS, AND LEATHER GOODS

Fodor'sChoice
★

Tani. Fashionable Upper West Side ladies love this shoe store for its huge selection and patient staff. Tani's selection is mostly classic-with-a-twist, and shoppers will find slightly off-the-radar brands such as Bensimon, Mugumi Ochi, and Butter. ⊠ *2020 Broadway, between 69th and 70th Sts., Upper West Side* 🕾 *212/873–4361* ⊕ *taninyc.com* Ⓜ *1, 2, 3 to 72nd St.*

Where to Eat

WORD OF MOUTH

"NYC has . . . almost any cuisine you can name. Do you want to try something trendy like Vietnamese sandwiches, go for upscale traditional French, or casual American . . . "

— nytraveler

Updated by
David Farley

Ready to take a bite out of New York? Hope you've come hungry. In a city where creativity is expressed in many ways, the food scene takes center stage, with literally thousands of ways to get an authentic taste of what Gotham is all about. Whether they're lining up at street stands, gobbling down legendary deli and diner grub, or chasing a coveted reservation at the latest celebrity-chef venue, New Yorkers are a demanding yet appreciative audience.

Every neighborhood offers temptations high, low, and in between, meaning there's truly something for every taste, whim, and budget. No matter how you approach dining out here, you can't go wrong. Planning a day of shopping among the glittering boutique flagships along 5th and Madison? Stop into one of the Upper East Side's storied restaurants for a repast among the "ladies who lunch." Clubbing in the Meatpacking District? Tuck into a meal at eateries as trendy as their patrons. Craving authentic ethnic? From food trucks to hidden joints, there are almost more choices than there are appetites. Recent years have also seen entire food categories, from ramen to meatballs to mac and cheese, riffed upon and turned into fetishistic obsessions.

Amid newfound economic realities, there's been a revived appreciation for value, meaning you can tap into wallet-friendly choices at every end of the spectrum. At many restaurants you'll also notice an almost religious reverence for seasonal cuisine. And don't forget—New York is still home to more celebrity chefs than any other city. Your chances of running into your favorite cookbook author, Food Network celeb, or paparazzi-friendly chef are higher, adding even more star wattage to a restaurant scene with an already through-the-roof glamour quotient. Ready, set, eat. Rest assured, this city will do its part to satisfy your appetite.

NEW YORK DINING PLANNER

EATING OUT STRATEGY

Where should we eat? With thousands of Manhattan eateries competing for your attention, it may seem like a daunting question. But fret not—our expert writers and editors have done most of the legwork. The selections here represent the best this city has to offer—from hot dogs to haute cuisine. Search "Best Bets" for top recommendations by price, cuisine, and experience. Sample local flavor in the neighborhood features. Or find a review quickly in the alphabetical listings. Dive in and enjoy!

CHILDREN

Though it's unusual to see children in the dining rooms of Manhattan's most elite restaurants, dining with youngsters in New York does not have to mean culinary exile. Many of the restaurants reviewed in this chapter are excellent choices for families, and are marked with a symbol.

RESERVATIONS

It's still a good idea to plan ahead. Some renowned restaurants are booked weeks or even months in advance. If that's the case, you can get lucky at the last minute if you're flexible—and friendly. Most restaurants keep a few tables open for walk-ins and VIPs. Show up for dinner early (5:30 pm) or late (after 10 pm), and politely inquire about any last-minute vacancies or cancellations. Occasionally, an eatery may take your credit-card number and ask you to call the day before your scheduled meal to reconfirm: don't forget or you could lose out, or possibly be charged for your oversight.

WHAT TO WEAR

When in the nation's style capital, do as the natives do: dress up to eat out. Whatever your style, dial it up a notch. Have some fun while you're at it. Pull out the clothes you've been saving for a special occasion and get glamorous. Unfair as it is, the way you look can influence how you're treated—and where you're seated. Generally speaking, jeans and a button-down shirt will suffice at most table-service restaurants in the $ to $$ range. Moving up from there, some pricier restaurants require jackets, and some insist on ties. In reviews, we note dress only when a jacket or jacket and tie are required. If you have doubts, call the restaurant and ask.

19

TIPPING AND TAXES

In most restaurants, tip the waiter 15%–20%. (To figure out a 20% tip quickly, just move the decimal point one place to the left on your total and double that amount.) Bills for parties of six or more sometimes include the tip already. Tip at least $1 per drink at the bar, and $1 for each coat checked. Never tip the maître d' unless you're out to impress your guests or expect to pay another visit soon.

SMOKING

Smoking is prohibited in all enclosed public spaces in New York City, including restaurants and bars.

HOURS

New Yorkers seem ready to eat at any hour. Many restaurants stay open between lunch and dinner, some offer late-night seating, and still others serve around the clock. Restaurants that serve breakfast often do so until noon or later. Restaurants in the East Village, the Lower East Side, SoHo, TriBeCa, and Greenwich Village are likely to remain open late, whereas Midtown spots and those in the Theater and Financial districts and uptown generally close earlier. Unless otherwise noted, the restaurants listed in this guide are open daily for lunch and dinner.

PRICES

If you're watching your budget, be sure to ask the price of the daily specials recited by the waiter. The charge for specials at some restaurants is noticeably out of line with the other prices on the menu. Beware of the $10 bottle of water; ask for tap water instead. And always review your bill.

If you eat early or late, you may be able to take advantage of a prix-fixe deal not offered at peak hours. Most upscale restaurants offer great lunch deals, with special menus at cut-rate prices designed to give customers a true taste of the place.

Credit cards are widely accepted, but many restaurants (particularly smaller ones downtown) accept only cash. If you plan to use a credit card, it's a good idea to confirm that it is acceptable when making reservations or before sitting down to eat.

Prices in the reviews are the average cost of a main course at dinner or, if dinner is not served, at lunch.

CHECK BEFORE YOU GO

The nature of the restaurant industry means that places open and close in a New York minute. It's always a good idea to phone ahead and make sure your restaurant is still turning tables.

19

BEST BETS FOR
NEW YORK CITY DINING

With thousands of restaurants to choose from, how will you decide where to eat? Fodor's writers and editors have selected their favorite restaurants by price, cuisine, and experience in the Best Bets lists below. You can also search by neighborhood for excellent eats—just peruse the following pages.

Fodor'sChoice★

A Voce, $$$, p. 413
Aldea, $$$, p. 414
Baoguette, $, p. 389
Babbo Ristorante, $$$, p. 400
Bar Boulud, $$$, p. 439
The Breslin Bar and Dining Room, $$$, p. 414
Burger Joint, $, p. 428
Candle 79, $$, p. 436
The City Bakery, $, p. 414
Clinton St. Baking Co., $$, p. 396
Cookshop, $$$, p. 410
Daniel, $$$$, p. 437
Danji, $$$, p. 428
DBGB Kitchen & Bar, $$, p. 389
Eleven Madison Park, $$$$, p. 416
Emporio, $$, p. 382
Fatty Crab, $$, p. 406
Freeman's, $$, p. 396
Gotham Bar & Grill, $$$$, p. 419
Grimaldi's, $, p. 447

Hundred Acres, $$$, p. 386
I Sodi, $$$, p. 407
Katz's Delicatessen, $, p. 397
L'Atelier de Joël Robuchon, $$$$, p. 422
Le Bernardin, $$$$, p. 431
Marea, $$$$, p. 442
Momofuku Ko, $$$$, p. 392
Momofuku Noodle Bar, $$, p. 393
North End Grill, $$$, p. 379
Northern Spy Food Co., $$, p. 393
Osteria Morini, $$, p. 387
Per Se, $$$$, p. 443
Perbacco, $$$, p. 394
Peter Luger, $$$$, p. 451
Saxon & Parole, $$$, p. 395
Shake Shack, $, p. 417
Tía Pol, $$, p. 411
Torrisi Italian Specialties, $$$, p. 384
Zabb Elee, $, p. 396

Best by Price

$

Baoguette, p. 389
Bubby's, p. 377
Burger Joint, p. 428
Cascabel Taquería, p. 436
City Bakery, p. 414
Eisenberg's, p. 415
Financier Patisserie, p. 376
Gray's Papaya, p. 402
'inoteca, p. 397
Katz's Delicatessen, p. 397
Mexicana Mama, p. 407
Shake Shack, p. 417

$$

Arturo's, p. 400
Back Forty, p. 388
Candle 79, p. 436
Emporio, p. 382
Fatty Crab, p. 406
Momofuku Noodle Bar, p. 393
Northern Spy Food Co., p. 393

Osteria Morini, p. 387
Tía Pol, p. 411

$$$

A Voce, p. 413
ABC Kitchen, p. 413
Babbo, p. 400
Balthazar, p. 385
Bar Boulud, p. 439
Craft, p. 415
Minetta Tavern, p. 403
The Modern and Bar Room, p. 432
Scarpetta, p. 412
The Standard Grill, p. 412

$$$$

Adour Alain Ducasse, p. 420
Eleven Madison Park, p. 416
Jean Georges, p. 441
L'Atelier de Joël Robuchon, p. 422
Le Bernardin, p. 431
Marea, p. 442
Per Se, p. 443

Best by Cuisine

AMERICAN

ABC Kitchen, p. 413
Cookshop, p. 410
Gramercy Tavern, p. 416
Hundred Acres, p. 386
Northern Spy Food Co., p. 393
Park Avenue Seasonal, p. 437
Per Se, p. 443

CHINESE

Grand Sichuan, p. 391
Great New York Noodletown, p. 380
Joe's Shanghai, p. 381
Shun Lee Palace, p. 424
Tasty Hand-Pulled Noodles, p. 381

FRENCH

Adour Alain Ducasse, p. 420
Bar Boulud, p. 439
Daniel, p. 437
Jean Georges, p. 441
Le Bernardin, p. 431
The Modern and Bar Room, p. 432

GREEK

Kefi, p. 442
Pylos, p. 395
Snack, p. 387

INDIAN

Tamarind, p. 417

ITALIAN

Babbo, p. 400
Emporio, p. 382
'ino, p. 406
'inoteca, p. 397
Lupa, p. 402
Marea, p. 442
Osteria Morini, p. 387
Perbacco, p. 394
Scarpetta, p. 412
Torrisi Italian Specialties, p. 384

JAPANESE

Ippudo, p. 392

Kuruma Zushi, p. 422
Sushi of Gari, p. 438
Sushi Yasuda, p. 424

MEDITERRANEAN

Aldea, p. 414
August, p. 404
Il Buco, p. 391
Picholine, p. 443

MEXICAN

Cascabel Taqueria, p. 436
Maya, p. 437
Mexicana Mama, p. 407
Toloache, p. 434

NEW AMERICAN

Craft, p. 415
Eleven Madison Park, p. 416
Hundred Acres, p. 386
The Red Cat, p. 410

PIZZA

Arturo's, p. 400
Co., p. 410
Esca, p. 429
Grimaldi's, p. 447
Keste Pizza & Vino, p. 402
Lombardi's, p. 383

SEAFOOD

Grand Central Oyster Bar & Restaurant, p. 421
The John Dory, p. 416
Marea, p. 442
Mary's Fish Camp, p. 407
Pearl Oyster Bar, p. 408

SPANISH

Boqueria, p. 414
Casa Mono, p. 418
Tía Pol, p. 411

STEAKHOUSE

BLT Prime, p. 418
BLT Steak, p. 421
Peter Luger's, p. 451
Porter House, p. 443
Sparks Steakhouse, p. 424

VIETNAMESE

Baoguette, p. 389

Best by Experience

BRUNCH

Balthazar, p. 385
Bubby's, p. 377
Cookshop, p. 410
Hundred Acres, p. 386
Sarabeth's Kitchen, p. 444

CELEB-SPOTTING

ABC Kitchen, p. 413
Balthazar, p. 385
The Breslin, p. 414
Café Boulud, p. 435
DBGB Kitchen & Bar, p. 389
Four Seasons, p. 421
Minetta Tavern, p. 403
Nobu, p. 379
Pastis, p. 412
The Standard Grill, p. 412

CHILD-FRIENDLY

Bubby's, p. 377
Carmine's, pp. 428, 440
City Bakery, p. 414
Fatty Crab Upper West Side, p. 441
Joe's Shanghai, p. 381
Lombardi's, p. 383
Odeon, p. 380
Serafina, p. 434

GREAT VIEW

Asiate, p. 438
Marea, p. 442
Michael Jordan's The Steakhouse NYC, p. 423
Per Se, p. 443
Porter House, p. 443

LATE-NIGHT DINING

Balthazar, p. 385
The Breslin, p. 414
DBGB Kitchen & Bar, p. 389
Emporio, p. 382
Fatty Crab, p. 406
Minetta Tavern, p. 403
Osteria Morini, p. 387
Pastis, p. 412
The Standard Grill, p. 412

WINE LIST

'21' Club, p. 425
Babbo, p. 400
Corton, p. 378
Del Posto, p. 411
'inoteca, p. 397
Marea, p. 442
The Modern and Bar Room, p. 432

19

LOWER MANHATTAN

A wave of development and attractive pricing have meant thousands of new residents in Lower Manhattan, fueling an up-and-coming— yet still slow-moving—neighborhood scene.

The most visible changes? Restaurants in and around the Financial District no longer adhere to banker's hours, and formal dining rooms have been outnumbered by casual cafés and wine bars. On the pedestrian-only Stone Street, throngs of young professionals gather for after-work drinks and dinner at nearby bistros, oyster bars, and steak houses.

To the north, Chinatown beckons adventurous diners with restaurants representing numerous regional cuisines of China, including Cantonese-, Szechuan-, Hunan-, Fujian-, Shanghai-, and Hong Kong–style cooking. Malaysian and Vietnamese restaurants also have taken root here, and the neighborhood continues to grow rapidly, encroaching into what was Little Italy.

To the west, TriBeCa still holds an air of exclusivity, though glamorous dining rooms in converted warehouses have now been joined by more casual spots with later hours.

TRIBECA BRUNCH

Iron Chef winner Marc Forgione serves indulgent brunch in the wood-and-brick dining room of his eponymous restaurant (✉ *134 Reade St., between West Broadway and Hudson ✛ 1:C2*). Try Eggs Benny lavished in a preserved-lemon Hollandaise, sliders featuring beer-braised suckling pig, and a seasonal mimosa made with fresh-squeezed juice. If you're looking for a more elegant atmosphere, try **Capsouto Frères** (✉ *451 Washington St., near Watts St.* ☎ *212/966–4900 ✛ 2:B5*), a landmark French bistro that makes the city's best sweet and savory soufflés. The praline soufflé and the three-cheese soufflé are favorites.

CHINATOWN CHOWDOWN

With more than 200 restaurants in just under 2 square miles, deciding where to eat is tricky, but these are some of our favorites.

Cantonese: For Hong Kong–style dim sum, head to **Ping's Seafood** (⊠ *22 Mott St., near Worth St.* ☎ *212/602–9988* ⊹ *2:F6*) or **HSF** (⊠ *46 Bowery, near Canal St.* ☎ *212/374–1319* ⊹ *2:F5*). Both spots are crowded but have addictive fare like turnip cakes, steamed pork buns, and fried sesame-seed balls. One of the best deals in Chinatown is at **Vanessa's Dumpling House** (⊠ *118 Eldridge St., near Broome St.* ☎ *212/625–8008* ⊹ *2:G4*), where sizzling pork-and-chive dumplings are four for a buck.

Malaysian: There's something for everyone at **New Malaysia** (⊠ *48 Bowery, near Canal St.* ☎ *212/964–0284* ⊹ *2:G5*); try roti flatbread with curry and delicious red-bean and coconut-milk drinks.

Shanghainese: The city's best soup dumplings—doughy pouches filled with ground pork and meaty broth—are ripe for the slurping at **Joe's Shanghai** (⊠ *9 Pell St., near Bowery* ☎ *212/233–8888* ⊹ *2:F5*).

Szechuan: Foodies go ga-ga for the twice-cooked pork in bean sauce and scallion pancakes at **Grand Sichuan** (⊠ *125 Canal St., at Chrystie St.* ☎ *212/625–9212* ⊹ *2:G5*). At the **Peking Duck House** (⊠ *28 Mott St., near Mosco St.* ☎ *212/227–1810* ⊹ *2:F5*), don't miss the stunning signature dish. Crispy-skin Peking duck comes with pancakes, scallions, cucumbers, and hoisin sauce.

FINANCIAL DISTRICT'S RESTO ROW

Nestled alongside skyscrapers and the towering New York Stock Exchange, Stone Street is a two-block restaurant oasis that feels more like a village than the center of the financial universe. After the market closes, Wall Streeters head to **Ulysses'** (⊠ *95 Pearl St., near Hanover Sq.* ☎ *212/482–0400* ⊹ *1:E4*), a popular pub with 19 beers on tap and more than 50 bottled beers.

Clerks might stop in for a broccoli rabe–and–sausage pie (they don't do slices) at **Adrienne's Pizza Bar** (⊠ *54 Stone St., near Hanover Sq.* ☎ *212/248–3838* ⊹ *1:E4*) while high-rolling brokers continue down the block to **Harry's Café and Steak** (⊠ *1 Hanover Sq., at Stone St.* ☎ *212/785–9200* ⊹ *1:E4*) for a dry-aged porterhouse and a reserve-collection cabernet from a 2,800-strong cellar. Those with a sweet tooth end up at **Financier Patisserie** (⊠ *62 Stone St., between Mill La. and Hanover Sq.* ☎ *212/344–5600* ⊹ *1:E4*).

DIM SUM DO'S AND DON'TS

Jing Fong
Weekends in Chinatown are synonymous with one thing: dim sum. There may be newer, trendier spots, but Jing Fong (⊠ *20 Elizabeth St., 2nd fl., between Bayard and Canal Sts.* ⊹ *2:F5*) is a classic spot worth visiting. Take the seats you're given (most likely at a communal table) and simply let your appetite guide your ordering from the jaw-dropping array of dishes that roll by on carts. Point at your choices, then hand over your card to be stamped; the total will be tallied at the end and you'll pay on the way out. Pace yourself—it's easy to get full fast. And don't be afraid to ask questions; the cart attendants often know more English than they let on! Top choices include shrimp folded inside a floppy giant noodle and topped with a squirt of sweet soy; plump spinach dumplings (one of the few choices for vegetarians), and the elusive, spongy barbecue pork buns—pounce if you find them, and you won't be sorry.

19

SOHO, NOLITA, AND LITTLE ITALY

In this high-rent neighborhood, dining options are somewhat limited, resulting in crowded restaurants with steep prices. But snacking is a great strategy for experiencing the local flavor without buyer's remorse.

Longtime New Yorkers lament that SoHo has evolved from a red-hot art district into a big-brand outdoor mall. Shoppers engulf the neighborhood on weekends like angry bees, turning Lafayette Street into a buzzing hive of commerce. As a result, popular spots can be tough to get into during prime times.

In NoLIta, the trendy next-door neighborhood of indie boutiques and restaurants, the spirit of old SoHo prevails. Modest eateries are squeezed between boutiques featuring products from up-and-coming designers.

If you want authentic Italian food, don't head south to Little Italy: most of the pasta factories along the main strip of Mulberry Street have developed reputations as tourist traps. As with SoHo, it's a better bet to snack your way through this area.

FRESH-BAKED

Follow the beguiling scent of fresh-baked bread to **Balthazar Bakery** (⊠ 80 Spring St., near Crosby St. ☎ 212/965–1785 ✛ 2:E4), where you'll find baguettes, boules, batards, brioche, and several other different breads. The bakery—an extension of Keith McNally's always-packed Balthazar restaurant— boasts an extensive menu of panini, sandwiches, quiches, and homemade soups, plus newly added fresh breakfast egg dishes. The pastry chefs also turn out custom-made pastries, cakes, and cookies. Try the berry noisette tart or coconut cake, or keep it simple with a few of Balthazar Bakery's buttery lemon or chocolate madeleines.

SOHO SIPS AND SNACKS

THREE QUICK BITES

Relax and refuel at one of these neighborhood haunts.

Apertivo at Emporio (✉ *231 Mott St., near Prince St.*
☎ *212/358–1707* ✛ *2:F3*): Visit this cozy Italian restaurant at happy hour, weekdays 5 to 7 pm, when cocktails and wine come with free snacks. The daily selection may include olives, ricotta frittata, cheeses, pizzas, and cubed Italian ham.

Cuban sandwich at Café Habana (✉ *17 Prince St., at Elizabeth St.* ☎ *212/625–2002* ✛ *2:F3*): This popular pan-Latin dive also boasts excellent Mexican-style grilled corn and café con leche (with milk). The Cuban sandwich features roasted pork, ham, Swiss cheese, pickles, and chipotle mayo.

Tacos at La Esquina (✉ *106 Kenmare St.* ☎ *646/613–7100* ✛ *2:F4*): Order tasty pulled chicken or char-grilled steak tacos and tortas to go from the counter-service taqueria, or squeeze into the small café around the corner for a bigger sit-down meal.

ELEVATE YOUR COCKTAIL CONSCIOUSNESS

The American cocktail renaissance is under way at **Pegu Club** (✉ *77 W. Houston St., near West Broadway* ☎ *212/473–7348* ✛ *2:D3*), where renowned mixologist Audrey Saunders developed impeccable modern cocktail recipes steeped in pre-Prohibition tradition.

Inspired by a 19th-century British officers' club in Burma, the intimate second-floor lounge has a colonial aura, outfitted with palm trees, dark woods, and low-slung brown velvet couches.

Since Pegu opened several years ago, many imitators have followed, but Saunders's libations still hold their own, with fresh-squeezed juices and house infusions in every cocktail. Watching the barkeeps in their natty vests and shirtsleeves ply their trade making drinks like an Earl Grey martini with tea-infused gin, or the Jamaican Firefly, featuring fresh ginger beer with rum and lime, makes the bar a prime perch. Ice is hand-chipped, bitters and syrups are brewed on the premises, and the results show in every glass.

"You have to look at well-crafted cocktails as fine cuisine with elements of sweet, sour, bitter, and spicy," Saunders says. "They're not just fruit and booze. You need spices, herbs, and other ingredients to add complexity."

AND FOR DESSERT . . .

MarieBelle (✉ *484 Broome St., between Wooster St. and West Broadway* ☎ *212/925–6999* ✛ *2:D4*). Slip into MarieBelle to experience chocolate nirvana in a Parisian-style café setting. At the front of the shop you'll find an assortment of artisanal chocolates filled with velvety ganache. But real chocoholics head to the Cacao Bar at the back of the store for MarieBelle's über-rich hot chocolate, crafted from ground cacao beans instead of cocoa powder, then mixed with boiling water (European-style) or steamed milk (American-style). For an unusual treat, try the spicy hot chocolate—it has a real kick to it. Tea lovers will be delighted by MarieBelle's diverse hand-blended selection. Not to worry if you're visiting during the late spring or summer: skip the hot chocolate and cool off with MarieBelle's Aztec iced chocolate—the warm-weather version of her decadent cacao elixir—or the house-made chocolate gelato.

19

EAST VILLAGE AND LOWER EAST SIDE

With luxury condos stretching as far east as Avenue C and the Bowery's glistening revamp, the East Village—once Manhattan's edgiest enclave—has become yet another high-rent neighborhood. Nearby, the Lower East Side, home to generations of immigrant newcomers, has nearly completed a similar transformation.

Both neighborhoods still offer some of the best meal deals in the city, and the influx of flush new residents has steadily raised the bar on high-quality eats. Legends like **Katz's** deli, coexist with high-end destinations featuring tasting menus and hard-to-score tables. There's something for every budget and craving, from yakitori parlors to midprice trattorias. St. Marks Place is the center of New York's downtown Little Tokyo, and 6th Street is its Indian row. On the Lower East Side, meanwhile, cute little bistros and some restaurant heavy hitters have been inching into new gentrified stretches south of Delancey Street. The neighborhoods have even given birth to their own homegrown star chefs like **Momofuku**'s David Chang and **wd~50**'s Wylie Dufresne.

TOP BUDGET EATS

Be careful with the incendiary hot sauce at **Mamoun's Falafel** (⊠ 22 St. Marks Pl., between 2nd and 3rd Aves. ☎ 212/674–8685 ✛ 3:G5), where tahini-topped pitas are packed with fresh, green-on-the-inside falafel balls. Gluttony reigns at **Crif Dogs** (⊠ 113 St. Marks Pl., at Ave. A ☎ 212/614–2728 ✛ 3:H5); indulge in a bacon-wrapped, deep-fried hot dog and chili-cheese tater tots. Next door, **Tuck Shop** (⊠ 115 St. Marks Pl., between Ave. A and Ave. B ☎ 212/979–5200 ✛ 3:H5) offers Australian street food. Try a spicy beef meat pie followed by a dense, sweet vanilla slice (vanilla custard surrounded by puff pastry and topped with icing).

RAMEN REVOLUTION

A Japanese ramen noodle revolution has stormed the East Village, starting with **Momofuku Noodle Bar** (✉ *171 1st Ave., between 10th and 11th Sts.* ☎ *212/777-7773* ✛ *3:H5*), David Chang's flagship restaurant. Chang's ramen features fatty slabs of Berkshire pork belly and shredded pork shoulder in savory broth topped with fresh vegetables and a slow-poached egg. At **Ippudo** (✉ *65 4th Ave., between 9th and 10th Sts.* ☎ *212/388-0088* ✛ *3:G5*), the first American branch of the Japanese chain, crowds wait more than two hours for noodles in a thick miso brew and a slick of spicy oil (not to mention the sleeper dish: peppery chicken wings). Japanese expats flock to **Rai Rai Ken** (✉ *214 E. 10th St., between 1st and 2nd Aves.* ☎ *212/477-7030* ✛ *3:H5*) for ramen sunk into one of three signature broths. **Minca** (✉ *536 E. 5th St., between Ave. A and Ave. B* ☎ *212/505-8001* ✛ *2:G2*) has received the least fanfare, but its ramen may very well be the best. Start your meal with light, panfried whole shrimp dumplings and then dive into the shoyu (soy sauce) pork ramen.

LATE-NIGHT EATS

From dirt cheap to stylish, the city's best late-night eats can be found right here. Grab a gargantuan slice at table-less **Artichoke Pizza** (✉ *328 E. 14th St., between 1st and 2nd Aves.* ☎ *212/228-2004* ✛ *3:H4*), where lines snake until 5 am for the artichoke-spinach slice, which tastes like cheesy dip on crackers. For authentic Ukrainian cuisine, 24-hour diner gem **Veselka** (✉ *144 2nd Ave., at 9th St.* ☎ *212/228-9682* ✛ *3:H5*) offers a solid burger and even better potato pierogi. Grab a chewy chocolate chip–M&M cookie for dessert. The swanky tapas restaurant and lounge **Stanton Social** (✉ *99 Stanton St., between Orchard and Ludlow Sts.* ☎ *212/995-0099* ✛ *2:G3*) offers shareable Kobe beef sliders, French onion soup dumplings, and fresh doughnut holes until 2 am nightly (3 on weekends).

AND FOR DESSERT . . .

The standing-only, workbenchlike tables at **Momofuku Milk Bar** (✉ *207 2nd Ave., at 13th St.* ☎ *212/254-3500* ✛ *3:G4*) provide clear views of pastry chef Christina Tosi tinkering with her constantly evolving menu of creations such as curiously flavored soft-serve ice cream (cereal-milk, lemon verbena) and Candy Bar Pie, a sweet bomb of caramel, peanut-butter nougat, and pretzels atop a chocolate-cookie crust. If taking a seat is preferred, scoot into the cozy couches and chairs at **Sugar Sweet Sunshine** (✉ *126 Rivington St., between Essex and Norfolk Sts.* ☎ *212/995-1960* ✛ *2:G3*), the brainchild of two former Magnolia Bakery employees. Sugar Sweet's cupcakes are far superior; try the chocolate-almond Gooey Gooey, or the cream cheese frosting–topped pumpkin flavor. The real star showstopper? Swoon-inducing banana pudding incorporating slices of ripe fruit and crumbled Nilla wafers suspended in decadent vanilla pudding.

19

GREENWICH VILLAGE

WITH WEST VILLAGE AND MEATPACKING DISTRICT

Dining styles collide on the West Side, with quaint, chef-driven eateries in Greenwich Village facing off against the Meatpacking District's massive, celebrity-fueled hot spots.

Francophiles and fashionistas flock to Pastis, a brasserie in the Meatpacking District, for its stylish scene and standout seared tuna Niçoise.

Greenwich Village's bohemian days may have faded with the Beatnik era, but the romantic allure of its tiny bistros, bars, and cafés remains. Around New York University, shabby-chic eateries and takeout joints line the streets and are patronized by a student clientele. Avoid heavily trafficked thoroughfares like Bleecker Street (unless you're tapping into the new artisan pizza craze), as most of the Village's culinary gems lie tucked away on side streets and alleyways, especially west of 7th Avenue, in the West Village. The vibe here is low-key and friendly, with patrons squeezed together at tiny tables in matchbox-size eateries.

For a glitzier scene, head to the Meatpacking District, which has been transformed in recent years from a gritty commercial warehouse area to the celebrity-chef–driven epicenter of the city's dining scene. The vibe is flashy, favored by actors, models, and their suitors.

PEANUT BUTTER & CO.

For the childhood classic kicked up a notch, head to Peanut Butter & Co. Sandwich Shop (✉ *240 Sullivan St., near W. 3rd St.* ☎ *212/677–3995* ⟡ *2:D2*). Stick with the standard PB&J, or go Proustian with any of the menu's 21 options like the Elvis (grilled with peanut butter, bananas, and honey), the Pregnant Lady (peanut butter and pickles), or the sandwich of the week.

BEST BAR SEATS: WEST VILLAGE

Belly up to the bar for dinner at these neighborhood institutions:

At **Babbo** (⊠ *110 Waverly Pl., between MacDougal St. and 6th Ave.* ☎ *212/777–0303* ✛ *2:C1*), if reservations are hard to come by, stake your place outside before opening and at 5:30 pm you'll have a decent shot of nabbing a seat or two at the bar, ideal for sampling Mario Batali's iconic dishes like squid-ink spaghetti with sausage.

Gotham Bar and Grill (⊠ *12 E. 12th St., between 5th Ave. and University Pl.* ☎ *212/620–4020* ✛ *3:E4*) is almost better known for its bar seating than its dining room. It's the place solo diners and couples alike sit at the long, deep bar top for a taste of attentive service (and generous pours) from knowledgeable bartenders paired with Chef Alfred Portale's iconic New American cuisine.

And at **Wallsé** (⊠ *344 W. 11th St., at Washington St.* ☎ *212/352–2300* ✛ *3:B6*), chef Kurt Guttenbrunner's modern-Austrian cuisine (think dishes like schnitzel and spaetzle, only with a twist) is best enjoyed at the U-shape bar, as is the impressive art collection with works by the likes of Julian Schnabel and the late Dennis Hopper.

PIZZA THREE WAYS IN THE WEST VILLAGE

AUTHENTIC NEAPOLITAN
At the back of narrow **Keste Pizza & Vino** (⊠ *271 Bleecker St., between 6th and 7th Aves.* ☎ *212/243–1500* ✛ *2:C2*) sits a beautiful, tiled, wood-fired oven that cooks Manhattan's most authentic Neapolitan pies at 1,000 degrees. Blistered and chewy around the edges, each pie gives way to a softer center pooled with San Marzano tomato sauce and imported buffalo mozzarella.

CLASSIC COAL OVEN
Founded in 1957, **Arturo's** (⊠ *106 W. Houston St., at Thompson St.* ☎ *212/677–3820* ✛ *2:D3*) is a double throwback: it's a jazz bar and friendly neighborhood coal-oven pizza restaurant where crackly-crusted pies are a guarantee. If you can brave the organized chaos and the usual wait, a gooey meatball pie awaits.

SLICE
Flavor reigns at **Bleecker Street Pizza** (⊠ *69 7th Ave. S, at Bleecker St.* ☎ *212/924–4466* ✛ *2:B2*), where the thin-crusted Nonna Maria is topped with garlicky marinara, grated mozzarella, fresh mozzarella, and freshly grated parmigiano-reggiano. You may not find a seat inside tiny **Joe's Pizza** (⊠ *7 Carmine St., at 6th Ave.* ☎ *212/366–1182* ✛ *2:C2*), but you will get one of the best versions of a purist's New York slice.

AND FOR DESSERT . . .

Sweet Revenge (⊠ *62 Carmine St., between Bedford St. and 7th Ave.* ☎ *212/242–2240* ⊕ *www. sweetrevengenyc.com* ✛ *2:C3*). Everyone loves beer, wine, and cupcakes, but only Sweet Revenge brings them all together in a cozy neighborhood spot. Vibrantly flavored and delicately rich, the cupcakes are the real draw. Nut-studded peanut butter–buttercream tops a moist, crumbly peanut-butter cake housing a chocolate ganache center you'll want to measure out in every bite. Pair it with the suggested Argentinean red or German Hefeweizen or combine one of the other 15 wines and beers with a special cupcake of the day, such as the Very Strawberry, with fresh strawberries baked into vanilla cake topped with strawberry cream-cheese frosting. There are also sandwiches and savory cakes, but indulgence is a dish best served sweet. Ten dollars gets you a glass of sangria or wine and a cupcake from 4 to 8 pm weekdays.

19

UNION SQUARE
WITH GRAMERCY, MURRAY HILL, AND FLATIRON DISTRICT

The blocks around Union Square and its open-air greenmarket are filled with upscale foodie havens featuring market-driven menus. But fancy seasonal fare isn't all the area offers: Curry Hill and Koreatown are just blocks away.

Some of the city's most popular restaurants, including **Craft** and **Union Square Cafe,** are in the area northwest of Union Square, called the Flatiron District. **Rosa Mexicano** has fabulous margaritas. The neighborhood is also a hot shopping destination, with plenty of refueling spots like City Bakery, a gourmet deli and sweets spot that's a standby for many New Yorkers.

Lexington Avenue between 27th and 29th streets is known as Curry Hill (it borders Murray Hill) for its wall-to-wall Indian restaurants, spice shops, and takeout joints. The area near Koreatown, on West 32nd Street, between 5th and 6th avenues, may look deserted, as eateries often lack visible signage—it's best to go with a specific spot in mind rather than try your luck window shopping.

BURGER BLISS

This area is prime burger turf. The **Stand4** (⊠ 24 E. 12th St., near University Pl. ☎ 212/488–5900 ✚ 3:F4) offers upscale fast fare in a sleek setting. We recommend the bacon-and-egg cheeseburger, topped with cheddar and hard-boiled-egg mayo. For an Old New York feel, try the classic burgers at the **Old Town Bar** (⊠ 45 E. 18th St., near Park Ave. S ☎ 212/529–6732 ✚ 3:F3), where they've been serving 'em up for more than 100 years. Or, if the weather is nice, head up to Madison Square Park, where burger lovers are always queued up at the original **Shake Shack** (⊠ 23rd St. near Madison Ave. ☎ 212/889–6600 ✚ 3:F2). Leave room for frozen custard.

THE GREENMARKET CHEF

The popular upscale restaurant Gramercy Tavern is famous the world over for its seasonal, produce-driven menu. Their top purveyor—the Union Square Greenmarket—is a stone's throw away, at the northwest corner of Union Square (Broadway at East 17th Street). Executive chef Michael Anthony is uniquely positioned to take advantage of this beloved New York City culinary treasure. "It's one of the most precious resources this city has," says Anthony, who, along with his staff, visits the market four times a week to pick up the very best raw ingredients for his top-rated eatery. "It's where we get our inspiration."

In addition to waving to fellow chefs who shop the market, he catches up with the many farmers he's befriended over the years. "They're cultivating more than a business," Anthony says. "They're cultivating a community."

Anthony's typically dressed in civilian clothing when he hits the market, but shoppers often sense his passion as he inspects and buys unusual produce. "They'll ask me, 'How do I use that? What does that taste like?'"

At some restaurants greenmarket finds are scrawled on a chalkboard or highlighted on the menu as daily specials. Anthony likes to maintain a bit of drama. "We want people to bite into our food and ask, 'What is this? Where did this come from?'"

The food at Gramercy Tavern is seductively simple, letting the ingredients speak for themselves. "When a dish is shouting with the flavors [of] soft, seductive sweet potatoes, roasted sweet shallots, or the very best organically raised New York State chicken, we know we're doing our job right."

TOP GREENMARKET SNACKS

On Friday—Chef Michael Anthony's day off from Gramercy Tavern—you'll typically find him back at the greenmarket, shopping for his personal "VIP customers"—his family. "If I stay focused, I can get through in half an hour," he says. Still, there are some worthy distractions. He rarely escapes without downing a cup of cider or a drinkable yogurt from Ronnybrook Farms, and a few samples of toasty Martin's pretzels. Then there's the nut-flecked granola from Hawthorne Valley Farms. "I'm lucky if that makes it home."

AND FOR DESSERT . . .

Max Brenner: Chocolate by the Bald Man (✉ *841 Broadway, near 13th St.* ☎ *212/388–0030* ✛ *3:F4*). Sure, it's an international chain, but if you're looking for a major chocolate fix, you can count on this place to provide your poison. Max Brenner: Chocolate by the Bald Man is a Willy Wonka–esque chocolate emporium filled with college kids, families, and tourists—chocolate lovers, one and all. The extensive chocoholic menu boasts flavored chocolate beverages in custom-made sipping "hug mugs," chocolate fondues, cookies, cakes, brownies, and ice creams, even chocolate pizzas. If the Max Brenner scene isn't for you, check out the more sophisticated **City Bakery** (✉ *3 W. 18th St., between 5th and 6th Aves.* ☎ *212/366–1414* ✛ *3:E3*) a few blocks to the north and west, where you can sip gourmet cocoa as thick as mud and nosh on crème brûlée tartlets with chocolate crusts or bag some addictively salty pretzel croissants to go.

19

MIDTOWN WEST AND CHELSEA

Big is the buzz in Times Square and neighboring hoods, where neon-lighted billboards, towering skyscrapers, and Broadway theaters play starring roles. But watch out for restaurant rip-offs in this urban-theme-park environment.

It's true that tourist traps abound on the Great White Way, but fortunately you needn't head far from Times Square to score a stellar meal. Just move away from the bright lights and unrelenting foot traffic that clogs the area. On calmer side streets and in adjoining Hell's Kitchen there are excellent dining options for budget travelers and expense-account diners alike. Some of the best steak houses and Italian restaurants are here, and many eateries offer budget pretheater dinners and prix-fixe lunch menus to draw in new business.

But if the constant hustle and bustle unsettles your stomach, head south to Chelsea, a calmer neighborhood filled with art galleries and casual eateries. Chelsea may not be a white-hot dining destination, but you can eat well if you know where to go.

STEAK WITH STYLE

The design at **Quality Meats** (⊠ 57 W. 58th St., near 6th Ave. ☎ 212/371-7777 ✛ 4:D1), pictured above, is butcher-shop inspired, with wood, stainless steel, and white marble. Sit at the bar to peruse the extensive menu of wines and single-malt scotches. Then retire to the dining room for sophisticated riffs on steak-house classics like beef Wellington. Steak aficionados should know that Midtown has high-quality meats on every block. Here are more sure bets: **Ben Benson's** (⊠ 123 W. 52nd St., near 6th Ave. ☎ 212/581-8888 ✛ 4:D2) and **Uncle Jack's** (⊠ 440 9th Ave., at 35th St. ☎ 212/244-0005 ✛ 4:B6).

DINING IN TIMES SQUARE

There are plenty of chain eateries here that charge a premium for a substandard, rushed meal. But we've narrowed the field, selecting the best spots for a range of experiences and prices—from fun family dining to pretheater favorites.

Unlike the mostly kitschy theme restaurants that occupy Times Square, the sleek **Blue Fin** (⊠ *1567 Broadway, near 47th St.* ☎ *212/918–1400* ✢ *4:C3*) seafood restaurant is a refreshing departure. Watch the crowds go by from the corner glass bar or head upstairs.

Plates of fresh antipasti are displayed right as you walk into **Bond 45** (⊠ *154 W. 45th St., between 6th and 7th Aves.* ☎ *212/869–4545* ✢ *4:C4*). This Italian eatery, with a dark-wood bar and leather-backed booths, serves a variety of pizzas, pastas, and steaks. With a separate pretheater menu, this Theater District hot spot is an ideal option for dining and then dashing to your show of choice.

Ça Va (⊠ *310 W. 44th St., between 8th and 9th Aves.* ☎ *212/803–4545* ✢ *4:B4*) in the new InterContinental Hotel is chef Todd English's paean to French brasserie cuisine. There's a nice-looking bar with good wines by the glass, and hearty dishes like cassoulet, braised pork shank, and halibut with roasted Provençale vegetables.

For family-style fun, you can't miss the retro, 1950s-style **Ellen's Stardust Diner** (⊠ *1650 Broadway, at 51st St.* ☎ *212/956–5151* ✢ *4:C3*), complete with a singing waitstaff. Enjoy all-American classics such as meat loaf and chicken potpie while your waiters and waitresses serenade you with Broadway tunes.

Havana Central (⊠ *151 W. 45th St., between 6th and 7th Aves.* ☎ *212/398–7440*) is a great place for reasonably priced group dining and for sampling Cuban-Latino standards like garlicky chicken and well-seasoned skirt steak with a cucumber-and-mango salad. There's also a full menu of tropical-flavored mojitos, including coconut, blueberry, and passion fruit.

A mixed crowd of tourists, theatergoers, and thespians frequents **Joe Allen Restaurant** (⊠ *326 W. 46th St., between 8th and 9th Aves.* ☎ *212/581–6464* ✢ *4:B3*), a pretheater favorite. This casual yet classy restaurant serves reliable American cuisine. Don't fret about missing the show—the Broadway-knowledgeable staff will make sure you get to the theater in time for the opening number.

Toloache (⊠ *251 W. 50th St., between Broadway and 8th Ave.* ☎ *212/581–1818* ✢ *4:B3*), a festive Mexican cantina, is a top foodie destination for its fresh ceviches, guacamoles, and standout dishes like the Negra Modelo–braised brisket taco or the quesadilla with black truffle and *huitlacoche* (corn fungus).

AND FOR DESSERT . . .

Kyotofu (⊠ *705 9th Ave., near 48th St.* ☎ *212/974–6012* ✢ *4:A3*). Even if you're not crazy about tofu, the soy-based delights at this Japanese dessert bar will make you reconsider the merits of the soybean. Kyotofu's signature sweet tofu with Kuromitsu black sugar syrup is so creamy and delicious, you'd think it was a traditional panna cotta. The strawberry shortcake with strawberry sake sorbet and the warm miso chocolate cake with chocolate soybean ganache and green-tea cream are two more totally compelling favorites. Kyotofu's menu is full of intriguing options, so your best bet, on your first visit, is to go for the Kaiseki prix-fixe, a three-course tasting menu that enables you to try six different mini-desserts. Their menu changes seasonally, and it also includes savory brunch, lunch, and dinner options as well as an extensive sake and shochu cocktail list.

19

MIDTOWN EAST/UPPER EAST SIDE

Power brokers like to seal their deals over lunch on the East Side, so that means more than a few suits and ties at the restaurants during the day.

At night Midtown's streets are relatively quiet, but the restaurants are filled with expense-account diners celebrating their successes. Some of the most formal dining rooms and most expensive meals in town can be found here, at restaurants like the landmark **Four Seasons** and **L'Atelier de Joël Robuchon** or the **Modern.**

Farther uptown, the Upper East Side is jam-packed with pricey neighborhood eateries that cater to the area's well-heeled residents, but a few, more reasonable choices are cropping up. Long viewed as an enclave of the privileged, these neighborhoods have plenty of elegant restaurants that serve the society "ladies who lunch" and bankers looking forward to a steak and single-malt scotch at the end of the day. However, visitors to Museum Mile and 5th Avenue shopping areas need not be put off. Whether you're looking to celebrate a special occasion or just want to grab a quick bite, you're sure to find something here for almost any budget.

URBAN PICNIC

For a uniquely New York experience, take a picnic lunch to one of the outdoor plazas that line Park Avenue from 51st to 53rd streets and seat yourself alongside scores of local office workers. (For architecture buffs, the Mies van der Rohe–designed Seagram Building is at 375 Park Avenue, at 52nd Street.) First, pick up your wares at the **Market at Grand Central Terminal** (Main Concourse, East), a trusted resource for gourmet goods on-the-go. Your menu could include fresh-baked bread from **Corrado Bread & Pastry**, olives or prosciutto from **Ceriello Fine Foods**, and fresh mozzarella from **Murray's Cheese.**

MUSEUM MUNCHING

	SAVE	SPLURGE
Museum of Modern Art	**La Bonne Soupe** (✉ 48 W. 55th St., between 5th and 6th Aves. ☎ 212/586–7650 ✛ 4:E2) specials include a bowl of soup with bread, salad, a glass of wine, and dessert for $19.50.	The Modern's **Bar Room** (✉ 9 W. 53rd St., near 5th Ave. ☎ 212/333–1220 ✛ 4:D2) offers fare like tarte flambé, flatbread topped with bacon, onion, and crème fraîche.
Neue Galerie	**Pintaile's** (✉ 26 E. 91st St., at Madison Ave. ☎ 212/722–1967 ✛ 6:F5) pizza has a thin crust and toppings like wild mushrooms and chorizo.	**Café Sabarsky** (✉ 1048 5th Ave., near 86th St. ☎ 212/288–0665 ✛ 6:E6) entices visitors with hearty fare, but desserts are the real draw.
Metropolitan Museum of Art	Belgian chain **Le Pain Quotidien** (✉ 1131 Madison Ave., between 84th and 85th Sts. ☎ 212/327–4900 ✛ 5:F1) has gourmet light fare, like sandwiches, and salads.	**E.A.T.** (✉ 1064 Madison Ave., between 80th and 81st Sts. ☎ 212/772–0022 ✛ 5:F2), Eli Zabar's upscale diner, is pricey, but devotees return for excellent food.
Museum of Art and Design	**AQ Café** (✉ 1800 Broadway, at Columbus Circle ☎ 212/462–0005) serves Swedish-inspired food like meatballs, herring, and house-cured gravlax, plus desserts.	The top floor of the museum houses **Robert** @ Mad (✉ 2 Columbus Circle ☎ 212/299–7730), with stellar views and a menu of treats like striped bass sashimi.

FORAGING IN CENTRAL PARK

There are plenty of pushcarts offering hot dogs and sodas, but if you're looking to soak up Central Park's magical ambience in an elegant setting, head for the **Central Park Boathouse Restaurant** (✉ E. 72nd St. at Park Dr. N ☎ 212/517–2233 ✛ 5:E3), which overlooks the gondola lake. There you can relax on the outdoor deck with a glass of wine and a cheese plate, or go for a more formal meal inside the restaurant. In warmer months the restaurant can get crowded: go for a late lunch or early-evening cocktail.

AND FOR DESSERT . . .

Junior's (✉ 107 E. 42nd St., Grand Central Terminal's Lower Dining Concourse ☎ 212/983–5257 ✛ 4:F4). The Grand Central Dining Concourse is not your typical food court—it contains outposts of some of the city's most popular edibles, including Junior's, a favorite of cheesecake lovers. This cheesecake is dense and moist. You can get it with cherries, strawberries, or other fruit on top, or you can have it with a swirl of raspberry, but the plain cheesecake is one of the best things about New York City. There's also a wonderful lemon coconut "cheesecake" that combines traditional cheesecake with lemon chiffon cake and lemon custard cream. If you want more than dessert, the restaurant serves a full sit-down menu of soups, sandwiches, and burgers, and there's another bakery counter on the main level of Grand Central near Track 36.

19

UPPER WEST SIDE/HARLEM

Anchoring the dining experience in this section of town are the high-end restaurants at the Time Warner Center, including renowned Per Se. Head farther uptown for cheaper eats and a burgeoning gourmet dining scene.

Dining room at Per Se in the Time Warner Center.

With Lincoln Center theatergoers, hungry shoppers, and visitors to Central Park nearby, chefs are finally waking up to the captive built-in audience of tourists and locals alike. The main avenues are indeed lined with restaurants, but until recently many of them have been mediocre. Now the better-known destination-dining spots beyond the Time Warner Center—among them **Jean Georges**, **Picholine**, **Telepan**, and **Dovetail**—have been joined by newcomers like **Salumeria Rossi**, **Fatty Crab**, and **Ed's Chowder**, all second or third restaurants from well-known chefs. Brunch is still a good bet, too. The flaky scones and fluffy omelets at **Sarabeth's**, not to mention blintzes and bagels at **Barney Greengrass**, are worth seeking out. For more adventurous eating, head up to Harlem for the city's best southern cooking.

HIDDEN GEM

Fairway Supermarket is a neighborhood institution, with a reputation for great prices on gourmet products—and shopping-cart jockeying down the narrow aisles. Upstairs is the respite of **Fairway Café** (⊠ 2127 Broadway, between 74th and 75th Sts. ☎ 212/944–9555 ⊹ 5:A3), a large, brick-walled room with windows overlooking Broadway. You can get a pastry and coffee to go, but there's a full menu of fairly priced entrées as well. The place is run by Mitchell London, who's known for his juicy, well-marbled steaks.

WHAT'S HOT IN HARLEM

Visitors in decades past may remember Harlem as an area scarred by crime and poverty. But times have changed: the Harlem of today is a vibrant community with excellent restaurants of all stripes. The bottom line? Harlem's ethnic eats are worth the trip.

Here are our top picks for savoring the multicultural flavor of the neighborhood:

Miss Mamie's Spoonbread Too (⊠ *366 W. 110th St., near Manhattan Ave.* ☎ *212/865–6744* ✥ *6:B2*) is a much-loved Southern spot that's known for its friendly staff, fried chicken, grits, and corn bread.

Native (⊠ *161 Lenox Ave., at 118th St.* ☎ *212/665–2525* ✥ *6:C1*) is a mildly Caribbean restaurant serving flavorful rice bowls and entrées that span a broad range of cuisines. With curry chicken, smoked salmon linguine, and Moroccan fried chicken with collard greens and mashed potatoes, the menu is all over the map but still delicious.

Sylvia's (⊠ *328 Lenox Ave., near 127th St.* ☎ *212/996–0660* ✥ *6:D1*) is a Harlem mainstay; they've been serving soul-food favorites like smothered chicken, barbecue ribs, collard greens, and mashed potatoes to locals, tourists, and college students since 1962.

For a more laidback soul food experience, try **Melba's** (⊠ *300 West 114th St. at 8th Ave.* ☎ *212/864–0660* ✥ *6:C1*) for excellent chicken and waffles; there's music some nights, too.

AND FOR DESSERT . . .

Levain Bakery (⊠ *167 W. 74th St., near Amsterdam Ave.* ☎ *212/874–6080* ✥ *5:B3*). A big cookie for the big city. Completely unpretentious and utterly delicious, Levain's cookies are rich and hefty. In fact, they clock in at 6 ounces each! Choose from the chocolate-chip walnut, dark-chocolate chocolate chip, dark-chocolate peanut-butter chip, or oatmeal raisin. Batches are baked fresh daily, and they taste best when they're warm and melty right out of the oven, so it's definitely worth seeking out this small basement bakery for a cookie craving. Levain also bakes artisanal breads, including banana chocolate chip and pumpkin ginger spice, sour cream coffee cake, chocolate-chip and cinnamon brioche, sourdough rolls stuffed with Valrhona chocolate, blueberry muffins, a variety of scones, and bomboloncini—their unique jelly doughnuts.

19

RESTAURANT REVIEWS

Listed alphabetically within neighborhoods.

LOWER MANHATTAN

FINANCIAL DISTRICT

Post-9/11 development and attractive pricing have meant thousands of new residents in Lower Manhattan, fueling an up-and-coming—yet still slow-moving—neighborhood scene. The most visible changes? Restaurants in and around the Financial District no longer adhere to banker's hours, and formal dining rooms have been outnumbered by casual cafés and wine bars. On the pedestrian-only Stone Street, throngs of young professionals gather for after-work drinks and dinner at nearby bistros, oyster bars, and steak houses.

$$
ITALIAN
☼
✕**Adrienne's Pizza Bar.** They don't do slices, but this local lunch favorite on restaurant-packed Stone Street is the place for salads and shareables like the broccoli rabe-and-sausage pie. $ *Average main: $17* ✉ *54 Stone St., near Hanover Sq., Financial District* ☎ *212/248-3838* ⊕ *www.adriennespizzabar.com* Ⓜ *R to Whitehall St.* ✛ *1:E4.*

$$$$
STEAKHOUSE
✕**Delmonico's.** The oldest continually operating restaurant in New York City (it opened in 1837), austere Delmonico's is steeped in cultural, political, and culinary history. Lobster Newburg and Baked Alaska were invented here—and are still served. Inside the stately mahogany-panel dining room, tuck into the classic Delmonico's steak, a 20-ounce boneless rib eye smothered with frizzled onions, and don't forget to order creamed spinach on the side. The cheesy spaetzle with pancetta is also sinfully sublime. The dining room gets busy early with an after-work Wall Street crowd, making reservations essential. $ *Average main: $37* ✉ *56 Beaver St., at William St., Financial District* ☎ *212/509-1144* ⊕ *www.delmonicosny.com* ⌖ *Reservations essential* ☽ *Closed Sun. No lunch Sat.* Ⓜ *2, 3 to Wall St.; R to Whitehall St./South Ferry; 4, 5 to Bowling Green* ✛ *1:D4.*

$
CAFÉ
✕**Financier Patisserie.** On the cobblestone pedestrian street that has become the Financial District's restaurant row, this charming patisserie serves excellent pastries and delicious savory foods, like mushroom bisque, salads, and hot or cold sandwiches (we have cravings for the panini pressed with prosciutto, fig jam, mascarpone, and arugula). After lunch, relax with a cappuccino and a *financier* (almond tea cake), or an elegant pastry. In warm weather, perch at an outdoor table and watch Manhattanites buzz by. There are locations all over town. $ *Average main: $7* ✉ *62 Stone St., between Mill La. and Hanover Sq., Lower Manhattan* ☎ *212/344-5600* ⊕ *www.financierpastries.com* ⌖ *Reservations not accepted* ☽ *Closed Sun. No dinner* Ⓜ *2, 3 to Wall St.; 4, 5 to Bowling Green* ✛ *1:E4.*

$$$
STEAKHOUSE
✕**Harry's Café and Steak.** Its noise-dampening acoustics and maze of underground nooks combine to make Harry's Steak—the fine-dining half of the restaurant (Harry's Café is more casual, but the menu is the same)—one of the city's most intimate steak houses. Settle in to one of the leather booths and start with a classic shrimp cocktail or the tomato

trio, starring thick beefsteak slices topped with bacon and blue cheese, mozzarella and basil, and shaved onion with ranch dressing. The star attraction—prime aged porterhouse for two—is nicely encrusted with sea salt and a good match for buttery mashed potatoes infused with sweet roasted shallots and thick steak sauce spooned from Mason jars. Weekend brunch is popular, too. ⑤ *Average main: $33* ✉ *1 Hanover Sq., between Stone and Pearl Sts., Financial District* ☎ *212/785–9200* ⊕ *www.harrysnyc.com* ⌕ *Reservations essential* ☉ *Closed Sun.* Ⓜ *4, 5 to Bowling Green; 2, 3 to Wall St.* ✛ *1:E4.*

$$$$ ✕ **SHO Shaun Hergatt.** This restaurant in the Setai complex downtown
MODERN befits the riches of nearby Wall Street, and though it launched at the
AMERICAN height of the 2008 recession, the decor screams all-out extravagance. After passing through a dramatic corridor composed of glass-encased wine bottles, diners enter a sprawling series of rooms adorned with framed silver rings, striated wood walls, and luxurious Asian-inspired fabrics. Australian chef Shaun Hergatt, often visible in the open kitchen, brings a light touch to the upscale cuisine in dishes like peekytoe crab with galangal gelée and sea urchin, and an ingot of three-day short rib over a rich parsnip puree that looks—and tastes—like a savory candy bar. Dinner is prix-fixe only; there are à la carte options at lunch. ⑤ *Average main: $85* ✉ *40 Broad St., the Setai, 2nd level, Financial District* ☎ *212/809–3993* ⊕ *www.shoshaunhergatt.com* ⌕ *Reservations essential* Ⓜ *R to Rector St., 2, 3, 4, 5 to Wall St. or J, M, Z to Broad St.* ✛ *1:D4.*

$ ✕ **Ulysses'.** Nestled alongside skyscrapers and the towering New York
AMERICAN Stock Exchange, Stone Street is a two-block restaurant oasis that feels more like a village than the center of the financial universe. After the market closes, Wall Streeters head to Ulysses', a popular pub with 19 beers on tap and more than 50 bottled beers. ⑤ *Average main: $8.50* ✉ *95 Pearl St., near Hanover Sq., Financial District* ☎ *212/482–0400* ⊕ *www.ulyssesfolkhouse.com* Ⓜ *4, 5 to Bowling Green* ✛ *1:E4.*

19

TRIBECA

TriBeCa still holds an air of exclusivity, though glamorous dining rooms in converted warehouses have been joined by more casual spots with later hours. This is a great neighborhood to stop for a meal on your way to Lower Manhattan's many attractions.

$$$ ✕ **Blaue Gans.** Chef Kurt Gutenbruner, alone at the top of the Austrian
AUSTRIAN food scene in New York, runs this sprawling brasserie like an all-day
☺ clubhouse. Pop in for a late morning or early afternoon snack—the coffee comes topped with schlag, the donuts filled with apricot jam. Or swing by in the evening for sausage, schnitzel, and beer at the bar. ⑤ *Average main: $25* ✉ *139 Duane St., near West Broadway, TriBeCa* ☎ *212/571–8880* ⊕ *www.kg-ny.com* Ⓜ *1, 2, 3, A, C to Chambers St.* ✛ *1:C1.*

$ ✕ **Bubby's.** Neighborhood crowds clamoring for coffee and freshly
AMERICAN squeezed juice line up for brunch at this TriBeCa mainstay, but Bub-
☺ by's is good for lunch and dinner, too if you're in the mood for eclectic comfort food like mac and cheese or fried chicken. The dining room is homey and comfortable, with big windows; in summer, patrons sit at tables outside with their dogs. Brunch options include just about

everything, including homemade granola, sour-cream pancakes with bananas and strawberries, and *huevos rancheros* with guacamole and grits. ⑤ *Average main: $17* ✉ *120 Hudson St., at N. Moore St., TriBeCa* ☎ *212/219–0666* ⊕ *www.bubbys.com* Ⓜ *1 to Franklin St.* ✛ *1:C1.*

$$$ ✕ **Capsouto Frères.** If you're looking for an elegant atmosphere, try Cap-
FRENCH   souto Frères, a landmark French bistro that makes the city's best sweet and savory soufflés. We love the praline soufflé with hazelnut crème anglaise. ⑤ *Average main: $26* ✉ *451 Washington St., near Watts St., TriBeCa* ☎ *212/966–4900* ⊕ *www.capsoutofreres.com* ⌂ *Reservations essential* Ⓜ *1 to Canal St.* ✛ *2:B4.*

$$$$ ✕ **Corton.** Restaurateur Drew Nieporent transformed the former Mon-
FRENCH   trachet space into a spare, elegant dining room. It's the perfect stage for young whiz-kid chef Paul Liebrandt's understated, mildly experi-mental cuisine. The walls are decorated with subtle white trompe-l'oeil designs of cherry blossoms and birds, but the real adornment is on the plate, where Liebrandt transports diners with dishes like his "from the garden" composition: an assemblage of nearly 20 vegetable com-ponents that redefines what produce can do. Heirloom eggs are pre-sented at the table in a basket, then spirited back to the kitchen for a slow poach before being served with trumpet mushrooms and serrano gelée. Desserts include chocolate tart with grapefruit and hazelnuts. The well-curated wine list has a cost-conscious selection of "country French" bottles. ⑤ *Average main: $85* ✉ *239 W. Broadway, between Walker and White Sts., TriBeCa* ☎ *212/219–2777* ⊕ *www.cortonnyc. com* ⌂ *Reservations essential* ♥ *Closed Sun. No lunch* Ⓜ *1 to Franklin St., A, C, E to Canal St.* ✛ *2:D5.*

$$$ ✕ **The Harrison.** It's been more than a decade since Jimmy Bradley opened
AMERICAN   the Harrison, following his success with the Red Cat in Chelsea, but it's still a quintessential neighborhood eatery. The warm, woody room serves as a relaxed backdrop for the seasonal American food, like English-cut lamb loin with baby carrots and fennel and malt-vinegar mayo. Desserts, including an ice cream–brownie sandwich with Saz-erac caramel, are at once accessible and sophisticated. ⑤ *Average main: $27* ✉ *355 Greenwich St., at Harrison St., TriBeCa* ☎ *212/274–9310* ⊕ *www.theharrison.com* ⌂ *Reservations essential* ♥ *No lunch* Ⓜ *1 to Franklin St.* ✛ *2:C6.*

$ ✕ **Kitchenette.** This small, comfy restaurant lives up to its name with
AMERICAN   tables so close together, you're likely to make new friends. Indeed,
ⓒ   the dining room pretty much feels like a breakfast nook, and the food tastes like your mom made it—provided she's a great cook. There are no frills, just solid cooking, friendly service, and a long line at peak times. At brunch don't miss the blackberry-cherry pancakes or the baked vanilla brûlée French toast. There's also an outpost uptown, in Harlem (✛ *6:A1*) ⑤ *Average main: $15* ✉ *156 Chambers St., near Greenwich St., TriBeCa* ☎ *212/267–6740* ⊕ *www.kitchenetterestaurant.com* Ⓜ *1, 2, 3, A, C to Chambers St.* ✛ *1:C2.*

$$ ✕ **Locanda Verde.** Chef Andrew Carmellini, an acolyte of Daniel Boulud,
ITALIAN   has definitely made a name for himself in New York City with this Rob-ert De Niro–backed restaurant, and then with the Dutch in SoHo. The space at Locanda Verde is warm and welcoming, with accents of brick

and wood and large windows that open to the street, weather permitting, while the menu is full of inspired Italian comfort food that hits the mark, especially the small plates like blue crab crostino with jalapeños and the mound of sheep's-milk ricotta scattered with sea salt and herbs that diners reminisce about. Several draft beers, along with more than a dozen wines by the glass, make an already hopping bar scene even more of a draw. ⑤ *Average main: $23.50* ✉ *377 Greenwich St., at N. Moore St., TriBeCa* ☎ *212/925–3797* ⊕ *www.locandaverdenyc.com* ⌑ *Reservations essential* Ⓜ *1 to Franklin St.* ✛ *1:B1*.

$$$
AMERICAN

✗ **Marc Forgione.** Chef Marc Forgione has restaurant success in his blood (his father was one of the New York food scene megastars with his 1980s restaurant, An American Place), but the son more than holds his own at this lovely neighborhood restaurant that continues to attract crowds for the ambitious, creative New American cuisine. The menu changes with the whims of the chef and the seasonal availability of produce, but whatever you order will be bold, flavorful, and inventive without a hint of preciousness. The bar hops with a blend of neighborhood locals and Wall Street boys loosening their ties after work, and almost every table feels like a cozy corner regardless of the right angles surrounding it. Meat dishes are excellent and well prepared but Forgione has a special way with seafood. His chili lobster appetizer, a take on a dish you'll find all over Asia, comes with Texas toast for mopping up the spicy, buttery sauce. Tartare (it could be kingfish, hamachi, or salmon, depending on the day) is accented with avocado in a pool of sweet, soy-lashed sauce, all accompanied by housemade chips. ⑤ *Average main: $29.50* ✉ *134 Reade St., between Hudson and Greenwich Sts., TriBeCa* ☎ *212/941–9401* ⊕ *www.marcforgione.com* ⌑ *Reservations essential* � *No lunch* Ⓜ *1, 2, 3 to Chambers St.* ✛ *1:C1*.

$$$
JAPANESE

✗ **Nobu.** At this huge, bustling TriBeCa dining room (or its sister location uptown), you might just spot a celeb or two. New York's most famous Japanese restaurant has gained a lot of competition in recent years, but this is still the destination for the innovative Japanese cuisine Nobu Matsuhisa made famous (even if the chef himself is rarely in attendance these days). Dishes like fresh yellowtail sashimi with jalapeño, rock-shrimp tempura, or miso-marinated Chilean sea bass continue to draw huge crowds. Put yourself in the hands of the chef by ordering the tasting menu, the *omakase*, specify how much you want to spend, and let the kitchen do the rest. (Can't get reservations? Try your luck at the first-come, first-served **Nobu Next Door** (literally next door), with a similar menu plus a sushi bar. There's also an option in Midtown: Nobu Fifty-Seven (✛ *4:D1*) ⑤ *Average main: $32* ✉ *105 Hudson St., at Franklin St., TriBeCa* ☎ *212/219–0500* ⊕ *www. myriadrestaurantgroup.com* ⌑ *Reservations essential* ☽ *No lunch weekends* Ⓜ *1 to Franklin St.* ✛ *1:B1*.

$$$
SEAFOOD
Fodor's Choice
★

✗ **North End Grill.** The movers and shakers who frequent this handsome, seafood-heavy restaurant in the Financial District are in good hands. Floyd Cardoz, who made a name for himself at the now-shuttered elevated Indian eatery, Tabla, mans the stoves, churning out inspired fare like memorable grilled octopus, pumpkin soup bobbing with crab, and succulent whole fish (for two). Carnivores can dig into a juicy Berkshire

19

pork chop or lamb loin topped with a minty chickpea puree. Order a Scotch cocktail and you'll fit right in with the Wall Street heavy hitters at the next table. ⑤ *Average main: $26 ⊠ 104 North End Ave., at Murray St., Financial District* ☎ *646/747–1600* ⊕ *www.northendgrillnyc.com* Ⓜ *1, 2, 3 to Chambers St.; E to World Trade Center* ✛ *1:A2.*

$$$
BISTRO
☾
✕**Odeon.** New Yorkers change hangouts faster than they can press speed-dial, but this spot has managed to maintain its quality and flair for more than 25 years. The neo–art-deco room is still packed nightly with revelers and the pleasant service and well-chosen wine list are always in style. The bistro-menu highlights include *frisée aux lardons* (bacon-enhanced frisée salad) with poached farm egg, grilled New York strip steak, and slow-cooked cod with baby leeks and fennel confit. ⑤ *Average main: $28 ⊠ 145 West Broadway, between Duane and Thomas Sts., TriBeCa* ☎ *212/233–0507* ⊕ *www.theodeonrestaurant. com* Ⓜ *1, 2, 3, A, C to Chambers St.* ✛ *2:D6.*

SOHO, NOLITA, LITTLE ITALY, AND CHINATOWN

CHINATOWN

Chinatown beckons adventurous diners with restaurants representing numerous regional cuisines of China, including Cantonese-, Szechuan-, Hunan-, Fujian-, Shanghai-, and Hong Kong–style cooking. Malaysian and Vietnamese restaurants also have taken root here, and the neighborhood continues to grow rapidly, encroaching into what was Little Italy.

$
SHANGHAINESE
✕**456 Shanghai Cuisine.** Come to this Chintown eatery for above-average Chinese fare, such as General Tsao's chicken, pork buns, and cold sesame noodles, but do yourself a favor and ask for an order of soup dumplings (*xiao long bao*) the second you sit down. You won't regret it. The dumplings, doughy and thin on the outside, encase morsels of crab swimming in a bold pork-y broth, and are truly a wonder of the culinary world—456 does them as good as (or better than) anyone in the city. ⑤ *Average main: $14 ⊠ 69 Mott St., between Canal and Bayard Sts., Chinatown* ☎ *212/964–0003* Ⓜ *J, N, Q, J to Canal St.* ✛ *2:F5.*

$
CHINESE
☾
✕**Great New York Noodletown.** Although the soups and noodles are unbeatable at this no-frills restaurant, what you should really order are the window decorations—the hanging lacquered ducks and roasted pork, which are listed on a simple board hung on the wall and superb served with pungent garlic-and-ginger sauce on the side. Seasonal specialties like duck with flowering chives and salt-baked soft-shell crabs are excellent. So is the *congee*, or rice porridge, available with any number of garnishes. Solo diners may end up at a communal table. Noodletown is open late—till 4 am on Friday and Saturday. ⑤ *Average main: $10 ⊠ 28 Bowery, at Bayard St., Chinatown* ☎ *212/349–0923* ▭ *No credit cards* Ⓜ *6, J, M, Z to Canal St.; B, D to Grand St.* ✛ *2:F5.*

$
CHINESE
☾
✕**Jing Fong.** On weekend mornings people pack this vast dim sum palace so be prepared to wait. Once your number is called you'll take the escalator up to the carnivalesque second-floor dining room, where servers push carts of steamed dumplings, barbecue pork buns, and shrimp balls. For adventurous eaters, there's chicken feet, tripe, and snails. Arrive early for the best selection, and save room for mango

pudding. ⑤ *Average main: $12* ✉ *20 Elizabeth St., 2nd fl., between Bayard and Canal Sts., Chinatown* ☎ *212/964–5256* Ⓜ *6, J, M, N, Q, R, Z to Canal St.* ✛ *2:F5.*

$ ✗ **Joe's Shanghai.** Joe opened his first Shanghai restaurant in Queens in
CHINESE 1995 but, buoyed by the accolades accorded his steamed soup dump-
Ⓒ lings—filled with a rich, fragrant broth and ground pork or pork-crab-
meat mixture—several Manhattan outposts soon followed. The trick
is to take a bite of the dumpling and slurp out the soup, then eat the
rest. There's almost always a wait, but the line moves fast. The soup
dumplings are a must, but you can fill out your order from the extensive
menu. There's another Joe's Shanghai in Midtown West (✉ *24 W. 56th
St., between 5th and 6th aves.* ✛ *4:E2; credit cards accepted).* ⑤ *Average main: $16* ✉ *9 Pell St., between the Bowery and Mott St., Chi-
natown* ☎ *212/233–8888* ⊕ *www.joeshanghairestaurants.com* ▭ *No
credit cards* Ⓜ *6, J, M, N, Q, R, Z to Canal St.* ✛ *2:F5.*

$ ✗ **New Malaysia.** For Southeast Asian favorites like roti flatbread with
MALAYSIAN curry and delicious red-bean and coconut-milk drinks, you can't beat
New Malaysia. ⑤ *Average main: $13* ✉ *48 Bowery, near Canal St.,
Chinatown* ☎ *212/964–0284* Ⓜ *B, D to Grand St.* ✛ *2:G5.*

$$ ✗ **Peking Duck House.** This Chinatown institution is the place to go in
CHINESE New York for authentic Peking duck. Although the restaurant offers
a full Chinese menu, everyone—and we mean everyone—orders the
duck. Begin, as most tables do, with an order of Shanghai soup dump-
lings, then move on to the bird. It's carved table-side with plenty of
fanfare—crisp burnished skin separated from moist flesh. Roll up the
duck, with hoisin and scallions, in tender steamed pancakes. The menu
at the Midtown East location (✉ *236 E. 53rd Street* ✛ *4:G2) is a bit
pricier.* ⑤ *Average main: $18* ✉ *28 Mott St., at Mosco St., Chinatown*
☎ *212/227–1810* ⊕ *www.pekingduckhousenyc.com* Ⓜ *6, J, M, N, Q,
R, Z to Canal St.* ✛ *2:F5.*

$ ✗ **Tasty Hand-Pulled Noodles.** The name says it all. And it doesn't lie. The
CHINESE open kitchen at this salt-of-the-earth Chinatown restaurant (located on
the charming Doyer Street), means you can watch the noodle slinger
in action while awaiting your bowl of, um, tasty hand-pulled noodles.
Just choose your ingredients—beef, pork, oxtail, eel, chicken, lamb, or
shrimp, among others—and prepare to eat the most delicious bowl of
$5 noodles since that last trip to Shanghai. ⑤ *Average main: $5* ✉ *1
Doyer St., at Bowery, Chinatown* ☎ *212/791–1817* ▭ *No credit cards*
Ⓜ *6, J, M, N, Q, R, W, Z to Canal St.* ✛ *2:F6.*

$ ✗ **Vanessa's Dumpling House.** One of the best deals in Chinatown can
CHINESE be found here, where sizzling pork-and-chive dumplings are four for a
buck. ⑤ *Average main: $8* ✉ *118 Eldridge St., near Broome St., China-
town* ☎ *212/625–8008* ✍ *Reservations not accepted* ▭ *No credit cards*
Ⓜ *B, D to Grand St.* ✛ *2:G4.*

$ ✗ **Xe Lua.** A good Vietnamese restaurant in Manhattan is hard to find,
VIETNAMESE which is why you should seek out Xe Lua, in Chinatown just below Little
Italy. Quick service and the marathon-length menu should satisfy any
palate, but the real standouts are the clay-pot dishes: cooked and served
in—you guessed it—a clay pot, the pork, chicken, veggies, or whatever
you order become slightly caramelized, giving a subtle sweetness to the

19

dish. The *pho* (the soupy national dish of Vietnam) is also a good bet, as the broth seems to have a bolder taste here than at other places. ⑤ *Average main: $11* ✉ *86 Mulberry St., between Canal and Bayard Sts., Chinatown* ☎ *212/577–8887* Ⓜ *N, Q, R, 6 to Canal St.* ✛ *2:F5.*

LITTLE ITALY

Little Italy is, these days, more about tourist trap pasta factories that just aren't very good. Don't despair, though, there is seriously good Italian food to be found in just about every neighborhood in Manhattan . . . and Brooklyn, too, of course. Right near by, in NoLita, check out Torrisi's and Rubirosa for some of the best Italian around.

NOLITA

In NoLIta, SoHo's trendy next-door neighborhood of indie boutiques and restaurants, the spirit of old SoHo prevails. Modest eateries are squeezed between boutiques featuring products from up-and-coming designers.

$ ╳**Café Gitane.** Specializing in simple salads and sandwiches, this French-FRENCH Moroccan café draws models and model-gazers to its rather cramped NoLIta location (which is cash-only) and the larger branch on the far edge of the West Village. The clientele and the waitstaff seem to have wandered in fresh off the runway. The scene is quietest in the morning, when there are flaky croissants and big bowls of café au lait. ⑤ *Average main: $14* ✉ *242 Mott St., near Prince St., NoLIta* ☎ *212/334–9552* ⊕ *www.cafegitanenyc.com* ⚰ *Reservations not accepted* ▭ *No credit cards* Ⓜ *6 to Spring St., N, R, W to Prince St.* ✛ *2:F3* ⑤ *Average main: $14* ✉ *Jane Hotel, 113 Jane St., near West St., Greenwich Village* ☎ *212/334–9552* Ⓜ *A, C, E, L to 14th St.–8th Ave.* ✛ *3:B5.*

$ ╳**Café Habana.** The Mexican-style grilled corn, liberally sprinkled with ECLECTIC chili powder, lime, and cotija cheese is undoubtedly worth getting your ☾ hands dirty at this hip luncheonette counter. Follow up with a classic Cuban sandwich (roast pork, ham, Swiss cheese, pickles, and chipotle mayo), fish tacos, or one of the innovative salads. Be prepared for a wait at lunchtime or on weekend afternoons. ⑤ *Average main: $12* ✉ *17 Prince St., at Elizabeth St., NoLIta* ☎ *212/625–2001* ⊕ *www. cafehabana.com* ⚰ *Reservations not accepted* Ⓜ *B, D, F, M to Broadway–Lafayette St.* ✛ *2:F3.*

$$ ╳**Emporio.** In a neighborhood where the long, boutique-lined blocks can ITALIAN sometimes feel deserted after dark, Emporio is a chic, welcoming hangout Fodor'sChoice with warmth to spare. The brick-lined front room is a gathering spot for ★ happy hour at the bar, where you'll find an appetizing selection of free small bites like frittata, white-bean salad, and ham-and-spinach *tramez-zini* (finger sandwiches). The centerpiece of the large, skylighted back room is a wood-fired oven that turns out crisp, thin-crusted pizzas topped with quality ingredients like prosciutto, buffalo mozzarella, and arugula. Service is solicitous but not speedy, so you can linger over a bottle of wine from the copious selection. House-made pastas like chewy *garganelli* with pork sausage and house-made *ragu*, and entrées like whole roasted fish with grilled lemon, are also excellent options. ⑤ *Average main: $18* ✉ *231 Mott St., between Prince and Spring Sts., NoLIta* ☎ *212/966–1234* Ⓜ *B, D, F, M, A, C, E to W. 4th St., 6 to Bleecker St.* ✛ *2:F3.*

$$ ✕ **La Esquina.** Anchoring a downtown corner under a bright neon sign,
MEXICAN La Esquina looks like nothing more than a fast-food taqueria, with
cheap tacos sold to-go until 2 in the morning. Just around the corner,
though, is a modestly priced café serving those same tacos along with
more ambitious fare like chiles rellenos (stuffed peppers) and *carne
asada* (grilled meat). The real hipster draw, however, is hidden from
sight: the basement brasserie, like a Mexican speakeasy, is accessible by
reservation only, through an unmarked door just inside the ground-floor
taqueria. Once inside, you'll discover a buzzy subterranean scene with
pretty people drinking potent margaritas, dining on upscale Mexican
fare. Prices downstairs are high, but portions are large. $ *Average main:*
$18 ✉ *106 Kenmare, between Cleveland Pl. and Lafayette St., NoLIta*
☎ *646/613–7100* ⊕ *esquinanyc.com/* Ⓜ *6 to Spring St.* ✛ *2:F4.*

$ ✕ **Lombardi's Pizza.** Brick walls, red-and-white checkered tablecloths,
PIZZA and the aroma of thin-crust pies emerging from the coal oven set the
☺ mood for dining on some of the best pizza in Manhattan. Lombardi's
has served pizza since 1905 (though not in the same location), and busi-
ness doesn't seem to have died down a bit. The mozzarella is always
fresh, resulting in an almost greaseless slice, and the toppings, such as
meatballs, pancetta, or imported anchovies, are also top quality. The
clam pizza, with freshly shucked clams, garlic oil, pecorino-Romano
cheese, and parsley, is well known among aficionados. $ *Average main:*
$16 ✉ *32 Spring St., at Mott St., NoLIta* ☎ *212/941–7994* ⊕ *www.*
firstpizza.com ▬ *No credit cards* Ⓜ *6 to Spring St.; B, D, F, M to Broad-*
way–Lafayette ✛ *2:F4.*

$$$ ✕ **Peasant.** The crowd at this rustic restaurant is stylishly urban. Inspired
ITALIAN by the proverbial "peasant" cuisine where meals were prepared in the
kitchen hearth, chef-owner Frank DeCarlo cooks all of his wonderful food in a bank of wood- or charcoal-burning ovens, from which
the heady aroma of garlic perfumes the room. Don't fill up on the
crusty bread and fresh ricotta or you'll miss out on flavorful Italian
fare like sizzling sardines that arrive in terra-cotta pots, or spit-roasted
leg of lamb with bitter *trevisano* lettuce and polenta. $ *Average main:*
$24.50 ✉ *194 Elizabeth St., between Spring and Prince Sts., NoLIta*
☎ *212/965–9511* ⊕ *www.peasantnyc.com* ✍ *Reservations essential*
☽ *Closed Mon. No lunch* Ⓜ *6 to Spring St.; R to Prince St.* ✛ *2:F3.*

$$$ ✕ **Public.** To start with, the space here is complex and sophisticated,
ECLECTIC with soaring ceilings and whitewashed brick walls, skylights, fireplaces,
three dining areas, and a vast bar. You've come for the food, though,
and you won't be disappointed. The menu flaunts its nonconformity,
and dishes like Australian barramundi fish, served with vanilla-celeriac
puree and braised garlic greens, demonstrates a light yet adventurous
touch. Brunch at Public is a local favorite, with exotic dishes like coco-
nut pancakes topped with fresh ricotta, mango, and lime syrup, and
a juicy venison burger. Standout desserts include a chocolate mousse
with tahini ice cream and sesame candy. $ *Average main: $25* ✉ *210*
Elizabeth St., between Prince and Spring Sts., NoLIta ☎ *212/343–7011*
⊕ *www.public-nyc.com* ☽ *No lunch weekdays* Ⓜ *6 to Spring St.; N, R*
to Prince St.; J, M to Bowery ✛ *2:F3.*

19

$$ ✕**Rubirosa.** Named for a jet-setting Dominican playboy, this NoLIta
ITALIAN restaurant is Latin and lascivious in name only. Owner Angelo "A. J."
Pappalardo has created an exciting Italian-American eatery that locals
have shown an insatiable appetite for (so be prepared to wait). The
kitchen isn't trying to reinvent anything here—just serve high-quality
classic Italian dishes. And that's exactly what they do so well: from
pasta with red sauce or a fork-tender veal chop Milanese to the thin-
crust pizza—the recipe for the last comes from Mr. Pappalardo's par-
ents, who have run the popular Staten Island pizza joint, Joe & Pat's,
since anyone can remember. You don't have to be a jet-setter or a play-
boy to love this place. Just come hungry. $ *Average main: $17* ✉ *235
Mulberry St., between Prince and Spring Sts., NoLIta* ☎ *212/965–0500*
Ⓜ *6 to Spring St.* ✚ *2:F3.*

$$$ ✕**Torrisi Italian Specialties.** Italian-American cuisine is back, and this hot
ITALIAN spot is helping bring locals back to Mulberry, a street otherwise flanked
Fodor's Choice by schlocky, mediocre Italian restaurants that have long attracted tour-
★ ists. Run by chefs Mario Carbone and Rich Torrisi (both of whom have
logged time in the kitchens of some of the city's most lauded Italian
eateries), this 25-seat restaurant isn't easy to get into, so plan ahead and
reserve online or by telephone for the nightly $65 seven-course, prix-
fixe dinner or for the decadent 20-course meal (for $125). Whatever the
case, come hungry, as you may be feasting on Italian-American staples
like devil's chicken, the crunchy pork chop, or spaghetti with clams.
If you want something less elaborate, head next door to Torrisi spin-
off, Parm, for great Italian-accented sandwiches. $ *Average main: $65*
✉ *250 Mulberry St., near Prince St., NoLIta* ☎ *212/965–0955* ⊕ *www.
torrisinyc.com* ⚏ *Reservations essential* Ⓜ *N to Prince St.* ✚ *2:F3.*

SOHO

Longtime New Yorkers lament that SoHo has evolved from a red-hot
art district into a big-brand outdoor mall. Shoppers engulf the neighborhood on weekends like angry bees, turning Lafayette Street into a
buzzing hive of commerce. As a result, popular spots can be tough to
get into during prime times.

$$$ ✕**Aquagrill.** A SoHo standard for fresh seafood, this lively neighbor-
SEAFOOD hood eatery also makes its own pastries and baked goods—including
the bread for its brunchtime challah French toast with cinnamon apples
and pecan butter. Fans rave about the lunchtime $23 prix-fixe Shucker
Special—a half-dozen oysters with homemade soup or chowder and a
salad. Dinner specialties include roasted Dungeness crab cake napoleon
with sundried tomato oil, and falafel-crusted salmon. Desserts are excel-
lent, too, especially the chocolate tasting plate with its molten chocolate
cake, milk chocolate ice cream, and white chocolate mousse. Service is
warm and welcoming. $ *Average main: $27* ✉ *210 Spring St., at 6th
Ave., SoHo* ☎ *212/274–0505* ⊕ *www.aquagrill.com* ⚏ *Reservations
essential* Ⓜ *C, E to Spring St.* ✚ *2:D4.*

$ ✕**Balthazar Bakery.** Follow the beguiling scent of fresh-baked bread to
CAFÉ Balthazar Bakery, next door to Keith McNally's always-packed Baltha-
zar restaurant. Choices include fresh baked baguettes and other varieties
of French breads, as well as gourmet sandwiches, soups, and memorable
pastries to take out (there is no seating). Try the berry noisette tart

or coconut cake, or keep it simple with an eggy cannele or a buttery lemon or chocolate madeleine. $ *Average main: $23* ✉ *80 Spring St., near Crosby St., SoHo* ☎ *212/965–1785* ⊕ *www.balthazarbakery.com* ⌂ *Reservations not accepted* ⊙ *Lunch only* Ⓜ *6 to Spring St.; N, R to Prince St.; B, D, F, M to Broadway–Lafayette* ✛ *2:E4.*

$$$ ✕ **Balthazar.** Even with long waits and excruciating noise levels, most
FRENCH out-of-towners agree that it's worth making reservations to experience restaurateur Keith McNally's flagship, a painstakingly accurate reproduction of a Parisian brasserie with an insider New York feel. Like the decor, entrées re-create French classics: Gruyère-topped onion soup, steak frites, and icy tiers of crab, oysters, and other pristine shellfish. Brunch is still one of the toughest tables in town. The best strategy to experience this perennial fave is to go at off-hours, or on weekdays for breakfast, to miss the crush. $ *Average main: $27.50* ✉ *80 Spring St., between Broadway and Crosby St., SoHo* ☎ *212/965–1414* ⊕ *www. balthazarny.com* ⌂ *Reservations essential* Ⓜ *6 to Spring St.; N, R to Prince St.; B, D, F, M to Broadway–Lafayette* ✛ *2:E4.*

$$$ ✕ **Blue Ribbon.** After 20 years, Blue Ribbon still has a reputation not just
MODERN for top-notch seafood and eclectic menu items, but also as a serious
AMERICAN late-night foodie hangout. Join the genial hubbub for midnight noshing, namely the beef marrow with oxtail marmalade and the renowned raw-bar platters. Trustafarians, literary types, chefs, designers—a good-looking gang—generally fill this dark box of a room until 4 am. The menu appears standard at first blush, but it's not. Try the duck club sandwich or the matzo-ball soup; the latter is a heady brew filled with the sacrilegious combo of seafood and traditional Jewish dumplings. $ *Average main: $32* ✉ *97 Sullivan St., between Prince and Spring Sts., SoHo* ☎ *212/274–0404* ⊕ *www.blueribbonrestaurants.com* ⌂ *Reservations not accepted* ⊙ *No lunch* Ⓜ *C, E to Spring St.; R to Prince St. ✛ 2:D3.*

$$$ ✕ **Blue Ribbon Sushi.** Sushi, like pizza, attracts plenty of opinionated
JAPANESE fanatics. Stick to the excellent raw fish and specials here if you're a purist. Or branch out and try one of the experimental rolls: the Blue Ribbon—lobster, *shiso* (Japanese basil), and black caviar—is popular. The dark, intimate nooks, minimalist design, and servers with downtown attitude attract a stylish crowd that doesn't mind waiting for a table or for chilled sake. $ *Average main: $24* ✉ *119 Sullivan St., between Prince and Spring Sts., SoHo* ☎ *212/343–0404* ⊕ *www. blueribbonrestaurants.com* ⌂ *Reservations not accepted* Ⓜ *C, E to Spring St.; R to Prince St. ✛ 2:D3.*

19

$$$ ✕ **The Dutch.** Perpetually packed with the "see and be seen" crowd, chef
AMERICAN Andrew Carmellini's homage to American cuisine is really an encapsulation of recent food and dining trends: there's an excellent burger (and at $17 it should be), a Kentucky-size bourbon collection behind the bar, greenmarket-driven comfort food dishes like fried chicken, and bacon paired with things you would have not likely seen a couple decades ago (in this case, scallops with bacon jam). And it all works well at this SoHo restaurant. So much so, you might consider returning for weekend brunch when the fried bologna sandwich or cornmeal flapjacks make appearances on the menu. $ *Average main: $25* ✉ *131 Sullivan St., at*

Prince St., SoHo ☎ *212/677–6200* ⌕ *Reservations essential* Ⓜ *C, E to Spring St.* ✛ *2:D3.*

$$$
MODERN
AMERICAN
Fodor's Choice
★

✕ **Hundred Acres.** The rustic, farmhouse-slash-greenhouse setting of Hundred Acres set the tone perfectly for the menu of market-driven creative comfort food, and neighborhood patrons keep coming back to enjoy it. Mains run the gamut from fish to meat: think Hampshire pork shank with polenta and rhubarb chutney; shrimp and grits; or a classic burger made from pasture-raised beef, topped with Vermont cheddar and served with fries and Vidalia onion mayonnaise. It's a cozy spot, but more relaxing at lunch. ⑤ *Average main: $26* ✉ *38 MacDougal St., between Houston and Prince Sts., SoHo* ☎ *212/475–7500* ⊕ *hundredacresnyc.com* Ⓜ *1 to Houston; C, E to Spring St.; N, R to Prince St.* ✛ *2:D3.*

$$
BISTRO

✕ **Lucky Strike.** Whether you're lucky enough to nab a table at this sceney SoHo bistro at 1 pm or 1 am, Lucky Strike always seems like the place to be. Bedecked in classic bistro trappings—copper hammered stools, mirrors with menu items scrawled on them—the restaurant would look just as perfect in the Bastille neighborhood of Paris as it does in this swanky part of the Big Apple. The kitchen offerings are a straightfoward affair: croque monsieur, grilled salmon, and salade Niçoise are old standbys, with a turkey burger thrown in to accommodate the *American* palate. ⑤ *Average main: $16* ✉ *59 Grand St., between W. Broadway and Wooster St., SoHo* ☎ *212/941–0772* Ⓜ *1 to Canal St.* ✛ *2:D4.*

$
MEXICAN
☺

✕ **Lupe's East LA Kitchen.** This cheap and cheerful Mexican dive, just on the western edge of fashionable SoHo, serves great heaping platters of barrio-style enchiladas filled with stewed beef, shrimp, and chicken mole. The Super Vegetarian Burrito has loyal vegetarian followers. If you're shopping in SoHo and looking for a cheap lunch without attitude, this is the place. ⑤ *Average main: $12* ✉ *110 6th Ave., near Watts St., SoHo* ☎ *212/966–1326* ⊕ *www.lupeskitchen.com* ⌕ *Reservations not accepted* ▭ *No credit cards* Ⓜ *A, C, E, 1 to Canal St.* ✛ *2:D4.*

$$$
SEAFOOD

✕ **Lure Fishbar.** Decorated like the clubby interior of a sleek luxury liner, Lure's menu offers oceanic fare prepared in multiple culinary styles. From the sushi bar, you can feast on options like the Lure House Roll— a shrimp-tempura roll crowned with spicy tuna and Japanese tartar sauce—or you can opt for creative dishes from the kitchen, like steamed branzino with oyster mushrooms, scallions, and ponzu sauce, or Manila clams over pancetta-studded linguine. For an all-American treat, you can't go wrong with a classic lobster roll on brioche. The dark subterranean bar is a good spot for cocktails and a snack. ⑤ *Average main: $29* ✉ *142 Mercer St., at Prince St., SoHo* ☎ *212/431–7676* ⊕ *www. lurefishbar.com* ☾ *No lunch weekends* Ⓜ *6 to Bleecker St.; B, D, F, M to Broadway–Lafayette St.; N, R to Prince St.* ✛ *2:E3.*

$
CAFÉ
☺

✕ **MarieBelle.** Practically invisible from the front of the chocolate emporium, the back entry to the Cacao Bar opens into a sweet, high-ceiling, 12-table hot-chocolate shop. Most people order the Aztec, European-style (that's 60% Colombian chocolate mixed with hot water—no cocoa powder here!). The first sip is startlingly rich but not too dense. American-style, made with milk, is sweeter. And not to worry if you're visiting in spring or summer: you can opt for Aztec iced chocolate—the warm-weather version of her decadent cacao elixir—or the house-made chocolate gelato. For more substantial snacking, choose a salad or sandwich from the dainty lunch menu. ⑤ *Average main: $12* ⊠ *484 Broome St., between West Broadway and Wooster St., SoHo* ☎ *212/925–6999* ⊕ *www.mariebelle.com* ⚲ *Reservations not accepted* ⊗ *No dinner* Ⓜ *6 to Spring St.; A, C, E to Canal St.* ✛ *2:D4.*

$$$ ✕ **The Mercer Kitchen.** Part of Alsatian superchef Jean-Georges Vongerich-
ASIAN FUSION ten's culinary empire, the celebrity-laden front room of this SoHo spot is as much about scene as it is cuisine. Which isn't a bad thing. Dishes here look toward Asia (as is the proclivity of Mr. Vongerichten), using simple ingredients and pairings to create deliciousness on the taste bud. Think scallops with lentils and pancetta or crispy squid with black-olive tartar sauce. It's all good enough to make you feign disinterest over the A-list celeb who just walked in. ⑤ *Average main: $28* ⊠ *99 Prince St., at Mercer St., SoHo* ☎ *212/966–5454* ⊕ *www.jean-georges.com* Ⓜ *6 to Spring St.; N, R to Prince St.* ✛ *2:E3.*

$$ ✕ **Osteria Morini.** Less formal than chef Michael White's other renowned
ITALIAN Italian restaurants (like Marea in Midtown West), the atmosphere at Osteria Morini is lively and upbeat, with communal tables at the center and a rock-and-roll soundtrack. The food still steals the show, though. Start with a selection of cheeses and cured meats, then move on to hearty pastas—a lusty *ragu* Bolognese, a ham- and cream-lashed *garganelli* with prosciutto and truffle butter, for example—and main courses like oven-baked polenta accompanied by either sausage or mushrooms. Waits can be long, so try to come early or late, or grab one of the few bar seats for an inventive cocktail or a glass of Italian wine. ⑤ *Average main: $24* ⊠ *218 Lafayette St., between Spring and Broome Sts., SoHo* ☎ *212/965–8777* ⊕ *www.osteriamorini.com* ⚲ *Reservations essential* ⊗ *No lunch weekends* Ⓜ *6 to Spring St.* ✛ *2:E4.*

$$$ ✕ **Raoul's.** One of the first trendy spots in SoHo, this arty French res-
FRENCH taurant has yet to lose its touch, either in the kitchen or with the atmosphere. Expect a chic bar scene—especially late at night—filled with beautiful people, amazing photos on every piece of available wall space, and a lovely back room that you reach through the kitchen. The winding stairs to the upstairs dining room are narrow and a bit treacherous if you're wearing your highest heels. Food-wise, it's bistro-inspired, with oysters and salads to start, and pastas, fish, and meat options for mains. ⑤ *Average main: $28.50* ⊠ *180 Prince St., between Sullivan and Thompson Sts., SoHo* ☎ *212/966–3518* ⊕ *www.raouls.com* ⊗ *No lunch* Ⓜ *C, E to Spring St.* ✛ *2:D3.*

$$ ✕ **Snack.** This SoHo cubbyhole may look like just another drop-in café,
GREEK but the food served inside will transport you to Greece. Typical mezes like tzakiki, taramosalata, hummus, and skordalia are several notches better than what you'd get elsewhere, but the menu options range beyond snacks: pop in at lunch for a braised-lamb sandwich or spinach pie, or linger in the evenings over votive-lighted tables and pastitsio or stuffed peppers. The light-filled West Village location, Snack Taverna, is somewhat roomier and also serves breakfast daily and brunch on weekends. ⑤ *Average main: $19* ⊠ *105 Thompson St., near Prince St., SoHo* ☎ *212/929–3499* ⊕ *www. snackny.com* ⚲ *Reservations not accepted* Ⓜ *C, E to Spring St.* ✛ *2:D3*

19

$ *Average main: $19* ✉ *63 Bedford St., at Morton St., West Village* 🕿 *212/929–3499* Ⓜ *B, D, F, M to W. 4th St.* ✛ *2:C2.*

$$ ✕ **Spring Street Natural.** When this SoHo spot first fired up its burners in
AMERICAN 1973, restaurants emphasizing organic, whole, and natural ingredients
were mostly limited to San Francisco and college towns. The dining
landscape may have caught up, but Spring Street Natural is still going
strong, powered by a loyal clientele who come here for healthy food
that actually tastes good. Start with the creamy organic hummus (and
warm pita bread) before moving on to pan-roasted free-range chicken
(accompanied by sweet potato–poblano pepper gratin) or the pancetta-
laced pumpkin ravioli. If you're too full for dessert, order a glass of
organic wine, sit back and stare out the floor-to-ceiling windows, gawk-
ing at the occasional celebrity and the SoHo shoppers. $ *Average main:*
$18 ✉ *62 Spring St., at Lafayette St., SoHo* 🕿 *212/966–0290* Ⓜ *6 to*
Spring St. ✛ *2:E4.*

EAST VILLAGE AND LOWER EAST SIDE

EAST VILLAGE

With luxury condos on Avenue C and the continued glamification of
the formerly seedy Bowery, the East Village—once Manhattan's edgiest
enclave—has become yet another high-rent neighborhood. But it still
offers some of the best meal deals in the city, and the influx of flush
new residents has steadily raised the bar on high-quality eats. There's
something for every budget and craving, from yakitori parlors to mid-
price trattorias. St. Marks Place is the center of New York's downtown
Little Tokyo, and 6th Street is its Indian row.

$ ✕ **Artichoke Pizza.** Grab a gargantuan slice at table-less Artichoke Pizza,
PIZZA where lines often snake in the wee hours for the artichoke-spinach
☺ slice, which tastes like cheesy dip on crackers. Those in the know opt
for the less greasy Margherita slice. There are locations in Chelsea and
Greenwich Village, too. $ *Average main: $4* ✉ *328 E. 14th St., between*
1st and 2nd Aves., East Village 🕿 *212/228–2004* ⬧ *Reservations not*
accepted Ⓜ *L to 1st Ave.* ✛ *3:H4.*

$$ ✕ **Back Forty.** Pioneering chef Peter Hoffman, a longtime leader in pro-
AMERICAN moting local, sustainable food, attracts a devoted crowd at this casual
restaurant that feels like a neighborhood joint. Despite Hoffman's pedigree, Back Forty displays plenty of humility. Prices on the short, rustic, greenmarket menu are moderate, and the homey decor features a
pastoral mural behind the bar and rusty farm tools on the walls. Begin
with an appetizer like the house charcuterie plate, washed down with a
fine house cocktail like the excellent, bourbon-based "Back Forty." The
simply prepared dinner selections include a perfect grilled trout; moist
pan-roasted chicken; and a wide array of seasonal sides, perhaps including roasted Brussels sprouts with maple-cider vinegar and lemon-thyme
butter. Don't miss the house-made doughnuts with seasonal glazes for
dessert. Brunch is served on Saturday, and there are frequent seasonal
"special events" like crab-boil dinners in summer. Weather permitting,
snag a table in the leafy garden out back. The new Back Forty West
(✛ 2:E3), on Prince Street, between Lafayette and Crosby, is garnering

equally stellar reviews. $ *Average main: $18.50* ⊠ *190 Ave. B, at 12th St., East Village* ☎ *212/388–1990* ⊕ *www.backfortynyc.com* ⊗ *No lunch Mon.–Sat.* Ⓜ *L to 1st Ave.* ✛ *3:H4.*

$ ✕ **Baoguette.** Vietnamese *banh mi* have taken New York by storm in
VIETNAMESE   the past couple of years, and Baoguette, a chainlet from restaurateur
Fodor'sChoice   Michael Hunh, is a great place to try these spicy, multilayered baguette
★   sandwiches. This is the flagship, decorated with raffia walls and large
photos of Vietnamese street scenes, and though there a few tables, the
majority of customers get their sandwiches to go. Try the namesake
Baoguette, layered with savory pâté, flavorful pulled pork, and aromatic
herbs, or the addictive Sloppy Bao, a sweet and savory sloppy joe with
curried beef, mango, and lemongrass. $ *Average main: $7* ⊠ *37 St.
Marks Pl., between 2nd and 3rd Aves., East Village* ☎ *212/380–1487*
⊕ *www.baoguette.com* ⟶ *Reservations not accepted* Ⓜ *R to 8th St./
NYU; 6 to Astor Pl./4th Ave.* ✛ *2:F1.*

$$ ✕ **Cafe Mogador.** An East Village dining institution if there ever was one,
MOROCCAN   Cafe Mogador is a frequent stop for locals and, for some, a hip place
to be seen. Since 1983, the restaurant has been serving above-average
Morrocan cuisine in a date-friendly candlelight atmosphere. Finish off
that creamy hummus before the chicken tagine arrives, nurse that glass
of Italian wine, and ponder the fact that most of the people around
you were 3-feet tall when this family-run restaurant first fired up its
couscous-cooking burners. $ *Average main: $14* ⊠ *101 St. Marks Pl.,
near 2nd Ave., East Village* ☎ *212/677–2226* ⊕ *www.cafemogador.com*
Ⓜ *F to 2nd Ave.; L to 1st Ave.* ✛ *2:G1.*

$$ ✕ **Chinatown Brasserie.** The large, bilevel dining room is exactly what
CHINESE   you'd expect from an upscale Chinese restaurant: sultry lighting, dark
cherry banquettes, and silk lanterns. The menu is what you'd expect
from Americanized Chinese food, but presentation and quality are elevated a few levels above a typical Chinatown eatery. Crispy Peking duck
is a specialty, sliced and presented on a long platter with the crackling
skin still attached, accompanied by fresh Mandarin pancakes, julienned
scallions, and pungent hoisin sauce. Dim sum is a big draw for those
who don't want to deal with the frenetic, more authentic experience
downtown. $ *Average main: $19.50* ⊠ *380 Lafayette St., at Great
Jones St., East Village* ☎ *212/533–7000* ⊕ *www.chinatownbrasserie.
com* Ⓜ *6 to Bleecker St.; B, D, F, M to Broadway–Lafayette St.* ✛ *2:E2.*

$ ✕ **Crif Dogs.** Gluttony reigns at Crif Dogs, where you can indulge in
FAST FOOD   creative—and delicious—hot dog creations. Try the Chihuahua, bacon-
☺   wrapped and layered with avocado and sour cream. There are vegetarian dogs, too, for those who are into that kind of thing. The tater
tots will banish all memories of the high school cafeteria. $ *Average
main: $5* ⊠ *113 St. Marks Pl., at Ave. A, East Village* ☎ *212/614–2728*
⊕ *www.crifdogs.com* Ⓜ *6 to Astor Pl.* ✛ *3:H5.*

$$ ✕ **DBGB Kitchen & Bar.** The most recent addition to Daniel Boulud's New
FRENCH   York City restaurant fleet, DBGB forgoes the white tablecloths, for-
Fodor'sChoice   mal service, and steep prices found at the famed chef's fancier digs,
★   and instead pays homage to the grittier, younger feel of its Lower East
Side location. (The name is a wink to the legendary rock club CBGB.)
Lined with shelves of pots, plates, and pans (not to mention copperware

19

donated by renowned chefs from around the world), the dining room gives way to a partially open kitchen where you can catch the chefs preparing Boulud's take on French- and German-inspired pub fare. The menu features 14 different varieties of sausages (the *tunisienne*, a spicy lamb-and-mint merguez, is a particular standout), decadently sinful burgers (the aptly named "piggy" burger, a juicy beef patty topped with a generous portion of pulled pork, jalapeño mayonnaise, and mustard-vinegar slaw on a cheddar bun—not for the weak-willed), and classic entrées like steak frites and lemon-and-rosemary roasted chicken. The $27 three-course, prix-fixe lunch is quite a steal. $ *Average main: $23* ✉ *299 Bowery, between Houston and 1st St., East Village* ☎ *212/933–5300* ⊕ *www.danielnyc.com* ⌕ *Reservations essential* ◷ *No lunch Mon.* Ⓜ *F to 2nd Ave.* ✛ *2:F2.*

$$$
AUSTRIAN

✕ **Edi & the Wolf.** For those who have always wanted to spend an evening in a countryside Austrian pub—and who hasn't?—but don't have the means to hop on a plane to Vienna, there's Edi & the Wolf, an outstanding restaurant deep in the section of the East Village called Alphabet City. The rustic interior (usually crammed with stylish thirtysomethings) is the perfect venue to sample dishes like honey-and-beer-accented ribs, pork belly–laced poached eggs, and, of course, Wiener schnitzel, which is refreshingly free of grease and super tender. The well-edited beer selection focuses on central Europe. Try the dark Czech brew, Krusovice. $ *Average main: $20* ✉ *102 Ave. C, at E. 7th St., East Village* ☎ *212/598–1040* Ⓜ *F to 2nd Ave.; L to 1st Ave.* ✛ *2:H1.*

$$
BRITISH

✕ **The Fat Radish.** The phrase "seasonal British" might have once seemed puzzling but with seasonal ingredients very much in vogue and British cuisine making a name for itself, this handsome, hip, and sceney Lower East Side (almost Chinatown) restaurant is very much of the moment. The menu is eclectic but full of excellent choices. Think monkfish vindaloo, a cheeseburger served with duck fat fries, and, as the name vaguely suggests, plenty of farm-to-table fresh veggie dishes. Match that with quality craft British brews and potent cocktails and you'll be championing English cuisine in no time. $ *Average main: $18* ✉ *17 Orchard St., near Canal St., Lower East Side* ☎ *212/300–4053* ⊕ *thefatradishnyc.com* Ⓜ *F to E. Broadway* ✛ *2:G5.*

$$
AMERICAN

✕ **Five Points.** Describing a menu in terms of "seasonal" and "market-driven" might be old news but chef Marc Meyer really makes the most of the greenmarket, and showcases it in a cozy, convivial dining room. Expect plump chilled oysters, exemplary Caesar salad, and splendid house-made pasta, followed by the likes of pan-seared day-boat halibut with cucumber gazpacho and chopped tomato salsa, and grilled baby lamb chops with rosemary potatoes, mint-yogurt sauce, and black-olive-stuffed tomato. Weekend brunch is one of the best in the city, and prices are quite friendly. Weekday lunch is served, too, usually without the wait that hungry stomachs have come to expect at other times. $ *Average main: $24* ✉ *31 Great Jones St., between Lafayette St. and Bowery, East Village* ☎ *212/253–5700* ⊕ *www.fivepointsrestaurant. com* ⌕ *Reservations essential* Ⓜ *6 to Bleecker St.; B, D, F, M to Broadway–Lafayette St.* ✛ *3:G6.*

$$$ ✕ **Gemma.** There's something almost formulaic about this restaurant
ITALIAN on the ground floor of the hip Bowery Hotel: from the rustic, wood-
bedecked interior to the stone-wall interior facade to the see-and-be-
seen crowd who frequent the place and the menu of above-average
Italian staples. But the food here is good and nabbing an outside table
may make you feel cooler than you are for a couple of hours, so what
difference does it make? Answer: only when it's time to pay the bill
and leave. Ⓢ *Average main: $19* ✉ *335 Bowery, at E. 3rd St., East Vil-*
lage ☎ *212/505–9100* ⊕ *theboweryhotel.com/dining* ⌨ *Reservations*
not accepted Ⓜ *F to 2nd Ave.* ✛ *2:F2.*

$$ ✕ **Gnocco.** Owners Pierluigi Palazzo and Gianluca Giavonetti named
ITALIAN their restaurant not after gnocchi but after a regional Italian specialty—
deep-fried dough bites typically served with Northern Italian sliced
meats like capicola, salami, and aged prosciutto. The *gnocco* are certainly good, but the menu has so many other options you'll be forgiven
if you skip them in favor of the salads, house-made pasta specials,
pizza topped with mozzarella, truffles, and mushrooms, and hearty
entrées like pork tenderloin in a balsamic emulsion with flakes of Grana
Padano cheese—preferably all enjoyed in the roomy, canopied garden
out back. Ⓢ *Average main: $20* ✉ *337 E. 10th St., between Aves. A and*
B, East Village ☎ *212/677–1913* ⊕ *www.gnocco.com* Ⓜ *L to 1st Ave.;*
6 to Astor Pl. ✛ *2:H1.*

$ ✕ **Grand Sichuan.** Yes, it's a local Chinese chainlet, and no, you don't
CHINESE come here for the ambience, but the food—like fiery Sichuan *dan dan*
noodles or crab soup dumplings—is good and inexpensive. Check the
website for other locations around town. Ⓢ *Average main: $17.50*
✉ *19–23 St. Marks Pl., near 3rd Ave., East Village* ☎ *212/529–4800*
⊕ *www.thegrandsichuan.com* Ⓜ *6 to Astor Pl.* ✛ *2:F1* ✉ *368 W. 46th*
St., Midtown West ☎ *212/969–9001* ✉ *229 9th Ave., at W. 24th St.,*
Chelsea ☎ *212/620–5200* Ⓜ *C, E to 23rd St.* ✛ *3:B2* ✉ *15 7th Ave. S,*
between Leroy and Carmine Sts., West Village ☎ *212/645–0222* Ⓜ *1 to*
Houston St.; A, B, C, D, E, F, V to W. 4th St. ✛ *2:C3.*

$$ ✕ **Hecho en Dumbo.** "Made in Dumbo"—referring to the restaurant's
MEXICAN former location in the Brooklyn neighborhood, DUMBO—specializes
in *antojitos*, or "little cravings." The result is something equivalent to
Mexican comfort food for the hip thirtysomethings who frequent this
restaurant on the ever-happening Bowery. Variations on the theme of
tacos may dominate the menu, but Hecho shines with house dishes like
roasted kid goat and wine-braised oxtail served over Oaxacan mole
sauce. Pair your meal with a tamarind margarita or sangria. Ⓢ *Average*
main: $15 ✉ *354 Bowery, between Great Jones and W. 4th Sts., East*
Village ☎ *212/937–4245* ⊕ *www.hechoendumbo.com* Ⓜ *6 to Astor Pl.*
✛ *2:F2.*

$$$ ✕ **Il Buco.** The unabashed clutter of vintage kitchen gadgets and table-
ITALIAN ware harks back to Il Buco's past as an antiques store and the effect is a
romantic country-house feel with excellent food. This is a favorite for a
cozy, intimate meal. The menu focuses on meat and produce from local
farms, with several excellent pasta choices, and a variety of Mediterranean
tapaslike appetizers. Call ahead to book the intimate wine cellar for dinner.
Ⓢ *Average main: $28* ✉ *47 Bond St., between Bowery and Lafayette St.,*

19

East Village ☎ *212/533–1932* ⊕ *www.ilbuco.com* ◎ *No lunch Sun.* Ⓜ *6 to Bleecker St.; B, D, F, M to Broadway–Lafayette St.* ✛ *2:F2.*

$
JAPANESE

✕ **Ippudo.** Crowds wait hours for the ramen noodles at Ippudo, the first American branch of the Japanese chain, and if you ask, loyal patrons will say it's all about the rich, pork-based broth—there is a vegetarian version available but it lacks the depth of flavor. Those really in the know, though, make sure to order the sleeper hit appetizers like the peppery chicken wings or the pork buns. It's not a hole in the wall ramen spot, so although a meal here is relatively inexpensive, it's not dirt cheap. ⑤ *Average main: $15* ⊠ *65 4th Ave., between 9th and 10th Sts., East Village* ☎ *212/388–0088* ⊕ *www.ippudony.com* ⬧ *Reservations not accepted* Ⓜ *6 to Astor Pl.* ✛ *3:G5.*

$$$$
JAPANESE

✕ **Jewel Bako.** Tiny Jewel Bako is arguably the best sushi restaurant in the East Village, gleaming in a minefield of cheap, often inferior sushi houses. The futuristic bamboo tunnel of a dining room is gorgeous, but try to nab a place at the sushi bar and put yourself in the hands of sushi master Yoshi Kousaka. The five-course *omakase*, or chef's menu, starts at $95. (A less-expensive sushi or sashimi *omakase* is $50.) You'll be served only what's freshest and best. ⑤ *Average main: $40* ⊠ *239 E. 5th St., between 2nd and 3rd Aves., East Village* ☎ *212/979–1012* ⬧ *Reservations essential* ◎ *Closed Sun. No lunch* Ⓜ *6 to Astor Pl.* ✛ *3:G6.*

$
MIDDLE EASTERN
☺

✕ **Mamoun's Falafel.** Bustling day and night, this hole-in-the-wall is the place to go for fast, hot, and delicious Middle Eastern food. Tahinitopped pitas are packed with fresh, green-on-the-inside falafel balls. Be warned: the hot sauce is incendiary. The original Mamoun's is still on MacDougal Street, near Washington Square Park in Greenwich Village. ⑤ *Average main: $7* ⊠ *22 St. Marks Pl., between 2nd and 3rd Aves., East Village* ☎ *212/387–7747* ⊕ *mamouns.com* ⬧ *Reservations not accepted* ▭ *No credit cards* Ⓜ *6 to Astor Pl.* ✛ *3:G5.*

$
JAPANESE

✕ **Minca.** It may have received less fanfare than some other East Village noodle bars, but the ramen at this tiny, cramped spot is among the best in the city; the fact that visiting Japanese students eat here is a good sign. Try to get a seat at the bar, where you can watch the chefs prepare your food. Start with homemade *gyoza* dumplings, then dive your spoon and chopsticks into one of the many types of ramen. The shoyu (soy sauce) Minca ramen is unfailingly good, but anything with pork is a good bet. ⑤ *Average main: $13* ⊠ *536 E. 5th St., between Ave. A and Ave. B, East Village* ☎ *212/505–8001* ⊕ *www.newyorkramen.com* ⬧ *Reservations not accepted* ▭ *No credit cards* Ⓜ *F to 2nd Ave.* ✛ *2:G2.*

$$$$
ASIAN
Fodor's Choice
★

✕ **Momofuku Ko.** A seasonal tasting menu full of clever combinations and esoteric ingredients explains the deafening buzz for James Beard Award–winning chef David Chang's most formal dining option. Ko's small, intimate space is sparsely furnished with a counter of blonde wood and only a dozen stools. Diners get to see Ko's chefs in action as they prepare all manner of inventive dishes, including a signature preparation of frozen foie-gras *torchon* grated over lychee fruits and white wine gelée. Reservations can be made only online, no more than 7 days ahead for dinner and 14 days ahead for lunch, and are extremely difficult to get. Log on at 10 am (credit-card number needed just to get in the system) when new reservations are available, and keep hitting reload. $ *Average main: $60* ⊠ *163 1st Ave., at E. 10th St., East Village* ⊕ *www.momofuku.com* ⌲ *Reservations essential* ⊙ *No lunch Mon.– Thurs.* Ⓜ *L to 1st Ave.; 6 to Astor Pl.* ✛ *3:H5.*

$$ ✕ **Momofuku Noodle Bar.** Chef-owner David Chang has created a shrine to ramen with this stylish 70-seat restaurant. His riff on the Japanese classic features *haute* ingredients like Berkshire pork, free-range chicken, and organic produce—though there are plenty of other innovative options on the menu. His modern take on pork buns with cucumber and scallions is phenomenal—worth the trip alone. Go early or late—the tiny restaurant is packed during regular mealtimes. The excellent fried-chicken meal, featuring triple-fried Korean-style chicken and Old Bay Southern-style, with a variety of accoutrements feeds 4 to 8 people and is available only by special reservations only on the website. $ *Average main: $15* ⊠ *171 1st Ave., between E. 10th and E. 11 Sts., East Village* ☎ *212/777–7773* ⊕ *www.momofuku.com/noodle* ⌲ *Reservations not accepted* Ⓜ *L to 1st Ave.* ✛ *3:H5.*

ASIAN
Fodor's Choice
★

$$ ✕ **Momofuku Ssäm Bar.** New York foodies have been salivating over chef David Chang's Asian-influenced fare since he opened his first restaurant, Momofuku, a Japanese noodle shop, in 2004, and Ssäm Bar, with a more extensive menu, is equally worth the raves. The restaurant is packed nightly with downtown diners cut from the same cloth as the pierced and tattooed waitstaff and cooks, and the no-reservation policy (except for large parties or special dinners) means you'll likely have to wait for a chance to try Chang's truly inventive flavor combinations. The menu is constantly changing but the not-to-be-missed riff on the classic Chinese steamed pork bun is almost always available. You can make reservations for the festive Bo Ssäm dinner (6 to 10 people), featuring a slow-roasted pork shoulder, oysters, kimchi, and a variety of sauces, or the rotisserie duck dinner (3 to 6 people) through their website. $ *Average main: $23* ⊠ *207 2nd Ave., at 13th St., East Village* ☎ *212/254–3500* ⊕ *www.momofuku.com/ssam* Ⓜ *L to 1st Ave.* ✛ *3:H4.*

ASIAN

19

$ ✕ **Motorino Pizza.** The Manhattan branch of the now-closed Williamsburg original has brought impossibly high standards—and the long lines to match—to a new borough. The authentic Neapolitan pies are made with glutinous, dough-friendly double-zero flour and San Marzano tomatoes, and the crusts are lightly charred. You can't go wrong with any of the signature traditional pizzas, like classic marinara; margherita with fresh tomatoes, mozzarella, and basil; or a pie with spicy sopressata sausage and garlic, but there are also seasonal selections featuring brussels sprouts and other vegetables, and brunch pizza (with egg and pancetta) on the weekends. Antipasti like octopus and fingerling potato salad with celery-chili oil, and cockle-clam crostini round out the menu. The weekday, lunchtime prix-fixe means pizza and salad for $12/person. $ *Average main: $15* ⊠ *349 E. 12th St., at 1st Ave., East Village* ☎ *212/777–2644* ⊕ *www.motorinopizza.com* ⌲ *Reservations not accepted* Ⓜ *L to 1st Ave.* ✛ *3:H4.*

PIZZA

$$ ✕ **Northern Spy Food Co.** A gem in the East Village, named for an apple variety, Northern Spy is run by two San Francisco transplants who have brought with them from the West Coast a fresh perspective on the farm-to-table movement. Start your meal with the freekeh risotto,

AMERICAN
Fodor's Choice
★

a traditional dish made with a quirky little-known grain, or a giant mound of shredded kale tossed with cheddar, pecorino, and toasted almonds. Main courses are winners, too—choose tender meatballs in marinara sauce, roast chicken for two, or baked polenta, eggs, and mushrooms topped with crème fraîche. There is also an interesting, reasonably priced list of wines and beers, and a selection of housemade desserts like chocolate cake with sea salt and caramel. ⑤ *Average main: $21.50* ⊠ *511 E. 12th St., between 1st Ave. and Ave. A, East Village* ☎ *212/228–5100* ⊕ *www.northernspyfoodco.com* ⊰ *Reservations not accepted* Ⓜ *L to 1st Ave.* ✛ *3:H4.*

$$
SOUTHERN
☀

✕ **Peels Restaurant.** Imagine a Southern-flared eatery in one of the hippest parts of Manhattan, and you might come up with Peels, a sceney grits-and-all spot from the people who gave NYC the überhip (and trendsetting) Freemans. As one might expect, the buttermilk-biscuit egg sandwich is a delightful way to start any day. And the buttery grits are done right. But Peels excels in more original fare: the andouille corn dogs with sweet Dijon mustard and the root-vegetable pot pie are good enough to name your next child Cletus. ⑤ *Average main: $25.50* ⊠ *325 Bowery, near 2nd St., East Village* ☎ *646/602–7015* ⊕ *peelsnyc.com* ⊰ *Reservations not accepted* Ⓜ *4, 6 to Bleecker St.* ✛ *3:G6.*

$$$
MODERN ITALIAN
Fodor'sChoice
★

✕ **Perbacco.** Diminutive and dimly lighted, with a rustic exposed-brick-wall interior, this quiet East Village spot looks, at first glance, like it could be an Italian restaurant in anywhere from Turin to Tucson. But this is not your padre's Italian eatery. No, *signore*. Imagine: crème brûlée of Parmigiano Reggiano? Or deconstructed carbonara served with deep-fried spaghetti? And it's good? That's right, it's *really* good. The culinary wizard behind the madness is Simone Bonelli, who transformed what was an ordinary Italian restaurant into a temple of creativity and indulgence when he came over from Modena's lauded Osteria Francescana a few years ago. Oh, don't worry, timid, unadventurous eaters: there are plenty of recognizable pasta and meat dishes on the menu as well. There's a three-course, $40 tasting menu in addition to the à la carte options. ⑤ *Average main: $25* ⊠ *234 E. 4th St., between Aves. A and B, East Village* ☎ *212/253–2038* Ⓜ *F to 2nd Ave.* ✛ *2:H2.*

$
ITALIAN

✕ **Porchetta.** Super-succulent Italian roast pork—dusted in fennel pollen and covered in crisp cracklin' skin—is the star attraction here. It is, in fact, just about the only thing this tiny spot offers. Order your pork in a sandwich or as a platter with stewed greens and roasted potatoes. There's not much room inside for dining on-site, but the benches out front are ideal when the weather cooperates. ⑤ *Average main: $10* ⊠ *110 E. 7th St., near 1st Ave., East Village* ☎ *212/777–2151* ⊕ *www.porchettanyc.com* ⊰ *Reservations not accepted* Ⓜ *6 to Astor Pl.* ✛ *3:H5.*

$$
AMERICAN

✕ **Prune.** There's just something very right-on about the food at Prune, a cozy treasure of a restaurant serving eclectic, well-executed American food from cult chef Gabrielle Hamilton. The choices change with the season, but you might find braised rabbit legs in vinegar sauce, whole grilled fish with fennel oil and chunky sea salt, or roasted marrow bones with parsley salad and toast points. If they're on the menu, try the pillowy, fried sweetbreads. There's usually a wait, and the quarters are very cramped, so don't expect to feel comfortable lingering at your rickety wooden table. Desserts, like ricotta ice cream with salted-caramel croutons, are irresistible, and on weekends lines form early for the restaurant's deservedly popular brunch. $ *Average main: $20* ⊠ *54 E. 1st St., between 1st and 2nd Aves., East Village* ☎ *212/677–6221* ⊕ *www. prunerestaurant.com* ☙ *Reservations essential* Ⓜ *F to 2nd Ave.* ✛ *2:G2.*

$$$
GREEK

✕**Pylos.** The perfect setting for a relaxed dinner or an intimate special occasion, this refined, light-filled East Village restaurant emphasizes rustic Greek cooking from all over Greece. There are delicious versions of hearty comfort food dishes like pastitsio and moussaka on the menu, but the lighter dishes—especially fish—let the flavors shine. There is an extensive selection of intriguing hot and cold mezes: start with the traditional trio of tzatkziki (garlicky yogurt dip), taramosalata (lemony fish roe dip), and melitzanosalta (an eggplant-based dip) and explore from there. Accompany your meal with a bottle from the all-Greek wine list; the light white Atlantis wine from the island of Santorini is particularly enjoyable—and affordable. $ *Average main: $25* ⊠ *128 E. 7th St., near Ave. A, East Village* ☎ *212/473–0220* ⊕ *www.pylosrestaurant.com* Ⓜ *F to 2nd Ave.; L to 1st Ave.* ✛ *3:H5.*

$$$
MODERN
AMERICAN
Fodor's Choice
★

✕**Saxon & Parole.** One of the hottest spots on this burgeoning stretch of the Bowery, this eatery may be named for two 19th century racehorses, but the food—and the extremely good-looking crowd—is nothing that you'd find in a barnyard. Settle into this cozy, sceney spot, order a cocktail, and peruse a menu loaded with the Zeitgeist dishes of New York dining: miso-glazed bone marrow, Brussels sprouts, pork belly, chicken liver mousse, and, of course, an overpriced-but-excellent burger. The kitchen executes it all to complete deliciousness. You may even forget you're in a restaurant named for racehorces. The bar scene is lively, too, so plan to come early for a cocktail. $ *Average main: $22* ⊠ *316 Bowery, at Bleecker St., East Village* ☎ *212/254–0350* ⊕ *saxonandparole. com* Ⓜ *B, D, F, M to Broadway–Lafayette* ✛ *2:F2.*

$$
AMERICAN

✕**The Smile.** Subterranean and almost hidden, the Smile will turn your frown upside down if you like hipsters, celebrities, and, most especially, hipster celebrities. Lounge among the fashionably conscious clientele (who are trying oh so hard to not look that way) and munch on breakfast-y items (breakfast is served until 4:30 pm) like chunky granola, giant sandwiches, or spaghetti with heirloom tomato sauce. Just be sure you wear shoes that scream "this season." $ *Average main: $15* ⊠ *26 Bond St., between Lafayette St. and Bowery, East Village* ☎ *646/ 329–5836* ⊕ *www.thesmilenyc.com* Ⓜ *B, D, F, M to Broadway–Lafayette; 6 to Astor Pl.* ✛ *2:E2.*

$
CAFÉ
☺

✕**Veniero's Pasticceria.** More than a century old, this bustling bakery-café sells every kind of Italian *dolce* (sweet), from cherry-topped cookies to creamy cannoli and flaky *sfogliatelle* pastry. A wine license means you can top off an evening with a bottle of red. $ *Average main: $5* ⊠ *342 E. 11th St., near 1st Ave., East Village* ☎ *212/674–7070* ⊕ *www. venierospastry.com* ☙ *Reservations not accepted* Ⓜ *6 to Astor Pl.; L to 1st Ave.* ✛ *3:H5.*

19

$ | **Veselka.** You can order potato pierogis 24 hours a day at this East
EASTERN | Village stalwart. The authentic Ukrainian cuisine slash diner food is the
EUROPEAN | perfect stick-to-your-ribs end to a night on the town. ⑤ *Average main:*
☾ | *$11* ✉ *144 2nd Ave., at 9th St., East Village* ☎ *212/228–9682* ⊕ *www.*
veselka.com ⌕ *Reservations not accepted* ⊟ *No credit cards* Ⓜ *6 to*
Astor Pl. ✛ *3:H5.*

$ | **Zabb Elee.** Don't expect to find pad Thai on the menu at this com-
THAI | fortable but simply bedecked subterranean East Village restaurant. An
Fodor'sChoice | outpost of a popular Queens restaurant of the same name, Zabb Elee
★ | features the cuisine of Isan, a region in northeastern Thailand that
emphasizes simplicity and spiciness. Order a plate of *larb*—ground meat
with mint, scallions, cilantro, and chili—or *som tam*, spicy papaya
salad, and tell the server the level of hotness you prefer (one means
mild, four means very spicy, and "Thai" means out-of-this-world hot).
⑤ *Average main: $9* ✉ *75 2nd Ave., Between E. 4 and E. 5th Sts., East*
Village ☎ *212/505–9533* Ⓜ *F to 2nd Ave.* ✛ *2:F1.*

$$ | **Zum Schneider.** Located in Alphabet City—in the wilds of the East
GERMAN | Village—this garrulous Teutonic spot will teach you the ABCs of beer
drinking and hearty eating. Grab a table outside among the young
hipsters who frequent the spot and get ready for some kraut-laden fun.
After quaffing a huge liter stein of the sudsy stuff you may want to eat,
and the menu, naturally, is a veritable sausage-palooza. In addition to
the usual meaty fare, such as Wiener schnitzel, goulash, there are, well,
more sausages. ⑤ *Average main: $16* ✉ *107 Ave. C, at E. 7th St., East*
Village ☎ *212/598–1098* ⊕ *www.zumschneider.com* Ⓜ *L to 1st Ave.; F*
to 2nd Ave. ✛ *2:H1.*

LOWER EAST SIDE

The Lower East Side, home to generations of immigrant newcomers,
is undergoing a transformation into a high-rent neighborhood. Cute
little bistros have been inching into newly gentrified stretches south of
Delancey Street. And the neighborhood has even given birth to its own
homegrown star chefs, wildly creative renegades with cultish followings
like **wd~50**'s Wylie Dufresne.

$$ | **Clinton St. Baking Co.** There once was a time when this Lower East
AMERICAN | Side restaurant was *the* place to come for brunch. Specifically, it was
Fodor'sChoice | *the* place to eat blueberry pancakes, which many regulars professed
★ | were the best in the city, if not the state, or the whole country. But all
that changed when owners Neil Kleinberg and DeDe Lahman opened
their beloved eatery for lunch and dinner. Oh, it's still a great place for
brunch, but now you can eat those pancakes (along with a good Black
Angus burger or a crab-cake sandwich) any time of day you like. February is pancake month, when, in addition to the blueberry pancakes,
every weekday brings a special incarnation of the pancake. ⑤ *Aver-*
age main: $17 ✉ *4 Clinton St., near E. Houston St., Lower East Side*
☎ *646/602–6263* ⊕ *clintonstreetbaking.com* Ⓜ *F to 2nd Ave.* ✛ *2:H2.*

$$ | **Freemans.** It's hard to believe now but there was once a time when
AMERICAN | New York restaurant interiors looked like they were trying hard not to
Fodor'sChoice | look cool, when there was no taxidermy or ironic tchotchkes littered
★ | around the room, when the menu wasn't filled with old-school (albeit
very good) lodge-ish dishes like hunter's stew, potted pork, and grilled

trout with an equally inspired cocktails menu. But we have Freemans to thank for that. Down a little-used alleyway on the Lower East Side, trendsetting Freemans is as hip and popular as when it opened in 2004. Just don't try too hard to look cool. The hot artichoke dip is still the best way to start any meal. ⓢ *Average main: $18* ⊠ *End of Freeman Alley, near Rivington, Lower East Side* ☎ *212/420–0012* ⊕ *www. freemansrestaurant.com* ⊕ *2:F3.*

ⓢ

ITALIAN

✕ **'inoteca.** The Italian terms on the menu may be unfamiliar (*tramezzini* just means soft bread sandwiches), but the food is not daunting in the least—this is real Italian comfort food. An Italian small-plates concept with an excellent by-the-glass wine list, this rustic eatery is perpetually packed. (Reservations are accepted for parties of six or more.) Come for cheese and charcuterie plates, the famous truffled egg toast, and delicious panini filled with cured meat, runny cheeses, and hot peppers. Menu staples include fresh salads and creative entrées like lentils, fennel, celery root, capers, and saffron, and roast lamb cannelloni with white beans, spinach, and pecorino with house-made sausage. ⓢ *Average main: $13* ⊠ *98 Rivington St., at Ludlow St., Lower East Side* ☎ *212/614–0473* ⊕ *www.inotecanyc.com* Ⓜ *F, J, M, Z to Delancey St.* ⊕ *2:G3.*

ⓢ

DELI

Fodor's Choice

★

✕ **Katz's Delicatessen.** Everything and nothing has changed at Katz's since it first opened in 1888, when the neighborhood was dominated by Jewish immigrants. The rows of Formica tables, the long self-service counter, and such signs as "Send a salami to your boy in the army" are all completely authentic. The lines still form for succulent hand-carved corned beef and pastrami sandwiches, soul-warming soups, juicy hot dogs, and crisp half-sour pickles. ⓢ *Average main: $15* ⊠ *205 E. Houston St., at Ludlow St., Lower East Side* ☎ *212/254–2246* ⊕ *www. katzdeli.com* Ⓜ *F to 2nd Ave.* ⊕ *2:G2.*

$$

GERMAN

✕ **Loreley Restaurant & Biergarten.** Once upon a time, beer gardens dotted the New York City landscape in the way that Starbucks does now, but after World War I and Prohibition, most of these outdoor drinking spots vanished. And then in 2003 came Loreley (which eventually kicked off a new beer garden craze in the city). But don't mistake this Lower East Side hotspot for a place where geriatrics in lederhosen swing their plus-size steins of beer to polka music. Instead, there's a better than good chance that you'll find a gaggle of hipsters nursing German craft beers while bobbing their heads to the new Radiohead album and munching on plate of sausage, meatballs, or schnitzel. The space out back may be more concrete than garden, but it's a pleasure on a mild evening. ⓢ *Average main: $15* ⊠ *7 Rivington St., near Bowery, Lower East Side* ☎ *212/253–7077* ⊕ *www.loreleynyc.com* Ⓜ *J to Bowery; B, D to Grand; F to 2nd Ave.* ⊕ *2:F3.*

19

ⓢ

CAFÉ

�え

✕ **Momofuku Milk Bar.** The standing-only, workbenchlike tables at Momofuku Milk Bar provide clear views of pastry chef Christina Tosi and her bakers tinkering with their evolving menu of creations, but your attention will quickly turn to your taste buds. Try curiously flavored soft-serve ice cream (cereal-milk, lemon verbena), Candy Bar Pie (a sweet bomb of caramel, peanut-butter nougat, and pretzels atop a chocolate-cookie crust), addictive cookies (try the compost cookies, with pretzels, chocolate chips, and/or whatever inspires the bakers that day), or any of the intriguing savories (the "Volcano" is a cheese and potato pastry that is impossible to eat daintily). There are also branches in Midtown, the Upper West Side, Williamsburg, and Carroll Gardens. ⑤ *Average main: $6* ✉ *251 E. 13th St., East Village* ☎ *347/577–9505* ⊕ *www.milkbarstore.com* ⌕ *Reservations not accepted* Ⓜ *L to 3rd Ave.* ✛ *3:G4.*

$$$
LATIN AMERICAN
✕**Rayuela.** There's a young, sexy vibe at this vibrant Lower East Side restaurant where diners come for creative Latin cuisine courtesy of Máximo Tejada, the chef who built his reputation cooking at the popular (now closed) Lucy's Latin Kitchen. The bilevel eatery has a dining area, a ceviche bar, and—growing in the center of the restaurant—an olive tree. Ceviches are excellent, and there are several to choose from, as well as a selection of tapas. The kitchen excels with fish but the rice dishes are worthy of acclaim, too. For maximum enjoyment, come early for a predinner drink at the bar: standout cocktails include the pisco made with sour lime juice and foamy egg white. Latin-inspired brunch is served on weekends. ⑤ *Average main: $27.50* ✉ *165 Allen St., between Rivington and Stanton Sts., Lower East Side* ☎ *212/253–8840* ⊕ *www.rayuelanyc.com* ☽ *No lunch* Ⓜ *F to 2nd Ave.; J, M, Z to Essex and Delancey Sts.* ✛ *2:G3.*

$$
BISTRO
☾
✕**Schiller's Liquor Bar.** It may not be as hard to get in as it was back in 2003 when Keith McNally first opened this sceney hangout on the Lower East Side but it still has the allure, with excellent bistro fare, sexy cocktails, and the kind of atmosphere that is as comfortable for celebrities or parents with strollers. This is vintage Parisian à la McNally: verdigris mirrored panels, forever-in-style subway tiles, a tin ceiling, and a checkered floor, while Cuban sandwiches and steak frites reveal a steady hand in the kitchen. This is also the place for a late-night bite, since the kitchen is open until midnight every night except Friday and Saturday, when food is served until 3 am. Breakfast is served weekdays until 4 pm, with brunch on the weekends. ⑤ *Average main: $20* ✉ *131 Rivington St., at Norfolk St., Lower East Side* ☎ *212/260–4555* ⊕ *www.schillersny.com* Ⓜ *F to Delancey St.; J, M, Z to Essex St.* ✛ *2:G3.*

$$
ECLECTIC
✕**The Stanton Social.** This swanky Lower East Side favorite lures the crowds with an expansive and eclectic small-plates menu, accompanied by a perfectly calibrated cocktail list. Come before 7 if you want to be able to hear your fellow diners speak, but the people-watching and shared dishes are good at any hour. Try the gooey, Gruyère-topped onion soup dumplings, juicy Kobe beef sliders, and wasabi-crusted salmon. Downstairs feels like a more traditional dining room, whereas the second level features a buzzy bar. The late-night lounge area, decorated with cherry-blossom wallpaper and red leather upholstery, turns more nightclubby the later it gets. Brunch—with options like spicy lobster Benedict, and appropriate cocktails—might blow your mind. Whatever time you come, save room for the fresh doughnuts. ⑤ *Average main: $20* ✉ *99 Stanton St., between Ludlow and Orchard Sts., Lower East Side* ☎ *212/995–0099* ⊕ *www.thestantonsocial.com* ⌕ *Reservations essential* ☽ *No lunch* Ⓜ *F to 2nd Ave.* ✛ *2:G3.*

$ ✕ **Sugar Sweet Sunshine.** The brainchild of two former Magnolia Bakery
CAFÉ employees, Sugar Sweet's cupcakes are far superior; try the chocolate-
☾ almond Gooey Gooey, or the cream cheese frosting–topped pumpkin
flavor. The real showstopper? Swoon-inducing banana pudding incorporating slices of ripe fruit and crumbled Nilla wafers suspended in
decadent vanilla pudding. Cupcakes are the perfect on-the-go treat but
if you prefer to hang out, there are cozy couches for lounging. $ *Aver-
age main: $5 ⊠ 126 Rivington St., between Essex and Norfolk Sts.,
Lower East Side* ☎ *212/995–1960* ⊕ *www.sugarsweetsunshine.com*
◿ *Reservations not accepted* Ⓜ *F to Delancey St.* ✛ *2:G3.*

$$$ ✕ **wd~50.** Chef Wylie Dufresne—the mad genius and early progenitor
MODERN of the molecular gastronomy trend—mixes colors, flavors, and tex-
AMERICAN tures with a masterful hand, and the staff encourages diners to feel at
ease trying the deconstructed interpretations of modern food. As of
May 2012, Dufresne is overhauling the entire menu, jettisoning the
popular dishes that have been on the menu for years, but there are
sure to be many intriguing tastes and concepts. Tasting menus only
will be available in the main dining room (a primary menu of about
12 dishes will be $155; a smaller menu will be available for $75);
select dishes will be available à la carte at the bar. $ *Average main:
$34 ⊠ 50 Clinton St., between Rivington and Stanton Sts., Lower East
Side* ☎ *212/477–2900* ⊕ *www.wd-50.com* ☾ *No lunch Wed.–Sun.* Ⓜ *F
to Delancey St.; J, M, Z to Essex St.* ✛ *2:H3.*

$ ✕ **The Meatball Shop.** New York's first full-service meatball restaurant has
ITALIAN a pedigree chef, a professional waitstaff, a wine list, and a hip crowd.
☾ And the meatballs, oh, the meatballs. Choose beef, pork, chicken, or
veggie, or "special" ball options that range from chili cheese balls to
Greek lamb balls to Buffalo chicken balls, then decide if you want
them served simple as is, in sliders or a hero, as a salad, or as a plat-
ter; all with an appropriate choice of sauce and cheese. The meatball
concept quickly caught on and there are now three locations: two in
Manhattan and one in Williamsburg. Mix-and-match ice-cream sand-
wiches—choose your flavor and cookie. They're the only dessert but
worth saving room for. $ *Average main: $9 ⊠ 84 Stanton St., near Allen
St., Lower East Side* ☎ *212/982–8895* ⊕ *www.themeatballshop.com*
◿ *Reservations not accepted* Ⓜ *F, V to 2nd Ave.* ✛ *2:G3.*

$ ✕ **Shopsin's.** Don't ask for substitutions or sauce on the side at New
ECLECTIC York's most eccentric eatery because Kenny Shopsin, owner and chef,
☾ really may toss you out or ban you for life; somehow the attitude is
part of the appeal here. Though the eclectic menu runs to literally hun-
dreds of items—from pumpkin pancakes to chilaquiles, and from chili
cheeseburgers to lamb-curry soups—even the strangest foods conjured
up in his tight diner kitchen taste pretty great. The mac-and-cheese
pancakes have loyal followers (they're even better with hot sauce). The
space in the Essex Market is tiny, so expect to wait. Parties of more than
four aren't accepted. $ *Average main: $16.50 ⊠ 120 Essex St., near
Rivington St., in Essex Market, Lower East Side* ☎ *No phone* ⊕ *www.
shopsins.com* ◿ *Reservations not accepted* ▭ *No credit cards* ☾ *Closed
Mon. and Tues. No dinner* Ⓜ *J, M, Z to Essex St* ✛ *2:G3.*

19

$
CAFÉ
☺
✕**Doughnut Plant.** If the cupcake craze is getting you down, head to the Doughnut Plant, where the all-American junk-food staple is elevated to high art. Fresh seasonal ingredients go into these decadent treats, with real fruit and imported chocolate mixed into the batter. Traditionalists will croon over the vanilla bean doughnut but there are plenty of exotic flavors to tempt taste buds: the dense, fudgy blackout is covered in crumb topping; carrot cake doughnuts have a cream-cheese filling. In the center are the ultimate handheld piece of cake. There's a second location in Chelsea, next to the Chelsea Hotel; doughnuts are also available around the city at Dean & Deluca and Zabars. ⓢ *Average main: $5* ⊠ *379 Grand St., near Essex St., Lower East Side* ☎ *212/505–3700* ⊕ *www.doughnutplant.com* ⌲ *Reservations not accepted* ⊟ *No credit cards* ⊙ *Closed Mon.* Ⓜ *F to Delancey St.* ✛ *2:G4.*

$
CHINESE
✕**Congee Village.** Don't be put off by the name—this boisterous Chinatown icon serves much more than rice porridge. Indeed, the menu is enormous, covering an encyclopedic range of unusual Cantonese classics. The bamboo-cloaked dining room is great with a group of people, but being wedged in at a communal table with a boisterous family is part of the experience. If you're feeling adventurous, try the duck tongues in XO sauce or salt-and-pepper frog, or stick to familiar classics. Either way, the porridge is a great way to start. ⓢ *Average main: $15* ⊠ *100 Allen St., near Delancey St., Lower East Side* ☎ *212/941–1818* ⊕ *www. congeevillagerestaurants.com* Ⓜ *F to Delancey St.* ✛ *2:G3.*

GREENWICH VILLAGE AND THE WEST VILLAGE

GREENWICH VILLAGE

Greenwich Village's bohemian days may have faded with the Beatnik era, but the romantic allure of its tiny bistros, bars, and cafés remains. Around New York University, shabby-chic eateries and take-out joints line the streets and are patronized by a student clientele. Avoid heavily trafficked thoroughfares like Bleecker Street (unless you're tapping into the new artisan pizza craze), as most of the Village's culinary gems lie tucked away on side streets and alleyways, especially west of 7th Avenue, in the West Village. The vibe here is low-key and friendly, with patrons squeezed together at tiny tables in matchbox-size eateries.

$$
PIZZA
☺
✕**Arturo's.** Few guidebooks list this classic New York pizzeria, but the jam-packed room and pleasantly smoky scent foreshadow a satisfying meal. There's a full menu of Italian classics, but don't be fooled: pizza is the main event. The thin-crust beauties are cooked in a coal oven, and emerge sizzling with simple toppings like pepperoni, sausage, and eggplant. Monday to Thursday you can call ahead to reserve a table; weekends, be prepared to wait and salivate. ⓢ *Average main: $18* ⊠ *106 W. Houston St., near Thompson St., Greenwich Village* ☎ *212/677–3820* ⊙ *No lunch* Ⓜ *1 to Houston St.; B, D, F, M to Broadway–Lafayette St.* ✛ *2:D3.*

$$$
ITALIAN
Fodor's Choice
★
✕**Babbo Ristorante.** It shouldn't take more than one bite of the ethereal homemade pasta or tender barbecued squab with roast beet farrotto for you to understand why it's so hard to get a reservation at Mario Batali's casually elegant restaurant. The menu strays widely from Italian

FOOD COURT RENAISSANCE

Everywhere you turn, a new food court is opening. But these are not shopping-mall-style clusters of franchised eateries. Because we're talking New York, you can expect high-quality dining, a boon for hungry pavement-pounders looking for food, fast—not fast food.

At the **Plaza Food Hall** (⊠ 1 W. 59th St., at 5th Ave. ☎ 212/986–9260 ✛ 4:E1) in the basement of the Plaza Hotel, celeb chef Todd English oversees a series of mini-restaurants, each with its own counter with seating ideal for a quick snack or a full-fledged meal. Entry is a little confusing; though the place is made up of individual food concepts, you'll be seated by a hostess at any available counter. One you're settled, get up and survey your choices, then sit down and place one order from your waiter. There's a glistening raw bar, a burger joint, and a wood-burning

pizza station where you can sample some of English's iconic pies, such as fig and prosciutto. It's one of the most varied and affordable daytime food options in an area of town that can still feel like a lunchtime wasteland.

The cavernous **Eataly** (⊠ 200 5th Ave., at 23rd St. ☎ 646/398–5100 ✛ 3:E2), from Mario Batali & Co., is a temple of all things Italian. Ignore the overpriced produce market by the front entrance and make a beeline for La Piazza for sandwiches made with meticulously sourced ingredients (you can eat them at the standup tables nearby); a full-service pizza and pasta restaurant; a raw bar and fish eatery; and a spot for quaffing wines by the glass and beers on tap. There's also a corridor that's a gourmand's dream, with Italian chocolates, coffees, gelati, and pastries.

standards and hits numerous high points, in particular with the "mint love letters": ravioli filled with pureed peas, ricotta, and fresh mint, finished with spicy lamb sausage ragout; and rabbit with Brussels sprouts, house-made pancetta, and carrot vinaigrette. This is the perfect spot for a raucous celebratory dinner with flowing wine and festive banter. But be forewarned: if anyone in your party is hard of hearing, or bothered by loud rock music, choose someplace more sedate. ⑤ *Average main: $29* ⊠ *110 Waverly Pl., between MacDougal St. and 6th Ave., Greenwich Village* ☎ *212/777–0303* ⊕ *www.babbonyc.com* ✍ *Reservations essential* ☽ *No lunch* Ⓜ *A, B, C, D, E, F, M to W. 4th St.* ✛ *2:C1.*

19

$ ✕ **Bleecker Street Pizza.** Flavor reigns at this bustling corner pizzeria. It's
PIZZA   the perfect place to stop for a stand-up slice at the counter: the thin-
☾   crusted Nonna Maria is topped with garlicky marinara, grated and fresh
mozzarella, and freshly grated parmigiano-reggiano. ⑤ *Average main: $4* ⊠ *69 7th Ave. S, at Bleecker St., Greenwich Village* ☎ *212/924–4466* ⊕ *bleekerstreetpizza.net* ✍ *Reservations not accepted* Ⓜ *A, B, C, D, E, F, M to W. 4th St.; 1 to Christopher St.* ✛ *2:C2.*

$$$ ✕ **Blue Hill.** This tasteful, sophisticated den of a restaurant—formerly a
MODERN   speakeasy—on a quiet side street maintains an impeccable reputation for
AMERICAN   excellence and consistency under the leadership of chef Dan Barber. The
Obamas even stopped by here for dinner, shutting down the street for one of their "date nights." Part of the slow food, sustainable agriculture

movement, Blue Hill mostly uses ingredients grown or raised within 200 miles, including the Four Season Farm at Stone Barns Center for Food and Agriculture, Barber's second culinary project in nearby Westchester County. The chefs produce precisely cooked and elegantly constructed food such as wild striped bass with potato-and-clam chowder and house-cured *guanciale* (pork jowl), and a smoked-tomato soup with American caviar. $ *Average main: $29* ✉ *75 Washington Pl., between Washington Sq. W. and 6th Ave., Greenwich Village* ☎ *212/539–1776* ⊕ *www.bluehillfarm.com* ⚮ *Reservations essential* ⊙ *No lunch* Ⓜ *A, B, C, D, E, F, M to W. 4th St.* ✛ *2:C1.*

$ ✕ **Gray's Papaya.** It's a stand-up, takeout dive. And, yes, limos do some-
AMERICAN   times stop here for these legendary hot dogs. These traditional, juicy all-beef dogs are delicious, and quite the economical meal. Gray's is also a good bet for appeasing fussy children. $ *Average main: $6* ✉ *402 6th Ave., at W. 8th St., Greenwich Village* ☎ *212/260–3532* ▬ *No credit cards* Ⓜ *A, B, C, D, E, F, V to W. 4th St.* ✛ *3:D5* ✉ *2090 Broadway, at 72nd St., Upper West Side* ☎ *212/799–0243* Ⓜ *1, 2, 3 to 72nd St.* ✛ *5:B4.*

$ ✕ **Keste Pizza & Vino.** At the back of the long, narrow Keste Pizza & Vino
PIZZA   restaurant is a beautiful, tiled, wood-fired oven that cooks Manhattan's most authentic Neapolitan pies at 1,000 degrees. Blistered and chewy around the edges, each pie gives way to a softer center pooled with San Marzano tomato sauce and imported buffalo mozzarella. $ *Average main: $14* ✉ *271 Bleecker St, between 6th and 7th Aves., West Village* ☎ *212/243–1500* ⊕ *www.kestepizzeria.com* ⚮ *Reservations not accepted* Ⓜ *A, B, C, D, E, F, M to W. 4th St.* ✛ *2:C2.*

$$ ✕ **Lupa.** Even the most hard-to-please connoisseurs have a soft spot
ITALIAN   for Lupa, Mario Batali and Joseph Bastianich's "downscale" Roman trattoria. Rough-hewn wood, great Italian wines, and simple preparations with top-quality ingredients define the restaurant, along with the "gentle" prices. People come repeatedly for dishes such as ricotta gnocchi with sweet-sausage ragout, house-made salumi, and sardines with golden raisins and pine nuts. $ *Average main: $22* ✉ *170 Thompson St., between Bleecker and W. Houston Sts., Greenwich Village* ☎ *212/982–5089* ⊕ *www.luparestaurant.com* Ⓜ *A, B, C, D, E, F, M to W. 4th St.* ✛ *2:D3.*

$$ ✕ **Mermaid Oyster Bar.** If you're craving a great raw bar, lobster roll, or
SEAFOOD   soft-shell crab sandwich (in season), Mermaid Oyster Bar gives nearby classics Mary's Fish Camp and Pearl Oyster Bar a run for their money. Chef Lawrence Edelman (who also helms the city's two Mermaid Inn locations) goes beyond the comfort-food classics, though, with an alluring menu of sophisticated dinner choices. Almost every dish is a winner here, but the lobster bisque laced with Manzanilla sherry and toasted pumpkin seeds, the blackened striped bass with roasted squash and Swiss chard, and the spicy seafood *bucatini fra diavolo* are all standouts. From the bar, try something from the list of perfect-pitch cocktails, like a Dark and Stormy, made with black rum and ginger beer, or a Pimm's cooler with refreshing pieces of fresh cucumber. $ *Average main: $21* ✉ *79 MacDougal St., at W. Houston St., Greenwich*

Village ☎ *212/260–0100* ⊕ *www. themermaidnyc.com* ☾ *No lunch* Ⓜ *1 to Houston St., A, C, E to Spring St.* ✛ *2:C2.*

$$$
MODERN
AMERICAN
✕ **Minetta Tavern.** By converting a moribund 80-year-old Italian restaurant into a cozy hot spot, restaurateur Keith McNally has created yet another hit. Try early and often to score reservations, so that you can sample creations like buttery trout *meunière*, bone marrow on

toast, expertly aged steaks, and the celebrated Black Label burger, a gorgeous assembly of meat topped with caramelized onions and—for the brave—an added layer of cheese. The bar room, with its original details intact, is great for people-watching. Landing a table in the back room, with its original mural depicting West Village life and wall-to-wall photos of famous and infamous customers from eras gone by, makes sweet-talking the reservationist worth your while. ⑤ *Average main: $26* ⊠ *113 MacDougal St., between Bleecker and West 3rd Sts., Greenwich Village* ☎ *212/475–3850* ⊕ *www. minettatavernny.com* ⌲ *Reservations essential* Ⓜ *A, B, C, D, E, F, M to W. 4th St.* ✛ *2:D2.*

$
INDIAN
✕ **Kati Roll Company.** You can think of a kati roll as a South Asian taco: griddled parathas stuffed with savory-spiced grilled meat, shrimp, paneer, chickpea mash, or spiced mashed potato. They're the only things sold at this tiny, popular lunch spot cheerfully festooned with Bollywood posters. This is an excellent and inexpensive lunch option, but be warned that lines often form at weekday lunch, and there are only a few seats, so a good plan is to take your kati roll to a nearby park bench. ⑤ *Average main: $6* ⊠ *99 MacDougal St., near Bleecker St., Greenwich Village* ☎ *212/730–4280* ⊕ *www.thekatirollcompany.com* ⌲ *Reservations not accepted* ▭ *No credit cards* Ⓜ *A, C, B, D, E, F, M to W. 4th St.* ✛ *2:D2* ⑤ *Average main: $6* ⊠ *49 W. 39th St., near 6th Ave., Midtown West* ☎ *212/730–4280* ⊕ *www.thekatirollcompany.com* Ⓜ *B, D, F, M to 42nd St.* ✛ *3:G2.*

$
AMERICAN
☺
✕ **Peanut Butter & Co. Sandwich Shop.** For a childhood classic kicked up a notch, head to Peanut Butter & Co. Sandwich Shop. You can go with a standard PB&J, or explore any of the menu's 21 options, including the Elvis (grilled with peanut butter, bananas, and honey), the Pregnant Lady (peanut butter and pickles), or the sandwich of the week, with expertly paired ingredients such as cherry jam, cream cheese, and Crunch Time peanut butter. ⑤ *Average main: $7* ⊠ *240 Sullivan St., near W. 3rd St., Greenwich Village* ☎ *212/677–3995* ⊕ *ilovepeanutbutter.com* ⌲ *Reservations not accepted* Ⓜ *A, B, C, D, E, F, M to W. 4th St.* ✛ *2:D2.*

$
MIDDLE EASTERN
✕ **Taïm.** There's a real chef behind this tiny sliver of a restaurant—New York's only gourmet falafel stand. Taïm means "tasty" in Hebrew, and Tel Aviv transplant Einat Admony's fried chickpea balls are delicious, and available in several beguiling flavors (try them infused with spicy

19

harissa sauce) along with a tantalizing display of à la carte salads (the carrots with Moroccan spices are a standout). A new location in NoLIta opened in spring 2012. $ *Average main: $8.75* ⊠ *222 Waverly Pl., near Perry St., West Village* ☎ *212/691–1287* ⊕ *www.taimfalafel.com* ⌔ *Reservations not accepted* ═ *No credit cards* Ⓜ *1 to Christopher St.* ⊕ *2:B1.*

WEST VILLAGE

$$$

MODERN ASIAN

✕ **Annisa.** After a fire gutted this chic West Village restaurant in 2009, celebrity chef and co-owner Anita Lo has bounced back stronger than ever. "Annisa" may mean "the women" in Arabic, but the food here is inspired by Asia. And it's top notch. Foie-gras soup dumplings, barbequed squid with basil and peanuts, and Japanese curry-spiked rabbit are just a few winning examples you might find on the menu. But be sure to save room for dessert: the pecan and salted butterscotch beignets with bourbon ice cream are good enough to make you enroll in the fire academy to protect the place from another fire. $ *Average main: $30* ⊠ *13 Barrow St., between W. 4th and 7th Ave. S, West Village* ☎ *212/741–6699* ⊕ *www.annisarestaurant.com* Ⓜ *1 to Christopher St.–Sheridan Sq.* ⊕ *2:C2.*

$$$

EUROPEAN

✕ **August.** Rustic simplicity is the theme at this bustling West Village eatery, where many of the dishes come from the wood-burning oven in the dining room. Fish is always a good choice here, be it baked skate or pan-roasted cod, and meaty entrées like the pork chop or dry-aged sirloin are excellently cooked. Starters are more inventive; try the tarte flambé, an Alsatian flat bread topped with onion, bacon, and crème fraîche. Wood-planed floors and an arched cork ceiling envelop the busy 40-seat dining room; you can also dine at the bar. For a quieter meal, ask for a table in the glass-enclosed 15-seat atrium in back. $ *Average main: $33.50* ⊠ *359 Bleecker St., at Charles St., West Village* ☎ *212/929–8727* ⊕ *www.augustny.com* ⌔ *Reservations essential* Ⓜ *1 to Christopher St./Sheridan Sq.; A, B, C, D, E, F, M to W. 4th St.* ⊕ *3:C6.*

$

ITALIAN

✕ **Barbuto.** Chef Jonathan Waxman specializes in rustic preparations like house-made duck sausage with creamy polenta, red-wine-braised short ribs, and pasta carbonara, though the menu changes daily, depending on what's available. Waxman's acclaimed roasted chicken is usually on the menu in one form or another. The airy space continues to get busy; it's particularly pleasant in nice weather when the giant garage-door-like windows open onto the street. $ *Average main: $16.50* ⊠ *775 Washington St., between Jane and W. 12th Sts., West Village* ☎ *212/924–9700* ⊕ *www.barbutonyc.com* Ⓜ *A, C, E, to 14th St.; L to 8th Ave.; 1 to Christopher St./Sheridan Sq.* ⊕ *3:B5.*

$$

ECLECTIC

✕ **Blue Ribbon Bakery.** A neighborhood standard for good, if expensive, food, this outpost of the Blue Ribbon empire has an eclectic menu featuring substantial sandwiches on homemade bread (freshly baked in the oven downstairs), small plates, legendary bread pudding, and entrées that span the globe, from hummus to grilled catfish with sauteed collards and sweet potatoes. The basement dining room is dark and intimate; upstairs is more open and light-filled, with large windows looking out onto a pretty West Village corner. Brunch is notoriously crowded. $ *Average main: $25* ⊠ *35 Downing St., at Bedford St., Greenwich*

Village ☎ *212/337–0404* ⊕ *www.blueribbonrestaurants.com* Ⓜ *1 to Houston St.; A, B, C, D, E, F, M to W. 4th St.* ✛ *2:C2.*

$$$ ✕ **Commerce.** This former speakeasy harks back to days gone by with its
MODERN Diego Rivera–style murals, vintage sconces, and restored subway tiles,
AMERICAN but the crowd really comes for chef Harold Moore's seasonal cuisine.
Appetizers range from a red cabbage, apple, and pecan salad to yuzu-
marinated hamachi ceviche. Entrées are just as vibrant: bright, sweet
peas offset pristine halibut, and the shareable roast chicken, presented
table-side, is served with foie-gras bread stuffing. Brunch has a Middle
Eastern influence, with scrambled eggs and hummus atop a pillowy
pita, and a mean *shakshuka*—baked eggs nestled in a pepper, onion,
and tomato sauce. Even the contents of the bread basket are a pleasure
here. For a quieter meal, choose one of the booths near the bar. ⑤ *Aver-
age main: $35.50* ⊠ *50 Commerce St., West Village* ☎ *212/524–2301*
⊕ *www.commercerestaurant.com* ☾ *No lunch* Ⓜ *1 to Christopher St./
Sheridan Sq.; A, B, C, D, E, F, M to W. 4th St.* ✛ *2:B2.*

$$$ ✕ **dell'anima.** Lines snake out the door of this neighborhood favorite so
ITALIAN it's a good idea to make a reservation. Once you're in, check out the
open kitchen, where the stylish crowd converges to watch chefs prepare
authentic Italian dishes with a modern twist. Starters might include
sweetbreads, bone marrow, or charred octopus with chorizo, while
traditional first courses like pasta alla carbonara with speck (smoked
and cured pork), egg, and pecorino are impeccable. The signature *pollo
al diavolo* (spicy chicken) with broccoli rabe, garlic, and chili is seared
with enough smoke and heat for all seasons. If you can't get a table,
head to the 10-seat bar and try one of the restaurant's 400 wines or
signature cocktails. Anfora, their wine bar next door, is good for an
after-dinner drink if you want to linger. Brunch is served on weekends. ⑤ *Average main: $26* ⊠ *38 8th Ave., at Jane St., West Village*
☎ *212/366–6633* ⊕ *www.dellanima.com* ☾ *No lunch weekdays* Ⓜ *A,
C, E to 14th St.; L to 8th Ave.* ✛ *3:C5.*

$$ ✕ **Ditch Plains.** Named for a surf spot in Montauk, this laid-back neigh-
SEAFOOD borhood restaurant serves an eclectic bill of beachfront fare—from
fish tacos, lobster rolls, and fish-and-chips to clam chowder and crab
dip. There are options for landlubbers and vegetarians, too. It's not
quite a beach shack, but the food and the setting, with an upbeat rock
soundtrack, are designed for conviviality, and the wine-list prices are
extremely friendly, with whole and half bottles sold just above cost.
Breakfast/brunch is served every day from 11 am. There is also a loca-
tion on the Upper West Side. ⑤ *Average main: $13* ⊠ *29 Bedford St.,
near Downing St., West Village* ☎ *212/633–0202* ⊕ *www.ditch-plains.
com* ⚏ *Reservations not accepted* Ⓜ *1 to Houston St.* ✛ *2:C3.*

$$ ✕ **Do Hwa.** If anyone in New York is responsible for making Korean
KOREAN food cool and user-friendly, it is the mother-daughter team behind this
perennially popular restaurant and its East Village sister, Dok Suni's.
Jenny Kwak and her mother, Myung Ja, serve home cooking in the
form of *kalbi jim* (braised short ribs), *bibimbop* (a spicy, mix-it-yourself
vegetable-and-rice dish), and other favorites that may not be as pungent
as they are in Little Korea but are satisfying nevertheless. ⑤ *Average
main: $22.50* ⊠ *55 Carmine St., between Bedford St. and 7th Ave., West*

19

Village ☎ *212/414–1224* ⊕ *www.dohwanyc.com* ⊘ *No lunch weekends* Ⓜ *1 to Houston St.; A, B, C, D, E, F, M to W. 4th St.* ✛ *2:C2.*

$ ✕ **Fatty Crab.** This rustic Malaysian cantina showcases the exciting cui-
MALAYSIAN sine of chef Zak Pelaccio, who spent years cooking at famous French
Fodor's Choice restaurants before escaping to Southeast Asia for a year, where he fell
★   in love with the flavors of the region. Start with the addictive pickled watermelon and crispy pork salad, an improbable combination
that's both refreshing and decadent. The can't-miss signature dish
is chili crab—cracked Dungeness crab in a pool of rich, spicy chili
sauce, served with bread for dipping. It's messy for sure, but worth
rolling up your sleeves. Friday and Saturday the kitchen is open until
2 am. There are other incarnations of the Fatty Crab around town
and in Brooklyn. ⑤ *Average main: $15* ✉ *643 Hudson St., between
Gansevoort and Horatio Sts., West Village* ☎ *212/352–3592* ⊕ *www.
fattycrab.com* ⌖ *Reservations not accepted* Ⓜ *A, C, E to 14th St.; L
to 8th Ave.* ✛ *3:B5.*

$$$ ✕ **Fedora.** Up until 2011, subterranean Fedora was an ancient, little-
ECLECTIC patronized restaurant with an even more ancient owner (of which the
restaurant was eponymously named). But charming Fedora—the old
Italian owner—has left the building and restauratuer Gabe Stulman
took over the spot, vowing to keep the place largely intact. At least
the decor. Now see-and-be-scene folk cram the long narrow space
munching on French Canadian–accented fare like garlic cream-topped
duck breast and scallops paired with bone marrow and sipping cock-
tails, including the signature Fedora Dorato, named for the erstwhile
owner: Scotch, Cynar, and Cocchi Americano. Fedora (the restaurant)
will never be the same and that's maybe a good thing. ⑤ *Average main:
$25* ✉ *239 W. 4th St., between Charles and W. 10th Sts., West Village*
☎ *646/449–9336* Ⓜ *1 to Christopher St./Sheridan Sq.* ✛ *2:B1.*

$$ ✕ **Frankies 570.** The Frankies—that is, owners and chefs Frank Falci-
ITALIAN nelli and Frank Castronovo—have a winning formula, and their fourth
New York restaurant, this one in the West Village, seems to exemplify
it best: serve hearty not-necessarily-by-the-book Italian-inflected fare
using local, organic, and humanely raised ingredients in a laid-back
atmosphere. Most menu items change seasonally but expect pasta dishes
with standout sauces like almond pesto or ravioli stuffed with sweet
potato. The large menu also includes crostini, fresh salads, cured meats,
and cheese plates. ⑤ *Average main: $18* ✉ *570 Hudson St., at W. 11th
St., West Village* ☎ *212/924–0818* ⊕ *frankiesspuntino.com* Ⓜ *C, E to
14th St.* ✛ *2:B1.*

$ ✕ **'ino.** 'Ino's the kind of place you'd find every excuse to frequent if
ITALIAN you lived in the neighborhood. Every inch of space is economized in
this cozy, brick-lined eatery, where the chefs turn out an astonishing
variety of fresh bruschetta, tramezzini (soft-bread sandwiches), and
panini—not to mention soups and salads—from the tiny kitchen. Grab
a newspaper from the ledge, take a seat at the bar, choose your snacks,
and sample something from the excellent selection of Italian wines by
the glass. Everything's delicious, but the truffled egg toast, available for
brunch or anytime, with an oozing yolk and gooey fontina cheese, is a
star attraction. There are Inoteca sister restaurants around the city as

well. $ *Average main: $10* ✉ *21 Bedford St., between Downing and W. Houston Sts., West Village* ☎ *212/989–5769* ⊕ *www.inotecanyc.com* ⌒ *Reservations not accepted* Ⓜ *A, B C, D, E, F, M to W. 4th St.; 1 to Varick St.* ✛ *2:C3.*

$$$
ITALIAN
Fodor's Choice
★

✕ **I Sodi.** In a city of what seems like a million Italian restaurants, this minimalist-designed Tuscan-focused eatery in the West Village is a real find. Spikey-haired owner Rita Sodi, a Florentine who formerly worked in the fashion industry, ensures the traditional fare coming from the kitchen is satisfying. The menu changes weekly based on seasonal ingredients but expect a bevy of pasta dishes topped with good stuff like duck ragout and artichoke-laced lasagna, as well as not-very-Lipitor-friendly pancetta-wrapped pork and rabbit. Hoist a glass of grappa at the end of the meal and be happy you're in the right place. $ *Average main: $25* ✉ *105 Christopher St., between Bleecker and Hudson Sts., West Village* ☎ *212/414–5774* ⊕ *www.isodinyc.com* Ⓜ *1 to Christopher St.–Sheridan Sq.* ✛ *2:B2.*

$$
MODERN
AMERICAN

✕ **The Little Owl.** This tiny neighborhood joint, with seating for 28 people, is exceptionally eager to please. The menu is congruently small, which actually makes it easier to decide what you want. And what you want are the pork-veal-beef-pecorino-cheese meatball "sliders" or miniburgers. The unusually juicy pork loin chop, served with Parmesan butter beans and wild dandelion greens, is gigantic, and hugely satisfying. Raspberry-filled beignets, served with a ramekin of warm Nutella, are otherworldly. $ *Average main: $24* ✉ *90 Bedford St., at Grove St., West Village* ☎ *212/741–4695* ⊕ *www.thelittleowlnyc.com* ⌒ *Reservations essential* Ⓜ *1 to Christopher St./Sheridan Sq.; A, B, C, D, E, F, M to W. 4th St.* ✛ *3:D6.*

$$
SEAFOOD

✕ **Mary's Fish Camp.** Diners still line up down the street before the restaurant opens for dinner to get a table at this small but bustling seafood shack. The result of a split between Pearl Oyster Bar's partners, Mary's is a more intimate space, but the two have similar menus: excellent fried oysters, chowders, and, of course, the sweet lobster roll with crisp fries, all of which will have you licking your fingers. The killer hot-fudge sundae is worth saving room for. The staff here are warm and friendly, too. This is the kind of place everyone wishes was in the neighborhood. $ *Average main: $21* ✉ *64 Charles St., at W. 4th St., West Village* ☎ *646/486–2185* ⊕ *marysfishcamp.com* ⌒ *Reservations not accepted* ⊘ *Closed Sun.* Ⓜ *1 to Christopher St./Sheridan Sq.* ✛ *2:B1.*

$
MEXICAN

✕ **Mexicana Mama.** This colorful, popular space serves vividly flavored fare, and the kitchen is serious enough to create four different salsas daily, including a rotating "special salsa" that incorporates an authentic Mexican chili. Several dishes come with your choice of salsa and filling. The tomato-habanero salsa is simply unforgettable; cream tames the habaneros, but only slightly. Three chili-roasted pork tacos are also filled with piquant Chihuahua cheese and black beans, and served over Mexican rice and avocado cubes. Quesadillas are made with fresh corn tortillas (for a change!), filled with that melted Chihuahua cheese and your choice of chicken, barbacoa beef, chicken mole, or a daily special vegetable filling. For dessert, look no further than the eggy flan in flavors like caramel or cinnamon. $ *Average main: $13* ✉ *525 Hudson*

19

St., near Charles St., West Village ☎ *212/924–4119* ▭ *No credit cards* ⊘ *Closed Mon.* Ⓜ *1 to Christopher St./Sheridan Sq.; A, B, C, D, E, F, M to W. 4th St.* ✛ *3:C6.*

$ ✕ **Moustache.** There's typically a crowd waiting outside for one of the
MIDDLE EASTERN   copper-top tables at this appealing Middle Eastern neighborhood restaurant. The focal point is the perfect pita that accompanies tasty salads like lemony chickpea and spinach, and hearty lentil and bulgur. Also delicious is *lahambajin,* spicy ground lamb on a crispy flat crust. For entrées, try the leg of lamb or *merguez* (sausage sandwiches. Service is slow but friendly. There's also a location in the East Village. Ⓢ *Average main: $11.50* ⊠ *90 Bedford St., between Barrow and Grove Sts., West Village* ☎ *212/229–2220* ⊕ *moustachepitza.com/* ⌱ *Reservations not accepted* ▭ *No credit cards* Ⓜ *1 to Christopher St./Sheridan Sq.* ✛ *2:B2.*

$$$ ✕ **Pearl Oyster Bar.** There have been many imitators and few real com-
SEAFOOD   petitors to this West Village seafood institution. Since 1997, Rebecca Charles has been serving arguably the best lobster roll in New York City in a no-frills space down charming, restaurant-lined Cornelia Street— which expanded next door to accommodate the throngs. But that's not the only reason you should cast your net here. Pan-roasted sea scallops and plus-size crab cakes may compete with the legendary lobster roll for your taste buds' attention. Ⓢ *Average main: $25* ⊠ *18 Cornelia St., between W. 4th and Bleecker Sts., West Village* ☎ *212/691–8211* ⊕ *www.pearloysterbar.com* ⊘ *Sundays* Ⓜ *A, B, C, D, E, F, M to W. 4th St.* ✛ *2:C2.*

$$$ ✕ **Perry St.** Pay no mind to the cars whizzing by on the nearby West
MODERN   Side Highway; inside, the clean lines of this austere dining room with
AMERICAN   its gauze-swaddled wraparound windows and straight-back cream banquettes get you to focus on the main event on your plate. Owner Jean-Georges Vongerichten's son Cedric is manning the stoves, turning out memorable dishes like black-pepper crab dumplings plated with snow peas. Fried chicken is served with mushroom spaetzle and ginger vinaigrette, and a retro char-grilled cheeseburger is lavished with Russian dressing and crispy onions. Vongerichten's restaurants can be pricey, but give the man credit for offering value-oriented prix-fixe specials at lunch and dinner: $32 and $38, respectively. Ⓢ *Average main: $26* ⊠ *176 Perry St., at West St., West Village* ☎ *212/352–1900* ⊕ *www. jean-georges.com* Ⓜ *1 to Christopher St./Sheridan Sq.* ✛ *2:A2.*

$$$ ✕ **RedFarm.** Conceived and run by Bruce Schoenfeld, an expert on Chi-
CHINESE   nese cuisine, and Joe Ng, known as the dumpling king of New York, this second-floor West Village restaurant specializes in—you guessed it—Chinese-style dumplings. At least partly. The menu focuses mostly on dim sum—small plates and snacks (often in dumpling form)—as well as Chinese-American dishes like three-chili chicken and chicken in garlic sauce. The lobster dumplings and the crab-and-pork soup dumplings are culinary wonders and nearly obligatory for first timers. But come with a wallet the size of China itself because the dishes add up. Ⓢ *Average main: $29* ⊠ *529 Hudson St., between W. 10th and Charles Sts., West Village* ☎ *212/792–9700* ⊕ *redfarmnyc.com* Ⓜ *1 to Christopher St.–Sheridan Sq.; C, E to 8th Ave.* ✛ *2:B2.*

$$$
BRITISH

✕**The Spotted Pig.** Part cozy English pub, part laid-back neighborhood hangout, part gastronome's lure, the Spotted Pig showcases the impeccable food of Londoner April Bloomfield (Mario Batali and his partners consulted). Pair the tang of radishes in a salad with plenty of Parmesan and arugula, or smoked haddock–and-corn chowder with homemade crackers for studies in contrasts in texture and flavor. Shoestring potatoes accompany their Roquefort cheeseburger. Chase it with a glass of foam-dripping Old Speckled Hen. ⑤ *Average main: $23* ✉ *314 W. 11th St, at Greenwich St., West Village* ☎ *212/620–0393* ⊕ *www. thespottedpig.com* ⚄ *Reservations not accepted* Ⓜ *A, C, E to 14th St.; L to 8th Ave.* ✛ *2:A1.*

$$$
AUSTRIAN

✕**Wallsé.** Kurt Gutenbrunner's modern Austrian menu at this neighborhood restaurant with a quasi–Wiener Werkstätte look is soulful and satisfying, with a strong emphasis on Austrian tradition and urban New York attitude. It's hard to argue with such dishes as Wiener schnitzel with potato-cucumber salad and lingonberries, or venison goulash with spaetzle and Brussels sprouts. Desserts do Vienna proud: apple-walnut strudel is served with apple sorbet. ⑤ *Average main: $32.50* ✉ *344 W. 11th St., at Washington St., West Village* ☎ *212/352–2300* ⊕ *www. wallse.com* ⚄ *Reservations essential* ⊘ *No lunch weekdays* Ⓜ *1 to Christopher St./Sheridan Sq.; A, C, E to 14th St.; L to 8th Ave.* ✛ *3:B6.*

$
AMERICAN
☺

✕**Westville.** If New York's neighborhoods were small country towns, they'd all have restaurants just like Westville. These adorable spots—with branches in the East Village and Chelsea—serve simple wholesome fare, at reasonable prices. There are decent burgers and chops, but the seasonal sides, which change daily based on what's fresh at the market, are the real star attraction. ⑤ *Average main: $11* ✉ *210 W. 10th St., near Bleecker St., West Village* ☎ *212/741–7971* ⊕ *www.westvillenyc. com* Ⓜ *1 to Christopher St.* ✛ *3:C6.*

$
AMERICAN

✕**Wilfie & Nell.** When a local magazine named this gastropub one of the best places in Manhattan to meet young, attractive singles, food became something of an afterthought. But don't ignore the menu of hearty pub grub at this rustic (and perpetually crowded) restaurant–bar. Grilled cheese on thick country bread, juicy Berkshire pork sliders, and creamy chicken liver pâté, all supplemented with a frothy Irish or English brew, are a few things you'd be missing. Then again, if you're lucky, you may eat well *and* find a date. ⑤ *Average main: $12* ✉ *228 W. 4th St., between W. 10th St. and 7th Ave. S, West Village* ☎ *212/242–2990* Ⓜ *1 to Christopher St./Sheridan Sq.* ✛ *2:B1.*

19

CHELSEA AND THE MEATPACKING DISTRICT

CHELSEA

Chelsea is a calm neighborhood filled with art galleries and casual eateries. Subway stops are few and far between once you get west of 8th Avenue, so be prepared to walk or take a cab. One of the neighborhood's main highlights is the High Line, an elevated park that towers over the neighborhood.

$$$
ASIAN

✕**Buddakan.** Few—if any—restaurants in Manhattan can rival the 16,000-square-foot Buddakan in terms of sheer magnitude and buoyant theatricality. And in a neighborhood whose eateries often get by on sizzle alone, the food here has real substance as well. Restaurateur Steven Starr outdid himself with this New York version of his Philadelphia original: the upstairs bar is a great end-of-day meet-up spot for pert cocktails and appetizers; the vast downstairs is like a dining hall in a medieval castle, complete with a communal table spanning the room. The kitchen prepares ethereal tuna spring rolls that are narrow flutes of ruby tuna tartare in a crisp fried shell, while edamame dumplings are light and delicate. The menu is large, made up of Asian specialties like black pepper beef, glazed black cod, and sizzling short ribs served with tender, wide noodles. Considering the droves of patrons, service is surprisingly attentive. $ *Average main: $27* ⊠ *75 9th Ave., between W. 15th and W, 16th Sts., Chelsea* ☎ *212/989–6699* ⊕ *www.buddakannyc. com* ⚓ *Reservations essential* ⊗ *No lunch* Ⓜ *A, C, E to 14th St.; L to 8th Ave.* ✛ *3:B4* $ *Average main: $27* ⊠ *220 W. 23rd St., between 7th and 8th aves., Chelsea* ☎ *212/675-9100.*

$ ╳**Co.** Co., or, as it's pronounced "Company," took the New York pizza
PIZZA scene by red-sauce storm when it opened in early 2009. Bread master Jim Lahey, who made a name for himself at the Sullivan Street Baking Company, crafts simple but memorable pies, with the crust playing a starring role. The simple Margherita (tomato sauce, mozzarella, basil) is a good start, but diners are always tempted by unorthodox pizzas like the carmelized-onion-walnut-puree pie or the bechamel-and-Parmesan-topped version. This Chelsea pizzeria is anything but half baked. $ *Average main: $15* ⊠ *230 9th Ave., at W. 24th St., Chelsea* ☎ *212/243–1105* Ⓜ *C, E to 23rd St.* ✛ *3:B2.*

$$$ ╳**Cookshop.** One of far-west Chelsea's first hot restaurants, Cookshop
AMERICAN (from the same team as Five Points and Hundred Acres) manages a
Fodor'sChoice casual elegance while focusing on seasonal, farm-fresh cuisine that con-
★ tinues to wow. Outdoor seating on 10th Avenue is quite peaceful in the evening; during the day you can survey a cross-section of gallery-hoppers and shoppers. Divine cocktails, made with fresh fruit juices, are veritable elixirs of well-being. Line up early for brunch; it's worth the wait for dishes like baked eggs over duck and Swiss chard, or the fluffiest pancakes in town. Dinner is also a triumph, with a variety of perfectly prepared dishes like whitefish with lemony asparagus and hen-of-the-woods mushrooms or a simply roasted chicken. $ *Average main: $25.50* ⊠ *156 10th Ave., at 20th St., Chelsea* ☎ *212/924–4440* ⊕ *www.cookshopny.com* Ⓜ *A, C, E to 23rd St.* ✛ *3:B3.*

$$$ ╳**The Red Cat.** Elegant yet unpretentious, a lovely neighborhood spot
NEW AMERICAN *and* a destination restaurant, the Red Cat and its American-meets-Mediterranean menu is a great place for a long chat with a friend, to celebrate an auspicious occasion, to have a business dinner, or just the kind of place to go for an excellent meal. The menu changes frequently, based on what's in season, but expect an eclectic menu of well-executed pastas, burgers, saffron-laced seafood, and meaty numbers. Factor in the affordable wine list and you'll most definitely feel like one lucky cat. $ *Average main: $25* ⊠ *227 10th Ave., between W. 23rd and W. 24th Sts., Chelsea* ☎ *212/242–1122* ⊕ *www.redcatrestaurants.com* Ⓜ *C, E to 23rd St.* ✛ *3:A2.*

$$ **Trestle on Tenth.** Cozy and warm
SWISS with an inviting exposed brick interior, this Swiss brasserie is a true west Chelsea neighborhood spot. Locals and gallery hoppers quaff foamy beers or glasses of wine from the reasonable list while awaiting hearty Alpine-inspired dishes. Crispy duck necks, calves' liver with potato *rosti* and butter lettuce with bacon are fan favorites here.

It's not art—for that hit up one of the many galleries in the neighborhood—but it will make you yearn for Alpine landscapes. [$] *Average main: $20* ⊠ *242 10th Ave., at W. 24th St., Chelsea* ☎ *212/645–5659* ⊕ *www.trestleontenth.com* Ⓜ *C, E to 23rd St.* ⊕ *3:B2.*

$$ **Tia Pol.** It may be small, dark, and somewhat out-of-the-way, but none
SPANISH of that stops this popular tapas bar from being packed most nights (a
Fodor's Choice sardine-can metaphor would be apt here), with good reason. This is
★ one of the best tapas spots in town, with a welcoming vibe, a dozen reasonably priced Spanish wines by the glass, and charm to spare. The tables and stools are small (and high), but the flavors are enormous. One of the most original tapas has become a signature here: bittersweet chocolate smeared on a baguette disc and topped with salty chorizo. *Patatas bravas* (rough-cut potatoes served with a dollop of spicy aioli) are so addictive, you won't want to share them. The pork loin, piquillo pepper, and mild tetilla cheese sandwich is scrumptious, and so is the Galician octopus terrine. In fact, everything on the menu is transportingly delicious. [$] *Average main: $12* ⊠ *205 10th Ave., between W. 22nd and W. 23rd Sts., Chelsea* ☎ *212/675–8805* ⊕ *www.tiapol.com* ⚑ *Reservations essential* ☾ *No lunch Mon.* Ⓜ *C, E to 23rd St.* ⊕ *3:A2.*

$$ **Tipsy Parson.** If New York's Chelsea neighborhood were magically
SOUTHERN transported to the American South, it might taste something like Tipsy Parsons, a hip Southern-accented eatery with a menu of artery-hardening delights. Named for a boozy Southern dessert, the TP and its menu are all about comfort in the belly and soul: fried pickles, homemade peanut butter with crackers, bourbon-laced chicken liver mousse, and seafood pot pie are designed to make you leave full and happy. The restaurant's close proximity to the High Line, the elevated park/greenway, means you can walk it all off afterward. [$] *Average main: $24* ⊠ *156 9th Ave., between W. 19th and W. 20th Sts., Chelsea* ☎ *212/620–4545* ⊕ *www.tipsyparson.com* Ⓜ *C, E to 8th Ave.* ⊕ *3:B3.*

MEATPACKING DISTRICT

For a glitzy scene, head to the Meatpacking District, which has transformed in recent years from a gritty commercial warehouse area to the celebrity-chef–driven epicenter of the city's dining scene. The vibe is flashy, favored by Europeans, actors, models, and their suitors.

$$$$ **Del Posto.** Much more formal than Babbo, Del Posto is Mario Batali's
ITALIAN grown-up venue (in partnership with Lidia and Joe Bastianich), and the dining room—with its sweeping staircase, formal decor, and live music from a baby grand—has the feel of an opulent hotel lobby. This is one

19

of the most consistently dazzling special-occasion spots in the city and the food is stellar. There are a variety of set menus to choose from (no à la carte): pitch-perfect risotto is made fresh to order for two people or more (and served in the oversize pan); meat dishes like roasted veal chops are standouts, and pastas are ethereal—all accompanied by old-world table-side service. For a smaller taste of the experience, come for a cocktail and sample the bargain bar menu. ⑤ *Average main: $50* ✉ *85 10th Ave., between W. 15th and W. 16th Sts., Meatpacking District* ☎ *212/497–8090* ⊕ *delposto.com* ☾ *No lunch Tues.–Sat.* Ⓜ *A, C, E to 14th St.; L to 8th Ave.* ✛ *3:A4.*

$$$
BISTRO
✕ **Pastis.** Long a mainstay in the Meatpacking District, Pastis looks like it was shipped in, tile by nicotine-stained tile, from Paris's Pigalle neighborhood. French favorites are front and center, including tooth-some steak frites with béarnaise, mussels steamed in Pernod, and tasty apple tartlet with phyllo crust, and there's a still a good chance you'll see a local celebrity or two. Tables outside in nice weather are prime real estate for people-watching. ⑤ *Average main: $27* ✉ *9 9th Ave., at Little W. 12th St., Meatpacking District* ☎ *212/929–4844* ⊕ *www.pastisny. com* Ⓜ *A, C, E to 14th St.; L to 8th Ave.* ✛ *3:B4.*

$$$
ITALIAN
✕ **Scarpetta.** Chef Scott Conant left L'Impero and Alto to open Scarpetta, a critical darling since day one, adjacent to the glitz of the Meatpacking District. Walk past the bar into the polished dining room, where orange belts loop around mirrors and a retractable roof ushers in natural light. For a rousing start, try the creamy, rich polenta and mushrooms before enjoying one of the house-made pastas, like the al dente tagliatelle laced with strands of tender lamb ragout or the signature *capretto* (baby goat). Save room for dessert: the Amadei chcocolate cake with burnt-caramel gelato brings à la mode to a whole new level. ⑤ *Average main: $29* ✉ *355 W. 14th St., at 9th Ave., Meatpacking District* ☎ *212/691–0555* ⊕ *www.scarpettanyc.com* ☾ *No lunch* Ⓜ *A, C, E to 14th St.; L to 8th Ave.* ✛ *3:B4.*

$$$
ASIAN
✕ **Spice Market.** Set in a cavernous space amid embroidered curtains and artifacts from Burma, India, and Malaysia, chef Jean-Georges Vongerichten's playful takes on Southeast Asian street food will keep you asking the waiters for information: what exactly was in that? Sometimes the playfulness works, sometimes it doesn't, but don't miss the steamed lobster with garlic, ginger, and dried chili, or the squid salad with papaya and cashews. ⑤ *Average main: $22* ✉ *403 W. 13th St., at 9th Ave., Meatpacking District* ☎ *212/675–2322* ⊕ *www.spicemarketnewyork. com/* ⟡ *Reservations essential* Ⓜ *A, C, E to 14th St.; L to 8th Ave.* ✛ *3:B4.*

$$$
AMERICAN
✕ **The Standard Grill.** Hotelier André Balasz created an instant scene for celebs, fashion-industry insiders, and the common folk, too, who all cluster at this buzzy restaurant inside the Standard Hotel. In warm weather the spacious outdoor seating area is perfect for sampling creative cocktails; the indoor bar has low lighting, and a raw bar and charcuterie station that works on overdrive to put out plates of oysters and Italian cured meats for the two dining rooms—the more casual one in front, with wainscoted walls and views of Washington Street, and the larger room in the back, with a floor whimsically made up of thousands

of glittering copper pennies. Chef Dan Silverman's food is comfort-luxe, with dishes like roast chicken for two in a cast-iron skillet and delicious moist trout with a currant-and-pine-nut relish. For dessert, there's a nearly obscene chocolate mousse that comes with four silicone spatulas in lieu of spoons. A late-night menu is offered until 4 am. $ *Average main: $57* ⊠ *848 Washington St., between Little W. 12th and 13th Sts., Meatpacking District* ☎ *212/645–4100* ⊕ *www.thestandardgrill.com* Ⓜ *A, C, E to 14th St./8th Ave., L to 14th St./8th Ave.* ✛ *3:4A.*

UNION SQUARE WITH THE FLATIRON DISTRICT AND GRAMERCY

FLATIRON DISTRICT

Some of the city's most popular restaurants are in the area northwest of Union Square, called the Flatiron District. The neighborhood is also a hot shopping destination, with plenty of refueling spots like City Bakery, a gourmet deli and sweets spot that's a standby for many New Yorkers.

$$$
ITALIAN
Fodor's Choice
★

✕ **A Voce.** Executive chef Missy Robbins has a passion for Italian cuisine, and it shows. The American-born Robbins honed her Italian chops in northern Italy at the highly acclaimed Agli Amici restaurant in Friuli and also spent five years as the executive chef at Chicago's Spiaggia. At A Voce, her menu is inspired by regional dishes from all over Italy. The pasta is prepared fresh every day, and Robbins's fish and meat dishes are exceptional. The *agnello in due modi* entrée is especially well prepared, with tender lamb chops and a flavorful vegetable soffrito. For dessert, try the Tuscan bomboloni doughnuts with dark-chocolate dipping sauce. A Voce's atmosphere is warm, and the 90-seat dining room has a retro Italian feel to it—walnut floors, pale green leather-top tables, and Eames chairs. There's additional seating on the patio when weather permits. $ *Average main: $27* ⊠ *41 Madison Ave., between 25th and 26th Sts., Flatiron District* ☎ *212/545–8555* ⊕ *www.avocerestaurant. com* Ⓜ *N, R to 23rd St.* ✛ *3:F2.*

$$$
AMERICAN

✕ **ABC Kitchen.** Jean-Georges Vongerichten's latest New York City restaurant is attached to posh housewares emporium ABC Carpet and Home, and it's one of the hottest reservations in the city. Much more than a shopping break, ABC Kitchen is more like a love letter to greenmarket cuisine. Underneath the exposed concrete beams, a chic crowd devours fresh, flavorful appetizers like the roasted carrot salad with avocado, crème fraiche, and toasted pumpkin seeds or candy-sweet baby Maine shrimp with a sprinkling of sea salt and horseradish. There are pizzas with whole wheat crust (try the clam or trumpet mushroom versions) and substantial entrées like a well-charred steak served with a lusty red wine–and-carrot puree or a pristine fillet of arctic char served with fractal-looking Romanesco cauliflower. The restaurant is committed to all the right causes—environmentalism, sustainability, supporting local farmers—all of which are announced in a near manifesto-length list on the back of the menu. Thankfully, ABC Kitchen pulls it off without seeming patronizing or preachy. $ *Average main: $27* ⊠ *35 E. 18th St., between Broadway and Park Ave. S, Flatiron* ☎ *212/475–5829*

19

⊕ *www.abckitchennyc.com* ⌲ *Reservations essential* Ⓜ *N, R, Q, 4, 5, 6 to 14th St./Union Square* ✛ *3:F3.*

$$$ ✕ **Aldea.** Bouley alumnus George Mendes has opened a restaurant that
MEDITERRANEAN   uses his Portuguese heritage as inspiration and rises to new heights.
Fodor's Choice   Although there are no bad seats in this sleek bilevel space decorated
★   with touches of wood, glass, and blue accents, watching Mendes work
in his spotless tiled kitchen from one of the seats at the chef's counter
in the back is undeniably exciting. *Petiscos* (small bites) like cubes of
crisp pork belly with apple cider and caramelized endive and an earthy
pork-and-duck terrine with sweet muscat gelée reveal sophisticated
cooking techniques and flavors presented in highly addictive packages.
A delicate matsutake mushroom broth floated with a slow-poached
egg is edged with a subtle brace of pine. On the $85 five-course chef's
tasting menu, the sea urchin on a crispy toast flat is a standout, as is
the duck confit with chorizo and crunchy duck-skin cracklings. Ⓢ *Average main: $31* ⊠ *31 W. 17th St., between 5th and 6th Aves., Flatiron
District* ☎ *212/675–7223* ⊕ *www.aldearestaurant.com* ⌲ *Reservations
essential* ⊘ *Closed Sun. No lunch Sat.* Ⓜ *N, R, Q, 4, 5, 6 to 14th St./
Union Sq.; F, M to 14th St. and 6th Ave.* ✛ *3:3E.*

$$ ✕ **Boqueria.** Perenially packed, this convivial tapas spot has leather ban-
SPANISH   quettes lining the main room, but if you want to make friends opt for
the communal table running down the center of the dining room—if
you can get a seat. There are a few spots at the bar, too. Fried quail
eggs and chorizo on roasted bread are even better than they sound, and
the mushroom and ham croquettes are a mainstay. Traditional churros
come with a thick hot chocolate for dipping. Ⓢ *Average main: $19* ⊠ *53
W. 19th St., between 5th and 6th Aves., Flatiron District* ☎ *212/255–
4160* ⊕ *www.boquerianyc.com* ⌲ *Reservations not accepted* Ⓜ *6, F, R,
M, W to 23rd St.* ✛ *3:E3.*

$$$ ✕ **The Breslin Bar and Dining Room.** A sceney meatopia inside the ever-
BRITISH   trendy Ace Hotel, the Breslin is not for the Lipitor crowd. English chef
Fodor's Choice   April Bloomfield, who also runs the John Dory right next door and the
★   excellent Spotted Pig in the West Village, hardens arteries with peanuts
fried in pork fat, whipped lardo on pizza bianca, blood sausage accom-
panied by a fried duck egg, and a delicious feta-topped lamb burger. The
dimly lighted, wood-bedecked interior is like a culinary womb, inspir-
ing thoughts of planting yourself there all day or night nursing pints of
cask-conditioned ale or Scotch-based cocktails. And you wouldn't be
the first (or last) to have actually done it. Ⓢ *Average main: $30* ⊠ *20
W. 29th St., at Broadway, Flatiron District* ☎ *212/679–1939* Ⓜ *N, R
to 28th St.* ✛ *3:E1.*

$ ✕ **The City Bakery.** This self-service bakery-restaurant has the urban aes-
AMERICAN   thetic to match its name. Chef-owner Maury Rubin's baked goods—
☺   giant cookies, addictively flaky, salty-sweet pretzel croissants, elegant
Fodor's Choice   caramel tarts—are unfailingly rich. A major draw is the salad bar. It
★   may seem overpriced, but the large selection of impeccably fresh food,
including whole sides of baked salmon, roasted vegetables, soups, and
several Asian-accented dishes, delivers bang for the buck. Much of the
produce comes from the nearby farmers' market. In winter the bakery
hosts a hot-chocolate festival; in summer it's lemonade time. Weekend

brunch includes limited table-side service. $ *Average main: $12* ⊠ *3 W. 18th St., between 5th and 6th Aves., Flatiron District* ☎ *212/366–1414* ⊕ *www.thecitybakery.com* ⌲ *Reservations not accepted* ☉ *No dinner* Ⓜ *L, N, Q, R, 4, 5, 6 to 14th St./Union Sq.; F, M to 14th St.* ✛ *3:E3.*

$$$ ✕ **Craft.** A meal here is like a luscious choose-your-own-adventure
MODERN game since every delectable dish comes à la carte, including sides for
AMERICAN your roasted guinea hen or braised monkfish. Craft is *Top Chef* head judge Tom Colicchio's flagship in a mini-empire of excellent restaurants around the country, including the upscale Craftbar and Craftsteak brands, as well as grab-and-go sandwich bars called 'wichcraft. Just about everything here is exceptionally prepared with little fuss, from simple yet intriguing starters (grilled French sardines) and sides (the justly famous variety of roasted mushrooms, including oysters, trumpets, chanterelles, and hen-of-the-woods) to desserts (warm chocolate tart with buttermilk ice cream, cinnamon custard, and cashews). The serene dining room of burnished dark wood and dangling radiant bulbs—is more welcoming than it sounds. $ *Average main: $33* ⊠ *43 E. 19th St., between Broadway and Park Ave. S, Flatiron District* ☎ *212/780–0880* ⊕ *www.craftrestaurant.com* ⌲ *Reservations essential* ☉ *No lunch* Ⓜ *L, N, Q, R, 4, 5, 6 to 14th St./Union Sq.* ✛ *3:F3.*

$$ ✕ **Craftbar.** The casual sibling to Tom Colicchio's Craft is a bargain
MODERN in comparison, but still not cheap, though the food continues to gar-
AMERICAN ner raves, and the service is consistently excellent. The menu features assertive seasonal cooking similar to what you can find at the upscale flagship just around the corner. The small-plates category on the menu elevates tiny nibbles like sausage-stuffed fried sage leaves or addictive fluffy salt-cod croquettes to temptations that make you forget the main course entirely. The rest of the menu is eclectic enough to satisfy. $ *Average main: $18* ⊠ *900 Broadway, between 19th and 20th Sts., Flatiron District* ☎ *212/461–4300* ⊕ *www.craftbarnyc.com* ⌲ *Reservations essential* Ⓜ *L, N, Q, R, 4, 5, 6 to 14th St./Union Sq.* ✛ *3:F3.*

$$$ ✕ **Eataly.** The cavernous Eataly, from Mario Batali & Co., is a temple
ITALIAN of all things Italian. Ignore the overpriced produce market by the front entrance and make a beeline for La Piazza for sandwiches made with meticulously sourced ingredients (you can eat at the standup tables nearby). There's also a full-service pizza and pasta restaurant, a raw bar and fish eatery, and a wine bar for quaffing wines by the glass and beers on tap. Gourmet Italian chocolates, coffees, gelati, and pastries are all delicious to take away, too, though none of this is cheap. Upstairs, the covered, roof-top birrerria is open in all weather and serves hearty Austrian and German food as well as Italian specialties, and excellent beer, of course. $ *Average main: $25* ⊠ *200 5th Ave., at 23rd St., Flatiron* ☎ *646/398–5100* ⊕ *eatalyny.com* ⌲ *Reservations not accepted* Ⓜ *F, M, N, R to 23rd St.* ✛ *3:E2.*

$ ✕ **Eisenberg's Sandwich Shop.** Since 1929 this narrow coffee shop with
AMERICAN its timeworn counter and cramped tables has provided the city with some of the best tuna-, chicken-, and egg-salad sandwiches. On chilly days Eisenberg's classic matzo-ball soup also really hits the spot. The lively and friendly staff use the cryptic language of soda jerks, in which "whiskey down" means rye toast and "Adam and Eve on a raft" means

19

two eggs on toast. Considering the mayhem in the place, it's a pleasant surprise that you always get your meal, quickly and precisely as ordered. $ *Average main: $8* ✉ *174 5th Ave, between E. 22nd and E. 23rd Sts., Flatiron District* ☎ *212/675–5096* ⊕ *www.eisenbergsnyc.com* ⌕ *Reservations not accepted* ◷ *No dinner* Ⓜ *R, 6 to 23rd St.* ✛ *3:E2.*

$$$$ ✕ **Eleven Madison Park.** Luxury, precision, and creativity are the driving

MODERN   forces at this internationally renowned restaurant overlooking Madison

AMERICAN   Park. Swiss-born chef Daniel Humm oversees the kitchen, concocting

Fodor's Choice   unexpected dishes that change often but may include sea urchin cap-

★   puccino, duck with lavender honey, and prawn roulade with apple, avocado, and lime. It's tasting menu–only format, and dishes are listed simply by their principal ingredients, giving Humm and Co. maximum latitude to work their magic on the plate. Reservations should be made two months in advance. $ *Average main: $55* ✉ *11 Madison Ave., at 24th St., Flatiron District* ☎ *212/889–0905* ⊕ *www.elevenmadisonpark. com* ⌕ *Reservations essential* ◷ *Closed Sun. No lunch Sat.* Ⓜ *N, R, 6 to 23rd St.* ✛ *3:F2.*

$$$$ ✕ **Gramercy Tavern.** Danny Meyer's intensely popular restaurant tops

AMERICAN   many a New Yorker's list of favorite dining spots. In front, the first-come, first-served tavern has a lighter menu—including a value-packed three-course prix-fixe—along with great craft beers and cocktails scrawled on a board at the bar. The more formal dining room has a prix-fixe American menu, where choices include seasonal dishes such as marinated sea scallops with pickled peppers and fresh grapes, and rack of lamb with sunchokes, hazelnuts, and exotic mushrooms. Meyer's restaurants—he owns several well-regarded eateries in the city—are renowned for their food and hospitality, and Gramercy Tavern sets the standard. $ *Average main: $35* ✉ *42 E. 20th St., between Broadway and Park Ave. S, Gramercy* ☎ *212/477–0777* ⊕ *www.gramercytavern. com* ⌕ *Reservations essential* Ⓜ *6, R to 23rd St.* ✛ *3:F3.*

$$ ✕ **The John Dory.** Chef April Bloomfield and former rock band man-

SEAFOOD   ager-turned-restaurateur Ken Friedman can do no wrong. Their third restaurant—after gastropub-y Spotted Pig and the Breslin—turns its attention to the sea. Fish tanks with brightly colored reefs and floor-to-ceiling windows create an eye-pleasing venue for the seafood feast that awaits those who snagged tables at this restaurant off the lobby of the hip Ace Hotel. The menu is dominated by small plates—chorizo-stuffed squid, an excellent lobster roll—but focuses on the crudo (raw) dishes. The happy-hour special of a half-dozen oysters or clams and a choice of sparkling wine or a pint of ale for $15 is the perfect start to an evening. $ *Average main: $19* ✉ *1196 Broadway, at W. 29th St., Flatiron District* ☎ *212/792–9000* ⊕ *thejohndory.com* ⌕ *Reservations not accepted* Ⓜ *N, R to 28th St.* ✛ *3:E1.*

$$$$ ✕ **Primehouse New York.** A sleek steakhouse from fabled restaurateur Ste-

STEAKHOUSE   phen Hanson, Primehouse does meat and does it well. There is steak tartare prepared table-side, and respectable dry-aged prime cuts, ranging from hanger steak ($21) to porterhouse for two ($96), as well as classic accompaniments like Caesar salad. For something lighter, try skate sautéed in lemon-brown-butter sauce, or the Berkshire pork chop with fig glaze and apple compote. The mod space has a cream-and-black motif that recalls the Jetsons' futuristic 1960s feel, interspersed with geometric M. C. Escher–like patterns. [$] *Average main: $49* ⊠ *381 Park Ave. S, at 27th St., Flatiron District* ☎ *212/824–2600* ⊕ *www.primehousenyc. com* Ⓜ *6, R to 28th St.* ✛ *3:F2.*

$$$

ITALIAN

✕ **SD26.** The charming father-daughter restaurant team of Tony and Marisa May closed uptown's San Domenico to open this more casual, yet still impressive, Italian spot. The cavernous main dining room, decorated with a constellation of pinpoint lights and ringed with more intimate tables and banquettes, speaks to a fresher, more modern approach than its predecessor. The food—pappardelle with wild boar ragout, smoked lobster with porcini mushrooms and orange segments—is a refreshing mix of classic and forward-thinking. Expect a personal greeting from either father or daughter before your meal comes to an end. [$] *Average main: $26* ⊠ *19 E. 26th St., between 5th and Madison Aves., Flatiron District* ☎ *212/265–5959* ⊕ *www.sd26ny.com* ⌣ *Reservations essential* Ⓜ *R to 23rd St. and 5th Ave.* ✛ *3:E2.*

$

AMERICAN

Fodor's Choice

★

✕ **Shake Shack.** Although there are other locations of Danny Meyer's patties 'n' shakes joint around town (including Brooklyn), this is where it all began. Here in Madison Square Park there's no indoor seating—just snaking outdoor lines. ■ **TIP→ Check the "Shack Cam" from their website to gauge your wait.** If it's raining, you may be in luck—inclement weather can mean shorter lines. Fresh Angus beef burgers are ground daily, and a single will run you from $3.75 to $4.75, depending on what you want on it. For a burger on-the-go, they're decidedly tasty. For a few more bucks you can order a double, a stacks, or a vegetarian 'Shroom Burger—a super-rich melty Muenster and cheddar cheese–stuffed, fried portobello, topped with lettuce, tomato, and Shack sauce. The menu also offers beef and bird (chicken) hot dogs, french fries, and a variety of delicious frozen custard desserts, and—of course—shakes! [$] *Average main: $5* ⊠ *Madison Square Park near Madison Ave. and E. 23rd St., Flatiron District* ☎ *212/889–6600* ⊕ *www.shakeshack.com* Ⓜ *N, R, 6 to 23rd St.* ✛ *3:F2.*

$$$

INDIAN

✕ **Tamarind.** Many consider Tamarind Manhattan's best Indian restaurant. Forsaking the usual brass, beads, sitar, and darkness, you'll find a lustrous skylighted dining room awash in soothing neutral colors and awaft with tantalizing fragrances. Your welcoming hosts, owner Avtar Walia and his nephew, general manager Gary, practically reinvent charm. The busy kitchen offers multiregional dishes, some familiar (tandoori chicken, a searing lamb vindaloo), some unique (succulent venison chops in a vigorously spiced cranberry sauce; she-crab soup with saffron, nutmeg, and ginger juice). The more intriguing a dish sounds, the better it turns out to be. [$] *Average main: $25* ⊠ *41–43 E. 22nd St., between Broadway and Park Ave. S, Flatiron District* ☎ *212/674–7400* ⊕ *www.tamarinde22.com* ⌣ *Reservations essential* Ⓜ *N, R, 6 to 23rd St.* ✛ *3:F2.*

GRAMERCY

This leafy, high-rent neighborhood is anchored by Gramercy Park, a locked, private park that takes up a city block. Access to the park is restricted to nearby residents and businesses, including guests of the Gramercy Park Hotel. With its historic homes and tucked-away bars

19

and restaurants, it is a scenic, interesting neighborhood for an afternoon stroll.

$$$$ ✕ **BLT Prime.** A masculine, vivacious space is the showcase for bold,
STEAKHOUSE appealing Franco-American cuisine. Menu specials are scrawled on a blackboard. Everything is served à la carte, and prices are high, but so is the quality of every dish. Former restaurant namesake Laurent Tourondel's signature steaming-hot Gruyère popovers remain on the menu. They're light and buttery with an addictive texture. Although there are poultry, veal, and lamb dishes on the menu—from lemon-rosemary chicken to a lamb T-bone—steaks are the main event. The dry-aged USDA prime steaks—pulled from a 30-foot-wide dry-aging room—are broiled at 1,700 degrees, spread lightly with herb butter and offered with a choice of sauce (the béarnaise is perfection). $ *Average main: $38* ✉ *111 E. 22nd St., between Lexington and Park Aves., Gramercy Park* ☎ *212/995–8500* ⊕ *www.bltprime.com* ⚶ *Reservations essential* ☾ *No lunch* Ⓜ *6, R to 23rd St.* ✛ *3:F3.*

$$ ✕ **Casa Mono.** Andy Nusser put in his time cooking Italian under Mario
SPANISH Batali at Babbo before an obsession with Spain landed him his own acclaimed Iberian niche. The perennially cramped and crowded Casa Mono sends its overflow to Bar Jamón, the annex wine-and-ham bar next door, where you can pick at plates of *jamón serrano* while awaiting the call for a prime seat at the Casa Mono counter overlooking the chef's open kitchen. Though most menu items are delectably shareable, of particular note are all things seared *à la plancha*, including blistered peppers and garlic-kissed mushrooms. Like his renowned mentor, Nusser has a weakness for the most neglected cuts of meat so check your food fears at the door and try the blood sausage, cockscombs, or tripe. $ *Average main: $17.50* ✉ *52 Irving Pl., at E. 17th St., Gramercy Park* ☎ *212/253–2773* ⊕ *www.casamononyc.com* Ⓜ *4, 5, 6, L, N, Q, R to Union Sq.* ✛ *3:G3.*

$$$$ ✕ **Maialino.** Named for its signature dish—suckling pig—the perpetually
ROMAN packed restaurant inside the Gramercy Park Hotel has benefited from New York diners' growing interest in all things Roman in the last couple years. But that's not to say that Maialino can't stand on its own. The suckling pig *is* worth every penny (and it's not cheap) for the taste of the crispy skin that gives way to juicy pork. But come hungry because if you haven't been to the Eternal City in a while; there's plenty to reintroduce your taste buds to La Dolce Vita: fried artichokes executed authentically enough you might think you're back in Rome's Jewish ghetto, spaghetti alla carbonara (made with *guanciale*—or pig cheek—just like in Rome), and the sausage-studded pasta dish *lumaconi alla Norcia*. It's enough to make a toast to the good life—that is, if your dining companions can hear you over the guffaws and chatter of the fashion models and bankers at surrounding tables. $ *Average main: $24* ✉ *2 Lexington Ave., at E. 21st St., Gramercy* ☎ *212/777–2410* ⊕ *www.maialinonyc. com/* ⚶ *Reservations essential* Ⓜ *6 to 23rd St.* ✛ *3:G3*

UNION SQUARE

The blocks around Union Square and its open-air greenmarket are filled with upscale foodie havens featuring market-driven menus. But fancy seasonal fare isn't all the area offers. With excellent shopping nearby, there are also plenty of spots to duck in for a quick lunch or snack on-the-go.

$$$$
AMERICAN
Fodor's Choice
★

✕**Gotham Bar & Grill.** A culinary landmark, Gotham Bar & Grill is every bit as thrilling as it was when it opened in 1984. Celebrated chef Alfred Portale, who made the blueprint for "architectural food"—that is, towers of stacked ingredients—builds on a foundation of simple, clean flavors. People come for Portale's transcendent preparations: no rack of lamb is tenderer, no seafood salad sweeter. The stellar 20,000-bottle cellar provides the perfect accompaniments—at a price. The three-course $25 prix-fixe lunch from noon to 2:30 weekdays is a steal, even if it's not as sophisticated as dinner. Desserts are also memorable. $ *Average main: $41* ✉ *12 E. 12th St., between 5th Ave. and University Pl., Union Square* ☎ *212/620–4020* ⊕ *www.gothambarandgrill.com* ⊗ *No lunch weekends* Ⓜ *L, N, Q, R, 4, 5, 6 to 14th St./Union Sq.* ✛ *3:E4.*

$
ASIAN

✕**Republic.** When Republic first opened, it was one of very few places to get an Asian-style noodle bowl with a stylish edge. Many have followed in its footsteps—and some are better—but for window shoppers, green-marketers, and anyone else in the Union Square area, this place gets the job done. The look is like a cross between a downtown art gallery and a Japanese school cafeteria, and the young waitstaff dressed in black T-shirts and jeans hold remote-control ordering devices to accelerate the already speedy service. Sit at the long, bluestone bar or at the picnic-style tables and order appetizers such as smoky grilled eggplant and luscious fried wontons. Entrées are all based on noodles or rice. Spicy coconut chicken soup and Vietnamese-style barbecued pork are menu standouts. $ *Average main: $12* ✉ *37 Union Sq. W, between E. 16th and E. 17th Sts., Union Square* ☎ *212/627–7172* ⊕ *www.thinknoodles. com* ⬤ *Reservations not accepted* Ⓜ *L, N, Q, R, 4, 5, 6 to 14th St./ Union Sq.* ✛ *3:F4.*

$$$
MODERN
MEXICAN

✕**Rosa Mexicano.** The idea that you can't find good south-of-the-border cuisine in the Big Apple is quickly fading, thanks in part to this Union Square restaurant (there are two other locations, at Lincoln Center and Midtown East). Although the spacious, colorfully lighted interior might tip you off that if authenticity is what you seek, look elsewhere, but if you're looking for high-quality, well-executed Mex-flavored fare, step right up, hombre. Start with an order of guac (made table-side) and dig in, moving on, perhaps, to the pork belly and scallop tacos, soul-comforting chicken tortilla pie, or the crispy pork shank. All of which taste better with a pomegranate margarita or three. $ *Average main: $28* ✉ *9 E. 18th St., between 5th Ave. and Union Sq., Flatiron* ☎ *212/533–3350* Ⓜ *R, N. Q, 4, 5, 6, L to 14th St./Union Sq.* ✛ *3:F3*

$$$
MODERN
AMERICAN

✕**Tocqueville.** Hidden just steps from busy Union Square, Tocqueville is a refined dining oasis that's a secret even to many New York foodies. Enter through the austere reception area, past the heavy curtains and a six-seat bar, and you'll find the intimate dining area where chef-owner Marco Moreira's signature starter is the unctuous sea urchin angel-hair carbonara. Main courses are steeped in French tradition, but with international flavors, like honey-glazed Peking duck breast and leg terrine, and curry-dusted Chatham cod. The three-course $24 prix-fixe lunch is the ultimate deal. $ *Average main: $28* ✉ *1 E. 15th St., between*

19

5th Ave. and Union Sq. W, Union Square ☎*212/647–1515* ⊕*www. tocquevillerestaurant.com* ♨*Reservations essential* Ⓜ*L, N, Q, R, 4, 5, 6 to 14th St./Union Sq.* ✛*3:F4.*

$$$ ✕**Union Square Cafe.** When he opened Union Square Cafe in 1985,
AMERICAN Danny Meyer changed the American restaurant landscape: his combination of upscale food and unpretentious but focused service sparked a revolution. Meyer might not be in the kitchen but this landmark spot still draws devotees with the crowd-pleasing menu, warm atmosphere, and, of course, the service. Wood paneling and white walls are hung with modern paintings; in addition to the three dining areas, there's a long bar ideal for solo diners. The cuisine is American with a thick Italian accent—hearty pastas, seafood, and an excellent roast chicken—and the lunchtime burger is a perennial favorite. ⑤*Average main: $28.50* ✉*21 E. 16th St., between 5th Ave. and Union Sq. W, Union Square* ☎*212/243–4020* ⊕*www.unionsquarecafe.com* ♨*Reservations essential* Ⓜ*L, N, Q, R, 4, 5, 6 to 14th St./Union Sq.* ✛*3:F4.*

$ ✕**Stand4.** A pioneer on the gourmet-burger scene, this spiffy full-service
BURGER restaurant serves its bespoke patties with a wide variety of upmar-
☾ ket toppings, from applewood-smoked bacon and onion marmalade to porcini-mushroom and green-peppercorn sauces. Even the classic burgers here are a better breed than most, fat and juicy on a great eggy bun—options include chicken, turkey, veggie, salmon, and "crabbie" burgers. Accompany your meal with a premium gelato milkshake, virgin or spiked. ⑤*Average main: $13.50* ✉*24 E. 12th St., near University Pl., Union Square* ☎*212/488–5900* ⊕*www.standburger.com* ♨*Reservations not accepted* Ⓜ*4, 5, 6, L, N, Q, R to Union Square* ✛*3:F4.*

MIDTOWN EAST WITH MURRAY HILL

MIDTOWN EAST

Midtown East's streets are relatively quiet at night and on weekends, but the restaurants are filled with expense-account diners celebrating their successes. Some of the most formal dining rooms and most expensive meals in town can be found here, at restaurants like the landmark **Four Seasons** and **L'Atelier de Joël Robuchon**.

$$$$ ✕**Adour Alain Ducasse.** Master chef Alain Ducasse added to his growing
MODERN FRENCH empire with the elegant, wine-focused Adour, in the equally sophisticated St. Regis Hotel, although a chef shuffle brought a new aide-de-camp to the kitchen in early 2012. Celebratory couples of all ages gravitate to the Left and Right Bank rooms, and a mix of tourists, shoppers, and businessmen settle on plush burgundy chairs and banquettes in the regal but relaxed main dining room. Deep pockets splurge on artfully arranged dishes, such as roasted chicken with mushrooms and herb butter, accompanied by Swiss-chard gratin. Sommeliers help decipher an international wine list (displayed on interactive computer screens at the bar) with bottles that range from $35 to $19,000. ⑤*Average main: $55* ✉*2 E. 55th St., near 5th Ave., Midtown East* ☎*212/710–2277* ⊕*www.adour-stregis.com* ♨*Reservations essential* ☾*No lunch* Ⓜ*E, M to 5th Ave./53rd St.; F to 57th St.* ✛*4:E2.*

$$$$ ✕ **Aquavit and Aquavit Café.** Celebrity chef and co-owner Marcus Samu-
SCANDINAVIAN elsson may no longer be in the kitchen here, but you'd never know it
from the impeccable cuisine and service at this fine-dining restaurant
and upscale café, now in the hands of able executive chef Marcus Jen-
mark. The elegant atmosphere features warm woods and modern decor
from a Scandinavian design team. In the café, try a two-course dinner
of daily "Swedish home cooking" specials, or order à la carte to try the
herring sampler, with boldly flavored selections like curry and apple,
and vodka-lime. The main dining room is prix-fixe only, with a three-
course dinner or a chef's tasting. ⑤ *Average main: $60 ✉ 65 E. 55th
St., between Madison and Park Aves., Midtown East ☎ 212/307–7311
⊕ www.aquavit.org ⌬ Reservations essential ⊗ No lunch Sat., except
in café* Ⓜ *E, M to 5th Ave./53rd St.* ✛ *4:F2.*

$$$ ✕ **BLT Steak.** Chef Laurent Tourondel is no longer involved with his
STEAKHOUSE namesake steak house, but this classy space, decked out in beige with
resin-top black tables, still draws crowds. As soon as you're settled,
puffy Gruyère popovers arrive still steaming. The no-muss, no-fuss
menu is nonetheless large, and so are the portions of supple crab cakes
with celery-infused mayonnaise and luscious ruby tuna tartare with
avocado, ramped up with soy-lime dressing. A veal chop crusted with
rosemary and Parmesan lends new depth to the meat. At lunch, the
quintessential BLT includes Kobe beef, foie gras, bacon, and tomato
on a split ciabatta bun, with a cute plastic pig toothpick indicating
desired doneness. Sides and desserts, like a killer peanut butter–choco-
late mousse with banana ice cream, are all superior. ⑤ *Average main:
$33 ✉ 106 E. 57th St., between Lexington and Park Aves., Midtown
East ☎ 212/752–7470 ⊕ www.bltsteak.com ⌬ Reservations essential
⊗ Closed Sun. No lunch Sat.* Ⓜ *4, 5, 6, N, R to 59th St./Lexington
Ave.* ✛ *4:F1.*

$$$$ ✕ **The Four Seasons.** The landmark Seagram Building houses one of
AMERICAN America's most famous restaurants, truly an only-in–New York experi-
ence. Owners Alex Von Bider and Julian Niccolini supervise the seating
chart like hawks, placing power players in finance, entertainment, and
New York society in prime positions for maximum visibility. The stark
Grill Room, birthplace of the power lunch, has one of the best bars in
New York. Illuminated trees and a gurgling Carrara marble pool char-
acterize the more romantic Pool Room. The menu changes seasonally;
there's a $65 prix-fixe pretheater dinner—a delicious indulgence. You
can't go wrong with classic dishes like Dover sole, filet mignon, or crispy
duck, but the restaurant moves with the times, so expect roving sea-
sonal specials featuring luxe ingredients and preparations. Finish with
pear William, Grand Marnier, or a chocolate soufflé. ⑤ *Average main:
$57 ✉ 99 E. 52nd St., between Park and Lexington Aves., Midtown
East ☎ 212/754–9494 ⊕ www.fourseasonsrestaurant.com ⌬ Reserva-
tions essential Jacket required ⊗ Closed Sun. No lunch Sat.* Ⓜ *E, M to
Lexington Ave./53rd St.; 6 to 51st St.* ✛ *4:F2.*

$$$ ✕ **Grand Central Oyster Bar & Restaurant.** Nestled deep in the belly of
SEAFOOD Grand Central Station, the Oyster Bar has been a worthy seafood desti-
nation since 1913. Sit at the counter for the fried-oyster po'boy, or slurp
an assortment of bracingly fresh oysters before having a steaming bowl

19

of clam chowder washed down with an ice-cold brew. Or experience the forgotten pleasure of fresh, unadorned seafood such as lobster with drawn butter or grilled herring in season. Avoid anything that sounds too complicated, like cream-smothered seafood pan roasts. ⑤ *Average main: $30* ⊠ *Grand Central Station, dining concourse, East 42nd St. at Vanderbilt Ave., Midtown East* ☎ *212/490–6650* ⊕ *www.oysterbarny. com* ⊘ *Closed Sun.* Ⓜ *4, 5, 6, 7, S to 42nd St./Grand Central* ✛ *4:F4.*

$$$$ ✕ **Kuruma Zushi.** Only a small sign in Japanese indicates the location
JAPANESE of this extraordinary restaurant that serves only sushi and sashimi. Bypass the tables, sit at the sushi bar, and put yourself in the hands of Toshishiro Uezu, the chef-owner. Among the selections are hard-to-find fish that Uezu imports directly from Japan. The most attentive, pampering service staff in the city completes the wildly expensive experience. The showstopping chef's *omakase* will cost you $250, but it's a multicourse feast you'll never forget. ⑤ *Average main: $155* ⊠ *7 E. 47th St., 2nd Floor, Midtown East* ☎ *212/317–2802* ⊕ *www.kurumazushi. com/* ⌕ *Reservations essential* ⊘ *Closed Sun.* Ⓜ *4, 5, 6, 7 to 42nd St./ Grand Central* ✛ *4:E3.*

$$$$ ✕ **L'Atelier de Joël Robuchon.** The New York branch of Joël Robuchon's
FRENCH luxurious restaurant, inside the Four Seasons Hotel, features essentially
Fodor's Choice the same food as the Paris original. And that, it turns out, is a very good
★ thing. The perfectionist chef has installed a longtime protégé to uphold the standards that can make a Robuchon meal a life-changing experience. Skip the regular-size appetizers and entrées. Instead, secure a seat at the pear-wood counter and cobble together your own small-plate feast. But be warned: with heady ingredients like Scottish langoustines (tempura fried), Osetra caviar atop crabmeat and coral gelée, and foie gras (paired with caramelized eel), Robuchon's little bites come at a steep price. ⑤ *Average main: $60* ⊠ *57 E. 57th St., between Madison and Park Aves., in the Four Seasons Hotel, Midtown East* ☎ *212/350– 6658* ⊕ *www.fourseasons.com/newyorkfs/dining.html* ⌕ *Reservations essential* ⊘ *No lunch* Ⓜ *4, 5, 6 to 59th St.* ✛ *4:F1.*

$$$$ ✕ **Le Cirque.** Impresario-owner Sirio Maccioni still presides over a dining
FRENCH room filled nightly with a who's who of political, business, and society circles—regulars who've table-hopped from Le Cirque's first incarnation to its latest, in a glass-enclosed atrium on the ground floor of the Bloomberg headquarters. Billowing silk, gauzy shades, and porcelain monkeys create a playful big-top effect. The menu strikes a balance between the creative and classic. Dover sole, filleted table-side, gives way to more avant-garde preparations like a duo of seared foie gras and sushi-grade tuna. Desserts, too, have a split personality, with the menu divided into the "classic" and "new." The foot-tall napoleon that seems to arrive at every second table is an old favorite, but newer creations like the praline tortellini with exotic fruit also satisfy high-society sweet tooths. Though jackets are still required in the dining room, things are more relaxed in the casual wine lounge. ⑤ *Average main: $59* ⊠ *151 E. 58th St., at Lexington Ave., Midtown East* ☎ *212/644–0202* ⊕ *www. lecirque.com* ⌕ *Reservations essential* ⊘ *Closed Sun. No lunch Sat.* Ⓜ *4, 5, 6, N, R to Lexington Ave./59th St.* ✛ *4:F1.*

$$$
STEAKHOUSE

⨉**Michael Jordan's The Steakhouse NYC.** Don't be dissuaded by the fact that this place is technically part of a chain: there's nowhere remotely like it. The handsomely appointed space in Grand Central Terminal, hung with gracious filigree chandeliers, overlooks one of the most famous interiors in America. Start with the stack of soft, toasted bread soldiers in a pool of hot Gorgonzola fondue. Pristine oysters make a great prelude for a prime dry-aged rib eye or a 2½-pound lobster, grilled, steamed, sautéed, or broiled. Sides, like creamy mac and cheese and a crispy rosemary hash-brown cake, are equally tempting. $ *Average main: $30* ⊠ *Grand Central Terminal, West Balcony, 23 Vanderbilt Ave., between E. 43rd and E. 44th Sts., Midtown East* ☎ *212/655–2300* ⊕ *www.michaeljordansnyc.com* ⌣ *Reservations essential* Ⓜ *4, 5, 6, 7 to 42nd St./Grand Central* ✛ *4:F4.*

$$
INDIAN

⨉**Mint Restaurant & Lounge.** With a delightful dining room splashed with bright colors and flattering lighting, and executive chef and owner Gary Sikka's brightly seasoned dishes, Mint has joined the ranks of the best Indian restaurants in town. The large menu includes rarely encountered specialties from Goa and Sikkim. Freshly grilled, moist ground lamb kebabs deliver a slow burn to the palate. Chili heat punctuates other spices in the lamb vindaloo, resulting in a well-rounded array of savory flavors. Finish with carrot pudding with saffron and coconut flakes. $ *Average main: $20* ⊠ *150 E. 50th St., Midtown East* ☎ *516/307–8677* ⊕ *mintny.com* Ⓜ *6, E, M to 51st St./Lexington Ave.* ✛ *4:G3.*

$$$
STEAKHOUSE

⨉**The Palm Restaurant.** They may have added tablecloths, but it would take more than that to hide the brusque, no-nonsense nature of this legendary steak house. The steak is always impeccable, and the Nova Scotia lobsters are so big—3 pounds and up—that there may not be room at the table for such classic side dishes as rich creamed spinach, served family-style for two or more. The "half-and-half" side combination of cottage-fried potatoes and fried onions is particularly addictive. There are other locations (the original, Palm 1, is on 2nd Ave, at 58th St., the Palm Too is right across the street on 2nd Avenue [✛ *4:G4*], there's one in the mid-'50s [✛ *4:C3*], one in TriBeca [✛ *1:B2*], and one in JFK), but because of its perch near the Theater District and Midtown businesses, this is the one with the most action. $ *Average main: $30* ⊠ *837 2nd Ave., between 44th and 45th Sts., Midtown East* ☎ *212/687–2953* ⊕ *www.thepalm.com* ◷ *Closed Sun. No lunch Sat.* Ⓜ *4, 5, 6, 7, S to Grand Central* ✛ *4:G4.*

$$
AMERICAN

⨉**P. J. Clarke's.** This East Side institution has been dispensing burgers and beer for more than a century. Despite renovations and several different owners over the years, the original P. J. Clarke's (there's also an offshoot in Midtown West and downtown at the World Financial Center [✛ *1:B2*]) maintains the beveled-glass and scuffed-wood look of an old-time saloon. Many of the bartenders and patrons are as much a fixture as the decor. More civilized at lunchtime, the bar area heaves with an after-work mob on weekday evenings. Pull up a stool if you can for superlative bar food, like clams casino and the signature burger smothered in creamy Béarnaise. $ *Average main: $18* ⊠ *915 3rd Ave., at 55th St., Midtown East* ☎ *212/285–1500* ⊕ *www.pjclarkes.com* Ⓜ *E to 53rd or 4, 65, to 59th* ✛ *4:G2* ⊠ *44 West 63rd St., at Broadway,*

19

Midtown West ☎ *212/957–9700* Ⓜ *1 to 66th St. or B, D, A, C, 2, 3 to 66 St.–Columbus Circle* ✛ *5:C5.*

$$$ ✕ **Shun Lee Palace.** If you want inexpensive Cantonese food without

CHINESE pretensions, head to Chinatown; but if you prefer to be pampered and don't mind spending a lot of money, this is the place. The cuisine is absolutely classic Chinese. Beijing panfried dumplings make a good starter, and rack of lamb Szechuan-style, grilled with scallions and garlic, is a popular entrée. Beijing duck is sure to please. Ⓢ *Average main: $28* ✉ *155 E. 55th St., between Lexington and 3rd Aves., Midtown East* ☎ *212/371–8844* ⊕ *www.shunleepalace.com* ⌘ *Reservations essential* Ⓜ *N, R, 4, 5, 6 to 59th St./Lexington Ave.* ✛ *4:G2.*

$$$$ ✕ **Sparks Steakhouse.** Magnums of wines that cost more than most peo-

STEAKHOUSE ple earn in a week festoon the large dining rooms of this classic New York steak house. Although seafood is given more than fair play on the menu, Sparks is really about dry-aged steak. The extra-thick lamb and veal chops are also noteworthy. Classic sides of hash browns, creamed spinach, sautéed mushrooms, and grilled onions are all you need to complete the experience. Ⓢ *Average main: $38* ✉ *210 E. 46th St., between 2nd and 3rd Aves., Midtown East* ☎ *212/687–4855* ⊕ *www. sparkssteakhouse.com* ⌘ *Reservations essential* ☾ *Closed Sun. No lunch Sat.* Ⓜ *4, 5, 6, 7, S to 42nd St./Grand Central* ✛ *4:G3.*

$$$ ✕ **Sushi Yasuda.** Devotees mourned the return of namesake chef

JAPANESE Naomichi Yasuda to Japan, but things are in able hands with his hand-picked successor, Misturu Tamura. Here, the sleek bamboo-lined interior is as elegant as the food. Whether using fish flown in daily from Japan or the creamiest sea urchin, the chef makes sushi so fresh and delicate, it melts in your mouth. A number of special appetizers change daily (crispy fried eel backbone is a surprising treat), and a fine selection of sake and beer complements the lovely food. Try to sit at the bar, which was hand-crafted by Yasuda out of imported Japanese materials. Ⓢ *Average main: $30* ✉ *204 E. 43rd St., between 2nd and 3rd Aves., Midtown East* ☎ *212/972–1001* ⊕ *www.sushiyasuda.com* ☾ *Closed Sun. No lunch Sat.* Ⓜ *4, 5, 6, 7 to 42nd St./Grand Central* ✛ *4:G4.*

MURRAY HILL

This area has a residential feel with plenty of bistros perfect for a casual meal. Lexington Avenue's "Curry Hill" section between East 27th and East 29th streets is also home to Indian spice shops, cafés, and restaurants.

$$ ✕ **2nd Ave Deli.** It may no longer be on 2nd Avenue, but the new incar-

DELI nation of this East Village institution—about a mile uptown, in midtown—is still delivering on its longtime traditional matzo-ball soup, overstuffed three-decker sandwiches filled with house-cured pastrami, and other old-world specialties. Hot open sandwiches, like juicy beef brisket served with gravy and french fries, may be a heart attack on a plate, but hey, you only live once. Even better, you can now get your fill of kasha *varnishkes*, carrot tzimmes, and potato kugel until the wee hours of the night. There's also an outpost on the Upper East Side. Ⓢ *Average main: $23* ✉ *162 E. 33rd St., between Lexington and 3rd Aves., Murray Hill* ☎ *212/689–9000* ⊕ *www.2ndavedeli.com/* Ⓜ *6 to 33rd St./Lexington Ave.* ✛ *4:G6.*

$$$ ✕**Artisanal.** This spacious brasserie is a shrine to cheese, the passion
BRASSERIE of chef-owner Terrance Brennan. Though service can be spotty, gas-
tronomes and business lunchers still flock here for the more than 150
cheeses—available for on-site sampling or retail sale—then stay to
enjoy their selections with one of 160 wines by the glass. Hot *fromage-*
imbued fare also is satisfying, with preparations like addictive *gougère*
cheese puffs, onion soup gratiné, and several types of fondue. For curd-
adverse customers, steak frites or selections from the raw bar should
satisfy. Ⓢ *Average main: $27* ✉ *2 Park Ave., at E. 32nd St., Murray Hill*
☎ *212/725–8585* ⊕ *www.artisanalbistro.com* ⌂ *Reservations essential*
Ⓜ *6 to 33rd St.* ✛ *3:F1.*

$$ ✕**Les Halles.** This local hangout, owned by Philippe Lajaunie since 1990
FRENCH and benefiting from the celebrity of former executive chef and writer
☯ Anthony Bourdain (although he has little to do with the restuarant
these days), is boisterous and unpretentious—just like a true French
brasserie. A good bet is steak frites—with fries regarded by some as the
best in New York. Other prime choices include crispy duck-leg confit
with frisée salad, blood sausage with caramelized apples, and steak
tartare, prepared table-side. Another Les Halles is in Lower Manhattan at 15 John Street (✛ *1:D3).* Ⓢ *Average main: $22* ✉ *411 Park Ave.
S, between E. 28th and E. 29th Sts., Murray Hill* ☎ *212/679–4111*
⊕ *www.leshalles.net* Ⓜ *6 to 28th St.* ✛ *3:F1.*

MIDTOWN WEST

Big is the buzz in Times Square and neighboring hoods in Midtown
West, where neon-lighted billboards, towering skyscrapers, and Broadway theaters play starring roles. But watch out for restaurant rip-offs
in this urban-theme-park environment.

It's true that tourist traps abound on the Great White Way, but fortunately you needn't head far from Times Square to score a stellar meal.
Just move away from the bright lights and unrelenting foot traffic that
clogs the area. On calmer side streets and in adjoining Hell's Kitchen
there are excellent dining options for budget travelers and expense-
account diners alike. Some of the best steak houses and Italian restaurants are here, and many eateries offer budget pretheater dinners and
prix-fixe lunch menus to draw in new business.

$$$$ ✕**'21' Club.** Tradition's the thing at this town-house landmark, a for-
AMERICAN mer speakeasy that opened in 1929. Chef John Greeley tries to satisfy
everyone with standards like the famous '21' burger and Dover sole
with brown butter, and more modern dishes, such as smoked Berkshire pork belly with savoy cabbage and green apples, but the food is
almost secondary to the restaurant's storied past. Belongings donated
by famous patrons—for example, John McEnroe's tennis racket or
Howard Hughes's model plane—hang from the ceiling. Men, a jacket
is required, but you can leave your tie at home. Ⓢ *Average main:
$40.50* ✉ *21 W. 52nd St., between 5th and 6th Aves., Midtown West*
☎ *212/582–7200* ⊕ *www.21club.com* 🏛 *Jacket required* ☾ *Closed Sun.
No lunch Sat.* Ⓜ *E, M to 53rd St./5th Ave.; B, D, F, M to 47th–50th
Sts./Rockefeller Center* ✛ *4:D2.*

19

$
SCANDINAVIAN

✕**AQ Kafé.** Just south of Central Park, AQ Kafé serves excellent take-out coffee and pastries and is a good spot for a fast sit-down lunch if you're in the mood for Swedish-inspired food like meatballs, herring, and house-cured gravlax, plus desserts, including a hazelnut-crusted cheesecake. ⓈAverage main: $12 ✉1800 Broadway, at Columbus Circle, Midtown West ☎212/541–6801 ⊕www.aqkafe.com ⓂA, B, C, D, 1 to 59th St.–Columbus Circle ✛4:B1.

$$$$
MODERN
AMERICAN

✕**Aureole.** An island of fine dining in the heart of bustling Times Square, Aureole is the second act of a New York classic from Charlie Palmer and his executive chef, Christoph Bellanca. From the street, a curved second-story corridor hosting the restaurant's storied wine collection beckons. A welcoming front bar room serves a more casual, yet refined, menu with dishes like a cheddar-bacon burger dolloped with pickled ramp mayonnaise. The dining room, with its abundance of flowers, is the place to hobnob with expense-account diners and pretheater revel-ers alike. For dinner, starters like the sea-scallop "sandwich" topped with foie gras and passion-fruit coulis is a treat, and the $110 "parallel tasting" offers the menu's greatest hits, with an optional wine pairing. There is no à la carte in the main dining room. ⓈAverage main: $50 ✉135 W. 42nd St., between Broadway and 6th Ave, Midtown West ☎212/319–1660 ⊕www.charliepalmer.com ⚑Reservations essential ⓂB, D, F, M to 42nd St./Bryant Park; 1, 2, 3, 9, N, R, Q to 42nd St./Times Sq. ✛4:D4.

$$$
SOUTHERN

✕**Bar Americain.** Celeb chef Bobby Flay's largest Manhattan restaurant is the soaring Bar Americain. The 200-seat two-story space looks like a dining room on a luxury liner (complete with a gift shop: you can purchase his many cookbooks in the front). This is not food for the faint-of-heart: Flay piles on the butter, cream, and endless varieties of bacon. Southern-inflected brasserie fare includes gold corn Johnny-cakes with barbecued pulled pork and cranberry butter, smoked chicken with hatch-green-chili spoon bread and black-pepper vinegar sauce, and roasted duck breast surrounded by dirty wild rice with bourbon-soaked pecans. Slightly naughtier are the éclairs piped with whiskey-infused pastry cream and burnished with a burnt-sugar glaze. Brunch, featuring dishes like biscuits and cream gravy with sausage and scrambled eggs, is delicious. ⓈAverage main: $34 ✉152 W. 52nd St., between 6th and 7th Aves., Midtown West ☎212/265–9700 ⊕www.baramericain.com ⚑Reservations essential ⓂB, D, E to 7th Ave.; 1, C, E to 50th St.; N, R to 49th St. ✛4:C2.

$$
ITALIAN

✕**Becco.** An ingenious concept makes Becco a prime Restaurant Row choice for time-constrained theatergoers. There are two pricing sce-narios: one includes an all-you-can-eat selection of antipasti and three pastas served hot out of pans that waiters circulate around the dining room; the other adds a generous entrée to the mix. The pasta selection changes daily, but often includes gnocchi, fresh ravioli, and fettuccine in a cream sauce. The entrées include braised veal shank, grilled double-cut pork chop, and rack of lamb, among other selections. ⓈAverage main: $23 ✉355 W. 46th St., between 8th and 9th Aves., Midtown West ☎212/397–7597 ⊕www.becco-nyc.com ⓂA, C, E to 42nd St. ✛4:B3.

$$$
BISTRO

X **Benoit.** Who needs to go to Paris when the world's most famous French chef, Alain Ducasse, can come to you? Ducasse imported his famous Right Bank bistro to the Big Apple in 2008 and it's been a hit with Gallic-loving eaters ever since. The decor—cozy red velour banquettes and wall lamps illuminating each table—is plucked straight from the City of Light. So is the menu, which doesn't reinvent anything as much as it replicates. And that's okay, especially when the fennel-inflected *loup de mer* (also known as sea bass) and the tender leg of lamb are so well executed. It's not exactly cheap for simple bistro fare. Then again, neither is a round-trip ticket to Paris. $ *Average main: $25* ✉ *60 W. 55th St., between 5th and 6th Aves., Midtown West* ☎ *646/943–373* ⊕ *www.benoitny.com* Ⓜ *B, D, E. to 7th Ave.; F to 57th St.* ✛ *4:D2.*

> **WORD OF MOUTH**
>
> "It's true that the downtown area is much more hip and trendy than midtown, but it doesn't mean you can't find good food in midtown—perhaps more traditional than 'hip.' For one, you might try the Bar Americain on West 52 St."
> —nytraveler

$$$$
STEAKHOUSE

X **Ben Benson's Steakhouse.** Among the most venerable steak houses around, Ben Benson's feels like a clubby hunting lodge. The gracefully choreographed, intensely focused staff will bring you only the finest dry-aged prime meats and only the freshest seafood, all classically prepared, teeming with familiar and beloved flavors. The trimmings are ravishing, too: comforting creamed spinach, sizzling onion rings, and decadent hash browns are essential. Power lunches were practically invented here; just being in the place makes you feel important. $ *Average main: $45* ✉ *123 W. 52nd St., between 6th and 7th Aves., Midtown West* ☎ *212/581–8888* ⊕ *www.benbensons.com* ⚑ *Reservations essential* ⊘ *No lunch weekends* Ⓜ *B, D, E to 7th Ave.; 1 to 50th St.; N, R to 49th St.* ✛ *4:D2.*

$$$
ITALIAN

X **Bond 45.** Plates of fresh antipasti are displayed right as you walk into Bond 45. This Italian eatery, with a dark-wood bar and leather-backed booths, serves a variety of pizzas, pastas, and steaks. With a separate pretheater menu, this Theater District hot spot is an ideal option for dining and then dashing to your show of choice. $ *Average main: $25* ✉ *154 W. 45th St., between 6th and 7th Aves., Midtown West* ☎ *212/869–4545* ⊕ *www.bond45.com* Ⓜ *A, C, E, N, Q, R, S, 1, 2, 3, 7 to 42nd St./Times Sq.* ✛ *4:C4.*

$$$
BRASSERIE

X **Brasserie Ruhlmann.** In a plush 120-seat dining room with just enough art deco touches to harmonize with its Rockefeller Center setting, the sublime French bistro cookery, courtesy of Laurent Tourondel, is on display. The room has a refined air but the staff is so friendly that the place could never be stuffy. Seventeen excellent wines are available by the glass, as well as 10 half bottles. A pristine raw bar, featuring a selection of pedigreed oysters, is a great way to begin, or opt for a blue crab salad over mache with a honey-lime vinaigrette. If it's on the menu, order braised rabbit nestled in mustard cream on a bed of fresh i, sprinkled with pitted cherries. Desserts like Floating Island—delicately baked meringue floating on a pond of crème anglaise—are

19

embellished by a tangled flurry of spun sugar. ⑤ *Average main: $28* ✉ *45 Rockefeller Plaza, 50th St. between 5th and 6th Aves., Midtown West* ☎ *212/974–2020* ⊕ *www.brasserieruhlmann.com* ⌕ *Reservations essential* Ⓜ *B, D, F, M to 47th–50th Sts./Rockefeller Center* ✛ *4:D3.*

$

BURGER

Fodor'sChoice

★

✕ **Burger Joint.** What's a college burger bar, done up in particleboard and rec-room decor straight out of a *Happy Days* episode, doing hidden inside a five-star Midtown hotel? This tongue-in-cheek lunch spot, tucked behind a heavy red velvet curtain in the Parker Meridien hotel, does such boisterous midweek business that lines often snake through the lobby (which means you're best off coming at noon or earlier). Stepping behind the curtain, you can find baseball cap–wearing, grease-spattered cooks dispensing paper-wrapped cheeseburgers and crisp, thin fries. Forget Kobe beef or foie gras—these burgers are straightforward, cheap, and delicious. ⑤ *Average main: $7* ✉ *118 W. 57th St., between 6th and 7th Aves., inside the Parker Meridien, Midtown West* ☎ *212/245–5000* ⊕ *www.parkermeridien.com* ▭ *No credit cards* Ⓜ *F, N, Q, R to 57th St.* ✛ *4:D1.*

$$

ITALIAN

☺

✕ **Carmine's.** Savvy New Yorkers line up early for the affordable family-style meals at this large, busy Midtown eatery. Family photos line the walls, and there's a convivial feeling amid all the Times Square hubbub. Don't be fooled: Carmine's may be huge, but it fills up with families carbo-loading for a day of sightseeing or a night of theater on Broadway. There are no reservations taken for parties of fewer than six people after 7 pm, but those who wait are rewarded with mountains of such popular, toothsome viands as fried calamari, linguine with white clam sauce, chicken parmigiana, and veal saltimbocca. ⑤ *Average main: $24* ✉ *200 W. 44th St., between Broadway and 8th Ave., Midtown West* ☎ *212/221–3800* ⊕ *www.carminesnyc.com* Ⓜ *A, C, E, N, Q, R, S, 1, 2, 3, 7 to 42nd St./Times Sq.* ✛ *4:C4.*

$$$

KOREAN

Fodor'sChoice

★

✕ **Danji.** Diminutive and dark, Danji is no ordinary Korean restaurant. Helmed by talented chef Hooni Kim, this Hell's Kitchen spot is a standout among the rows of restaurants that attract theater-going tourists in the neighborhood. That's because Kim's take on Korean cuisine is inventive and inspired. The menu is split in two, and both sides contain a number of winnning dishes. Start with the scallion and pepper pancake and the trio of kimchi from the "traditional" side of the page, then set your taste buds singing with Korean chicken wings and unctuous pork-belly sliders from the "modern" side of the menu. Then count your blessings that you're not eating a mediocre meal like the rest of the out-of-town visitors in the neighorhood. ⑤ *Average main: $14* ✉ *346 W. 52nd St., between 8th and 9th Aves., Midtown West* ☎ *212/586–2880* Ⓜ *C, E to 50th St.* ✛ *4:B2.*

$$$

FRENCH

✕ **DB Bistro Moderne.** Daniel Boulud's "casual bistro" (it's neither, actually) consists of two elegantly appointed dining rooms. The menu features classic dishes like Nantucket Bay scallops or hanger steak exquisitely prepared. Ever the trendsetter, Boulud's $32 db hamburger, available at lunch and dinner, and stuffed with braised short ribs, foie gras, and black truffles, is the patty credited with kick-starting the whole gourmet burger trend. Yes, it's worth every penny. ⑤ *Average main: $31* ✉ *55 W. 44th St., between 5th and 6th Aves., Midtown*

West ☎ *212/391–2400* ⊕ *www.danielnyc.com* ⌕ *Reservations essential* ⊙ *No lunch Sun.* Ⓜ *B, D, F, M to 42nd St./Bryant Park; 7 to 5th Ave./ Bryant Park* ✛ *4:D4.*

$$
AMERICAN
☾

✕ **Ellen's Stardust Diner.** If you haven't had enough Broadway singing and dancing, you'll get a kick out of Ellen's, a retro, 1950s-style diner, complete with a singing waitstaff. The menu focuses on all-American classics like meat loaf and chicken potpie, and the waiters and waitresses serenading you have the talent to prove this restaurant is right on Broadway. It's the kind of over-the-top family-style fun that you'd expect from the close-to Times Square location. Ⓢ *Average main: $20* ✉ *1650 Broadway, at 51st Street, Midtown West* ☎ *212/956–5151* ⊕ *www.ellensstardustdiner.com* Ⓜ *1 to 50th St.* ✛ *4:C3.*

$$$
SEAFOOD

✕ **Esca.** The name is Italian for "bait," and this restaurant, courtesy of partners Mario Batali, Joe Bastianich, and longtime chef David Pasternack, lures diners in with delectable raw preparations called *crudo*— such as tilefish with orange and Sardinian oil or pink snapper with a sprinkle of crunchy red clay salt—and hooks them with such entrées as whole, salt-crusted *branzino*, sea bass for two, or *bucatini* pasta with spicy baby octopus. The menu changes daily. Bastianich is in charge of the wine cellar, so you can expect an adventurous list of Italian bottles. Ⓢ *Average main: $30* ✉ *402 W. 43rd St., at 9th Ave., Midtown West* ☎ *212/564–7272* ⊕ *www.esca-nyc.com* ⌕ *Reservations essential* ⊙ *No lunch Sun.* Ⓜ *A, C, E to 42nd St.* ✛ *4:A4.*

$
AMERICAN

✕ **Five Napkin Burger.** This perennially packed Hell's Kitchen burger place/brasserie has been a magnet for burger lovers since day one. Bottles of Maker's Mark line the sleek, alluringly lighted bar in the back, a collection of antique butcher's scales hangs on a tile wall near the kitchen, and meat hooks dangle from the ceiling between the light fixtures. Though there are many menu distractions—deep-fried pickles, warm artichoke dip, to name a few—the main attractions are the juicy burgers, like the original 10-ounce chuck with a tangle of onions, Gruyère cheese, and rosemary aioli. There's a patty variety for everyone, including a ground lamb *kofta* and an onion ring–topped ahi tuna burger. For dessert, have an über-thick black-and-white malted milkshake. Ⓢ *Average main: $16* ✉ *630 9th Ave., at 45th St, Midtown West* ☎ *212/757–2277* ⊕ *www.5napkinburger.com* Ⓜ *A, C, E to 42nd St./8th Ave.* ✛ *4:B4.*

$
KOREAN

✕ **Gahm Mi Oak.** The deconstructed industrial design, inexpensive 24-hour menu, and late-night hours attract a young, stylish crowd— there are even photos on the menu to help bleary-eyed revelers order. Every item on the limited menu goes well with *soju*, a Korean spirit, or beer. Korean-style fried mung-bean pancakes with scallions, onions, carrots, and ground pork are addictive, and the kimchi is renowned. Try the *sul long tang*, a milky ox-bone soup with thin slices of beef, rice, and noodles that is reputed to be an effective hangover cure. Ⓢ *Average main: $14* ✉ *43 W. 32nd St., between 5th Ave. and Broadway, Midtown West* ☎ *212/695–4113* ⌕ *Reservations not accepted* Ⓜ *B, D, F, N, Q, R, M to 34th St./Herald Sq.* ✛ *3:E1.*

$$$
FRENCH

✕ **Gordon Ramsay at The London and Maze.** With more than a dozen restaurants around the world—and an ever-busy TV schedule—you're not

19

likely to find British chef Gordon Ramsay at his eponymous Midtown restaurant. What you will find, however, are Ramsay's trembling aco-lytes producing flawless facsimiles of his classically muted haute cuisine. The flagship fine-dining restaurant is an exorbitant time commitment, with menus that start at $110 for three courses and stretch to $150 for seven. It is hidden behind opaque glass doors just beyond the compara-tively casual, and much more reasonably priced, Maze. The lower-key annex, in a silver-gray dining room, specializes in elegant small-plate cuisine (often very small). Although dinner is a mix-and-match affair, Maze's $39 prix-fixe three-course lunch is one of the top bargains in Midtown. Ⓢ *Average main: $24* ⊠ *151 W. 54th St., between 6th and 7th Aves., Midtown West* ☎ *212/468–8889* ⊕ *www.gordonramsay.com/* ⊘ *No lunch. No dinner Sun. and Mon.* Ⓜ *B, D, E to 7th Ave.; N, Q, R to 57th St.* ✛ *4:D2.*

$ ✕ **Havana Central.** This is a great place for reasonably priced group din-
CUBAN   ing and for sampling Cuban-Latino standards like garlicky chicken and well-seasoned skirt steak with a cucumber-and-mango salad. There's a full menu of tropical-flavored mojitos, including coconut, blue-berry, and passion fruit. Ⓢ *Average main: $18. 50* ⊠ *151 W. 46th St., between 6th and 7th Aves., Midtown West* ☎ *212/398–7440* ⊕ *www. havanacentral.com* Ⓜ *N, Q, R to 49th St.; B, D, F, M to 47th–50th Sts./ Rockefeller Center* ✛ *4:C3.*

$ ✕ **Kyotofu.** Even if you're not crazy about tofu, the soy-based delights at
JAPANESE   Kyotofu—New York's preeminent dessert bar—will make you recon-
ⓒ   sider the merits of the soybean. Kyotofu's signature sweet tofu with Kuromitsu black sugar syrup is so creamy and delicious, you'd think it was a traditional panna cotta. The strawberry shortcake with straw-berry sake sorbet and the warm miso chocolate cake with chocolate soybean ganache and green-tea cream are two more totally compelling favorites. Kyotofu's menu is full of intriguing options, so your best bet, on your first visit, is to go for the Kaiseki prix-fixe, a three-course tasting menu that enables you to try six different mini-desserts. The menu changes seasonally, and it also includes savory brunch, lunch, and dinner options as well as desserts, and an extensive sake and sho-chu cocktail list. Ⓢ *Average main: $15* ⊠ *705 9th Ave., near 48th St., Midtown West* ☎ *212/974–6012* ⊕ *www.kyotofu-nyc.com* Ⓜ *C, E to 50th St.* ✛ *4:A3.*

$$ ✕ **La Bonne Soupe.** The La Bonne Soupe special includes a bowl of soup
FRENCH   with bread, salad, a beverage (house wine, beer, soda, or coffee), and dessert for $19.50. À la carte options include bistro classics like crepes, omelets, salads, quiche, and croque madame and monsieur. Expect a bustling, lively crowd, and often a line at lunchtime. Ⓢ *Average main: $15* ⊠ *48 W. 55th St., between 5th and 6th Aves., Midtown West* ☎ *212/586–7650* ⊕ *www.labonnesoupe.com* Ⓜ *F to 57th St.* ✛ *4:E2.*

$$$ ✕ **The Lambs Club.** Restaurateur Geoffrey Zakarian's opulent supper club
MODERN   on the ground floor of the Chatwal Hotel features superb art-deco
AMERICAN   detailing, blood-red leather banquettes, and a roaring fireplace in an refurbished antique grill. Cocktails are concocted by hipster mixolo-gist Sasha Petraske, who eschews experimental in favor of classics like the sidecar and the martini, done well. The food is typical Zakarian,

meaning New American cuisine with luxe touches in dishes like veal sweetbreads with peppered jus and grilled treviso lettuce, or seared scallops with porcini mushrooms and Indian-spiced sauce. Desserts, like double-chocolate ginger cake with poached pears, are worth the splurge. The lunchtime menu is padded with appealing choices, but the sleeper meal here is breakfast. Dishes like a house-made biscuit with fried egg, bacon, and cheddar, or fluffy lemon-ricotta pancakes, may just fill you up for the rest of the day. $ *Average main: $35.50* ⊠ *132 W. 44th St., between 6th Ave. and Broadway, Midtown West* ☎ *212/997–5262* ⊕ *www.thelambsclub.com* Ⓜ *1, 2, 3 to 42nd St., B, D, F, M to 47th–50th Sts./Rockefeller Center* ✛ *4:D4.*

$$$$ ✕ **Le Bernardin.** Owner Maguy LeCoze presides over the teak-panel
FRENCH dining room at this trendsetting French seafood restaurant, and chef-
Fodor'sChoice partner Eric Ripert works magic with anything that swims—preferring
★ at times not to cook it at all. Deceptively simple dishes such as poached lobster in rich coconut-ginger soup or crispy spiced black bass in a Peking duck bouillon are typical of his style. It's widely agreed that there's no beating Le Bernardin for thrilling cuisine, seafood or otherwise, coupled with some of the finest desserts in town and a wine list as deep as the Atlantic. It's prix fixe only, and there are nonfish options (pasta and meat) by request. $ *Average main: $155* ⊠ *155 W. 51st St., between 6th and 7th Aves., Midtown West* ☎ *212/554–1515* ⊕ *www. le-bernardin.com* ⓐ *Jacket required* ⊘ *Closed Sun. No lunch Sat.* Ⓜ *1 to 50th St.; R to 49th St.; B, D, F, M to 47th–50th Sts./Rockefeller Center* ✛ *4:C2.*

$ ✕ **Le Pain Quotidien.** This international Belgian chain brings its home-
BAKERY land ingredients with it, treating New Yorkers to crusty organic breads, jams, chocolate, and other specialty products. You can grab a snack to go or stay and eat breakfast, lunch, or dinner at communal or private tables with waiter service. Come for a steaming latte and croissant in the morning or a *tartine* (open-faced sandwich) at noon. There are more than 20 locations throughout Manhattan, including in Central Park. $ *Average main: $13* ⊠ *1271 Ave. of the Americas, at 50th St., Midtown West* ☎ *646/462–4165* ⊕ *www.lepainquotidien.com* Ⓜ *B, D, F, V to 47–50th Sts./Rockefeller Center* ✛ *4:C1 .*

$$ ✕ **Lugo Caffé.** The area around Madison Square Garden is a restaurant
ITALIAN wasteland with the rare sparkling exception of Lugo Caffé, founded by an Italian menswear line. Locals rejoiced at the introduction of this spacious Italian "brasserie" offering comfort food with a *dolce vita* twist all day long. Stop by for an espresso and pastry in the morning. Later, a single menu presents lunch, *aperitivo*, and dinner options, which include grazing portions of salumi, cheeses, and vegetable dishes like eggplant caponata, Tuscan bean salad, and grilled zucchini with pine nuts. Fuller meals of Neapolitan-style pizzas, house-made pastas, and grilled meats and fish also are commendable. $ *Average main: $24* ⊠ *1 Penn Plaza, 33rd St. and 8th Ave., Midtown West* ☎ *212/760–2700* ⊕ *www.lugocaffe.com* ⊘ *Closed Sun. (except on some MSG sports game days)* Ⓜ *A, C, E to 34th St.; 1, 2, 3 to 34th St.* ✛ *4:C6.*

$$$ ✕ **Má Pêche.** Starkly decorated and set in the basement of the Cham-
ASIAN bers Hotel, Má Pêche is just blocks from MoMA. And as the largest

19

restaurant in David Chang's empire, you have a better shot of nabbing a seat. The menus are a bit more refined than those at Momofuku Noodle Bar and Ssam Bar, with elegantly composed plates that might include lamb shank accompanied by eggplant, raisins, and rice, or seared swordfish with black beans, braised celery, and crisped shallots. At lunchtime, there are also tasty banh mi filled with pork and vegetables. On the way out you can pick up sweets from the uptown offshoot of Momofuku Milk Bar, like the addictive, buttery Crack Pie or intriguingly flavored soft-serve. $ *Average main: $25 ⊠ 15 West 56th St., between 5th and 6th Aves., Midtown West* 212/757–5878 *www. momofuku.com/ma-peche* ♥ *No lunch Sun.* Ⓜ *F to 57th St.* ✢ *4:E1.*

$$ ✕ **Marseille.** With great food and a convenient location near several
MEDITERRANEAN Broadway theaters, Marseille is perpetually packed. The Mediterranean creations are continually impressive, including the bouillabaisse, the signature dish of the region for which the restaurant is named—a mélange of mussels, shrimp, and white fish in a fragrant broth, topped with a garlicky crouton and served with rouille on the side. Leave room for the spongy beignets with chocolate and raspberry dipping sauces. $ *Average main: $22 ⊠ 630 9th Ave., at W. 44th St., Midtown West* 212/333–2323 *www.marseillenyc.com* ☙ *Reservations essential* Ⓜ *A, C, E to 42nd St./Port Authority Bus Terminal* ✢ *4:B4.*

$$$ ✕ **The Modern and Bar Room.** Both spots competing for the title of the
FRENCH country's best museum restaurant sit side by side on the ground floor of the New York MoMA. The Modern, run by restaurateur Danny Meyer, is two restaurants in one, and both offer the dazzling food of Alsatian chef Gabriel Kreuther. The formal dining room features a view of the museum's sculpture garden and an ambitious, pricey, prix-fixe menu with standouts like chorizo-crusted codfish with white coco-bean puree. The far more accessible and popular Bar Room lies just beyond a partition, and this is where you can find a dizzying collection of shareable plates, like the refreshing arctic char tartare and oysters with leeks and caviar. Two or three make a fine if extravagant afternoon snack—double that number and you have a full meal. $ *Average main: $45 ⊠ 9 W. 53rd St., between 5th and 6th Aves., Midtown West* 212/333–1220 *www.themodernnyc.com* ♥ *Closed Sun.* Ⓜ *E, M to 5th Ave./53rd St.* ✢ *4:D2.*

$$$ ✕ **Oceana.** Entering Oceana is like walking into the dressy stateroom
SEAFOOD of a modern luxury ocean liner. Floor-to-ceiling windows look out both north and west, and the arrestingly designed raw bar backed with Mediterranean-hue ceramics offers stunningly fresh choices. You would expect gorgeous oysters at a restaurant called Oceana, and you get them: they're so full flavored that they transcend their chilliness. Chef Ben Pollinger has all the skill and confidence necessary to serve some of the most vivid and delicious seafood in town. A "contemporary appetizer" section features items like marinated cucumber with cucumber, apple, and toasted spices. Grilled whole fish like halibut, swordfish, and crispy wild striped bass are served with a perfect rotating roster of sauces like classic romesco and grilled pineapple salsa. Thai-style red snapper comes with tender silk squash, crisp jicama, and a kaffir-saffron broth. $ *Average main: $32 ⊠ 120 West 49th St., at 6th Ave., Midtown*

West ☎ *212/759–5941* ⊕ *www.oceanarestaurant.com* ⌖ *Reservations essential* Ⓜ *E, M to 53rd St./5th Ave.* ✛ *4:D3.*

$$$ ╳ **Plataforma Churrascaria Rodizio.** This sprawling, boisterous shrine to
BRAZILIAN meat, with its all-you-can-eat prix-fixe menu, is best experienced with
a group of ravenous friends. A *caipirinha,* featuring cachaça sugarcane
liquor, sugar, and lime, will kick things off nicely. Follow up with a
trip to the salad bar piled with vegetables, meats, and cheeses. But
restrain yourself—there's a parade of all manner of grilled meats and
poultry, from pork ribs to chicken hearts, delivered to the table on
long skewers until you beg for mercy. ⑤ *Average main: $33* ✉ *316 W.
49th St., between 8th and 9th Aves., Midtown West* ☎ *212/245–0505*
⊕ *www.plataformaonline.com* ⌖ *Reservations essential* Ⓜ *C, E to 50th
St.* ✛ *4:B3.*

$$ ╳ **Plaza Food Hall by Todd English.** At the Plaza Food Hall in the base-
ECLECTIC ment of the Plaza Hotel, celeb chef Todd English oversees a series of
mini-restaurants, each with its own counter with seating ideal for a
quick snack or a full-fledged meal. Entry is a little confusing; though
the place is made up of individual food concepts, you'll be seated by
a hostess at any available counter. One you're settled, get up and survey your choices, then sit down and place one order from your waiter.
There's a glistening raw bar, a burger joint, and a wood-burning pizza
station where you can sample some of English's iconic pies, such as fig
and prosciutto. It's one of the most varied and affordable daytime food
options in an area of town that can still feel like a lunchtime wasteland. ⑤ *Average main: $18* ✉ *1 W. 59th St., at 5th Ave., Midtown West*
☎ *212/986–9260* ⊕ *theplazafoodhall.com* Ⓜ *N, Q, R to 5th Ave./59th
St.* ✛ *4:E1.*

$$$ ╳ **Quality Meats.** The design at Quality Meats is inspired by classic New
STEAKHOUSE York City butcher shops in its use of warm wood, stainless steel, and
white marble. Sit at the bar to peruse the extensive menu of wines and sin-
gle-malt scotches. Then retire to the dining room for sophisticated riffs on
steak-house classics like beef Wellington. ⑤ *Average main: $36.50* ✉ *57
W. 58th St., near 6th Ave., Midtown West* ☎ *212/371–7777* ⊕ *www.
qualitymeatsnyc.com* ⌖ *Reservations essential* ☾ *No lunch on week-
ends* Ⓜ *F to 57th St.* ✛ *4:D1.*

$$$ ╳ **Seäsonal Restaurant and Weinbar.** Partners and executive chefs Wolf-
AUSTRIAN gang Ban and Eduard Frauneder have brought something *neu* to Mid-
town: a swanky Austrian-German restaurant and Weinbar. With its
sculptural ceiling lighting, elliptical bar, and contemporary Austrian
and German art, Seäsonal feels more "downtown" than you'd expect
from such central Midtown digs. The cuisine is sophisticated and contemporary, yet still steeped in regional traditions. The chefs are committed to using fresh, seasonal ingredients and, whenever possible, locally
sourced products. Appetizers like the foie-gras terrine and the cheese
ravioli with smoked chanterelle mushrooms delight with their contrasting lightness and intensity of flavor. Mains, such as the pumpkin seed–
crusted black sea bass with butternut squash and black truffles, and
the classic Wiener schnitzel served with a crescent potato-cucumber
salad, will pleasure your palate with simple but striking flavor combinations. Seäsonal's Weinbar features a distinctive selection of wines

19

from emerging Austrian and German winemakers—definitely the right place for your Riesling fix. ⑤ *Average main: $27* ✉ *132 W. 58th St., Midtown West* ☎ *212/957–5550* ⊕ *www.seasonalnyc.com* Ⓜ *F to 57th St./6th Ave.* ✛ *4:D1.*

$$
ITALIAN

✗ **Serafina.** The thin-crust pizzas, antipasti, salads, and typical main courses make this a fine neighborhood eatery but not worth a special trip. Come for a casually upscale meal, if you're feeling peckish; the outdoor terrace at the midtown location is popular despite the fact that the tables are just steps from busy Broadway. ⑤ *Average main: $17* ✉ *210 W. 55th St., at Broadway, Midtown West* ☎ *212/315–1700* ⊕ *www.serafinarestaurant.com* Ⓜ *N, Q, R, W to 57th St./7th Ave.* ✛ *4:C2.*

$
BURGER
Fodor's Choice
★

✗ **Shake Shack.** Local restaurant legend Danny Meyer has gone a little low-brow with his fast-ish food venture, Shake Shack—and New Yorkers are loving it. Area-wise, this Theater District location is the largest and with the most seating, but be warned: lines still snake out the door, especially at prime mealtimes. ⑤ *Average main: $6* ✉ *691 8th Ave., at W. 44th St., Midtown West* ☎ *646/435–0135* ⊕ *www.shakeshacknyc.com* Ⓜ *1, 2, 3, A, C, E, S to 42nd St./Times Sq.* ✛ *4:C4.*

$$
ITALIAN

✗ **Sosa Borella.** This is one of the Theater District's top spots for reliable food at a reasonable cost. The bi-level, casual Argentinian-Italian eatery is an inviting and friendly space where diners choose from a wide range of options. The lunch menu features staples like warm sandwiches and entrée-size salads, whereas the dinner menu is slightly gussied up with meat, fish, and pasta dishes (the rich agnolotti with lamb Bolognese sauce, topped with a wedge of grilled pecorino cheese, is a must-try). The freshly baked bread served at the beginning of the meal with pesto dipping sauce is a nice touch as you wait for your meal. The service can be slow at times, so leave yourself plenty of time before the show. ⑤ *Average main: $25* ✉ *832 8th Ave., between 50th and 51st Sts., Midtown West* ☎ *212/262–8282* ⊕ *www.sosaborella.com* Ⓜ *C, E, 1 to 50th St.* ✛ *4:B3.*

$$
MEXICAN

✗ **Toloache.** Make a quick detour off heavily trafficked Broadway into this pleasantly bustling Mexican cantina for one of the best dining options around Times Square. The bi-level eatery has a festive, celebratory vibe, with several seating options: bar, balcony, main dining room, and ceviche bar. Foodies flock here for three types of guacamole (traditional, fruited, and spicy), a trio of well-executed ceviches, and dishes like the Mexico City–style tacos with Negra Modelo–braised brisket, and quesadillas studded with black truffle and *huitlacoche* (a corn fungus). There's an extensive tequila selection—upward of 100 brands. Adventurous palates will be drawn to tacos featuring chili-studded dried grasshoppers, lobes of seared foie gras, and caramelized veal sweetbreads. ⑤ *Average main: $18.50* ✉ *251 W. 50th St., near 8th Ave., Midtown West* ☎ *212/581–1818* ⊕ *www.toloachenyc.com* Ⓜ *1, C, E to 50th St.; N, R to 49th St.* ✛ *4:B3.*

$$$$
STEAKHOUSE

✗ **Uncle Jack's Steakhouse.** Surpassing even its celebrated flagship restaurant in Bayside, Queens, Uncle Jack's soars directly into the pantheon of the best steak houses in Manhattan. As in most great steakhouses, you can feel the testosterone throbbing all through the place. The space is vast and gorgeously appointed, and service is swift and focused.

USDA prime steaks are dry-aged for 21 days. Australian lobster tails are so enormous, they have to be served carved, yet the flesh is meltingly tender. $ *Average main: $67* ⊠ *440 9th Ave., between W. 34th and W. 35th Sts., Midtown West* ☎ *212/244–0005* ⊕ *www.unclejacks. com* ☒ *Reservations essential* ⊙ *No lunch weekends* Ⓜ *A, C, E to 34th St./Penn Station* ✛ *4:B6.*

UPPER EAST SIDE

The Upper East Side is jam-packed with pricey neighborhood eateries that cater to the area's well-heeled residents. Long viewed as an enclave of the privileged, these neighborhoods have plenty of elegant restaurants that serve the society "ladies who lunch" and bankers looking forward to a steak and single-malt scotch at the end of the day. However, visitors to Museum Mile and 5th Avenue shopping areas need not be put off. Whether you're looking to celebrate a special occasion or just want to grab a quick bite, you're sure to find something here for almost any budget.

$$$$ ✕ **Alloro.** Italian chef Salvatore Corea and his wife, Gina, a native New
ITALIAN Yorker, are living their dream of opening an old-fashioned family-run restaurant here on the Upper East Side. It's not Corea's first New York restaurant endeavor—he's opened three other successful venues in the city (Cacio e Pepe, Spiga, and Bocca), but Alloro is his first venture with his wife, and judging by the friendly vibe and the delicious dishes coming out of Corea's *cucina,* it's working swimmingly well. Chef Corea's creative take on traditional, regional Italian cuisines leads the way for delicious dishes, like *creamy Parmesan risotto with Lambrusco-wine caramel.* Both the sliced rib eye over corn puree and the fillet of sole in pumpkin-Amaretto crust are fantastic. Gluten-free pasta selections are also available. $ *Average main: $38* ⊠ *307 E. 77th St., near 2nd Ave., Upper East Side* ☎ *212/535–2866* ⊕ *www.alloronyc.com* Ⓜ *6 to 77th St.* ✛ *5:H2.*

$$$$ ✕ **Café Boulud.** Manhattan's who's who in business, politics, and the art
FRENCH world come to hobnob at Daniel Boulud's café-in-name-only, where the food and service are top-notch. The menu, overseen by Boulud protégé Gavin Kaysen, is divided into four parts: under La Tradition you can find classic French dishes such as roasted duck breast Montmorency with cherry chutney, green Swiss chard, and baby turnips; Le Potager tempts with lemon ricotta ravioli; La Saison follows the rhythms of the season; and Le Voyage reinterprets cuisines of the world. Start with a drink at the chic Bar Pleiades. $ *Average main: $36* ⊠ *20 E. 76th St., between 5th and Madison Aves., in the Surrey Hotel, Upper East Side* ☎ *212/772–2600* ⊕ *www.danielnyc.com* ☒ *Reservations essential* Ⓜ *6 to 77th St.* ✛ *5:F3.*

$$ ✕ **Café d'Alsace.** Unusually comfortable burgundy banquettes, huge
BRASSERIE antiqued mirrors, and low lighting that makes everyone look fabulous characterize this Alsatian gem. Start with a house cocktail—say, L'Alsacien, in which the aperitif Belle de Brillet meets cognac, pear, and fresh lemon in a happy union. Standouts include the *tarte flambé,* a *fromage blanc*–topped flat bread scattered with tawny caramelized onions and hunks of bacon. The *choucroute garnie* entrée comes in

19

a cast-iron kettle that keeps it piping hot. Sausages, smoked pork breast, and pork belly are so carefully braised that everything comes out in perfect harmony. Delicious bread pudding is studded with strawberries. $ *Average main: $22* ⊠ *1695 2nd Ave., at E. 88th St., Upper East Side* ☎ *212/722–5133* ⊕ *www.cafedalsace.com* Ⓜ *4, 5, 6 to 86th St.* ⊹ *6:G6.*

WORD OF MOUTH

"My wife and I love to go to the Grand Central Oyster Bar and have a dozen oysters, bottle of champagne, chowder and split a fish entree and then head to the Campbell Apartment for cocktails. Great way to spend an evening."
—ksucat

$$ ✕ **Café Sabarsky.** Luxurious Vien-
AUSTRIAN   nese coffee, cakes, strudels, and Sacher tortes lure museumgoers and anyone craving an old-world café fix. Hearty entrées like sausage and goulash are also served but it's the sweets that are worth the calories. $ *Average main: $18* ⊠ *1048 5th Ave., near 86th St., in Neue Galerie, Upper East Side* ☎ *212/240–9557* ⊕ *kg-ny.com* ⌖ *Reservations not accepted* Ⓜ *4, 5, 6 to 86th St.* ⊹ *6:E6.*

$$ ✕ **Candle 79.** The Upper East Side may seem like an unlikely place for
VEGETARIAN   gourmet vegan fare, but the people behind Candle 79 have found a
Fodor's Choice   formula that would work in any neighborhood. The elegant, bi-level
★   space, done in warm, autumnal tones with touches of wood and rich fabric, is far from the health-food stereotype. Try for a second-floor table overlooking the street, and refresh yourself with an inventive cocktail. Appetizers like rice balls with tempeh bacon may sound like hippie throwbacks, but they taste more like well-executed trattoria fare. Signature dishes include the seitan piccata, which replaces the usual protein with a vegetarian substitute and is so well made and well seasoned that you would never miss the meat. Salads, soups, desserts, and entrées are all stunningly fresh and made with local, organic, seasonal produce. There's also an impressive list of organic wines and sakes. $ *Average main: $21.50* ⊠ *154 E. 79th St., at Lexington Ave., Upper East Side* ☎ *212/537–7179* ⊕ *www.candle79.com* Ⓜ *6 to 77th St./Lexington Ave.* ⊹ *5:G2.*

$ ✕ **Cascabel Taqueria.** One of New York's top-rated taquerias is in an
MEXICAN   unexpected neighborhood. At Cascabel, the wrestling-theme decor is a whimsical backdrop for some seriously delicious, reasonably priced Mexican food—something sorely lacking in New York, and especially on the Upper East Side. Tacos, which come two to an order, are inventive without veering too far from the comfort-food norm. The *camarón* scatters plump roasted wild shrimp among fresh oregano, garlic oil, and black beans. The beef tongue is slow braised, then topped with spring onion and serrano chilies, nothing like the stuff you'll find in a deli sandwich containing the same principal ingredient. There's also fresh, creamy guacamole with house-fried chips, pert tortilla soup with queso fresco cheese and chicken, and dinner-only platters like adobe-marinated Berkshire pork butt with cucumbers and an alluring onion-tamarind mixture. At lunchtime, one of Cascabel's sandwiches—shredded chicken with mango and smashed avocado, for one—hit the spot with an ice-cold Mexican beer. Inside seating is limited, but in temperate

weather the outdoor tables expand your possibilities. $ *Average main: $13.25* ⊠ *1538 2nd Ave., between 80th and 81st Sts., Upper East Side* ☎ *212/717–8226* ⊕ *www.nyctacos.com* ☽ *No dinner Sun.* ✛ *5:H2.*

$$$ ✕ **Central Park Boathouse Restaurant.** There are plenty of pushcarts offer-
AMERICAN ing hot dogs and sodas, but if you're looking to soak up Central Park's magical ambience in an elegant setting, head for the Central Park Boat-house, which overlooks the gondola lake. There you can relax on the outdoor deck with a glass of wine and a cheese plate, or go for a more formal meal inside the restaurant. In warmer months the res-taurant can get crowded: go for a late lunch or early-evening cocktail. $ *Average main: $30* ⊠ *E. 72nd St., at Park Dr. N, Upper East Side* ☎ *212/517–2233* ⊕ *www.thecentralparkboathouse.com* ⌲ *Reserva-tions not accepted* Ⓜ *B, C to 72nd St.* ✛ *5:E3.*

$$$$ ✕ **Daniel.** Celebrity-chef Daniel Boulud has created one of the most ele-
FRENCH gant dining experiences in Manhattan. The prix-fixe–only menu (there
Fodor's Choice are à la carte selections in the elegant lounge and bar) is predominantly
★ French, with such modern classics as turbot on Himalayan salt with an ale-and-gingerbread sauce, and a duo of dry-aged Black Angus beef featuring meltingly tender red wine–braised short ribs and seared rib eye with black trumpet mushrooms and Gorgonzola cream. Equally impressive are the serious artwork, professional service, extensive wine list, and masterful cocktails. Don't forget the decadent desserts and overflowing cheese trolley. A three-course vegetarian menu is also avail-able. $ *Average main: $60* ⊠ *60 E. 65th St., between Madison and Park Aves., Upper East Side* ☎ *212/288–0033* ⊕ *www.danielnyc.com* ⌲ *Reservations essential* ⌂ *Jacket required* ☽ *Closed Sun. No lunch* Ⓜ *6 to 68th St./Hunter College* ✛ *5:F5.*

$$ ✕ **Maya.** The upscale-hacienda appearance of this justifiably popular
MEXICAN restaurant showcases some of the best Mexican food in the city, cour-tesy of pioneering Mexican chef Richard Sandoval. Begin with a fresh mango mojito, then tuck into delicious roasted corn soup with *huitla-coche* dumplings, stuffed poblano peppers, and smoky filet mignon taco with jalapeño escabeche. Finish with caramelized goat's-milk crepes and cinnamon ice cream, and you'll leave wearing a big grin. $ *Average main: $24* ⊠ *1191 1st Ave., between E. 64th and E. 65th Sts., Upper East Side* ☎ *212/585–1818* ⊕ *www.modernmexican.com* ☽ *No lunch* Ⓜ *6 to 68th St./Hunter College* ✛ *5:H5.*

$$$ ✕ **Park Avenue Seasonal.** New York's most self-consciously seasonal res-
AMERICAN taurant swaps out much more than its menu as temperatures change. Four times a year the restaurant—the formerly staid Park Avenue Café—shuts its doors for a head-to-toe makeover, switching, for instance, from a summery blond-wood beach-house motif to dark-wood-and-copper fall-foliage tones. Chef Craig Koketsu's seasonal food lives up to the striking surroundings. Summer brings a bounty of fresh-shucked corn, with a big, juicy veal chop and heirloom tomatoes. Come autumn the kitchen turns its focus to mushrooms, truffles (on a flaky halibut fillet accompanied by a brioche-crusted poached egg), and game (local quail, big venison chops scattered with pomegranate and pumpkin seeds). Desserts, by award-winning pastry chef Richard Leach, include hard-to-resist elegant creations like sweet-corn ice cream

19

with rhubarb, warm caramel, and popcorn. [$] *Average main: $38.50* ⊠ *100 E. 63rd St., at Park Ave., Upper East Side* ☎ *212/644–1900* ⊕ *www.parkavenyc.com* ⌖ *Reservations essential* [M] *F to Lexington Ave./63rd St.; 4, 5, 6 to 59th St.; N, R to 5th Ave./59th St.* ✛ *5:F6.*

$$ [JAPANESE] ✕ **Sushi of Gari.** Options at this popular sushi restaurant range from the ordinary (California roll) to such exotic choices as tuna with creamy tofu sauce, miso-marinated cod, or Japanese yellowtail with jalapeño. Japanese noodles (udon or soba) and meat dishes such as teriyaki and negimaki (scallions rolled in

thinly sliced beef) are well prepared. Reservations are recommended. Another location at 370 Columbus Avenue (✛ *5:B2*) gives Upper West Siders their udon fix. [$] *Average main: $24* ⊠ *402 E. 78th St., at 1st Ave., Upper East Side* ☎ *212/517–5340* ⊕ *www.sushiofgari.com* ⊘ *No lunch* [M] *6 to 77th St.* ✛ *5:H2.*

UPPER WEST SIDE

Anchoring the dining experience in this section of town are the high-end restaurants at the Time Warner Center, which some call a "fine-dining food court." Head farther uptown for cheaper eats, but also a burgeoning gourmet dining scene.

With Lincoln Center theatergoers, hungry shoppers, and visitors to Central Park nearby, chefs are finally waking up to the captive built-in audience of tourists and locals alike. The main avenues are indeed lined with restaurants, but until recently many of them have been mediocre. Now the better-known destination-dining spots beyond the Time Warner Center—among them **Jean-Georges, Picholine, Telepan,** and **Dovetail**—have been joined by newcomers like **Salumeria Rossi, Fatty Crab,** and **Ed's Chowder,** all second or third restaurants from well-known chefs. Brunch is still a good bet, too. The flaky scones and fluffy omelets at **Sarabeth's,** not to mention blintzes and bagels at **Barney Greengrass,** are worth seeking out.

$$$$ [ASIAN] ✕ **Asiate.** The unparalleled view is reason enough to visit Asiate's pristine dining room, perched on the 35th floor of the Time Warner Center in the Mandarin Oriental Hotel. Artfully positioned tables and minimalist decor help direct eyes to the windows, which peer over Central Park. At night crystalline lights reflect in the glass, creating a magical effect. Young chef Brandon Kida creates contemporary dishes with an Asian influence. One of his signature dishes is soba noodles with Osetra caviar and wasabi cream; another standout is Wagyu beef tenderloin with smoked potato puree and braised short rib. Professional, attentive service helps foster an atmosphere of dreamlike luxury. The

restaurant has prix-fixe menus only, and an illustrious wine collection housing 2,000 bottles. $ *Average main: $85* ⊠ *80 Columbus Circle, 35th fl., at W. 60th St., inside the Mandarin Oriental, Upper West Side* ☎ *212/805–8881* ⊕ *www.mandarinoriental.com* Ⓜ *A, B, C, D, 1 to 59th St./Columbus Circle* ✛ *5:C6.*

$$$
FRENCH
Fodor'sChoice
★

✕**Bar Boulud.** Acclaimed French chef Daniel Boulud, known for upscale New York City eateries Daniel and Café Boulud, shows diners his more casual side with this lively contemporary bistro and wine bar. The long, narrow space accommodates 100 people and has a 14-seat round table for special wine-theme tastings. An additional level has three rooms for larger parties. The menu emphasizes charcuterie, including terrines and pâtés designed by Parisian charcutier Gilles Verot, who arranged just to work with Boulud, as well as traditional French bistro dishes like steak frites and *poulet rôti à l'ail* (roast chicken with garlic mashed potatoes). The 500-bottle wine list is heavy on wines from Burgundy and the Rhône Valley. Wallet watchers won't feel left out: a pretheater three-course menu starts at $42, and weekend brunch has two hearty courses plus coffee and dessert for $42. $ *Average main: $25.50* ⊠ *1900 Broadway, between 63rd and 64th Sts., Upper West Side* ☎ *212/595–0303* ⊕ *www.barboulud.com* Ⓜ *1 to 66th St./Lincoln Center; 1, A, C, B, D to 59th St./Columbus Circle* ✛ *5:B5.*

$$
AMERICAN

✕**Barney Greengrass.** At this New York Jewish landmark brusque waiters send out stellar smoked salmon, sturgeon, and whitefish to a happy crowd packed to the gills at small Formica tables. Split a fish platter with bagels, cream cheese, and other fixings, or get your velvety nova scrambled with eggs and buttery caramelized onions. If you're still hungry, go for a plate of cheese blintzes or the to-die-for chopped liver. Beware: the weekend brunch wait can exceed an hour. $ *Average main: $18* ⊠ *541 Amsterdam Ave., between W. 86th and W. 87th Sts., Upper West Side* ☎ *212/724–4707* ⊕ *www.barneygreengrass.com* ⌦ *Reservations not accepted* ▭ *No credit cards* ⊗ *Closed Mon. No dinner* Ⓜ *1, B, C to 86th St.* ✛ *6:B6.*

19

$
DINER

✕**Big Nick's Burger Joint & Pizza Joint.** This cramped, 24-hour neighborhood diner is decorated with photographs of the celebrities who've visited, but the primary draw is the burgers, which are huge and juicy. The endless menu lists every conceivable burger topping, from avocado and bacon to Greek tzatziki sauce. The classic Bistro Burger has mushrooms, Swiss, and fried onions on toasted challah bread. $ *Average main: $11* ⊠ *2175 Broadway, between W. 76th and W. 77th Sts., Upper West Side* ☎ *212/362–9238* ⊕ *www.bignicksnyc.com* Ⓜ *1 to 79th St.; 1, 2, 3 to 72nd St.* ✛ *5:A3.*

$
CAFÉ

✕**Bouchon Bakery.** Never mind that you're in the middle of a shopping mall under a Samsung sign; soups and sandwiches don't get much more luxurious than this. Acclaimed chef Thomas Keller's low-key lunch spot (one floor down from his extravagant flagship, Per Se) draws long lines for good reason. Share a mason jar of salmon rillettes—an unctuous spread of cooked and smoked salmon folded around crème fraîche and butter—then move on to one of the fork-and-knife open-faced tartines, like the tuna niçoise. When a sandwich has this much pedigree, $13.50 is actually a bargain. Grab dessert to go, a fresh macaroon or éclair, from the nearby bakery window. $ *Average main: $14* ✉ *10 Columbus Circle, Time Warner Center, 3rd floor, Upper West Side* ☎ *212/823–9366* ⊕ *www.bouchonbakery.com* Ⓜ *1, A, B, C, D to 59th St./Columbus Circle* ✛ *5:C6.*

$$$
FRENCH

✕ **Café Luxembourg.** The old soul of the Lincoln Center neighborhood seems to inhabit the tiled and mirrored walls of this lively, cramped restaurant, where West End Avenue regulars—including lots of on-air talent from nearby ABC News—are greeted with kisses, and musicians and audience members pack the room after a concert. The bar's always hopping, and the menu (served until 11 pm Sunday through Tuesday and until midnight from Wednesday through Saturday) includes dishes like steak tartare and lobster roll, alongside dishes with a more contemporary spin like pan-seared trout with haricots verts, hazelnuts, and tomato-caper compote. $ *Average main: $28* ✉ *200 W. 70th St., between Amsterdam and West End Aves., Upper West Side* ☎ *212/873–7411* ⊕ *www.cafeluxembourg.com* ⚞ *Reservations essential* Ⓜ *1, 2, 3, B, C to 72nd St.* ✛ *5:A4.*

$$$
ITALIAN
☺

✕ **Carmine's.** Set on a nondescript block of Broadway, this branch of the Italian family-style mainstay is a favorite for families celebrating special occasions, pre-prom groups of teens, and plain old folks who come for the tried-and-true menu items like fried calamari, linguine with white clam sauce, chicken parmigiana, and veal saltimbocca, all served in mountainous portions. Family photos line the walls, there's a groaning antipasti table filled with savory meats, cheese, and salads, and there's a convivial feeling amid the organized chaos. On weekends, only parties of six or more can make dinner reservations. $ *Average main: $26* ✉ *2450 Broadway, between 90th and 91st Sts., Upper West Side* ☎ *212/362–2200* ⊕ *www.carminesnyc.com/* Ⓜ *1, 2, 3, to 96th St./Broadway* ✛ *6:A5.*

$$$$
AMERICAN

✕ **Dovetail.** Inside Dovetail, chef-owner John Fraser's subdued town house and restaurant, cream-color walls and maple panels create a warm, soothing atmosphere, and a recent expansion allows for more dining-room space and a larger bar area. The menu, which changes daily, features refined but hearty dishes. Seek solace from winter temperatures with the earthy gnocchi topped with matsutake mushrooms, poppy seeds, and lemon. Tender lamb is heightened by potatoes, artichokes, and olives. The savory feast continues with pastry chef Michael Shelkowitz's Earl Grey pumpkin cake with lemon curd and cinnamon-toast ice cream. $ *Average main: $37* ✉ *103 W. 77th St., at Columbus Ave., Upper West Side* ☎ *212/362–3800* ⊕ *www.dovetailnyc.com* ☽ *No lunch Mon.–Thurs., Sat., or Sun.* Ⓜ *1 to 79th St.; B, C to 81st St./Museum of Natural History* ✛ *5:B3.*

$$
AMERICAN

✕ **Fairway Café.** Fairway Supermarket is a neighborhood institution, living up to its reputation for great prices on gourmet products—and shopping-cart jockeying down the narrow aisles. Upstairs, though, is the respite of Fairway Café, a large, brick-walled room with windows overlooking Broadway. Up front you can grab a pastry and coffee to go, but there's a full menu of fairly priced entrées as well. The place is run by Mitchell London, who's known for his juicy, well-marbled steaks—try the rib eye and you may never go back to Brooklyn's Peter

Luger steak house again. $ *Average main: $20* ✉ *2127 Broadway, between 74th and 75th Sts., Upper West Side* ☎ *212/994–9555* ⊕ *www. fairwaymarket.com* Ⓜ *1, 2, 3 to 72nd St.* ✛ *5:A3.*

$$
ASIAN FUSION
✕ **Fatty Crab.** The uptown branch of Zac Pelaccio's downtown Malaysian street-food joint has two major advantages over its downtown sibling: more seats and a reservations line. Other than that, the menu mimics the Hudson Street locale's laundry list of crowd-pleasing favorites, like coconut-rich short rib Rendang and soft buns filled with Berkshire pork, cilantro, and savory sauce. Perhaps in deference to the child-toting population in the neighborhood, there's spacious outdoor seating perfect for parking strollers. $ *Average main: $21.50* ✉ *2170 Broadway, between 76th and 77th Sts., Upper West Side* ☎ *212/496–2722* ⊕ *www. fattycrab.com* Ⓜ *1 to 79th St./Broadway* ✛ *5:A3.*

$$
MEDITERRANEAN
✕ **Fishtag.** Upper West Siders aren't going to be throwing chef Michael Psilakis and his Greek-heavy Mediterranean fare back into the water any time soon. At Anthos, a big-box Midtown eatery that shuttered a few years ago, Psilakis was lauded for his prowess on the grill. He brings the same skills to Fishtag with dishes like grilled striped bass and grilled swordfish. Fanatics of Anthos's insanely good lamb burger can breathe easy, as it's on the menu here. The wine list is long and categorized with subtitles like "Funky & Earthy" and "Explosive & Bold" and brew imbibers will declare Fishtag a good catch when they see 20 craft beers on the menu. $ *Average main: $19* ✉ *222 W. 79th St., between Broadway and Amsterdam Ave., Upper West Side* ☎ *212/362–7470* Ⓜ *1 to 79th St.* ✛ *5:A2.*

$$$
SPANISH
✕ **GastroArte.** Aside from the Lower East Side restaurant wd-50, the so-called "molecular gastronomy" hasn't really taken off in New York. But leave it to a Spaniard, chef Jesus Nunez, to bring inventive and, at times, sensually perplexing cuisine to the Upper West Side, a neighborhood that was once a culinary graveyard. Imagine: an "egg" that is actually cauliflower, a deconstructed Spanish omelet that is served in a glass, and "edible dirt" that is actually a falafel. With such culinary trickery, it's a good thing there are plenty of strong cocktails on the menu (and a long list of Spanish wine). $ *Average main: $27* ✉ *141 W. 69th St., at Broadway, Upper West Side* ☎ *646/692–8762* Ⓜ *1, 2, 3 to 72nd St.* ✛ *5:B4.*

19

$$
AMERICAN
✕ **Isabella's.** Set in the shadow of the Museum of Natural History, Isabella's has been a brunch-and-beyond stalwart for decades. Lunch is less crowded, a great time to try neighborhood-institution salads like the seafood-loaded Cobb or grilled artichoke hearts with parmesan and lemon-thyme vinaigrette. Another winner: the crab-cake sandwich layered with lush avocado. $ *Average main: $20* ✉ *359 Columbus Ave., at 77th St., Upper West Side* ☎ *212/724–2100* ⊕ *www.isabellas.com* Ⓜ *1 to 79th St.* ✛ *5:B3.*

$$$$
FRENCH
✕ **Jean Georges.** This culinary temple in the Trump International Hotel and Towers focuses wholly on *chef célèbre* Jean-Georges Vongerichten's spectacular creations. Some approach the limits of the taste universe, like foie-gras brûlée with spiced fig jam and ice-wine reduction. Others are models of simplicity, like slow-cooked cod with warm vegetable vinaigrette. Exceedingly personalized service and a well-selected wine list contribute to an unforgettable meal, as do tattooed celeb pastry chef

Johnny Iuzzini's rock-and-roll desserts, like a lemon ice cream filled with house-made pop rocks. It's prix fixe only. For Jean Georges on a budget, try the prix-fixe lunch in the front room, Nougatine. $ *Average main: $100* ⊠ *1 Central Park W, at W. 59th St., Upper West Side* ☎ *212/299–3900* ⊕ *www.jean-georges.com* ⌂ *Reservations essential Jacket required* ⊗ *Closed Sun.* Ⓜ *A, B, C, D, 1 to 59th St./Columbus Circle* ✛ *5:C6.*

$ ✕**Kefi.** Michael Psilakis's homage to his grandmother's Greek cooking
GREEK   has moved to an expansive space a few blocks north of the now-closed original location. Among the mezes, the meatballs with roasted garlic, olives, and tomato is a standout; the flavorful roast chicken, potatoes, red peppers, garlic, and thyme makes for a winning entrée, and the béchamel-rich Kefi mac and cheese is irresistible. Reasonable prices make it easy to stick around for a piece of traditional walnut cake with walnut ice cream. $ *Average main: $13.95* ⊠ *505 Columbus Ave., between 84th and 85th Sts., Upper West Side* ☎ *212/873–0200* ⊕ *www.kefirestaurant. com* ⊗ *No lunch Mon.* Ⓜ *1 to 86th St.; B, C to 86th St.* ✛ *5:B1.*

$ ✕**Levain Bakery.** Completely unpretentious and utterly delicious, Levain
BAKERY   Bakery's cookies are rich and hefty. In fact, they clock in at 6 ounces
⊗   each! Choose from the chocolate-chip walnut, dark-chocolate chocolate chip, dark-chocolate peanut-butter chip, or oatmeal raisin. Batches are baked fresh daily, and they taste best when they're warm and melty right out of the oven, so it's definitely worth seeking out this small basement bakery for a cookie craving. Levain's also bakes artisanal breads, including banana chocolate chip and pumpkin ginger spice, sour cream coffee cake, chocolate-chip and cinnamon brioche, sourdough rolls stuffed with Valrhona chocolate, blueberry muffins, a variety of scones, and *bombol-oncini*—their unique jelly doughnuts. $ *Average main: $9* ⊠ *167 W. 74th St., near Amsterdam Ave., Upper West Side* ☎ *212/874–6080* ⊕ *www. levainbakery.com* ⊗ *No dinner* Ⓜ *1, 2, 3 to 72nd St.* ✛ *5:B3.*

$$$$ ✕**Marea.** Carefully sourced, meticulously prepared fish and seafood
ITALIAN   take center stage at this glossy, well-pedigreed restaurant. Large pic-
Fodor's Choice   ture windows in the dining room offer expansive views of Central Park
★   South, and silver-dipped shells on pedestals decorate the dining room. No expense is spared in importing the very best of the ocean's bounty, beginning with an entire menu of *crudo* dishes—think scallops with orange, wild fennel, and arugula—that is rapidly becoming the restaurant's signature and can be enjoyed in the main dining room or an eight-seat bar at the end of the front room's shimmering onyx wall. You'd be remiss, though, if you skipped the pastas that made chef Michael White famous at the East Side's Convivio (and at his expanding empire, which includes Osteria Morini in NoLita and Ai Fiori in the new Setai Hotel). They're served here in lusty iterations like rich fusilli with octopus and bone marrow and spaghetti with sea urchin. Whole fish like roasted turbot and salt-baked snapper are equally showstopping. Service is flawless, and even the dishware-scalloped china embossed with the restaurant's name—tiny shell-shape espresso cups—is special. $ *Average main: $41* ⊠ *240 Central Park S, between Broadway and 7th Ave., Midtown West* ☎ *212/582–5100* ⊕ *www.marea-nyc.com* ⌂ *Reserva-tions essential* Ⓜ *A, B, C, D, 1 to Columbus Circle* ✛ *4:B1.*

$$ ✕ **Nice Matin.** If the Upper West Side and the French Riviera collided,
BISTRO   it might look a little bit like Nice Matin. This is a longtime neighbor-
🕓   hood favorite, particularly in the warm weather months, when regu-
lars plant themselves at sidewalk tables and gawk at passersby while
munching on Gallic fare like monkfish wading in sweet potato puree
and garlicky mussels, and, of course, steak frites. The novel-size wine
list boasts more than 2,000 bottles, so bring your reading glasses. And
be sure to dress for the people-watching occasion, particularly at the
popular weekend brunch. ⑤ *Average main: $24* ⊠ *201 W. 79th St., at
Amsterdam Ave., Upper West Side* ☎ *212/873–6423* ⊕ *nicematinnyc.
com* Ⓜ *1 to 79th St.* ✛ *5:A2.*

$$$$ ✕ **Per Se.** The New York interpretation of what many consider America's
AMERICAN   finest restaurant, Napa Valley's French Laundry, Per Se is chef Thomas
Fodor'sChoice   Keller's Broadway stage. Keller equally embraces French technique, a
★   religious fervor for seasonality, and a witty playfulness that speaks to
his confidence in the kitchen. The large dining room is understated and
elegant, with touches of wood, towering florals, and—the best design
touch of all—sweeping windows with views of Central Park. Keller's
dishes are now world renowned, such as his tiny cones of tuna tartare
topped with crème fraîche, and "oysters and pearls," delicate tiny mol-
lusks suspended in a creamy custard with tapioca. Dessert service is a
multicourse celebration of all things sweet, including a choice of 27
house-made chocolates and, of course, treats to take home. Waiters,
who can, and may, recite the provenance of the tiniest turnip, are also
some of the nicest, most disarming servers in town. There's also a new
à la carte "salon" menu available in the front bar room, but let's face
it: if you manage to snag a reservation, there's nothing else to do but
submit to the $275 prix-fixe. ⑤ *Average main: $76.50* ⊠ *Time Warner
Center, 10 Columbus Circle, 4th Floor, at W. 60th St., Upper West
Side* ☎ *212/823–9335* ⊕ *www.perseny.com* ⌔ *Reservations essential*
🏛 *Jacket required* ⊗ *No lunch Mon.–Thurs.* Ⓜ *A, B, C, D, 1 to 59th
St./Columbus Circle* ✛ *5:C6.*

$$$$ ✕ **Picholine.** Terrence Brennan's classic French restaurant, has main-
MEDITERRANEAN   tained its dignified atmosphere over the years, as well as the emphasis
on contemporary Mediterranean cuisine, sourced from artisanal farm-
ers and food producers. The menu is divided into four relatively small
sections: Preludes, Pastas, Day Boats, and the Land, and you are invited
to construct your own tasting by selecting three or four sections. The
Picholine take on chicken Kiev is particularly brilliant: an heirloom
chicken breast is pressed into a fat juicy tube and rolled in crushed corn-
flakes before it is deep-fried. Slice into the soft cylinder and it spills its
luscious "liquid foie gras" filling. Don't miss the famous cheese course,
which Brennan practically invented here. ⑤ *Average main: $42* ⊠ *35
W. 64th St., between Broadway and Central Park W, Upper West Side*
☎ *212/724–8585* ⊕ *www.picholinenyc.com* ⌔ *Reservations essential*
⊗ *No lunch. Closed Sun.* Ⓜ *1 to 66th St./Lincoln Center* ✛ *5:C5.*

$$$$ ✕ **Porter House New York.** With clubby interiors by Jeffrey Beers and an
STEAKHOUSE   adjoining lounge area, Porter House marks the splashy return to the
scene of former Windows on the World chef Michael Lomonaco. Fill-
ing the meat-and-potatoes slot in the Time Warner Center's upscale

19

"Restaurant Collection," the masculine throwback highlights American wines and pedigreed super-size meat. The neighborhood, long under-served on the steak-house front, has quickly warmed to Lomonaco's simple, solid American fare. Begin with his smoky clams casino or rich roasted marrow bones. Steaks are huge and expertly seasoned, and come with the usual battery of à la carte sides—creamed spinach, roasted mushrooms, and truffle mashed potatoes. ⑤ *Average main: $40* ✉ *10 Columbus Circle, at 60th St., 4th floor, Upper West Side* ☎ *212/823–9500* ⊕ *www.porterhousenewyork.com* Ⓜ *1, A, B, C, D to 59th St./Columbus Circle* ✧ *5:C6.*

$ ✕ **Salumeria Rosi Parmacotto.** Just up the block from Gray's Papaya is
ITALIAN this compact temple to a whole different subset of cured meats. Chef Cesare Casella has created a showcase for dozens of varieties of pro-sciutto, coppa, mortadella, and more, carved from a professional slicer for consumption on the spot or as indulgent takeout. There's also a more ambitious menu, including salads and a lusty osso buco over creamy mashed potatoes. If you're lucky, you might catch a glimpse of the avuncular chef with his signature rosemary sprig peeking out from his breast pocket. ⑤ *Average main: $13* ✉ *283 Amsterdam Ave., between 73rd and 74th Sts., Upper West Side* ☎ *212/877–4800* ⊕ *www. salumeriarosi.com* Ⓜ *1, 2, 3 to 72nd St.* ✧ *5:B3.*

$$ ✕ **Sarabeth's Kitchen.** Lining up for brunch here is as much an Upper
AMERICAN West Side tradition as taking a sunny Sunday afternoon stroll in nearby Riverside Park. Locals love the bric-a-brac-filled restaurant for sweet morning-time dishes like lemon ricotta pancakes, as well as for the comforting dinners. The afternoon tea includes buttery scones with Sarabeth's signature jams, savory nibbles, and outstanding baked goods. Dinner entrées include chicken potpie and truffle mac and cheese. There are several other locations around town. ⑤ *Average main: $18* ✉ *423 Amsterdam Ave., at W. 80th St., Upper West Side* ☎ *800/773–7378* ⊕ *www.sarabeth.com* Ⓜ *1 to 79th St.* ✧ *5:B2.*

$ ✕ **Shake Shack.** The Upper West Side location of Danny Meyer's Shake
BURGER Shack is an eat-in joint just across Columbus Avenue from the Ameri-
Fodor's Choice can Museum of Natural History. Although the lines may be long at
★ lunchtime, the grub is good and well priced. ⑤ *Average main: $6* ✉ *366 Columbus Ave., at W. 77th St., Upper West Side* ☎ *646/747–8770* ⊕ *www.shakeshacknyc.com* Ⓜ *B, C to 81st St.* ✧ *5:B2.*

$$$ ✕ **Telepan.** Chef-owner Bill Telepan is a regular at the neighborhood
AMERICAN greenmarket, and it shows in his seasonal, produce-driven menu, which is divided into three courses: appetizers of salads, light fish dishes, and soups; middle courses of eggs, pasta, or vegetables; and main courses of meat and fish. A trio of tiny *amuses-bouches* such as wild mushroom cappuccino arrives to tease your palate, and the servers are well versed on the wine list. The menu features brook trout served on celery-root blini with green-apple sour cream, a well-deserved favorite, as is any-thing on the menu that contains eggs, like the "egg-in-a-hole" served with spinach and hen-of-the-woods mushrooms. For dessert, a crunchy peanut-butter and milk-chocolate gianduja duo with peanut-brittle ice cream is sublime. ⑤ *Average main: $28.50* ✉ *72 W. 69th St., between Columbus Ave. and Central Park W, Upper West Side* ☎ *212/580–4300*

⊕ *www.telepan-ny.com* ⊗ *No lunch Mon. and Tues.* Ⓜ *1 to 66th St./ Lincoln Center; 1, 2, 3 to 72nd St.; B, C to 72nd St.* ✛ *5:B4.*

HARLEM

For more adventurous eating, head up to Harlem for the city's best Southern cooking. This is a neighborhood that takes pride in its cooking, and in addition to plates of collard greens, mac and cheese and smothered chicken, an infusion of wine bars, restaurants, and lounges is changing the landscape. This is where renowned chef Marcus Samuelsson now lives and recently opened his high-profile restaurant, Red Rooster, helping to encourage the beginning of a new Harlem dining renaissance.

$$
BISTRO

✕ **Chez Lucienne.** French Harlem? Not exactly, but Chez Lucienne is about as close as you'll get to France without leaving the comfortable confines of this historic neighborhood. And if you can't get into the Red Rooster next door, then grab a seat at the baby blue banquette or relax at an outdoor table where locals come to sip coffee or wine, dogs at their side. The menu looks to Lyon with classics like sauteed foie gras and steak au poivre by a chef who logged time in the kitchen with famed chef Daniel Boulud. Ⓢ *Average main: $18* ⊠ *308 Lenox Ave., between W. 125th and W. 126th Sts., Harlem* ☏ *212/289–5555* ⊕ *www. chezlucienne.com* Ⓜ *2, 3 to 116th St.* ✛ *6:D1.*

$
SOUTHERN
☺

✕ **Miss Mamie's Spoonbread Too.** Miss Mamie's Spoonbread Too is a much-loved Southern spot that's known for its friendly staff as well as its fried chicken, grits, and cornbread. Local politicians are sometimes seen rubbing elbows with the Columbia University students who gather here. Ⓢ *Average main: $15* ⊠ *366 W. 110th St., near Manhattan Ave., Harlem* ☏ *212/865–0700* ⊕ *www.spoonbreadinc.com* Ⓜ *B, C to 110th St.* ✛ *6:B2.*

$
ECLECTIC

✕ **Native.** Mildly Caribbean is just one way to describe the food at Native, where the menu features flavorful rice bowls and entrées that span a broad range of cuisines. Favorites include the curry chicken, smoked salmon linguine, and Moroccan fried chicken with collard greens and mashed potatoes, this eatery manages to be all over the map and still find its way. Ⓢ *Average main: $16* ⊠ *161 Lenox Ave., at 118th St., Harlem* ☏ *212/665–2525* ⊕ *www.harlemnativenyc.com* ⊟ *No credit cards* ⊗ *No lunch* Ⓜ *2, 3 to 116th St.* ✛ *6:C1.*

$$$
AMERICAN

✕ **Red Rooster Harlem.** Marcus Samuelsson, who earned his celebrity chefdom at Aquavit in Midtown for his take on Ethiopian-accented Scandinavian cuisine (fusing the food of his birthplace with that of where he grew up), moves way uptown to Harlem, where he has created a culinary hot spot for the ages. The comfort food menu jumps all over the place, reflecting the ethnic diversity that is modern-day New York City (and the patrons who regularly come here), from plantain-loaded oxtail to fried chicken to the tender meatballs (with lingonberry sauce) that he served at Aquavit. Expect a wait for Sunday brunch, with its gospel music, boozy cocktails, and modern takes on dishes like chicken and waffles. Ⓢ *Average main: $26* ⊠ *310 Lenox Ave., between 125th and 126th, Harlem* ☏ *212/792–9001* ⊕ *www.redroosterharlem.com* Ⓜ *2, 3 to 125th St.* ✛ *6:D1.*

19

$$ ✗ **Sylvia's.** This Harlem mainstay has been serving soul-food favorites

SOUTHERN like smothered chicken, barbecue ribs, collard greens, and mashed pota-

☺ toes to a dedicated crowd of locals, tourists, and college students since 1962. The food is so popular that owner Sylvia Woods bottles her sig-nature sauces and spices for the masses, available for purchase at the restaurant and online. Some say it's overly touristy—and the bus loads attest, but it's still an experience. $ *Average main: $24* ⊠ *328 Lenox Ave., near 127th St., Harlem* ☎ *212/996–0660* ⊕ *www.sylviassoulfood. com* ✛ *6:D1.*

BROOKLYN

BRIGHTON BEACH

$$ ✗ **Tatiana Grill.** It's open year-round, but Tatiana's, right on the board-

RUSSIAN walk, really bustles in the summer when the outdoor tables fill with Russian-speaking couples and families. The menu has pages and pages of options that range from sushi to Ukrainian dishes. The excellent Greek salad is a refreshing choice after a day at the beach, and the grilled chicken skewers are simple but good. $ *Average main: $15* ⊠ *3152 Brighton 6th St., on boardwalk, Brooklyn* ☎ *718/891–5151* Ⓜ *B, Q to Brighton Beach* ⊕ *www.tatianagrill.com/.*

BROOKLYN HEIGHTS

$$ ✗ **Henry's End.** At this nearly 40-year-old neighborhood favorite, the

AMERICAN casual decor belies the quality of the food and wine. Wild game such as elk, kangaroo, and ostrich take center stage during the Wild Game Festival in the late fall and winter months; seasonal seafood and foraged vegetables star in the springtime. If duck is your thing, there are usually several preparations on the menu. $ *Average main: $18.50* ⊠ *44 Henry St., near Cranberry St., Brooklyn Heights, Brooklyn* ☎ *718/834–1776* ⊕ *www.henrysend.com* ☺ *No lunch* Ⓜ *2, 3 to Clark St.; A, C to High St.*

$$ ✗ **Noodle Pudding.** The name is bad, but the food is great at this cozy

ITALIAN Brooklyn Heights restaurant that serves excellent Italian fare. Locals especially rave about the osso buco served with goat-cheese polenta. It gets crowded, but that means it's noisy enough that you can bring the kids. Reservations are accepted only for parties of six or more. $ *Average main: $18* ⊠ *38 Henry St., near Cranberry St., Brooklyn Heights, Brooklyn* ☎ *718/625–3737* ▭ *No credit cards* ☺ *No lunch* Ⓜ *A, C to High St.; 2, 3 to Clark St.*

CARROLL GARDENS

$$ ✗ **Buttermilk Channel.** This cozy restaurant is like a spirited slice of down-

AMERICAN home Americana. Locals swear by comfort-food mainstays with empha-sis on local and organic, especially the all-time fave: buttermilk-fried chicken with cheddar waffles. Other standouts include the house-made charcuterie and snacks like handmade mozzarella. Specials include a Monday night, three-course dinner for $25. It's a bit of a trek if you're taking the subway. $ *Average main: $19* ⊠ *524 Court St., at Huntington St., Carroll Gardens, Brooklyn* ☎ *718/852–8490* ⊕ *www. buttermilkchannelnyc.com* ☺ *No lunch weekdays* Ⓜ *F to Carroll St.*

$$ ✕ **Char No. 4.** With 300-plus whiskeys to choose from—the focus is
AMERICAN on American labels—Char No. 4 is a connoisseur's dream (the name
refers to barrels in which the golden liquor is aged). To complement
your tipple, there are updated dishes from south of the Mason-Dixon
line. Many of the appetizers involve bacon; don't miss the thick-cut
bacon with peas and carrots, the BLT, or the cheese curds with pimento
sauce. $ *Average main: $20* ⊠ *196 Smith St., Carroll Gardens, Brook-
lyn* ☏ *718/643–2106* ⊕ *www.charno4.com* ⊙ *No lunch Mon.–Thurs.*
Ⓜ *F to Bergen St.*

$$$ ✕ **SAUL restaurant.** Owner Saul Bolton, who logged time in the kitchens
AMERICAN of Le Bernardin and Bouley, was one of the first to include seasonal
local ingredients on his plates. More than a decade later, this Smith
Street restaurant is still a favorite eating destination for the culinary
cognoscenti. Saul is particularly good at mixing surf and turf, in dishes
like caramelized scallops paired with chorizo and grilled octopus with
slow-roasted pork belly—the resulting delights are well executed without being overly precious. $ *Average main: $30.50* ⊠ *140 Smith St.,
near Bergen, Carroll Gardens, Brooklyn* ☏ *718/935–9844* ⊕ *www.
saulrestaurant.com* ⊙ *No lunch* Ⓜ *F to Bergen St.*

CONEY ISLAND

$ ✕ **Nathan's Famous.** No visit to Coney Island would be truly complete
AMERICAN without a hot dog from this stand that first opened in 1916. The fries
are darn good, too. On the Fourth of July thousands come to see their
world-famous hot dog–eating contest; the record stands at 68 in 10
minutes. $ *Average main: $4* ⊠ *1310 Surf Ave., at Stillwell Ave., Coney
Island* ☏ *718/946–2705* ⊕ *www.nathansfamous.com/* Ⓜ *D, F, N, Q to
Coney Island–Stillwell Ave.*

DOWNTOWN BROOKLYN

$$$$ ✕ **Brooklyn Fare.** At Brooklyn's only restaurant with three coveted
ECLECTIC Michelin stars, local star chef César Ramirez and his sous-chefs offer a
culinary performance during three nightly seatings. At each, 20 dainty,
often seafood-focused concoctions are presented to 18 diners seated at
a semicircular steel counter. Dishes might include king salmon parfait
with basil gelée, avocado, maple syrup, and mustard; or fresh tofu
and king crab blended with matsutake mushrooms and dashi sauce.
It's BYOB. Getting a reservation is a complicated ordeal so plan in
advance. $ *Average main: $135* ⊠ *200 Schermerhorn St., near Hoyt
St., Downtown* ☏ *718/243–0050* ⊕ *www.brooklynfare.com* ⊜ *Reservations essential* ⊙ *Closed Sun. and Mon. No lunch* Ⓜ *A, C to Hoyt–
Schermerhorn; 2, 3 to Hoyt St.; 4, 5 to Nevins St.; B, M, Q, R to
Dekalb Ave.*

DUMBO

$ ✕ **Grimaldi's.** This classic New York–style parlor serves excellent pizza
PIZZA pies from its coal ovens. Although sometimes inconsistent, when they're
Fodor's Choice good, the thin crisp crust is slightly blackened and the fresh mozzarella
★ oozes satisfyingly. Grimaldi's popularity allows them to be picky: no
slices, no reservations, no credit cards; and there are usually no empty
tables so expect a wait. Impatient foodies have been known to phone
in a to-go order, swoop past the lines, and then enjoy their pizza in the

19

nearby Brooklyn Bridge Park. ⑤ *Average main: $14* ⊠ *19 Old Fulton St., between Front and Water Sts., DUMBO* ☎ *718/858–4300* ⊕ *www. grimaldis.com* ⚲ *Reservations not accepted* ⊟ *No credit cards* Ⓜ *A, C to High St.; 2, 3 to Clark St.; F to York St.*

$ ✕ **Rice.** Students and loft-dwelling artists frequent this vegetarian-
ECLECTIC   friendly, "world cuisine" restaurant with its small, exposed-brick dining
☯   room and friendly vibe. The inspired range of healthful, global dishes range from Indian chicken curry and Jamaican jerk to Thai beef salad and ratatouille; the vegetarian meatballs are particularly good. Choose from a variety of rices that include Basmati, Thai black, and Bhutanese red to accompany your meal. The DUMBO location has outdoor seating in back. ⑤ *Average main: $11* ⊠ *81 Washington St., at York St., DUMBO, Brooklyn* ☎ *718/222–9880* ⊕ *www.riceny.com* ⊟ *No credit cards* Ⓜ *F to York St.*

$$$$ ✕ **River Café.** The River Café's incredible views of the Manhattan skyline
MODERN   across the way, lush flowers, and live piano music make it a waterfront
AMERICAN   favorite for romantic meals, marriage proposals, fancy birthdays, and special celebrations. The menu offers a contemporary take on local and exotic ingredients—it's fixed-price-only at dinner; lunch has à la carte options. For the ultimate experience, snag a window seat and try the chef's six-course tasting menu ($125 per person). Gentlemen: jackets are required after 5 pm. ⑤ *Average main: $100* ⊠ *1 Water St., near Old Fulton St., DUMBO* ☎ *718/522–5200* ⊕ *www.rivercafe.com* Ⓜ *F to York St.; A, C to High St.; 2, 3 to Clark St.*

$$ ✕ **Vinegar Hill House.** In an offbeat enclave on the edge of DUMBO called
MODERN   Vinegar Hill, this relative newcomer to Brooklyn's dining scene has
AMERICAN   formed a fiercely loyal following. Foodies trek out to the rustic-chic dining room for well-prepared seasonal food and cozy ambience. Favorites include the moist, crispy-skinned cast-iron chicken and the oven-roasted octopus. ⑤ *Average main: $23.50* ⊠ *72 Hudson Ave., between Front and Water Sts., DUMBO* ☎ *718/522–1018* ⊕ *www.vinegarhillhouse. com* ⚲ *Reservations not accepted* ☯ *No lunch weekdays* Ⓜ *F to York St.*

FORT GREENE

$$ ✕ **The General Greene.** Hearty, locally sourced fare keeps the crowds
AMERICAN   happy these days no matter where you are, but this neighborhood darling outdoes much of the competition. Start with buttermilk biscuits or seven-spice onion rings, then move on to fried chicken, a whole trout, or short-rib Stroganoff with organic rigatoni. Vegetable sides like steamed red kale or brussel sprouts with bacon and mushrooms are just the other side of virtuous. Waiting for a table is part of the experience, especially for weekend brunch, as are the cocktails and the famous salted-caramel sundae. ⑤ *Average main: $18* ⊠ *229 DeKalb Ave., Fort Greene, Brooklyn* ☎ *718/222–1510* ⊕ *www.thegeneralgreene.com* Ⓜ *C to Lafayette Ave.; B, M, Q, R to DeKalb Ave.*

$$ ✕ **No. 7.** Perch at the marble-topped bar or lounge at one of the ban-
MODERN   quettes in the back at this buzzy neighborhood bistro lighted up by Edi-
AMERICAN   son bulbs. The frequently changing menu takes American classics and throws them for a global spin. The result is a nouveau fusion that pulls in droves of local diners and makes vegetarians happy. Highlights might include anything from crispy eggplant with tofu in a tomato vinaigrette

to skirt steak with baked potato, Chinese sausage, and chimichurri sauce. Brunch dishes are similarly innovative but delicious—think fried eggs with nachos and jalapeños, or pork loin with fried eggs, buttermilk pancake, and pineapple maple syrup. $ *Average main: $20* ⊠ *7 Greene Ave., Fort Greene, Brooklyn* ☎ *718/522–6370* ⊕ *www.no7restaurant. com* ⊘ *No lunch weekdays; bar only Mon.* Ⓜ *C to Lafayette Ave; 2, 3, 4, 5, B, Q to Atlantic Ave.*

$$ ✕ **Stonehome Wine Bar and Restaurant.** Just down the street from BAM,
MODERN Stonehome is the place to go before or after a show for sophisticated
AMERICAN food and wine at reasonable prices. This dimly lighted basement hideaway has excellent tasting flights—three samples for $18—and 35 wines by the glass, perfect to pair with cheese, charcuterie, and housemade pâtés. The small and uncomplicated menu focues on market-fresh new American fare like pan-roasted chicken with cheddar grits and greens. The back garden is a delight when the weather is fine. $ *Average main: $19* ⊠ *87 Lafayette Ave., at S. Portland Ave., Fort Greene, Brooklyn* ☎ *718/624–9443* ⊕ *www.stonehomewinebar.com* ⊘ *No lunch* Ⓜ *C to Lafayette Ave.*

$$ ✕ **Roman's.** When the masterminds behind Marlow & Sons opened
ITALIAN this locavore Italian restaurant in Fort Greene, neighborhood foodies rejoiced, and the consistently excellent food, convivial atmosphere, and friendly service has them still clamoring for a table or a spot at the refinished marble bar. The dinner menu changes nightly and showcases small plates like roasted rabbit loins with lentils. Weekend brunch is a hit— don't skip the homemade doughnuts. $ *Average main: $16.50* ⊠ *243 Dekalb Ave., near Vanderbilt Ave., Fort Greene, Brooklyn* ☎ *718/622– 5300* ⊕ *www.romansnyc.com* ⚱ *Reservations not accepted* ⊘ *No lunch on weekdays* Ⓜ *C to Lafayette Ave.*

PARK SLOPE AND PROSPECT HEIGHTS

$$ ✕ **al di là.** This Northern Italian hot spot has been consistently packed
ITALIAN since it first opened back in 1998, and it's easy to understand why: affordable prices, a relaxed and charming environment, and simple yet soulfully comforting dishes such as the red beet and ricotta ravioli in a butter and poppy seed sauce, braised rabbit, or hanger steak. The no-reservations policy ensures that the place always has a buzz around it from waiting patrons. $ *Average main: $21* ⊠ *248 5th Ave., at Carroll St., Park Slope, Brooklyn* ☎ *718/783–4565* ⊕ *www.aldilatrattoria.com* ⚱ *Reservations not accepted* ⊘ *No lunch Tues.* Ⓜ *F to 15th St.–Prospect Park; R to Union St.*

$ ✕ **Franny's.** Though many swear by Grimaldi's for the borough's best
PIZZA pie, this Park Slope pizza shop has developed quite a following of its own. The crisp, thin-crust pizzas run the gamut from a "naked" pie with olive oil and salt to their justly talked up clam-and-garlic iteration. Many of the toppings are seasonal and locally sourced. $ *Average main: $16* ⊠ *295 Flatbush Ave., Park Slope, Brooklyn* ☎ *718/230–0221* ⊕ *www.frannysbrooklyn.com* ⚱ *Reservations not accepted* ⊘ *No lunch weekdays* Ⓜ *B, Q to 7th Ave.; 2, 3 to Bergen St., 4, 5, N, R to Pacific St.*

$ ✕ **Tom's Restaurant.** For friendly service and great diner fare and excellent
AMERICAN fluffy lemon-ricotta pancakes served with homemade flavored butters, head three blocks north of the Brooklyn Museum to this family-owned

19

restaurant, which opened in 1936. Lines are long on weekends. $ *Average main: $8* ⊠ *782 Washington Ave., at Sterling Pl., Prospect Heights, Brooklyn* 🕾 *718/636–9738* 🍴 *Reservations not accepted* ▭ *No credit cards* ☽ *No dinner* Ⓜ *2, 3 to Grand Army Plaza.*

WILLIAMSBURG

$$
AMERICAN

✕ **Diner.** Tucked inside a 1927 dining car, this restaurant serves simple seasonal fare and so many specials that your waiter will scrawl their names on the paper tablecloth to help you remember them all. It's more upscale than the name implies but still casual. Save room for the intense flourless chocolate cake. $ *Average main: $20* ⊠ *85 Broadway, at Berry St., Williamsburg, Brooklyn* 🕾 *718/486–3077* ⊕ *www. dinernyc.com* 🍴 *Reservations not accepted* Ⓜ *J, M, Z to Marcy Ave.; L to Bedford Ave.*

$$$
MODERN
AMERICAN

✕ **Dressler.** Williamsburg has become one of the tastiest parts of the Big Apple and handsome, dark-wood-and-exposed-brick bedecked restaurants like Dressler are exactly what have given the neighborhood its culinary star status. Famed, old-school steak house Peter Luger may be just across the street, but food-loving hipsters are hitting Dressler for American seasonal cuisine like house-smoked sturgeon and braised veal cheeks. And if that's not enough to make a hipster's skinny jeans tighter, the legendary burger from sister restaurant, Dumont, is also on the menu. $ *Average main: $30.50* ⊠ *149 Broadway, between Bedford and Driggs Aves., Williamsburg, Brooklyn* 🕾 *718/384–6343* ⊕ *www. dresslernyc.com* Ⓜ *J, M, Z to Marcy Ave.; L to Bedford Ave.*

$$
AMERICAN

✕ **DuMont.** Slide into a candlelight leather booth or sit outside in the charming back garden and peruse the menu of seasonal salads, pasta, and main courses. This is the place for inspired cocktails and cuisine in a laid-back atmosphere. Classic menu items include a swoon-inducing mac 'n cheese and juicy burgers that inspired a separate restaurant, Dumont Burger, nearby (314 Bedford Avenue). $ *Average main: $20* ⊠ *432 Union Ave., between Metropolitan Ave. and Devoe St., Williamsburg, Brooklyn* 🕾 *718/486–7717* ⊕ *www.dumontrestaurant.com* Ⓜ *L to Lorimer St.*

$$
ASIAN

✕ **Fatty 'Cue.** The decibel level in the series of low-lighted, low-ceilinged rooms is often as high as the enjoyment level of the people chowing down on deliciously juicy smoked fare with a Southeast Asian twist. Locally sourced meats and fish are thrown into two Ole Hickory smokers and rubbed with unique flavors, resulting in a delicious medley of snacks and more substantial dishes. Favorites include pork ribs with smoked-fish palm syrup and Indonesian long pepper, and the beef brisket with chili jam, aioli, bao (a Vietnamese steamed bun filled with meat or vegetables), pickled red onion, and bone broth. This is the original Fatty 'Cue, itself an offshoot of Fatty Crab; there are now multiple locations of each, as well as several Fatty Snack kiosks (Battery Park and World Financial Center Plaza) and a Fatty Snack pullcart in Central Park. $ *Average main: $16* ⊠ *91 S. 6th St., at Berry St., Williamsburg, Brooklyn* 🕾 *718/599–3090* ⊕ *www.fattycue.com* Ⓜ *L to Bedford Ave.*

$
BARBECUE

✕ **Fette Sau.** It might seem odd to go to a former auto-body repair shop to eat meat, but the funky building and outside courtyard seem just right for the serious 'cue served here. A huge wood-and-gas smoker delivers well-smoked brisket, sausages, ribs, and even duck, all ordered by the pound. Avoid the disappointing salads and sides, and instead choose from among the more than 40 American whiskeys and 10 micro-brews. Come early, as tables fill up quickly, and even with 700 pounds of meat a night, the good stuff sometimes runs out by 9 pm. There's limited indoor seating. $ *Average main: $11.50* ✉ *354 Metropolitan Ave., between Havemeyer and Roebling Sts., Williamsburg, Brooklyn* ☎ *718/963–3404* ⊕ *fettesaubbq.com* ⌂ *Reservations not accepted* ⊙ *No lunch weekdays* Ⓜ *L to Lorimer St.*

$ ✕ **La Superior.** Serving some of Brooklyn's best Mexican grub this side
MEXICAN   of the Red Hook ball fields, La Superior is Mexican street food with a Williamsburg ethic. The service is slapdash and the decor is unremarkable, but the food—from beef-tongue tacos to pescadillas (fish quesadillas)—really delivers. Don't be surprised if your waiter has a seat at your table while discussing the menu. $ *Average main: $10* ✉ *295 Berry St., Williamsburg, Brooklyn* ☎ *718/388–5988* ⊕ *lasuperiornyc. com* ⌂ *Reservations not accepted* ▭ *No credit cards* Ⓜ *L to Bedford Ave.; J, M, Z to Marcy Ave.*

$$ ✕ **Marlow & Sons.** It may look like a gourmet food store but it's also a
AMERICAN   restaurant with a wood-paneled dining room, started by the people behind Diner next door, and Roman's in Fort Greene. Start with oysters or a wedge of tortilla Española, or choose one of many daily specials. Don't miss the adventurous cocktails, so good they'll almost make you forget about the uncomfortable wooden seats. After dinner, you can shop for delicacies like wildflower honey and aromatic bitters. $ *Average main: $23* ✉ *81 Broadway, at Berry St., Williamsburg, Brooklyn* ☎ *718/384–1441* ⊕ *www.marlowandsons.com* ⌂ *Reservations not accepted* Ⓜ *J, M, Z to Marcy Ave.; L to Bedford Ave.*

$$$$ ✕ **Peter Luger Steak House.** Long before Brooklyn was chic, even the
STEAKHOUSE   snobbiest Manhattanites flocked to Peter Luger's. Other steak houses
Fodor'sChoice   have more elegant ambience, bigger wine lists, and less brusque ser-
★   vice, but the meat here makes the trip undeniably worth it. Three tips: bring a meat-eating buddy or several (individual steaks are available, but porterhouse is served only for two, three, or four), make a reservation (prime slots fill up more than a month in advance), and bring lots of cash—Luger's doesn't take plastic. The lunch-only burger is beloved among locals. $ *Average main: $50* ✉ *178 Broadway, at Driggs Ave., Williamsburg, Brooklyn* ☎ *718/387–7400* ⊕ *www.peterluger.com* ⌂ *Reservations essential* ▭ *No credit cards* Ⓜ *J, M, Z to Marcy Ave.*

$$ ✕ **Roberta's.** Roberta's has done something no other restaurant in Brook-
PIZZA   lyn's Bushwick can do: not only get Manhattan-dwelling food lovers
Fodor'sChoice   to get on the subway and go across the East River but to come to the
★   buddingly hip neighborhood of Bushwick, which lies just beyond Williamsburg. Rustic-looking Roberta's is worth the trek. The menu, which is something like "Brooklyn Italian" for its emphasis on using very local ingredients (there's a garden on the roof!) changes regularly but expect duck-prosciutto pizza, goat-spiked pasta, and variations on the theme of snout-to-tail dining. And, of course, a super cool soundtrack that's music to any hipster's ears. $ *Average main: $20* ✉ *261 Moore St., at*

19

Bogart St., Bushwick, Brooklyn ☎ *718/417–1118* ⊕ *www.peterluger. com* ⚷ *Reservations essential* ⊟ *No credit cards* Ⓜ *L to Morgan Ave.*

$$
AMERICAN

✕ **Rye.** Delicious bistro classics and creative American fare are on the menu at this dark, moody speakeasy-style hideaway on a little-trodden block. Enter through the unmarked door and you'll find yourself in a world of leather cushions, pressed-tin ceilings, dark wood, mosaic floors, and a 100-year-old oak bar. The signature meatloaf sandwich is daydream-worthy, served with crispy buttermilk onions and horseradish sauce. Cocktails are also excellent; try the Havemayer with overproof rye whiskey. Reservations are accepted only for parties of six or more. ⑤ *Average main: $25* ⊠ *247 S. 1st St., at Havemeyer St., Williamsburg, Brooklyn* ☎ *718/218–8047* ⊕ *www.ryerestaurant.com* ⊘ *No lunch weekdays* Ⓜ *L to Lorimer St.; J, M, Z to Marcy Ave.*

QUEENS

ASTORIA

$
EASTERN
EUROPEAN

✕ **Bohemian Hall & Beer Garden.** If your favorite outdoor activities include drinking beer and eating kielbasa, you'll love this place. The last survivor of the more than 800 beer gardens that once graced New York, this popular spot offers imported Czech beers and Central-European eats like pierogi and schnitzel. Get there early to avoid long lines. Just drinking? Bring cash, as credit cards are reserved for orders from the kitchen. Bad weather? Don't worry: indoor seating is available. ⑤ *Average main: $16* ⊠ *29–19 24th Ave., between 29th and 31st Sts., Astoria* ☎ *718/728–9278* ⊕ *www.bohemianhall.com/* Ⓜ *N to Astoria Blvd.*

$
MIDDLE EASTERN

✕ **Kabab Café.** Middle-Eastern restaurants are a dime a dozen in NYC, but Egyptian-Mediterranean spots are a rarer find, attracting foodies like celebrity chef Anthony Bourdain. This charming yet eccentric 16-seat café, which excels at interesting home-style dishes, is a true hidden treasure. The menu changes nightly, but exceedingly tender lamb stuffed with pomegranate is always great. ⑤ *Average main: $16* ⊠ *25–12 Steinway St., Astoria, Queens* ☎ *718/728–9858* ⚷ *Reservations not accepted* ⊟ *No credit cards* ⊘ *Closed Mon.* Ⓜ *N to Astoria– Ditmars Blvd.*

$
GREEK

✕ **Taverna Kyclades.** The current powerhouse of Hellenic eats in the neighborhood, Taverna Kyclades offers Greek classics at a higher level than you'd expect, given the simple decor and unassuming location. Fried calamari and grilled octopus make appearances at rock-bottom prices, despite their obvious quality, as do more out-of-the-ordinary dishes like "caviar dip" and swordfish kebabs. Be prepared to wait for a table at peak times, as they don't take reservations. ⑤ *Average main: $11.50* ⊠ *33–07 Ditmars Blvd., Astoria, Queens* ☎ *718/545–8666* ⊕ *tavernakyclades.com* ⚷ *Reservations not accepted* Ⓜ *N to Astoria– Ditmars Blvd.*

JACKSON HEIGHTS

$
INDIAN

✕ **Jackson Diner.** Neighborhood folk and Manhattanites alike flock to Jackson Diner for the spicy, authentic fare served in generous portions. Popular choices include chicken tandoori, South Indian lentil doughnuts in a tangy broth, and any of the curry dishes, as well as the many

The 7 Train: A Foodie's Favorite Subway

19

Manhattan may be known for its fine four-star restaurants, but food lovers know there's one train line to take to some of the best eats in the city. The 7 train snakes its way through the middle of Queens, and conveniently through some of the best eating neighborhoods in New York. Because the tracks are elevated, it's easy to get a handle on your surroundings—and to know where to find the train once your explorations are through.

Irish expats have long settled in the adjoining neighborhoods of Woodside and Sunnyside (near the 61st Street stop), the site of many great Gaelic bars and a few restaurants. Get a proper Irish breakfast, including black and white pudding, at the casual **Stop Inn** (✉ 6022 Roosevelt Ave., Woodside ☎ 718/779–0290). At **Donovan's Pub** (✉ 5724 Roosevelt Ave., at 58th St., Woodside ☎ 718/429–9339) ask for extra napkins and get one of the best burgers in New York City, nicely charred and served with home-cut steak fries.

But the main reason foodies flock to Woodside is for the Thai restaurant **SriPraPhai** (✉ 64–13 39th Ave., Woodside ☎ 718/899–9599), pronounced See-PRA-pie, widely considered the best Thai restaurant in New York. Don't miss the crispy watercress salad and the *larb* (ground pork with mint, lime juice, and onions). It's closed on Wednesday.

At either the 74th Street or 82nd Street stop, diverse Jackson Heights offers not only outstanding Indian restaurants but also many other Southeast Asian spots and fantastic eats from all over Latin America. Named after a town in Puebla, Mexico, **Taqueria Coatzingo** (✉ 76–05 Roosevelt Ave., Jackson Heights ☎ 718/424–1977) has deeply flavorful mole poblano, but those in the know stick to daily handwritten specials like *Pipian en Puerco Rojo*—pork cooked in red pumpkin-seed sauce. **El Chivito de Oro III** (✉ 84–02 37th Ave., Jackson Heights ☎ 718/424–0600), a Uruguayan diner, serves up parades of grilled meats called *parrilladas*—easily enough for two. Since many Uraguayans are of Italian heritage, Chivito also serves delicate pastas.

The 7 train may save the best for last: at the end of the line is Flushing, home to the second-largest Chinatown in the United States. (First is San Francisco's.) Wide streets have few tourists and many interesting stores and restaurants, making the long trip worth it. The standout is **Spicy and Tasty** (✉ 39–07 Prince St., at 39th Ave., Flushing ☎ 718/359–1601), which lives up to its name with numbing Szechuan peppercorns and slicks of red chili oil. Tea-smoked duck has crispy skin and smoky, salty meat. Eggplant with garlic sauce tastes of ginger, tomatoes, and red chilies. Cool it all down with a Tsingtao beer.

A few tips: Bring cash, because not many of these restaurants accept credit cards. Be prepared to encounter language difficulties, as English speakers are in the minority. In Manhattan, catch the 7 train at Times Square or Grand Central Terminal.

—Nina Callaway

vegetarian specialties. $ *Average main: $15* ✉ *37–47 74th St., between Roosevelt and 37th Aves., Jackson Heights* ☎ *718/672–1232* Ⓜ *7 to 74th St./Broadway.*

$ ✕ **Spicy Mina.** Since 2003, fans of Mina Azad's Bangladeshi food have
ASIAN eagerly followed her career. They mourned when her Sunnyside restaurant closed, and cheered when she briefly popped up again, cooking in Manhattan. Now they trek to the border of Jackson Heights and Woodside to wait patiently through spotty service while she prepares elaborately spiced feasts from scratch, an anomaly in a sea of steam-table buffet restaurants. It's also BYOB. $ *Average main: $15* ✉ *64–23 Broadway, Woodside* ☎ *718/205–2340* ⊕ *spicymina.shuchinta.com* Ⓜ *G, R, M to 65th St.*

THE BRONX

$$ ✕ **Antonio's Trattoria.** Antonio's bills itself as "an Italian restaurant serv-
ITALIAN ing simple food," but that's underselling it by far. Fantastic classic Italian fare is dished out here; do not miss the baked clams, the house-made ravioli, and the excellent pizzas. It's a bit off the main Arthur Avenue strip, but worth the trek. $ *Average main: $20* ✉ *2370 Belmont Ave., Belmont, Bronx* ☎ *718/733–6630* ⊕ *antoniostrattoria.com* ⊗ *Closed Mon.* Ⓜ *B, D to 182nd.*

$ ✕ **Zero Otto Nove.** Though insiders who can get a table swear by Rao's
ITALIAN on 114th in Manhattan, Zero Otto Nove chugs along as one of the best Italian restaurants north of 96th Street. The draw? Wood-oven-fired pizza, perfectly chewy and larded with buffalo mozzarella. The San Matteo, which adds broccoli rabe to the mix, is just as addictive as the plain Jane margherita. $ *Average main: $15* ✉ *2357 Arthur Ave., Belmont, Bronx* ☎ *718/220–1027* ⊕ *www.roberto089.com/* ⟋ *Reservations not accepted* ⊗ *Closed Mon.* Ⓜ *B, D to 182nd.*

New York City Dining and Lodging Atlas

KEY

□ Hotels
■ Restaurants
▣ Restaurant in Hotel

Ⓜ 1,2,3,A,B,C ← Station
NYC MTA Subway

Where to Stay

WORD OF MOUTH

"Murray Hill is on the east side, more near midtown. I'm partial to the UWS (having lived there for several years!) but I think you'll enjoy the neighborhood feel there. Plus, there's great proximity to both Central Park and Riverside Park, and Columbus Circle."

—TarheelsInNj

Updated
by Adeena
Sussman

There are more hotel rooms than ever in New York City, as exciting new properties continue to open their doors not only in Manhattan proper, but in Brooklyn and the outer boroughs as well. But does that mean that New York is cheap? Well, we wouldn't say *cheap*, but you can still find some deals, especially if you're not set on a specific property or neighborhood, and if you don't mind a few extra minutes of commuting time.

Hotels continue to slash rates based on market sensitivity—especially if you and all of those other Internet-savvy room shoppers are willing to wait until the last minute. That said, if you want to stay in a specific place and the rate seems reasonable, book it—it's just as likely to go up, especially during peak seasons (spring and fall).

And how to choose? The first thing to consider is location (check out our "Where Should I Stay?" chart). Many New York City visitors insist on staying in the hectic Midtown area—and options are improving there—but other neighborhoods are often just as convenient. Less-touristy areas, such as Gramercy, the Lower East Side, the Upper West Side—even Brooklyn—offer a far more realistic sense of New York life.

Also consider timing: the least expensive months to book rooms in the city are January and February. If you're flexible on dates, ask the reservationist if there's a cheaper time to stay during your preferred traveling month—that way you can avoid peak dates, like Fashion Week and the New York City Marathon. And be sure to ask about possible weekend packages that could include a third night free. (The Financial District in particular can be a discount gold mine on the weekend.)

Another source of bargains? Chain hotels. Many have moved into the city, offering reasonable room rates. In addition to favorites like the Sheraton, Hilton, and Hyatt brands, there are Best Westerns, Days Inns, and Comfort Inns. These rates aren't as low as you'll find outside Manhattan, but they're certainly getting closer.

WHERE SHOULD I STAY?

	Neighborhood Vibe	Pros	Cons
Brooklyn	Brooklyn has a bit of everything so it depends on where you end up. Williamsburg is all about hipsters, while downtown Brooklyn and around are quite residential.	You'll find generally smaller boutique-style hotels with personalized service and character, and rates worth traveling for. Plus, a whole new borough to explore.	If you're out late in the city and you want to get back to Brooklyn, it's either the subway or a relatively pricey taxi.
Lower Manhattan	Mostly skyscraper hotels in an area that buzzes with activity during weekday hours but can be eerily quiet at night.	Low crime area; easy subway access to uptown sights; great walking paths along the waterfront and in Battery Park.	Construction and congestion near World Trade Center site; limited choice of restaurants and shopping.
SoHo and Little Italy (with NoLIta)	Swanky, high-end hotels with hip restaurants and lounges patronized by New Yorkers and travelers alike.	Scores of upscale clothing boutiques and art galleries nearby; safe area for meandering walks; easy subway access.	Not budget-friendly; streets are crowded on weekends; few major monuments nearby.
Greenwich Village and the West Village	Hotels in this part of town are few and far between. The ones that are here are small and boutiquey.	Easy subway access to anywhere in town; great shopping, dining, and drinking venues.	Winding streets can be tough to navigate; most hotels are on the pricey side.
Chelsea (with the Meatpacking District)	More hotels are opening in one of the city's trendiest restaurant and nightlife areas.	See and be seen, and lots of great shopping.	This is a trendy and pricey neighborhood for hotels. Most hotel bars are a real scene.
Union Square, with the Flatiron District and Gramercy	A residential area where you'll get a feel for what it's really like to live in the city.	Patches of calm respite from the hustle-and-bustle of downtown and Midtown; low crime area.	Limited subway access; Gramercy may be too quiet for some.
East Village and the Lower East Side	The epicenter of edgy New York, great for travelers looking to party.	Great low-cost options for young generation. Great restaurants and independent boutiques.	One of the least subway-accessible Manhattan 'hoods; expect late-night noise.
Midtown East and West, and Murray Hill	Mostly big-name hotel chains and luxury business suites around Times Square; lots of tourists.	Near Broadway theaters; budget options are available in chain hotels and indies alike.	Streets are often packed with pedestrians; area around Port Authority can feel gritty. Murray Hill is pretty quiet.
Upper East Side	Well-heeled residential neighborhood near many museums.	Removed from Midtown hustle; near tourist attractions like Central Park.	Streets are quiet after 9 pm; few budget dining options; limited subway access (just the 6 line).
Upper West Side	Hotels in a residential neighborhood near Central Park, Lincoln Center, and some museums.	Lovely tree-lined streets; laid-back neighborhood eateries.	Weekend trains can be slow; most hotels are on the pricey side.

20

BEST BETS FOR NEW YORK CITY LODGING

Fodor's offers a selective listing of high-quality lodging in every price range, from the city's best budget motel to its most sophisticated luxury hotel. Here we've compiled our top picks by price and experience.

Fodor'sChoice★

Ace Hotel, $, p. 486
Crosby Street Hotel, $$$, p. 480
The Inn at Irving Place, $$$, p. 489
Inn on 23rd, $, p. 484
James Hotel, $$$, p. 481
Library Hotel, $$, p. 491
Mandarin Oriental, $$$$, p. 501
The Peninsula, $$$$, p. 492
The Plaza Hotel, $$$$, p. 501
Ritz-Carlton New York, Central Park, $$$$, p. 503
The St. Regis, $$$$, p. 493
The Standard, $, p. 485

Best by Price

$

Ace Hotel, p. 486
Best Western Plus President Hotel, p. 496
Carlton Arms, p. 489
The Herald Square Hotel, p. 494
Hotel Beacon, p. 509
Hotel Metro, p. 498

Inn on 23rd, p. 484
La Quinta Inn, p. 500
Pod Hotel, p. 492

$$

Casablanca Hotel, p. 497
Holiday Inn SoHo, p. 480
Library Hotel, p. 491
The Mansfield, p. 501
The Maritime Hotel, p. 485
The Michelangelo, p. 501
Room Mate Grace, p. 503
The Standard, p. 485
Thompson LES, p. 483
W Hotel New York, p. 494
Yotel, p. 506

$$$

Gramercy Park Hotel, p. 489
The Inn at Irving Place, p. 489
The James Hotel New York, p. 481
The Mercer, p. 481

$$$$

The Carlyle, p. 506
The Chatwal, p. 497

Mandarin Oriental, p. 501
The Mark, p. 507
The Peninsula, p. 492
Ritz-Carlton New York, Central Park, p. 503
The St. Regis, p. 493

Best by Experience

BEST BEDS

Four Seasons, p. 490
Ink48, p. 500
The Inn at Irving Place, p. 489
The Mansfield, p. 501
The Mark, p. 507
The Nolitan Hotel, p. 480
Ritz-Carltons, pp. 479, 503
The Setai Fifth Avenue, p. 493

BEST FOR BUSINESS

Bryant Park Hotel, p. 497
The Chatwal, p. 497
The Peninsula, p. 492
Ritz-Carlton New York, Battery Park, p. 479
The Setai Fifth Avenue, p. 493

Trump International Hotel and Towers, p. 509

BEST CELEBRITY RETREAT

Ace Hotel, p. 486
Four Seasons, p. 490
The Lowell, p. 507
Mandarin Oriental, p. 501
The Mark, p. 507
The Mercer, p. 481
The Standard, p. 485

BEST CONCIERGE

Four Seasons, p. 490
Le Parker Meridien, p. 500
The London NYC, p. 500
Mandarin Oriental, p. 501
Ritz-Carlton New York, Battery Park, p. 479

BEST GYM

The Grand Hyatt New York, p. 491
The James Hotel New York, p. 481
Le Parker Meridien, p. 500
The London NYC, p. 500
The Mark, p. 507
Trump International Hotel and Towers, p. 509

20

PLANNER

STRATEGY

Manhattan has hundreds of hotels, so making a choice may seem daunting. But fret not—our expert writers and editors have done most of the legwork. The 120-plus selections here represent the best this city has to offer—from the best budget motels to the sleekest designer boutiques. Scan "Best Bets" on the following pages for top recommendations by price and experience. Or find a review quickly in the listings—search by neighborhood, then alphabetically. Happy hunting!

NEED A RESERVATION?

Hotel reservations are an absolute necessity when planning your trip to New York—although rooms are easier to come by these days. Competition for clients also means properties must undergo frequent improvements, especially during July and August, so when booking, ask about any renovations, lest you get a room within earshot of construction. In this ever-changing city travelers can find themselves temporarily, and most inconveniently, without commonplace amenities such as room service or spa access if their hotel is upgrading.

SERVICES

Unless otherwise noted in the individual descriptions, all the hotels listed have private baths, central heating, air-conditioning, and private phones. Almost all hotels have data ports and phones with voice mail, as well as valet service. Many now have wireless Internet (Wi-Fi) available, although it's not always free. Most large hotels have video or high-speed checkout capability, and many can arrange babysitting. Pools are a rarity, but most properties have gyms or health clubs, and sometimes full-scale spas; hotels without facilities usually have arrangements for guests at nearby gyms, sometimes for a fee.

PARKING

Bringing a car to Manhattan can add significantly to your expenses. Many properties in all price ranges do have parking facilities, but they are often at independent garages that charge as much as $20 or more per day, and valet parking can cost up to $60 a day. The city's exorbitant 18.375% parking tax can turn any car you drive into the Big Apple into a lemon.

FAMILY TRAVEL

New York has gone to great lengths to attract family vacationers, and hotels have followed the family-friendly trend. Some properties provide such diversions as Web TV and in-room video games; others have suites with kitchenettes and foldout sofa beds. Most full-service Manhattan hotels provide rollaway beds, babysitting, and stroller rental, but be sure to make arrangements when booking the room, not when you arrive.

DOES SIZE MATTER?

If room size is important to you, ask the reservationist how many square feet a room has, not just if it's big. A hotel room in New York is considered quite large if it's 500 square feet. Very large rooms, such as those at the Four Seasons, are 600 square feet. To stay anywhere larger you'll have to get a multiroom suite. Small rooms are a tight 150 to 200 square feet, and sometimes even less. Very small rooms are less than 100 square feet; you'll find these at inns and lodges, and they're sold as a single for only one person. There are studio apartments in the city that are 250 square feet and include a kitchen; 1,000 square feet is considered a huge abode in this very compact and crowded urban playland.

PRICES

There's no denying that New York City hotels are expensive, but rates run the full range. For high-end hotels like the Mandarin Oriental at Central Park, prices start at $895 a night for a standard room in high season, which runs from September through December. At the low end of the spending spectrum, a bunk at the Jane starts at $99 for a single. But don't be put off by the prices printed here—many hotels slash their rates significantly for promotions and Web-only deals.

Prices in the reviews are the lowest cost of a standard double room in high season.

HOTEL REVIEWS

Listed alphabetically within neighborhoods. Please visit Fodors.com for expanded reviews.

BROOKLYN

DOWNTOWN BROOKLYN AND COBBLE HILL

$$
HOTEL
🖻
Fodor'sChoice
★

Aloft New York Brooklyn. A funky boutique in the heart of downtown Brooklyn, the Aloft is a lively yet comfortable space, with the re:mix lounge pumping world music in the lobby and relatively spacious rooms upstairs, with the quality beds the Starwood properties are known for. **Pros:** pet-, family- and kid-friendly; good subway access; fab rooftop bar; reasonable prices; guests have access to Sheraton's indoor swimming pool and room service. **Cons:** rumored construction on back side of hotel could mean noisy construction in years to come. **TripAdvisor:** "comfy and trendy," "good looks," "great staff." ⑤ *Rooms from: $319* ✉ *216 Duffield St., between Willoughby St. and Fulton Mall, Downtown Brooklyn* ☎ *718/256-3833* ⊕ *www.alofthotel.com* ⤵ *170 rooms, 6 suites* ⦿*No meals* Ⓜ *A, C, F, R to Jay St./MetroTech; 2, 3 to Hoyt St.*

$$
HOTEL

New York Marriott at the Brooklyn Bridge. You'll find, like many New Yorkers before you, that one virtue of staying in Brooklyn is all the extra space; what Manhattan hotel has room for an Olympic-length lap pool, an 1,100-car garage, and even a dedicated kosher kitchen? **Pros:** near some of New York's hipper neighborhoods; traditional-style full-service hotel, stylish rooms. **Cons:** on a busy street in downtown Brooklyn. **TripAdvisor:** "great location," "quiet stay," "outstanding views." ⑤ *Rooms from: $369* ✉ *333 Adams St., between Johnson and Willoughby Sts., Downtown Brooklyn* ☎ *718/246-7000* ⊕ *www.marriott.com/nycbk* ⤵ *668 rooms, 25 suites* Ⓜ *2, 3, 4, 5 to Borough Hall.*

$
HOTEL

Nu Hotel Brooklyn. The hip-yet-affordable Nu, on one of Brooklyn's main nightlife and shopping streets, is perfect for visitors seeking a manageable taste of outer-borough New York—and the staff is eager

20

to highlight the neighborhood's charms. **Pros:** great Brooklyn launching pad; knowledgeable staff; fitness center open 24 hours. **Cons:** it's a subway or cab ride to anything in Manhattan; bar area can be a little too quiet; limited in-room amenities. **TripAdvisor:** "very good service," "nice room," "hip hotel." ⑤ *Rooms from: $251* ⊠ *85 Smith St., Cobble Hill* ☏ *718/852–8585* ⊕ *www.nuhotelbrooklyn.com* ↩ *93 rooms* ⑩| *No meals* Ⓜ *F to Bergen St.; A, C, G to Hoyt-Schermerhorn.*

WILLIAMSBURG

$ ▦ **Hotel Le Jolie.** This no-frills favorite has excellent service and is conve-
HOTEL   nient not only to the arts, culture, and dining scenes that Williamsburg has become known for—but also to several subway lines and the Bronx-Queens Expressway, in case you want to get into the city. **Pros:** good value; free parking on a first-come, first-served basis; convenient part of Brooklyn. **Cons:** location next to highway can mean noise; can feel remote even though convenient to subways. **TripAdvisor:** "a Williamsburg Brooklyn jewel," "nice small hotel," "good service." ⑤ *Rooms from: $199* ⊠ *235 Meeker Ave., between Lorimer and Union Aves., Williamsburg* ☏ *718/625–2100* ⊕ *www.hotellejolie.com* ↩ *52 rooms, 2 suites* ⑩| *Breakfast* Ⓜ *L to Lorimer St.*

$$ ▦ **Hotel Williamsburg, New York.** With funky design details like an under-
HOTEL   foot, glass-encased river in the lobby (and a fireplace), and a plum location overlooking Brooklyn's McCarren Park—and an arrangement to rescreen the park's summer music festival at the spacious rooftop bar—the Hotel Williamsburg succeeds in scenester savvy, though it could be more user friendly. **Pros:** high hip factor; in-house restaurant/bar, complimentary coffee/tea/water on request; close to main thoroughfare Bedford Avenue. **Cons:** gym is shared with children's playroom; potential for noise from concerts in McCarren Park; some room details like electrical outlet placement are not user-friendly. **TripAdvisor:** "cozy room," "nice," "overpriced." ⑤ *Rooms from: $299* ⊠ *160 N. 12th St., between Bedford St. and Bary St., Williamsburg* ☏ *718/218–7500* ⊕ *www.hwbrooklyn.com* ↩ *64 rooms* ⑩| *No meals* Ⓜ *L to Bedford Ave.*

LOWER MANHATTAN

FINANCIAL DISTRICT

$ ▦ **Gild Hall.** Captains of Industry, here's a boutique hotel for you: oper-
HOTEL   ated by the owners of the several Thompson hotels around the United States and elsewhere, Gild Hall aggressively courts those clientele with a Y chromosome: beds have padded leather headboards and tartan throw blankets. **Pros:** central Financial District location; eye-popping lobby; stylish room design. **Cons:** small rooms for the price; untraditional location. **TripAdvisor:** "Wall Street wonder," "quiet," "British prep school with Hollywood style." ⑤ *Rooms from: $275* ⊠ *15 Gold St., at Platt St., Financial District* ☏ *212/232–7700, 800/268–0700* ⊕ *www. thompsonhotels.com* ↩ *126 rooms* ⑩| *Breakfast* Ⓜ *2, 3, 4, 5, 6, A, C to Fulton St./Broadway-Nassau* ✛ *1:E3.*

$$ ▦ **The W New York Downtown.** In the heart of the Financial District, this
HOTEL   W outpost juxtaposes the gritty feel of the Financial District with sleek

surfaces. **Pros:** near popular tourist attractions; restaurant offers some surprisingly affordable fare; modern workout room. **Cons:** scaffolding-dense neighborhood; construction of World Trade Center nearby; partially obstructed views; not family-friendly. **TripAdvisor:** "great service and great beds," "trendy rooms," "painfully hip." ⑤ *Rooms from: $409* ✉ *123 Washington St., at Albany St., Financial District* ☎ *646/826–8600* ⊕ *www.starwoodhotels.com* ⤴ *85 rooms* ⦿ *No meals* Ⓜ *1, N, R to Rector St.* ✛ *1:C4.*

TRIBECA

$ ⬚ **The Cosmopolitan Hotel.** For a bargain room in a great downtown
HOTEL   neighborhood, it's hard to beat this cost-conscious favorite. **Pros:** friendly staff; great location for power shoppers. **Cons:** noisy location; spartan rooms; slow elevators; no gym. **TripAdvisor:** "very good service," "very well-priced hotel for the basics," "great location." ⑤ *Rooms from: $255* ✉ *95 West Broadway, at Chambers St., TriBeCa* ☎ *212/566–1900* ⊕ *www.cosmohotel.com* ⤴ *125 rooms* ⦿ *No meals* Ⓜ *1, 2, 3, A, C to Chambers St.* ✛ *1:C2.*

$$$ ⬚ **Duane Street Hotel.** Amid TriBeCa's historic warehouses and trendy
HOTEL   art galleries sits the Duane Street Hotel, a fashionable addition to the neighborhood. **Pros:** great location; in-room spa treatments available through Euphoria Spa TriBeCa. **Cons:** noisy; off-site gym. **TripAdvisor:** "great décor and service," "Tribecatastic," "staff was top notch." ⑤ *Rooms from: $430* ✉ *130 Duane St., TriBeCa* ☎ *212/964–4600* ⊕ *www.duanestreethotel.com* ⤴ *45 rooms* ⦿ *No meals* Ⓜ *1, 2, 3 to Chambers St.; A, C to Chambers St.* ✛ *2:D6.*

$$$ ⬚ **The Greenwich Hotel.** You talkin' to me? Yes, Robert De Niro is an
HOTEL   owner of the Greenwich Hotel in TriBeCa, De Niro's backyard and a neighborhood he's helped put on the map as a culinary and cultural benchmark. **Pros:** varied yet clever room decoration; great restaurant. **Cons:** odd lobby; price is high for what you get. **TripAdvisor:** "quiet," "romantic," "consistently beautiful and comfortable." ⑤ *Rooms from: $525* ✉ *377 Greenwich St., TriBeCa* ☎ *212/941–8900* ⊕ *www. thegreenwichhotel.com* ⤴ *88 rooms, 13 suites* ⦿ *No meals* Ⓜ *1 to Franklin St.* ✛ *2:C6.*

$$$ ⬚ **The Ritz-Carlton New York, Battery Park.** If you're staying this far down-
HOTEL   town, the Ritz is your top choice. **Pros:** excellent service; best base for downtown exploring; pet- and kid-friendly; Liberty views. **Cons:** removed from Midtown tourist sights; limited nighttime activities; few neighborhood options for dining and entertainment. **TripAdvisor:** "right priced luxury," "great service," "quiet." ⑤ *Rooms from: $545* ✉ *2 West St., at Battery Park, Battery Park* ☎ *212/344–0800, 800/241–3333* ⊕ *www.ritzcarlton.com/batterypark* ⤴ *298 rooms, 39 suites* ⦿ *No meals* Ⓜ *1, R, J to Rector St.* ✛ *1:C5.*

$$ ⬚ **Smyth Tribeca.** Resting almost on top of a convenient subway stop,
HOTEL   this thoroughly modern hotel makes TriBeCa a welcoming landing spot for visitors. **Pros:** great service; good restaurant; excellent subway access. **Cons:** Wi-Fi not free; only a frosted glass partition divides bathroom from sleeping area, limiting privacy; bathrooms could have better lighting. **TripAdvisor:** "above and beyond expectations," "nice room," "beautiful hotel." ⑤ *Rooms from: $299* ✉ *85 W. Broadway,*

20

between Chambers and Warren Sts., TriBeCa ☎ 212/587–7000 ⊕ www.thompsonhotels.com ➷ 84 rooms, 16 suites �‖ No meals Ⓜ 1, 2, 3 to Chambers St. ✛ 1:C2.

WORD OF MOUTH

"[The SoHo Grand] is definitely funky, yet nice. The bar is always packed but a good place to people watch. I have found the rooms small but comfortable and the staff helpful. I find it less pretentious that some 'W' hotels at which I have stayed." —A2

$$$ 🚇 **Tribeca Grand.** Still popular
HOTEL with the glitterati, the scene at the Tribeca Grand centers on the eight-story atrium's Church Lounge bar and café. **Pros:** great dining and bar scene; central downtown location; fun social atrium; pet-friendly.
Cons: rooms get noise from restaurant below; bathroom has slightly cold design. **TripAdvisor:** "flawless service," "hip and happening," "terrific location." Ⓢ Rooms from: $499 ✉ 2 Ave. of the Americas (6th Ave.), between Walker and White Sts., TriBeCa ☎ 212/519–6600, 800/965–3000 🖷 212/519-6700 ⊕ www.tribecagrand.com ➷ 197 rooms, 6 suites �‖ No meals Ⓜ A, C, E to Canal St. ✛ 2:D5.

SOHO AND NOLITA

NOLITA

$$ 🚇 **The Nolitan Hotel.** A welcome addition to an underserved neighbor-
HOTEL hood, the Nolitan combines a hip, slightly gritty, city feel with some luxe touches, but rooms are as small as you'd find downtown in NoLIta. **Pros:** cool vibe; fun location convenient to lower Manhattan and Brooklyn. **Cons:** blasé concierge; gym access five-minute walk away; street noise from other balconies can be aggressive. **TripAdvisor:** "chic done well," "helpful staff," "neighborhood gem." Ⓢ Rooms from: $409 ✉ 30 Kenmare St., NoLIta ☎ 212/925–2555 ➷ 55 rooms �‖ No meals Ⓜ 6 to Spring St. ✛ 2:F4.

SOHO

$$ 🚇 **60 Thompson.** It may no longer be the center of the universe, scene-
HOTEL wise, but that's been a blessing for guests at 60 Thompson, improving the service and toning down the attitude of hotel staffers. **Pros:** supercentral for SoHo nightlife; good gym; some rooms have balconies. **Cons:** not family-oriented; no pets allowed. **TripAdvisor:** "comfortable," "very helpful staff," "glamorous." Ⓢ Rooms from: $425 ✉ 60 Thompson St., between Broome and Spring Sts., SoHo ☎ 212/431–0400, 877/431–0400 ⊕ www.thompsonhotels.com ➷ 92 rooms, 8 suites �‖ No meals Ⓜ C, E to Spring St. ✛ 2:D4.

$$$ 🚇 **Crosby Street Hotel.** The first branch of the U.K.'s Firmdale Hotels to
HOTEL open in the United States, 60 Crosby is in a class of its own. **Pros:** unique
Fodor's Choice design; big, bright rooms; great bar. **Cons:** breakfast not included; small
★ gym. **TripAdvisor:** "the best showers ever," "stunning style," "classy."
Ⓢ Rooms from: $495 ✉ 79 Crosby St., between Prince and Spring Sts., SoHo ☎ 212/226–6400 ⊕ www.firmdale.com ➷ 86 rooms �‖ No meals Ⓜ 6 to Spring St., R to Prince St. ✛ 2:E3.

$$ 🚇 **Holiday Inn SoHo.** "SoHo" and "Holiday Inn" may not sound right
HOTEL together, but here they are. **Pros:** well-priced SoHo solution; well-trained

staff. **Cons:** nothing stylish; closer to Chinatown than to SoHo. **TripAdvisor:** "great first-time NYC experience," "conveniently located," "very welcoming." $ *Rooms from: $270* ⊠ *138 Lafayette St., near Canal St., SoHo* ☎ *212/966–8898, 800/465–4329* ⊕ *www.hidowntown-nyc. com* ⤴ *215 rooms, 12 suites* ⦶ *No meals* Ⓜ *6, M, N, Q, R to Canal St.* ✛ *2:E5.*

$$$
HOTEL
☪
Fodor's Choice
★

The James Hotel New York. A favorite of creative-types, businesspeople, fashionistas, and deep-pocketed regular Joes, the James, right on the edge of SoHo, never sacrifices comfort for style, so it's no wonder there's a high percentage of return customers. **Pros:** stellar service; fabulous views. **Cons:** the upstairs Jimmy bar is expensive and sometimes too-cool-for-school. **TripAdvisor:** "amazing staff," "an apartment in the city," "warm and intimate." $ *Rooms from: $539* ⊠ *27 Grand St., between Thompson and 6th Ave., SoHo* ☎ *212/465–2000* ⊕ *www. jameshotel.com* ⤴ *114 rooms* ⦶ *No meals* Ⓜ *1 to Canal St.* ✛ *2:D4.*

$$$
HOTEL

The Mercer. Owner André Balazs has a knack for dating Hollywood starlets and channeling a neighborhood sensibility, and here it's SoHo loft all the way. **Pros:** great location; sophisticated design touches; celebrity sightings in lobby. **Cons:** service inconsistent; some tiny rooms. **TripAdvisor:** "very stylish property with good service," "great Village location," "classically cool." $ *Rooms from: $595* ⊠ *147 Mercer St., at Prince St., SoHo* ☎ *212/966–6060, 888/918–6060* ⊕ *www.mercerhotel. com* ⤴ *67 rooms, 8 suites* ⦶ *No meals* Ⓜ *R to Prince St.* ✛ *2:E3.*

$$$
HOTEL
Fodor's Choice
★

Mondrian Soho. Snazzy style and a chic SoHo vibe make the Mondrian a winner for anyone looking for a real downtown–New York experience. **Pros:** great design; friendly to electronics addicts. **Cons:** dark elevators; standard rooms are small; restaurant in flux; charge for Internet. **TripAdvisor:** "good staff," "a Soho oasis," "hip décor and crowd." $ *Rooms from: $455* ⊠ *9 Crosby St., SoHo* ☎ *212/389–1000* 🖶 *212/389–1001* ⊕ *www.mondriansoho.com* ⤴ *270 rooms* ⦶ *No meals* Ⓜ *N, Q, R, 6 to Canal St.* ✛ *2:E4.*

$$
HOTEL

SoHo Grand. The SoHo Grand defines what SoHo is today—once pioneering, now expensive, and with a vaguely creative vibe. **Pros:** fashionable, laid-back sophistication; great service; surprisingly discreet setting; diverse eating and drinking options. **Cons:** closer to Canal Street than prime SoHo; rooms on small side. **TripAdvisor:** "downtown chic," "outstanding service," "great atmosphere." $ *Rooms from: $329* ⊠ *310 West Broadway, at Grand St., SoHo* ☎ *212/965–3000, 800/965–3000* ⊕ *www.sohogrand.com* ⤴ *341 rooms, 12 suites* ⦶ *No meals* Ⓜ *6, J, M, N, Q, R to Canal St.* ✛ *2:D4.*

20

EAST VILLAGE AND THE LOWER EAST SIDE

EAST VILLAGE

$$
HOTEL
Fodor's Choice
★

The Bowery Hotel. The Bowery Hotel is like an English hunting lodge in Manhattan, warmed by rich floor-to-ceiling tapestries, fireplaces, and chandeliers—and there's no shortage of British, who flock to the property; the only thing missing is a trusty hound. **Pros:** quirky, fun location; happening bar and lobby-lounge area; celebrity sightings; interesting views. **Cons:** gritty neighbors; rooms aren't luxurious. **TripAdvisor:**

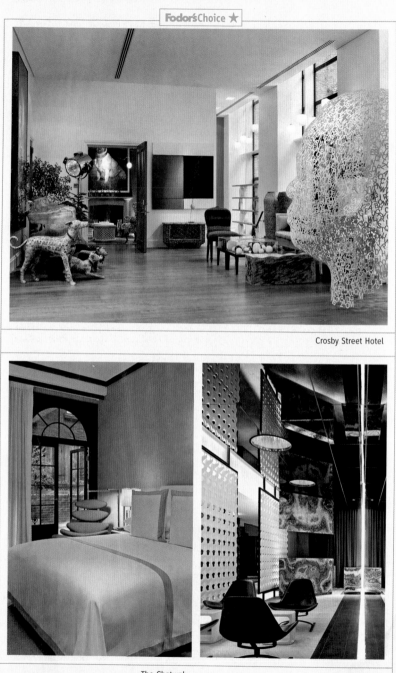

Crosby Street Hotel

The Chatwal

The Standard

"fun," "absolutely boutique," "lovely late 1800s charm." ⑤ *Rooms from: $425* ✉ *335 Bowery, at 3rd St., East Village* ☎ *212/505–9100* ⊕ *www.theboweryhotel.com* ↘ *135 rooms, 25 suites* �‖ *Breakfast* Ⓜ *6 to Bleecker; B, D, F, M to Broadway/Lafayette* ✛ *2:F2.*

$$$ ⛢ **Standard East Village.** A jarring, 21-story glass-and-steel finger rising
HOTEL up in the low-rise East Village, this hotel was never going to pass under the radar—and that's guaranteed now that Andre Balasz and company have taken over. **Pros:** stylish rooms; central location. **Cons:** out of character with the area; restaurant seems constantly in flux. **TripAdvisor:** "great vibe," "trendy," "an East Village experience." ⑤ *Rooms from: $525* ✉ *25 Cooper Sq., between E. 5th and E. 6th Sts., East Village* ☎ *212/475–5700* ⊕ *eastvillage.standardhotels.com/* ↘ *145 rooms* �‖ *No meals* Ⓜ *6 to Astor Pl.; R to 8th. St./NYU* ✛ *2:F2.*

LOWER EAST SIDE

$$ ⛢ **Hotel on Rivington.** A pioneer when it opened back in 2004, this glass-
HOTEL walled hotel on the Lower East Side is still a go-to choice, especially if being in the thick of the neighborhood's nightlife and dining action is a priority. **Pros:** cool location and vibe; huge windows with wonderful New York views; many rooms have balconies. **Cons:** feels like a club on weekends; spotty service; small rooms and suites. **TripAdvisor:** "great hotel in trendy neighborhood," "unique," "wonderful staff." ⑤ *Rooms from: $400* ✉ *107 Rivington St., between Ludlow and Essex Sts., Lower East Side* ☎ *212/475–2600, 800/915–1537* ⊕ *www.hotelonrivington.com* ↘ *96 rooms, 14 suites* �‖ *No meals* Ⓜ *F, J, M, Z to Delancey/Essex Sts.* ✛ *2:G3.*

$$ ⛢ **Thompson LES.** With its smoked glass tower and central location, the
HOTEL Thompson LES is a great embodiment of the neighborhood inhabits: hip, but friendly when you get to know it. **Pros:** in the heart of downtown; great views from suites. **Cons:** occasionally snobby staff; rooms stylish but dark. **TripAdvisor:** "modern," "highly recommend," "right location, great service." ⑤ *Rooms from: $299* ✉ *190 Allen St., between Houston and Stanton Sts., Lower East Side* ☎ *212/460–5300* ⊕ *www.thompsonhotels.com* ↘ *141 rooms* �‖ *No meals* Ⓜ *F, J, M, Z to Delancey/Essex Sts.* ✛ *2:G3.*

GREENWICH VILLAGE AND THE WEST VILLAGE

GREENWICH VILLAGE

$ ⛢ **Washington Square Hotel.** This low-key hotel in Greenwich Village is
HOTEL popular with visiting New York University parents—the location near Washington Square Park and its magnificent arch (and just down the street from Mario Batali's Babbo restaurant) is just a bonus. **Pros:** park-front location; deluxe rooms are charming; great hotel bar. **Cons:** NYU students everywhere in the neighborhood; rooms are small. **TripAdvisor:** "old world charm," "almost perfect," "clean and comfortable." ⑤ *Rooms from: $225* ✉ *103 Waverly Pl., at MacDougal St., Greenwich Village* ☎ *212/777–9515, 800/222–0418* ⊕ *www.wshotel.com* ↘ *160 rooms* �‖ *Breakfast* Ⓜ *A, B, C, D, E, F, M to W. 4th St./Washington Sq.* ✛ *2:D1.*

20

WEST VILLAGE

$ **The Jane.** To some, it's impossibly chic; to others, the rooms are remi-
HOTEL   niscent of Sing Sing—welcome to the Jane hotel, a sister property to
the hip Bowery Hotel on the Lower East Side. **Pros:** cheap; hot bar
scene; amazing decor in lounge; great branch of weekend brunch favorite Café Gitane; convenient neighborhood for downtown sightseeing.
Cons: impossibly tiny standard rooms; shared bathrooms; noise from
the bar. **TripAdvisor:** "great character," "cool eccentric," "good things
in small packages." ⑤ *Rooms from: $125* ✉ *113 Jane St., at West St.,
West Village* ☎ *212/924–6700* ⊕ *www.thejanenyc.com* ⇨ *150 rooms,
40 suites* ⦿*No meals* Ⓜ *A, C, E, L to 14th St. and 8th Ave.* ✦ *3:B5.*

CHELSEA AND THE MEATPACKING DISTRICT

CHELSEA

$ **Chelsea Lodge.** Popular with Europeans and budget-conscious visitors,
HOTEL   the Chelsea Lodge is a great location for guests who don't insist on a lot
of amenities. **Pros:** on a gorgeous Chelsea block; residential feel; great
bang for the buck. **Cons:** not romantic; shared bathrooms not right
for everyone. **TripAdvisor:** "quaint little hotel," "comfy and cozy,"
"great base for exploring Manhattan." ⑤ *Rooms from: $134* ✉ *318 W.
20th St., between 8th and 9th Aves., Chelsea* ☎ *212/243–4499* ⊕ *www.
chelsealodge.com* ⇨ *22 rooms, 2 with bath; 4 suites* ⦿*No meals* Ⓜ *C,
E to 23rd St.; 1 to 18th St.* ✦ *3:C3.*

$$ **The GEM Hotel Chelsea.** At this stylish, well-priced boutique hotel the
HOTEL   modern rooms are small but designed to make the most of limited space.
Pros: great Chelsea location; close to several subway lines. **Cons:** gym
and business center, both on the lower level, feel like a work in progress;
rooms may be too small for some. **TripAdvisor:** "nice adult hotel," "a
small gem," "great value in NYC." ⑤ *Rooms from: $329* ✉ *300 W.
22nd St., between 8th and 9th Aves., Chelsea* ☎ *212/675–1911* ⊕ *www.
thegemhotel.com* ⇨ *81 rooms* ⦿*No meals* Ⓜ *C, E to 23rd St.; 1 to
23rd St.* ✦ *3:C3.*

$ **Hilton New York Fashion District.** This addition to the Hilton chain is
HOTEL   part of the emerging Fashion District neighborhood, previously known
as the garment district, on the upper edge of Chelsea, and fashion is the
theme here—the lobby is done in rich textiles with multicolor spools
mounted on a white board behind the front desk. **Pros:** reasonable
prices for a great location. **Cons:** small closets; trying to be trendier
than it is. **TripAdvisor:** "nice but small room," "great staff," "excellent
service." ⑤ *Rooms from: $249* ✉ *152 W. 26th St., between 6th and 7th
Aves., Chelsea* ☎ *212/858–5888* ▤ *212/858–5889* ⊕ *www1.hilton.com*
⇨ *280 rooms* ⦿*No meals* Ⓜ *1, 2, 3, A, C, E, B, D, F V, N, Q, R, W
to 34th St./Penn Station* ✦ *3:D2.*

$ **The Inn on 23rd.** Friendly innkeepers Annette and Barry Fisherman
B&B/INN   welcome guests to this five-floor, 19th-century building, which also comes
☺   with its own cat/mascot. **Pros:** charming innkeepers; comfy and relaxed
Fodor'sChoice   library; affordable, given location. **Cons:** few business services; some
★   older amenities; beware if you have cat allergies. **TripAdvisor:** "more

bed than breakfast," "perfect property," "excellent accommodation." ⑤ *Rooms from: $279* ✉ *131 W. 23rd St., between 6th and 7th Aves., Chelsea* ☎ *212/463–0330* ⊕ *www. innon23rd.com* ⤴ *13 rooms, 1 suite* ⦿| *Breakfast* Ⓜ *F, M to 23rd St.* ⊕ *3:D2.*

$$ 🏨 **The Maritime Hotel.** The Maritime's white-ceramic tower, the former HQ for the National Maritime Union, was the first luxury hotel to be built in the Chelsea gallery district and the property still feels a bit nautical: the small rooms resemble modern ship's cabins, with burnished teak paneling, sea-blue drapes and bed accents, and 5-foot "portholes" that face the Hudson

HOTEL

WORD OF MOUTH

"The Gansevoort (and its location) is young, hip, and fun but can also be loud. The rooftop bar is extremely popular; there are often lines outside the hotel to get into the bar at night. The rooms are nice, albeit not large. I live in Manhattan but have still stayed there on a couple of occasions for bachelor parties of friends. The few times I've hung out by the pool, we met several other Manhattanites who were staying there as a one- or two-day getaway from their apartment. —JarredK

River skyline. **Pros:** fun rooms with big porthole windows; great location near Chelsea Market and the Chelsea galleries. **Cons:** Street noise; small rooms. **TripAdvisor:** "quirky and elegant," "very pleasant," "peace and quiet in the city." ⑤ *Rooms from: $425* ✉ *363 W. 16th St., at 9th Ave., Chelsea* ☎ *212/242–4300* ⊕ *www.themaritimehotel.com* ⤴ *121 rooms, 5 suites* Ⓜ *A, C, E to 14th St.* ⊕ *3:B3.*

MEATPACKING DISTRICT

$$ 🏨 **Hotel Gansevoort.** Though the nearby Standard New York has stolen some of its thunder, there's plenty to draw guests to this chic Meatpacking District pioneer, starting with the sleek rooms that overlook the city or the Hudson River and the rooftop deck with a 45-foot heated pool that remains a draw for locals and tourists alike. **Pros:** rooftop pool; wonderful art collection; great location for restaurants and shopping. **Cons:** location can seem too trendy, especially at night; service can be slipshod. **TripAdvisor:** "best experience I ever had," "amazing customer service," "excellent location." ⑤ *Rooms from: $425* ✉ *18 9th Ave., at 13th St., Meatpacking District* ⊕ *www.hotelgansevoort. com* ⤴ *166 rooms, 21 suites* ⦿| *Breakfast* Ⓜ *A, C, E, L to 14th St. and 8th Ave.* ⊕ *3:B4.*

HOTEL

20

$$ 🏨 **The Standard.** André Balazs's architectural statement on the West Side is still one of New York's hottest hotels. **Pros:** beautiful building; beautiful people; impressive restaurant space. **Cons:** noisy at night; tight rooms; can be too sceney. **TripAdvisor:** "no other hotel like it," "very cool," "a lot of silly fun." ⑤ *Rooms from: $395* ✉ *848 Washington St., between W. 13th and Little W. 12th Sts., Meatpacking District* ☎ *212/645–4646* ⊕ *www.standardhotels.com* ⤴ *338 rooms and studios* ⦿| *No meals* Ⓜ *A, C, E, L to 14th St. and 8th Ave.* ⊕ *3:B4.*

HOTEL

Fodor's Choice

★

UNION SQUARE, FLATIRON DISTRICT, AND GRAMERCY

FLATIRON DISTRICT

$ **Ace Hotel.** Stepping into Ace Hotel is something of a revelation:
HOTEL you'll immediately be hit with the thought that is not an ordinary bou-
Fodor'sChoice tique hotel. **Pros:** in-house restaurants are destination worthy in their
★ own right; supercool but friendly vibe. **Cons:** dark lobby; caters to a
young crowd; may be too sceney for some; neighborhood itself isn't the
most exciting. **TripAdvisor:** "beautiful hotel," "trendy," "hip joint."
⑤ *Rooms from: $259* ✉ *20 W. 29th St., at Broadway, Flatiron District*
☎ *212/679–2222* ⊕ *www.acehotel.com* ⤳ *251 rooms, 11 suites* ⋔⃞*No
meals* Ⓜ *N, R to 28th St.; 1 to 28th St.* ✛ *3:E1.*

$$ **The Eventi.** The newest Kimpton property to grace New York City,
HOTEL the Eventi adds a touch of hotel style just below Penn Station in an
☾ area desperately in need of new hotel options. **Pros:** great location;
fun dining options; nice gym. **Cons:** crowded lobby; dark rooms. **Trip-
Advisor:** "clean and modern," "good staff," "nice rooms." ⑤ *Rooms
from: $350* ✉ *851 Avenue of the Americas, at 30th St., Flatiron Dis-
trict* ☎ *866/996–8396* ⊕ *www.eventihotel.com* ⤳ *236 rooms, 56 suites*
⋔⃞*No meals* Ⓜ *N, R to 28th St.* ✛ *3:D1*

$$$ **Gansevoort Park.** A downtown-hip hotel on the edge of lower Mid-
HOTEL town, the Gansevoort Park improves upon its hard-living Meatpack-
ing District sibling by several degrees. **Pros:** happening bar; location
convenient to Union Square; friendly staff. **Cons:** if you want peace
and quiet this hotel is not for you. **TripAdvisor:** "stylish yet luxurious," "almost perfect," "friendly staff." ⑤ *Rooms from: $475* ✉ *420
Park Avenue South, at 29th Street, Flatiron District* ☎ *212/317-2900*
⊕ *www.gansevoortpark.com* ⤳ *212 rooms, 37 suites* ⋔⃞*No meals* Ⓜ *6
to 28th St.* ✛ *3:F1.*

$$$ **Hotel Giraffe.** The decade-old Giraffe remains a consistent property
HOTEL with friendly service, large rooms, and lots of repeat customers, particu-
larly business travelers. **Pros:** rooftop terrace for guests; quiet hotel. **Cons:**
street noise near lower levels; pricey for the quality you get. **TripAdvisor:**
"a really lovely hotel," "great location," "wouldn't change a thing."
⑤ *Rooms from: $449* ✉ *365 Park Ave. S, at E. 26th St., Flatiron District*
☎ *212/685–7700, 877/296–0009* ⊕ *www.hotelgiraffe.com* ⤳ *52 rooms,
21 suites* ⋔⃞*Breakfast* Ⓜ *6 to 28th St.* ✛ *3:F2.*

$$$$ **Hotel Lola.** Opened in late 2011, the Lola is the laid-back new girl
HOTEL in town, just around the corner from the latest Gansevoort hotel and
convenient to the action without being smack in the middle of it. **Pros:**
up and coming neighborhood; trendy but not over the top; cozy single
rooms are a great option if you're traveling alone. **Cons:** dark entry-
way; lower floors lack views and can feel a bit basement-y. **TripAdvisor:**
"quiet rooms," "nice facility," "hip Midtown digs." ⑤ *Rooms from:
$475* ✉ *29 E. 29th St., between Park and Madison Aves., Flatiron
District* ☎ *212/689–1900* ⤳ *276 rooms* ⋔⃞*No meals* Ⓜ *6 to 28th St.*
✛ *3:F1*

$ **Park South Hotel.** In this beautifully transformed 1906 office building,
HOTEL rooms feel smartly contemporary, though they've retained some period
details, but request one that doesn't overlook noisy 27th Street or is
too close to the bar on the ground floor—ask instead for a view of the

Hotel Hot Spots

Some of the city's most stylish bars and lounges are in hotels. These boîtes occasionally require crossing a velvet-roped entrance, but most extend automatic entry to hotel guests.

Downtown, the swank bar at the **Mondrian** (⇨ SoHo) is a treat, and the Jimmy bar at the **James Hotel** (⇨ SoHo) hotel has some of the best views in town. On the Lower East Side, the Lobby Bar in the **Bowery Hotel** (⇨ Lower East Side) is a Wes Anderson movie come to life, with worn velvet furniture, Persian rugs, an assortment of taxidermy, and a back patio that harbors some of the most coveted summertime tables in the neighborhood.

Mega-hotelier Ian Schrager's properties are design temples, with chic lounges favored by jet-setters and locals alike. The new "haute Bohemian" **Gramercy Park Hotel** (⇨ Gramercy) is Schrager's latest offering, with its popular—and pricey—Rose Bar and Jade Bar. The hotel also has a private members- and guests-only Roof Club. The **Ace Hotel** (⇨ Flatiron) is the sweet spot du jour, with one bar in the eclectic lobby and another at the trendy Breslin restaurant. The **Standard** (⇨ Meatpacking District) has a happening bar scene at the Standard Grill. The 18th-floor lounge is a tough row to hoe unless

you're a friend of the owner, but downstairs you can also sip suds in the outdoor beer garden, which is more egalitarian, and frankly, more fun—they even have Ping-Pong. It's also open year-round now.

In Midtown, the art deco–designed **Chatwal** (⇨ Midtown West) has a hopping lobby scene with drinks by cocktail guru Sasha Petraske and an elegant second-floor bar decorated with whimsical touches that are a paean to classic New York (look for the shimmering light fixtures shaped like the Chrysler Building).

Print at the Ink48 (⇨ Midtown West) is an elegant place to catch an early bite and a drink—later you can dance to views of both the Hudson to the west and the glittering city on the other side. The **Room Mate Grace** (⇨ Midtown West) in Times Square has a bar that's adjacent to its lobby-level pool; you can see all the underwater action through voyeur windows above the bar. Just make sure to pay attention at the end of the evening, or you might be the hotel's next swimming sensation. At the **Mandarin Oriental** on Columbus Circle (⇨ Midtown West), the 35th-floor lounge is the place to soak in views of Central Park. Come summertime, **Yotel** (⇨ Midtown West) offers one of the city's most expansive outdoor patios, with happening DJs and Latin-inspired cocktails.

20

Chrysler Building. **Pros:** free breakfast and Internet; turndown service; good value. **Cons:** rooms can feel a bit worn; small bathrooms and small rooms. **TripAdvisor:** "great bar," "best stay in NYC," "polite." ⑤ *Rooms from: $269* ✉ *124 E. 28th St., between Lexington and Park Aves., Flatiron District* ☏ *212/448–0888, 800/315–4642* ⊕ *www.parksouthhotel.com* ⤵ *139 rooms, 2 suites* ⏁ *Breakfast* Ⓜ *6 to 28th St.* ✛ *3:F2.*

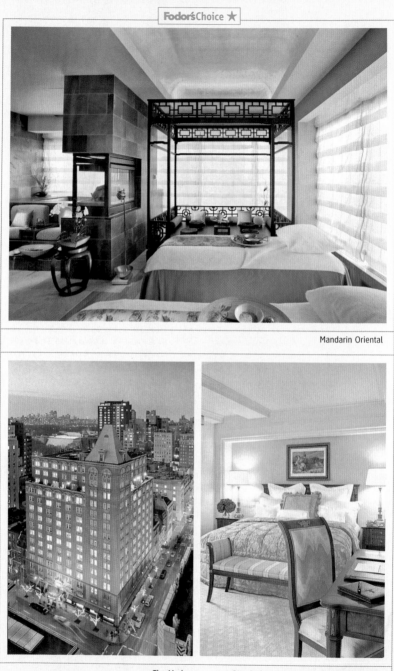

Mandarin Oriental

The Mark   Ritz-Carlton New York, Central Park South

GRAMERCY PARK

$ | **Carlton Arms.** Europeans and students know about the chipper, winning attitude of this friendly, no-frills hotel, where the rooms are painted by artists on a rotating basis. **Pros:** rock-bottom prices; friendly attitude; quieter residential Murray Hill location. **Cons:** no elevator; many rooms have shared baths. **TripAdvisor:** "excellent location," "very quirky and fantastic," "good choice for arty budget travelers." $ *Rooms from: $130 ⊠ 160 E. 25th St., at 3rd Ave., Gramercy ☎ 212/684–8337, 212/679–0680 for reservations ⊕ www.carltonarms.com ↴ 54 rooms, 20 with bath Ⓜ R to 28th St. ✛ 3:G2.*

HOTEL

$$$ | **Gramercy Park Hotel.** Ian Schrager, boutique hotelier extraordinaire, designed this property with the fruits of his hard-won wisdom: the contemporary art that's scattered throughout includes works by Andy Warhol, and there's Basquiat in the lobby, which has a chic, hushed quality; upstairs, the rooms go for fabulousness over comfort, with draped velvet, studded leather, and very red drapes. **Pros:** trendy bar scene; opulent rooms; great restaurant; park-side location. **Cons:** inconsistent service; form-over-function rooms; expensive bar. **TripAdvisor:** "great neighborhood feel," "a NYC gem," "excellent service." $ *Rooms from: $595 ⊠ 2 Lexington Ave., at Gramercy Park, Gramercy Park ☎ 212/920–3300 ⊕ www.gramercyparkhotel.com ↴ 139 rooms, 46 suites Ⓜ 6 to 23rd St. ✛ 3:G3.*

HOTEL

$$$ | **The Inn at Irving Place.** Fantasies of Old New York—Manhattan straight from the pages of Edith Wharton and Henry James, an era of genteel brick town houses and Tiffany lamps—spring to life at this discreet, romantic 20-room inn. **Pros:** romantic; charming property; big rooms; excellent breakfast and tea service; Mario Batali's Casa Mono is downstairs. **Cons:** rooms aren't flawless, with imperfections like older grouting; street noise. **TripAdvisor:** "quiet and serene," "genuine delight," "quirky hotel in a great neighborhood." $ *Rooms from: $449 ⊠ 56 Irving Pl., between E. 17th and E. 18th Sts., Gramercy Park ☎ 212/533–4600, 800/685–1447 ⊕ www.innatirving.com ↴ 5 rooms, 6 suites ⦿ Multiple meal plans Ⓜ 4, 5, 6, L, N, Q, R to 14th St./Union Sq. ✛ 3:G3.*

HOTEL
Fodor'sChoice
★

$$ | **Marcel at Gramercy.** The chic, affordable Marcel gives guests both style and substance in a prime location. **Pros:** outdoor patio has spectacular views of the city; good value. **Cons:** elevators are slow. **TripAdvisor:** "a NY treasure," "very enjoyable," "top hotel with top staff." $ *Rooms from: $299 ⊠ 201 E. 24th St., Gramercy Park ☎ 212/696–3800 ⊕ www.themarcelatgramercy.com ↴ 133 rooms, 2 suites ⦿ No meals Ⓜ 6 to 23rd St. ✛ 3:G2.*

HOTEL

UNION SQUARE

$$$$ | **W New York Union Square.** The W chain's iconic New York City property continues to attract a mix of trendsetters and tourists, thanks to the downtown location and its funky style. **Pros:** fashionable location; great restaurant. **Cons:** noisy lobby; expensive Wi-Fi. **TripAdvisor:** "wonderful hotel," "great staff," "quiet." $ *Rooms from: $650 ⊠ 201 Park Ave. S, at E. 17th St., Union Square ☎ 212/253–9119, 877/946–8357 ⊕ www.whotels.com ↴ 254 rooms, 16 suites ⦿ No meals Ⓜ 4, 5, 6, L, N, Q, R to 14th St./Union Sq. ✛ 3:F3.*

HOTEL

20

MIDTOWN EAST AND MURRAY HILL

MIDTOWN EAST

$$ **70 Park Avenue.** A recent multimillion-dollar refresh has brought new
HOTEL   life to this Midtown business-traveler favorite, infusing the lobby and
rooms with a bright color palette and modern furniture. **Pros:** weekday
wine reception; polite service; simple, not overdesigned rooms and hotel
layout. **Cons:** small rooms; small fitness center. **TripAdvisor:** "always a
pleasure," "great location," "wonderful staff." ⑤ *Rooms from: $299*
✉ *70 Park Ave., at 38th St., Midtown East* ☎ *212/973–2401, 800/707–
2752* ⊕ *www.70parkave.com* ⤳ *201 rooms, 4 suites* ⑩ *No meals* Ⓜ *6
to 33rd St.* ✛ *4:F5.*

$$ **Affinia 50.** This popular hotel attracts business travelers but it's also
HOTEL   comfortable for families or leisure travelers—especially the studios and
☾   suites, which have plenty of space to stretch out in, with full kitchens and a clean, playful design that incorporates oversize chairs and
couches. **Pros:** apartment-style living; large rooms; good value; kid-
and pet-friendly. **Cons:** pricey Wi-Fi. **TripAdvisor:** "feels like home,"
"great place for families," "the very best experience." ⑤ *Rooms from:
$314* ✉ *155 E. 50th St., at 3rd Ave., Midtown East* ☎ *212/751–5710,
800/637–8483* ⊕ *www.affinia.com* ⤳ *75 rooms, 134 suites* Ⓜ *6 to 51st
St./Lexington Ave.; E, M to Lexington–3rd Aves./53rd St.* ✛ *4:G3.*

$$ **The Alex.** Often overlooked in a part of the city that's heavy with
HOTEL   office buildings, the Alex is a sleek little oasis of style on Manhattan's
East Side. **Pros:** all suites have kitchens; good service; on-site fitness
facilities. **Cons:** cramped lobby; small bathrooms; expensive Wi-Fi.
TripAdvisor: "beautiful modern hotel," "very cool," "I wanted to
move in." ⑤ *Rooms from: $405* ✉ *205 E. 45th St., between 2nd and
3rd Aves., Midtown East* ☎ *212/867–5100* ⊕ *www.thealexhotel.com*
⤳ *73 rooms, 130 suites* ⑩ *No meals* Ⓜ *4, 5, 6, 7, S to 42nd St./Grand
Central* ✛ *4:G4.*

$$$ **The Benjamin.** NYC is often called the City That Never Sleeps, but if
HOTEL   a good night's rest is essential for your visit, the Benjamin may be your
☾   choice accommodation—with a menu of 12 pillows to choose from
(including buckwheat, water, and Swedish memory varieties), white-
noise machines, and 400-thread-count sheets, they've got it covered.
Pros: sleep-friendly; great location; gracious staff; kitchenettes in big
rooms, pets stay for free. **Cons:** paid Internet and Wi-Fi; boring views;
dull neighborhood after dark. **TripAdvisor:** "a well kept secret," "great
staff," "just perfect." ⑤ *Rooms from: $459* ✉ *125 E. 50th St., at Lex-
ington Ave., Midtown East* ☎ *212/715–2500* ⊕ *www.thebenjamin.com*
⤳ *109 rooms, 100 suites* ⑩ *No meals* Ⓜ *6 to 51st St./Lexington Ave.;
E, M to Lexington–3rd Aves./53rd St.* ✛ *4:F3.*

$$$$ **Four Seasons Hotel.** It's the Four Seasons, and for better or worse,
HOTEL   it remains the blueprint for what a Manhattan luxury hotel should
be—sure, that also means it's outrageously expensive, but you get a
fair amount of bang for your buck, including stellar service that goes
to the ends of the earth for guests, an imposing lobby done in marble
and blond wood, and a well-connected concierge who can get reservations at most of New York's hot tables. **Pros:** spacious and comfortable
rooms; perfect concierge and staff service; afternoon tea in the lobby

lounge. **Cons:** pricey; confusing room controls; some furniture could use updating. **TripAdvisor:** "great accommodations," "unparalleled personalized service," "retreat within the concrete jungle." ⑤ *Rooms from: $950* ⊠ *57 E. 57th St., between Park and Madison Aves., Midtown East* ☎ *212/758–5700, 800/487–3769* ⊕ *www.fourseasons.com* ⟿ *300 rooms, 68 suites* ⑩ *No meals* Ⓜ *4, 5, 6, N, Q, R to 59th St./Lexington Ave.* ✛ *4:F1.*

$$ **The Gotham Hotel.** This sleek, skinny hotel has a lot going for it, but
HOTEL   a clincher for some is the fact that every single room has an outdoor space. **Pros:** welcoming staff; central location; every room has a balcony. **Cons:** no on-site gym. **TripAdvisor:** "pure romance," "wonderful gem in Times Square," "great staff." ⑤ *Rooms from: $350* ⊠ *16 E. 46 St., between 5th and Madison Aves., Midtown East* ☎ *212/490–8500* ⊕ *www.thegothamhotelny.com* ⟿ *66 rooms* Ⓜ *B, D, F, M to 47th–50th Sts./Rockefeller Center* ✛ *4:ED3.*

$$$ **Grand Hyatt New York.** A top-to-bottom renovation has reinvented this
HOTEL   historic Grand Central mainstay into a sleek, modern behemoth, making it a desireable central hub once again. **Pros:** Comfy beds, light-filled gym on a high floor; refreshing modern design; large, well-planned rooms. **Cons:** no in-room minibar; Wi-Fi not free. **TripAdvisor:** "great location and service," "comfortable rooms," "beautiful indoor areas." ⑤ *Rooms from: $359* ⊠ *109 E. 42nd St., between Park and Lexington Aves., Midtown East* ☎ *212/833–1234, 800/233–1234* ⊕ *www.grandnewyork. hyatt.com* ⟿ *51 suites, 1,255 rooms* ⑩ *No meals* ✛ *4:F4.*

$$$ **Hotel Elysée.** A relative bargain given its location, this intimate hotel is
HOTEL   a favorite for travelers looking for great location without breaking the bank. **Pros:** complimentary snacks and Wi-Fi; individually decorated rooms; cute library. **Cons:** underwhelming lobby; slightly outdated decor. **TripAdvisor:** "very comfortable," "wonderful staff," "value and charm." ⑤ *Rooms from: $495* ⊠ *60 E. 54th St., between Madison and Park Aves., Midtown East* ☎ *212/753–1066, 800/535–9733* ⊕ *www. elyseehotel.com* ⟿ *87 rooms, 16 suites* ⑩ *Breakfast* Ⓜ *E, M to 5th Ave.* ✛ *4:F2.*

$$$ **The Kitano.** As you might guess from the name, the Kitano imports
HOTEL   much of its sensibility from Japan, with touches that include a bilingual concierge and a high-concept Japanese restaurant. **Pros:** extra soundproofing in guest rooms; cute mezzanine bar area; guest pass to great local New York Sports Club; good value. **Cons:** lower-floor views are limited; expensive restaurant. **TripAdvisor:** "attractive property," "a serene and lovely place," "simple luxury." ⑤ *Rooms from: $449* ⊠ *66 Park Ave., at E. 38th St., Midtown East* ☎ *212/885–7000, 800/548–2666* ⊕ *www.kitano.com* ⟿ *149 rooms, 18 suites* ⑩ *No meals* Ⓜ *6 to 33rd St.* ✛ *4:F5.*

$$ **Library Hotel Manhattan.** Bookishly handsome, this stately landmark
HOTEL   brownstone, built in 1900, is inspired by the nearby New York Public
Fodor's Choice   Library—each of its 10 floors is dedicated to one of the 10 categories of
★   the Dewey Decimal System and stocked with art and books relevant to a subtopic such as erotica, astronomy, or biography—let your interests guide your choice. **Pros:** fun rooftop bar; playful book themes; stylish rooms. **Cons:** rooftop sometimes reserved for events; more books in

20

rooms themselves would be nice. **TripAdvisor:** "great service," "small stylish hotel," "clean and comfortable." $ *Rooms from: $379* ⊠ *299 Madison Ave., at E. 41st Street, Midtown East* ☎ *212/983–4500, 212/983–4500* ⊕ *www.libraryhotel.com* ⤴ *60 rooms* |◯| *Breakfast* Ⓜ *4, 5, 6, 7, S to 42nd St./Grand Central* ✛ *4:E4.*

$$$ 🏨 **Loews Regency Hotel.** The snazzy lobby sums up the focus of this Park
HOTEL Avenue hotel: good service and lots of space. **Pros:** friendly and helpful staff; relatively quiet; good for pets; updated fitness center. **Cons:** expensive Internet. **TripAdvisor:** "comfortable room," "lovely," "a trip down memory lane." $ *Rooms from: $509* ⊠ *540 Park Ave., at E. 61st St., Midtown East* ☎ *800/235–6397, 800/233–2356* ⊕ *www.loewshotels. com/* ⤴ *267 rooms, 87 suites* Ⓜ *4, 5, 6, N, Q, R to 59th St./Lexington Ave.* ✛ *5:F6.*

$$ 🏨 **Millennium UN Plaza.** This hotel in this sky-high tower near the United
HOTEL Nations starts on the 28th floor, which means there are breathtaking views—ask for a room facing west, toward Manhattan—and the multilingual staff caters to a discerning clientele that includes heads of state. **Pros:** unbeatable East River and city views; good value; great front-door and bell staff. **Cons:** a walk to the subway; pricey Internet access. **TripAdvisor:** "big rooms and quiet location," "superb views," "scenic oasis as advertised." $ *Rooms from: $315* ⊠ *1 United Nations Plaza, at E. 44th St. and 1st Ave., Midtown East* ☎ *212/758–1234, 866/866–8086* ⊕ *www.millenniumhotels.com* ⤴ *382 rooms, 45 suites* |◯| *No meals* Ⓜ *4, 5, 6, 7, S to 42nd St./Grand Central* ✛ *4:H4.*

$$$ 🏨 **New York Palace.** From the moment you enter the gilded gates of these
HOTEL connected mansions, originally built in the 1880s by railroad baron Henry Villard, you know you're somewhere special; there's a reason this is called the Palace. **Pros:** gorgeous courtyard with 15th-century Italian-style motifs; great service; unmatched views of St. Patrick's Cathedral. **Cons:** high prices; harried staff. **TripAdvisor:** "beautiful hotel," "faultless experience," "great staff." $ *Rooms from: $599* ⊠ *455 Madison Ave., at E. 50th St., Midtown East* ☎ *212/888–7000, 800/697–2522* ⊕ *www.newyorkpalace.com* ⤴ *804 rooms, 88 suites* |◯| *No meals* Ⓜ *6 to 51st St./Lexington Ave.; E, M to Lexington–3rd Aves./53rd St.* ✛ *4:E3.*

$$$$ 🏨 **The Peninsula.** Stepping through the Peninsula's Beaux Arts facade
HOTEL onto the grand staircase overhung with a monumental chandelier,
Fodor'sChoice you know you're in for a glitzy treat. **Pros:** brilliant service; fabulous
★ rooms, with the best lighting of all city hotels (good angles, easy to use); unforgettable rooftop bar. **Cons:** expensive. **TripAdvisor:** "attentive service," "excellent all around," "simply luxurious." $ *Rooms from: $975* ⊠ *700 5th Ave., at 55th St., Midtown East* ☎ *212/956–2888, 800/262–9467* ⊕ *www.peninsula.com* ⤴ *185 rooms, 54 suites* |◯| *No meals* Ⓜ *E, M to 5th Ave.* ✛ *4:E2.*

$ 🏨 **The Pod Hotel.** This is the hotel that made bunk beds cool again. **Pros:**
HOTEL great prices; fun design. **Cons:** if you're prone to claustrophobia, you may want to reconsider. **TripAdvisor:** "great atmosphere," "funky and functional," "all around nice place." $ *Rooms from: $159* ⊠ *230 E. 51st St., between 2nd and 3rd Aves., Midtown East* ☎ *212/355–0300, 800/742–5945* ⊕ *www.thepodhotel.com* ⤴ *347 rooms, 195 with bath*

‖⃝ *No meals* Ⓜ *6 to 51st St./Lexington Ave.; E, M to Lexington–3rd Aves./53rd St.* ✢ *4:G2.*

$ ⊞ **Roger Smith.** This quirky choice is one of the better budget buys in
HOTEL   the city and the art-filled rooms, matched by the murals in the lobby, are homey and comfortable, with down pillows and quilts on the beds. **Pros:** good location near Grand Central; intimate atmosphere; free Wi-Fi. **Cons:** street noise; small bathrooms. **TripAdvisor:** "friendly staff," "eclectic and historical," "home away from home." Ⓢ *Rooms from: $299* ✉ *501 Lexington Ave., between E. 47th and E. 48th Sts., Midtown East* ☎ *212/755–1400, 800/445–0277* ⊕ *www.rogersmith. com* ✑ *102 rooms, 28 suites* ‖⃝ *No meals* Ⓜ *6 to 51st St./Lexington Ave.; E, M to Lexington–3rd Aves./53rd St.* ✢ *4:F3.*

$ ⊞ **The Roosevelt Hotel.** Named after Teddy, not Franklin, this Midtown
HOTEL   icon just steps from Grand Central has an ornate lobby with cushy couches and an old-school bar with heavy wood detailing that makes the place feel like it's from another time, and it should—the property dates from 1924. **Pros:** great public areas; big bathrooms. **Cons:** dated decor; limited in-room amenities. **TripAdvisor:** "friendly staff," "a New York icon," "perfect place to stay." Ⓢ *Rooms from: $299* ✉ *45 E. 45th St., at Madison Ave., Midtown East* ☎ *888/833–3969* ⊕ *www. theroosevelthotel.com* ✑ *1,015 rooms, 24 suites* ‖⃝ *No meals* Ⓜ *4, 5, 6 to Grand Central/42nd St.* ✢ *4:F4.*

$$$ ⊞ **The Setai Fifth Avenue.** Setting new standards for luxury, the towering,
HOTEL   limestone-clad Setai was conceived as an opulent crash pad for wealthy
★   overseas tourists, captains of industry on long-term stays, and anyone in need of some serious pampering. **Pros:** attentive service; gorgeous spa; great location. **Cons:** street noise reported by guests on lower floors. **TripAdvisor:** "a high quality of service," "simply brilliant and out-standing," "truly a leading world hotel." Ⓢ *Rooms from: $595* ✉ *400 5th Ave., Midtown East* ☎ *212/695–4005* ⊕ *www.setaififthavenue.com* ✑ *157 rooms, 57 suites* ‖⃝ *No meals* Ⓜ *B, D, F, V to 34th St./Penn Station* ✢ *4:E5.*

$$$$ ⊞ **The Sherry-Netherland.** The Sherry is a stately part of the New York
HOTEL   landscape so it may come as a surprise to learn that it's essentially a tall, luxurious apartment building that also has 50 hotel rooms and suites. **Pros:** gorgeous lobby; commanding, impeccable location; Cipriani access. **Cons:** small check-in area; rooms vary in taste and decor; non-suites are on the small side; interior rooms lack views; guests sometimes feel the cold shoulder from the full-time residents. **TripAdvisor:** "first class all the way," "old-time New York at its best," "100% genuine and wonderful." Ⓢ *Rooms from: $649* ✉ *781 5th Ave., at E. 59th St., Mid-town East* ☎ *212/355–2800, 800/247–4377* ⊕ *www.sherrynetherland. com* ✑ *30 rooms, 20 suites* ‖⃝ *Breakfast* Ⓜ *N, R, Q to 5th Ave.* ✢ *5:E6.*

$$$$ ⊞ **The St. Regis.** World-class from head to toe, this 5th Avenue Beaux
HOTEL   Arts landmark comes as close to flawless as any hotel in New York.
Fodor'sChoice   **Pros:** rooms combine true luxury with helpful technology; easy-access
★   butler service; superb in-house dining; prestigious location. **Cons:** expensive; too serious for families seeking fun. **TripAdvisor:** "excellent concierge," "a legend in the heart of Manhattan," "expensive but spe-cial." Ⓢ *Rooms from: $895* ✉ *2 E. 55th St., at 5th Ave., Midtown East*

20

☎ 888/625–4988, 877/787–3447 ⊕ *www.stregis.com* ⤴ *164 rooms, 65 suites* ▮◯▮ *No meals* Ⓜ *E, M to 5th Ave.* ✛ *4:E2.*

$$ 📠 **Hilton Manhattan East.** This traditional-style, 20-story Tudor City hotel
HOTEL is a stone's throw from the United Nations and Grand Central Termi-
nal, making it fairly convenient but not very glamorous. **Pros:** near
UN; some balconies; convenient location for getting to major sights.
Cons: long walk to subway. **TripAdvisor:** "a cozy property," "service
is good," "nice accommodations." Ⓢ *Rooms from: $405* ✉ *304 E.
42nd St., between 1st and 2nd Aves., Midtown East* ☎ *212/986–8800,
800/879–8836* ⊕ *www.hilton.com* ⤴ *286 rooms, 14 suites* ▮◯▮ *No meals*
Ⓜ *4, 5, 6, 7, S to 42nd St./Grand Central* ✛ *4:G4.*

$$$ 📠 **Waldorf-Astoria.** The Waldorf is undeniably historic, and presidents
HOTEL usually stay here thanks to the security of the drive-in entrance, but we'd
recommend having a cocktail at the classic Bull and Bear Bar downstairs
rather than spending the night in one of the small standard rooms,
which top out at a cozy 250 square feet and can feel a bit oppressive
with their extensive floral patterns. **Pros:** historic art-deco building filled
with NYC's aristocratic, gangster, and jazz histories; best Waldorf salad
in town; knowledgeable doormen. **Cons:** rooms not up to date; more
about the name than the experience; in-hotel Starbucks costs twice as
much as ones around the corner. **TripAdvisor:** "great service and location," "worth every penny," "you pay for history." Ⓢ *Rooms from:
$549* ✉ *301 Park Ave., between E. 49th and E. 50th Sts., Midtown East*
☎ *212/355–3000, 800/925–3673* ⊕ *www.waldorfastoria.com* ⤴ *1,176
rooms, 276 suites* ▮◯▮ *No meals* Ⓜ *6 to 51st St./Lexington Ave.; E, M to
Lexington–3rd Aves./53rd St.* ✛ *4:F3.*

$$ 📠 **W Hotel New York.** A hopping bar and sunken lounge in the reception
HOTEL area, superfunky decor touches like window boxes filled with grass, and
guest rooms that hew to the classic W formula—they're small and they
look good—this is a quintessential W property. **Pros:** central location;
great-looking rooms; Bliss Spa in hotel. **Cons:** thin walls; small rooms;
inconsistent service. **TripAdvisor:** "excellent service," "very modern,"
"cozy." Ⓢ *Rooms from: $279* ✉ *541 Lexington Ave., between E. 49th
and E. 50th Sts., Midtown East* ☎ *212/755–1200, 877/946–8357*
⊕ *www.whotels.com* ⤴ *629 rooms, 62 suites* ▮◯▮ *No meals* Ⓜ *6 to 51st
St./Lexington Ave.; E, M to Lexington–3rd Aves./53rd St.* ✛ *4:F3.*

MURRAY HILL

$$$ 📠 **The Carlton Hotel.** From the two-story lobby designed by David
HOTEL Rockwell to still-intact, original 1904 Beaux Arts details such as the
stained-glass dome (created by workers from the Tiffany glass factory),
a 40-foot ceiling in the lobby, and a soaring two-story crystal chandelier, the Carlton is a refurbished gem. **Pros:** spectacular lobby; stylish
rooms. **Cons:** expensive bar; small rooms. **TripAdvisor:** "elegant," "a
sanctuary," "wonderful service." Ⓢ *Rooms from: $459* ✉ *88 Madison
Ave., between E. 28th and E. 29th Sts., Murray Hill* ☎ *212/532–4100,
800/601–8500* ⊕ *www.carltonhotelny.com* ⤴ *294 rooms, 22 suites* Ⓜ *6
to 28th St.* ✛ *3:F1.*

$ 📠 **The Herald Square Hotel.** The sculpted cherubs on the facade and the
HOTEL vintage magazine covers adorning the common areas give good hints
that the great value Herald Square Hotel used to be *Life* magazine's

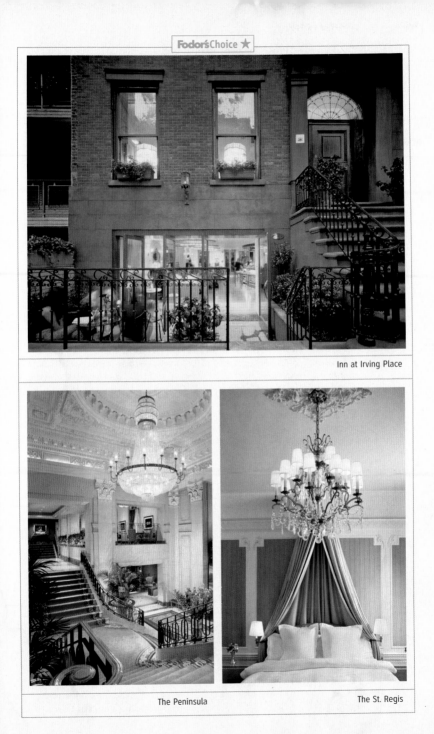

Fodor'sChoice ★

Inn at Irving Place

The Peninsula

The St. Regis

headquarters. **Pros:** cheap; centrally located. **Cons:** unattractive lobby; readers report inconsistent service. **TripAdvisor:** "wonderful staff," "superb," "comfortable beds." ⑤ *Rooms from: $199* ✉ *19 W. 31st St., between 5th Ave. and Broadway, Murray Hill* ☎ *212/279–4017, 800/727–1888* ⊕ *www.heraldsquarehotel.com* ⟿ *120 rooms* ❙❍❙ *No meals* Ⓜ *B, D, F, N, Q, R, M to 34th St./Herald Sq.* ⊹ *3:E1.*

MIDTOWN WEST

$ 🏨 **6 Columbus.** A boutique-style hotel nestled in the shadow of the towering Time Warner center, 6 Columbus—part of the ever-proliferating Thompson Hotels group—offers the vibe and amenities of downtown lodging with the convenience of a more central Midtown location. **Pros:** convenient location; fun in-hotel restaurant; reasonably priced for neighborhood; family-friendly. **Cons:** rooms on lower floors facing 58th Street can be noisy. **TripAdvisor:** "friendly service," "charming and sophisticated," "incredible room." ⑤ *Rooms from: $295* ✉ *6 Columbus Circle, on 58th St. between 8th and 9th Aves., Midtown West* ☎ *212/204–3000* ⊕ *www.thompsonhotels.com* ⟿ *72 rooms, 16 suites* ❙❍❙ *No meals* Ⓜ *1, A, B, C, D to 59th St./Columbus Circle* ⊹ *4:B1.*

$$$ 🏨 **The Algonquin.** One of the Manhattan's most historic properties, the HOTEL Algonquin is a landmark of literary history. The hotel has been closed for renovations but is expected to reopen in mid-2012. **TripAdvisor:** "super location," "character rather than cutting edge," "a piece of NY history." ⑤ *Rooms from: $550* ✉ *59 W. 44th St., between 5th and 6th Aves., Midtown West* ☎ *212/840–6800, 800/555–8000* ⊕ *www. algonquinhotel.com* ⟿ *150 rooms, 24 suites* ❙❍❙ *No meals* Ⓜ *B, D, F, M to 42nd St.* ⊹ *4:D4.*

$ 🏨 **Belvedere Hotel.** The Belvedere's main draw is the Times Square/The-HOTEL ater District location more than its rooms, which tend to be dark and don't stand out design-wise, although they're spacious and have kitchenettes with a microwave, mini-refrigerator, and coffeemaker. **Pros:** good rates available; renovated rooms are good value. **Cons:** can be loud with street noise; slow elevators. **TripAdvisor:** "great accommodation," "excellent location," "clean." ⑤ *Rooms from: $239* ✉ *319 W. 48th St., between 8th and 9th Aves., Midtown West* ☎ *212/245–7000, 888/468–3558* ⊕ *www.belvederehotelnyc.com* ⟿ *328 rooms, 1 suite* ❙❍❙ *No meals* Ⓜ *C, E to 50th St.* ⊹ *4:B3.*

$ 🏨 **Best Western Plus President Hotel.** After a $15 million renovation that HOTEL transformed it from a ho-hum Best Western, the President is the only politically themed hotel in the city, starting with the purple color scheme, a combination of Republican red and Democratic blue. **Pros:** sleek rooms for the price; convenient location; unique theme. **Cons:** cramped lobby; dark bathrooms; poor views. **TripAdvisor:** "always a pleasant stay," "breakfast is excellent," "small and practical." ⑤ *Rooms from: $249* ✉ *234 W. 48th St., between 8th Ave. and Broadway, Times Square* ☎ *212/246–8800, 800/828–4667* ⊕ *www.thepresidenthotel.com* ⟿ *334 rooms* ❙❍❙ *No meals* Ⓜ *C, E to 50th St.* ⊹ *4:C3.*

$$$ 🏨 **The Blakely New York.** It may be a tried-and-true design motif, but HOTEL it's hard to resist the English gentlemen's club when it's done right. **Pros:** all rooms have kitchenettes; central location; good-size rooms;

acclaimed restaurant. **Cons:** rooms facing 54th Street can be noisy; some rooms have little natural light; expensive. **TripAdvisor:** "comfortable," "New York elegance," "spacious room." ⑤ *Rooms from: $525* ✉ *136 W. 55th St., between 6th and 7th Aves., Midtown West* ☎ *212/245–1800, 800/735–0710* ⊕ *www.blakelynewyork.com* ⚓ *60 rooms, 58 suites* ⓄⱰ *No meals* Ⓜ *N, Q, R to 57th St.* ✛ *4:C2.*

$$ 📺 **Bryant Park Hotel.** A New York landmark in brown brick, towering
HOTEL over the New York Public Library and Bryant Park, this sleekly modern hotel is still a Midtown hot spot. **Pros:** gorgeous building; fashionable crowd and setting; across from Bryant Park. **Cons:** expensive; Cellar Bar frequently booked for events. **TripAdvisor:** "excellent location," "my home in NYC," "staff were great." ⑤ *Rooms from: $445* ✉ *40 W. 40th St., between 5th and 6th Aves., Midtown West* ☎ *212/869–0100, 877/640–9300* ⊕ *www.bryantparkhotel.com* ⚓ *114 rooms, 14 suites* ⓄⱰ *No meals* Ⓜ *B, D, F, M to 42nd St.; 7 to 5th Ave.* ✛ *4:D5.*

$$ 📺 **Casablanca Hotel.** A favorite for the comfortable rooms and great
HOTEL location, the Casablanca evokes the sultry Mediterranean. **Pros:** great
Fodor's Choice access to the Theater District; all rooms are smoke-free. **Cons:** exercise
★ facilities at nearby New York Sports Club, not on premises; heavy tourist foot traffic. **TripAdvisor:** "very accommodating," "a true oasis," "stay here for the location and service." ⑤ *Rooms from: $439* ✉ *147 W. 43rd St., Midtown West* ☎ *212/869–1212* ⊕ *www.casablancahotel. com* ⚓ *48 rooms* Ⓜ *1, 2, 3, 7, N, Q, R, S to Times Sq./42nd St.* ✛ *4:C4.*

$$$$ 📺 **The Chatwal New York.** A lavishly refurbished reincarnation of a classic
HOTEL Manhattan theater club that lay fallow for decades, the Chatwal New
Fodor's Choice York delivers the luxury experience in style, with the price tag to match.
★ **Pros:** gorgeous lobby; state-of-the-art room controls and amenities; excellent service. **Cons:** expensive—some visitors may find justifying such high prices for a Times Square locale difficult. **TripAdvisor:** "excellent staff," "impeccable service," "almost perfect eye candy." ⑤ *Rooms from: $695* ✉ *130 W. 44th St., between 5th and 6th Aves., Midtown West* ☎ *212/764–6200* ⊕ *www.thechatwalny.com* ⚓ *76 rooms* ⓄⱰ *No meals* Ⓜ *B, D, F, M, 7 to 42nd St./Bryant Park* ✛ *4:C4.*

$$ 📺 **City Club Hotel.** The City Club's ocean-liner-inspired rooms are brisk,
HOTEL bright, and masculine: they're also about the same size as a room on a cruise ship—that means tight quarters, matey, no matter how much you enjoy sharing space with Jonathan Adler ceramics. **Pros:** free Wi-Fi; great restaurant; personal service. **Cons:** no gym; occasioanally dim lighting; tiny lobby. **TripAdvisor:** "perfect boutique hotel," "a magnificent city gem," "Times Square convenience." ⑤ *Rooms from: $400* ✉ *55 W. 44th St., between 5th and 6th Aves., Midtown West* ☎ *212/921–5500* ⊕ *www.cityclubhotel.com* ⚓ *62 rooms, 3 suites* ⓄⱰ *No meals* Ⓜ *B, D, F, N, R, M, 1, 2, 3, 9 to 42nd St.; 7 to 5th Ave.* ✛ *4:D4.*

$ 📺 **The Distrikt.** Rising high above Port Authority, the Distrikt tries to
HOTEL approximate the boutique hotel experience in an area of town better known for its bus depot and, for the most part, it succeeds. **Pros:** great central location; friendly staff; good Midtown views from higher floors. **Cons:** on a gritty block right across from Port Authority; noisy on lower floors. **TripAdvisor:** "great service," "a room with a view," "fabulous staff." ⑤ *Rooms from: $279* ✉ *342 W. 40th St., between 8th*

20

and 9th Aves., Midtown West ☎ *212/706–6100* ⊕ *www.distrikthotel. com* ☞ *155 rooms* |◉| *No meals* Ⓜ *A, C, W to 42nd St./8th Ave.* ✣ *4:B5.*

$$ 🏨 **DoubleTree Suites by Hilton Hotel New York City–Times Square.** Space is the
HOTEL   big draw at this Times Square top dog, where rooms are twice the size
☾   of New York City's average; one-bedroom suites are about 400 square
feet and have double vanities, mini-refrigerators, microwaves, and iPod
docks. **Pros:** free 24-hour gym and Wi-Fi in public areas; extremely
helpful, informed concierge; convenient to the Theater District; very
quiet considering the Times Square location. **Cons:** paid Wi-Fi in guest
rooms; pricey for a DoubleTree. **TripAdvisor:** "consistent," "great ser-
vice," "it doesn't get any better." Ⓢ *Rooms from: $349* ✉ *1568 Broad-
way, at 47th St., Midtown West* ☎ *212/719–1600* ⊕ *www.doubletree1.
hilton.com* ☞ *460 rooms* |◉| *No meals* Ⓜ *B, D, F, M to 42nd St.* ✣ *4:C3.*

$$ 🏨 **Dream New York.** Part hotel, part Kafkaesque dream, this Midtown
HOTEL   experience is brought to you by hotelier Vikram Chatwal, and it spe-
cializes in style over comfort, but despite some over-the-top design features—and noise from the scenesters headed to the rooftop bar—it's
quite livable. **Pros:** Ava Lounge penthouse bar; large spa; up-to-the-
minute electronics. **Cons:** small rooms; spotty service. **TripAdvisor:**
"comfortable and friendly," "hip property," "unique look and feel."
Ⓢ *Rooms from: $279* ✉ *210 W. 55th St., at Broadway, Midtown West*
☎ *212/247–2000* ⊕ *www.dreamny.com* ☞ *204 rooms, 12 suites* Ⓜ *N,
Q, R to 57th St.* ✣ *4:C2.*

$$$ 🏨 **Hilton Times Square.** A glass-and-steel skyscraper atop a 335,000-square-
HOTEL   foot retail complex that includes a movie theater and Madame Tus-
saud's Wax Museum, the Hilton Times Square soars 44 stories above
Manhattan and overlooks New York City's famous skyline and the
Hudson River. **Pros:** great location for Times Square entertainment;
convenient to public transportation; big rooms. **Cons:** impersonal feel;
nickel-and-dime charges and overpriced food and drink, including a $26
buffet breakfast. **TripAdvisor:** "awesome staff," "close to the action,"
"nice room." Ⓢ *Rooms from: $549* ✉ *234 W. 42nd St., between 7th and
8th Aves., Midtown West* ☎ *212/840–8222, 800/445–8667* ⊕ *www.
hilton.com* ☞ *460 rooms, 2 suites* |◉| *No meals* Ⓜ *1, 2, 3, 7, N, Q, R,
S to 42nd St./Times Sq.* ✣ *4:C4.*

$ 🏨 **Holiday Inn New York City Midtown.** Business travelers, tourists, and
HOTEL   families all appreciate this good value option a stone's throw from Penn
station, and understand that it's not the most exciting hotel experience.
Pros: good value; friendly and efficient service; location in the thick of it.
Cons: small workout room; not much character. **TripAdvisor:** "friendly
staff," "a room with a view," "comfortable and quiet." Ⓢ *Rooms from:
$199* ✉ *30 W. 31st St., between 5th Ave. and Broadway, Midtown
West* ☎ *212/695–7401* ⊕ *www.holidayinn.com* ☞ *120 rooms, 2 suites*
|◉| *No meals* ✣ *3:E1.*

$ 🏨 **Hotel Metro.** With mirrored columns and elegant black-and-white
HOTEL   photos in the lobby, the Hotel Metro feels distinctively retro. **Pros:** com-
plimentary coffee and tea 24/7; renovated exercise room has flat-screen
TVs; free Wi-Fi in rooms. **Cons:** noise seeps from outside; rooms are
tasteful but spartan. **TripAdvisor:** "a vintage art deco gem," "comfort
with a view," "excellent facilities and location." Ⓢ *Rooms from: $275*

CLOSE UP

Romantic Retreats

As the English explorer Sir Walter Raleigh once wrote, "Romance is a love affair in other than domestic surroundings." Indeed, many high-end hotels seem custom-built for romance, with plush feather beds, silky linens, and ultrasoft robes. But some properties go above and beyond in catering to couples, offering services like bath butlers and in-room massages. Here's our pick of the city's best spots for an intimate getaway.

At the **Ritz-Carlton New York, Battery Park** (⇨ *Lower Manhattan*), your wish is their command. Take advantage of lower-than-normal weekend rates to book a Liberty Suite, with sweeping views of the Statue of Liberty. With a quick call to the concierge you can arrange to have champagne and strawberries waiting in your room when you arrive. A bath butler can then fill your marble tub with a potion of bath oils and flower petals. If you're here in February, don't miss a trip to the penthouse Chocolate Bar, with its aphrodisiac chocolate-and-champagne buffet.

The **Inn at Irving Place** (⇨ *Union Square/Gramercy*) does romance the old-fashioned way, with four-poster beds, fireplaces, fur throws, and plenty of privacy in an elegant 1800s brownstone. The complimentary breakfast is served on fine bone china either in the cozy sitting room or in bed.

Few things are as romantic as taking a bath, and at the Carlye (⇨ *Upper East Side*) every room has one. Fill the tub with steaming water and some Kiehl's bubble bath, take a soak, then lounge with your lover in a plush terrycloth robe while looking out at some of the City's best views. The 23,000-square-foot Bliss Spa at **W New York** (⇨ *Midtown East and Upper East Side*), on Lexington Avenue, is an urban oasis, with men's and women's lounges, a gym, and a full menu of facial and body treatments, massage, waxing, and nail services. Couples can spend a full day being pampered and pedicured in the spa or unwind in their rooms with an in-room massage, offered 24 hours a day.

All the rooms at the **Library Hotel** (⇨ *Midtown East and Upper East Side*) have an inviting charm that makes them a good choice for a romantic weekend away, but if you're looking for a little mood reading, ask for the Erotic Literature room or the Love Room, curated by Dr. Ruth.

20

✉ *45 W. 35th St., between 5th and 6th Aves., Midtown West* ☎ *212/947 2500* ⊕ *www.hotelmetronyc.com* ⤳ *181 rooms* ⦿| *Breakfast* Ⓜ *B, D, F, N, Q, R, M to 34th St./Herald Sq.* ✛ *4:D6.*

$$$
HOTEL
🏨 **Hudson New York Hotel.** Manna from heaven for budget fashionistas when it opened, the Hudson is starting to show its age. **Pros:** fabulous, elegant bar; gorgeous Francesco Clemente fresco in lobby; breathtaking Sky Terrace. **Cons:** staff can be condescending; tiny rooms; worn furnishings; overpriced cocktails. **TripAdvisor:** "too cool," "a different experience," "great place to stay." Ⓢ *Rooms from: $499* ✉ *356 W. 58th St., between 8th and 9th Aves., Midtown West* ☎ *212/554–6000* ⊕ *www.hudsonhotel.com* ⤳ *1,000 rooms, 2 suites* ⦿| *No meals* Ⓜ *1, A, B, C, D to 59th St./Columbus Circle* ✛ *4:B1.*

$ **Ink48.** If you want convenience to central Midtown but some remove
HOTEL from the hustle and bustle (not to mention a breathtaking rooftop
space), this Kimpton property is an excellent option. **Pros:** friendly staff;
great views; large rooms; beautiful rooftop. **Cons:** off-the-beaten-track
location; lobby can feel overly quiet at times; street noise. **TripAdvisor:**
"Hell's Kitchen gem," "great service," "best time ever." *[$] Rooms from:
$259 ✉ 653 11th Ave., at W. 48th St., Midtown West ☎ 212/757–0088
⊕ www.ink48.com ⇨ 195 rooms, 27 suites ⦿No meals Ⓜ C, E to
50th St. ✦ 4:A3.*

$$$ **InterContinental New York Times Square.** A central location mere blocks
HOTEL from the heart of Broadway, Times Square, and restaurant-rich Hell's
Kitchen makes the city's newest InterContinental a conveniently located
draw. **Pros:** central for transportation and entertainment; in-house res-
taurant helmed by celebrity chef; attentive staff. **Cons:** fee for Inter-
net. **TripAdvisor:** "very clean," "excellent location with great views,"
"beautiful hotel." *[$] Rooms from: $539 ✉ 300 W. 44th St., between
8th and 9th aves., Midtown West ☎ 877/331–5888 ☎ 212/315–2535
⊕ www.interconny.com ⇨ 518 rooms, 29 suites ⦿No meals Ⓜ A, C,
E to 42nd St./Port Authority Bus Terminal ✦ 4:B4.*

$$$ **Jumeirah Essex House.** When the Jumeirah Hotel Group took over this
HOTEL famed property right across from Central Park South, in 2007, they
did a $90 million refurbishment and the luxury hotel still looks fresh
several years on. **Pros:** great service; amazing views; impressive restaurant. **Cons:** overly complex room gadgetry; expensive bar. **TripAdvisor:** "very friendly," "great location," "a perfect stay." *[$] Rooms from:
$469 ✉ 160 Central Park S, between 6th and 7th Aves., Midtown West
☎ 212/247–0300, 800/937–8461 ⊕ www.jumeirahessexhouse.com
⇨ 515 rooms, 70 suites ⦿No meals Ⓜ F, N, R, Q to 57th St. ✦ 4:C1.*

$ **La Quinta Inn Manhattan.** Smack in the middle of Koreatown and
HOTEL close to Penn Station, this budget-friendly hotel in a cheerful old Beaux
Arts building may be one of the best deals in town. **Pros:** self-check-in
machines; gift shop on the premises for necessities. **Cons:** no room service; no frills. **TripAdvisor:** "comfy beds," "central location," "clean
and comfortable." *[$] Rooms from: $225 ✉ 17 W. 32nd St., between 5th
Ave. and Broadway, Midtown West ☎ 212/736–1600 ⊕ www.lq.com
⇨ 182 rooms ⦿Breakfast Ⓜ B, D, F, N, Q, R, M to 34th St./Herald
Sq. ✦ 4:E6.*

$$$ **Le Parker Meridien.** A splash of kookiness in otherwise staid Midtown,
HOTEL the Parker Meridian is a mix of a dependable large hotel with elements
of whimsy that keeps visitors coming back. **Pros:** lively, animated spirit;
best hotel gym in the city; fun eating options; tech-friendly rooms.
Cons: lobby is a public space; small bathrooms. **TripAdvisor:** "bril-
liant service," "a very comfortable stay," "cozy room." *[$] Rooms from:
$529 ✉ 119 W. 56th St., between 6th and 7th Aves., Midtown West
☎ 212/245–5000, 800/543–4300 ⊕ www.parkermeridien.com ⇨ 511
rooms, 215 suites ⦿No meals Ⓜ B, D, E, N, Q, R to 57th St. ✦ 4:D1.*

$$$ **The London NYC.** Stylish and sophisticated, the London NYC merges
HOTEL the flair of both of its namesake cities, with the added bonus of Gor-
don Ramsay's first stateside restaurant. **Pros:** posh atmosphere without prissiness; Gordon Ramsay restaurants; great fitness club. **Cons:**

inconsistent service; no bathtubs in most rooms; expensive dining options. **TripAdvisor:** "sophisticated and spacious," "great staff," "amazing stay." $ *Rooms from: $499* ⊠ *151 W. 54th St., between 6th and 7th Aves., Midtown West* ☎ *866/690–2029* ⊕ *www.thelondonnyc. com* ⤳ *561 suites* ⦿*No meals* Ⓜ *B, D, E to 7th Ave.; N, Q, R to 57th St.* ✣ *4:C2.*

$$$$
HOTEL
Fodor's Choice
★

Ⓣ **Mandarin Oriental.** The Mandarin's cavernous lobby, on the 35th floor of the Time Warner Center, oozes with luxury, setting the tone for the rest of the hotel experience. **Pros:** fantastic pool views; all the resources of the Time Warner Center; expansive suites. **Cons:** Trump hotel blocks some of the park views; expensive; mall-like surroundings. **TripAdvisor:** "perfect," "luxury and location," "incredible view." $ *Rooms from: $895* ⊠ *80 Columbus Circle, at 60th St., Midtown West* ☎ *212/805–8800* ⊕ *www.mandarinoriental.com/newyork* ⤳ *202 rooms, 46 suites* ⦿*No meals* Ⓜ *A, B, C, D, 1 to 59th St./Columbus Circle* ✣ *5:C6.*

$$
HOTEL

Ⓣ **The Mansfield.** They sweat the small stuff at the Mansfield: Wi-Fi is free, bathroom products are from Aveda, and even the key cards are snazzily embossed with scenes of old-timey New York. **Pros:** complimentary Wi-Fi; business center; 24-hour gym; great bar. **Cons:** small bathrooms; air conditioners are window units. **TripAdvisor:** "charming," "amazing experience," "great service." $ *Rooms from: $399* ⊠ *12 W. 44th St., between 5th and 6th Aves., Midtown West* ☎ *800/255–5167* ⊕ *www.mansfieldhotel.com* ⤳ *124 rooms, 25 suites* ⦿*No meals* Ⓜ *B, D, F, M to 42nd St.* ✣ *4:E4.*

$$
HOTEL

Ⓣ **The Michelangelo.** Italophiles will feel like they've been transported to the good life in the Mediterranean at this deluxe hotel, where the long, wide lobby lounge is clad with multihue marble and Veronese-style oil paintings. **Pros:** good location and restaurant; spacious rooms. **Cons:** noisy air-conditioning units; some rooms have limited views; small closets; in-room fixtures need some updating. **TripAdvisor:** "excellent staff," "incredible find," "perfect location and amenities." $ *Rooms from: $399* ⊠ *152 W. 51st St., at 7th Ave., Midtown West* ☎ *212/765–1900, 800/237–0990* ⊕ *www.michelangelohotel.com* ⤳ *123 rooms, 56 suites* ⦿*Breakfast* Ⓜ *B, D, E to 7th Ave.; 1 to 50th St.; B, D, F, M to 47th–50th Sts./Rockefeller Center* ✣ *4:C3.*

$$
HOTEL

Ⓣ **Muse Hotel.** Surrealist prints and busts of Thalia, the muse of comedy, adorn the lobby of this polished Kimpton property that pleases guests looking for a Midtown boutique hotel experience. **Pros:** contemporary interiors; good Midtown location; pet-friendly. **Cons:** street noise; small gym. **TripAdvisor:** "a friendly place in the big city," "perfect getaway for tired parents," "fabulous service." $ *Rooms from: $429* ⊠ *130 W. 46th St., between 6th and 7th Aves., Midtown West* ☎ *212/485–2400, 877/692–6873* ⊕ *www.themusehotel.com* ⤳ *200 rooms, 19 suites* ⦿*No meals* Ⓜ *B, D, F, M to 47th–50th Sts./Rockefeller Center* ✣ *4:C4.*

$$$$
HOTEL

Ⓣ **The Plaza.** Eloise's adopted home on the corner of Central Park, the Plaza is back in the hotel game after a $450 million renovation in 2008 in which some, but not all, of the rooms were turned into condos; the hotel once again hosts all manner of dignitaries, moneymakers, and royalty, as befits one of New York's most storied hotels. **Pros:** historic property; great hotel bar; lavish rooms. **Cons:** rooms aren't that big for

20

Ace Hotel

Library Hotel

Inn on 23rd

the money; Oak Room restaurant is pricey and inconsistent. **TripAdvisor:** "a beautiful grand hotel," "classic hotel with great location," "romantic." Ⓢ *Rooms from: $745 ⊠ 768 5th Ave., at Central Park, Midtown West ☎ 212/759–3000 ⊕ www.theplaza.com ⊲ 282 rooms, 102 suites* ◎| *No meals* Ⓜ *N, R to 59th St.* ✛ *4:E1.*

$$$
HOTEL

Renaissance Hotel. After a shift from all-business to a more design-centric approach, the Renaissance is enjoying a renaissance of its own. **Pros:** contemporary design; latest in-room technology. **Cons:** rooms can be a bit noisy; high occupancy means rooms can wear out fast. **TripAdvisor:** "fantastic hotel in a superb location," "great boutique feel," "excellent in every way." Ⓢ *Rooms from: $539 ⊠ 714 7th Ave., between W. 47th and W. 48th Sts., Midtown West ☎ 212/765–7676, 800/628–5222 ⊕ www.renaissancehotels.com ⊲ 305 rooms, 5 suites* ◎| *No meals* Ⓜ *R to 49th St.; 1 to 50th St.* ✛ *4:C3.*

$$$$
HOTEL
☾
Fodor's Choice
★

The Ritz-Carlton New York, Central Park. It's all about the park views here, though the above-and-beyond service, accommodating to a fault, makes this renowned property popular with celebs and other demanding guests. **Pros:** great concierge; personalized service; stellar location; views. **Cons:** pricey; limited common areas. **TripAdvisor:** "total experience is over the top," "fantastic staff," "location makes the difference." Ⓢ *Rooms from: $895 ⊠ 50 Central Park S, at 6th Ave., Midtown West ☎ 212/308–9100, 866/671–6008 ⊕ www.ritzcarlton.com ⊲ 259 rooms, 47 suites* ◎| *No meals* Ⓜ *F, M to 57th St.* ✛ *4:D1.*

$$
HOTEL
☾

Room Mate Grace. A favorite of European visitors and business travelers who work in fashion and entertainment, Grace delivers high-design lodgings on a budget. **Pros:** free, ample continental breakfast; friendly, helpful staff. **Cons:** small rooms; little in-room privacy (no door separating shower from main room). **TripAdvisor:** "cool hotel in amazing location," "huge room," "fun and funky place." Ⓢ *Rooms from: $319 ⊠ 125 W. 45th St., Midtown West ☎ 212/354–2323 ⊕ www.roommatehotels.com ⊲ 139 rooms* ◎| *Breakfast* Ⓜ *B, D, F, M to 42nd St.* ✛ *4:D4.*

$$$
HOTEL

The Royalton. Back in the 1990s, the Royalton's lobby bar was one of the prime meeting spots for local A-listers, and a complete redesign simply attracts a new generation of movers and shakers, so you'll have to run the gauntlet of the bustling lounge before you get to your room—but the efficient check-in and helpful staff ensure that things go smoothly. **Pros:** hip lobby scene; luxe beds and bathrooms; helpful service. **Cons:** dark hallways; lighting verges on eye-strainingly dim. **TripAdvisor:** "helpful staff," "slick and modern yet comfy," "treated like royalty." Ⓢ *Rooms from: $549 ⊠ 44 W. 44th St., between 5th and 6th Aves., Midtown West ☎ 212/869–4400, 800/697–1791 ⊕ www.royaltonhotel.com ⊲ 141 rooms, 27 suites* ◎| *No meals* Ⓜ *B, D, F, M to 42nd St.* ✛ *4:D4.*

$$
HOTEL

The Shoreham. Location is everything—and the Shoreham has one of the best, with MoMA within walking distance, and Central Park, Times Square, and Rockefeller all nearby. **Pros:** stylish decor; tech-friendly. **Cons:** not designed for families. **TripAdvisor:** "expectations exceeded," "very modern," "boutique hotel with personal attitude." Ⓢ *Rooms from: $399 ⊠ 33 W. 55th St., between 5th and 6th Aves., Midtown West*

20

Kids in Tow

Many New York hotels go out of their way to accommodate families, with special amenities and family-size rooms. However, a hotel claiming that it's child-friendly doesn't always translate to true kid-welcoming style. Ask if cribs come with linens, whether there are high chairs and children's menus in the dining room, and if there are in-house babysitters. Some hotels will even clear out the minibar (for bottle or baby-food storage), baby-proof a room, or provide baby-proofing materials. Here are some of the top picks for traveling with kids.

IN THE BAG. At Aloft hotels in Harlem and Brooklyn, kids receive a sleeping bag, coloring tools, and even popcorn in their own bag. And many rooms at Aloft New York Brooklyn can be conjoined to create family-friendly suites.

SUITE LIFE. Space is at a premium in New York hotels, and if you have more than two people in a standard room, you'll really start to feel the squeeze. The answer? A suite, where you can spread out in style. The **Embassy Suites New York** (⇨ TriBeCa), a tried-and-true family option, is even more kid-friendly in New York, because it's in the same building as a multiplex movie theater and several reasonably priced dining options. With renovated, spacious suites, **Affinia 50** (⇨ Midtown East and Upper East Side) is the family hotel of choice on the residential East Side.

PURE PAMPERING. Just because you have children in tow doesn't mean your dream of a pampering vacation needs to go down the drain. Several top New York hotels go out of their way to accommodate families. The **Mandarin-Oriental** (⇨ Midtown West) offers complimentary kids' DVDs and

video games, and free coloring books and crayons for kids.

FUN FLAVOR. Room Mate Grace (⇨ Midtown West) might make the perfect respite if you have teens in tow. There's a funky lobby pool, a kiosk that stocks sweets with which to fill the in-room refrigerators, and rooms with bunk beds that levitate out of the walls and have their own plasma TVs. At the hip **Hotel on Rivington** (⇨ East Village and Lower East Side) a special family suite has two full bedrooms, one with two sets of bunk beds and a big bin of toys, two full baths, and a Japanese tub. Bonus points: the hotel is across from Economy Candy.

KID KARMA. Family-friendly **Le Parker Meridien** (⇨ Midtown West and Chelsea) has a large pool, a restaurant that serves decadent breakfast foods such as chocolate French toast until 3 pm, and a casual dining spot, Burger Joint, that serves nothing but burgers and shakes.

KID-SIZE. At the 70 Park, the Eventi, and the Ink48 (all Kimpton Hotels) kids get their own minisize animal-print robes (also available for purchase) so they can feel just like their grown-up travel companions. TEA FOR TWO. At the Plaza, fanciful children of all ages will revel in dress-up clothes, formal tea service, and film screenings that are all part of the Eloise-theme experiences that seek to re-create the fictional character's time at the iconic hotel.

☎ *212/247–6700, 877/847–4444* ⊕ *www.shorehamhotel.com* ⤳ *174 rooms, 37 suites* ⦿⧘ *Breakfast* Ⓜ *E, M to 5th Ave.* ✛ *4:D2.*

$$$
HOTEL

⬚ **Sofitel Luxury Hotel.** With bilingual signage throughout the hotel, plenty of velvet in the lobby, and European modern design in the rooms—blond-wood and fresh flowers—the Sofitel brings a Gallic flair to Midwtown West. **Pros:** central location; great beds. **Cons:** pricey; room views vary. **TripAdvisor:** "flawless experience," "elegant," "perfect hotel in perfect location." Ⓢ *Rooms from: $500* ✉ *45 W. 44th St., between 5th and 6th Aves., Midtown West* ☎ *212/354–8844* ⊕ *www. sofitel.com* ⤳ *346 rooms, 52 suites* ⦿⧘ *No meals* Ⓜ *B, D, F, M to 42nd St.* ✛ *4:E4.*

$
HOTEL

⬚ **The Time Hotel.** One of the neighborhood's first boutique hotels, this spot half a block from the din of Times Square tempers trendiness with a touch of humor. **Pros:** acclaimed and popular Serafina restaurant downstairs; surprisingly quiet for Times Square location; good turndown service. **Cons:** decor makes the rooms a little dated; service is inconsistent; water pressure is lacking. **TripAdvisor:** "the best location," "vibrant," "close to perfection." Ⓢ *Rooms from: $275* ✉ *224 W. 49th St., between Broadway and 8th Ave., Midtown West* ☎ *212/246–5252, 877/846–3692* ⊕ *www.thetimeny.com* ⤳ *164 rooms, 29 suites* ⦿⧘ *No meals* Ⓜ *1, C, E to 50th St.* ✛ *4:C3.*

$$
HOTEL

⬚ **W Times Square.** Although it opened back in 2001, the W Times Square still stands out in the the craziness of Time Square, thanks to its iconic, 57-story exterior—and if you want to be in the thick of the action, this is a fun place to stay. **Pros:** bustling nightlife and happy-hour scene; sleek rooms. **Cons:** if you want quiet, head elsewhere; no bathtubs in the smaller rooms. **TripAdvisor:** "fine views," "most helpful staff," "comfortable stay." Ⓢ *Rooms from: $329* ✉ *1567 Broadway, at W. 47th St., Midtown West* ☎ *212/930–7400, 877/946–8357* ⊕ *www. whotels.com* ⤳ *466 rooms, 43 suites* ⦿⧘ *No meals* Ⓜ *1, 2, 3, 7, N, Q, R, S to 42nd St./Times Sq.* ✛ *4:C3.*

$$
HOTEL

⬚ **Warwick.** This grande dame was built by William Randolph Hearst for his mistress, Hollywood actress Marion Davies and it's hosted many from Tinseltown since then, including Cary Grant in the Presidential Suite for 12 years. **Pros:** excellent restaurant and bar; historic property; spacious suites. **Cons:** some rooms could use a refresh; no a/c in the hallways. **TripAdvisor:** "charming," "good accommodation," "wonderful customer service." Ⓢ *Rooms from: $299* ✉ *65 W. 54th St., at 6th Ave., Midtown West* ☎ *212/247–2700, 800/223–4099* ⊕ *www. warwickhotelny.com* ⤳ *359 rooms, 66 suites* ⦿⧘ *No meals* Ⓜ *E, M to 57th St.; N, Q, R, W to 57th St.* ✛ *4:D2.*

$
HOTEL
☾

⬚ **Wellington Hotel.** A few blocks south of Central Park and Columbus Circle, the Wellington is a good base for visitors who want to see the sights in Midtown and the Upper West Side. **Pros:** central location; chipper, helpful staff; good for big families. **Cons:** Dark, often-small bathrooms; limited breakfast. **TripAdvisor:** "clean," "polite staff," "perfect hotel for a short city break." Ⓢ *Rooms from: $265* ✉ *871 7th Ave., at W. 55th St., Midtown West* ☎ *212/247–3900, 800/652–1212* ⊕ *www. wellingtonhotel.com* ⤳ *515 rooms, 85 suites* ⦿⧘ *Breakfast* Ⓜ *N, Q, R to 57th St.* ✛ *4:C2.*

20

$$ **Westin New York at Times Square.** This giant Midtown hotel has every-
HOTEL thing you'd expect, at fairly reasonable prices, though without much
style. **Pros:** busy Times Square location; big rooms; great gym. **Cons:**
busy Times Square location; small bathroom sinks; some rooms need to
be refreshed. **TripAdvisor:** "convenient and comfortable," "great Wes-
tin service," "ideal location." $ *Rooms from: $319* ✉ *270 W. 43rd St.,
at 8th Ave., Midtown West* ☎ *212/201–2700, 866/837–4183* ⊕ *www.
westinny.com* ↷ *863 rooms, 29 suites* ❑ *No meals* Ⓜ *A, C, E to 42nd
St./Times Sq.* ✛ *4:B4.*

$$ **Yotel.** Look beyond the gimmicks (a luggage-storing robot, the futur-
HOTEL istic white design scheme) of this Midtown West hotel and you'll dis-
Fodor's Choice cover one of New York's best-run, most functional lodgings, though
★ note that it's pretty far west. **Pros:** great value; everything brand-new;
access to West Side piers and Javits Center. **Cons:** rooms may be small
for some; limited luggage storage and hanging space; 10th Avenue may
be stretching "Times Square" a bit far for some. **TripAdvisor:** "very nice
trendy hotel," "outstanding service in an eclectic atmosphere," "great
food." $ *Rooms from: $299* ✉ *570 10th Ave., at 42nd Street, Midtown
West* ☎ *646/449–7700* ↷ *111 rooms, 3 suites* ❑ *Breakfast* Ⓜ *A, C, E
to 42nd St./Times Sq.* ✛ *4:A4.*

UPPER EAST SIDE

$$$$ **The Carlyle, A Rosewood Hotel.** On the well-heeled corner of Madison
HOTEL Avenue and 75th Street, the Carlyle's fusion of venerable elegance and
Manhattan swank calls for the aplomb of entering a Chanel boutique:
walk in chin-high, wallet out, and ready to be impressed. **Pros:** perhaps NYC's best Central Park views; refined service; delightful array
of dining and bar options, great chic shopping in the neighborhood;
great bathtubs. **Cons:** removed from tourist Manhattan; stuffy vibe
may not work for families; every room is different, limiting consistency.
TripAdvisor: "classic hotel with excellent service," "shabby without
the chic," "proper old-fashioned excellence." $ *Rooms from: $800*
✉ *35 E. 76th St., between Madison and Park Aves., Upper East Side*
☎ *212/744–1600* ⊕ *www.thecarlyle.com* ↷ *124 rooms, 64 suites* ❑ *No
meals* Ⓜ *6 to 77th St.* ✛ *5:F3.*

$ **The Franklin.** The best luxury boutique hotel north of 57th Street, the
HOTEL Franklin, in a nine-story town house, is a gem nestled in a decidedly
residential neighborhood. **Pros:** neighborhood-y location; free Wi-Fi.
Cons: far from many NYC tourist sights except Museum Mile; small
rooms. **TripAdvisor:** "great little find," "comfortable room," "gorgeous." $ *Rooms from: $279* ✉ *164 E. 87th St., between Lexington and 3rd Aves., Upper East Side* ☎ *212/369–1000, 800/607–4009*
⊕ *www.franklinhotel.com* ↷ *50 rooms* ❑ *Breakfast* Ⓜ *4, 5, 6 to 86th
St.* ✛ *6:G6.*

$$$$ **Hôtel Plaza Athénée.** Positioned unobtrusively by Central Park on the
HOTEL Upper East Side, the Plaza Athénée (now related in name only to its Parisian cousin) makes stellar service a priority, with a personal sit-down
check-in off to the side of the lobby, and extravagant in-room dining
service with an old-world feel: white tablecloths, candles, and flowers
are part of the deal. **Pros:** discerning service; fabulous hotel bar. **Cons:**

lobby can feel dark; Wi-Fi costs extra; expensive. **TripAdvisor:** "very lovely," "amazing location and service," "great accommodations." $ *Rooms from: $965* ✉ *37 E. 64th St., at Madison Ave., Upper East Side* ☎ *212/734–9100, 212/606–4600* ⊕ *www.plaza-athenee.com* ⤴ *117 rooms, 25 suites* ⊚ *Breakfast* Ⓜ *6 to 68th St./Hunter College* ✣ *5:F5.*

$$$ ⚏ **Hotel Wales.** A favorite for in-the-know travelers, the Wales is pleasant if unassuming in a sedate neighbhorhood. **Pros:** on-site fitness facilities; great neighborhood feel; roof garden. **Cons:** the best rooms, with views of Central Park, are still being upgraded in 2012 **TripAdvisor:** "charming," "pleasant small hotel," "elegant." $ *Rooms from: $395* ✉ *1295 Madison Ave., between E. 92nd and E. 93rd Sts., Upper East Side* ☎ *212/876–6000, 212/876–6000* ⊕ *www.waleshotel.com* ⤴ *46 rooms, 43 suites* ⊚ *No meals* Ⓜ *4, 5, 6 to 86th St.* ✣ *6:F5.*

HOTEL
☺

$$$$ ⚏ **The Lowell.** This old-money refuge was built as an upscale apartment hotel in the 1920s and it still delivers genteel sophistication and pampering service in an unbeatable location. **Pros:** great location; service with a personal touch; charming decor. **Cons:** cramped lobby; expensive. **TripAdvisor:** "warm and cozy," "charming hotel with great service," "a quiet and professional oasis." $ *Rooms from: $750* ✉ *28 E. 63rd St., between Madison and Park Aves., Upper East Side* ☎ *212/838–1400, 800/221–4444* ⊕ *www.lowellhotel.com* ⤴ *23 rooms, 49 suites* ⊚ *No meals* Ⓜ *4, 5, 6, N, R to 59th St./Lexington Ave.; F to 63rd St./Lexington Ave.* ✣ *5:F6.*

HOTEL

$$$$ ⚏ **The Mark.** If you took every Upper East Side real estate fantasy and condensed it into a modern hotel, you'd come up with the Mark, the perfect representation of uptown panache infused with a healthy dose of downtown chic. **Pros:** hip design; cavernous closet space; great service; scene-making restaurant and bar. **Cons:** expensive; limited budget-dining options in neighborhood. **TripAdvisor:** "very comfortable," "epitome of chic," "first class all the way." $ *Rooms from: $650* ✉ *25 E. 77th St., at Madison Ave., Upper East Side* ☎ *212/744–4300* ⊕ *www.themarkhotel.com* ⤴ *100 rooms* ⊚ *No meals* Ⓜ *6 to 77th St./Lexington Ave.* ✣ *5:F2.*

HOTEL
Fodor's Choice
★

20

UPPER WEST SIDE

$ ⚏ **The Empire Hotel.** In a prime Upper West Side spot, the sophisticated Empire Hotel attracts locals for the breathtaking views from the rooftop pool and lounge area, underneath the hotel's iconic red neon sign, while guests appreciate the rooms, which are a comfortable and chic escape from the bustle of the city. **Pros:** great location next to Lincoln

HOTEL

Lodging Alternatives

APARTMENT RENTALS VS. SUITE HOTELS

For your trip to New York, you may want a little more space than the city's typically tiny hotel rooms provide. Some travelers consider apartment rentals, but we recommend hotel suites instead. Why? First, apartment rentals of less than 30 days are now—with some very limited exceptions—illegal in New York City. Furthermore, apartment-rental scams are prevalent. In some published reports, potential guests have arrived to find that the apartment they rented does not exist, or that they are paying for an illegal sublet. In some cases, travelers have lost their deposit money, or their prepaid rent (note: never wire money to an individual's account).

There are a few reputable providers of short-term rentals, *noted below*. But many Fodorites have turned to suite hotels and bed-and-breakfasts with apartmentlike accommodations to guard themselves from possible scams. We've noted some of their most enthusiastic recommendations.

Local rental agencies that arrange rentals of furnished apartments:

Abode Limited *800/835–8880, 212/472–2000* ⊕ *www.abodenyc.com.*

Manhattan Getaways ☎ *212/956–2010* ⊕ *www.manhattangetaways. com.*

Suite suggestions from **Fodor's Forums** (⊕ *www.fodors.com/forums*):

"For a week or less, there's no need to risk being scammed or renting something illegal by renting a private apt. There are *loads* of suite hotels and B&Bs at all price levels that will provide the space and convenience of an apartment, many with the amenities of a hotel including the ability to be able to read reviews of them before you book and know what you're getting. **Affinia** (⊕ *www.Affinia.com*) is a group of seven suite hotels at various prices that's well regarded. **Milburn Hotel** (⊕ *www.milburnhotel.com*) and the **Salisbury Hotel** (⊕ *www. nycsalisbury.com*) are some of the more popular independent budget options." —mclaurie

BED-AND-BREAKFASTS

B&Bs booked through a service may be either hosted (you're the guest in someone's quarters) or unhosted (you have full use of someone's vacated apartment, including kitchen privileges). Reservation services:

Bed-and-Breakfast Network of New York ✉ *134 W. 32nd St., Suite 602, between 6th and 7th Aves.* ☎ *212/645–8134, 800/900–8134* ⊕ *www.bedandbreakfastnetwork.com.*

City Lights Bed-and-Breakfast ☎ *212/737–7049* ⊕ *www. citylightsbedandbreakfast.com.*

"**West Eleventh** (⊕ *www.westeleventh.com*) and **Abingdon Guest House** (⊕ *www.abingdonguesthouse. com*) are two of many B&Bs in the village with some charm, but are only good for two people." —mclaurie

"Also try **B&B Manhattan** (⊕ *www. bandbmanhattan.com*) which has very nice studio and 1-bed apartments in Chelsea and GV. A friend stayed with them last year and liked it a lot." —tomassocroccante

Center and just blocks from Central Park; beautiful rooftop pool and bar; nice turndown service. **Cons:** rooftop bar brings lots of foot traffic through hotel lobby, plus noise to some rooms; some rooms could use a refresh; bathrooms are nicely designed but tiny; pool is quite small. **TripAdvisor:** "great staff," "excellent location," "hip hotel." ⑤ *Rooms from: $229* ✉ *44 W. 63rd St., at Columbus Ave., Upper West Side, New York* ☎ *212/265–7401* ⊕ *www.empirehotelnyc.com* ⟿ *50 suites, 370 rooms* ⦿ *No meals* Ⓜ *1, A, B, C to 59th St./Columbus Circle* ✛ *5:C5.*

$$
HOTEL

▦ **The Excelsior Hotel.** Directly across the street from the American Museum of Natural History, this well-kept, old-school spot is comfortable but has occasionally inconsistent staff. **Pros:** excellent neighborhoody Upper West Side location near Central Park; foodie mecca Zabar's, and burger joint Shake Shack; tranquil environment. **Cons:** spotty front-desk staff; rooms are inconsistent; Wi-Fi is not free. **TripAdvisor:** "fantastic location," "beautiful old hotel," "comfortable room." ⑤ *Rooms from: $329* ✉ *45 W. 81st St., between Central Park W and Columbus Ave., Upper West Side, New York* ☎ *212/362–9200, 212/362–9200* ⊕ *www.excelsiorhotelny.com* ⟿ *118 rooms, 80 suites* ⦿ *No meals* Ⓜ *B, C to 81st St.* ✛ *5:C2.*

$
HOTEL

▦ **Hotel Beacon.** A neighborhood favorite for a reason, the Upper West Side's best buy for the price is three blocks from Central Park, 10 blocks from Lincoln Center, and footsteps from the neighborhood's best gourmet grocery stores—Zabar's, Fairway, and Citarella. **Pros:** kitchenettes in all rooms; heart of UWS location; affordable; great service. **Cons:** rooms emphasize comfort over style; gym passes to local Equinox $20/day per guest. **TripAdvisor:** "like having your own Manhattan apartment," "first class all the way," "brilliant hotel." ⑤ *Rooms from: $245* ✉ *2130 Broadway, at W. 75th St., Upper West Side, New York* ☎ *212/787–1100, 800/572–4969* ⊕ *www.beaconhotel.com* ⟿ *134 rooms, 133 suites* ⦿ *No meals* Ⓜ *1, 2, 3 to 72nd St.* ✛ *5:A3.*

$$
HOTEL

▦ **The Lucerne.** Service is the strong suit at this landmark-faceded hotel, whose exterior has more pizzazz than the predictable guest rooms decorated with their dark-wood reproduction furniture and chintz bedspreads. **Pros:** free Wi-Fi; clean; great gym; close to Central Park. **Cons:** inconsistent room size; some guests report uncomfortable pillows. **TripAdvisor:** "Midtown chic," "nice room," "luxurious stay." ⑤ *Rooms from: $299* ✉ *201 W. 79th St., at Amsterdam Ave., Upper West Side, New York* ☎ *212/875–1000, 800/492–8122* ⊕ *www.thelucernehotel.com* ⟿ *142 rooms, 42 suites* ⦿ *No meals* Ⓜ *1 to 79th St.* ✛ *5:A2.*

20

$
HOTEL

▦ **On the Ave Hotel.** At this tranquil Upper West Side property just off Broadway, decor is tasteful and modern and service is purposeful and professional. **Pros:** great dining options; excellent value. **Cons:** small charges add up; location not ideal for all NYC visitors. **TripAdvisor:** "wonderful hotel," "pleasant surprise," "great time on the West side." ⑤ *Rooms from: $259* ✉ *2178 Broadway, at W. 77th St., Upper West Side, New York* ☎ *800/509–7598* ⊕ *www.ontheave-nyc.com* ⟿ *250 rooms, 32 suites* ⦿ *No meals* Ⓜ *1 to 79th St.* ✛ *5:A3.*

$$$$
HOTEL

▦ **Trump International Hotel and Towers.** This iconic New York property with incomparable views of Central Park has interior design and decor—much conceived with the help of the Donald's equally famous daughter, Ivanka—in line with the rest of the property's stellar standards for service and attention to detail. **Pros:** fine service; stellar views; discerning treatment. **Cons:** expensive. **TripAdvisor:** "location and luxury," "amazing friendly service," "a quiet home in the city." ⑤ *Rooms from: $825* ⊠ *1 Central Park W, between W. 59th and W. 60th Sts., Upper West Side, New York* ☎ *212/586–8422, 888/448–7867* ⊕ *www.trumpintl.com* ⤳ *33 rooms, 143 suites* ⦿ *No meals* Ⓜ *1, A, B, C, D to 59th St./Columbus Circle* ⊕ *5:C6.*

HARLEM

$ 🖼 **Aloft Harlem.** A reasonably priced option in an increasingly popular
HOTEL area of Harlem (Marcus Samuelsson's hot Red Rooster restaurant is within walking distance), this branch of the Aloft chain delivers with cheerful service and a fun atmosphere, once you get past the confusing front entrance. **Pros:** good room size for the price; convenient to subways, ever-increasing local shopping, and dining options. **Cons:** rooms have minimal space for hanging clothes; rooms get some streeet noise. **TripAdvisor:** "awesome hotel and staff," "great service," "trendy." ⑤ *Rooms from: $199* ⊠ *2296 Frederick Douglass Blvd., between W. 124th and W. 125th Sts., Harlem, New York* ☎ *212/749–4000* ⊕ *www.aloftharlem.com* ⤳ *124 rooms* ⦿ *No meals* Ⓜ *A, B, C, D to 125th St.* ⊕ *6:B1.*

Travel Smart
New York City

WORD OF MOUTH

"When riding the subways go to the first car and look through the window in front door. Kids and adults like watching the tracks, lights, and stations zip by."

—Aduchamp1

GETTING HERE AND AROUND

New York City packs a staggering range of sights and activities into the 322 square miles of its five boroughs. You'll probably want to focus most of your visit in Manhattan, but with more time, taking a trip to the "outer" boroughs (meaning Brooklyn, Queens, the Bronx, and Staten Island) is worthwhile.

If you're flying into one of the three major airports that service New York—John F. Kennedy (JFK), LaGuardia, or Newark, which is in New Jersey—pick your mode of transportation for getting to Manhattan before your plane lands. The route tourists typically take is to hire a car or wait in the taxi line, but those aren't necessarily the best choices, especially if arriving during rush hour. Public transportation is inexpensive and should be considered, especially if you are traveling light and without young children.

Once you're in Manhattan, getting around can be a breeze when you get the hang of the subway system. When not in a rush, just walk—it's the best way to discover the true New York. Not quite sure where you are or how to get where you're headed? Ask a local. You may be surprised at how friendly the city's inhabitants are, debunking their reputation for rudeness. In the same getting-there-is-half-the-fun spirit, find water, land, and air journeys to see the city from a whole new perspective.

▌ AIR TRAVEL

Generally, more international flights go in and out of John F. Kennedy Airport, more domestic flights go in and out of LaGuardia Airport, and Newark Airport serves both domestic and international travelers.

Airlines and Airports **Airline and Airport Links.com** (⊕ *www.airlineandairportlinks.com*) has links to many of the world's airlines and airports.

Airline Security Issues **The Transportation Security Administration** (⊕ *www.tsa.gov*) has answers for almost every question that might come up.

AIRPORTS

The major air gateways to New York City are LaGuardia Airport (LGA) and JFK International Airport (JFK) in the borough of Queens, and Newark Liberty International Airport (EWR) in New Jersey.

■ TIP→ Long layovers don't have to be only about sitting around or shopping. These days they can be about burning off vacation calories. Check out www.airportgyms.com for lists of health clubs that are in or near many U.S. and Canadian airports.

Airport Information **JFK International Airport** ☎ *718/244–4444* ⊕ *www.jfkairport. com*. **LaGuardia Airport** ☎ *718/533–3400* ⊕ *www.laguardiaairport.com*. **Newark Liberty International Airport** ☎ *973/961–6000, 888/397–4636* ⊕ *www.newarkairport.com*.

TRANSFERS—CAR SERVICES

Car services can be a great deal because the driver will often meet you on the concourse or in the baggage-claim area and help you with your luggage. The flat rates and tolls are often comparable to taxi fares, but some car services will charge for parking and waiting time at the airport. To eliminate these expenses, other car services require that you telephone their dispatcher when you land so they can send the next available car to pick you up. New York City Taxi and Limousine Commission rules require that all car services be licensed and pick up riders only by prior arrangement; if possible, call 24 hours in advance for reservations, or at least a half day before your flight's departure. Drivers of nonlicensed vehicles (gypsy cabs) often solicit fares outside the terminal in baggage-claim areas. Don't take them: you run the risk of an unsafe ride, and you'll definitely pay more than the going rate.

⇨ *For phone numbers, see Taxi Travel.*

TRANSFERS — TAXIS AND SHUTTLES

Outside the baggage-claim area at each of New York's major airports are taxi stands where a uniformed dispatcher helps passengers find taxis (⇨ *Taxi Travel*). Cabs are not permitted to pick up fares anywhere else in the arrivals area, so if you want a taxi, take your place in line. Shuttle services generally pick up passengers from a designated spot along the curb.

New York Airport Service runs buses between JFK and LaGuardia airports, and buses from those airports to Grand Central Terminal, Port Authority Bus Terminal, Penn Station, Bryant Park, and hotels between 23rd and 63rd streets in Manhattan. Fares cost between $12 and $15 one-way and $21 to $27 round-trip. Buses operate from 6:05 am to 11 pm from the airport; between 5 am and 10 pm going to the airport.

SuperShuttle vans travel to and from Manhattan to JFK, LaGuardia, and Newark. These blue vans will stop at your home, office, or hotel. There are courtesy phones at the airports. For travel to the airport, the company recommends that you make your request 24 hours in advance. Fares range from $15 to $23 per person. ■TIP→ A shuttle is less expensive than a cab, but factor in extra time for the shuttle's other pick-ups/drop-offs along the way.

Shuttle Service **New York Airport Service** ☎ *718/875-8200* ⊕ *www.nyairportservice. com.* **SuperShuttle** ☎ *800/258-3826* ⊕ *www. supershuttle.com.*

TRANSFERS FROM JFK INTERNATIONAL AIRPORT

Taxis charge a flat fee of $45 plus tolls (which may be as much as $6) to Manhattan only, and take 35–60 minutes. Prices are roughly $20–$55 for trips to most other locations in New York City. You should also tip the driver.

JFK's clean and fast AirTrain ($5) connects JFK Airport to the New York City Subway and the Long Island Railroad (LIRR)—both of which will take you to Manhattan. The monorail system runs 24 hours. Take it from your terminal at JFK to Howard Beach Station, where you will find the A subway train to take you through Brooklyn and into Manhattan. Alternately, take the AirTrain to Jamaica Station/Sutphin Blvd. to catch either the E subway train, which goes through Queens to Midtown Manhattan, or the LIRR to Queens and Manhattan's Penn Station. ■TIP→ Not sure which train to take? Check Hopstop.com for the best route to your destination. Travel between JFK and Midtown Manhattan via the A or E trains takes less than an hour and costs $2.25 in subway fare plus $5 for the AirTrain. The LIRR travels between Penn Station and JFK in around 30 minutes, for a total cost of about $13. When traveling from Manhattan to the Howard Beach station, be sure to take the A train marked "Far Rockaway" or "Rockaway Park," not "Lefferts Boulevard."

JFK Transfer Information **AirTrain JFK** ☎ *718/244-4444* ⊕ *www.airtrainjfk.com.* **Long Island Railroad** ⊠ *Queens* ☎ *718/217-5477* ⊕ *www.mta.info/lirr/.*

TRANSFERS FROM LAGUARDIA AIRPORT

Taxis cost $21–$30 plus tip and tolls (which may be as high as $6) to most destinations in New York City, and take at least 20–40 minutes.

For $2.25 (pay with a Metrocard or exact change only) you can ride the M-60 public bus to 106th Street and Broadway on Manhattan's Upper West Side, with connections en route to the Q-48 bus (which will take you to the Main Street subway station in Queens, where you can transfer to the 7 train) and several New York City Subway lines (where you can catch the N, Q, 2, 3, 4, 5, 6, A, B, C, D trains). Allow at least 90 minutes for the entire trip to Midtown.

TRANSFERS FROM NEWARK AIRPORT

Taxis to Manhattan cost $50–$70 plus tolls and tip and take 20 to 45 minutes. "Share and Save" group rates are available for up to four passengers between 8 am and midnight—make arrangements with the airport's taxi dispatcher. If you're heading to the airport from Manhattan, there's a $15 surcharge on top of the normal taxi rate.

AirTrain Newark, an elevated light rail system that connects passengers from their airline terminal to New Jersey Transit and Amtrak trains at the Newark Liberty International Airport Station, is an efficient and low-cost way to get to New York City. Total travel time to Penn Station in Manhattan is approximately 30 minutes and costs $12.50. AirTrain runs every 3 minutes from 5 am to midnight and every 15 minutes from midnight to 5 am.

Budget-conscious travelers can take the AirTrain to Newark's Penn Station (which takes five minutes) and then connect to a PATH train, a rail link between the West Side of New York City and New Jersey urban communities, which run to Manhattan 24 hours a day. PATH trains run every 10 minutes on weekdays, every 15 to 30 minutes on weeknights and weekends. After stopping at Christopher Street, one line travels along 6th Avenue, making stops at West 9th Street, West 14th Street, West 23rd Street, and West 33rd Street. Other PATH trains connect Newark Penn Station with the World Trade Center site. PATH train fare is $2.

Coach USA with Olympia Trails buses leave for Grand Central Terminal and Penn Station in Manhattan about every 15 to 30 minutes until midnight. The trip takes roughly 45 minutes, and the fare is $16. Headed from the Port Authority or Grand Central Terminal to Newark, buses run every 20 to 30 minutes. The trip takes 55 to 65 minutes

Newark Airport Information AirTrain Newark ☎ 888/397-4636 ⊕ www.panynj. gov/airports/ewr-airtrain.html. **Coach USA** ☎ 877/894-9155 ⊕ www.coachusa.com. **PATH Trains** ☎ 800/234-7284 ⊕ www.panynj.gov/ path.

TRANSFERS BETWEEN AIRPORTS

There are several transportation options for connecting to and from area airports including shuttles, AirTrain and mass transportation, and car service or taxi. New York Airport Service runs buses between JFK and LaGuardia airports. AirTrain provides detailed, up-to-the-minute recorded information on how to reach your destination from any of New York's airports. Note that if you arrive after midnight at any airport, you may wait a long time for a taxi. Consider calling a car service, as there is no shuttle service at that time.

Contacts AirTrain ☎ 800/247-7433 ⊕ www. panynj.gov/airtrain.

▌ BOAT TRAVEL

The Staten Island Ferry runs across New York Harbor between Whitehall Street next to Battery Park in Lower Manhattan and St. George terminal in Staten Island. The free 25-minute ride gives you a view of the Financial District skyscrapers, the Statue of Liberty, and Ellis Island.

New York Water Taxi, in addition to serving commuters, shuttles tourists to the city's many waterfront attractions between the West and East sides and Lower Manhattan (including the 9/11 Memorial), the South Street Seaport, and Brooklyn's waterfront parks.

The Hop-On/Hop-Off one-day pass ticket is $26; the Hop-On/Hop-Off +9/11 Memorial pass (which allows passengers to visit the 9/11 Memorial as part of their sightseeing package) is also $26.

Information New York Water Taxi (*NYWT*). ☎ 212/742-1969 ⊕ www.nywatertaxi.com. **Staten Island Ferry** ⊕ www.siferry.com.

▌ BUS TRAVEL

Most city buses follow easy-to-understand routes along the Manhattan street grid. Routes go up or down the north–south avenues, or east and west on the major two-way crosstown streets: 96th,

86th, 79th, 72nd, 57th, 42nd, 34th, 23rd, and 14th. Usually bus routes operate 24 hours, but service is infrequent late at night. Traffic jams can make rides maddeningly slow, especially along 5th Avenue in Midtown and the Upper East Side. Certain bus routes provide "limited-stop service" during weekday rush hours, which saves travel time by stopping only at major cross streets and transfer points. A sign posted at the front of the bus indicates that it has limited service; ask the driver whether the bus stops near where you want to go before boarding.

To find a bus stop, look for a light-blue sign (green for a limited bus) on a green pole; bus numbers and routes are listed, with the stop's name underneath.

Bus fare is the same as subway fare: $2.25. MetroCards (⇨ *Public Transportation Travel*) allow you one free transfer between buses or from bus to subway; when using coins on the bus, you can ask the driver for a free transfer coupon, good for one change to an intersecting route. Legal transfer points are listed on the back of the slip. Transfers generally have time limits of two hours.

Route maps and schedules are posted at many bus stops in Manhattan, at major stops throughout the other boroughs, and at MTA.info. Each of the five boroughs of New York has a separate bus map; they're available from some station booths, but rarely on buses. The best places to obtain them are the MTA booth in the Times Square Information Center, the information kiosks in Grand Central Terminal and Penn Station, or at the MTA's website.

Pay your bus fare when you board, with exact change in coins (no pennies, and no change is given) or with a MetroCard.

Most buses that travel outside the city feed into the Port Authority Bus Terminal, on 8th Avenue between West 40th and 42nd streets. You must purchase your ticket at a ticket counter, not from the bus driver, so give yourself enough time to wait in a line. Several bus lines serving northern

New Jersey and Rockland County, New York, make daily stops at the George Washington Bridge Bus Station from 5 am to 1 am. The station is connected to the 175th Street Station on the A line of the subway, which travels down the West Side of Manhattan.

A variety of discount bus services, including BoltBus and Vamoose Bus, offer direct routes from cities such as Philadelphia, Boston, and Washington, D.C., with the majority of destinations lying along the East Coast. These budget options, priced from about $20 one-way, depart from locations throughout the city.

Buses in New York Metropolitan Transit Authority (MTA) Travel Information Line ☎ *511* ⊕ *www.mta.info.*

Buses to New York Adirondack, Pine Hill & New York Trailways ☎ *800/225–6815* ⊕ *www.trailways.com.* BoltBus ☎ *877/265–8287* ⊕ *www.boltbus.com.* Coach ☎ *800/631–8405* ⊕ *www.coachusa.com.* Greyhound Lines Inc. ☎ *800/231–2222* ⊕ *www.greyhound.com.* New Jersey Transit ☎ *973/275–5555* ⊕ *www.njtransit.com.* Vamoose Bus ☎ *877/393–2828* ⊕ *www.vamoosebus.com.*

Bus Stations George Washington Bridge Bus Station ✉ *4211 Broadway, between 178th and 179th Sts., Washington Heights* ☎ *800/221–9903* ⊕ *www.panynj.gov.* The Port Authority of New York and New Jersey ✉ *625 8th Ave., at 42nd St., Midtown West* ☎ *212/564–8484* ⊕ *www.panynj.gov.*

▮ CAR TRAVEL

If you plan to drive into Manhattan, try to avoid the morning and evening rush hours and lunch hour. The deterioration of the bridges to Manhattan, especially those spanning the East River, means that repairs will be ongoing for the next few years. Tune in to traffic reports on the radio (i.e., WCBS 880 or 1010 WINS on the AM radio dial) before you set off, and don't be surprised if a bridge is partially closed or entirely blocked with traffic.

Driving within Manhattan can be a nightmare of gridlocked streets, obnoxious drivers and bicyclists, and seemingly suicidal jaywalkers. Narrow and one-way streets are common, particularly downtown, and can make driving even more difficult. The most congested streets of the city lie between 14th and 59th streets and 3rd and 8th avenues.

GASOLINE

Gas stations are few and far between in Manhattan. If you can, fill up at stations outside the city, where prices are from 10¢ to 50¢ cheaper per gallon. In Manhattan, you can refuel at stations along the West Side Highway and 11th Avenue south of West 57th Street and along East Houston Street. Some gas stations in New York require you to pump your own gas; others provide attendants.

PARKING

Free parking is difficult to find in Midtown and on weekday evenings and weekends in other neighborhoods. If you find a spot on the street, check parking signs carefully, and scour the curb for a faded yellow line, the bane of every driver's existence. Violators may be towed away or ticketed literally within minutes. If you do drive, use your car sparingly in Manhattan. Instead, park it in a guarded parking garage for at least several hours; hourly rates (which can be as much as $23 for two hours) decrease somewhat if a car is left for a significant amount of time. ■TIP→ Best Parking (⊕ www. nyc.bestparking.com) will help you find the cheapest parking-lot options for your visit; search by neighborhood, address, or attraction.

CAR RENTALS

When you reserve a car, ask about cancellation penalties, taxes, drop-off charges (if you're planning to pick up the car in one city and leave it in another), and surcharges (for being under or over a certain age, for additional drivers, or for driving across state or country borders or beyond a specific distance from your point of rental). All these things can add substantially to your costs. Request car seats and extras such as GPS when you book.

Rates are sometimes—but not always—better if you book in advance or reserve through a rental agency's website. There are other reasons to book ahead, though: for popular destinations, during busy times of the year, or to ensure that you get certain types of cars (vans, SUVs, exotic sports cars).

■TIP→ Make sure that a confirmed reservation guarantees you a car. Agencies sometimes overbook, particularly for busy weekends and holiday periods.

Rates in New York City are around $50–$125 a day and $250–$425 a week for an economy car with air-conditioning, automatic transmission, and unlimited mileage. This includes the state tax on car rentals, which is 19.87%. Rental costs are lower just outside New York City, specifically in such places as Hoboken, New Jersey, and Yonkers, New York.

CAR-RENTAL INSURANCE

If you own a car and carry comprehensive car insurance for both collision and liability, your personal auto insurance will probably cover a rental, but read your policy's fine print to be sure. If you don't have auto insurance, then you should probably buy the collision- or loss-damage waiver (CDW or LDW) from the rental company. This eliminates your liability for damage to the car. Some credit cards offer CDW coverage, but it's usually supplemental to your own insurance and rarely covers SUVs, minivans, luxury models, and the like. If your coverage is secondary, you may still be liable for loss-of-use costs from the car-rental company (again, read the fine print). But no credit-card insurance is valid unless you use that card for *all* transactions, from reserving to paying the final bill.

■TIP→ Diners Club offers primary CDW coverage on all rentals reserved and paid for with the card. This means that Diners Club's company—not your own car insurance—pays in case of an accident. It doesn't mean that your car-insurance company won't raise your rates once it discovers you had an accident.

You may also be offered supplemental liability coverage. The car-rental company is required to carry a minimal level of liability coverage insuring all renters, but it's rarely enough to cover claims in a really serious accident if you're at fault. Your own auto-insurance policy will protect you if you own a car; if you don't, you have to decide whether you are willing to take the risk.

U.S. rental companies sell CDWs and LDWs for about $20 to $40 a day; supplemental liability is usually more than $10 a day. The car-rental company may offer you all sorts of other policies, but they're rarely worth the cost. Personal accident insurance, which is basic hospitalization coverage, is an especially egregious rip-off if you already have health insurance.

■ TIP→ You can decline the insurance from the rental company and purchase it through a third-party provider such as Travel Guard (*www.travelguard.com*)—$9 per day for $35,000 of coverage. That's sometimes just under half the price of the CDW offered by some car-rental companies.

▌PUBLIC TRANSPORTATION

When it comes to getting around New York, you have your pick of transportation in almost every neighborhood. The subway and bus networks are extensive, especially in Manhattan, although getting across town can take some extra maneuvering. If you're not pressed for time, take a public bus (⇨ *Bus Travel*); they generally are slower than subways, but you can also see the city as you travel. Yellow cabs (⇨ *Taxi Travel*) are abundant, except during the evening rush hour, when many drivers' shifts change. Like a taxi ride, the subway (⇨ *Subway Travel*) is a true New York City experience; it's also often the quickest way to get around. But

New York is really a walking town, and depending on the time of day, the weather, and your destination, hoofing it could be the easiest and most enjoyable option.

During weekday rush hours (from 7:30 am to 9:30 am and 5 pm to 7 pm) avoid the Midtown area if you can—subways and streets will be jammed, and travel time on buses and taxis can easily double.

Subway and bus fares are $2.50 for a single ride ticket or $2.25 per ride if you buy a MetroCard for two or more rides or pay with coins on the bus. Reduced fares are available for senior citizens and people with disabilities during nonrush hours.

You pay for mass transit with a Metro-Card, a plastic card with a magnetic strip. As you swipe the card through a subway turnstile or insert it in a bus's card reader, the cost of the fare is automatically deducted. With the MetroCard, you can transfer free from bus to subway, subway to bus, or bus to bus, within a two-hour period.

MetroCards are sold at all subway stations and at some stores—look for an "Authorized Sales Agent" sign. The MTA sells two kinds of MetroCards: unlimited-ride and pay-per-ride. Seven-day unlimited-ride MetroCards ($29) allow bus and subway travel for a week. If you will ride more than 13 times, this is the card to get.

Unlike unlimited-ride cards, pay-per-ride MetroCards can be shared between riders. (Unlimited-ride MetroCards can be used only once at the same station or bus route in an 18-minute period.)

You can buy or add money to an existing MetroCard at a MetroCard vending machine, available at most subway station entrances (usually near the station booth). The machines accept major credit cards and ATM or debit cards. Many also accept cash, but note that the maximum amount of change they will return is $6.

Schedule and Route Information **Metropolitan Transit Authority (MTA) Travel Information Line.** Metropolitan Transit Authority (MTA) Travel Information Line ☎ 511 ⊕ *www.mta.info.*

■ SUBWAY TRAVEL

The subway system operates on more than 840 miles of track 24 hours a day and serves nearly all the places you're likely to visit. It's cheaper than a cab, and during the workweek it's often faster than either taxis or buses. The trains are well lighted and air-conditioned. Still, the New York subway is hardly problem-free. Many trains are crowded, the older ones are noisy, the air-conditioning can break, and platforms can be dingy and damp. Homeless people sometimes take refuge from the elements by riding the trains, and panhandlers head there for a captive audience. Although trains usually run frequently, especially during rush hours, you never know when some incident somewhere on the line may stall traffic. In addition, subway construction sometimes causes delays or limitation of service, especially on weekends.

Most subway entrances are at street corners and are marked by lampposts with an illuminated Metropolitan Transit Authority (MTA) logo or globe-shape green or red lights—green means the station is open 24 hours and red means the station closes at night (though colors don't always correspond to reality). Subway lines are designated by numbers and letters, such as the 3 line or the A line. Some lines run "express" and skip stops, and others are "locals" and make all stops. Each station entrance has a sign indicating the lines that run through the station. Some entrances are also marked "uptown only" or "downtown only." Before entering subway stations, read the signs carefully. One of the most frequent mistakes visitors make is taking the train in the wrong direction. Maps of the full subway system are posted in every train car and usually on the subway platform (though these are sometimes out of date). You can usually pick up free maps at station booths.

For the most up-to-date information on subway lines, call the MTA's Travel Information Center or visit its website. The website Hopstop is a good source for figuring out the best line to take to reach your destination. Alternatively, ask a station agent.

You can transfer between subway lines an unlimited number of times at any of the numerous stations where lines intersect. If you use a MetroCard (⇨ *Public Transportation*) to pay your fare, you can also transfer to intersecting MTA bus routes for free. Such transfers generally have time limits of two hours.

Pay your subway fare at the turnstile, using a MetroCard bought at the station booth or from a vending machine.

Subway Information **Hopstop** ⊕ *www. hopstop.com.* **Metropolitan Transportation Authority (MTA) Travel Information Line** ☎ *511* ⊕ *www.mta.info.* **MTA Lost Property Office** ☎ *511.*

■ TAXI TRAVEL

Yellow cabs are in abundance almost everywhere in Manhattan, cruising the streets looking for fares. They are usually easy to hail on the street or from a cabstand in front of major hotels, though finding one at rush hour or in the rain can take some time. Even if you're stuck in a downpour or at the airport, do not accept a ride from a gypsy cab. If a cab is not yellow and does not have a numbered aqua-color plastic medallion riveted to the hood, you could be putting yourself in danger by getting into the car.

You can see whether a taxi is available by checking its rooftop light. If the center panel is lighted and the side panels are dark, the driver is ready to take passengers. Once the meter is engaged (and if it isn't, alert your driver; you'll seldom benefit from negotiating an off-the-record ride), the fare is $2.50 just for entering the vehicle and 40¢ for each unit thereafter. A unit is defined as either 0.20 mile when the cab's cruising at 6 mph or faster or as 60 seconds when the cab is either not moving or moving at less than 16 mph. A 50¢ night surcharge is added between 8 pm and 6 am, and a much-maligned $1 weekday surcharge is tacked on between 4 pm and 8 pm.

One taxi can hold a maximum of four passengers (an additional passenger under the age of seven is allowed if the child sits on someone's lap). There is no charge for extra passengers. You must pay any bridge or tunnel tolls incurred during your trip (a driver will usually pay the toll himself to keep moving quickly, but that amount will be added to the fare when the ride is over). Taxi drivers expect a 15% to 20% tip.

To avoid unhappy taxi experiences, try to know where you want to go and how to get there before you hail a cab. ■ TIP→ Know the specific cross streets of your destination (for instance, "5th Avenue and 42nd Street") before you enter a cab; a quick call to your destination will give you cross-street information, as will a glance at a map. Also, speak simply and clearly to make sure the driver has heard you correctly. When you leave the cab, remember to take your receipt. It includes the cab's medallion number, which can help you track the cabbie down in the event that you lose your possessions in the cab or if, after the fact, you want to report an unpleasant ride.

Taxis can be extremely difficult (if not impossible) to find in many parts of Brooklyn, Queens, the Bronx, and Staten Island, but a proposal to bring legal street hail service to all five boroughs may soon change that. In the meantime, you may have no choice but to call a car service. Always determine the fee beforehand when using a car service sedan; a 10%–15% tip is customary above that.

Taxi Companies **Carmel Car Service**
☎ 212/666-6666, 866/666-6666 ⊕ www. carmelcarservice.com. **Dial 7 Car Service**
☎ 212/777-7777 ⊕ www.dial7.com. **London Towncars** ⊠ Long Island City ☎ 212/988-9700, 800/221-4009 ⊕ www.londontowncars. com.

▌ TRAIN TRAVEL

⇨ For information about traveling by subway within New York City, see Subway Travel.

Metro-North Railroad trains take passengers from Grand Central Terminal to points north of New York City, both in New York State and Connecticut. Amtrak trains from across the United States arrive at Penn Station. For trains from New York City to Long Island and New Jersey, take the Long Island Railroad and New Jersey Transit, respectively; both operate from Penn Station. The PATH trains offer service to Newark, Jersey City, and Hoboken. All of these trains generally run on schedule, although occasional delays occur.

Information **Amtrak** ☎ 800/872-7245 ⊕ www.amtrak.com. **Long Island Rail Road** ☎ 511 ⊕ www.mta.info/lirr. **Metro-North Railroad** ☎ 212/532-4900 ⊕ www.mta.info/ mnr. **New Jersey Transit** ☎ 973/275-5555 ⊕ www.njtransit.com. **PATH** ☎ 800/234-7284 ⊕ www.pathrail.com.

Train Stations **Grand Central Terminal** ⊠ 87 E. 42nd St., at Park Ave., Midtown East ⊕ www. grandcentralterminal.com. **Penn Station** ⊠ W. 31st to W. 33rd Sts., between 7th and 8th Aves., Midtown West.

ESSENTIALS

■ COMMUNICATIONS

INTERNET

You can check your email or surf the Internet at cafés, copy centers, libraries, and most hotels. By far the best equipped and probably most convenient is Cyber Café in Times Square, which has dozens of computers plus scanners, color printers, and camera chip readers; it's open from 8 am to 11 pm on weekdays and 11 am to 11 pm on weekends. The organization NYCwireless keeps track of free Wi-Fi hot spots in the New York area, while websites like JiWire and HotSpotr help you find Wi-Fi hot spots in cafés, hotels, libraries, parks, and other locations throughout the city.

Contacts **JiWire** ⊕ www.jiwire.com. **NYCwireless** ⊕ www.nycwireless.net.

Internet Cafés **Cybercafe** ✉ 250 W. 49th St., between 8th Ave. and Broadway, Midtown West ☎ 212/333–4109 ⊕ www.cyber-cafe.com.

Other Internet Locations **New York Public Library–Mid-Manhattan Library** ✉ 455 5th Ave., at E. 40th St., Midtown East ☎ 212/340–0863 ⊕ www.nypl.org.

■ DISABILITIES AND ACCESSIBILITY

New York has come a long way in making life easier for people with disabilities. At most street corners curb cuts allow wheelchairs to roll along unimpeded. Many restaurants, shops, and movie theaters with step-up entrances have wheelchair ramps. And though some New Yorkers may rush past those in need of assistance, you'll find plenty of people who are more than happy to help you get around. Hospital Audiences maintains a website with information on the accessibility of many landmarks and attractions. Big Apple Greeter's Access Program offers tours of New York City tailored to visitors' personal preferences. If you need to rent a wheelchair while you are in New York, Big Apple Mobility will deliver to your hotel (or other preferred location) for a $20 fee.

Local Resources **Big Apple Greeter** ☎ 212/669–8519 ⊕ www.bigapplegreeter.org Ⓜ 4, 5, 6, to Brooklyn Bridge-City Hall. **Big Apple Mobility** ☎ 212/662–4548 ⊕ www. bigapplemobility.com. **Hospital Audiences** ✉ 548 Broadway, 3rd Fl ☎ 212/575–7676 ⊕ www.hospaud.org.

LODGING

Despite the Americans with Disabilities Act, the definition of accessibility seems to differ from hotel to hotel. Some properties may be accessible by ADA standards for people with mobility problems but not for people with hearing or vision impairments, for example.

If you have mobility problems, ask for the lowest floor on which accessible services are offered. If you have a hearing impairment, check whether the hotel has devices to alert you visually to the ring of the telephone, a knock at the door, and a fire/emergency alarm. Some hotels provide these devices without charge. Discuss your needs with hotel personnel if this equipment isn't available, so that a staff member can personally alert you in the event of an emergency.

If you're bringing a guide dog, get authorization ahead of time and write down the name of the person with whom you spoke.

RESERVATIONS

When discussing accessibility with an operator or reservations agent, ask hard questions. Are there any stairs, inside *or* out? Are there grab bars next to the toilet *and* in the shower/tub? How wide is the doorway to the room? To the bathroom? For the most extensive facilities meeting the latest legal specifications, opt for newer accommodations. If you reserve through a toll-free number, consider also calling the hotel's local number to confirm the information from the central reservations office. Get confirmation in writing when you can.

SIGHTS AND ATTRACTIONS

Most public facilities in New York City, whether museums, parks, or theaters, are wheelchair-accessible. Some attractions have tours or programs for people with mobility, sight, or hearing impairments.

TRANSPORTATION

Although the city is working to retrofit stations to comply with the ADA, not all stations are accessible. Accessible stations are clearly marked on subway and rail maps. Visitors in wheelchairs will have better success with public buses, all of which have wheelchair lifts and "kneelers" at the front to facilitate getting on and off. Bus drivers will provide assistance.

Reduced fares are available to disabled passengers; if you're paying with cash, you will need to present a Medicare card or Paratransit card. You may also apply for a Temporary Reduced Fare Metrocard in advance of your visit. Visitors to the city are also eligible for the same Access-a-Ride program benefits as New York City residents. Drivers with disabilities may use windshield cards from their own state or Canadian province to park in designated handicapped spaces.

The U.S. Department of Transportation Aviation Consumer Protection Division's online publication *New Horizons: Information for the Air Traveler with a Disability* offers advice for travelers with a disability, and outlines basic rights. Visit Disability.gov for general information.

Information and Complaints **Reduced Fare Metrocard** ☎ 511 ⊕ *www.mta.info/ accessibility/transit.htm.* **U.S. Department of Transportation Aviation Consumer Protection Division** (⊕ *airconsumer.dot.gov/ publications/horizons.htm.*)

▌ GAY AND LESBIAN TRAVEL

Attitudes toward same-sex couples are very tolerant in Manhattan and many parts of Brooklyn. Chelsea, Greenwich Village, and Hell's Kitchen are the most prominently gay neighborhoods, but gay men and lesbians feel right at home almost everywhere. The world's oldest gay-pride parade takes place on 5th Avenue the last Sunday in June.

PUBLICATIONS

For listings of gay events and places, check out *Next* and the *Gay City News,* both distributed free on the street and in many bars and shops throughout Manhattan. Magazines *Paper* and *Time Out New York* have a gay-friendly take on what's happening in the city.

Local Information **Gay & Lesbian Switchboard of NY** ☎ 212/989-0999, 888/843-4564 ⊕ *www.glnh.org.* **Lesbian, Gay, Bisexual & Transgender Community Center** ✉ 208 W. 13th St., between 7th and 8th Aves., Greenwich Village ☎ 212/620-7310 ⊕ *www.gaycenter.org.*

Gay Publications **Gay City News** ☎ 646/452-2502 ⊕ *www.gaycitynews.com.* **Next** ☎ 212/627-0165 ⊕ *www.nextmagazine. com.*

Gay- and Lesbian-Friendly Travel Agencies **Different Roads Travel** ☎ 760/325-6964, 800/429-8747 ✎ *lgernert@tzell.com.* **Flying Dutchmen Travel.** Serves gay and lesbian travelers. ☎ 707/546-9888, 800/225-5759 ⊕ *www.flyingdutchmentravel.com.*

▌ KIDS IN NEW YORK

For listings of children's events, consult *New York* magazine and *Time Out New York Kids.* The Friday *New York Times* Arts section also includes children's activities. Other good sources on happenings for youngsters are the monthly magazines *New York Family* and *NY Metro Parents,* both available free at toy stores, children's museums, and other places where parents and children are found. The website Parents Connect includes listings of what's going on. If you have access to cable television, check the local all-news channel New York 1, where you'll find a spot aired several times daily that covers current and noteworthy children's events. *Fodor's New York City with Kids* (available in bookstores everywhere) can help you plan your days together.

Publications and Websites New York magazine ⊕ *nymag.com/family/kids/*. **NY Metro Parents** ⊕ *www.nymetroparents.com*. **Parents Connect** ⊕ *www.parentsconnect. com*. **Time Out New York Kids** ⊕ *timeoutnewyorkkids.com*.

LODGING

Before you consider using a cot or fold-out couch for your child, ask just how large your hotel room is—New York City rooms tend to be small. Most hotels in New York allow children under a certain age to stay in their parents' room at no extra charge, but others charge for them as extra adults; be sure to find out the cutoff age for children's discounts.

PUBLIC TRANSPORTATION

Children shorter than 44 inches ride for free on MTA buses and subways. If you're pushing a stroller, don't struggle through a subway turnstile; ask the station agent to buzz you through the gate (the attendant will ask you to swipe your MetroCard through the turnstile nearest the gate). Keep a sharp eye on young ones while in the subway; at some stations there is a gap between the train doors and the platform.

▮ MONEY

In New York, it's easy to get swept up in a debt-inducing cyclone of $60-per-person dinners, $100 theater tickets, $20 nightclub covers, and $300 hotel rooms. But one of the good things about the city is that you can spend in some areas and save in others. Within Manhattan, a cup of coffee can cost from 75¢ to $4, a pint of beer from $5 to $8, and a sandwich from $6 to $10. Generally, prices in the outer boroughs are lower than those in Manhattan.

The most generously bequeathed treasure of the city is the arts. The stated admission fee at the Metropolitan Museum of Art is a suggestion; those who can't afford it can donate a lesser amount and not be snubbed. Many other museums in town have special times during which admission is free. The Museum of Modern Art, for instance, is free on Friday 4–8. In summer a handful of free music, theater, and dance performances, as well as films (usually screened outdoors) fill the calendar each day.

Prices throughout this guide are given for adults. Substantially reduced fees are typically available for children, students, and senior citizens.

CREDIT CARDS

The following abbreviations are used: AE, American Express; D, Discover; DC, Diners Club; MC, MasterCard; and V, Visa.

Record all your credit-card numbers—as well as the phone numbers to call if your cards are lost or stolen—in a safe place, so you're prepared should something go wrong. Both MasterCard and Visa have general numbers you can call if your card is lost, but you're better off calling the number of your issuing bank, since MasterCard and Visa usually just transfer you to your bank; your bank's number is usually printed on your card.

Reporting Lost Cards American Express ☎ *800/528–4800 in U.S.* ⊕ *www. americanexpress.com*. **Diners Club** ☎ *800/234–6377* ⊕ *www.dinersclub.com*. **Discover** ☎ *800/347–2683 in U.S.,* ⊕ *www. discovercard.com*. **MasterCard** ☎ *800/627–8372* ⊕ *www.mastercard.com*. **Visa** ☎ *800/847–2911* ⊕ *www.visa.com*.

TRAVELER'S CHECKS AND CARDS

Both Citibank (under the Visa brand) and American Express issue traveler's checks in the United States, but Amex is better known and more widely accepted; you can also avoid hefty surcharges by cashing Amex checks at Amex offices. Whatever you do, keep track of all the serial numbers in case the checks are lost or stolen.

Contacts American Express ☎ *800/528–4800* ⊕ *www.americanexpress.com.*

▌RESTROOMS

Seinfeld fans might recall George Costanza's claim that if you named any given coordinates in New York City, he could instantly name the closest and most worthy public restroom in the vicinity. Regrettably, unless you're traveling with your own George, public restrooms in New York are few and far between.

If you find yourself in need of a restroom, head for Midtown department stores, museums, or the lobbies of large hotels to find the cleanest bathrooms. Public atriums, such as those at the Citicorp Center and Trump Tower, also provide good public facilities, as do Bryant Park and the many Starbucks coffee shops in the city (although it has been reported that—due to lines and maintenance costs—many Starbucks are converting their public restrooms to employee-only facilities). If you're in the area, the Times Square Information Center, on Broadway between 46th and 47th streets, can be a godsend.

Restaurants usually allow only their patrons to use their restrooms, but if you're dressed well and look as if you belong, you can often just sail right in. And if you're too self-conscious for this brand of nonchalance, just ask the host or hostess nicely. Be aware that cinemas, Broadway theaters, and concert halls have limited amenities, and there are often long lines before performances and during intermissions.

Find a Loo The Bathroom Diaries. The Bathroom Diaries is flush with unsanitized info on restrooms the world over—each one located, reviewed, and rated. ⊕ *www. thebathroomdiaries.com.*

▌SAFETY

New York City is one of the safest large cities in the country. However, do not let yourself be lulled into a false sense of security. As in any large city, travelers in New York remain particularly easy marks for pickpockets and hustlers.

After the September 11, 2001, terrorist attacks security was heightened throughout the city. Never leave any bags unattended, and expect to have yourself and your possessions inspected thoroughly in such places as airports, sports stadiums, museums, and city buildings.

Ignore the panhandlers on the streets and subways, people who offer to hail you a cab (they often appear at Penn Station, the Port Authority, and Grand Central), and limousine and gypsy-cab drivers who (illegally) offer you a ride.

Keep jewelry out of sight on the street; better yet, leave valuables at home. Don't carry wallets, smartphones, or other gadgets in your back pockets, and make sure bags and purses stay closed.

Avoid deserted blocks in unfamiliar neighborhoods. A brisk, purposeful pace helps deter trouble wherever you go.

The subway runs around the clock and is generally well trafficked until midnight (and until at least 2 am on Friday and Saturday nights), and overall it is very safe. If you do take the subway late at night, ride in the center car, with the conductor, and wait on the center of the platform. Watch out for unsavory characters lurking around the inside or outside of stations.

When waiting for a train, stand far away from the edge of the subway platform, especially when trains are entering or leaving the station. Once the train pulls into the station, avoid empty cars. While on the train don't engage in verbal exchanges with aggressive riders. If a fellow passenger makes you nervous while on the train, trust your instincts and change cars.

When disembarking, stick with the crowd until you reach the street.

Travelers Aid International helps crime victims, stranded travelers, and wayward children, and works closely with the police.

■TIP→ Distribute your cash, credit cards, IDs, and other valuables between a deep front pocket, an inside jacket or vest pocket, and a hidden money pouch. Don't reach for the money pouch once you're in public.

Information **Travelers Aid International** ⊠ *JFK International Airport, Terminal 4, Queens* ☎ *202/546–1127* ⊕ *www.travelersaid.org* ⊠ *Newark International Airport, Terminal B, Newark, New Jersey* ☎ *973/623–5052.*

■ SENIOR-CITIZEN TRAVEL

The Metropolitan Transit Authority (MTA) offers lower fares for passengers 65 and over.

To qualify for age-related discounts, mention your senior-citizen status up front when booking hotel reservations (not when checking out). Be sure to have identification on hand. When renting a car, ask about promotional car-rental discounts, which can be cheaper than senior-citizen rates.

Educational Programs **Road Scholar** ☎ *800/454–5768, 978/323–4141 international callers, 877/426–2167 TTY* ⊕ *www.roadscholar. org.*

Information **MTA Reduced Fare info** ☎ *511* ⊕ *www.mta.info/nyct/fare/rfindex.htm.*

■ SPORTS AND THE OUTDOORS

The City of New York's Parks & Recreation division lists all of the recreational facilities and activities available through New York's Parks Department. The sports section of *Time Out New York,* sold at most newsstands, lists upcoming events, times, dates, and ticket information.

Contact Information **Department of Parks & Recreation** ☎ *311 in New York City, 212/639–9675* ⊕ *www.nycgovparks.org.*

BASEBALL
The subway will get you directly to stadiums of both New York–area major-league teams. In 2009, the New York Mets moved from Shea Stadium to the neighboring, newly constructed Citi Field, at the next-to-last stop on the 7 train, in Queens; the New York Yankees also got a new home at the new Yankee Stadium. Affiliated with the Mets since 2001, the minor-league Brooklyn Cyclones are named for Coney Island's famous wooden roller coaster. They play 38 home games at KeySpan Park, next to the boardwalk, with views of the Atlantic over the right-field wall and views of historic Astroland over the left-field wall. Most people make a day of it, with time at the beach and amusement rides before an evening game. Take the D, F, or Q subway to the end of the line, and walk one block to the right of the original Nathan's Famous hot dog stand.

For another fun, family-oriented experience, check out the Staten Island Yankees, one of New York's minor-league teams, which warms up many future New York Yankees players. The stadium, a five-minute walk from the Staten Island Ferry terminal, has magnificent panoramic views of Lower Manhattan and the Statue of Liberty.

Contact Information **Brooklyn Cyclones** ⊠ *1904 Surf Ave., at 19th St., Coney Island, Brooklyn* ☎ *718/449–8497* ⊕ *www. brooklyncyclones.com* Ⓜ *D, F, Q to Stillwell Ave.* **Citi Field** ⊠ *Roosevelt Ave. off Grand Central Pkwy., Flushing, Queens* ☎ *718/507–8499* ⊕ *www.mets.com* Ⓜ *7 to Mets/Willets Pt.* **Staten Island Yankees** ⊠ *Richmond County Bank Ballpark at St. George, 75 Richmond Terr., Staten Island* ☎ *718/720–9265* ⊕ *www. siyanks.com.* **Yankee Stadium** ⊠ *161st St. at River Ave., Bronx* ☎ *718/293–6000* ⊕ *www. yankees.com* Ⓜ *B, D, 4 to 161st St.–Yankee Stadium.*

BASKETBALL

The New York Knicks arouse intense hometown passions, which means tickets for home games at Madison Square Garden are hard to come by. At this writing, the New Jersey Nets are scheduled to become the Brooklyn Nets in September 2012; they'll move from their home at the Meadowlands in the Izod Center to Barclays Center of Brooklyn. The men's basketball season runs from late October through April. Try StubHub to score tickets. The New York Liberty, a member of the Women's NBA, had its first season in 1997; some of the team's more high-profile players are already legendary. The season runs from mid-May through August, with home games played at Madison Square Garden.

If the professional games are sold out, try to attend a college game where New York stalwarts Fordham, Hofstra, and St. John's compete against national top 25 teams during invitational tournaments.

Contact Information Brooklyn Nets ☎ 201/935–3900 box office, 800/765–6387 ⊕ www.nba.com/nets. **Madison Square Garden** ✉ 4 Pennsylvania Plaza ☎ 212/465–6741 ⊕ www.thegarden.com. **New York Knicks** ☎ 212/465–5867 ⊕ www.nba.com/knicks. **New York Liberty** ☎ 212/465–6766 tickets, 212/564–9622 fan hotline ⊕ www.wnba.com/liberty.

BICYCLING

Central Park has a 6-mile circular drive with a couple of decent climbs. It's closed to automobile traffic from 10 am to 3 pm (except the southeast portion between 6th Avenue and East 72nd Street) and 7 pm to 7 am on weekdays, and from 7 pm Friday to 7 am Monday. On holidays it's closed to automobile traffic from 7 pm the night before until 7 am the day after.

The bike lane along the Hudson River Park's esplanade parallels the waterfront from West 59th Street south to the esplanade of Battery Park City. The lane also heads north, connecting with the bike path in Riverside Park and the promenade between West 72nd and West 110th streets, and continuing all the way to the George Washington Bridge. A new two-way bike lane was installed in June 2012 along the park's Terrace Drive, a popular route across the park at 72nd Street. From Battery Park it's a quick ride to the Wall Street area, which is deserted on weekends, and over to South Street and a bike lane along the East River.

The 3.3-mile circular drive in Brooklyn's Prospect Park is closed to cars year-round except from 7 am to 9 am and 5 pm to 7 pm on weekdays. It has a long, gradual hill that tops off near the Grand Army Plaza entrance. (Biking around Manhattan streets next to the dense traffic is best left to messengers and seasoned cyclists.)

Bike Rentals Bicycle Rentals at Loeb Boathouse ✉ Midpark near E. 74th St., East 72nd St. & Park Dr. North, Central Park ☎ 212/517–2233 Ⓜ 6 to 68th St./Hunter College. **Bicycles NYC** ✉ 1400 3rd Ave., between E. 79th and E. 80th Sts., Upper East Side ☎ 212/794–2929 ⊕ www.bicyclesnyc.com Ⓜ 4, 5, 6 to 86th St.. **Pedal Pusher Bike Shop** ✉ 1306 2nd Ave., at E. 69th St., Upper East Side ☎ 212/288–5592 ⊕ www.pedalpusherbikeshop.com Ⓜ 6 to 68th St./Hunter College. **Toga Bike Shop** ✉ 110 West End Ave., at W. 64th St., Upper West Side ☎ 212/799–9625 ⊕ www.togabikes.com Ⓜ 1 to 66th St..

GROUP BIKE RIDES

For organized rides with other cyclists, call or email before you come to New York. Bike New York runs a five-borough bike ride in May. The Five Borough Bicycle Club organizes day and weekend rides. The New York Cycle Club sponsors weekend rides for every level of ability. Time's Up!, a nonprofit environmental group, leads free recreational rides at least twice a month for cyclists as well as skaters; the Central Park Moonlight Ride, departing from Columbus Circle at 10 pm the first Friday of every month, is a favorite.

Contact Information Bike New York ☎ 212/870–2080 ⊕ www.bikenewyork.org.

Five Borough Bike Club ☎ *347/688–2925*
⊕ *www.5bbc.org.* **New York Cycle Club**
☎ *212/828–5711* ⊕ *www.nycc.org.* **Time's Up!**
☎ *212/802–8222* ⊕ *times-up.org.*

BOATING AND KAYAKING

Central Park has rowboats (plus one Venetian gondola for glides in the moonlight) on the 22-acre Central Park Lake. Rent your rowboat at Loeb Boathouse, near East 74th Street, from March through October; gondola rides are available only in summer and can be reserved ($30 per half hour). In summer at the Pier 96 Boathouse in Midtown West, you can take a sturdy kayak out for a paddle for free on weekends and weekday evenings from mid-May through mid-October. Beginners learn to paddle in the calmer embayment area closest to shore until they feel ready to venture farther out into open water. More experienced kayakers can partake in the three-hour trips conducted every weekend and on holiday mornings. Because of high demand, there is a lottery to determine who gets to go out each morning; to be entered, you must be at the pier to sign up before 8 am. No reservations are taken in advance. Manhattan Kayak Company gives lessons for all levels and runs trips on the Hudson River between May and late September, including a fun New York After Dark tour for $80.

Contact Information Loeb Boathouse ⊠ *Midpark near E. 74th St., Central Park* ☎ *212/517–2233* ⊕ *www. thecentralparkboathouse.com* Ⓜ *6 to 68th St./ Hunter College.* **Manhattan Kayak Company** ⊠ *The Boathouse, Pier 66, W., 26th St. at 12th Ave., Chelsea* ☎ *212/924–1788* ⊕ *www. manhattankayak.com* Ⓜ *C, E to 23rd St..* **Pier 96 Boathouse** ⊠ *56th St. at the Hudson River, Midtown West* ⊕ *www.downtownboathouse.org* Ⓜ *1, A, C, E to 59th St..*

FOOTBALL

The football season runs from September through December. The enormously popular New York Giants play at the MetLife Stadium. Most seats for Giants games are sold on a season-ticket basis—and there's a long waiting list for those. However, single tickets are occasionally available at the stadium box office or on ticket resale sites like StubHub. The New York Jets also play at MetLife Stadium. Although Jets tickets are not as scarce as those for the Giants, most are snapped up by fans before the season opener.

Contact Information New York Giants ☎ *201/935–8222 for tickets* ⊕ *www.giants. com.* **New York Jets** ☎ *800/469–5387 for tickets* ⊕ *www.newyorkjets.com.*

ICE-SKATING

The outdoor rink in Rockefeller Center, open from October through early April, is much smaller in real life than it appears on TV and in movies—though it *is* as beautiful, especially when Rock Center's enormous Christmas tree towers above it. Tickets are first come, first served, so be prepared to wait—especially around the holidays. Skating rates are $12–$16 and skate rentals are $9.

The city's outdoor rinks, open from roughly November through March, all have their own character. Central Park's beautifully situated Wollman Rink offers skating until long after dark beneath the lights of the city. Be prepared for daytime crowds on weekends. The Lasker Rink, at the north end of Central Park, is smaller and usually less crowded than Wollman. Chelsea Piers' Sky Rink has two year-round indoor rinks overlooking the Hudson. Skate rentals are available at all rinks. Citi Pond at Bryant Park offers free skating, not including the cost of skate rental, from late October through February, from 8 am to 10 pm from Sunday through Thursday and from 8 am to midnight Friday and Saturday. A $20 Citi Pond Fastpass (available online, includes skate rental) allows you to skip the line. ■TIP➔ Head to the Standard Hotel's teeny ice rink in the Meatpacking District from noon to 1 am in winter. The scene is cool and the cocktails are hot! Skate tickets are $12 and skate rental is $3.

Contact Information **Bryant Park** ⊠ *6th Ave. between W. 40th and W. 42nd Sts., 1065 Ave. of the Americas, Midtown West* ☎ *212/661–6640* ⊕ *citipondatbryantpark.com* Ⓜ *B, D, F to 42nd St.*. **Lasker Rink** ⊠ *Midpark near E. 106th St., 2 Lenox Ave., Central Park* ☎ *917/492–3856* ⊕ *www.laskerrink.com* Ⓜ *B, C to 103rd St.*. **Rockefeller Center** ⊠ *50th St. at 5th Ave., lower plaza, Midtown West* ☎ *212/332–7654* ⊕ *www.therinkatrockcenter.com* Ⓜ *B, D, F to 47th–50th Sts./Rockefeller Center; E, V to 5th Ave.–53rd St.*. **Sky Rink** ⊠ *Pier 61, W. 23rd St. & the Hudson River, Chelsea* ☎ *212/336–6100* ⊕ *www.chelseapiers.com/sr01.htm* Ⓜ *C, E to 23rd St.*. **Trump Wollman Skating Rink** ⊠ *North of 6th Ave. and Central Park South entrance, between 62nd and 63rd Sts.* ☎ *212/439–6900* ⊕ *www.wollmanskatingrink. com* Ⓜ *A, B, C, D, 1 to 59th St./Columbus Circle.*

JOGGING

All kinds of New Yorkers jog, some with dogs or babies in tow, so you'll always have company on the regular jogging routes. What's not recommended is setting out on a lonely park path at dusk. Jog when and where everybody else does. On Manhattan streets, roughly 20 north–south blocks make a mile.

In Manhattan, Central Park is the busiest spot, specifically along the 1.6-mile path circling the Jacqueline Kennedy Onassis Reservoir, where you jog in a counterclockwise direction. A runners' lane has been designated along the park roads; the entire loop road is a hilly 6 miles. A good 1.75-mile route starts at the former Tavern on the Green (now closed) along the West Drive, heads south around the bottom of the park to the East Drive, and circles back west on the 72nd Street park road to your starting point. Riverside Park, along the Hudson River bank in Manhattan, is glorious at sunset. You can cover 4½ miles by running from West 72nd to 116th Street and back, and the Greenbelt trail extends 4 more miles north to the George Washington Bridge at 181st Street. Other favorite Manhattan circuits are the Battery Park City esplanade (about 2 miles), which connects to the Hudson

River Park (about 1½ miles), and the East River Esplanade (just over 3 miles from East 63rd to East 125th streets).

STUDENTS IN NEW YORK

New York is home to such major schools as Columbia University, New York University, Fordham University, and the City College of New York. With other colleges scattered throughout the five boroughs, as well as a huge population of public and private high-schoolers, it's no wonder the city is rife with student discounts. Wherever you go, especially museums, sightseeing attractions, and performances, identify yourself as a student up front and ask if a discount is available. However, be prepared to show your ID as proof of enrollment and/or age.

A great program made available to children between the ages of 13 and 18 (or anyone in middle or high school) is High 5 for the Arts. Tickets to a wide variety of performances are sold for $5 online or by phone. Write or call to receive a free catalog of events, check it out online, or pick up a catalog at any New York public library or at High 5's offices.

IDs and Services **High 5 for the Arts** ⊠ *520 8th Ave., at 36th St., Midtown* ☎ *212/750–0555* ⊕ *www.highfivetix.org*. **STA Travel** ☎ *212/627–3111, 800/781–4040 24-hr service center* ⊕ *www.sta.com*.

TAXES

A sales tax of 8.875% applies to almost everything you can buy retail, including restaurant meals. However, prescription drugs and nonprepared food bought in grocery stores are exempt. Clothing and footwear costing less than $110 does not incur the sales tax.

TIPPING

The customary tipping rate for taxi drivers is 15%–20%, with a minimum of $2; bellhops are usually given $2 per bag in luxury hotels, $1 per bag elsewhere. Hotel maids should be tipped $2 per day of your stay. A doorman who hails or helps you into a cab can be tipped $1–$2. You should also tip your hotel concierge for services rendered; the size of the tip depends on the difficulty of your request, as well as the quality of the concierge's work. Waiters should be tipped 15%–20%, though at higher-end restaurants, a solid 20% is more the norm. Tip $1 per drink you order at the bar.

▌ VISITOR INFORMATION

The Grand Central Partnership (a sort of civic Good Samaritans' group) has installed a number of information booths in and around Grand Central Terminal (there's one near Vanderbilt Avenue and East 43rd Street). They're loaded with maps and helpful brochures on attractions throughout the city and staffed by friendly, knowledgeable, multilingual New Yorkers.

NYC & Company's Times Square Visitors Center is decked out with lots of fun and helpful tools like multilingual kiosks. The bureau also has a Midtown visitor center on 7th Avenue and runs kiosks in Lower Manhattan at City Hall Park and at Federal Hall National Memorial at 26 Wall Street; in Chinatown at the triangle where Canal, Walker, and Baxter streets meet; and in Harlem at the Apollo Theater at 253 West 125th Street.

> ### THE FODORS.COM CONNECTION
>
> Before your trip, be sure to check out what fellow travelers are saying in Talk on www.fodors.com.

The Downtown Alliance has information on the area encompassing City Hall south to Battery Park, and from the East River to West Street. For a free booklet listing New York City attractions and tour packages, contact the New York State Division of Tourism.

CONTACTS

City Information Downtown Alliance ☎ 212/566–6700 ⊕ www.downtownny.com. **Grand Central Partnership** ☎ 212/883–2420 ⊕ www.grandcentralpartnership.org. **NYC & Company Convention & Visitors Bureau** ✉ 810 7th Ave., between W. 52nd and W. 53rd Sts., 3rd fl., Midtown West ☎ 212/484–1200 ⊕ www.nycgo.com. **Times Square Information Center** ✉ 1560 Broadway, between 46th and 47th Sts., Midtown West ☎ 212/768–1560 ⊕ www.timessquarenyc.org Ⓜ N, Q, R, S, 1, 2, 3, 7 to 42nd St./Times Square.

Statewide Information New York State Division of Tourism ☎ 800/225–5697 ⊕ www.iloveny.com.

INDEX

PHOTO CREDITS

1, Songquan Deng/Shutterstock. 3, Liberty Helicopters, Inc. Chapter 1: Experience New York City: 6-7, Rudy Sulgan/age fotostock. 8, Luc Novovitch/age Fotostock. 9 (left), LHB Photo/Alamy. 9 (right), Oote Boe Photography/Alamy. 12, Ace Stock Limited/Alamy. 14, Alija/iStockphoto. 16 (left), Rome and Greece gallery by Xuan Che http://www.flickr.com/photos/rosemania/2157661526/Attribution License. 16 (top center), Kord.com/age fotostock. 16 (top right), New York. MoMA by Tomas Fano http://www.flickr. com/photos/tomasfano/2713778452/Attribution-ShareAlike License. 16 (bottom), Doug Scott/age foto-stock. 17 (top left), SuperStock/age fotostock. 17 (bottom left), Craig Chesek/AMNH. 17 (right), Picture-Quest. 18, Jeff Greenberg/Alamy. 20, Black Star/Alamy. 21 (left), David H. Wells/age fotostock. 21 (right), Richard Levine/Alamy. 23, 110613-N-TT977-235 by http://www.flickr.com/photos/thejoint-staff/5830275495/Attribution License. 24, Brooklyn Bridge Park Etienne Frossard/www.brooklynbridge-parknyc.org. 25 (left), Frances M. Roberts/Alamy. 25 (right), Union Square by adactio http://www.flickr. com/photos/adactio/3817931108/Attribution-License.29 (left), David Berkowitz/Flickr. 29 (right), emi-lydickinsonridesabmx/Flickr. 30, Corbis . 31, Photodisc . 33 (top), Liberty Helicopters, Inc. 33 (bottom), Joshua Haviv/shutterstock. 35 (top), Library of Congress Prints and Photographs Division. 35 (bottom), Library of Congress Prints and Photographs Division. Chapter 2: Lower Manhattan: 37, Bill Grove/iStockphoto. 39, Heeb Christian. 40, Chuck Pefley/Alamy. 44, Silverstein Properties. 45 (top), White House Photo/Alamy. 45 (bottom), Sondra Paulson/iStockphoto. 46 (top left), Fireball erupting in the South Tower by Robert http://www.flickr.com/photos/themachinestops/88181088/Attribution-ShareAlike License. 46 (top right), Jim Watson/CHINFO, Navy Visual News Service (Public Domain), via Wikimedia Commons. 46 (bottom), RodneyRamsey/Flickr. 47 (left), Jim Watson/CHINFO, Navy Visual News Service (Public Domain), via Wikimedia Commons. 47 (center), Peter Comitini/Flickr. 47 (right), Denise Gould (Public Domain), via Wikimedia Commons. 48-49 (top), Silverstein Properties. 48 (bottom), Silver-stein Properties. 49 (bottom left and bottom right), Joe Woolhead/Silverstein Properties. 50 (top left), Luca Cepparo/iStockphoto. 50 (top right), FaceMePLS/Flickr. 50 (bottom left), p_c_w/Flickr. 50 (bottom right), cytech/Flickr. 54-55, kropic1/Shutterstock. 57, Estormiz/Wikimedia Commons. Chapter 3: SoHo, NoLIta, Little Italy, and Chinatown: 59, Art Kowalsky/Alamy. 61, Ambient Images Inc./Alamy. 62, Yadid Levy/Alamy. 64-65, Renault Philippe/age fotostock. 67, OK Harris Works of Art. 69, Philip Lange/Shutterstock. Chapter 4: The East Village and the Lower East Side: 71, Jeff Greenberg/Alamy. 73, peyri/Flickr. 74, New York. East Village. Stop the Violence. E 12TH St by http://www.flickr.com/photos/tomasfano/2710315445/Attribution-ShareAlike License. Chapter 5: Greenwich Village and the West Village: 79, wdstock/iStock-photo. 81, Tenement Houses Overlooking Washington Square Park, New York City by http://www.flickr.com/photos/43533334@N07/5139725894/Attribution License. 82, wdstock/iStockphoto. 83, Ambient Images Inc./Alamy. 86, PCL/Alamy. Chapter 6: Chelsea and the Meatpacking District: 89, David Berko-witz/Flickr. 91, Black Star/Alamy. 92, By Gryffindor [CC-BY-SA-3.0 (www.creativecommons.org/licenses/by-sa/3.0)], via Wikimedia Commons. 94-95, Kord.com/age fotostock. 97, Kokyat Choong/Alamy. Chap-ter 7: Union Square, the Flatiron District, and Gramercy Park: 101, David Shankbone/Wikipedia.org. 103, Kord.com/age fotostock. 104, Yadid Levy/Alamy. 105, Russell Kord/Alamy. 107, naphtalina/iStockphoto. 108, IMG_0776 by Jan-Erik Finnberg http://www.flickr.com/photos/wheany/2233336954/Attribution-NonCommercial License. Chapter 8: Midtown East: 111, Kord.com. 113, Jaap Hart/iStockphoto. 114, svlumagraphica/iStockphoto. 116, Rudy Sulgan/age fotostock. 119, Stuart Monk/iStockphoto/Think-stock. 121, Sylvain Grandadam/age fotostock. 122, Empire State Sunset by Eric E Yang http://www.flickr.com/photos/midweekpost/142493669/Attribution License. Chapter 9: Midtown West: 125, Times Square - New York by Céline http://www.flickr.com/photos/pepsiline/4247882387/Attribution-ShareAlike License. 127, Bruno Perousse/age fotostock. 128, (c) Mirceani | Dreamstime.com. 131, New York. Radio City Music Hall by Tomas Fano http://www.flickr.com/photos/tomasfano/2738549430/Attribution-ShareAlike License. 132, oversnap/iStockphoto. 136, New York. MoMA by Tomas Fano http://www.flickr.com/photos/tomasfano/2713778452/Attribution-ShareAlike License. Chapter 10: The Upper East Side: 139, Nicholas Pitt/Alamy. 141, JayLazarin/iStockphoto. 142, Janine Wiedel Photolibrary/Alamy. 145, Doug Scott/age fotostock. 146, Geoffrey Clements. 148, Brooks Walker. 149, Renaud Visage/age fotostock. 150 (top), Renaud Visage/age fotostock. 150 (center), Metropolitan Museum of Art. 150 (bot-tom), An East Greek Late Archaic Alabastron in the Form of a Kore by http://www.flickr.com/photos/antiquitiesproject/5515795335/Attribution License. 152 (top), the new American wing by Kristen Bonardi Rapp http://www.flickr.com/photos/gezellig-girl/3835837758/Attribution-ShareAlike License. 152 (bot-tom), Metropolitan Museum of Art. 153, Wild Bill Studio/Metropolitan Museum of Art. 154 (top and bottom), Metropolitan Museum of Art. Chapter 11: Central Park: 157 and 158 (top), Piero Ribelli. 158 (center), Rudy Sulgan/age fotostock. 158 (bottom), Library of Congress Prints & Photographs Division. 159 (left), Chase Guttman. 159 (right), Sandra Baker/Alamy. 160, Worldscapes/age fotostock. 161 (left), Chris Lee. 161 (right), Michal Daniel. 162, Peter Arnold, Inc./Alamy. 163 (left), Craig Hale/iStockphoto.

163 (right), Agency Jon Arnold Images/age fotostock.164 (top left), Walter Bibikow/age fotostock. 164 (top right), Terraxplorer/iStockphoto. 164 (bottom), Sandra Baker/Alamy. 165 (top left), Darren Green Photography/Alamy. 165 (top right), Chuck Pefley/Alamy. 165 (bottom), Chase Guttman. 166, Piero Ribelli. 167 (left), Sandra Baker/Alamy. 167 (right), Piero Ribelli. 168-169 (bottom), gary718/Shutterstock. 168 (top left), Peter Arnold, Inc./Alamy. 168 (top right), TNT Magazine/Alamy. 169 (top left), Chuck Pefley/Alamy. 169 (top right), LMR Group/Alamy. 170 (left), Piero Ribelli. 170 (right), Jon Arnold/ Agency Jon Arnold Images. 171, by Christian http://www.flickr.com/photos/ottosv/3757952801/Attribution-ShareAlike License. 172, Mario Savoia/iStockphoto. Chapter 12: The Upper West Side: 173, Kord. com/age fotostock. 175, Momos/Wikimedia Commons. 176, Kord.com/age fotostock. 178, Ken Ross/ viestiphoto. 179, Ken Ross/viestiphoto. 180 (top left), (c) Sepavo | Dreamstime.com. 180 (top right), Craig Chesek/AMNH. 180 (bottom), Dennis Finnin/AMNH. 182, American Museum of Natural History. 183 and 184, Denis Finnin/AMNH. 185 (top), C. Chesek/AMNH. 185 (bottom), D. Finnin/C. Chesek/ AMNH. Chapter 13: Harlem: 189, Cristian Baitg/iStockphoto. 191, Joe Malone/Agency Jon Arnold Images/age fotostock. 192, SuperStock/age fotostock. 195, Rieger /age footstock. Chapter 14: Brooklyn: 197, Jeff Greenberg/age fotostock. 199, SuperStock/age fotostock. 200, Ace Stock Limited/Alamy. 201, Brooklyn Bridge Park Julienne Schaer/www.brooklynbridgeparknyc.org. 204-205, Brooklyn Bridge Park Etienne Frossard/www.brooklynbridgeparknyc.org. 210, michele lugaresi/iStockphoto. 217, Colin D. Young/Shutterstock. Chapter 15: Queens, the Bronx, and Staten Island: 219, Sylvain Grandadam. 221, Michel Friang/Alamy. 222, Siobhan O'Hare. 229, Doug Milner. 235, Johnny Stockshooter. Chapter 16: The Performing Arts: 237, Jazz at Lincoln Center. 238, JPEG Manhattan, New York City by Jazz Guy http://www.flickr.com/photos/flickr4jazz/4027850338/Attribution License. 243, Brian Palmer. 248, Ted Pink / Alamy. 255, Brian Stanton. Chapter 17: Nightlife: 261, Michael Belardo/Alamy. 262, Louis Armstrong Centennial Band At Birdland, New York City By Jazz Guy Http://Www.Flickr.Com/Photos/ Flickr4jazz/3668870123/Attribution-Noncommercial License. 269, Francisco Rosario. 274, Beirut @ Bowery Ballroom by Tammy Lohttp://www.flickr.com/photos/tammylo/489390788/Attribution-License. Chapter 18: Shopping: 287, Bruno Perousse/age fotostock. 288, Richard Levine/Alamy. 298, Piero Ribelli. 299 (left), Balthazar SoHo by Eduardo Pavon http://www.flickr.com/photos/tomateverde/3663227269/ Attribution-NonCommercial-ShareAlike License. 299 (right), Jonathan Adler. 308 (bottom), Sigerson Morrison. 308 (top), Yadid Levy/Alamy. 309, Yadid Levy/Alamy. 316 (top), Las Venus. 316 (bottom), Sugar Sweet Sunshine Bakery. 317 (top), Frock. 317 (bottom), LowerEastSideny.com. 320, Frances Roberts/Alamy. 321 (top), Amy's Bread. 321 (bottom), Cynthia Rowley. 326 and 327, Piero Ribelli. 334 (top), Piero Ribelli. 334 (bottom), Louis Vuitton. 335, 344 and 345, Piero Ribelli. Chapter 19: Where to Eat: 353, Mimi Giboin. 354, Ace Stock Limited/Alamy. 360, Dina Litovsky/Stregoica Photography. 361, Dim sum by Kent Wang http://www.flickr.com/photos/kentwang/2788560928/Attribution-ShareAlike License. 362, Dina Litovsky/Stregoica Photography. 363, pravin.premkumar/Flickr. 364, Dina Litovsky/Stregoica Photography. 365 (left), Chickpea. 365 (right), Noah Kalina. 366, Dina Litovsky/Stregoica Photography. 367, Visual Mercenary Group. 368, Frances M. Roberts/Alamy. 369, nicasaurusrex/Flickr. 370, Quality Meats. 371, Courtesy of Kyotofu. 372, The Modern. 373, Rachel from Cupcakes Take the Cake/Flickr. 374, Per Se. 375 (left), Frances Roberts/Alamy. 375 (right), Pamela Weekes. Chapter 20: Where to Stay: 471, Arcaid/Alamy. 472, On The Ave Hotel. 482 (top), Simon Brown/Firmdale Hotels. 482 (bottom left), Courtesy of The Chatwal / Photographer Phillip Ennis. 482 (bottom right), Courtesy of The Standard. 488 (top), Courtesy Of Mandarin Oriental. 488 (bottom left), Photographed by Todd Eberle Courtesy of The Mark Hotel. 488 (bottom right), Courtesy of The Ritz-Carlton New York, Central Park. 495, (all) Roy Wright. 502 (top), Courtesy of Ace Hotel/Eric Laignel. 502 (bottom left), Courtesy Of Library Hotel. 502 (bottom right), Claudia Hehr Photography.

NOTES

NOTES

ABOUT OUR WRITERS

Lynne Arany is the author of *Little Museums*, contributor to *The New York Times*, and editor of *New Mexico: A Guide for the Eyes*. Travel has drawn her to the art-nouveau wonders of Budapest, Barcelona's Barri Gòtic, Glasgow's fine tearooms, polka dancing in Tamazulapan, and rambles throughout Mexico and the U.S., yet she remains forever in thrall to those five special boroughs known as New York City.

Alexander Basek is a food and travel writer based in New York City. His work has appeared in *Travel + Leisure*, *the New York Post*, and *Time Out New York*. He has a very passionate opinion about the best way to get to LaGuardia Airport.

Arthur Bovino is senior editor of the Eat and Dine section of *The Daily Meal*. His writing and photography have appeared in *Rough Guides* and *The New York Times*.

Having written or updated Fodor's guides to destinations as far-flung as Finland, Fiji, and Australia (where he once lived), Robert Brenner relished the opportunity to explore hometown landmarks he normally rushed past. He won't rush past them again.

Samantha Chapnick is a travel journalist and a digital-content expert. She's the founder of the Nickelodeon Best Blog in New York City (Parents Connect award winner) and kidcityny.com. Her writing has appeared in *ForbesTraveler.com*, *Robb Report*, *New York Family*, *Rough Guides*, and *Frommer's*.

David Farley is the author of the award-winning travel memoir *An Irreverent Curiosity* and writes about food and travel for *AFAR* magazine, the *New York Times*, and *National Geographic Traveler*. He teaches writing at New York University.

Irish-born writer Jacinta O'Halloran, a former in-house editor at Fodor's, has been calling New York City home for more than 15 years. She can walk the part (i.e., fast) and talk the part (i.e., when she's mad at cabdrivers, ordering bagels, or giving directions) of a local, but she still sees and feels the city like a visitor (i.e., she still looks up!).

Born and raised in Croatia, Anja Mutić is a New York–based travel writer who has been globetrotting on various assignments since 2000. Her writing has appeared in *The Washington Post, BBC Travel, New York* magazine, and *ShermansTravel*, among other publications. After more than 10 years in Brooklyn, she is still having a love affair with it. Anja blogs about her travels at *www.everthenomad.com*.

John Rambow, a former in-house editor at Fodor's, has written for *Travel + Leisure*, *Fast Company*, *Budget Travel*, and *New York* magazines, as well as several blogs and guidebooks. From a base in Queens, he aims to stay on top of all the amazing things happening throughout the whole city. His website is *www.johnrambow.com*.

Adeena Sussman is a write based in New York City. She is the restaurant critic for *Manhattan Magazine*, and has contributed articles and recipes to magazines including *Gourmet, Martha Stewart Living, Food and Wine, Cooking Light, Self, Sunset*, and *Time Out New York*. Her website is *www.adeenasussman.com*.

Christina Valhouli edits the award-winning website *iTraveliShop.com*, which covers luxury travel and shopping around the world. She is the former staff travel writer at